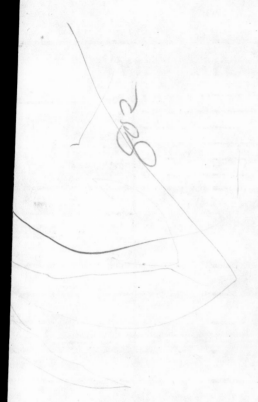

Ideas and Patterns in Literature

A series of literature anthologies accompanied by Student Guides

A Teacher's Edition of each Student Guide is available.

THE AUTHOR

*Allan Glatthorn is principal of the Abington High School
in Pennsylvania, where he was formerly chairman
of the English department and Coordinator of Language Arts.
He is a member of the President's National Council
on the Humanities. Dr. Glatthorn was a John Hay Fellow
at the University of Chicago and an Alfred
North Whitehead Fellow at Harvard*

*Richard S. Hootman has been an English teacher
and department chairman in high school and is now teaching English
and rhetoric at the University of Iowa*

*C. F. Main, who contributed the sections on The Poetry
of Robert Frost and Eight Ways of Thinking About Poetry,
is Professor of English at Rutgers University.
Dr. Main is an adviser to the Educational Testing Service
and a member of the committee on the Graduate
Record Examination in Literature*

GENERAL EDITOR

*Edgar H. Knapp has taught at secondary schools in New England,
New York, and New Jersey and is now Associate Professor
of English and Education at The Pennsylvania State University.
He is the author of Introduction to Poetry*

*William G. Leary is Professor of English at California State College
at Los Angeles. He is the author of Thought and Statement
and other texts for colleges and high school
and has delivered a series of television lectures on Shakespeare*

CONSULTANTS

*Delores Minor is Supervisor of High School English
in the Detroit public schools*

*James Hocker Mason, an authority on Latin-American
and Asiatic literatures in translation, is Professor of English
at Indiana State University at Terre Haute*

*Sylvia King contributed the section on African Voices.
She has studied African art and culture both
in this country and in Africa*

ALLAN GLATTHORN

RICHARD S. HOOTMAN

C. F. MAIN

IDEAS and PATTERNS in Literature II

GENERAL EDITORS:

Edgar H. Knapp

William G. Leary

CONSULTANTS:

Delores Minor, James Hocker Mason, Sylvia King

Harcourt Brace Jovanovich

New York   Chicago   San Francisco   Atlanta   Dallas   and   London

ACKNOWLEDGMENTS: *For permission to reprint copyrighted material, grateful acknowledgment is made to the following publishers, authors, and agents:*

The American Scholar: "The Beard of Joseph Palmer" by Stewart Holbrook from *The American Scholar*, Vol. 13, No. 4, Autumn, 1944, copyright © 1944 by the United Chapters of Phi Beta Kappa.

Ashley Famous Agency, Inc., and CBS Films, Inc.: "The Shelter" by Rod Serling from *The Twilight Zone* Series, copyright © 1961 by Cayuga Productions, Inc. CAUTION: The use of the play in present form must be confined to study and reference. It may not be presented publicly in any manner without written permission of CBS Films, Inc.

Atheneum Publishers: From "From Hero to Celebrity" from *The Image* by Daniel J. Boorstin, copyright © 1961 by Daniel J. Boorstin.

Bantam Books, Inc., and Francisco H-Pinzon Jiménez: "Dawning" by Juan Ramon Jiménez, translated by Willis Barnstone, from *Modern European Poetry* edited by Willis Barnstone, copyright © 1966 by Bantam Books, Inc.

Brandt & Brandt: "You Can't Do That" by John P. Marquand, copyright 1935 by The Curtis Publishing Company; copyright renewed © 1962 by John P. Marquand, Jr., and Christina M. Welch.

George Braziller, Inc.: "The Power of Laughter: Weapon Against Evil" from *The Green Crow* by Sean O'Casey, copyright © 1956 by Sean O'Casey.

City Lights Books: "The Dunce" by Jacques Prévert from *Pocketbooks Series*, translated by John Dixon Hunt, copyright © 1947 by Les Editions du Point du Jour.

Collins-Knowlton-Wing, Inc.: "Spoils" from *Collected Poems* by Robert Graves, copyright © 1955 by Robert Graves.

The Condé Nast Publications Inc.: "Meihem in ce Klasrum" by Dolton Edwards from *Astounding Science Fiction* (now *ANALOG Science Fiction–Science Fact*) copyright © 1946 by Street & Smith Publications, Inc.

Thomas Y. Crowell Company: "Through the Tunnel" by Doris Lessing. Originally appeared in *The New Yorker*, copyright © 1955 by Doris Lessing; from *The Habit of Loving*, Thomas Y. Crowell Company, New York, copyright © 1957 by Doris Lessing.

Crown Publishers, Inc.: "Up-Country" by Abioseh Nicol from *An African Treasury* by Langston Hughes, © 1960 by Langston Hughes.

Katherine Cuestas: "Poem" (retitled: "Soil") by Katherine Cuestas.

Curtis Brown, Ltd.: "Bill Trapp's Silence" from *Beetlecreek* by William Demby, copyright © 1950 by William Demby. "The Private Dining Room" from *Verses from 1929 On* by Ogden Nash, copyright © 1951 by Ogden Nash.

J. M. Dent & Sons, Ltd.: "The Dark House" from *Collected Poems* by Gerald Bullett.

Doubleday & Company, Inc.: "The Ant and the Grasshopper," copyright 1924 by W. Somerset Maugham, from *Cosmopolitans* by W. Somerset Maugham. "After the Fireworks," "At Kamakura," and "Loneliness" by Shiki; "Spring Rain," "In the House," "The Great Buddha at Nara," and "The Mushroom" by Issa from *An Introduction to Haiku* by Harold G. Henderson, copyright © 1958 by Harold G. Henderson. "The Bat," copyright 1938 by Theodore Roethke, from *The Collected Poems of Theodore Roethke*. "A Visit to Grandmother's," copyright © 1964 by William Melvin Kelley, from *Dancers on the Shore* by William Melvin Kelley. "Those Two Boys" from *Tobogganing on Parnassus* by Franklin P. Adams, copyright 1911 by Doubleday & Company, Inc.

E. P. Dutton & Co., Inc.: "The Ching-Ting Mountain" from *The Works of Li Po*, translated into English by Shigeyoshi Obata, copyright 1928; renewal 1950 by E. P. Dutton & Co., Inc. "In the Field Forever" from *Ungainly Things* by Robert Wallace, copyright © 1968 by Robert Wallace.

Sidney L. Eaton: "Spare Fast" by Sidney L. Eaton. All rights reserved.

Farrar, Straus & Giroux, Inc.: "The Snake and the Crocodile" from *The Dark Child* by Camara Laye, copyright 1954 by Camara Laye.

Angel Flores: "Just Lather, That's All" by Hernando Telléz, translated by Donald Yates, as included in *Great Spanish Short Stories* selected by Angel Flores.

Gloria Fuertes and Harcourt, Brace & World, Inc.: "The Picture" by Gloria Fuertes, translated by George Kearns, from *Que Estas en la Tierra* by Gloria Fuertes, published in 1961 in the Coleccion Colliure, Barcelona. English translation, copyright © 1970 by Harcourt, Brace & World, Inc.

Editions Gallimard and Marguerite Yourcenar: "Waiting for the Barbarians" by C. P. Cavafy, translated by Grace Frick from the French translation by Marguerite Yourcenar in *Presentation Critique de Constantine Cavafy.* © Editions Gallimard 1958.

Harcourt Brace Jovanovich, Inc.: "Shooting an Elephant" from *Shooting an Elephant and Other Essays* by George Orwell, copyright 1945, 1946, 1949, 1950 by Sonia Brownell Orwell. From "Politics and the English Language" from *Shooting an Elephant and Other Essays* by George Orwell, copyright 1945, 1946, 1949, 1950 by Sonia Brownell Orwell. *Animal Farm* by George Orwell, copyright 1946 by Harcourt Brace Jovanovich, Inc. "This for the Moon — Yes?" from *Slabs of the Sunburnt West* by Carl Sandburg, copyright 1922 by Harcourt Brace Jovanovich, Inc.; renewed 1950 by Carl Sandburg. "who knows if the moon's a balloon" by E. E. Cummings, copyright 1925 by E. E. Cummings, from his volume, *Poems 1923–1954.* "The Dream" and "A Slander" by Anton Chekhov, translated by Nathalie Wollard, copyright © 1970 by Harcourt Brace Jovanovich, Inc.

Harper & Row, Publishers, Inc.: "the ballad of late Annie," copyright 1949 by Gwendolyn Brooks Blakely; "The Bean Eaters" and "Old Mary," copyright © 1959 by Gwendolyn Brooks; "Of Robert Frost," copyright © 1963 by Gwendolyn Brooks Blakely; from *Selected Poems* (1963) by Gwendolyn Brooks. "Fifteen" from *The Rescued Year* by William Stafford, copyright © 1964 by William E. Stafford. "Player Piano" from *The Carpentered Hen and Other Tame Creatures* by John Updike, copyright 1954 by John Updike, originally appeared in *The New Yorker.* Pp. 126–44 of "Edmund G. Ross" from *Profiles in Courage* by John F. Kennedy, copyright © 1955 by John F. Kennedy. "Happy Childhood Tales" by Robert Benchley from *The Benchley Roundup* selected by Nathaniel Benchley, copyright 1932 by Robert C. Benchley. Pp. 79–80 (retitled: "The Fight") from *Black Boy* by Richard Wright, copyright 1937 by Richard Wright; renewed 1965 by Ellen Wright.

Harvard University Press and the Trustees of Amherst College: "Bee, I'm Expecting You" and "The Wind Begun to Rock the Grass" by Emily Dickinson from *The Poems of Emily Dickinson,* edited by Thomas H. Johnson, copyright 1951, 1955 by the President and Fellows of Harvard College.

Thor Heyerdahl: "Kon-Tiki" by Thor Heyerdahl from *Natural History* Magazine.

Hill and Wang, Inc.: "Friendship" from *The Night Visitor and Other Stories* by B. Traven, copyright © 1966 by B. Traven. "Around Us, Dawning" from *Idandre and Other Poems* by Wole Soyinka, © Wole Soyinka 1967.

Holt, Rinehart and Winston, Inc.: "Once by the Pacific," "Willful Homing," "Dust of Snow," "To the Thawing Wind," "Tree at my Window," "Desert Places," "Design," "Two Tramps in Mudtime," and "The Need of Being Versed in Country Things" from *Complete Poems of Robert Frost,* copyright 1923, 1928, 1934 by Holt, Rinehart and Winston, Inc., copyright 1936, 1942, 1951, © 1956, 1962 by Robert Frost, copyright © 1964 by Lesley Frost Ballantine. "Mending Wall," "The Road Not Taken," "Stopping by Woods on a Snowy Evening," "The Figure in the Doorway" and "Come In" from *Complete Poems of Robert Frost,* copyright 1916, 1923, 1928, 1930, 1939 by Holt, Rinehart and Winston, Inc., copyright 1936, 1942, 1944, 1951, © 1956, 1958 by Robert Frost, copyright © 1964, 1967 by Lesley Frost Ballantine. "My dreams are of a field afar" from *The Collected Poems of A. E. Housman,* copyright 1936 by Barclays Bank Ltd., copyright © 1964 by Robert E. Symons. "I Counsel You Beware" from *The Collected Poems of A. E. Housman,* copyright 1936 by Barclays Bank Ltd., copyright © 1964 by Robert E. Symons. "Loveliest of Trees" from "A Shropshire Lad" — Authorised Edition — from *The Collected Poems of A. E. Housman,* copyright 1939, 1940, © 1959 by Holt, Rinehart and Winston, Inc., copyright © 1967 by Robert E. Symons.

Illinois Bell Telephone Company and Gwendolyn Brooks Blakely: From "Speaking of Poetry" by Gwendolyn Brooks from the *Illinois Bell News,* February–March 1965.

Indiana University Press: "On the high upland plain," part 7 of "Brooklyn, Iowa, and West" from *Poems 1930–1960* by Josephine Miles. "Africa's Plea" by Roland Tombekai Dempster from *Poems from Black Africa* edited by Langston Hughes.

Denys Johnson-Davies and Tayeb Salih: "A Handful of Dates" by Tayeb Salih, translated by Denys Johnson-Davies, from *Encounter,* January 1966. (To be published in a volume entitled, *Wedding of Zein and Other Stories* by Tayeb Salih.)

Alfred A. Knopf, Inc.: "Little Lyric (Of Great Importance)," copyright 1942 by Langston Hughes, from *Selected Poems* by Langston Hughes.

J. B. Lippincott Company: "Sherrel" by Whit Burnett from *The Seas of God, Great Stories of the Human Spirit by Forty-nine Famous Authors,* edited by Whit Burnett, copyright 1944 by Whit Burnett.

Littauer and Wilkinson and Vance Packard: "America the Beautiful — and Its Desecraters" by Vance Packard from *The Atlantic Monthly,* August 1961, copyright © 1961 by The Atlantic Monthly Company, Boston, Massachusetts 02116.

Little, Brown and Company: "Perseus" from *Mythology* by Edith Hamilton, copyright 1942 by Edith Hamilton. "The Purist" by Ogden Nash, copyright 1935 by The Curtis Publishing Company, from *Verses from 1929 On* by Ogden Nash. "The Termite" by Ogden Nash, copyright 1942 by The Curtis Publishing Company, from *Verses from 1929 On* by Ogden Nash.

The Macmillan Company: "Song of Expiation," "Song of the Telegraph" and "Song of a Wandering Story-Teller" from *The Unwritten Song, Volume 1,* by Willard R. Trask, copyright © by Willard R. Trask 1966. "The Wind" from *Collected Poems* by James Stephens, copyright 1915 by The Macmillan Company; renewed 1943 by James Stephens. "John and Jane" from *Collected Poems* by Thomas Hardy, copyright 1925 by The Macmillan Company.

McGraw-Hill Book Company: "The Fox and the Crow" by La Fontaine, translated by George Kearns, and "Inscription for the Grave of a Dog" by Simonides, translated by George Kearns in *Literature of the World* edited by Thelma G. James et al. "The Ant" from *Light Armour* by Richard Armour, copyright 1954 by Richard Armour.

William Peyton Marin: "In Tribute to Robert Frost" from a speech by John F. Kennedy upon receiving the honorary degree of Doctor of Laws at Amherst College, Amherst, Massachusetts, October 26, 1963.

New Directions Publishing Corporation, Agents for the Estate of Federico Garcia Lorca, and Harcourt, Brace & World, Inc.: "The Dance," "The Horseman," and "In a Poor Neighborhood: Córdoba," translated by George Kearns, from *Orbras Completas* by Federico Garcia Lorca, © Aguilar. All rights reserved. English translations, copyright © 1970 by Harcourt, Brace & World, Inc.

New Directions Publishing Corporation: "Meditatio" from *Personae* by Ezra Pound, copyright 1926, 1954 by Ezra Pound. "Mother Goose" from *Collected Shorter Poems* by Kenneth Rexroth, copyright 1956 by New Directions. "Poem" (As the Cat) from *Collected Earlier Poems* by William Carlos Williams, copyright 1938 by William Carlos Williams.

W. W. Norton & Company, Inc.: "Bad News" from *Virgil's Machines, Poems* by Joel Sloman, copyright © 1966 by Joel Sloman.

Harold Ober Associates Incorporated: "The New Road," copyright © 1930 by Pearl S. Buck, from *The First Wife* by Pearl S. Buck. Originally appeared in *Asia* Magazine, May 1930. "Island" from *Selected Poems* by Langston Hughes, copyright © 1959 by Langston Hughes.

Preuves: "The Fetish Tree" by Jean Pliya, translated by Robert Baldich.

Random House, Inc.: Antigone, by Jean Anouilh, adapted and translated by Lewis Galantiere, copyright 1946 by Random House, Inc., from the Modern Library volume, *Four Contemporary French Plays.* CAUTION: Professionals and amateurs are hereby warned that all the plays in this volume, being fully protected under the Copyright Laws of the United States of America, the British Commonwealth, including the Dominion of Canada, and all other countries of the Berne and Universal Copyright Conventions, are subject to royalty. All rights, including professional, amateur, motion picture, recitation, lecturing, public reading, radio and television broadcasting, and the rights of translation into foreign languages, are strictly reserved. All inquiries should be addressed to Random House, Inc. "The Bird and the Machine," © copyright 1955 by Loren Eiseley, from *The Immense Journey,* by Loren Eiseley. "The Monkey" by Vladislav Khodasevich from *Two Centuries of Russian Verse* edited by Avrahm Yarmolinsky, copyright 1949, © 1962, 1966 by Avrahm Yarmolinsky. "Elegy for J.F.K." from *About the House* by W. H. Auden, © copyright 1965 by W. H. Auden. "Stop All the Clocks," copyright 1940 and renewed 1968 by W. H. Auden, from *Collected Shorter Poems 1927–1957* by W. H. Auden. "O What Is That Sound," copyright 1937 and renewed 1965 by W. H. Auden, from *Collected Shorter Poems 1927–1957* by W. H. Auden.

Paul R. Reynolds, Inc., 599 Fifth Avenue, New York, New York 10017: "The Iron Lady" by Conrad Richter, copyright © 1956 by The Curtis Publishing Company, Inc.

Paul R. Reynolds, Inc. and The Southern Methodist University Press, Dallas, Texas: "Antaeus" by Borden Deal, copyright © 1961 by The Southern Methodist University Press, from a 1961 issue of *Southwest Review.*

William Saroyan: "Where I Come From People Are Polite" from *The Saroyan Special: Best Stories of William Saroyan,* copyright 1948 by William Saroyan.

Scholastic Magazines, Inc.: "Indian Business" by Eric Howard from *Story in America 1933–1934* edited by Whit Burnett, copyright 1933 by Story Magazine, Inc. "What Are You Talking About?" by S. I. Hayakawa from *Literary Cavalcade,* copyright 1949 by Scholastic Magazines, Inc.

Charles Scribner's Sons: "A Day's Wait" from *Winner Take Nothing* by Ernest Hemingway, copyright 1933 Charles Scribner's Sons; renewal copyright © 1961 Mary Hemingway. "Quality" from *The Inn of Tranquility* by John Galsworthy, copyright 1912 Charles Scribner's Sons; renewal copyright 1940.

Charles Scribner's Sons and The Society of Authors as the literary representative of the late A. E. Housman: "Infant Innocence" by A. E. Housman from *My Brother, A. E. Housman* by Laurence Housman, copyright 1937, 1938 Laurence Housman; renewal copyright © 1965, 1966 Lloyds Bank Limited.

The Society of Authors as the literary representative of the Literary Trustees of Walter de la Mare: "Napoleon" by Walter de la Mare.

Irving Shepard: "To Build a Fire" from *Lost Faces* by Jack London.

The Stackpole Company: "The Talking Skull" from *African Genesis* by Leo Frobenius and Douglas Fox.

Helen Thurber: "The Greatest Man in the World" by James Thurber, copyright © 1935 James Thurber, copyright © 1963 Helen W. Thurber and Rosemary Thurber Sauers, from *The Middle-Aged Man on the Flying Trapeze* by James Thurber, published by Harper & Row. Originally appeared in *The New Yorker.* "The Moth and the Star" by James Thurber, copyright © 1940 James Thurber, from *Fables for Our Time* by James Thurber, published by Harper & Row. Originally appeared in *The New Yorker.* "The Fox and the Crow" by James Thurber, copyright © 1956 James Thurber, from *Further Fables for Our Time* by James Thurber, published by Simon and Schuster. Originally appeared in *The New Yorker.*

University of California Press: "The Panther" from *Selected Poems of Rilke*, translated by C. F. MacIntyre.

The University of Chicago Press: From *The Iliad of Homer*, translated with an introduction by Richmond Lattimore, copyright 1951 by The University of Chicago.

The University of Michigan Press: "Sky Diving" from *The Stride of Time* by Richmond Lattimore, copyright © by The University of Michigan 1966.

University of North Carolina Press: "John Henry" from *John Henry* by Guy B. Johnson.

The Vanguard Press: "B. Wordsworth" from *Miguel Street* by V. S. Naipaul, © V. S. Naipaul MCMLIX.

The Viking Press, Inc.: "Flight" from *The Long Valley* by John Steinbeck, copyright 1938, © 1966 by John Steinbeck. "The Storyteller" from *The Complete Short Stories of Saki* by H. H. Munro. All Rights Reserved. "First Lesson" from *Letter from a Distant Land* by Philip Booth, copyright © 1957 by Philip Booth. "Interior" from *The Portable Dorothy Parker*, copyright 1928, 1956 by Dorothy Parker. "Village Spa" from *Times Three* by Phyllis McGinley, copyright 1946 by Phyllis McGinley. Originally appeared in *The New Yorker.*

PICTURE CREDITS: p. xviii, reprinted with permission from *The New York Review of Books*, copyright © 1966 The New York Review; p. 76, George A. Lucas Collection, The Maryland Institute College of Art, courtesy of The Baltimore Museum of Art; p. 124, copr. © 1948 James Thurber from *The Beast in Me—and Other Animals* published by Harcourt, Brace & World, originally printed in *The New Yorker.* p. 166, George M. Cushing, Photography; p. 186, courtesy James L. Wells; p. 222, Collection Nelson Gallery, Atkins Museum (Gift of Mr. and Mrs. Robert B. Fizzell), Kansas City, Missouri; p. 264, from the collection of Mrs. Norman B. Woolworth; p. 326, Robert Emmett Bright from Rapho Guillumette Pictures; p. 330, Turin, Museum of Antiquities, courtesy American Heritage Publishing Co.; p. 408, Fogg Art Museum, Harvard University, Bequest of Meta and Paul J. Sachs; p. 478, Joslyn Art Museum, Omaha, Nebraska; p. 526, Giraudon; p. 582, from the Collection of R. Sturgis Ingersoll, photo Philadelphia Museum of Art.

Contents

BOOK ONE

PART 1   George Orwell   *Themes*
         Animal Farm   1

PART 2   **Man and the State**   77
Pearl Buck   The New Road   79   *Power Struggle*
Eric Howard   Indian Business   92
Guy de Maupassant   Two Friends   95
George Orwell   Shooting an Elephant   100
C. P. Cavafy   Waiting for the Barbarians   108

PART 3   **Animal Fables**   111
Aesop   The Dog and His Shadow   113
Aesop   The Mouse from the City and
         the Mouse from the Country   113
Aesop   The Crab and Her Son   114
Jean de La Fontaine   The Grasshopper and the Ant   115

James Thurber   The Moth and the Star   116

The Fox and the Crow:
Three Versions   117

I. Aesop

II. Thurber

III. La Fontaine

Somerset Maugham   The Ant and the Grasshopper   119

Jean de La Fontaine   The Old Man and His Donkey   123

PART 4   **The Power of Laughter**   125

Sean O'Casey   FROM The Power of Laughter:
Weapon Against Evil   127

Anton Chekhov   A Slander   129

Saki   The Storyteller   133

Robert Benchley   Happy Childhood Tales   139

Dolton Edwards   Meihem in ce Klasrum   142

Richard Armour   The Ant   145

Ogden Nash   The Termite   145

Franklin P. Adams   Those Two Boys   146

Langston Hughes   Little Lyric
(Of Great Importance)   147

Ogden Nash   The Purist   147

PART 5   **Language in Action**   149

Alphonse Daudet   The Last Lesson   151

Ernest Hemingway   A Day's Wait   155

S. I. Hayakawa   What Are You Talking About?   159

George Orwell   FROM Politics and
the English Language   162

BOOK TWO

PART 1   The Poetry of Robert Frost   167

FROST AS A POET OF NATURE   170

Robert Frost   Dust of Snow   170

The Need of Being Versed
   in Country Things   171

Tree at My Window   172

Once by the Pacific   172

To the Thawing Wind   173

Design   173

FROST'S INDIVIDUALISM   174

Robert Frost   The Figure in the Doorway   175

Mending Wall   176

Willful Homing   177

Two Tramps in Mud Time   178

Desert Places   180

THREE FAMOUS FROST POEMS   181

Robert Frost   The Road Not Taken   181

Stopping by Woods
   on a Snowy Evening   182

Come In   183

John F. Kennedy   In Tribute to Robert Frost   184

PART 2   Eight Ways of Thinking
About Poetry 187

ONE: A POEM IS A SURPRISE 189

A. E. Housman   I Counsel You Beware 190

E. E. Cummings   Who Knows If the Moon's
a Balloon 190

Emily Dickinson The Wind Begun to Rock 191

TWO: A POEM MAKES A SOUND 192

James Stephens   The Wind 193

John Updike   Player Piano 193

Ogden Nash   The Private Dining Room 194

THREE: A POEM IS SILENT 195

Joel Sloman   Bad News 196

Thomas Hardy   John and Jane 196

Walter de la Mare   Napoleon 197

Anonymous   White Was the Sheet 197

FOUR: A POEM HAS A SPEAKER 197

Emily Dickinson   Bee! 198

Carl Sandburg   This — for the Moon — Yes? 198

Anonymous   Epitaph for a Dog 199

William Stafford   Fifteen 199

FIVE: A POEM IS A GAME 200

Dorothy Parker   Interior 200

Richmond Lattimore   Sky Diving 201

William Carlos
Williams   Poem 202

Kenneth Rexroth   Mother Goose 202

SIX: A POEM IS UNTRUE   203

Sidney L. Eaton   Spare Fast   204
Philip Booth   First Lesson   205
Langston Hughes   Island   205
W. H. Auden   Stop All the Clocks   206

SEVEN: A POEM IS AN EXPERIENCE   206

Josephine Miles   On the High Upland Plain   207
Gerald Bullett   The Dark House   207
William Wordsworth   Old Man Traveling   208

EIGHT: A POEM IS TRUE   209

Ezra Pound   Meditatio   209
W. H. Auden   Elegy for J.F.K.   210
Walt Whitman   When I Heard
   the Learn'd Astronomer   210
A. E. Housman   Loveliest of Trees   211
Theodore Roethke   The Bat   211
Katherine Cuestas   Soil   212

A POETIC TRADITION: THE SONNET   213

William Shakespeare   No Longer Mourn for Me
   When I Am Dead   215
William Wordsworth   Composed upon
   Westminster Bridge   215
Robert Graves   Spoils   216
Phyllis McGinley   Village Spa   216

A POET OF TODAY:
GWENDOLYN BROOKS   217

Gwendolyn Brooks   The Bean Eaters   217

the ballad of late Annie   218

Old Mary   218

Of Robert Frost   219

An Interview
with Gwendolyn Brooks   219

PART 3   Individualism   223

William Saroyan   Where I Come From
People Are Polite   225

John F. Kennedy   Edmund G. Ross   233

Stewart H. Holbrook   The Beard of Joseph Palmer   244

John Galsworthy   Quality   252

William Demby   Bill Trapp's Silence   259

PART 4   Man and Nature   265

Borden Deal   Antaeus   267

Jack London   To Build a Fire   277

Thor Heyerdahl   Kon-Tiki   293

Loren Eiseley   The Bird and the Machine   306

Vance Packard   America the Beautiful —
and Its Desecraters   315

BOOK THREE

PART 1   William Shakespeare
Julius Caesar   327

PART 2   Problems of Conscience   409

Whit Burnett	Sherrel	411
B. Traven	Friendship	419
John P. Marquand	You Can't Do That	429
Anton Chekhov	The Dream	453
Rod Serling	The Shelter	458

PART 3   Conflicts   479

Richard Wright	The Fight	481
Doris Lessing	Through the Tunnel	484
John Steinbeck	Flight	494
William Melvin Kelley	A Visit to Grandmother	513

FIVE POEMS OF CONFLICT

William Blake	A Poison Tree	522
Stephen Crane	A Man Said to the Universe	522
A. E. Housman	My Dreams Are of a Field Afar	523
Emily Dickinson	Success Is Counted Sweetest	523
W. H. Auden	O What Is That Sound	524

PART 4   The Hero in Literature   527

I: THE HERO OF MYTH

Edith Hamilton	Perseus	529

II: BETWEEN MYTH AND ROMANCE

Homer	FROM The Iliad (Book 22)	537

III: THE HERO OF ROMANCE

Alfred, Lord Tennyson	Morte d'Arthur	546

IV: THE FOLK HERO

Anonymous	John Henry	554

V: THE COMMON MAN AS HERO

Conrad Richter　The Iron Lady　556

VI: THE IRONIC HERO

James Thurber　The Greatest Man in the World　571

VII: THE HERO AND THE MASS MEDIA

Daniel Boorstin　From Hero to Celebrity　579

BOOK FOUR

Readings in World Literature

DRAMA　583

Jean Anouilh　Antigone　585

SHORT STORIES　633

V. S. Naipaul　B. Wordsworth　633
Giovanni Boccaccio　The Falcon　640
Hernando Téllez　Just Lather, That's All　644

AFRICAN VOICES　649

Camara Laye　The Snake and the Crocodile　650
Tayeb Salih　A Handful of Dates　670
Anonymous　The Talking Skull　675
Jean Pliya　The Fetish Tree　676
Hottentot　Praise Songs for the Baboon　691
Pygmy　Song of Expiation　692
Ewe　Song of the Telegraph　692
Baule　Song of the Wandering Storyteller　692
Abioseh Nicol　Up-Country　693
Roland Tombekai　Africa's Plea　694
Dempster
Wole Soyinka　Around Us, Dawning　695

POETRY 696

ORIENTAL POETRY

Li Po	The Ching-ting Mountain	698
Anonymous	Anxiety of a Young Girl to Get Married 698	
Issa	Four Haiku 699	
Shiki	Three Haiku 700	

GREEK AND ROMAN POETRY

Simonides	Inscription for the Grave of a Dog 701
Paul the Silentiary	An Unknown Grave 701
Anonymous	For the Spartans Who Died at Thermopylae 702
Theocritus	A Gift for Pan 702
Lucilius	Mycilla's Hair 703
Catullus	At the Grave of His Brother 703
Martial	To Chloë 704
Martial	A Hinted Wish 704

EUROPEAN POETRY

François Villon	Ballad from the Gibbet 705
Juan Ramon Jiménez	Dawning 706
Federico Garcia Lorca	The Dance 707
Federico Garcia Lorca	In a Poor Neighborhood: Córdoba 707
Federico Garcia Lorca	The Horseman 708
Gloria Fuertes	The Picture 709
Rainer Maria Rilke	The Panther 710
Jacques Prévert	The Dunce 710
Vladislav Khodasevich	The Monkey 711

Index 713

Ideas and Patterns in Literature

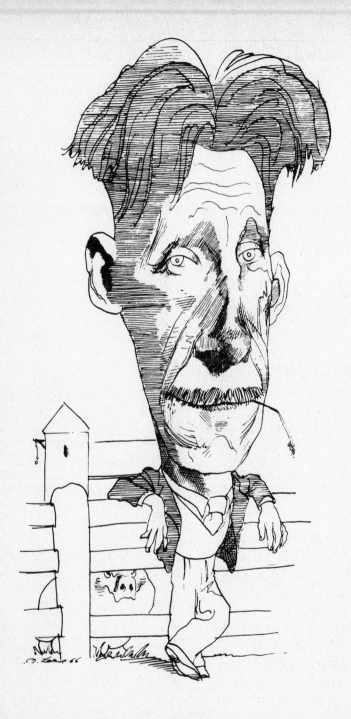

George Orwell as the proprietor of Animal Farm,
a caricature by David Levine.

ANIMAL FARM

George Orwell

In November 1917, the Russian people rose up against the oppressive rule of the Czar. One group, the Bolsheviks, quickly seized control of the government, suppressed all rival groups and opposition, and imposed upon the people a government patterned on their own political ideas. The leader of the Bolsheviks, Nikolai Lenin, dominated the new government for a few years and firmly established it in power. When he died in 1923, a bloody struggle for power developed between two of his lieutenants, Leon Trotsky and Joseph Stalin. Stalin, the more ruthless, single-minded, and determined of the two, won the struggle, and drove Trotsky to Mexico, where he was finally assassinated. Stalin then continued to strengthen his control of the central machinery of the Communist

Party. Thus, the Communist Party ruled Russia, and Stalin ruled the Communist Party.

Stalin carried out a reign of terror that exceeded the oppression of the Czar. Secret police were everywhere, spying, searching, arresting, finding evidence of treason even where there was none. Thousands were imprisoned and thousands were executed, among them high-ranking Party members and military men. Often the most prominent prisoners were tortured and brainwashed into reciting horrifying "confessions" of imaginary crimes in elaborate public trials. Purge followed purge as Stalin did away with everyone he felt might be a threat to him.

Many of the events in George Orwell's Animal Farm are similar to events which followed the Russian Revolution. But Orwell's story is primarily a fable, not a history. We do not read Animal Farm to learn what happened after the Russian Revolution. We cannot say that one pig in the story is Stalin, another pig Lenin. Like all writers of fables, Orwell has used animal characters to show something about human nature.

The essential problems of Animal Farm are those of all popular revolutions. Who should rule and who is capable of ruling? Are people always ruled by the most ruthless and aggressive among them? Are force and fear the necessary tools of government? How can people see through the high-sounding words of leaders who manipulate language to deceive them?

Animal Farm is a satire of politics and power which grew out of Orwell's awareness that the leadership of a "popular" government could be as selfish and treacherous as that of a dictatorship. The politics of Animal Farm could be the politics of any government which suppresses the rights and voices of its people to increase the powers of its leaders.

George Orwell was an enemy of totalitarianism — government which maintains its power through force and ruthless suppression of all opposition. He said of his own writing:

Every line of serious work that I have written since 1936 has been written, directly or indirectly, against totalitarianism. . . . Animal Farm was the first book in which I tried, with full consciousness of what I was doing, to fuse political purpose and artistic purpose into one whole.

Animal Farm

Mr Jones
Old Major
General Animals
Rebellious ideas of Old Major

CHAPTER 1

Mr. Jones, of the Manor Farm, had locked the hen houses for the night, but was too drunk to remember to shut the popholes. With the ring of light from his lantern dancing from side to side, he lurched across the yard, kicked off his boots at the back door, drew himself a last glass of beer from the barrel in the scullery,[1] and made his way up to bed, where Mrs. Jones was already snoring.

As soon as the light in the bedroom went out there was a stirring and a fluttering all through the farm buildings. Word had gone round during the day that old Major, the prize Middle White boar, had had a strange dream on the previous night and wished to communicate it to the other animals. It had been agreed that they should all meet in the big barn as soon as Mr. Jones was safely out of the way. Old Major (so he was always called, though the name under which he had been exhibited was Willingdon Beauty) was so highly regarded on the farm that everyone was quite ready to lose an hour's sleep in order to hear what he had to say.

At one end of the big barn, on a sort of raised platform, Major was already ensconced on his bed of straw, under a lantern which hung from a beam. He was twelve years old and had lately grown rather stout, but he was still a majestic-looking pig, with a wise and benevolent appearance in spite of the fact that his tushes [2] had never been cut. Before long the other animals began to arrive and make themselves comfortable after their different fashions. First came the three dogs, Bluebell, Jessie, and Pincher, and then the pigs, who settled down in the straw immediately in front of the platform. The hens perched themselves on the window-sills, the

---

[1] *scullery:* a room where kitchen utensils are kept.
[2] *tushes:* long, pointed teeth.

pigeons fluttered up to the rafters, the sheep and cows lay down behind the pigs and began to chew the cud. The two cart horses, Boxer and Clover, came in together, walking very slowly and setting down their vast, hairy hoofs with great care lest there should be some small animal concealed in the straw. Clover was a stout, motherly mare approaching middle life, who had never quite got her figure back after her fourth foal. Boxer was an enormous beast, nearly eighteen hands high, and as strong as any two ordinary horses put together. A white stripe down his nose gave him a somewhat stupid appearance, and in fact he was not of first-rate intelligence, but he was universally respected for his steadiness of character and tremendous powers of work. After the horses came Muriel, the white goat, and Benjamin, the donkey. Benjamin was the oldest animal on the farm, and the worst tempered. He seldom talked, and when he did, it was usually to make some cynical remark — for instance, he would say that God had given him a tail to keep the flies off, but that he would sooner have had no tail and no flies. Alone among the animals on the farm, he never laughed. If asked why, he would say that he saw nothing to laugh at. Nevertheless, without openly admitting it, he was devoted to Boxer; the two of them usually spent their Sundays together in the small paddock [3] beyond the orchard, grazing side by side and never speaking.

The two horses had just lain down when a brood of ducklings, which had lost their mother, filed into the barn, cheeping feebly and wandering from side to side to find some place where they would not be trodden on. Clover made a sort of wall round them with her great foreleg, and the ducklings nestled down inside it and promptly fell asleep. At the last moment Mollie, the foolish, pretty white mare who drew Mr. Jones's trap, came mincing daintily in, chewing at a lump of sugar. She took a place near the front and began flirting her white mane, hoping to draw attention to the red ribbons it was plaited with. Last of all came the cat, who looked round, as usual, for the warmest place, and finally squeezed herself in between Boxer and Clover; there she purred contentedly throughout Major's speech without listening to a word of what he was saying.

All the animals were now present except Moses, the tame raven, who slept on a perch behind the back door. When Major saw that

---

[3] *paddock*: pasture for exercising horses.

they had all made themselves comfortable and were waiting atten-tively, he cleared his throat and began:

"Comrades, you have heard already about the strange dream that I had last night. But I will come to the dream later. I have some-thing else to say first. I do not think, comrades, that I shall be with you for many months longer, and before I die, I feel it my duty to pass on to you such wisdom as I have acquired. I have had a long life, I have had much time for thought as I lay alone in my stall, and I think I may say that I understand the nature of life on this earth as well as any animal now living. It is about this that I wish to speak to you.

"Now, comrades, what is the nature of this life of ours? Let us face it: our lives are miserable, laborious, and short. We are born, we are given just so much food as will keep the breath in our bodies, and those of us who are capable of it are forced to work to the last atom of our strength; and the very instant that our usefulness has come to an end we are slaughtered with hideous cruelty. No animal in England knows the meaning of happiness or leisure after he is a year old. No animal in England is free. The life of an animal is misery and slavery: that is the plain truth.

"But is this simply part of the order of nature? Is it because this land of ours is so poor that it cannot afford a decent life to those who dwell upon it? No, comrades, a thousand times no! The soil of England is fertile, its climate is good, it is capable of affording food in abundance to an enormously greater number of animals than now inhabit it. This single farm of ours would support a dozen horses, twenty cows, hundreds of sheep — and all of them living in a comfort and a dignity that are now almost beyond our imagining. Why then do we continue in this miserable condition? Because nearly the whole of the produce of our labor is stolen from us by human beings. There, comrades, is the answer to all our problems. It is summed up in a single word — Man. Man is the only real enemy we have. Remove Man from the scene, and the root cause of hunger and overwork is abolished for ever.

"Man is the only creature that consumes without producing. He does not give milk, he does not lay eggs, he is too weak to pull the plow, he cannot run fast enough to catch rabbits. Yet he is lord of all the animals. He sets them to work, he gives back to them the bare minimum that will prevent them from starving, and the rest he keeps for himself. Our labor tills the soil, our dung fertilizes it, and yet there is not one of us that owns more than his bare skin. You cows that I see before me, how many thousands of gallons of milk have you given during this last year? And what has happened to that milk which should have been breeding up sturdy calves? Every drop of it has gone down the throats of our enemies. And you hens, how many eggs have you laid in this last year, and how many of those eggs ever hatched into chickens? The rest have all gone to market to bring in money for Jones and his men. And you, Clover, where are those four foals you bore, who should have been the support and pleasure of your old age? Each was sold at a year old — you will never see one of them again. In return for your four confinements and all your labor in the fields, what have you ever had except your bare rations and a stall?

"And even the miserable lives we lead are not allowed to reach their natural span. For myself I do not grumble, for I am one of the lucky ones. I am twelve years old and have had over four hundred children. Such is the natural life of a pig. But no animal escapes the cruel knife in the end. You young porkers who are sitting in front of me, every one of you will scream your lives out at the block within a year. To that horror we all must come — cows, pigs, hens, sheep, everyone. Even the horses and the dogs have no better fate. You, Boxer, the very day that those great muscles of yours lose their power, Jones will sell you to the knacker,[4] who will cut your throat and boil you down for the foxhounds. As for the dogs, when they grow old and toothless, Jones ties a brick around their necks and drowns them in the nearest pond.

"Is it not crystal clear, then, comrades, that all the evils of this life of ours spring from the tyranny of human beings? Only get rid of Man, and the produce of our labor would be our own. Almost overnight we could become rich and free. What then must we do? Why, work night and day, body and soul, for the overthrow of the human race! That is my message to you, comrades: Rebellion! I do not know when that Rebellion will come, it might be in a week or in a hundred years, but I know, as surely as I see this straw beneath my feet, that sooner or later justice will be done. Fix your eyes on that, comrades, throughout the short remainder of your lives! And above all, pass on this message of mine to those who come after you, so

---

[4] *knacker:* man who slaughters old horses for their hides, meat, etc.

that future generations shall carry on the struggle until it is victorious.

"And remember, comrades, your resolution must never falter. No argument must lead you astray. Never listen when they tell you that Man and the animals have a common interest, that the prosperity of the one is the prosperity of the others. It is all lies. Man serves the interests of no creature except himself. And among us animals let there be perfect unity, perfect comradeship in the struggle. All men are enemies. All animals are comrades."

At this moment there was a tremendous uproar. While Major was speaking four large rats had crept out of their holes and were sitting on their hindquarters, listening to him. The dogs had suddenly caught sight of them, and it was only by a swift dash for their holes that the rats saved their lives. Major raised his trotter for silence.

"Comrades," he said, "here is a point that must be settled. The wild creatures, such as rats and rabbits — are they our friends or our enemies? Let us put it to the vote. I propose this question to the meeting: Are rats comrades?"

The vote was taken at once, and it was agreed by an overwhelming majority that rats were comrades. There were only four dissentients, the three dogs and the cat, who was afterward discovered to have voted on both sides. Major continued:

"I have little more to say. I merely repeat, remember always your duty of enmity toward Man and all his ways. Whatever goes upon two legs is an enemy. Whatever goes upon four legs, or has wings, is a friend. And remember also that in fighting against Man, we must not come to resemble him. Even when you have conquered him, do not adopt his vices. No animal must ever live in a house, or sleep in a bed, or wear clothes, or drink alcohol, or smoke tobacco, or touch money, or engage in trade. All the habits of Man are evil. And, above all, no animal must ever tyrannize over his own kind. Weak or strong, clever or simple, we are all brothers. No animal must ever kill any other animal. All animals are equal.

"And now, comrades, I will tell you about my dream of last night. I cannot describe that dream to you. It was a dream of the earth as it will be when Man has vanished. But it reminded me of something that I had long forgotten. Many years ago, when I was a little pig, my mother and the other sows used to sing an old song of which they knew only the tune and the first three words. I had known that tune in my infancy, but it had long since passed out of my mind. Last night, however, it came back to me in my dream. And what is more, the words of the song also came back — words, I am certain, which were sung by the animals of long ago and have been lost to memory for generations. I will sing you that song now, comrades. I am old and my voice is hoarse, but when I have taught you the tune, you can sing it better for yourselves. It is called *Beasts of England.*"

Old Major cleared his throat and began to sing. As he had said, his voice was hoarse, but he sang well enough, and it was a stirring tune, something between "Clementine" and "La Cucaracha." The words ran:

> Beasts of England, beasts of Ireland,
> Beasts of every land and clime,
> Hearken to my joyful tidings
> Of the golden future time.
>
> Soon or late the day is coming,
> Tyrant Man shall be o'erthrown,
> And the fruitful fields of England
> Shall be trod by beasts alone.
>
> Rings shall vanish from our noses,
> And the harness from our back,
> Bit and spur shall rust forever,
> Cruel whips no more shall crack.
>
> Riches more than mind can picture,
> Wheat and barley, oats and hay,
> Clover, beans, and mangel-wurzels [5]
> Shall be ours upon that day.
>
> Bright will shine the fields of England,
> Purer shall its waters be,
> Sweeter yet shall blow its breezes
> On the day that sets us free.
>
> For that day we all must labor,
> Though we die before it break;
> Cows and horses, geese and turkeys,
> All must toil for freedom's sake.

---

[5] *mangel-wurzels:* European beets fed to cattle.

Beasts of England, beasts of Ireland,
Beasts of every land and clime,
Hearken well and spread my tidings
Of the golden future time.

The singing of this song threw the animals into the wildest excitement. Almost before Major had reached the end, they had begun singing it for themselves. Even the stupidest of them had already picked up the tune and a few of the words, and as for the clever ones, such as the pigs and dogs, they had the entire song by heart within a few minutes. And then, after a few preliminary tries, the whole farm burst out into *Beasts of England* in tremendous unison. The cows lowed it, the dogs whined it, the sheep bleated it, the horses whinnied it, the ducks quacked it. They were so delighted with the song that they sang it right through five times in succession, and might have continued singing it all night if they had not been interrupted.

Unfortunately, the uproar awoke Mr. Jones, who sprang out of bed, making sure that there was a fox in the yard. He seized the gun which always stood in a corner of his bedroom, and let fly a charge of number 6 shot into the darkness. The pellets buried themselves in the wall of the barn and the meeting broke up hurriedly. Everyone fled to his own sleeping place. The birds jumped on to their perches, the animals settled down in the straw, and the whole farm was asleep in a moment.

The Takeover

CHAPTER 2

Three nights later old Major died peacefully in his sleep. His body was buried at the foot of the orchard.

This was early in March. During the next three months there was much secret activity. Major's speech had given to the more intelligent animals on the farm a completely new outlook on life. They did not know when the Rebellion predicted by Major would take place, they had no reason for thinking that it would be within their own lifetime, but they saw clearly that it was their duty to prepare for it. The work of teaching and organizing the others fell naturally upon the pigs, who were generally recognized as being the cleverest of the animals. Pre-eminent among the pigs were two young boars named Snowball and Napoleon, whom Mr. Jones was breeding up for sale. Napoleon was a large, rather fierce-looking Berkshire boar, the only Berkshire on the farm, not much of a talker, but with a reputation for getting his own way. Snowball was a more vivacious pig than Napoleon, quicker in speech and more inventive, but was not considered to have the same depth of character. All the other male pigs on the farm were porkers. The best known among them was a small fat pig named Squealer, with very round cheeks, twinkling eyes, nimble movements, and a shrill voice. He was a brilliant talker, and when he was arguing some difficult point he had a way of skipping from side to side and whisking his tail which was somehow very persuasive. The others said of Squealer that he could turn black into white.

These three had elaborated old Major's teachings into a complete system of thought, to which they gave the name of Animalism. Several nights a week, after Mr. Jones was asleep, they held secret meetings in the barn and expounded the principles of Animalism to the others. At the beginning they met with much stupidity and apathy. Some of the animals talked of the duty of loyalty to Mr. Jones, whom they referred to as "Master," or made elementary remarks such as "Mr. Jones feeds us. If he were gone, we should starve to death." Others asked such questions as "Why should we care what happens after we are dead?" or "If this Rebellion is to happen anyway, what difference does it make whether we work for it or not?" and the pigs had great difficulty in making them see that this was contrary to the spirit of Animalism. The stupidest questions of all were asked by Mollie, the white mare. The very first question she asked Snowball was: "Will there still be sugar after the Rebellion?"

"No," said Snowball firmly. "We have no means of making sugar on this farm. Besides, you do not need sugar. You will have all the oats and hay you want."

"And shall I still be allowed to wear ribbons in my mane?" asked Mollie.

"Comrade," said Snowball, "those ribbons that you are so devoted to are the badge of slavery. Can you not understand that liberty is worth more than ribbons?"

Mollie agreed, but she did not sound very convinced.

The pigs had an even harder struggle to counteract the lies put about by Moses, the tame raven. Moses, who was Mr. Jones's special pet, was a spy and a tale-bearer, but he was also a clever talker. He claimed to know of the existence of a mysterious country called Sugarcandy Mountain, to which all animals went when they died. It was situated somewhere up in the sky, a little distance beyond the clouds, Moses said. In Sugarcandy Mountain it was Sunday seven days a week, clover was in season all the year round, and lump sugar and linseed cake grew on the hedges. The animals hated Moses because he told tales and did no work, but some of them believed in Sugarcandy Mountain, and the pigs had to argue very hard to persuade them that there was no such place.

Their most faithful disciples were the two cart horses, Boxer and Clover. These two had great difficulty in thinking anything out for themselves, but having once accepted the pigs as their teachers, they absorbed everything that they were told, and passed it on to the other animals by simple arguments. They were unfailing in their attendance at the secret meetings in the barn and led the singing of *Beasts of England*, with which the meetings always ended.

Now, as it turned out, the Rebellion was achieved much earlier and more easily than anyone had expected. In past years Mr. Jones, although a hard master, had been a capable farmer, but of late he had fallen on evil days. He had become much disheartened after losing money in a lawsuit, and had taken to drinking more than was good for him. For whole days at a time he would lounge in his Windsor chair in the kitchen, reading the newspapers, drinking, and occasionally feeding Moses on crusts of bread soaked in beer. His men were idle and dishonest, the fields were full of weeds, the buildings wanted roofing, the hedges were neglected, and the animals were underfed.

June came and the hay was almost ready for cutting. On Midsummer's Eve, which was a Saturday, Mr. Jones went into Willingdon and got so drunk at the Red Lion that he did not come back till midday on Sunday. The men had milked the cows in the early morning and then had gone out rabbiting, without bothering to feed the animals. When Mr. Jones got back he immediately went to sleep on the drawing-room sofa with the *News of the World* over his face, so that when evening came, the animals were still unfed. At last they could stand it no longer. One of the cows broke in the door of the store shed with her horn and all the animals began to help themselves from the bins. It was just then that Mr. Jones woke

up. The next moment he and his four men were in the store shed
with whips in their hands, lashing out in all directions. This was
more than the hungry animals could bear. With one accord, though
nothing of the kind had been planned beforehand, they flung themselves upon their tormentors. Jones and his men suddenly found
themselves being butted and kicked from all sides. The situation was
quite out of their control. They had never seen animals behave like
this before, and this sudden uprising of creatures whom they were
used to thrashing and maltreating just as they chose frightened them
almost out of their wits. After only a moment or two they gave up
trying to defend themselves and took to their heels. A minute later
all five of them were in full flight down the cart-track that led to the
main road, with the animals pursuing them in triumph.

Mrs. Jones looked out of the bedroom window, saw what was
happening, hurriedly flung a few possessions into a carpetbag, and
slipped out of the farm by another way. Moses sprang off his perch
and flapped after her, croaking loudly. Meanwhile the animals had
chased Jones and his men out on to the road and slammed the five-
barred gate behind them. And so, almost before they knew what was
happening, the Rebellion had been successfully carried through:
Jones was expelled, and the Manor Farm was theirs.

For the first few minutes the animals could hardly believe in their
good fortune. Their first act was to gallop in a body right round
the boundaries of the farm, as though to make quite sure that no
human being was hiding anywhere upon it; then they raced back to
the farm buildings to wipe out the last traces of Jones's hated reign.
The harness room at the end of the stables was broken open; the
bits, the nose rings, the dog chains, the cruel knives were all flung
down the well. The reins, the halters, the blinkers, the degrading
nosebags, were thrown on to the rubbish fire which was burning in
the yard. So were the whips. All the animals capered with joy when
they saw the whips going up in flames. Snowball also threw on to
the fire the ribbons with which the horses' manes and tails had
usually been decorated on market days.

"Ribbons," he said, "should be considered as clothes, which are
the mark of a human being. All animals should go naked."

When Boxer heard this he fetched the small straw hat which he
wore in summer to keep the flies out of his ears, and flung it on to
the fire with the rest.

In a very little while the animals had destroyed everything that reminded them of Mr. Jones. Napoleon then led them back to the store shed and served out a double ration of corn [1] to everybody, with two biscuits for each dog. Then they sang *Beasts of England* from end to end seven times running, and after that they settled down for the night and slept as they had never slept before.

But they woke at dawn as usual, and suddenly remembering the glorious thing that had happened, they all raced out into the pasture together. A little way down the pasture there was a knoll that commanded a view of most of the farm. The animals rushed to the top of it and gazed round them in the clear morning light. Yes, it was theirs — everything that they could see was theirs! In the ecstasy of that thought they gamboled round and round, they hurled themselves into the air in great leaps of excitement. They rolled in the dew, they cropped mouthfuls of the sweet summer grass, they kicked up clods of the black earth and snuffed its rich scent. Then they made a tour of inspection of the whole farm and surveyed with speechless admiration the plowland, the hayfield, the orchard, the pool, the spinney.[2] It was as though they had never seen these things before, and even now they could hardly believe that it was all their own.

Then they filed back to the farm buildings and halted in silence outside the door of the farmhouse. That was theirs too, but they were frightened to go inside. After a moment, however, Snowball and Napoleon butted the door open with their shoulders and the animals entered in single file, walking with the utmost care for fear of disturbing anything. They tiptoed from room to room, afraid to speak above a whisper and gazing with a kind of awe at the unbelievable luxury, at the beds with their feather mattresses, the looking-glasses, the horsehair sofa, the Brussels carpet, the lithograph of Queen Victoria over the drawing-room mantelpiece. They were just coming down the stairs when Mollie was discovered to be missing. Going back, the others found that she had remained behind in the best bedroom. She had taken a piece of blue ribbon from Mrs. Jones's dressing-table, and was holding it against her shoulder and admiring herself in the glass in a very foolish manner. The others reproached her sharply, and they went outside. Some

---

corn: in Britain, any cereal plant, chiefly grain.
spinney: a small wood or thicket.

hams hanging in the kitchen were taken out for burial, and the barrel of beer in the scullery was stove in with a kick from Boxer's hoof, otherwise nothing in the house was touched. A unanimous resolution was passed on the spot that the farmhouse should be preserved as a museum. All were agreed that no animal must ever live there.

The animals had their breakfast, and then Snowball and Napoleon called them together again.

"Comrades," said Snowball, "it is half-past six, and we have a long day before us. Today we begin the hay harvest. But there is another matter that must be attended to first."

The pigs now revealed that during the past three months they had taught themselves to read and write from an old spelling book which had belonged to Mr. Jones's children and which had been thrown on the rubbish heap. Napoleon sent for pots of black and white paint and led the way down to the five-barred gate that gave on to the main road. Then Snowball (for it was Snowball who was best at writing) took a brush between the two knuckles of his trotter, painted out MANOR FARM from the top bar of the gate and in its place painted ANIMAL FARM. This was to be the name of the farm from now onward. After this they went back to the farm buildings, where Snowball and Napoleon sent for a ladder, which they caused to be set against the end wall of the big barn. They explained that by their studies of the past three months the pigs had succeeded in reducing the principles of Animalism to Seven Commandments. These Seven Commandments would now be inscribed on the wall; they would form an unalterable law by which all the animals on Animal Farm must live for ever after. With some difficulty (for it is not easy for a pig to balance himself on a ladder) Snowball climbed up and set to work, with Squealer a few rungs below him holding the paint pot. The Commandments were written on the tarred wall in great white letters that could be read thirty yards away. They ran thus:

THE SEVEN COMMANDMENTS

1. Whatever goes upon two legs is an enemy. ~ better than other
2. Whatever goes upon four legs, or has wings, is a friend.
3. No animal shall wear clothes. - better for pigs to wear cloth

[handwritten: shared + earned by giving to the rockets Do not giving]

4. No animal shall sleep in a bed. — *without sheet*
5. No animal shall drink alcohol. — *to excess*
6. No animal shall kill any other animal. — *without a reason*
7. All animals are equal. — *some are more equal on their part.*

It was very neatly written, and except that "friend" was written "freind" and one of the S's was the wrong way round, the spelling was correct all the way through. Snowball read it aloud for the benefit of the others. All the animals nodded in complete agreement, and the cleverer ones at once began to learn the Commandments by heart.

"Now, comrades," cried Snowball, throwing down the paintbrush, "to the hayfield! Let us make it a point of honor to get in the harvest more quickly than Jones and his men could do."

But at this moment the three cows, who had seemed uneasy for some time past, set up a loud lowing. They had not been milked for twenty-four hours, and their udders were almost bursting. After a little thought, the pigs sent for buckets and milked the cows fairly successfully, their trotters being well adapted to this task. Soon there were five buckets of frothing creamy milk at which many of the animals looked with considerable interest.

"What is going to happen to all that milk?" said someone.

"Jones used sometimes to mix some of it in our mash," said one of the hens.

"Never mind the milk, comrades!" cried Napoleon, placing himself in front of the buckets. "That will be attended to. The harvest is more important. Comrade Snowball will lead the way. I shall follow in a few minutes. Forward, comrades! The hay is waiting."

So the animals trooped down to the hayfield to begin the harvest, and when they came back in the evening, it was noticed that the milk had disappeared.

[handwritten: Joint power]

CHAPTER 3

How they toiled and sweated to get the hay in! But their efforts were rewarded, for the harvest was an even bigger success than they had hoped.

Sometimes the work was hard; the implements had been designed

for human beings and not for animals, and it was a great drawback
that no animal was able to use any tool that involved standing on
his hind legs. But the pigs were so clever that they could think of
a way round every difficulty. As for the horses, they knew every inch
of the field, and in fact understood the business of mowing and rak-
ing far better than Jones and his men had ever done. The pigs did
not actually work, but directed and supervised the others. With
their superior knowledge it was natural that they should assume
the leadership. Boxer and Clover would harness themselves to the
cutter or the horserake (no bits or reins were needed in these days,
of course) and tramp steadily round and round the field with a pig
walking behind and calling out "Gee up, comrade!" or "Whoa back,
comrade!" as the case might be. And every animal down to the hum-
blest worked at turning the hay and gathering it. Even the ducks
and hens toiled to and fro all day in the sun, carrying tiny wisps of
hay in their beaks. In the end they finished the harvest in two days'
less time than it had usually taken Jones and his men. Moreover, it
was the biggest harvest that the farm had ever seen. There was no
wastage whatever; the hens and ducks with their sharp eyes had
gathered up the very last stalk. And not an animal on the farm had
stolen so much as a mouthful.

All through that summer the work of the farm went like clockwork. The animals were happy as they had never conceived it possible to be. Every mouthful of food was an acute positive pleasure,
now that it was truly their own food, produced by themselves and
for themselves, not doled out to them by a grudging master. With
the worthless parasitical human beings gone, there was more for
everyone to eat. There was more leisure too, inexperienced though
the animals were. They met with many difficulties — for instance,
later in the year, when they harvested the corn, they had to tread
it out in the ancient style and blow away the chaff with their breath,
since the farm possessed no threshing machine — but the pigs with
their cleverness and Boxer with his tremendous muscles always
pulled them through. Boxer was the admiration of everybody. He
had been a hard worker even in Jones's time, but now he seemed
more like three horses than one; there were days when the entire
work of the farm seemed to rest on his mighty shoulders. From
morning to night he was pushing and pulling, always at the spot
where the work was hardest. He had made an arrangement with one

of the cockerels to call him in the mornings half an hour earlier than anyone else, and would put in some volunteer labor at whatever seemed to be most needed, before the regular day's work began. His answer to every problem, every setback, was "I will work harder!" — which he had adopted as his personal motto.

But everyone worked according to his capacity. The hens and ducks, for instance, saved five bushels of corn at the harvest by gathering up the stray grains. Nobody stole, nobody grumbled over his rations, the quarreling and biting and jealousy which had been normal features of life in the old days had almost disappeared. Nobody shirked — or almost nobody. Mollie, it was true, was not good at getting up in the mornings, and had a way of leaving work early on the ground that there was a stone in her hoof. And the behavior of the cat was somewhat peculiar. It was soon noticed that when there was work to be done the cat could never be found. She would vanish for hours on end, and then reappear at mealtimes, or in the evening after work was over, as though nothing had happened. But she always made such excellent excuses, and purred so affectionately, that it was impossible not to believe in her good intentions. Old Benjamin, the donkey, seemed quite unchanged since the Rebellion. He did his work in the same slow obstinate way as he had done it in Jones's time, never shirking and never volunteering for extra work either. About the Rebellion and its results he would express no opinion. When asked whether he was not happier now that Jones was gone, he would say only "Donkeys live a long time. None of you has ever seen a dead donkey," and the others had to be content with this cryptic answer.

On Sundays there was no work. Breakfast was an hour later than usual, and after breakfast there was a ceremony which was observed every week without fail. First came the hoisting of the flag. Snowball had found in the harness room an old green tablecloth of Mrs. Jones's and had painted on it a hoof and a horn in white. This was run up the flagstaff in the farmhouse garden every Sunday morning. The flag [1] was green, Snowball explained, to represent the green fields of England, while the hoof and horn signified the future Republic of the Animals which would arise when the human race had been finally overthrown. After the hoisting of the flag all the animals trooped into the big barn for a general assembly which was

---

[1] *flag:* The Soviet flag has a yellow hammer and sickle on a red background.

known as the Meeting. Here the work of the coming week was
planned out and resolutions were put forward and debated. It was
always the pigs who put forward the resolutions. The other animals
understood how to vote, but could never think of any resolutions
of their own. Snowball and Napoleon were by far the most active
in the debates. But it was noticed that these two were never in
agreement: whatever suggestion either of them made, the other
could be counted on to oppose it. Even when it was resolved — a
thing no one could object to in itself — to set aside the small paddock behind the orchard as a home of rest for animals who were
past work, there was a stormy debate over the correct retiring age
for each class of animal. The Meeting always ended with the singing
of *Beasts of England,* and the afternoon was given up to recreation.

The pigs had set aside the harness room as a headquarters for
themselves. Here, in the evenings, they studied blacksmithing,[2]
carpentering, and other necessary arts from books which they had
brought out of the farmhouse. Snowball also busied himself with
organizing the other animals into what he called Animal Committees. He was indefatigable at this. He formed the Egg Production
Committee for the hens, the Clean Tails League for the cows, the
Wild Comrades' Re-education Committee (the object of this was to
tame the rats and rabbits), the Whiter Wool Movement for the
sheep, and various others, besides instituting classes in reading and
writing. On the whole, these projects were a failure. The attempt to
tame the wild creatures, for instance, broke down almost immediately. They continued to behave very much as before, and when
treated with generosity, simply took advantage of it. The cat joined
the Re-education Committee and was very active in it for some days.
She was seen one day sitting on a roof and talking to some sparrows
who were just out of her reach. She was telling them that all animals
were now comrades and that any sparrow who chose could come
and perch on her paw, but the sparrows kept their distance.

The reading and writing classes, however, were a great success. By
the autumn almost every animal on the farm was literate in some
degree.

As for the pigs, they could already read and write perfectly. The
dogs learned to read fairly well, but were not interested in reading

---

[2] *blacksmithing:* working with iron, particularly to shoe horses.

anything except the Seven Commandments. Muriel, the goat, could read somewhat better than the dogs, and sometimes used to read to the others in the evenings from scraps of newspaper which she found on the rubbish heap. Benjamin could read as well as any pig, but never exercised his faculty. So far as he knew, he said, there was nothing worth reading. Clover learned the whole alphabet but could not put words together. Boxer could not get beyond the letter D. He would trace out A, B, C, D, in the dust with his great hoof, and then would stand staring at the letters with his ears back, sometimes shaking his forelock, trying with all his might to remember what came next and never succeeding. On several occasions, indeed, he did learn E, F, G, H, but by the time he knew them, it was always discovered that he had forgotten A, B, C, and D. Finally he decided to be content with the first four letters, and used to write them out once or twice every day to refresh his memory. Mollie refused to learn any but the six letters which spelled her own name. She would form these very neatly out of pieces of twig, and would then decorate them with a flower or two and walk round them admiring them.

None of the other animals on the farm could get further than the letter A. It was also found that the stupider animals, such as the sheep, hens, and ducks, were unable to learn the Seven Commandments by heart. After much thought Snowball declared that the Seven Commandments could in effect be reduced to a single maxim, namely: "Four legs good, two legs bad." This, he said, contained the essential principle of Animalism. Whoever had thoroughly grasped it would be safe from human influences. The birds at first objected, since it seemed to them that they also had two legs, but Snowball proved to them that this was not so.

"A bird's wing, comrades," he said, "is an organ of propulsion and not of manipulation. It should therefore be regarded as a leg. The distinguishing mark of man is the *hand*, the instrument with which he does all his mischief."

The birds did not understand Snowball's long words, but they accepted his explanation, and all the humbler animals set to work to learn the new maxim by heart. FOUR LEGS GOOD, TWO LEGS BAD, was inscribed on the end wall of the barn, above the Seven Commandments and in bigger letters. When they had once got it by heart, the sheep developed a great liking for this maxim, and often

as they lay in the field they would all start bleating "Four legs good,
two legs bad! Four legs good, two legs bad!" and keep it up for hours
on end, never growing tired of it.

Napoleon took no interest in Snowball's committees. He said that
the education of the young was more important than anything that
could be done for those who were already grown up. It happened
that Jessie and Bluebell had both whelped soon after the hay harvest, giving birth between them to nine sturdy puppies. As soon as
they were weaned, Napoleon took them away from their mothers,
saying that he would make himself responsible for their education.
He took them up into a loft which could only be reached by a ladder from the harness room, and there kept them in such seclusion
that the rest of the farm soon forgot their existence.

The mystery of where the milk went to was soon cleared up. It
was mixed every day into the pigs' mash. The early apples were now
ripening, and the grass of the orchard was littered with windfalls.
The animals had assumed as a matter of course that these would
be shared out equally; one day, however, the order went forth that
all the windfalls were to be collected and brought to the harness
room for the use of the pigs. At this some of the other animals murmured, but it was no use. All the pigs were in full agreement on
this point, even Snowball and Napoleon. Squealer was sent to make
the necessary explanations to the others.

"Comrades!" he cried. "You do not imagine, I hope, that we pigs
are doing this in a spirit of selfishness and privilege? Many of us
actually dislike milk and apples. I dislike them myself. Our sole object in taking these things is to preserve our health. Milk and apples (this has been proved by Science, comrades) contain substances
absolutely necessary to the well-being of a pig. We pigs are brain-
workers. The whole management and organization of this farm
depend on us. Day and night we are watching over your welfare.
It is for *your* sake that we drink that milk and eat those apples. Do
you know what would happen if we pigs failed in our duty? Jones
would come back! Yes, Jones would come back! Surely, comrades,"
cried Squealer almost pleadingly, skipping from side to side and
whisking his tail, "surely there is no one among you who wants to
see Jones come back?"

Now if there was one thing that the animals were completely
certain of, it was that they did not want Jones back. When it was

put to them in this light, they had no more to say. The importance of keeping the pigs in good health was all too obvious. So it was agreed without further argument that the milk and the windfall apples (and also the main crop of apples when they ripened) should be reserved for the pigs alone.

BATTLE OF COWSHED
CHAPTER 4

By the late summer the news of what had happened on Animal Farm had spread across half the county. Every day Snowball and Napoleon sent out flights of pigeons whose instructions were to mingle with the animals on neighboring farms, tell them the story of the Rebellion, and teach them the tune of *Beasts of England*.

Most of this time Mr. Jones had spent sitting in the taproom of the Red Lion at Willingdon, complaining to anyone who would listen of the monstrous injustice he had suffered in being turned out of his property by a pack of good-for-nothing animals. The other farmers sympathized in principle, but they did not at first give him much help. At heart, each of them was secretly wondering whether he could not somehow turn Jones's misfortune to his own advantage. It was lucky that the owners of the two farms which adjoined Animal Farm were on permanently bad terms. One of them, which was named Foxwood, was a large, neglected, old-fashioned farm, much overgrown by woodland, with all its pastures worn out and its hedges in a disgraceful condition. Its owner, Mr. Pilkington, was an easy-going gentleman farmer who spent most of his time in fishing or hunting according to the season. The other farm, which was called Pinchfield, was smaller and better kept. Its owner was a Mr. Frederick, a tough, shrewd man, perpetually involved in lawsuits and with a name for driving hard bargains. These two disliked each other so much that it was difficult for them to come to any agreement, even in defense of their own interests.

Nevertheless, they were both thoroughly frightened by the rebellion on Animal Farm, and very anxious to prevent their own animals from learning too much about it. At first they pretended to laugh to scorn the idea of animals managing a farm for themselves. The whole thing would be over in a fortnight,[1] they said. They put it

---
[1] *fortnight:* two weeks.

about that the animals on the Manor Farm (they insisted on calling it the Manor Farm; they would not tolerate the name "Animal Farm") were perpetually fighting among themselves and were also rapidly starving to death. When time passed and the animals had evidently not starved to death, Frederick and Pilkington changed their tune and began to talk of the terrible wickedness that now flourished on Animal Farm. It was given out that the animals there practiced cannibalism, tortured one another with red-hot horseshoes, and had their females in common. This was what came of rebelling against the laws of nature, Frederick and Pilkington said.

However, these stories were never fully believed. Rumors of a wonderful farm, where the human beings had been turned out and the animals managed their own affairs, continued to circulate in vague and distorted forms, and throughout that year a wave of rebelliousness ran through the countryside. Bulls which had always been tractable suddenly turned savage, sheep broke down hedges and devoured the clover, cows kicked the pail over, hunters refused their fences and shot their riders on to the other side. Above all, the tune and even the words of *Beasts of England* were known everywhere. It had spread with astonishing speed. The human beings could not contain their rage when they heard this song, though they pretended to think it merely ridiculous. They could not understand, they said, how even animals could bring themselves to sing such contemptible rubbish. Any animal caught singing it was given a flogging on the spot. And yet the song was irrepressible. The blackbirds whistled it in the hedges, the pigeons cooed it in the elms, it got into the din of the smithies [2] and the tune of the church bells. And when the human beings listened to it, they secretly trembled, hearing in it a prophecy of their future doom.

Early in October, when the corn was cut and stacked and some of it was already threshed, a flight of pigeons came whirling through the air and alighted in the yard of Animal Farm in the wildest excitement. Jones and all his men, with half a dozen others from Foxwood and Pinchfield, had entered the five-barred gate and were coming up the cart-track that led to the farm. They were all carrying sticks, except Jones, who was marching ahead with a gun in his hand. Obviously they were going to attempt the recapture of the farm.

---

[2] *smithies:* blacksmiths' shops.

This had long been expected, and all preparations had been made. Snowball, who had studied an old book of Julius Caesar's campaigns which he had found in the farmhouse, was in charge of the defensive operations. He gave his orders quickly, and in a couple of minutes every animal was at his post.

As the human beings approached the farm buildings, Snowball launched his first attack. All the pigeons, to the number of thirty-five, flew to and fro over the men's heads and muted upon them from mid-air; and while the men were dealing with this, the geese, who had been hiding behind the hedge, rushed out and pecked viciously at the calves of their legs. However, this was only a light skirmishing maneuver, intended to create a little disorder, and the men easily drove the geese off with their sticks. Snowball now launched his second line of attack. Muriel, Benjamin, and all the sheep, with Snowball at the head of them, rushed forward and prodded and butted the men from every side, while Benjamin turned around and lashed at them with his small hoofs. But once again the men, with their sticks and their hobnailed boots, were too strong for them; and suddenly, at a squeal from Snowball, which was the signal for retreat, all the animals turned and fled through the gateway into the yard.

The men gave a shout of triumph. They saw, as they imagined, their enemies in flight, and they rushed after them in disorder. This was just what Snowball had intended. As soon as they were well inside the yard, the three horses, the three cows, and the rest of the pigs, who had been lying in ambush in the cowshed, suddenly emerged in their rear, cutting them off. Snowball now gave the signal for the charge. He himself dashed straight for Jones. Jones saw him coming, raised his gun and fired. The pellets scored bloody streaks along Snowball's back, and a sheep dropped dead. Without halting for an instant, Snowball flung his fifteen stone [3] against Jones's legs. Jones was hurled into a pile of dung and his gun flew out of his hands. But the most terrifying spectacle of all was Boxer, rearing up on his hind legs and striking out with his great iron-shod hoofs like a stallion. His very first blow took a stable-lad from Foxwood on the skull and stretched him lifeless in the mud. At the sight, several men dropped their sticks and tried to run. Panic overtook them, and the next moment all the animals together were

---

[3] *stone:* British measure of weight, equal to 14 pounds.

chasing them round and round the yard. They were gored, kicked, bitten, trampled on. There was not an animal on the farm that did not take vengeance on them after his own fashion. Even the cat suddenly leaped off a roof onto a cowman's shoulders and sank her claws in his neck, at which he yelled horribly. At a moment when the opening was clear, the men were glad enough to rush out of the yard and make a bolt for the main road. And so within five minutes of their invasion they were in ignominious retreat by the same way as they had come, with a flock of geese hissing after them and pecking at their calves all the way.

All the men were gone except one. Back in the yard Boxer was pawing with his hoof at the stable-lad who lay face down in the mud, trying to turn him over. The boy did not stir.

"He is dead," said Boxer sorrowfully. "I had no intention of doing that. I forgot that I was wearing iron shoes. Who will believe that I did not do this on purpose?"

"No sentimentality, comrade!" cried Snowball, from whose wounds the blood was still dripping. "War is war. The only good human being is a dead one."

"I have no wish to take life, not even human life," repeated Boxer, and his eyes were full of tears.

"Where is Mollie?" exclaimed somebody.

Mollie in fact was missing. For a moment there was great alarm; it was feared that the men might have harmed her in some way, or even carried her off with them. In the end, however, she was found hiding in her stall with her head buried among the hay in the manger. She had taken to flight as soon as the gun went off. And when the others came back from looking for her, it was to find that the stable-lad, who in fact was only stunned, had already recovered and made off.

The animals had now reassembled in the wildest excitement, each recounting his own exploits in the battle at the top of his voice. An impromptu celebration of the victory was held immediately. The flag was run up and *Beasts of England* was sung a number of times, then the sheep who had been killed was given a solemn funeral, a hawthorn bush being planted on her grave. At the grave-side Snowball made a little speech, emphasizing the need for all animals to be ready to die for Animal Farm if need be.

The animals decided unanimously to create a military decoration,

"Animal Hero, First Class," which was conferred there and then on Snowball and Boxer. It consisted of a brass medal (they were really some old horse brasses which had been found in the harness room), to be worn on Sundays and holidays. There was also "Animal Hero, Second Class," which was conferred posthumously on the dead sheep.

There was much discussion as to what the battle should be called. In the end, it was named the Battle of the Cowshed, since that was where the ambush had been sprung. Mr. Jones's gun had been found lying in the mud, and it was known that there was a supply of cartridges in the farmhouse. It was decided to set the gun up at the foot of the flagstaff, like a piece of artillery, and to fire it twice a year — once on October the twelfth, the anniversary of the Battle of the Cowshed, and once on Midsummer Day, the anniversary of the Rebellion.

Beginning of the end

CHAPTER 5

of Animalism

As winter drew on, Mollie became more and more troublesome. She was late for work every morning and excused herself by saying that she had overslept, and she complained of mysterious pains, although her appetite was excellent. On every kind of pretext she would run away from work and go to the drinking pool, where she would stand foolishly gazing at her own reflection in the water. But there were also rumors of something more serious. One day as Mollie strolled blithely into the yard, flirting her long tail and chewing at a stalk of hay, Clover took her aside.

"Mollie," she said, "I have something very serious to say to you. This morning I saw you looking over the hedge that divides Animal Farm from Foxwood. One of Mr. Pilkington's men was standing on the other side of the hedge. And — I was a long way away, but I am almost certain I saw this — he was talking to you and you were allowing him to stroke your nose. What does that mean, Mollie?"

"He didn't! I wasn't! It isn't true!" cried Mollie, beginning to prance about and paw the ground.

"Mollie! Look me in the face. Do you give me your word of honor that that man was not stroking your nose?"

"It isn't true!" repeated Mollie, but she could not look Clover in the face, and the next moment she took to her heels and galloped away into the field.

A thought struck Clover. Without saying anything to the others, she went to Mollie's stall and turned over the straw with her hoof. Hidden under the straw was a little pile of lump sugar and several bunches of ribbon of different colors.

Three days later Mollie disappeared. For some weeks nothing was known of her whereabouts, then the pigeons reported that they had seen her on the other side of Willingdon. She was between the shafts of a smart dogcart painted red and black, which was standing outside a public house. A fat red-faced man in check breeches and gaiters,[1] who looked like a publican,[2] was stroking her nose and feeding her with sugar. Her coat was newly clipped, and she wore a scarlet ribbon round her forelock. She appeared to be enjoying herself, so the pigeons said. None of the animals ever mentioned Mollie again.

In January there came bitterly hard weather. The earth was like iron, and nothing could be done in the fields. Many meetings were held in the big barn, and the pigs occupied themselves with planning out the work of the coming season. It had come to be accepted that the pigs, who were manifestly cleverer than the other animals, should decide all questions of farm policy, though their decisions had to be ratified by a majority vote. This arrangement would have worked well enough if it had not been for the disputes between Snowball and Napoleon. These two disagreed at every point where disagreement was possible. If one of them suggested sowing a bigger acreage with barley, the other was certain to demand a bigger acreage of oats, and if one of them said that such and such a field was just right for cabbages, the other would declare that it was useless for anything except roots. Each had his own following, and there were some violent debates. At the Meetings Snowball often won over the majority by his brilliant speeches, but Napoleon was better at canvassing support for himself in between times. He was especially successful with the sheep. Of late the sheep had taken to bleating "Four legs good, two legs bad" both in and out of season, and they often interrupted the Meeting with this. It was noticed

---

[1] *breeches and gaiters:* country trousers worn to the knee with leather or canvas covers to the foot.
[2] *publican:* a saloon-keeper.

that they were especially liable to break into "Four legs good, two legs bad" at crucial moments in Snowball's speeches. Snowball had made a close study of some back numbers of the *Farmer and Stock-breeder* which he had found in the farmhouse, and was full of plans for innovations and improvements. He talked learnedly about field-drains, silage, and basic slag, and had worked out a complicated scheme for all the animals to drop their dung directly in the fields, at a different spot every day, to save the labor of cartage. Napoleon produced no schemes of his own, but said quietly that Snowball's would come to nothing, and seemed to be biding his time. But of all their controversies, none was so bitter as the one that took place over the windmill.

In the long pasture, not far from the farm buildings, there was a small knoll which was the highest point on the farm. After survey-ing the ground, Snowball declared that this was just the place for a windmill, which could be made to operate a dynamo and supply the farm with electric power. This would light the stalls and warm them in winter, and would also run a circular saw, a chaff-cutter, a mangel-slicer, and an electric milking machine. The animals had never heard of anything of this kind before (for the farm was an old-fashioned one and had only the most primitive machinery), and they listened in astonishment while Snowball conjured up pictures of fantastic machines which would do their work for them while they grazed at their ease in the fields or improved their minds with reading and conversation.

Within a few weeks Snowball's plans for the windmill were fully worked out. The mechanical details came mostly from three books which had belonged to Mr. Jones — *One Thousand Useful Things to Do About the House*, *Every Man His Own Bricklayer*, and *Electricity for Beginners*. Snowball used as his study a shed which had once been used for incubators [3] and had a smooth wooden floor, suitable for drawing on. He was closeted there for hours at a time. With his books held open by a stone, and with a piece of chalk gripped between the knuckles of his trotter, he would move rapidly to and fro, drawing in line after line and uttering little whimpers of excitement. Gradually the plans grew into a complicated mass of cranks and cogwheels, covering more than half the floor, which the other animals found completely unintelligible but very impressive.

---

[3] *incubators:* apparatus kept warm to hatch eggs.

All of them came to look at Snowball's drawings at least once a day. Even the hens and ducks came, and were at pains not to tread on the chalk marks. Only Napoleon held aloof. He had declared himself against the windmill from the start. One day, however, he arrived unexpectedly to examine the plans. He walked heavily round the shed, looked closely at every detail of the plans and snuffed at them once or twice, then stood for a little while contemplating them out of the corner of his eye; then suddenly he lifted his leg, urinated over the plans, and walked out without uttering a word.

The whole farm was deeply divided on the subject of the windmill. Snowball did not deny that to build it would be a difficult business. Stone would have to be carried and built up into walls, then the sails [4] would have to be made and after that there would be need for dynamos and cables. (How these were to be procured, Snowball did not say.) But he maintained that it could all be done in a year. And thereafter, he declared, so much labor would be saved that the animals would only need to work three days a week. Napoleon, on the other hand, argued that the great need of the moment was to increase food production, and that if they wasted time on the windmill they would all starve to death. The animals formed themselves into two factions under the slogan, "Vote for Snowball and the three-day week" and "Vote for Napoleon and the full manger." Benjamin was the only animal who did not side with either faction. He refused to believe either that food would become more plentiful or that the windmill would save work. Windmill or no windmill, he said, life would go on as it had always gone on — that is, badly.

Apart from the disputes over the windmill, there was the question of the defense of the farm. It was fully realized that though the human beings had been defeated in the Battle of the Cowshed they might make another and more determined attempt to recapture the farm and reinstate Mr. Jones. They had all the more reason for doing so because the news of their defeat had spread across the countryside and made the animals on the neighboring farms more restive than ever. As usual, Snowball and Napoleon were in disagreement. According to Napoleon, what the animals must do was to procure firearms and train themselves in the use of them. According to Snowball, they must send out more and more pigeons

---

[4] *sails*: the broad part of the arm of a windmill.

and stir up rebellion among the animals on the other farms. The one argued that if they could not defend themselves they were bound to be conquered, the other argued that if rebellions happened everywhere they would have no need to defend themselves. The animals listened first to Napoleon, then to Snowball, and could not make up their minds which was right; indeed, they always found themselves in agreement with the one who was speaking at the moment.

/ At last the day came when Snowball's plans were completed. At the Meeting on the following Sunday the question of whether or not to begin work on the windmill was to be put to the vote. When the animals had assembled in the big barn, Snowball stood up and, though occasionally interrupted by bleating from the sheep, set forth his reasons for advocating the building of the windmill. Then Napoleon stood up to reply. He said very quietly that the windmill was nonsense and that he advised nobody to vote for it, and promptly sat down again; he had spoken for barely thirty seconds, and seemed almost indifferent as to the effect he produced. At this Snowball sprang to his feet, and shouting down the sheep, who had begun bleating again, broke into a passionate appeal in favor of the windmill. Until now the animals had been about equally divided in their sympathies, but in a moment Snowball's eloquence had carried them away. In glowing sentences he painted a picture of Animal Farm as it might be when sordid labor was lifted from the animals' backs. His imagination had now run far beyond chaff-cutters and turnip-slicers. Electricity, he said, could operate threshing machines, plows, harrows, rollers, and reapers and binders, besides supplying every stall with its own electric light, hot and cold water, and an electric heater. By the time he had finished speaking, there was no doubt as to which way the vote would go. But just at this moment Napoleon stood up and, casting a peculiar sidelong look at Snowball, uttered a high-pitched whimper of a kind no one had ever heard him utter before.

At this there was a terrible baying sound outside, and nine enormous dogs wearing brass-studded collars came bounding into the barn. They dashed straight for Snowball, who only sprang from his place just in time to escape their snapping jaws. In a moment he was out of the door and they were after him. Too amazed and frightened to speak, all the animals crowded through the door to watch the chase. Snowball was racing across the long pasture that led to the road. He was running as only a pig can run, but the dogs were close on his heels. Suddenly he slipped and it seemed certain that they had him. Then he was up again, running faster than ever, then the dogs were gaining on him again. One of them all but closed his jaws on Snowball's tail, but Snowball whisked it free just in time. Then he put on an extra spurt and, with a few inches to spare, slipped through a hole in the hedge and was seen no more.

Silent and terrified, the animals crept back into the barn. In a moment the dogs came bounding back. At first no one had been able to imagine where these creatures came from, but the problem was soon solved: they were the puppies whom Napoleon had taken away from their mothers and reared privately. Though not yet full-grown, they were huge dogs, and as fierce-looking as wolves. They kept close to Napoleon. It was noticed that they wagged their tails to him in the same way as the other dogs had been used to do to Mr. Jones.

Napoleon, with the dogs following him, now mounted on to the raised portion of the floor where Major had previously stood to deliver his speech. He announced that from now on the Sunday-morning Meetings would come to an end. They were unnecessary, he said, and wasted time. In future all questions relating to the working of the farm would be settled by a special committee of pigs, presided over by himself. These would meet in private and afterward communicate their decisions to the others. The animals would still assemble on Sunday mornings to salute the flag, sing *Beasts of England*, and receive their orders for the week; but there would be no more debates.

In spite of the shock that Snowball's expulsion had given them, the animals were dismayed by this announcement. Several of them would have protested if they could have found the right arguments. Even Boxer was vaguely troubled. He set his ears back, shook his forelock several times, and tried hard to marshal his thoughts; but in the end he could not think of anything to say. Some of the pigs themselves, however, were more articulate. Four young porkers in the front row uttered shrill squeals of disapproval, and all four of them sprang to their feet and began speaking at once. But suddenly the dogs sitting round Napoleon let out deep, menacing growls, and the pigs fell silent and sat down again. Then the sheep broke out into a tremendous bleating of "Four legs good, two legs bad!" which went on for nearly a quarter of an hour and put an end to any chance of discussion.

Afterward Squealer was sent round the farm to explain the new arrangement to the others.

"Comrades," he said, "I trust that every animal here appreciates the sacrifice that Comrade Napoleon has made in taking this extra labor upon himself. Do not imagine, comrades, that leadership is a pleasure! On the contrary, it is a deep and heavy responsibility. No one believes more firmly than Comrade Napoleon that all animals are equal. He would be only too happy to let you make your decisions for yourselves. But sometimes you might make the wrong decisions, comrades, and then where should we be? Suppose you had decided to follow Snowball, with his moonshine of windmills — Snowball, who, as we now know, was no better than a criminal?"

"He fought bravely at the Battle of the Cowshed," said somebody.

"Bravery is not enough," said Squealer. "Loyalty and obedience are more important. And as to the Battle of the Cowshed, I believe the time will come when we shall find that Snowball's part in it was much exaggerated. Discipline, comrades, iron discipline! That is the watchword for today. One false step, and our enemies would be upon us. Surely, comrades, you do not want Jones back?"

Once again this argument was unanswerable. Certainly the animals did not want Jones back; if the holding of debates on Sunday mornings was liable to bring him back, then the debates must stop. Boxer, who had now had time to think things over, voiced the general feeling by saying: "If Comrade Napoleon says it, it must be right." And from then on he adopted the maxim, "Napoleon is always right," in addition to his private motto of "I will work harder."

By this time the weather had broken and the spring plowing had begun. The shed where Snowball had drawn his plans of the windmill had been shut up, and it was assumed that the plans had been rubbed off the floor. Every Sunday morning at ten o'clock the animals assembled in the big barn to receive their orders for the week. The skull of old Major, now clean of flesh, had been disinterred from the orchard and set upon a stump at the foot of the flagstaff, beside the gun. After the hoisting of the flag, the animals were required to file past the skull in a reverent manner before entering the barn. Nowadays they did not sit all together as they had done in the past. Napoleon, with Squealer and another pig named Minimus, who had a remarkable gift for composing songs and poems, sat on the front of the raised platform, with the nine young dogs forming a semicircle around them and the other pigs sitting behind. The rest of the animals sat facing them in the main body of the barn. Napoleon read out the orders for the week in a gruff soldierly style, and after a single singing of *Beasts of England,* all the animals dispersed.

On the third Sunday after Snowball's expulsion, the animals were somewhat surprised to hear Napoleon announce that the windmill was to be built after all. He did not give any reason for having changed his mind, but merely warned the animals that this extra task would mean very hard work; it might even be necessary to reduce their rations. The plans, however, had all been prepared, down to the last detail. A special committee of pigs had been at work upon them for the past three weeks. The building of the windmill, with various other improvements, was expected to take two years.

That evening Squealer explained privately to the other animals that Napoleon had never in reality been opposed to the windmill. On the contrary, it was he who had advocated it in the beginning, and the plan which Snowball had drawn on the floor of the incubator shed had actually been stolen from among Napoleon's papers. The windmill was, in fact, Napoleon's own creation. Why, then, asked somebody, had he spoken so strongly against it? Here Squealer looked very sly. That, he said, was Comrade Napoleon's cunning. He had *seemed* to oppose the windmill, simply as a maneuver to get rid of Snowball, who was a dangerous character and a bad influence. Now that Snowball was out of the way, the plan could go forward without his interference. This, said Squealer, was something called tactics. He repeated a number of times, "Tactics, comrades, tactics!" skipping round and whisking his tail with a merry laugh. The animals were not certain what the word meant, but Squealer spoke so persuasively, and the three dogs who happened to be with him growled so threateningly, that they accepted his explanation without further questions.

A new set of Rules
CHAPTER 6

All that year the animals worked like slaves. But they were happy in their work; they grudged no effort or sacrifice, well aware that everything that they did was for the benefit of themselves and those of their kind who would come after them, and not for a pack of idle, thieving human beings.

Throughout the spring and summer they worked a sixty-hour week, and in August Napoleon announced that there would be work on Sunday afternoons as well. This work was strictly voluntary, but any animal who absented himself from it would have his rations reduced by half. Even so, it was found necessary to leave certain tasks undone. The harvest was a little less successful than in the previous year, and two fields which should have been sown with roots in the early summer were not sown because the plowing had not been completed early enough. It was possible to foresee that the coming winter would be a hard one.

The windmill presented unexpected difficulties. There was a good quarry [1] of limestone on the farm, and plenty of sand and cement had been found in one of the outhouses, so that all the materials for building were at hand. But the problem the animals could not at first solve was how to break up the stone into pieces of suitable size. There seemed no way of doing this except with picks and crowbars, which no animal could use, because no animal could stand on his hind legs. Only after weeks of vain effort did the right idea occur to somebody — namely, to utilize the force of gravity. Huge boulders, far too big to be used as they were, were lying all over the bed of the quarry. The animals lashed ropes round these, and then all together, cows, horses, sheep, any animal that could lay hold of the rope — even the pigs sometimes joined in at critical moments — they dragged them with desperate slowness up the slope to the top of the quarry, where they were toppled over the edge, to shatter to pieces below. Transporting the stone when it was once broken was comparatively simple. The horses carried it off in cartloads, the sheep dragged single blocks, even Muriel and Benjamin yoked themselves into an old governess cart and did their share. By late sum-

---

[1] *quarry*: an excavation from which stone is taken.

mer a sufficient store of stone had accumulated, and then the building began, under the superintendence of the pigs.

But it was a slow, laborious process. Frequently it took a whole day of exhausting effort to drag a single boulder to the top of the quarry, and sometimes when it was pushed over the edge it failed to break. Nothing could have been achieved without Boxer, whose strength seemed equal to that of all the rest of the animals put together. When the boulder began to slip and the animals cried out in despair at finding themselves dragged down the hill, it was always Boxer who strained himself against the rope and brought the boulder to a stop. To see him toiling up the slope inch by inch, his breath coming fast, the tips of his hoofs clawing at the ground, and his great sides matted with sweat, filled everyone with admiration. Clover warned him sometimes to be careful not to overstrain himself, but Boxer would never listen to her. His two slogans, "I will work harder" and "Napoleon is always right," seemed to him a sufficient answer to all problems. He had made arrangements with the cockerel to call him three quarters of an hour earlier in the mornings instead of half an hour. And in his spare moments, of which there were not many nowadays, he would go alone to the quarry, collect a load of broken stone, and drag it down to the site of the windmill unassisted.

The animals were not badly off throughout that summer, in spite of the hardness of their work. If they had no more food than they had had in Jones's day, at least they did not have less. The advantage of only having to feed themselves, and not having to support five extravagant human beings as well, was so great that it would have taken a lot of failures to outweigh it. And in many ways the animal method of doing things was more efficient and saved labor. Such jobs as weeding, for instance, could be done with a thoroughness impossible to human beings. And again, since no animal now stole, it was unnecessary to fence off pasture from arable land, which saved a lot of labor on the upkeep of hedges and gates. Nevertheless, as the summer wore on, various unforeseen shortages began to make themselves felt. There was need of paraffin oil, nails, string, dog biscuits, and iron for the horses' shoes, none of which could be produced on the farm. Later there would also be need for seeds and artificial manures, besides various tools and, finally the machinery for the windmill. How these were to be procured, no one was able to imagine.

One Sunday morning, when the animals assembled to receive their orders, Napoleon announced that he had decided upon a new policy. From now onward Animal Farm would engage in trade with the neighboring farms: not, of course, for any commercial purpose, but simply in order to obtain certain materials which were urgently necessary. The needs of the windmill must override everything else, he said. He was therefore making arrangements to sell a stack of hay and part of the current year's wheat crop, and later on, if more money were needed, it would have to be made up by the sale of eggs, for which there was always a market in Willingdon. The hens, said Napoleon, should welcome this sacrifice as their own special contribution toward the building of the windmill.

Once again the animals were conscious of a vague uneasiness. Never to have any dealings with human beings, never to engage in trade, never to make use of money — had not these been among the earliest resolutions passed at that first triumphant Meeting after Jones was expelled? All the animals remembered passing such resolutions, or at least they thought that they remembered it. The four young pigs who had protested when Napoleon abolished the Meetings raised their voices timidly, but they were promptly silenced by a tremendous growling from the dogs. Then, as usual, the sheep broke into "Four legs good, two legs bad!" and the momentary awkwardness was smoothed over. Finally Napoleon raised his trotter for silence and announced that he had already made all the arrangements. There would be no need for any of the animals to come in contact with human beings, which would clearly be most undesirable. He intended to take the whole burden upon his own shoulders. A Mr. Whymper, a solicitor [2] living in Willingdon, had agreed to act as intermediary between Animal Farm and the outside world, and would visit the farm every Monday morning to receive his instructions. Napoleon ended his speech with his usual cry of "Long live Animal Farm!" and after the singing of *Beasts of England* the animals were dismissed.

Afterward Squealer made a round of the farm and set the animals' minds at rest. He assured them that the resolution against en-

[2] *solicitor*: a lawyer.

gaging in trade and using money had never been passed, or even suggested. It was pure imagination, probably traceable in the beginning to lies circulated by Snowball. A few animals still felt faintly doubtful, but Squealer asked them shrewdly, "Are you certain that this is not something that you have dreamed, comrades? Have you any record of such a resolution? Is it written down anywhere?" And since it was certainly true that nothing of the kind existed in writing, the animals were satisfied that they had been mistaken.

Every Monday Mr. Whymper visited the farm as had been arranged. He was a sly-looking little man with side whiskers, a solicitor in a very small way of business, but sharp enough to have realized earlier than anyone else that Animal Farm would need a broker [3] and that the commissions would be worth having. The animals watched his coming and going with a kind of dread, and avoided him as much as possible. Nevertheless, the sight of Napoleon, on all fours, delivering orders to Whymper, who stood on two legs, roused their pride and partly reconciled them to the new arrangement. Their relations with the human race were now not quite the same as they had been before. The human beings did not hate Animal Farm any less now that it was prospering; indeed, they hated it more than ever. Every human being held it as an article of faith that the farm would go bankrupt sooner or later, and, above all, that the windmill would be a failure. They would meet in the public houses and prove to one another by means of diagrams that the windmill was bound to fall down, or that if it did stand up, then that it would never work. And yet, against their will, they had developed a certain respect for the efficiency with which the animals were managing their own affairs. One symptom of this was that they had begun to call Animal Farm by its proper name and ceased to pretend that it was called the Manor Farm. They had also dropped their championship of Jones, who had given up hope of getting his farm back and gone to live in another part of the county. Except through Whymper, there was as yet no contact between Animal Farm and the outside world, but there were constant rumors that Napoleon was about to enter into a definite business agreement either with Mr. Pilkington of Foxwood or with Mr. Frederick of Pinchfield — but never, it was noticed, with both simultaneously.

It was about this time that the pigs suddenly moved into the

---

[3] *broker:* one who buys and sells for another and is paid by commissions.

farmhouse and took up their residence there. Again the animals seemed to remember that a resolution against this had been passed in the early days, and again Squealer was able to convince them that this was not the case. It was absolutely necessary, he said, that the pigs, who were the brains of the farm, should have a quiet place to work in. It was also more suited to the dignity of the Leader (for of late he had taken to speaking of Napoleon under the title of "Leader") to live in a house than in a mere sty. Nevertheless, some of the animals were disturbed when they heard that the pigs not only took their meals in the kitchen and used the drawing room as a recreation room, but also slept in the beds. Boxer passed it off as usual with "Napoleon is always right!", but Clover, who thought she remembered a definite ruling against beds, went to the end of the barn and tried to puzzle out the Seven Commandments which were inscribed there. Finding herself unable to read more than individual letters, she fetched Muriel.

"Muriel," she said, "read me the Fourth Commandment. Does it not say something about never sleeping in a bed?"

With some difficulty Muriel spelled it out.

"It says, 'No animal shall sleep in a bed *with sheets,'*" she announced finally.

Curiously enough, Clover had not remembered that the Fourth Commandment mentioned sheets, but as it was there on the wall, it must have done so. And Squealer, who happened to be passing at this moment, attended by two or three dogs, was able to put the whole matter in its proper perspective.

"You have heard then, comrades," he said, "that we pigs now sleep in the beds of the farmhouse? And why not? You did not suppose, surely, that there was ever a ruling against *beds?* A bed merely means a place to sleep in. A pile of straw in a stall is a bed, properly regarded. The rule was against *sheets,* which are a human invention. We have removed the sheets from the farmhouse beds, and sleep between blankets. And very comfortable beds they are too! But not more comfortable than we need, I can tell you, comrades, with all the brainwork we have to do nowadays. You would not rob us of our repose, would you, comrades? You would not have us too tired to carry out our duties? Surely none of you wishes to see Jones back?"

The animals reassured him on this point immediately, and no

more was said about the pigs sleeping in the farmhouse beds. And when, some days afterward, it was announced that from now on the pigs would get up an hour later in the mornings than the other animals, no complaint was made about that either.

By the autumn the animals were tired but happy. They had had a hard year, and after the sale of part of the hay and corn, the stores of food for the winter were none too plentiful, but the windmill compensated for everything. It was almost half built now. After the harvest there was a stretch of clear dry weather, and the animals toiled harder than ever, thinking it well worthwhile to plod to and fro all day with blocks of stone if by doing so they could raise the walls another foot. Boxer would even come out at nights and work for an hour or two on his own by the light of the harvest moon. In their spare moments the animals would walk round and round the half-finished mill, admiring the strength and perpendicularity of its walls and marveling that they should ever have been able to build anything so imposing. Only old Benjamin refused to grow enthusiastic about the windmill, though, as usual, he would utter nothing beyond the cryptic remark that donkeys live a long time.

November came, with raging southwest winds. Building had to stop because it was now too wet to mix the cement. Finally there came a night when the gale was so violent that the farm buildings rocked on their foundations and several tiles were blown off the roof of the barn. The hens woke up squawking with terror because they had all dreamed simultaneously of hearing a gun go off in the distance. In the morning the animals came out of their stalls to find that the flagstaff had been blown down and an elm tree at the foot of the orchard had been plucked up like a radish. They had just noticed this when a cry of despair broke from every animal's throat. A terrible sight had met their eyes. The windmill was in ruins.

With one accord they dashed down to the spot. Napoleon, who seldom moved out of a walk, raced ahead of them all. Yes, there it lay, the fruit of all their struggles, leveled to its foundations, the stones they had broken and carried so laboriously scattered all around. Unable at first to speak, they stood gazing mournfully at the litter of fallen stone. Napoleon paced to and fro in silence, occasionally snuffing at the ground. His tail had grown rigid and twitched sharply from side to side, a sign in him of intense mental activity. Suddenly he halted as though his mind were made up.

"Comrades," he said quietly, "do you know who is responsible for this? Do you know the enemy who has come in the night and over-thrown our windmill? SNOWBALL!" he suddenly roared in a voice of thunder. "Snowball has done this thing! In sheer malignity, think-ing to set back our plans and avenge himself for his ignominious expulsion, this traitor has crept here under cover of night and de-stroyed our work of nearly a year. Comrades, here and now I pro-nounce the death sentence upon Snowball. 'Animal Hero, Second Class,' and half a bushel of apples to any animal who brings him to justice. A full bushel to anyone who captures him alive!"

The animals were shocked beyond measure to learn that even Snowball could be guilty of such an action. There was a cry of indig-nation, and everyone began thinking out ways of catching Snowball if he should ever come back. Almost immediately the footprints of a pig were discovered in the grass at a little distance from the knoll. They could only be traced for a few yards, but appeared to lead to a hole in the hedge. Napoleon snuffed deeply at them and pro-nounced them to be Snowball's. He gave it as his opinion that Snowball had probably come from the direction of Foxwood Farm.

"No more delays, comrades!" cried Napoleon when the footprints had been examined. "There is work to be done. This very morning we begin rebuilding the windmill, and we will build all through the winter, rain or shine. We will teach this miserable traitor that he cannot undo our work so easily. Remember, comrades, there must be no alteration in our plans: they shall be carried out to the day. Forward, comrades! Long live the windmill! Long live Animal Farm!" *Exelution*

CHAPTER 7

It was a bitter winter. The stormy weather was followed by sleet and snow, and then by a hard frost which did not break till well into February. The animals carried on as best they could with the rebuilding of the windmill, well knowing that the outside world was watching them and that the envious human beings would rejoice and triumph if the mill were not finished on time.

Out of spite, the human beings pretended not to believe that it was Snowball who had destroyed the windmill: they said that it had fallen down because the walls were too thin. The animals knew that this was not the case. Still, it had been decided to build the walls three feet thick this time instead of eighteen inches as before, which meant collecting much larger quantities of stone. For a long time the quarry was full of snowdrifts and nothing could be done. Some progress was made in the dry frosty weather that followed, but it was cruel work, and the animals could not feel so hopeful about it as they had felt before. They were always cold, and usually hungry as well. But Boxer and Clover never lost heart. Squealer made excellent speeches on the joy of service and the dignity of labor, but the other animals found more inspiration in Boxer's strength and his never-failing cry of "I will work harder!"

In January food fell short. The corn ration was drastically reduced, and it was announced that an extra potato ration would be issued to make up for it. Then it was discovered that the greater part of the potato crop had been frosted in the clamps,[1] which had not been covered thickly enough. The potatoes had become soft and discolored, and only a few were edible. For days at a time the animals had nothing to eat but chaff and mangels. Starvation seemed to stare them in the face.

It was vitally necessary to conceal this fact from the outside world. Emboldened by the collapse of the windmill, the human beings were inventing fresh lies about Animal Farm. Once again it was being put about that all the animals were dying of famine and disease, and that they were continually fighting among themselves and had resorted to cannibalism and infanticide. Napoleon was well aware of the bad results that might follow if the real facts of the food situation were known, and he decided to make use of Mr. Whymper to spread a contrary impression. Hitherto the animals had had little or no contact with Whymper on his weekly visits; now, however, a few selected animals, mostly sheep, were instructed to remark casually in his hearing that rations had been increased. In addition, Napoleon ordered the almost empty bins in the store shed to be filled nearly to the brim with sand, which was then covered up with what remained of the grain and meal. On some suitable pretext Whymper was led through the store shed and allowed to catch a glimpse of the bins. He was deceived, and continued to report to the outside world that there was no food shortage on Animal Farm.

---

[1] *clamps:* produce covered with straw.

Nevertheless, toward the end of January it became obvious that it would be necessary to procure some more grain from somewhere. In these days Napoleon rarely appeared in public, but spent all his time in the farmhouse, which was guarded at each door by fierce-looking dogs. When he did emerge, it was in a ceremonial manner, with an escort of six dogs who closely surrounded him and growled if anyone came too near. Frequently he did not even appear on Sunday mornings, but issued his orders through one of the other pigs, usually Squealer.

One Sunday morning Squealer announced that the hens, who had just come in to lay again, must surrender their eggs. Napoleon had accepted, through Whymper, a contract for four hundred eggs a week. The price of these would pay for enough grain and meal to keep the farm going till summer came on and conditions were easier.

When the hens heard this, they raised a terrible outcry. They had been warned earlier that this sacrifice might be necessary, but had not believed that it would really happen. They were just getting their clutches [2] ready for the spring sitting, and they protested that to take the eggs away now was murder. For the first time since the expulsion of Jones, there was something resembling a rebellion. Led by three young black Minorca pullets, the hens made a determined effort to thwart Napoleon's wishes. Their method was to fly up to the rafters and there lay their eggs, which smashed to pieces on the floor. Napoleon acted swiftly and ruthlessly. He ordered the hens' rations to be stopped, and decreed that any animal giving so much as a grain of corn to a hen should be punished by death. The dogs saw to it that these orders were carried out. For five days the hens held out; then they capitulated and went back to their nesting boxes. Nine hens had died in the meantime. Their bodies were buried in the orchard, and it was given out that they had died of coccidiosis.[3] Whymper heard nothing of this affair, and the eggs were duly delivered, a grocer's van driving up to the farm once a week to take them away.

All this while no more had been seen of Snowball. He was rumored to be hiding on one of the neighboring farms, either Fox-

---

[2] *clutches:* numbers of eggs laid at one time.
[3] *coccidiosis* (kok·sid′ē·ō′sis): highly infectious disease of animals, especially birds.

wood or Pinchfield. Napoleon was by this time on slightly better terms with the other farmers than before. It happened that there was in the yard a pile of timber which had been stacked there ten years earlier when a beech spinney was cleared. It was well seasoned, and Whymper had advised Napoleon to sell it; both Mr. Pilkington and Mr. Frederick were anxious to buy it. Napoleon was hesitating between the two, unable to make up his mind. It was noticed that whenever he seemed on the point of coming to an agreement with Frederick, Snowball was declared to be in hiding at Foxwood, while, when he inclined toward Pilkington, Snowball was said to be at Pinchfield.

Suddenly, early in the spring, an alarming thing was discovered. Snowball was secretly frequenting the farm by night! The animals were so disturbed that they could hardly sleep in their stalls. Every night, it was said, he came creeping in under cover of darkness and performed all kinds of mischief. He stole the corn, he upset the milk pails, he broke the eggs, he trampled the seedbeds, he gnawed the bark off the fruit trees. Whenever anything went wrong it became usual to attribute it to Snowball. If a window was broken or a drain was blocked up, someone was certain to say that Snowball had come in the night and done it, and when the key of the store shed was lost, the whole farm was convinced that Snowball had thrown it down the well. Curiously enough, they went on believing this even after the mislaid key was found under a sack of meal. The cows declared unanimously that Snowball crept into their stalls and milked them in their sleep. The rats, which had been troublesome that winter, were also said to be in league with Snowball.

Napoleon decreed that there should be a full investigation into Snowball's activities. With his dogs in attendance, he set out and made a careful tour of inspection of the farm buildings, the other animals following at a respectful distance. At every few steps Napoleon stopped and snuffed the ground for traces of Snowball's footsteps, which, he said, he could detect by the smell. He snuffed in every corner, in the barn, in the cowshed, in the hen houses, in the vegetable garden, and found traces of Snowball almost everywhere. He would put his snout to the ground, give several deep sniffs, and exclaim in a terrible voice, "Snowball! He has been here! I can smell him distinctly!" and at the word "Snowball" all the dogs let out blood-curdling growls and showed their side teeth.

The animals were thoroughly frightened. It seemed to them as though Snowball were some kind of invisible influence pervading the air about them and menacing them with all kinds of dangers. In the evening Squealer called them together, and with an alarmed expression on his face told them that he had some serious news to report.

"Comrades!" cried Squealer, making little nervous skips, "a most terrible thing has been discovered. Snowball has sold himself to Frederick of Pinchfield Farm, who is even now plotting to attack us and take our farm away from us! Snowball is to act as his guide when the attack begins. But there is worse than that. We had thought that Snowball's rebellion was caused simply by his vanity and ambition. But we were wrong, comrades. Do you know what the real reason was? Snowball was in league with Jones from the very start! He was Jones's secret agent all the time. It has all been proved by documents which he left behind him and which we have only just discovered. To my mind this explains a great deal, comrades. Did we not see for ourselves how he attempted — fortunately without success — to get us defeated and destroyed at the Battle of the Cowshed?"

The animals were stupefied. This was a wickedness far outdoing Snowball's destruction of the windmill. But it was some minutes before they could fully take it in. They all remembered, or thought they remembered, how they had seen Snowball charging ahead of them at the Battle of the Cowshed, how he had rallied and encouraged them at every turn, and how he had not paused for an instant even when the pellets from Jones's gun had wounded his back. At first it was a little difficult to see how this fitted in with his being on Jones's side. Even Boxer, who seldom asked questions, was puzzled. He lay down, tucked his fore hoofs beneath him, shut his eyes, and with a hard effort managed to formulate his thoughts.

"I do not believe that," he said. "Snowball fought bravely at the Battle of the Cowshed. I saw him myself. Did we not give him 'Animal Hero, First Class,' immediately afterward?"

"That was our mistake, comrade. For we know now — it is all written down in the secret documents that we have found — that in reality he was trying to lure us to our doom."

"But he was wounded," said Boxer. "We all saw him running with blood."

"That was part of the arrangement!" cried Squealer. "Jones's shot only grazed him. I could show you this in his own writing, if you were able to read it. The plot was for Snowball, at the critical moment, to give the signal for flight and leave the field to the enemy. And he very nearly succeeded — I will even say, comrades, he *would* have succeeded if it had not been for our heroic Leader, Comrade Napoleon. Do you not remember how, just at the moment when Jones and his men had got inside the yard, Snowball suddenly turned and fled, and many animals followed him? And do you not remember, too, that it was just at that moment, when panic was spreading and all seemed lost, that Comrade Napoleon sprang forward with a cry of 'Death to Humanity!' and sank his teeth in Jones's leg? Surely you remember *that*, comrades?" exclaimed Squealer, frisking from side to side.

Now when Squealer described the scene so graphically, it seemed to the animals that they did remember it. At any rate, they remembered that at the critical moment of the battle Snowball had turned to flee. But Boxer was still a little uneasy.

"I do not believe that Snowball was a traitor at the beginning," he said finally. "What he has done since is different. But I believe that at the Battle of the Cowshed he was a good comrade."

"Our Leader, Comrade Napoleon," announced Squealer, speaking very slowly and firmly, "has stated categorically — categorically, comrade — that Snowball was Jones's agent from the very beginning — yes, and from long before the Rebellion was ever thought of."

"Ah, that is different!" said Boxer. "If Comrade Napoleon says it, it must be right."

"That is the true spirit, comrade!" cried Squealer, but it was noticed he cast a very ugly look at Boxer with his little twinkling eyes. He turned to go, then paused and added impressively: "I warn every animal on this farm to keep his eyes very wide open. For we have reason to think that some of Snowball's secret agents are lurking among us at this moment!"

Four days later, in the late afternoon, Napoleon ordered all the animals to assemble in the yard. When they were all gathered together, Napoleon emerged from the farmhouse, wearing both his medals (for he had recently awarded himself "Animal Hero, First Class," and "Animal Hero, Second Class"), with his nine huge dogs frisking around him and uttering growls that sent shivers down all the animals' spines. They all cowered silently in their places, seeming to know in advance that some terrible thing was about to happen.

Napoleon stood sternly surveying his audience; then he uttered a high-pitched whimper. Immediately the dogs bounded forward, seized four of the pigs by the ear and dragged them, squealing with pain and terror, to Napoleon's feet. The pigs' ears were bleeding, the dogs had tasted blood, and for a few moments they appeared to go quite mad. To the amazement of everybody, three of them flung themselves upon Boxer. Boxer saw them coming and put out his great hoof, caught a dog in mid-air, and pinned him to the ground. The dog shrieked for mercy and the other two fled with their tails between their legs. Boxer looked at Napoleon to know whether he should crush the dog to death or let it go. Napoleon appeared to change countenance, and sharply ordered Boxer to let the dog go, whereat Boxer lifted his hoof, and the dog slunk away, bruised and howling.

Presently the tumult died down. The four pigs waited, trembling, with guilt written on every line of their countenances. Napoleon now called upon them to confess their crimes. They were the same four pigs as had protested when Napoleon abolished the Sunday Meetings. Without any further prompting they confessed that they had been secretly in touch with Snowball ever since his expulsion, that they had collaborated with him in destroying the windmill, and that they had entered into an agreement with him to hand over Animal Farm to Mr. Frederick. They added that Snowball had privately admitted to them that he had been Jones's secret agent for years past. When they had finished their confession, the dogs promptly tore their throats out, and in a terrible voice Napoleon demanded whether any other animal had anything to confess.

The three hens who had been the ringleaders in the attempted rebellion over the eggs now came forward and stated that Snowball had appeared to them in a dream and incited them to disobey Napoleon's orders. They, too, were slaughtered. Then a goose came forward and confessed to having secreted six ears of corn during the last year's harvest and eaten them in the night. Then a sheep confessed to having urinated in the drinking pool — urged to do this, so she said, by Snowball — and two other sheep confessed to having murdered an old ram, an especially devoted follower of Napoleon, by chasing him round and round a bonfire when he was suffering from a cough. They were all slain on the spot. And so the tale of confessions and executions went on, until there was a pile of corpses lying before Napoleon's feet and the air was heavy with the smell of blood, which had been unknown there since the expulsion of Jones.

When it was all over, the remaining animals, except for the pigs and dogs, crept away in a body. They were shaken and miserable. They did not know which was more shocking — the treachery of the animals who had leagued themselves with Snowball, or the cruel retribution they had just witnessed. In the old days there had often been scenes of bloodshed equally terrible, but it seemed to all of them that it was far worse now that it was happening among themselves. Since Jones had left the farm, until today, no animal had killed another animal. Not even a rat had been killed. They had made their way on to the little knoll where the half-finished windmill stood, and with one accord they all lay down as though huddling together for warmth — Clover, Muriel, Benjamin, the cows, the sheep, and a whole flock of geese and hens — everyone, indeed, except the cat, who had suddenly disappeared just before Napoleon ordered the animals to assemble. For some time nobody spoke. Only Boxer remained on his feet. He fidgeted to and fro, swishing his long black tail against his sides and occasionally uttering a little whinny of surprise. Finally he said:

"I do not understand it. I would not have believed that such things could happen on our farm. It must be due to some fault in ourselves. The solution, as I see it, is to work harder. From now onward I shall get up a full hour earlier in the mornings."

And he moved off at his lumbering trot and made for the quarry. Having got there, he collected two successive loads of stone and dragged them down to the windmill before retiring for the night.

The animals huddled about Clover, not speaking. The knoll where they were lying gave them a wide prospect across the countryside. Most of Animal Farm was within their view — the long pasture stretching down to the main road, the hayfield, the spinney, the drinking pool, the plowed fields where the young wheat was thick and green, and the red roofs of the farm buildings with the smoke curling from the chimneys. It was a clear spring evening. The grass and the bursting hedges were gilded by the level rays of the sun.

Never had the farm — and with a kind of surprise they remembered that it was their own farm, every inch of it their own property — appeared to the animals so desirable a place. As Clover looked down the hillside her eyes filled with tears. If she could have spoken her thoughts, it would have been to say that this was not what they had aimed at when they had set themselves years ago to work for the overthrow of the human race. These scenes of terror and slaughter were not what they had looked forward to on that night when old Major first stirred them to rebellion. If she herself had had any picture of the future, it had been of a society of animals set free from hunger and the whip, all equal, each working according to his capacity, the strong protecting the weak, as she had protected the lost brood of ducklings with her foreleg on the night of Major's speech. Instead — she did not know why — they had come to a time when no one dared speak his mind, when fierce, growling dogs roamed everywhere, and when you had to watch your comrades torn to pieces after confessing to shocking crimes. There was no thought of rebellion or disobedience in her mind. She knew that, even as things were, they were far better off than they had been in the days of Jones, and that before all else it was needful to prevent the return of the human beings. Whatever happened she would remain faithful, work hard, carry out the orders that were given to her, and accept the leadership of Napoleon. But still, it was not for this that she and all the other animals had hoped and toiled. It was not for this that they had built the windmill and faced the bullets of Jones's gun. Such were her thoughts, though she lacked the words to express them.

At last, feeling this to be in some way a substitute for the words she was unable to find, she began to sing *Beasts of England*. The other animals sitting around her took it up, and they sang it three times over — very tunefully, but slowly and mournfully, in a way they had never sung it before.

They had just finished singing it for the third time when Squealer, attended by two dogs, approached them with the air of having something important to say. He announced that, by a special decree of Comrade Napoleon, *Beasts of England* had been abolished. From now onward it was forbidden to sing it.

The animals were taken aback.

"Why?" cried Muriel.

"It's no longer needed, comrade," said Squealer stiffly. *"Beasts of England* was the song of the Rebellion. But the Rebellion is now completed. The execution of the traitors this afternoon was the final act. The enemy both external and internal has been defeated. In *Beasts of England* we expressed our longing for a better society in days to come. But that society has now been established. Clearly this song has no longer any purpose."

Frightened though they were, some of the animals might possibly have protested, but at this moment the sheep set up their usual bleating of "Four legs good, two legs bad," which went on for several minutes and put an end to the discussion.

So *Beasts of England* was heard no more. In its place Minimus, the poet, had composed another song which began:

> Animal Farm, Animal Farm,
> Never through me shalt thou come to harm!

and this was sung every Sunday morning after the hoisting of the flag. But somehow neither the words nor the tune ever seemed to the animals to come up to *Beasts of England*.

Commandments fall

CHAPTER 8

A few days later, when the terror caused by the executions had died down, some of the animals remembered — or thought they remembered — that the Sixth Commandment decreed "No animal shall kill any other animal." And though no one cared to mention it in the hearing of the pigs or the dogs, it was felt that the killings which had taken place did not square with this. Clover asked Benjamin to read her the Sixth Commandment, and when Benjamin, as usual, said that he refused to meddle in such matters, she fetched Muriel. Muriel read the Commandment for her. It ran: "No animal shall kill any other animal *without cause*." Somehow or other, the last two words had slipped out of the animals' memory. But they saw now that the Commandment had not been violated, for clearly there was good reason for killing the traitors who had leagued themselves with Snowball.

Throughout the year the animals worked even harder than they had worked in the previous year. To rebuild the windmill, with walls twice as thick as before, and to finish it by the appointed date, together with the regular work of the farm, was a tremendous labor. There were times when it seemed to the animals that they worked longer hours and fed no better than they had done in Jones's day. On Sunday mornings Squealer, holding down a long strip of paper with his trotter, would read out to them lists of figures proving that the production of every class of foodstuff had increased by two hundred percent, three hundred percent, or five hundred percent, as the case might be. The animals saw no reason to disbelieve him, especially as they could no longer remember very clearly what conditions had been like before the Rebellion. All the same, there were days when they felt that they would sooner have had less figures and more food.

All orders were now issued through Squealer or one of the other pigs. Napoleon himself was not seen in public as often as once in a fortnight. When he did appear, he was attended not only by his retinue of dogs but by a black cockerel who marched in front of him and acted as a kind of trumpeter, letting out a loud "cock-a-doodle-doo" before Napoleon spoke. Even in the farmhouse, it was said, Napoleon inhabited separate apartments from the others. He took his meals alone, with two dogs to wait upon him, and always ate from the Crown Derby dinner service which had been in the glass cupboard in the drawing-room. It was also announced that the gun would be fired every year on Napoleon's birthday, as well as on the other two anniversaries.

Napoleon was now never spoken of simply as "Napoleon." He was always referred to in formal style as "our Leader, Comrade Napoleon," and the pigs liked to invent for him such titles as Father of All Animals, Terror of Mankind, Protector of the Sheepfold, Ducklings' Friend, and the like. In his speeches, Squealer would talk with the tears rolling down his cheeks of Napoleon's wisdom, the goodness of his heart, and the deep love he bore to all animals everywhere, even and especially the unhappy animals who still lived in ignorance and slavery on other farms. It had become usual to give Napoleon the credit for every successful achievement and every stroke of good fortune. You would often hear one hen remark to another, "Under the guidance of our Leader, Comrade Napoleon, I have laid five eggs in six days"; or two cows, enjoying a drink at the pool, would exclaim, "Thanks to the leadership of Comrade

Napoleon, how excellent this water tastes!" The general feeling on the farm was well expressed in a poem entitled "Comrade Napoleon," which was composed by Minimus and which ran as follows:

> Friend of fatherless!
> Fountain of happiness!
> Lord of the swill bucket! Oh, how my soul is on
> Fire when I gaze at thy
> Calm and commanding eye,
> Like the sun in the sky,
> Comrade Napoleon!
>
> Thou are the giver of
> All that thy creatures love,
> Full belly twice a day, clean straw to roll upon;
> Every beast great or small
> Sleeps at peace in his stall,
> Thou watchest over all,
> Comrade Napoleon!
>
> Had I a sucking pig,
> Ere he had grown as big
> Even as a pint bottle or as a rolling pin,
> He should have learned to be
> Faithful and true to thee,
> Yes, his first squeak should be
> "Comrade Napoleon!"

Napoleon approved of this poem and caused it to be inscribed on the wall of the big barn, at the opposite end from the Seven Commandments. It was surmounted by a portrait of Napoleon, in profile, executed by Squealer in white paint.

Meanwhile, through the agency of Whymper, Napoleon was engaged in complicated negotiations with Frederick and Pilkington. The pile of timber was still unsold. Of the two, Frederick was the more anxious to get hold of it, but he would not offer a reasonable price. At the same time there were renewed rumors that Frederick and his men were plotting to attack Animal Farm and to destroy the windmill, the building of which had aroused furious jealousy in him. Snowball was known to be still skulking on Pinchfield Farm. In the middle of the summer the animals were alarmed to hear that three hens had come forward and confessed that, inspired by Snowball, they had entered into a plot to murder Napoleon. They were executed immediately, and fresh precautions for Napoleon's safety were taken. Four dogs guarded his bed at night, one at each corner, and a young pig named Pinkeye was given the task of tasting all his food before he ate it, lest it should be poisoned.

At about the same time it was given out that Napoleon had arranged to sell the pile of timber to Mr. Pilkington; he was also going to enter into a regular agreement for the exchange of certain products between Animal Farm and Foxwood. The relations between Napoleon and Pilkington, though they were only conducted through Whymper, were now almost friendly. The animals distrusted Pilkington, as a human being, but greatly preferred him to Frederick, whom they both feared and hated. As the summer wore on, and the windmill neared completion, the rumors of an impending treacherous attack grew stronger and stronger. Frederick, it was said, intended to bring against them twenty men all armed with guns, and he had already bribed the magistrates and police, so that if he could once get hold of the title deeds of Animal Farm they would ask no questions. Moreover, terrible stories were leaking out from Pinchfield about the cruelties that Frederick practiced upon his animals. He had flogged an old horse to death, he starved his cows, he had killed a dog by throwing it into the furnace, he amused himself in the evenings by making cocks fight with splinters of razor blade tied to their spurs. The animals' blood boiled with rage when they heard of these things being done to their comrades, and sometimes they clamored to be allowed to go out in a body and attack Pinchfield Farm, drive out the humans, and set the animals free. But Squealer counseled them to avoid rash actions and trust in Comrade Napoleon's strategy.

Nevertheless, feeling against Frederick continued to run high. One Sunday morning Napoleon appeared in the barn and explained that he had never at any time contemplated selling the pile of timber to Frederick; he considered it beneath his dignity, he said, to have dealings with scoundrels of that description. The pigeons who were still sent out to spread tidings of the Rebellion were forbidden to set foot anywhere on Foxwood, and were also ordered to drop their former slogan of "Death to Humanity" in favor of "Death to Frederick." In the late summer yet another of Snowball's machinations was laid bare. The wheat crop was full of weeds, and it was discovered that on one of his nocturnal visits Snowball had mixed weed seeds with the seed corn. A gander who had been privy to the plot had confessed his guilt to Squealer and immediately committed suicide by swallowing deadly nightshade berries. The animals now also learned that Snowball had never — as many of them had believed hitherto — received the order of "Animal Hero, First Class." This was merely a legend which had been spread sometime after the Battle of the Cowshed by Snowball himself. So far from being decorated, he had been censured for showing cowardice in the battle. Once again some of the animals heard this with a certain bewilderment, but Squealer was soon able to convince them that their memories had been at fault.

In the autumn, by a tremendous, exhausting effort — for the harvest had to be gathered at almost the same time — the windmill was finished. The machinery had still to be installed, and Whymper was negotiating the purchase of it, but the structure was completed. In the teeth of every difficulty, in spite of inexperience, of primitive implements, of bad luck and of Snowball's treachery, the work had been finished punctually to the very day! Tired out but proud, the animals walked round and round their masterpiece, which appeared even more beautiful in their eyes than when it had been built the first time. Moreover, the walls were twice as thick as before. Nothing short of explosives would lay them low this time! And when they thought of how they had labored, what discouragements they had overcome, and the enormous difference that would be made in their lives when the sails were turning and the dynamos running — when they thought of all this, their tiredness forsook them and they gamboled round and round the windmill, uttering cries of triumph. Napoleon himself, attended by his dogs and his cockerel, came down to inspect the completed work; he personally congratulated the animals on their achievement, and announced that the mill would be named Napoleon Mill.

Two days later the animals were called together for a special meeting in the barn. They were struck dumb with surprise when Napoleon announced that he had sold the pile of timber to Frederick. Tomorrow Frederick's wagons would arrive and begin carting it away. Throughout the whole period of his seeming friendship with Pilkington, Napoleon had really been in secret agreement with Frederick.

All relations with Foxwood had been broken off; insulting messages had been sent to Pilkington. The pigeons had been told to avoid Pinchfield Farm and to alter their slogan from "Death to Frederick" to "Death to Pilkington." At the same time Napoleon assured the animals that the stories of an impending attack on Animal Farm were completely untrue, and that the tales about Frederick's cruelty to his own animals had been greatly exaggerated. All these rumors had probably originated with Snowball and his agents. It now appeared that Snowball was not, after all, hiding on Pinchfield Farm, and in fact had never been there in his life: he was living — in considerable luxury, so it was said — at Foxwood, and had in reality been a pensioner [1] of Pilkington for years past.

The pigs were in ecstasies over Napoleon's cunning. By seeming to be friendly with Pilkington he had forced Frederick to raise his price by twelve pounds.[2] But the superior quality of Napoleon's mind, said Squealer, was shown in the fact that he trusted nobody, not even Frederick. Frederick had wanted to pay for the timber with something called a check, which, it seemed, was a piece of paper with a promise to pay written upon it. But Napoleon was too clever for him. He had demanded payment in real five-pound notes, which were to be handed over before the timber was removed. Already Frederick had paid up; and the sum he had paid was just enough to buy the machinery for the windmill.

Meanwhile the timber was being carted away at high speed. When it was all gone, another special meeting was held in the barn for the animals to inspect Frederick's banknotes. Smiling beatifically, and wearing both his decorations, Napoleon reposed on a bed of straw on the platform, with the money at his side, neatly piled on a china dish from the farmhouse kitchen. The animals filed slowly past, and each gazed his fill. And Boxer put out his nose to sniff at the banknotes, and the flimsy white things stirred and rustled in his breath.

Three days later there was a terrible hullabaloo. Whymper, his face deadly pale, came racing up the path on his bicycle, flung it down in the yard and rushed straight into the farmhouse. The next moment a choking roar of rage sounded from Napoleon's apartments. The news of what had happened sped around the farm like wildfire. The banknotes were forgeries! Frederick had got the timber for nothing!

---

[1] *pensioner:* one who depends on the bounty of another.
[2] *pounds:* British unit of currency.

Napoleon called the animals together immediately and in a terrible voice pronounced the death sentence upon Frederick. When captured, he said, Frederick should be boiled alive. At the same time he warned them that after this treacherous deed the worst was to be expected. Frederick and his men might make their long-expected attack at any moment. Sentinels were placed at all the approaches to the farm. In addition, four pigeons were sent to Foxwood with a conciliatory [3] message, which it was hoped might re-establish good relations with Pilkington.

The very next morning the attack came. The animals were at breakfast when the lookouts came racing in with the news that Frederick and his followers had already come through the five-barred gate. Boldly enough the animals sallied forth to meet them, but this time they did not have the easy victory that they had had in the Battle of the Cowshed. There were fifteen men, with half a dozen guns between them, and they opened fire as soon as they got within fifty yards. The animals could not face the terrible explosions and the stinging pellets, and in spite of the efforts of Napoleon and Boxer to rally them, they were soon driven back. A number of them were already wounded. They took refuge in the farm buildings and peeped cautiously out from chinks and knotholes. The whole of the big pasture, including the windmill, was in the hands of the enemy. For the moment even Napoleon seemed at a loss. He paced up and down without a word, his tail rigid and twitching. Wistful glances were sent in the direction of Foxwood. If Pilkington and his men would help them, the day might yet be won. But at this moment the four pigeons, who had been sent out on the day before, returned, one of them bearing a scrap of paper from Pilkington. On it was penciled the words: "Serves you right."

Meanwhile Frederick and his men had halted about the windmill. The animals watched them, and a murmur of dismay went around. Two of the men had produced a crowbar and a sledge hammer. They were going to knock the windmill down.

"Impossible!" cried Napoleon. "We have built the walls far too thick for that. They could not knock it down in a week. Courage, comrades!"

But Benjamin was watching the movements of the men intently. The two with the hammer and the crowbar were drilling a hole near

---

[3] *conciliatory* (kən·sil′ē·ə·tôr′ē) : friendly, offering favorable terms.

the base of the windmill. Slowly, and with an air almost of amuse-ment, Benjamin nodded his long muzzle.

"I thought so," he said. "Do you not see what they are doing? In another moment they are going to pack blasting powder into that hole."

Terrified, the animals waited. It was impossible now to venture out of the shelter of the buildings. After a few minutes the men were seen to be running in all directions. Then there was a deafen-ing roar. The pigeons swirled into the air, and all the animals, except Napoleon, flung themselves flat on their bellies and hid their faces. When they got up again, a huge cloud of black smoke was hanging where the windmill had been. Slowly the breeze drifted it away. The windmill had ceased to exist!

At this sight the animals' courage returned to them. The fear and despair they had felt a moment earlier were drowned in their rage against this vile, contemptible act. A mighty cry for vengeance went up, and without waiting for further orders they charged forth in a body and made straight for the enemy. This time they did not heed the cruel pellets that swept over them like hail. It was a savage, bitter battle. The men fired again and again, and, when the animals got to close quarters, lashed out with their sticks and their heavy boots. A cow, three sheep, and two geese were killed, and nearly everyone was wounded. Even Napoleon, who was directing opera-tions from the rear, had the tip of his tail chipped by a pellet. But the men did not go unscathed either. Three of them had their heads broken by blows from Boxer's hoofs, another was gored in the belly by a cow's horn, another had his trousers nearly torn off by Jes-sie and Bluebell. And when the nine dogs of Napoleon's own bodyguard, whom he had instructed to make a detour under cover of the hedge, suddenly appeared on the men's flank, baying fero-ciously, panic overtook them. They saw that they were in danger of being surrounded. Frederick shouted to his men to get out while the going was good, and the next moment the cowardly enemy was running for dear life. The animals chased them right down to the bottom of the field, and got in some last kicks at them as they forced their way through the thorn hedge.

They had won, but they were weary and bleeding. Slowly they began to limp back toward the farm. The sight of their dead com-rades stretched upon the grass moved some of them to tears. And for a little while they halted in sorrowful silence at the place where the windmill had once stood. Yes, it was gone; almost the last trace of their labor was gone! Even the foundations were partially destroyed. And in rebuilding it they could not this time, as before, make use of the fallen stones. This time the stones had vanished too. The force of the explosion had flung them to distances of hundreds of yards. It was as though the windmill had never been.

As they approached the farm Squealer, who had unaccountably been absent during the fighting, came skipping toward them, whisking his tail and beaming with satisfaction. And the animals heard, from the direction of the farm buildings, the solemn booming of a gun.

"What is that gun firing for?" said Boxer.

"To celebrate our victory!" cried Squealer.

"What victory?" said Boxer. His knees were bleeding, he had lost a shoe and split his hoof, and a dozen pellets had lodged themselves in his hind leg.

"What victory, comrade? Have we not driven the enemy off our soil — the sacred soil of Animal Farm?"

"But they have destroyed the windmill. And we had worked on it for two years!"

"What matter? We will build another windmill. We will build six windmills if we feel like it. You do not appreciate, comrade, the mighty thing that we have done. The enemy was in occupation of this very ground that we stand upon. And now — thanks to the leadership of Comrade Napoleon — we have won every inch of it back again!"

"Then we have won back what we had before," said Boxer.

"That is our victory," said Squealer.

They limped into the yard. The pellets under the skin of Boxer's leg smarted painfully. He saw ahead of him the heavy labor of rebuilding the windmill from the foundations, and already in imagination he braced himself for the task. But for the first time it occurred to him that he was eleven years old and that perhaps his great muscles were not quite what they had once been.

But when the animals saw the green flag flying, and heard the gun firing again — seven times it was fired in all — and heard the speech that Napoleon made, congratulating them on their conduct, it did seem to them after all that they had won a great victory. The ani-

mals slain in the battle were given a solemn funeral. Boxer and
Clover pulled the wagon which served as a hearse, and Napoleon
himself walked at the head of the procession. Two whole days were
given over to celebrations. There were songs, speeches, and more
firing of the gun, and a special gift of an apple was bestowed on
every animal, with two ounces of corn for each bird and three biscuits for each dog. It was announced that the battle would be called
the Battle of the Windmill, and that Napoleon had created a new
decoration, the Order of the Green Banner, which he had conferred upon himself. In the general rejoicings the unfortunate affair
of the banknotes was forgotten.

It was a few days later than this that the pigs came upon a case
of whisky in the cellars of the farmhouse. It had been overlooked at
the time when the house was first occupied. That night there came
from the farmhouse the sound of loud singing, in which, to everyone's surprise, the strains of *Beasts of England* were mixed up. At
about half-past nine Napoleon, wearing an old bowler hat of Mr.
Jones's, was distinctly seen to emerge from the back door, gallop
rapidly round the yard, and disappear indoors again. But in the
morning a deep silence hung over the farmhouse. Not a pig appeared to be stirring. It was nearly nine o'clock when Squealer made
his appearance, walking slowly and dejectedly, his eyes dull, his tail
hanging limply behind him, and with every appearance of being
seriously ill. He called the animals together and told them that he
had a terrible piece of news to impart. Comrade Napoleon was
dying!

A cry of lamentation went up. Straw was laid down outside the
doors of the farmhouse, and the animals walked on tiptoe. With
tears in their eyes they asked one another what they should do if
their Leader were taken away from them. A rumor went around that
Snowball had after all contrived to introduce poison into Napoleon's
food. At eleven o'clock Squealer came out to make another announcement. As his last act upon earth, Comrade Napoleon had
pronounced a solemn decree: the drinking of alcohol was to be
punished by death.

By the evening, however, Napoleon appeared to be somewhat better, and the following morning Squealer was able to tell them that
he was well on the way to recovery. By the evening of that day
Napoleon was back at work, and on the next day it was learned that

he had instructed Whymper to purchase in Willingdon some book-lets on brewing and distilling.[4] A week later Napoleon gave orders that the small paddock beyond the orchard, which it had previously been intended to set aside as a grazing ground for animals who were past work, was to be plowed up. It was given out that the pasture was exhausted and needed reseeding, but it soon became known that Napoleon intended to sow it with barley.

About this time there occurred a strange incident which hardly anyone was able to understand. One night at about twelve o'clock there was a loud crash in the yard, and the animals rushed out of their stalls. It was a moonlit night. At the foot of the end wall of the big barn, where the Seven Commandments were written, there lay a ladder broken in two pieces. Squealer, temporarily stunned, was sprawling beside it, and near at hand there lay a lantern, a paintbrush, and an overturned pot of white paint. The dogs imme-diately made a ring around Squealer, and escorted him back to the farmhouse as soon as he was able to walk. None of the animals could form any idea as to what this meant, except old Benjamin, who nodded his muzzle with a knowing air, and seemed to under-stand, but would say nothing.

But a few days later Muriel, reading over the Seven Command-ments to herself, noticed that there was yet another of them which the animals had remembered wrong. They had thought the Fifth Commandment was "No animal shall drink alcohol," but there were two words that they had forgotten. Actually the Command-ment read: "No animal shall drink alcohol *to excess*."

Boxer Betrayed

CHAPTER 9

Boxer's split hoof was a long time in healing. They had started the rebuilding of the windmill the day after the victory celebrations were ended. Boxer refused to take even a day off work, and made it a point of honor not to let it be seen that he was in pain. In the evenings he would admit privately to Clover that the hoof troubled him a great deal. Clover treated the hoof with poultices [1] of herbs which she prepared by chewing them, and both she and Benjamin

---

[4] *brewing and distilling*: processes in producing beer and liquor.

[1] *poultices*: a moist application to a wound.

urged Boxer to work less hard. "A horse's lungs do not last for ever," she said to him. But Boxer would not listen. He had, he said, only one real ambition left — to see the windmill well under way before he reached the age for retirement.

At the beginning, when the laws of Animal Farm were first formulated, the retiring age had been fixed for horses and pigs at twelve, for cows at fourteen, for dogs at nine, for sheep at seven, and for hens and geese at five. Liberal old-age pensions had been agreed upon. As yet no animal had actually retired on pension, but of late the subject had been discussed more and more. Now that the small field beyond the orchard had been set aside for barley, it was rumored that a corner of the large pasture was to be fenced off and turned into a grazing ground for superannuated [2] animals. For a horse, it was said, the pension would be five pounds of corn a day and, in winter, fifteen pounds of hay, with a carrot or possibly an apple on public holidays. Boxer's twelfth birthday was due in the late summer of the following year.

Meanwhile life was hard. The winter was as cold as the last one had been, and food was even shorter. Once again all rations were reduced, except those of the pigs and the dogs. A too rigid equality in rations, Squealer explained, would have been contrary to the principles of Animalism. In any case he had no difficulty in proving to the other animals that they were *not* in reality short of food, whatever the appearances might be. For the time being, certainly, it had been found necessary to make a readjustment of rations (Squealer always spoke of it as a "readjustment," never as a "reduction"), but in comparison with the days of Jones, the improvement was enormous. Reading out the figures in a shrill, rapid voice, he proved to them in detail that they had more oats, more hay, more turnips than they had had in Jones's day, that they worked shorter hours, that their drinking water was of better quality, that they lived longer, that a larger proportion of their young ones survived infancy, and that they had more straw in their stalls and suffered less from fleas. The animals believed every word of it. Truth to tell, Jones and all he stood for had almost faded out of their memories. They knew that life nowadays was harsh and bare, that they were often hungry and often cold, and that they were usually working when they were not asleep. But doubtless it had been worse in the old

---

[2] *superannuated*: too old to be useful.

days. They were glad to believe so. Besides, in those days they had been slaves and now they were free, and that made all the difference, as Squealer did not fail to point out.

There were many more mouths to feed now. In the autumn the four sows had all littered about simultaneously, producing thirty-one young pigs between them. The young pigs were piebald,[3] and as Napoleon was the only boar on the farm, it was possible to guess at their parentage. It was announced that later, when bricks and timber had been purchased, a schoolroom would be built in the farmhouse garden. For the time being, the young pigs were given their instruction by Napoleon himself in the farmhouse kitchen. They took their exercise in the garden, and were discouraged from playing with the other young animals. About this time, too, it was laid down as a rule that when a pig and any other animal met on the path, the other animal must stand aside and also that all pigs, of whatever degree, were to have the privilege of wearing green ribbons on their tails on Sundays.

The farm had had a fairly successful year, but was still short of money. There were the bricks, sand, and lime for the schoolroom to be purchased, and it would also be necessary to begin saving up again for the machinery for the windmill. Then there were lamp oil and candles for the house, sugar for Napoleon's own table (he forbade this to the other pigs, on the ground that it made them fat), and all the usual replacements such as tools, nails, string, coal, wire, scrap iron, and dog biscuits. A stump of hay and part of the potato crop were sold off, and the contract for eggs was increased to six hundred a week, so that that year the hens barely hatched enough chicks to keep their numbers at the same level. Rations, reduced in December, were reduced again in February, and lanterns in the stalls were forbidden to save oil. But the pigs seemed comfortable enough, and in fact were putting on weight if anything. One afternoon in late February a warm, rich, appetizing scent, such as the animals had never smelled before, wafted itself across the yard from the little brewhouse, which had been disused in Jones's time, and which stood beyond the kitchen. Someone said it was the smell of cooking barley. The animals sniffed the air hungrily and wondered whether a warm mash was being prepared for their supper. But no warm mash appeared, and on the following Sunday it was an-

---

[3] *piebald:* black-and-white spotted.

nounced that from now onward all barley would be reserved for the pigs. The field beyond the orchard had already been sown with barley. And the news soon leaked out that every pig was now receiving a ration of a pint of beer daily, with half a gallon for Napoleon himself, which was always served to him in the Crown Derby soup tureen.

But if there were hardships to be borne, they were partly offset by the fact that life nowadays had a greater dignity than it had had before. There were more songs, more speeches, more processions. Napoleon had commanded that once a week there should be held something called a Spontaneous Demonstration, the object of which was to celebrate the struggles and triumphs of Animal Farm. At the appointed time the animals would leave their work and march round the precincts of the farm in military formation, with the pigs leading, then the horses, then the cows, then the sheep, and then the poultry. The dogs flanked the procession and at the head of all marched Napoleon's black cockerel. Boxer and Clover always carried between them a green banner marked with the hoof and the horn and the caption, "Long live Comrade Napoleon!" Afterward there were recitations of poems composed in Napoleon's honor, and a speech by Squealer giving particulars of the latest increases in the production of foodstuffs, and on occasion a shot was fired from the gun. The sheep were the greatest devotees of the Spontaneous Demonstration, and if anyone complained (as a few animals sometimes did, when no pigs or dogs were near) that they wasted time and meant a lot of standing about in the cold, the sheep were sure to silence him with a tremendous bleating of "Four legs good, two legs bad!" But by and large the animals enjoyed these celebrations. They found it comforting to be reminded that, after all, they were truly their own masters and that the work they did was for their own benefit. So that, what with the songs, the processions, Squealer's lists of figures, the thunder of the gun, the crowing of the cockerel, and the fluttering of the flag, they were able to forget that their bellies were empty, at least part of the time.

In April, Animal Farm was proclaimed a Republic, and it became necessary to elect a President. There was only one candidate, Napoleon, who was elected unanimously. On the same day it was given out that fresh documents had been discovered which revealed further details about Snowball's complicity with Jones. It now ap-

peared that Snowball had not, as the animals had previously imagined, merely attempted to lose the Battle of the Cowshed by
means of a stratagem, but had been openly fighting on Jones's side.
In fact, it was he who had actually been the leader of the human
forces, and had charged into battle with the words "Long live Humanity!" on his lips. The wounds on Snowball's back, which a few
of the animals still remembered to have seen, had been inflicted by
Napoleon's teeth.

In the middle of the summer Moses the raven suddenly reappeared on the farm, after an absence of several years. He was quite
unchanged, still did no work, and talked in the same strain as ever
about Sugarcandy Mountain. He would perch on a stump, flap his
black wings, and talk by the hour to anyone who would listen. "Up
there, comrades," he would say solemnly, pointing to the sky with
his large beak — "up there, just on the other side of that dark cloud
that you can see — there it lies, Sugarcandy Mountain, that happy
country where we poor animals shall rest for ever from our labors!"
He even claimed to have been there on one of his higher flights and
to have seen the everlasting fields of clover and the linseed cake and
lump sugar growing on the hedges. Many of the animals believed
him. Their lives now, they reasoned, were hungry and laborious; was
it not right and just that a better world should exist somewhere
else? A thing that was difficult to determine was the attitude of the
pigs toward Moses. They all declared contemptuously that his
stories about Sugarcandy Mountain were lies, and yet they allowed
him to remain on the farm, not working, with an allowance of a
gill [4] of beer a day.

After his hoof had healed up, Boxer worked harder than ever. Indeed, all the animals worked like slaves that year. Apart from the
regular work of the farm, and the rebuilding of the windmill, there
was the schoolhouse for the young pigs, which was started in March.
Sometimes the long hours on insufficient food were hard to bear, but
Boxer never faltered. In nothing that he said or did was there any
sign that his strength was not what it had been. It was only his
appearance that was a little altered; his hide was less shiny than it
had used to be, and his great haunches seemed to have shrunken.
The others said, "Boxer will pick up when the spring grass comes
on," but the spring came and Boxer grew no fatter. Sometimes on

---

[4] *gill:* quarter-pint.

the slope leading to the top of the quarry, when he braced his muscles against the weight of some vast boulder, it seemed that nothing kept him on his feet except the will to continue. At such times his lips were seen to form the words, "I will work harder"; he had no voice left. Once again Clover and Benjamin warned him to take care of his health, but Boxer paid no attention. His twelfth birthday was approaching. He did not care what happened so long as a good store of stone was accumulated before he went on pension.

Late one evening in the summer, a sudden rumor ran around the farm that something had happened to Boxer. He had gone out alone to drag a load of stone down to the windmill. And sure enough, the rumor was true. A few minutes later two pigeons came racing in with the news: "Boxer has fallen! He is lying on his side and can't get up!"

About half the animals on the farm rushed out to the knoll where the windmill stood. There lay Boxer, between the shafts of the cart, his neck stretched out, unable even to raise his head. His eyes were glazed, his sides matted with sweat. A thin stream of blood had trickled out of his mouth. Clover dropped to her knees at his side.

"Boxer!" she cried, "how are you?"

"It is my lung," said Boxer in a weak voice. "It does not matter. I think you will be able to finish the windmill without me. There is a pretty good store of stone accumulated. I had only another month to go in any case. To tell you the truth, I had been looking forward to my retirement. And perhaps, as Benjamin is growing old too, they will let him retire at the same time and be a companion to me."

"We must get help at once," said Clover. "Run, somebody, and tell Squealer what has happened."

All the other animals immediately raced back to the farmhouse to give Squealer the news. Only Clover remained, and Benjamin, who lay down at Boxer's side, and, without speaking, kept the flies off him with his long tail. After about a quarter of an hour Squealer appeared, full of sympathy and concern. He said that Comrade Napoleon had learned with the very deepest distress of this misfortune to one of the most loyal workers on the farm, and was already making arrangements to send Boxer to be treated in the hospital at Willingdon. The animals felt a little uneasy at this. Except for Mollie and Snowball, no other animal had ever left the farm, and they did not like to think of their sick comrade in the hands of human beings. However, Squealer easily convinced them that the veterinary surgeon in Willingdon could treat Boxer's case more satisfactorily than could be done on the farm. And about half an hour later, when Boxer had somewhat recovered, he was with difficulty got on to his feet, and managed to limp back to his stall, where Clover and Benjamin had prepared a good bed of straw for him.

For the next two days Boxer remained in his stall. The pigs had sent out a large bottle of pink medicine which they had found in the medicine chest in the bathroom, and Clover administered it to Boxer twice a day after meals. In the evenings she lay in his stall and talked to him, while Benjamin kept the flies off him. Boxer professed not to be sorry for what had happened. If he made a good recovery, he might expect to live another three years, and he looked forward to the peaceful days that he would spend in the corner of the big pasture. It would be the first time that he had had leisure to study and improve his mind. He intended, he said, to devote the rest of his life to learning the remaining twenty-two letters of the alphabet.

However, Benjamin and Clover could only be with Boxer after working hours, and it was in the middle of the day when the van came to take him away. The animals were all at work weeding turnips under the supervision of a pig, when they were astonished to see Benjamin come galloping from the direction of the farm buildings, braying at the top of his voice. It was the first time that they had ever seen Benjamin excited — indeed, it was the first time that anyone had ever seen him gallop. "Quick, quick!" he shouted. "Come at once! They're taking Boxer away!" Without waiting for orders from the pig, the animals broke off work and raced back to the farm buildings. Sure enough, there in the yard was a large closed van, drawn by two horses, with lettering on its side and a sly-looking man in a low-crowned bowler hat sitting on the driver's seat. And Boxer's stall was empty.

The animals crowded around the van. "Good-by, Boxer!" they chorused, "good-by!"

"Fools! Fools!" shouted Benjamin, prancing around them and stamping the earth with his small hoofs. "Fools! Do you not see what is written on the side of that van?"

That gave the animals pause, and there was a hush. Muriel began to spell out the words. But Benjamin pushed her aside and in the midst of a deadly silence he read:

" 'Alfred Simmonds, Horse Slaughterer and Glue Boiler, Willingdon. Dealer in Hides and Bone-Meal. Kennels Supplied.' Do you not understand what that means? They are taking Boxer to the knacker's!"

A cry of horror burst from all the animals. At this moment the man on the box whipped up his horses and the van moved out of the yard at a smart trot. All the animals followed, crying out at the tops of their voices. Clover forced her way to the front. The van began to gather speed. Clover tried to stir her stout limbs to a gallop, and achieved a canter. "Boxer!" she cried. "Boxer! Boxer! Boxer!" And just at this moment, as though he had heard the uproar outside, Boxer's face, with the white stripe down his nose, appeared at the small window at the back of the van.

"Boxer!" cried Clover in a terrible voice. "Boxer! Get out! Get out quickly! They're taking you to your death!"

All the animals took up the cry of "Get out, Boxer, get out!" But the van was already gathering speed and drawing away from them. It was uncertain whether Boxer had understood what Clover had said. But a moment later his face disappeared from the window, and there was the sound of a tremendous drumming of hoofs inside the van. He was trying to kick his way out. The time had been when a few kicks from Boxer's hoofs would have smashed the van to matchwood. But alas! his strength had left him, and in a few moments the sound of drumming hoofs grew fainter and died away. In desperation the animals began appealing to the two horses which drew the van to stop. "Comrades, comrades!" they shouted. "Don't take your own brother to his death!" But the stupid brutes, too ignorant to realize what was happening, merely set back their ears and quickened their pace. Boxer's face did not reappear at the window. Too late, someone thought of racing ahead and shutting the five-barred gate, but in another moment the van was through it and rapidly disappearing down the road. Boxer was never seen again.

Three days later it was announced that he had died in the hospital at Willingdon, in spite of receiving every attention a horse could have. Squealer came to announce the news to the others. He had, he said, been present during Boxer's last hours.

"It was the most affecting sight I have ever seen!" said Squealer, lifting his trotter and wiping away a tear. "I was at his bedside at the very last. And at the end, almost too weak to speak, he whispered in my ear that his sole sorrow was to have passed on before the windmill was finished. 'Forward, comrades!' he whispered. 'Forward in the name of the Rebellion. Long live Animal Farm! Long live Comrade Napoleon! Napoleon is always right.' Those were his very last words, comrades."

Here Squealer's demeanor suddenly changed. He fell silent for a moment, and his little eyes darted suspicious glances from side to side before he proceeded.

It had come to his knowledge, he said, that a foolish and wicked rumor had been circulated at the time of Boxer's removal. Some of the animals had noticed that the van which took Boxer away was marked "Horse Slaughterer," and had actually jumped to the conclusion that Boxer was being sent to the knacker's. It was almost unbelievable, said Squealer, that any animal could be so stupid. Surely, he cried indignantly, whisking his tail and skipping from side to side, surely they knew their beloved Leader, Comrade Napoleon, better than that? But the explanation was really very simple. The van had previously been the property of the knacker, and had been bought by the veterinary surgeon, who had not yet painted the old name out. That was how the mistake had arisen.

The animals were enormously relieved to hear this. And when Squealer went on to give further graphic details of Boxer's deathbed, the admirable care he had received, and the expensive medicines for which Napoleon had paid without a thought as to the cost, their last doubts disappeared, and the sorrow that they felt for their comrade's death was tempered by the thought that at least he had died happy.

Napoleon himself appeared at the meeting on the following Sunday morning and pronounced a short oration in Boxer's honor. It had not been possible, he said, to bring back their lamented comrade's remains for interment on the farm, but he had ordered a large wreath to be made from the laurels in the farmhouse garden and sent down to be placed on Boxer's grave. And in a few days' time the pigs intended to hold a memorial banquet in Boxer's honor. Napoleon ended his speech with a reminder of Boxer's two favorite maxims, "I will work harder" and "Comrade Napoleon is always right" — maxims, he said, which every animal would do well to adopt as his own.

On the day appointed for the banquet, a grocer's van drove up from Willingdon and delivered a large wooden crate at the farmhouse. That night there was the sound of uproarious singing, which was followed by what sounded like a violent quarrel and ended at about eleven o'clock with a tremendous crash of glass. No one stirred in the farmhouse before noon on the following day, and the word went around that from somewhere or other the pigs had acquired the money to buy themselves another case of whisky.

Return of Humanism

CHAPTER 10

Years passed. The seasons came and went, the short animal lives fled by. A time came when there was no one who remembered the olds days before the Rebellion, except Clover, Benjamin, Moses the raven, and a number of the pigs.

Muriel was dead; Bluebell, Jessie, and Pincher were dead. Jones too was dead — he had died in an inebriates' home [1] in another part of the country. Snowball was forgotten, Boxer was forgotten, except by the few who had known him. Clover was an old stout mare now, stiff in the joints and with a tendency to rheumy eyes. She was two years past the retiring age, but in fact no animal had ever actually retired. The talk of setting aside a corner of the pasture for superannuated animals had long since been dropped. Napoleon was now a mature boar of twenty-four stone. Squealer was so fat that he could with difficulty see out of his eyes. Only old Benjamin was much the same as ever, except for being a little grayer about the muzzle, and, since Boxer's death, more morose and taciturn [2] than ever.

There were many more creatures on the farm now, though the increase was not so great as had been expected in earlier years. Many animals had been born to whom the Rebellion was only a dim tradition, passed on by word of mouth, and others had been bought who had never heard mention of such a thing before their arrival. The farm possessed three horses now besides Clover. They were fine upstanding beasts, willing workers and good comrades, but very stupid.

---

[1] *inebriates' home:* institution for habitual alcoholics.
[2] *taciturn* (tas′ə·tûrn) : habitually silent.

None of them proved able to learn the alphabet beyond the letter B. They accepted everything that they were told about the Rebellion and the principles of Animalism, especially from Clover, for whom they had an almost filial[3] respect; but it was doubtful whether they understood very much of it.

The farm was more prosperous now, and better organized: it had even been enlarged by two fields which had been bought from Mr. Pilkington. The windmill had been successfully completed at last, and the farm possessed a threshing machine and a hay elevator of its own, and various new buildings had been added to it. Whymper had bought himself a dogcart. The windmill, however, had not after all been used for generating electric power. It was used for milling corn, and brought in a handsome money profit. The animals were hard at work building yet another windmill; when that one was finished, so it was said, the dynamos would be installed. But the luxuries of which Snowball had once taught the animals to dream, the stalls with electric light and hot and cold water, and the three-day week, were no longer talked about. Napoleon had denounced such ideas as contrary to the spirit of Animalism. The truest happiness, he said, lay in working hard and living frugally.

Somehow it seemed as though the farm had grown richer without making the animals themselves any richer — except, of course, for the pigs and the dogs. Perhaps this was partly because there were so many pigs and so many dogs. It was not that these creatures did not work, after their fashion. There was, as Squealer was never tired of explaining, endless work in the supervision and organization of the farm. Much of this work was of a kind that the other animals were too ignorant to understand. For example, Squealer told them that the pigs had to expend enormous labors every day upon mysterious things called "files," "reports," "minutes," and "memoranda." These were large sheets of paper which had to be closely covered with writing, and as soon as they were so covered, they were burned in the furnace. This was of the highest importance for the welfare of the farm, Squealer said. But still, neither pigs nor dogs produced any food by their own labor; and there were very many of them, and their appetites were always good.

As for the others, their life, so far as they knew, was as it had always been. They were generally hungry, they slept on straw, they

---

[3] filial: befitting a son or daughter.

drank from the pool, they labored in the fields; in winter they were troubled by the cold, and in summer by the flies. Sometimes the older ones among them racked their dim memories and tried to determine whether in the early days of the Rebellion, when Jones's expulsion was still recent, things had been better or worse than now. They could not remember. There was nothing with which they could compare their present lives: they had nothing to go upon except Squealer's lists of figures, which invariably demonstrated that everything was getting better and better. The animals found the problem insoluble; in any case, they had little time for speculating on such things now. Only old Benjamin professed to remember every detail of his long life and to know that things never had been, nor ever could be much better or much worse — hunger, hardship, and disappointment being, so he said, the unalterable law of life.

And yet the animals never gave up hope. More, they never lost, even for an instant, their sense of honor and privilege in being members of Animal Farm. They were still the only farm in the whole county — in all England! — owned and operated by animals. Not one of them, not even the youngest, not even the newcomers who had been brought from farms ten or twenty miles away, ever ceased to marvel at that. And when they heard the gun booming and saw the green flag fluttering at the masthead, their hearts swelled with imperishable pride, and the talk turned always toward the old heroic days, the expulsion of Jones, the writing of the Seven Commandments, the great battles in which the human invaders had been defeated. None of the old dreams had been abandoned. The Republic of the Animals which Major had foretold, when the green fields of England should be untrodden by human feet, was still believed in. Some day it was coming: it might not be soon, it might not be within the lifetime of any animal now living, but still it was coming. Even the tune of *Beasts of England* was perhaps hummed secretly here and there: at any rate, it was a fact that every animal on the farm knew it, though no one would have dared to sing it aloud. It might be that their lives were hard and that not all of their hopes had been fulfilled, but they were conscious that they were not as other animals. If they went hungry, it was not from feeding tyrannical human beings; if they worked hard, at least they worked for themselves. No creature among them went upon two legs. No creature called any other creature "Master." All animals were equal.

One day in early summer Squealer ordered the sheep to follow him, and led them out to a piece of waste ground at the other end of the farm, which had become overgrown with birch saplings. The sheep spent the whole day there browsing at the leaves under Squealer's supervision. In the evening he returned to the farmhouse himself, but, as it was warm weather, told the sheep to stay where they were. It ended by their remaining there for a whole week, during which time the other animals saw nothing of them. Squealer was with them for the greater part of every day. He was, he said, teaching them to sing a new song, for which privacy was needed.

It was just after the sheep had returned, on a pleasant evening when the animals had finished work and were making their way back to the farm buildings, that the terrified neighing of a horse sounded from the yard. Startled, the animals stopped in their tracks. It was Clover's voice. She neighed again, and all the animals broke into a gallop and rushed into the yard. Then they saw what Clover had seen.

It was a pig walking on his hind legs.

Yes, it was Squealer. A little awkwardly, as though not quite used to supporting his considerable bulk in that position, but with perfect balance, he was strolling across the yard. And a moment later, out from the door of the farmhouse came a long file of pigs, all walking on their hind legs. Some did it better than others, one or two were even a trifle unsteady and looked as though they would have liked the support of a stick, but every one of them made his way right round the yard successfully. And finally there was a tremendous baying of dogs and a shrill crowing from the black cockerel, and out came Napoleon himself, majestically upright, casting haughty glances from side to side, and with his dogs gamboling round him.

He carried a whip in his trotter.

There was a deadly silence. Amazed, terrified, huddling together, the animals watched the long line of pigs march slowly round the yard. It was as though the world had turned upside-down. Then there came a moment when the first shock had worn off and when, in spite of everything — in spite of their terror of the dogs, and of the habit, developed through long years, of never complaining, never criticizing, no matter what happened — they might have uttered some word of protest. But just at that moment, as though at a signal, all the sheep burst out into a tremendous bleating of —

"Four legs good, two legs *better!* Four legs good, two legs *better!* Four legs good, two legs *better!*"

It went on for five minutes without stopping. And by the time the sheep had quieted down, the chance to utter any protest had passed, for the pigs had marched back into the farmhouse.

Benjamin felt a nose nuzzling at his shoulder. He looked around. It was Clover. Her old eyes looked dimmer than ever. Without saying anything, she tugged gently at his mane and led him round to the end of the big barn, where the Seven Commandments were written. For a minute or two they stood gazing at the tarred wall with its white lettering.

"My sight is failing," she said finally. "Even when I was young I could not have read what was written there. But it appears to me that the wall looks different. Are the Seven Commandments the same as they used to be, Benjamin?"

For once Benjamin consented to break his rule, and he read out to her what was written on the wall. There was nothing there now except a single Commandment. It ran:

ALL ANIMALS ARE EQUAL
BUT SOME ANIMALS ARE MORE EQUAL THAN OTHERS

After that it did not seem strange when next day the pigs who were supervising the work of the farm all carried whips in their trotters. It did not seem strange to learn that the pigs had bought themselves a wireless set, were arranging to install a telephone, and had taken out subscriptions to *John Bull*, *Tit-Bits*, and the *Daily Mirror*. It did not seem strange when Napoleon was seen strolling in the farmhouse garden with a pipe in his mouth — no, not even when the pigs took Mr. Jones's clothes out of the wardrobes and put them on, Napoleon himself appearing in a black coat, ratcatcher breeches, and leather leggings, while his favorite sow appeared in the watered silk dress which Mrs. Jones had been used to wear on Sundays.

A week later, in the afternoon, a number of dogcarts drove up to the farm. A deputation of neighboring farmers had been invited to make a tour of inspection. They were shown all over the farm, and expressed great admiration for everything they saw, especially the windmill. The animals were weeding the turnip field. They worked diligently, hardly raising their faces from the ground, and not knowing whether to be more frightened of the pigs or of the human visitors.

That evening loud laughter and bursts of singing came from the farmhouse. And suddenly, at the sound of the mingled voices, the animals were stricken with curiosity. What could be happening in there, now that for the first time animals and human beings were meeting on terms of equality? With one accord they began to creep as quietly as possible into the farmhouse garden.

At the gate they paused, half frightened to go on, but Clover led the way in. They tiptoed up to the house, and such animals as were tall enough peered in at the dining-room window. There, around the long table, sat half a dozen farmers and half a dozen of the more eminent pigs, Napoleon himself occupying the seat of honor at the head of the table. The pigs appeared completely at ease in their chairs. The company had been enjoying a game of cards, but had broken off for the moment, evidently in order to drink a toast. A large jug was circulating, and the mugs were being refilled with beer. No one noticed the wondering faces of the animals that gazed in at the window.

Mr. Pilkington, of Foxwood, had stood up, his mug in his hand. In a moment, he said, he would ask the present company to drink a toast. But before doing so, there were a few words that he felt it incumbent upon him to say.

It was a source of great satisfaction to him, he said — and, he was sure, to all others present — to feel that a long period of mistrust and misunderstanding had now come to an end. There had been a time — not that he, or any of the present company, had shared such sentiments — but there had been a time when the respected proprietors of Animal Farm had been regarded, he would not say with hostility, but perhaps with a certain measure of misgiving, by their human neighbors. Unfortunate incidents had occurred, mistaken ideas had been current. It had been felt that the existence of a farm owned and operated by pigs was somehow abnormal and was liable to have an unsettling effect in the neighborhood. Too many farmers had assumed, without due inquiry, that on such a farm a spirit of license and indiscipline would prevail. They had been nervous about the effects upon their own animals, or even upon their human employees. But all such doubts were now dispelled. Today he and his friends had visited Animal Farm and inspected every inch of it with their own eyes, and what did they find? Not only the most up-to-date methods, but a discipline and an orderliness which should be an example to all farmers everywhere. He believed that he was right in saying that the lower animals on Animal Farm did more work and received less food than any animals in the county. Indeed, he and his fellow-visitors today had observed many features which they intended to introduce on their own farms immediately.

He would end his remarks, he said, by emphasizing once again the friendly feelings that subsisted, and ought to subsist, between Animal Farm and its neighbors. Between pigs and human beings there was not, and there need not be, any clash of interests whatever. Their struggles and their difficulties were one. Was not the labor problem the same everywhere? Here it became apparent that Mr. Pilkington was about to spring some carefully prepared witticism on the company, but for a moment he was too overcome by amusement to be able to utter it. After much choking, during which his various chins turned purple, he managed to get it out: "If you have your lower animals to contend with," he said, "we have our lower classes!" This *bon mot* [4] set the table in a roar, and Mr. Pilkington once again congratulated the pigs on the low rations, the long working hours, and the general absence of pampering which he had observed on Animal Farm.

And now, he said finally, he would ask the company to rise to their feet and make certain that their glasses were full. "Gentlemen," concluded Mr. Pilkington, "gentlemen, I give you a toast: To the prosperity of Animal Farm!"

There was enthusiastic cheering and stamping of feet. Napoleon was so gratified that he left his place and came around the table to clink his mug against Mr. Pilkington's before emptying it. When the cheering had died down, Napoleon, who had remained on his feet, intimated that he too had a few words to say.

Like all of Napoleon's speeches, it was short and to the point. He too, he said, was happy that the period of misunderstanding was at an end. For a long time there had been rumors — circulated, he had reason to think, by some malignant enemy — that there was something subversive and even revolutionary in the outlook of himself and his colleagues. They had been credited with attempting to stir up rebellion among the animals on neighboring farms. Nothing

---

[4] *bon mot:* clever saying (French).

could be further from the truth! Their sole wish, now and in the past, was to live at peace and in normal business relations with their neighbors. This farm which he had the honor to control, he added, was a cooperative enterprise. The title deeds, which were in his own possession, were owned by the pigs jointly.

He did not believe, he said, that any of the old suspicions still lingered, but certain changes had been made recently in the routine of the farm which should have the effect of promoting confidence still further. Hitherto the animals on the farm had had a rather foolish custom of addressing one another as "Comrade." This was to be suppressed. There had also been a very strange custom, whose origin was unknown, of marching every Sunday morning past a boar's skull which was nailed to a post in the garden. This, too, would be suppressed, and the skull had already been buried. His visitors might have observed, too, the green flag which flew from the masthead. If so, they would perhaps have noted that the white hoof and horn with which it had previously been marked had now been removed. It would be a plain green flag from now onward.

He had only one criticism, he said, to make of Mr. Pilkington's excellent and neighborly speech. Mr. Pilkington had referred throughout to "Animal Farm." He could not of course know — for he, Napoleon, was only now for the first time announcing it — that the name "Animal Farm" had been abolished. Henceforward the farm was to be known as "The Manor Farm" — which, he believed, was its correct and original name.

"Gentlemen," concluded Napoleon, "I will give you the same toast as before, but in a different form. Fill your glasses to the brim. Gentlemen, here is my toast: To the prosperity of The Manor Farm!"

There was the same hearty cheering as before, and the mugs were emptied to the dregs. But as the animals outside gazed at the scene, it seemed to them that some strange thing was happening. What was it that had altered in the faces of the pigs? Clover's old dim eyes flitted from one face to another. Some of them had five chins, some had four, some had three. But what was it that seemed to be melting and changing? Then, the applause having come to an end, the company took up their cards and continued the game that had been interrupted, and the animals crept silently away.

But they had not gone twenty yards when they stopped short.

An uproar of voices was coming from the farmhouse. They rushed back and looked through the window again. Yes, a violent quarrel was in progress. There were shoutings, bangings on the table, sharp suspicious glances, furious denials. The source of the trouble appeared to be that Napoleon and Mr. Pilkington had each played an ace of spades simultaneously.

Twelve voices were shouting in anger, and they were all alike. No question, now, what had happened to the faces of the pigs. The creatures outside looked from pig to man, and from man to pig, and from pig to man again; but already it was impossible to say which was which.

"Grand Stairway in the Palace of Justice,"
a lithograph by Daumier.

MAN AND
THE STATE

*"All animals are equal, but some
animals are more equal than others."*
       GEORGE ORWELL, *Animal Farm*

Literature is devoted to hard questions, not to easy answers. One of the problems that has always faced man, and will always face him, is the relation of the individual to the State. When does the State unfairly encroach upon the rights of the individual? When must the individual stand up for his rights? When must he put his own desires aside and look to the common good?

In Animal Farm you have already seen a strong examination of one aspect of the State in the modern world. George Orwell found the relationship of the rulers to the ruled to be much like that in his own schooldays: "a continuous triumph of the strong over the weak." But the problem of Man and the State is far from peculiar to our own times; it is reflected later in this book by the problems faced by Brutus in Julius Caesar and by Antigone in Jean Anouilh's version of the Greek tragedy. In fact, you will find again and again, in stories, essays, poems, and plays, the problems of individuals in relation to government.

We can read every day in the newspapers of new rebellions and protests against governments in all parts of the world. Often the protest is against a colonial government ruling an underdeveloped people "for their own good." Often we read of struggles in the new nations of the world where tribal loyalties and older traditions conflict with twentieth-century ideas of government.

In our modern world, the government is often an alien force — or at least seems so. And yet, without governments, can men live in any but the most primitive conditions? Why does man need the State? What would an ideal State be like? When a conflict does arise between Man and the State, who is to decide where justice lies?

Questions such as these have absorbed writers for thousands of years. They form the focus of the following stories, essays, and poems.

China has been a land of revolution for many years. Pearl Buck's story "The New Road" is about the impact of a revolutionary state upon its people, especially upon the old.

The New Road

PEARL BUCK

Lu Chen kept a hot-water shop on the corner of the street of the North Gate, where the alley of the Hwang family intersects it. As everyone knows, that was one of the chief places in the whole length of that street. Not only did the silk shops fling out their banners of orange silk but down the alley of the Hwangs lived other great families. A score of times a day, the clerks idling about the dim shops sent the tea coolie for pots of scalding water to brew the tea that they sipped the whole day through. A score of times a day, the ladies of the alley, gambling delicately as a pastime in one another's houses, sent their slaves to get water from Lu Chen. It was a thriving business and had been a thriving business even in his grandfather's time, when an emperor had lived but a few miles away and that very street had ended in a prince's pleasure grounds.

From his father Lu Chen had received the shop, together with a rice sack full of silver dollars. The rice sack had been emptied to pay for his wedding, but gradually it had been filled again to pay for the schooling and then the wedding of his son. Now, after this last emptying, it was a fifth full again, and Lu Chen's grandchild ran about the shop, terrifying the old man with his venturesome spirit and his curiosity regarding the copper caldrons built into the earthen ovens.

"When I was a child," Lu Chen proclaimed at least daily to his small grandson, "I never ran near the caldrons. I obeyed my grandfather and did not eternally run about like a small chicken."

Of this the grandson understood nothing. He was as yet too young to speak clearly, but he was able to understand that he was the center of his grandfather's heart, and he continued to stagger about near the ovens under the old man's agitated eye. He had become

79

accustomed, of course, to being lifted suddenly by the collar of his small coat and to dangling in the air while his grandfather set him in the inner room.

"I cannot understand this child of yours," remarked Lu Chen to his tall young son. "When will you teach him obedience?"

Lu Chen's son, who had been inclined to idleness and discontent ever since finishing his fourth year at the government middle school, shrugged his shoulders in reply and said half petulantly, "We do not so worship obedience these days."

Lu Chen glanced at him sharply. He would never acknowledge that his son was at all idle. Even at night, when he lay within the curtains of his bamboo bed beside his wife, he would not acknowledge it.

Sometimes she said: "The boy has not enough to do. The shop is small, and there is really only one man's work. If you would only rest now — are you not fifty years old? — and allow our son to manage the business, it would be better. He is twenty years old, and he feels no responsibility for his rice or for the rice of his wife and the child. You do everything. Why did you send him to school if he is to be idle?"

Lu Chen threw back the thick, blue, cotton-stuffed quilt. This talk of giving up his work in the shop always stifled him. The real reason why he had allowed his son to continue in school year after year was that he might have the shop to himself.

"That bigger caldron," he muttered, "is never so bright as I could wish. I have said to him a dozen times, 'Take the ash from the oven and wet it a little and smear it upon the copper and, when it is dried —' but he never will do it."

"Because you are never satisfied when he does," said his wife. She was a large, stout-bodied woman; Lu Chen's small, dried figure scarcely lifted the quilt at all in comparison with the mound of her flesh beneath it.

"He will not do it as I command him," he said in a loud voice.

"You are never satisfied," she replied calmly.

This calmness of hers irritated him more than any anger. He sat upright and stared down at her placid face. Through the coarse linen curtains the light of the bean-oil lamp shone with a vague flicker; he could see her drowsy eyes and her full, expressionless lips.

"I do as my father taught me," he said shrilly.

"Ah, well," she murmured. "Let us sleep. What does it matter?"

He panted a moment and lay down.

"You care nothing for the shop," he said at last. It was the gravest accusation he could think of.

But she did not answer. She was asleep, and her loud, tranquil breathing filled the recesses of the curtains.

The next morning he rose very early and himself scoured the inside of the two caldrons until they reflected his lean brown face. He would have liked to let them remain empty until his son awoke and so show him how they could be made to look. But he dared not, since the slaves and servants came early for hot water for their mistresses' baths. He filled the caldrons, therefore, with water from the earthen jars and lighted the fires beneath them. Soon the steam was bubbling up from under the water-soaked wooden covers. He had filled and refilled the caldrons three times before his son sauntered in, rubbing his eyes, his blue cotton gown half buttoned around him and his hair on end. Lu Chen gave him a sharp look.

"When I was young," he said, "I rose early and scoured the caldrons and lighted the fires beneath them, and my father slept."

"These are the days of the Revolution," said the young man lightly. Lu Chen snorted and spat upon the ground. "These are the days of disobedient sons and of idle young men," he said. "What will your son be, seeing that you do not yet earn your rice?"

But the young man only smiled and, buttoning his coat slowly, went to the caldron nearest him and dipped into a basin water wherewith to wash.

Lu Chen watched him, his face quivering. "It is only for you that I value the shop," he said at last. "It is that the business may go to you and the child after you. This hot-water shop has stood here sixty years. It is well known. All my father's life and my life and your life have come from it — and now the child's."

"There is talk of the new road now," said the young man, wringing a steaming cloth from the water and wiping his face.

That was the first time Lu Chen heard of the new road. It meant nothing to him then. His son was always away, always full of talk of new things, ever since the Revolution had come into the city. What the Revolution was Lu Chen did not clearly perceive. There had certainly been days when his business was very poor and when the great shops had been closed for fear of looting and when the families he regularly supplied had moved away to Shanghai. His business then had been reduced to the petty filling of tin teakettles for the poorer people, who haggled over a copper penny. People said it was the Revolution, and he had become anxious and cursed it in his heart. Then suddenly soldiers were everywhere, and they bought water most recklessly. That was when he began filling up the rice sack again. That was the Revolution, too. He was mightily puzzled, but he no longer cursed it. Then the great shops opened and the old families came back and soldiers drifted away again and things were much as they had been except that prices were high, so that he could raise the price of water too and was relieved.

"These revolutions," he said to his son one morning, "what are they about? You have been to school — do you know? It has been a great stir. I am glad it is over."

At that the son raised his eyebrows. "Over?" he repeated. "It is only begun. Wait. This city will be the capital of the country, and then everything will be greatly changed."

The old man shook his head. "Change? There is never great change. Emperors and kings and presidents or what-not, people must drink tea and must bathe — these go on forever."

Well, but this new road? On the very day his son had mentioned it, that impudent young slave girl from the third alley down had turned up the corner of her lip at him and said: "I hear talk from our master of a great new road sixty feet wide. What then of your caldrons, Lu Chen?"

Lu Chen's arm was bare to the elbow and wrinkled and reddened by the continued steam from the water. He scarcely felt the heat. But now, as the slave girl spoke, he dipped his bamboo dipper more deeply into the water and grunted. His hand trembled and slopped a little water over the edge of the caldron into the hot coals of the fire. A hiss rose from them. He did not speak but made a pretense of stirring up the fire. He was not going to speak to that silly creature. Yet, after she had gone, he remembered that she was a slave in the house of Ling and that, since the eldest son of Ling was an official, there might indeed be talk of the road. He gazed about on the gray brick walls of his little shop in a sort of terror. They were darkened with smoke and dampness and had cracks that he could remember even from childhood. Sixty feet wide? Why, it would mean the whole shop ripped away!

"I will ask such a price that they cannot buy it," he thought. "Such a price — " He cast about in himself for a sum enormous enough to stagger a government. "I will ask ten thousand dollars!"

He was happy then. Who would pay ten thousand dollars for this twelve square feet of space and the two caldrons? Where was so much money in the world? Why, when his father had been a young man, the Prince Ming-yuan had built a palace for that. He laughed a little and was more lenient with his son and forgot the new road and daily preserved the life of the child from the caldrons. Everything was as before.

One morning midway to noon he sat down to rest and drink a little tea. He always brewed his own tea after the fifth emptying of the caldrons, just before he began to fill them again for the noon call. In this interval, when people had bought for the morning tea and the hour had not yet approached for the midday meal, he could enjoy a little leisure. He took the grandchild on his knee and let him drink also and smiled to see him grasp the bowl in two hands and drink, staring gravely over the rim.

All at once there was a sharp rap like a sword-cut at the door. Lu Chen set the child down carefully and moved the teapot out of his reach. Then he went to the door and, fumbling a little, drew back the wooden bar. A man stood there in a gray cotton uniform. He was a young officer of some sort, with an arrogant eye, but he scarcely looked at Lu Chen.

"Sir," said Lu Chen a little timidly, since the young officer carried a gun and a belt stuffed with cartridges. But he was interrupted.

"The new road passes your shop. What is your name, old man?" The officer rapidly consulted a sheet of paper drawn from his pocket. "Ah, yes, Lu! Thirty feet off your house. Fifteen days from today your shop must be gone. Else we will tear it down for you." He folded the paper carelessly and put it back into his pocket. Then he turned to go away. At his heels were three common soldiers, and they turned also and fell into step. Lu Chen could not speak. He swallowed, but his throat was dry. No sound came forth. One of the soldiers glanced back at him, a curious, pitying glance. That pity suddenly released the knot in Lu Chen's throat.

"Ten thousand dollars!" he called hoarsely after the young officer.

The officer halted instantly and wheeled about. "What is that?" he said sharply.

"The price of the shop is ten thousand dollars," faltered Lu Chen. The young officer grasped his gun, and Lu Chen shrank in alarm behind the door and closed it. But the young man would not have it. He walked back and thrust his gun so suddenly against the door that Lu Chen staggered and bumped into the child, who began to cry. Every time in the child's whole life that he had cried, Lu Chen had rushed to him. But now he did not even hear. He was gazing fixedly at the young officer, murmuring over and over, unconsciously, "Ten thousand dollars, ten thousand dollars."

The officer stared at him and then broke into a chilly laughter. "It is your contribution, then, to the new capital," he said, and, shouting a sharp command, he went away.

Contribution? What contribution? The child lay on the earthen floor, wailing. He was used to lying wherever he had fallen, since someone always picked him up, but now no one came. Lu Chen stood looking out through the door after the young man's figure. His heart lagged in his body so that he could scarcely draw his breath. Give up his shop, his life? What was all this talk of a new capital? It was none of his business. He turned and, seeing the child, dazedly picked him up and put him on his feet. Then, with the child in his arms, he sat down. Why, the shop was the child's! No one could take it away. Anger rose up in him and relieved him then, since it drove out his fear. He never would give up the shop — never! He would sit there in it until they tore the last tile from over his head. He set the child on the floor again and bustled mightily and filled the caldron and started roaring fires, so that within the hour the water bubbled and steamed and lifted the wooden covers. He was very sharp with his customers, and when the impudent slave girl came with her cheeks pink and her black eyes saucy, he skimped her a little on water and would not fill the kettle for all her scolding.

"It will be a good thing for us all when the new road comes and takes away your shop, old robber," she flung at him when she saw that he would give her no more.

"Nothing can be taken from me," he shouted after her and, when her mocking laugh came back to him, he shouted again, "That for the new road!" And he spat.

After a while the door opened, and his son came in.

"What of the new road?" he asked indolently, feeling of the teapot to see whether it was still hot.

"Now then," said Lu Chen. "You still return for your food, do you? Where have you been today?"

"But it is true of the new road," said the boy, sipping the half-cold tea from the spout of the pot. "Quite true. It comes straight past us. The shop — 'thirty feet off' — will leave but half of the two bedrooms at the back."

Lu Chen stared unbelievingly. He was all at once so angry that his eyes grew dim. He raised his hand and knocked the teapot from his son's hand, and it fell upon the ground and broke into three pieces.

"You stand there," Lu Chen muttered thickly, "you stand there and drink tea — " and, seeing the young man's astonished face, he began to weep and walked as fast as he could into the room where he slept and crawled into the bed and drew the curtains.

In the morning, when he rose, he was still angry with his son. When the young man ate his rice, innocently, Lu Chen twitched his eyebrows and muttered: "Yes, you eat and your son eats, but you do not think where the money is to come from." But for all of this he did not believe that they would really take away his shop, and he went on about his work as before.

The eleventh day after he was warned by the officer, his wife came to him with unwonted consternation on her face. "It is true that the road is coming," she said. "If you look up the street, you will see a sight. What shall we do?" She began to weep softly, her large face scarcely disturbed.

Lu Chen, seeing her, felt himself quivering. He went to the door and gazed up the street. Always the street had been so narrow, so winding, so darkened with the overhanging shop signs of varnished wood and colored silk, that one could see for only a few feet. But now there was the strange light of the sun shining upon the damp cobbles. A score of feet away all the signs were gone, and men were tearing down houses. Heaps of age-stained bricks and tiles lay on the street, and caravans of donkeys with baskets across their backs stood waiting to carry them away. The same officer that he had seen was walking about, and behind him followed four angry women, their hair streaming down their backs. They were cursing and wailing, and Lu could hear them say, "We have no life left, no life left — our homes are gone!"

Lu went into the shop then and shut the door and barred it. He sat down on the short wooden bench behind the caldron, his knees shaking, his mind in a maze. Inexorably the road was coming. The child ran out of the inner room and leaned against his knee, but Lu beheld him apathetically. The child, seeing his remote gaze, looked roguishly up and touched the great caldron with a tentative finger. But Lu, for the first time in his life, did not cry out at him. A dim thought went through his mind. "Burned? It is nothing. You will starve at last."

There was a thunderous knock at the door at that moment, and Lu's heart leaped. With his whole body taut, he went to remove the bar. It was the officer in a very clean new uniform, and behind him stood the three soldiers. No one could dream from their appearance that they had been bitterly cursed but a few moments ago, so sure and confident did they seem. Lu, looking at them, suddenly felt that he was a very old man and that it was best for him to die.

"Four days," said the officer, "and your shop must be gone. Tear it down yourself, and you will have the materials. Otherwise we will confiscate it."

"But the money?" faltered Lu Chen.

"Money?" repeated the officer sharply, tapping his shining leather boot with a small stick he carried.

"The price is ten thousand dollars," said Lu Chen a little more firmly, gathering himself together.

The officer gave a sharp, short laugh.

"There is no money," he replied, each word as clear and cold as steel. "You are presenting this to the Republic." Lu Chen looked wildly about. Surely there was some redress. Surely someone would help him.

He begin to scream out in a broken, shrill voice to the passers on the street. "Do you see this, sirs? I am to be robbed — robbed by the Republic! Who is this Republic? Will it give me food and my wife and my child — "

He felt himself twitched slightly by the coat. The soldier who had looked back at him the other day whispered hurriedly, "Do not anger the officer — it will be worse." Aloud he said: "Do not complain, old man! In any case your shop would have to go. In the new day that is coming we shall not want hot-water shops. Hot water will come pouring forth from the self-going pipes."

Lu Chen would have answered him, but was at that moment

pulled backward by his son, who stood there in front of him, facing the officer. The young man spoke anxiously, courteously: "Sir, forgive an old man who cannot understand that the Revolution has come and brought new light. I will answer for him. We will pull down the house, sir. It is an honor for us to sacrifice all we have to the country."

The red anger that had been rising over the officer's face faded: he gave a short nod and walked quickly away.

The young man barred the door against the curious, half-pitying crowd that had gathered to see the scene. Then he stood against the door and faced Lu Chen. Lu Chen had never seen him thus, firm and decided. "Shall we all be killed then?" he demanded. "Are we to die for the sake of a shop?"

"In any case we shall starve," said Lu Chen, seating himself on the other side of the table, opposite his wife. She had continued to weep the whole time, without noise or disturbance, merely wiping the large tears from her cheeks with the corner of her blue jacket.

"I have found work," said his son. "I am to be an overseer of workmen on the new road."

Lu Chen looked up at him, then, without any hope in his heart. "Even you, my son?" he whispered.

The young man pushed back his hair restlessly from his forehead. "Father, there is no use in fighting against it. It will come. Think of it, a great new road sweeping through our city! Automobiles, passing to and fro! Once at school I saw a picture of a street in a foreign city — big shops and automobiles rushing back and forth. Only *we* have wheelbarrows and rikshas and donkeys crowding against one another in the streets. Why, these streets were made a thousand years ago. Are we never to have new ones?"

"What is the use of automobiles?" muttered Lu Chen. He had seen them often in these past weeks, crowding, pushing, insistent, making people rush to doorways and side alleys. He hated them. "Our ancestors," he began.

But the young man snapped his fingers. "That for them!" he cried. "I shall get fifty dollars a month from the new road."

Fifty dollars a month? Lu Chen was stunned. He had never seen such an amount of money. He was diverted a little, and his wife stopped crying.

"Where will so much come from?" he asked, half fearfully.

"The new government has promised it," replied his son in a complacent tone.

"I shall buy myself a new black sateen coat," the young man's mother said, a light beginning to break over her face. And then, after an interval during which she thought about the coat, she gave a rumbling, hoarse laugh.

But to Lu Chen, when he had pondered the matter, it seemed that there was no hope for his shop, now that it was no longer their only means of support. He sat all day without lighting the fire, and the great caldrons for the first time in threescore years were cold.

When people came to buy water, he said: "There is no more need. You are to have pipes. Until then heat your own water."

The saucy slave girl stuck out her tongue at him, a small, red tongue, as red as a cherry, but he shook his head at her without anger or interest.

The next day his son asked, "Shall we not call the masons to tear down the house, lest we lose everything?"

That roused him a little. "No," he cried. "Since they will rob me, let them rob me utterly." And for four days he sat in his house, refusing to eat, refusing even to open his door, although he heard approaching nearer and nearer the destruction — the crash of fallen bricks, the groaning of timbers placed centuries ago and now lowered to the ground, the weeping of many people like himself, whose homes were thus demolished.

On the morning of the fifteenth day there was a great knock upon his door. He rose at once to open it. There stood a dozen men, armed with picks and axes. He faced them. "You come to destroy my shop? I am helpless. Here it is." And he sat down again upon his bench while they crowded in. There was not one touch of sympathy in their faces. In this fashion they had already destroyed hundreds of shops and homes, and to them, he saw very clearly, he was only an old man and one more troublesome than others.

His wife and his son and his son's wife and child had gone away that morning to a friend's house, and they had taken with them everything except the bench whereon Lu Chen sat and the two caldrons. His son had said: "Come with me, Father. I have prepared a place — I have rented a little house. They advanced me some money on the first month." But Lu Chen had shaken his head stubbornly and sat still as they went out.

There were the great copper caldrons, firmly embedded in the clay of the ovens. Two workmen hacked at them with pickaxes. "My grandfather put those in," he said suddenly. "There are no such workmen nowadays."

But he said nothing more while they took the tiles from the roof and the light began to seep down between the rafters. At last they took the rafters, and he sat there within four walls with the noonday sunshine beating on him. He was sick and faint, but he sat on through the long afternoon, and, when evening came, he still sat there, his shop a heap of bricks and tiles and broken rafters about him. The two caldrons stood up naked out of the ruins. People stared at him curiously but said nothing, and he sat on.

At last, when it was almost dark, his son came and took him by the hand. "The child will not eat because you have not come, Father," he said kindly, and then Lu Chen rose, like a very old man, and, holding his son's hand, went with him.

They made their dwelling, then, in a little thatched house just inside the North Gate, where there are fields and empty lands. Lu Chen, who all his life had lived in the bustle of the streets, could not endure the silence. He could not bear to look out across the blankness of the fields. He sat all day in the little bedroom that belonged to him and his wife, scarcely thinking. Since there was no need for him to work any more, he became very soon an old, old man. His son brought home at the end of the month fifty round silver dollars and showed them exultantly.

"It is more than the shop ever yielded," he cried. He was no longer indolent and careless, and he wore a clean gray uniform buttoned neatly about him.

But Lu Chen only muttered, "Those two big caldrons used to hold at least twenty gallons of river water."

One day his wife, as placid again in this house as she had ever been, showed him her new sateen coat, smoothing it over her great bosom. But he only stared at her. "My mother," he said heavily, "once had a gray coat that was bound in silk." And he fell to musing again.

No one could make him go out of the door. He sat day after day, his hair getting quite white and his lined face loosening from its former busy tenseness. His eyes, which had always been narrow and watchful and snapping, grew dull and hidden behind the veil of dimness that belongs to old people. Only the child sometimes beguiled him for a brief moment.

It was the child at last who beguiled him beyond the door. He had sat all through the shortening days of early winter, gazing out of the small window of his room. His day was marked off into the three periods of his meals, and at night he slept fitfully, sometimes still in his chair with his head on the table.

There came then, after a week of rain, one of the mild, deceptive days that are an interlude of autumn before the intense cold sets in. He had been conscious all morning of the soft, damp heat. The sun, shining obliquely through gray clouds, lighted up the landscape. He was restless, and he pushed open the window. The fresh smell of earth and moisture rose up. "I could have caught a caldronful of the rainwater," he said, sniffing the dampness. Rainwater in the old days could be sold at a high price.

Just then the child came tugging at his hand. "Out, out!" he cried, laughing. "Come and play!"

Lu Chen felt a stirring in him. Well, he would go out just a little, perhaps. And, rising slowly, he took the child's hand and went out. It was very warm, and the sun felt heartening to him. He straightened himself with an effort and began to walk toward some houses near by. He would just go and learn what news there might be. Not for a long time had he heard any. His son was busy all day, and as for the women, who would talk with a woman?

The child was chattering, and a small cheeping of autumn insects filled the air. It was almost like spring. He looked about curiously. Where was he, exactly? There was the North Gate yonder. Ah, that would be the end of the street where his shop had been. He would just go and look at it. Could he bear it? He walked a little more quickly.

Then he turned a corner, and the street lay before him. The street? What was this? A great wide sweep of emptiness, straight through the heart of the city! On all sides the same narrow, winding, dark streets and alleys that he had always known and, straight through them, like the clean swath of a sword-blade, this new road!

He stared along it, suddenly smitten with fright. Why, it was enormous — what would they ever do with a road like this? The men working on it were like midges — like ants. All the people in the world could go up and down it and not jostle one another. There were people standing about, like himself, subdued and silent. Some poignancy in their expression drew his interest. "You lived here?" he hinted to a thin-faced man who stood near him. The man nodded slowly. "The house was all I had," he said. "A good house, built in the time of the Mings. It had ten rooms. I live in a hut now. You see, the house was all I had — I rented the rooms."

Lu Chen nodded. "I had a shop — a hot-water shop," he said with difficulty. He would have liked to say more; it was on his tongue to say, "There were two huge copper caldrons." But the man was not listening. He stood staring down the vast new roadway.

Someone drew near, and Lu Chen saw it was his son. The young man broke into a smile and came running. "My father!" he cried. And then, "Father, what do you think of it?"

The old man's lips trembled. He felt that he might either laugh or weep. "It — looks as if a mighty storm had swept through the city," he answered.

But the young man only laughed and said eagerly: "See, Father, this is my bit of the work. Look, at the side there will be pavements, and, in the middle, room for the electric cars and on both sides great space for vehicles of all sorts — room for everything! People from the whole world walking and riding on this road — the road through the new capital!" Someone called him, and he walked away, bustling a little.

Lu Chen stood still, gazing up the road. Infinitely wide, it stretched on both sides of him, infinitely long it extended into the distance. How far did it go, he asked himself solemnly. He had never seen anything in his life like it for space and straightness. Far at the other end, as far as his eyes could pierce, it went on and on, astounding, magnificent, new! Well, here was a thing. Not even emperors had made a road like this! He looked down at the little child beside him. This child, he supposed, would take the road for granted. The young always took things for granted — the way his son had taken the destruction of the shop, for instance. For the first time he did not use the word "robbery" in his mind when he thought of his shop. Instead, this question occurred to him: Had it taken this new road to make his son a man? He perceived that, as he had cared for his shop, so his son cared for the road. He continued to stand with the child, looking up it soberly, absorbed, pondering its import. This Revolution — this new road! Where did it lead?

impression — how many changes

In the following story, as in "The New Road," traditional values are threatened by progress in the form of government agents and control. The setting, however, is not a culture on the other side of the earth but an Indian reservation in the United States.

Indian Business

ERIC HOWARD

Seganitso Begay whacked his pony and rode swiftly down the valley of green corn, beside the wash.[1] In his heart was the rhythm of his pony's flying feet; on his lips a song. The sun shone on the silver buttons that ornamented his green velvet blouse, gleamed on the bracelet encircling his wrist, and flashed from his glistening copper skin.

To be alive was good. To ride far on a day like this, with the sun shining, the sky cloudless and the tall buttes of red rock rising into its blue, was to live. Yet Seganitso Begay, having known this life since first he could walk, did not consciously think of his well-being. Health and strength and freedom were normal; he accepted them as he accepted the swift grace of his pony. Reflection did not mar the harmony of his being. Even the song he sang was but an accompaniment to the rhythm of living.

He did not think of yesterday or tomorrow. He did not dream of the day after. He lived. Rich blood coursed through his young veins, as through the veins of his pony. He was a part of his pony, as his pony was a part of all life. The sun which warmed them likewise warmed the cottonwoods in the wash and brought the corn to its full stature. All this was one. All was one. So ran the song he alternately hummed and sang in a high falsetto. So the elders had said, long ago. The sun's warmth, the growing corn, the tall trees, the spirited pony — all, and much more, moved in the eternal rhythm of life. Seganitso Begay, likewise.

---

[1] *wash:* dry bed of a stream.

Philosophy was unnecessary. He lived it.

If he thought at all, as he rode, his thoughts were pleasing pictures. He was going to a "sing," where the maidens would be. He saw the smiling, shy, white-toothed girl he had shyly greeted, at the trader's, in the time of the planting. She would be there. He would take his place in the chorus, with his friends. The water drum would carry the rhythm of the dance far across the land, and the songs of the chanting chorus, as their bodies swayed together, would lift up his heart.

Then he would leave the singers and allow himself to be seen among those who watched the dancing. She would see him, that maiden of the clear eyes and the smiling lips; her mother would see him. They would talk, perhaps, but he would not heed their talk. It was the way of a man to be indifferent, to be sought, not to seek. But his mother owned many sheep, and he himself was well and favorably known among the people of the high mesa. She would seek him out — of that he was sure — and she would lead him into the firelit circle of the dance. He would feign indifference, while his heart pounded in his breast at the touch of her hand on his arm. She would laugh shyly, and he would know that she had chosen him from among all others.

Life went on like a long ride through beautiful scenes. He let his fancy wander — to the clean new hogan of cedar where they would dwell, into a future idyllic and delightful, indefinite and sublime.

The vision was more than he could bear. He burst into a wild song of delight, of love, of triumph. He rode the trail of beauty. Beauty was before him, all around him, above him. Beauty was everywhere, in her and in him, in all the world they knew.

His voice rose to an exultant cry. "*Nizhuni! Nizhuni! Nizhuni!*" (Beautiful) he sang.

Then, abruptly, he halted. A car was coming down the road, and he pulled his pony to one side, waiting.

Even at a little distance he recognized the car and its occupants. They were two white men from the Agency, government farmers, sent out to help the Indians with their crops. Seganitso Begay's face clouded, became impassive, lost its lyrical light. He did not know what happened when he encountered white men, but a mask seemed to veil his countenance. He remembered, long ago, they had come for him, to take him to school, and his mother had hidden him until the officers had departed. Later, she had moved into a deep canyon, where there was feed and water but where white men did not come. And he had grown up, taught only by his uncles. He had never been to school; his hair had never been cut. There was a wild pride in his bearing, unlike the air of the boys who had been taken away. He was strong and fearless; he had never known the command of a superior, only the directions of his soft-voiced mother and the counsel of his wise uncles. He was respectful toward the old, gentle with children.

"Where are you going?" demanded the man at the wheel of the car, in Navajo that was harsh and unpleasant.

Seganitso Begay gestured vaguely. "Over there," he said.

The driver turned to his companion. "Going to a 'sing,' " he said disgustedly. "I knew it! Just when I told them to tend to their crops, the whole flock of them pick up and start for a 'sing.' You can't do a thing with these savages."

Although the words were in English, Seganitso Begay caught their meaning. His face was stern and sullen.

The white man shook his fist at him. "You'd better turn right around and take care of your corn!" he insisted.

The Indian rode close to the car. "Smoke?" he asked, using one of the few English words he knew.

Ungraciously, the white man extended a package of cigarettes. As the Indian lighted one, the farmer proceeded to lecture him about his crop.

"I go over there," said Seganitso Begay, gesturing. "I go on Indian business."

He turned and rode away, leaving the white men cursing.

For some time, as always after such an encounter, the young man's heart was troubled. Always those men came, to interrupt the smooth flow of life. Just when one was most enjoying all that was good and beautiful, they would appear.

But he did not think too long about it. His pony broke into a lope, and again he was riding fleetly and rhythmically on the trail of beauty, in the pathway of the sun.

Soon he began to sing again, and pleasing pictures accompanied him on the way.

When two races meet, one must triumph.

"*Nizhuni! Nizhuni! Nizhuni!*" he sang.

During the Franco-Prussian War (1870–71), German armies surrounded the city of Paris. At the time of the following story, the French people were near starvation, and the ordinary business of the city had come to a stop. Against this historical background, Guy de Maupassant, one of the early masters of the short story, tells a tale of two plain citizens caught up in the cruelty of war.

[handwritten: setting - Paris, Jan. 1870-1871] *[handwritten: characters: M. Morrissott, M. Sauvage]*

Two Friends

GUY DE MAUPASSANT

Paris was blockaded, desolate, famished. The sparrows were few, and anything that was to be had was good to eat.

On a bright morning in January, M. Morissot a watchmaker by trade but idler through circumstances, was walking along the boulevard, sad, hungry, with his hands in the pockets of his uniform trousers, when he came face to face with a brother-in-arms whom he recognized as an old-time friend. *[handwritten margin: Past - not in uniform, war.]*

Before the war Morissot could be seen at daybreak every Sunday, trudging along with a cane in one hand and a tin box on his back. He would take the train to Colombes and walk from there to the Isle of Marante, where he would fish until dark.

It was there he had met M. Sauvage, who kept a little notion store in the Rue Notre Dame de Lorette, a jovial fellow and passionately fond of fishing like himself. A warm friendship had sprung up between these two, and they would fish side by side all day, very often without saying a word. Some days, when everything looked fresh and new and the beautiful spring sun gladdened every heart, M. Morissot would exclaim:

"How delightful!" and M. Sauvage would answer:

"There is nothing to equal it."

Then again on a fall evening, when the glorious setting sun, spreading its golden mantle on the already tinted leaves, would throw strange shadows around the two friends, Sauvage would say:

"What a grand picture!"

"It beats the boulevard!" would answer Morissot. But they understood each other quite as well without speaking.

The two friends had greeted each other warmly and had resumed their walk side by side, both thinking deeply of the past and present events. They entered a café, and when a glass had been placed before each, Sauvage sighed:

"What terrible events, my friend!"

"And what weather!" said Morissot sadly. "This is the first nice day we have had this year. Do you remember our fishing excursions?"

"Do I! Alas, when shall we go again!"

They emerged from the café, feeling rather dizzy — that light-headed effect which alcohol has on an empty stomach. The balmy air had made Sauvage exuberant, and he exclaimed:

"Suppose we go!"

"Where?"

"Fishing."

"Fishing! Where?"

"To our old spot, to Colombes. The French soldiers are stationed near there, and I know Colonel Dumoulin will give us a pass."

"It's a go; I am with you."

An hour after, having supplied themselves with their fishing tackle, they arrived at the colonel's villa. He had smiled at their request and had given them a pass in due form.

At about eleven o'clock they reached the advance guard and, after presenting their pass, walked through Colombes and found themselves very near their destination. Argenteuil,[1] across the way, and the great plains toward Nanterre were all deserted. Solitary, the hill rose clearly above the plains, a splendid point of observation.

"See," said Sauvage, pointing to the hills, "the Prussians are there."

Prussians! They had never seen one, but they knew that they were all around Paris, invisible and powerful, plundering, devastating and slaughtering. To their superstitious terror they added a deep hatred for this unknown and victorious people.

"What if we should meet some?" said Morissot.

"We would ask them to join us," said Sauvage in true Parisian style.

---

[1] Argenteuil (ár·zhán·tœ′y′).

Still they hesitated to advance. The silence frightened them. Finally Sauvage picked up courage.

"Come, let us go on cautiously."

They proceeded slowly, hiding behind bushes, looking anxiously on every side, listening to every sound. A bare strip of land had to be crossed before reaching the river. They started to run. At last they reached the bank and sank into the bushes, breathless, but relieved.

Morissot thought he heard someone walking. He listened attentively, but no, he heard no sound. They were indeed alone! The little island shielded them from view. The house where the restaurant used to be seemed deserted; feeling reassured, they settled themselves for a good day's sport.

Sauvage caught the first fish, Morissot the second, and every minute they would bring one out which they would place in a net at their feet. It was indeed miraculous! They felt that supreme joy which one feels after having been deprived for months of a pleasant pastime. They had forgotten everything, even the war!

Suddenly they heard a rumbling sound, and the earth shook beneath them. It was the cannon on Mont Valérien. Morissot looked up and saw a trail of smoke, which was instantly followed by another explosion. Then they followed in quick succession.

"They are at it again," said Sauvage, shrugging his shoulders. Morissot, who was naturally peaceful, felt a sudden, uncontrollable anger.

"Stupid fools! What pleasure can they find in killing each other?"

"They are worse than brutes!"

"It will always be thus as long as we have governments."

"Well, such is life!"

"You mean death!" said Morissot, laughing.

They continued to discuss the different political problems, while the cannon on Mont Valérien sent death and desolation among the French.

Suddenly they started. They had heard a step behind them. They turned and beheld four big men in dark uniforms, with guns pointed right at them. Their fishing lines dropped out of their hands and floated away with the current.

In a few minutes the Prussian soldiers had bound them, cast them into a boat, and rowed across the river to the island which our friends had thought deserted. They soon found out their mistake when they reached the house, behind which stood a score or more of soldiers. A big burly officer, seated astride a chair, smoking an immense pipe, addressed them in excellent French:

"Well, gentlemen, have you made a good haul?"

Just then a soldier deposited at his feet the netful of fish which he had taken care to take along with him. The officer smiled and said:

"I see you have done pretty well, but let us change the subject. You are evidently sent to spy upon me. You pretended to fish so as to put me off the scent, but I am not so simple. I have caught you and shall have you shot. I am sorry, but war is war. As you passed the advance guard, you certainly must have the password; give it to me, and I will set you free."

The two friends stood side by side, pale and slightly trembling, but they answered nothing.

"No one will ever know. You will go back home quietly, and the secret will disappear with you. If you refuse, it is instant death! Choose!"

They remained motionless, silent. The Prussian officer calmly pointed to the river.

"In five minutes you will be at the bottom of this river! Surely you have a family, friends, waiting for you?"

Still they kept silent. The cannon rumbled incessantly. The officer gave orders in his own tongue, then moved his chair away from the prisoners. A squad of men advanced within twenty feet of them, ready for command.

"I give you one minute, not a second more!"

Suddenly approaching the two Frenchmen, the officer took Morissot aside and whispered:

"Quick, the password. Your friend will not know; he will think I changed my mind." Morissot said nothing.

Then, taking Sauvage aside, he asked him the same thing, but he also was silent. The officer gave further orders, and the men leveled their guns. At that moment Morissot's eyes rested on the netful of fish lying in the grass a few feet away. The sight made him faint and, though he struggled against it, his eyes filled with tears. Then, turning to his friend:

"Farewell, Monsieur Sauvage!"

"Farewell, Monsieur Morissot!"

They stood for a minute hand in hand, trembling with emotion which they were unable to control.

"Fire!" commanded the officer.

The squad of men fired as one. Sauvage fell straight on his face. Morissot, who was taller, swayed, pivoted, and fell across his friend's body, his face to the sky, while blood flowed freely from the wound in the breast. The officer gave further orders, and his men disappeared. They came back presently with ropes and stones, which they tied to the feet of the two friends, and four of them carried them to the edge of the river. They swung them and threw them in as far as they could. The bodies, weighted by stones, sank immediately. A splash, a few ripples and the water resumed its usual calmness. The only thing to be seen was a little blood floating on the surface. The officer calmly retraced his steps toward the house, muttering:

"The fish will get even now."

He perceived the netful of fish, picked it up, smiled, and called:

"Wilhelm!"

A soldier in a white uniform approached. The officer handed him the fish, saying:

"Fry these little things while they are still alive; they will make a delicious meal."

And, having resumed his position on the chair, he puffed away at his pipe.

As a young man not long out of school, George Orwell, the author of Animal Farm, *served as a police officer of the British government in Burma. In this role, he was an agent of a foreign nation and so a chief target for Burmese hostility. In "Shooting an Elephant," Orwell describes his discovery of the real motives behind the actions of officials who represent a powerful but unpopular government. Those who are ruled can shape the actions of their rulers, as Orwell discovered one hot day under the pressure of an excited mob.*

Shooting an Elephant

GEORGE ORWELL

In Moulmein, in Lower Burma, I was hated by large numbers of people — the only time in my life that I have been important enough for this to happen to me. I was subdivisional police officer of the town, and in an aimless, petty kind of way, anti-European feeling was very bitter. No one had the guts to raise a riot, but if a European woman went through the bazaars alone, somebody would probably spit betel juice over her dress. As a police officer I was an obvious target and was baited whenever it seemed safe to do so. When a nimble Burman tripped me up on the football field and the referee (another Burman) looked the other way, the crowd yelled with hideous laughter. This happened more than once. In the end the sneering yellow faces of young men that met me everywhere, the insults hooted after me when I was at a safe distance, got badly on my nerves. The young Buddhist priests were the worst of all. There were several thousands of them in the town, and none of them seemed to have anything to do except stand on street corners and jeer at Europeans.

All this was perplexing and upsetting. For at that time I had already made up my mind that imperialism [1] was an evil thing and the sooner I chucked up my job and got out of it the better. Theo-

---

[1] *imperialism:* a form of government in which one nation controls other peoples and territories. In Orwell's day, Burma was part of the British Empire.

retically — and secretly, of course — I was all for the Burmese and all against their oppressors, the British. As for the job I was doing, I hated it more bitterly than I can perhaps make clear. In a job like that you see the dirty work of Empire at close quarters. The wretched prisoners huddling in the stinking cages of the lockups, the gray, cowed faces of the long-term convicts, the scarred buttocks of the men who had been flogged with bamboos — all these oppressed me with an intolerable sense of guilt. But I could get nothing into perspective. I was young and ill-educated, and I had had to think out my problems in the utter silence that is imposed on every Englishman in the East. I did not even know that the British Empire is dying, still less did I know that it is a great deal better than the younger empires that are going to supplant it. All I knew was that I was stuck between my hatred of the empire I served and my rage against the evil-spirited little beasts who tried to make my job impossible. With one part of my mind I thought of the British Raj as an unbreakable tyranny, as something clamped down, *in saecula saeculorum*,[2] upon the will of prostrate peoples; with another part I thought that the greatest joy in the world would be to drive a bayonet into a Buddhist priest's guts. Feelings like these are the normal byproducts of imperialism; ask any Anglo-Indian official, if you can catch him off duty.

One day something happened which in a roundabout way was enlightening. It was a tiny incident in itself, but it gave me a better glimpse than I had had before of the real nature of imperialism — the real motives for which despotic governments act. Early one morning the subinspector at a police station the other end of the town rang me up on the phone and said that an elephant was ravaging the bazaar. Would I please come and do something about it? I did not know what I could do, but I wanted to see what was happening and I got on to a pony and started out. I took my rifle, an old .44 Winchester and much too small to kill an elephant, but I thought the noise might be useful *in terrorem*.[3] Various Burmans stopped me on the way and told me about the elephant's doings. It was not, of course, a wild elephant but a tame one which had gone "must." [4] It had been chained up, as tame elephants always

2 *in saecula saeculorum:* forever and ever.
3 *in terrorem:* for terror.
4 *"must":* a dangerous state of frenzy.

are when their attack of "must" is due, but on the previous night it had broken its chain and escaped. Its mahout,[5] the only person who could manage it when it was in that state, had set out in pursuit but had taken the wrong direction and was now twelve hours' journey away, and in the morning the elephant had suddenly reappeared in the town. The Burmese population had no weapons and were quite helpless against it. It had already destroyed somebody's bamboo hut, killed a cow, and raided some fruit stalls and devoured the stock; also it had met the municipal rubbish van and, when the driver jumped out and took to his heels, had turned the van over and inflicted violences upon it.

The Burmese subinspector and some Indian constables were waiting for me in the quarter where the elephant had been seen. It was a very poor quarter, a labyrinth [6] of squalid bamboo huts, thatched with palm leaf, winding all over a steep hillside. I remember that it was a cloudy, stuffy morning at the beginning of the rains. We began questioning the people as to where the elephant had gone and, as usual, failed to get any definite information. That is invariably the case in the East; a story always sounds clear enough at a distance, but the nearer you get to the scene of events, the vaguer it becomes. Some of the people said that the elephant had gone in one direction, some said that he had gone in another, some professed not even to have heard of any elephant. I had almost made up my mind that the whole story was a pack of lies, when we heard yells a little distance away. There was a loud, scandalized cry of "Go away, child! Go away this instant!" and an old woman with a switch in her hand came round the corner of a hut, violently shooing away a crowd of naked children. Some more women followed, clicking their tongues and exclaiming; evidently there was something that the children ought not to have seen. I rounded the hut and saw a man's dead body sprawling in the mud. He was an Indian, a black Dravidian [7] coolie, almost naked, and he could not have been dead many minutes. The people said that the elephant had come suddenly upon him round the corner of the hut, caught him with its trunk, put its foot on his back, and ground him into the earth. This was the rainy season and the ground was soft, and his face had

---

[5] *mahout* (mə·hout') : elephant's keeper and driver.
[6] *labyrinth* (lab'ə·rinth) : a confusing network of streets or passageways; a maze.
[7] *Dravidian*: a people of southern India.

scored a trench a foot deep and a couple of yards long. He was lying on his belly with arms crucified and head sharply twisted to one side. His face was coated with mud, the eyes wide open, the teeth bared and grinning with an expression of unendurable agony. (Never tell me, by the way, that the dead look peaceful. Most of the corpses I have seen looked devilish.) The friction of the great beast's foot had stripped the skin from his back as neatly as one skins a rabbit. As soon as I saw the dead man, I sent an orderly to a friend's house nearby to borrow an elephant rifle. I had already sent back the pony, not wanting it to go mad with fright and throw me if it smelled the elephant.

The orderly came back in a few minutes with a rifle and five cartridges, and meanwhile some Burmans had arrived and told us that the elephant was in the paddy fields below, only a few hundred yards away. As I started forward, practically the whole population of the quarter flocked out of the houses and followed me. They had seen the rifle and were all shouting excitedly that I was going to shoot the elephant. They had not shown much interest in the elephant when he was merely ravaging their homes, but it was different now that he was going to be shot. It was a bit of fun to them, as it would be to an English crowd; besides they wanted the meat. It made me vaguely uneasy. I had no intention of shooting the elephant — I had merely sent for the rifle to defend myself if necessary — and it is always unnerving to have a crowd following you. I marched down the hill, looking and feeling a fool, with the rifle over my shoulder and an ever-growing army of people jostling at my heels. At the bottom, when you got away from the huts, there was a metaled [8] road and beyond that a miry waste of paddy fields a thousand yards across, not yet plowed but soggy from the first rains and dotted with coarse grass. The elephant was standing eight yards from the road, his left side toward us. He took not the slightest notice of the crowd's approach. He was tearing up bunches of grass, beating them against his knees to clean them, and stuffing them into his mouth.

I had halted on the road. As soon as I saw the elephant, I knew with perfect certainty that I ought not to shoot him. It is a serious matter to shoot a working elephant — it is comparable to destroying a huge and costly piece of machinery — and obviously one ought

[8] *metaled:* paved.

not to do it if it can possibly be avoided. And at that distance, peacefully eating, the elephant looked no more dangerous than a cow. I thought then and I think now that his attack of "must" was already passing off; in which case he would merely wander harmlessly about until the mahout came back and caught him. Moreover, I did not in the least want to shoot him. I decided that I would watch him for a little while to make sure that he did not turn savage again, and then go home.

But at that moment I glanced around at the crowd that had followed me. It was an immense crowd, two thousand at the least and growing every minute. It blocked the road for a long distance on either side. I looked at the sea of yellow faces above the garish clothes — faces all happy and excited over this bit of fun, all certain that the elephant was going to be shot. They were watching me as they would watch a conjurer about to perform a trick. They did not like me, but with the magical rifle in my hands I was momentarily worth watching. And suddenly I realized that I should have to shoot the elephant after all. The people expected it of me, and I had got to do it; I could feel their two thousand wills pressing me forward, irresistibly. And it was at this moment, as I stood there with the rifle in my hands, that I first grasped the hollowness, the futility of the white man's dominion in the East. Here was I, the white man with his gun, standing in front of the unarmed native crowd — seemingly the leading actor of the piece — but in reality I was only an absurd puppet pushed to and fro by the will of those yellow faces behind. I perceived in this moment that when the white man turns tyrant, it is his own freedom that he destroys. He becomes a sort of hollow, posing dummy, the conventionalized figure of a sahib.[9] For it is the condition of his rule that he shall spend his life in trying to impress the "natives," and so in every crisis he has got to do what the "natives" expect of him. He wears a mask, and his face grows to fit it. I had got to shoot the elephant. I had committed myself to doing it when I sent for the rifle. A sahib has got to act like a sahib; he has got to appear resolute, to know his own mind and do definite things. To come all that way, rifle in hand, with two thousand people marching at my heels, and then to trail feebly away, having done nothing — no, that was impossible. The crowd would laugh at me. And my whole life, every white man's

---

[9] *sahib*: native term for a European in the Far East.

life in the East, was one long struggle not to be laughed at.

But I did not want to shoot the elephant. I watched him beating his bunch of grass against his knees, with that preoccupied grand-motherly air that elephants have. It seemed to me that it would be murder to shoot him. At that age I was not squeamish about killing animals, but I had never shot an elephant and never wanted to. (Somehow it always seems worse to kill a *large* animal.) Besides, there was the beast's owner to be considered. Alive, the elephant was worth at least a hundred pounds; dead, he would only be worth the value of his tusks, five pounds, possibly. But I had got to act quickly. I turned to some experienced-looking Burmans who had been there when we arrived and asked them how the elephant had been behaving. They all said the same thing: he took no notice of you if you left him alone, but he might charge if you went too close to him.

It was perfectly clear to me what I ought to do. I ought to walk up to within, say, twenty-five yards of the elephant and test his be-havior. If he charged, I could shoot; if he took no notice of me, it would be safe to leave him until the mahout came back. But also I knew that I was going to do no such thing. I was a poor shot with a rifle, and the ground was soft mud into which one would sink at every step. If the elephant charged and I missed him, I should have about as much chance as a toad under a steamroller. But even then I was not thinking particularly of my own skin, only of the watchful yellow faces behind. For at that moment, with the crowd watching me, I was not afraid in the ordinary sense, as I would have been if I had been alone. A white man mustn't be frightened in front of "natives"; and so, in general, he isn't frightened. The sole thought in my mind was that if anything went wrong, those two thousand Burmans would see me pursued, caught, trampled on, and reduced to a grinning corpse like that Indian up the hill. And if that hap-pened, it was quite probable that some of them would laugh. That would never do. There was only one alternative. I shoved the car-tridges into the magazine and lay down on the road to get a better aim.

The crowd grew very still, and a deep, low, happy sigh, as of peo-ple who see the theater curtain go up at last, breathed from in-numerable throats. They were going to have their bit of fun after all. The rifle was a beautiful German thing with cross-hair sights. I did not then know that in shooting an elephant, one would shoot to cut an imaginary bar running from earhole to earhole. I ought, therefore, as the elephant was sideways on, to have aimed straight at his earhole; actually I aimed several inches in front of this, thinking the brain would be further forward.

When I pulled the trigger, I did not hear the bang or feel the kick — one never does when a shot goes home — but I heard the devilish roar of glee that went up from the crowd. In that instant, in too short a time, one would have thought, even for the bullet to get fhere, a mysterious, terrible change had come over the elephant. He neither stirred nor fell, but every line of his body had altered. He looked suddenly stricken, shrunken, immensely old, as though the frightful impact of the bullet had paralyzed him without knocking him down. At last, after what seemed a long time — it might have been five seconds, I dare say — he sagged flabbily to his knees. His mouth slobbered. An enormous senility seemed to have settled upon him. One could have imagined him thousands of years old. I fired again into the same spot. At the second shot he did not collapse but climbed with desperate slowness to his feet and stood weakly upright, with legs sagging and head drooping. I fired a third time. That was the shot that did for him. You could see the agony of it jolt his whole body and knock the last remnant of strength from his legs. But in falling, he seemed for a moment to rise, for as his hind legs collapsed beneath him he seemed to tower upward like a huge rock toppling, his trunk reaching skyward like a tree. He trumpeted, for the first and only time. And then down he came, his belly toward me, with a crash that seemed to shake the ground even where I lay.

I got up. The Burmans were already racing past me across the mud. It was obvious that the elephant would never rise again, but he was not dead. He was breathing very rhythmically with long rattling gasps, his great mound of a side painfully rising and falling. His mouth was wide open — I could see far down into caverns of pale pink throat. I waited a long time for him to die, but his breathing did not weaken. Finally I fired my two remaining shots into the spot where I thought his heart must be. The thick blood welled out of him like red velvet, but still he did not die. His body did not even jerk when the shots hit him, the tortured breathing continued without a pause. He was dying, very slowly and in great agony, but in some world remote from me where not even a bullet could damage him further. I felt that I had got to put an end to that dreadful noise. It seemed dreadful to see the great beast lying there, powerless to move and yet powerless to die, and not even to be able to finish him. I sent back for my small rifle and poured shot after shot into his heart and down his throat. They seemed to make no impression. The tortured gasps continued as steadily as the ticking of a clock.

In the end I could not stand it any longer and went away. I heard later that it took him half an hour to die. Burmans were bringing dahs [10] and baskets even before I left, and I was told they had stripped his body almost to the bones by the afternoon.

Afterward, of course, there were endless discussions about the shooting of the elephant. The owner was furious, but he was only an Indian and could do nothing. Besides, legally I had done the right thing, for a mad elephant has to be killed, like a mad dog, if its owner fails to control it. Among the Europeans opinion was divided. The older men said I was right, the younger men said it was a shame to shoot an elephant for killing a coolie, because an elephant was worth more than any coolie. And afterward I was very glad that the coolie had been killed; it put me legally in the right, and it gave me a sufficient pretext for shooting the elephant. I often wondered whether any of the others grasped that I had done it solely to avoid looking a fool.

---

[10] *dahs*: large knives.

A state with a senate, an emperor, consuls, and praetors suggests ancient Rome, which was finally conquered by barbarians after being demoralized by centuries of luxury and corruption. The people of Rome, like the people of any dying empire, must have long expected the coming of their conquerors and awaited them with a kind of desperate excitement. Perhaps many of them even looked forward to their coming as a release from the dull and weary patterns of their own empty lives.

Waiting for the Barbarians

C. P. CAVAFY

"What are we waiting for,
All of us gathered together like this in the Square?"

"The Barbarians are due to arrive today."

"Why is the Senate at a standstill?
Why do the Senators sit without making laws?"

"Because the Barbarians are coming today.
What laws would the Senate pass now?
When the Barbarians get here *they* will make the laws."

"Why has our Emperor sat since dawn
Solemnly enthroned at the City gates,   10
And wearing his crown?"

"That's because the Barbarians are on their way.
The Emperor is ready to receive their chief,
And has even had a scroll prepared
Conferring honors and titles upon him."

"Why have our two consuls and our praetors come forth
In their heavily embroidered scarlet togas?
And why are they decked with amethyst bracelets,
And rings sparkling with emeralds?
Why do they carry their choicest staffs   20
So finely carved?"

"Oh, that's all for the Barbarians, coming today;
Costly things like these will dazzle Barbarians."

"And why are our gifted orators
Not holding forth with their usual eloquence?"

"Because the Barbarians are coming today,
And *they* won't value long speeches or fine rhetoric."

"Now why, so suddenly, this commotion and concern?
How troubled the faces have become!
Why are streets and squares emptying so fast,   30
And why does everyone head for home, looking so somber?"

"It's because night is falling,
And the Barbarians have not come.
Some folk just in from the frontiers say
That now there aren't any Barbarians any more."

"So now what will become of us, without Barbarians?
For they were, after all, a kind of solution."

A page from the sketchbook of the
16th century German artist Albrecht Dürer.

Sterling and Francine Clark Art Institute, Williamstown, Mass.

ANIMAL FABLES

*"Lectures bore us, but we gladly
    turn
To fables, where amused we
    learn."*
          JEAN DE LA FONTAINE

"The pigs now revealed that during the past three months they
had taught themselves to read and write from an old spelling
book. . . . Napoleon sent for pots of black and white paint. . . .
Then Snowball (for it was Snowball who was best at writing) took
a brush between the two knuckles of his trotter, painted out MANOR
FARM from the top bar of the gate and in its place painted ANIMAL
FARM."

Only in a particular kind of story do pigs read and write and paint
signs with brushes held in their trotters. This kind of story, an animal fable, comes from one of the oldest traditions in the world.
Storytellers discovered long ago that we can often see our own traits
more clearly in animals than in human characters.

Animals have been used to express all sorts of human experiences.
The ancient Egyptians used sculptures of the Sphinx, which had
the head of a man on the body of a lion, to communicate their religious feelings. The ancient Greek writer Aesop, to whom we attribute many famous fables, relied on the folk tradition of using animals to illustrate human follies.

In Animal Farm, George Orwell used animal characters to comment on modern politics. He warned democracy of the human tendency to blindly follow unscrupulous leaders. The writers of the
fables which follow are also concerned with human blindness and

failing. Animal characters add humor to the stories and make truth, which is often unpleasant, easier to swallow.

The simplicity of fables makes them easy reading, but subjects such as man's pride or vanity are not simple at all. From the humor and satire of fables come truths about the way men act and react. Fables are really lessons disguised in delight.

Aesop's life is more a matter of legend than of history. Scholars have no way of knowing to what extent Aesop borrowed from Oriental folk tales and to what extent his fables were original. According to legend, he was a slave who was later freed by a master who appreciated his gift for storytelling.

The Dog and His Shadow

AESOP

A dog was crossing a bridge with a piece of meat in his mouth. He looked down and saw his reflection in the water and thought he saw another dog with a bigger piece of meat. He jumped to snatch the meat from the mouth of the other dog. Of course, his own meat fell in the water, so he had neither.

MORAL: *This story shows what happens to those who want more than they have.* |Greed|

dog- gov't , meat- people

The Mouse from the City — adjust
and the Mouse from the Country

AESOP

A mouse who lived on a farm invited a mouse who lived in the city to come and dine with him. The city mouse accepted the invitation, but when he arrived, he found that all there was to eat was some raw grain in a barn. He said to his host: "You live very crudely, my friend. In the city we have all sorts of good things to eat. Let's go back to town for dinner."

So they went back to the city, and when they arrived, the city mouse showed his friend a meal of bread and dates, cheese, fruit, and honey. The country mouse was amazed and began to regret his own way of life.

They were just about to begin their dinner when a door suddenly opened, and the timid mice were so frightened that they scampered into a hole. When they came out and were just about to dine once more, the door opened again and they had to run and hide a second time.

The country mouse was disgusted. "Good-by, my friend," he said. "You may enjoy yourself and have all you want to eat. But you pay a heavy price for it by living in danger. I would rather go back to my barn and eat raw grain than have to live in fear all the time."

MORAL: *It is better to live a simple life but a peaceful one than to live in luxury and fear.*

The Crab and Her Son

AESOP

A mother crab kept nagging at her son to walk straight, not sideways. "All right, Mother," the son replied, "you walk straight yourself, and I'll follow your example."

MORAL: *Those who teach others to walk straight should be able to do so themselves.*

It is a long leap from the ancient world of Aesop to the elegant and fashionable world of seventeenth-century France. In the French court at this time, nobles wore huge powdered wigs and elaborate costumes, while on the fringe of this life a writer named Jean de La Fontaine quietly observed the strange antics of fashionable people and wrote little stories about them. To avoid offending powerful people in the court, La Fontaine often used animal characters instead of human characters.

Grasshopper - aurisocrat - not planning
Ant -

The Grasshopper and the Ant

JEAN DE LA FONTAINE

The Grasshopper just sang a song
All the easy summer long.
When at last the winter came,
She had nothing to her name:
Not even a fragment of a fly
To eat, or insect. She began to cry
And begged her neighbor, Ant, in vain,
To lend her just a bit of grain
Until the Spring. "I'll pay you back!"
She cried, "I promise you won't lack   10
— On the solemn word of an Animal! —
The interest nor the principal."

"Neither a borrower nor a lender be,"
Replied the Ant. "Just look at me:
When days were warm, I kept to my task.
What were *you* doing — if I may ask?"

"Day and night, night and day,
I sang and sang and sang away!"

"Sang? How nice! Now take the chance,
Dear Grasshopper, to learn to dance!"   20

It is not quite so long a leap from the fables of La Fontaine to the fables of James Thurber, a modern writer and artist who drew his own cartoons. Unlike most earlier writers of fables, Thurber was not a moralist. In fact, his fables are often parodies (satires of writing) of solemn attempts to teach dull moral lessons in fable form. The "moral" of a Thurber fable is made with a light touch, half laughing at itself and everyone. Thurber suggests that it is best not to take things (and especially people) too seriously.

The Moth and the Star

JAMES THURBER

A young and impressionable moth once set his heart on a certain star. He told his mother about this, and she counseled him to set his heart on a bridge lamp instead. "Stars aren't the thing to hang around," she said. "Lamps are the thing to hang around." "You get somewhere that way," said the moth's father. "You don't get anywhere chasing stars." But the moth would not heed the words of either parent. Every evening at dusk when the star came out, he would start flying toward it, and every morning at dawn he would crawl back home worn out with his vain endeavor. One day his father said to him, "You haven't burned a wing in months, boy, and it looks to me as if you were never going to. All your brothers have been badly burned flying around street lamps, and all your sisters have been terribly singed flying around house lamps. Come on, now, get out of here and get yourself scorched! A big strapping moth like you without a mark on him!"

The moth left his father's house, but he would not fly around street lamps and he would not fly around house lamps. He went right on trying to reach the star, which was four and one-third light years, or twenty-five trillion miles, away. The moth thought it was just caught in the top branches of an elm. He never did reach the star, but he went right on trying, night after night, and when he was a very, very old moth, he began to think that he really had reached the star, and he went around saying so. This gave him a deep and lasting pleasure, and he lived to a great old age.

MORAL: Who flies afar from the sphere of our sorrow is here today and here tomorrow.

Vanity is a favorite subject for writers of fables. Men of all ages have been susceptible to flattery. All of us have some trait or talent that can be puffed up by flattery to convince us, for a moment, how marvelous we are. "The Fox and the Crow" has never lost its point though told and retold for over two thousand years. Compare these three versions of the same fable by Aesop, Thurber, and La Fontaine.

The Fox and the Crow: Three Versions

A crow was sitting in a tree holding in his beak a piece of meat that he had stolen. A fox came by and decided to get the piece of meat. So the fox stopped under the tree and began to tell the crow how <u>handsome</u> he was. He said that the crow ought to be King of all the birds and that he *could* be King if only he had a <u>voice</u> worthy of a ruler. The crow was so eager to show that he had such a voice that he opened his beak and the meat fell to the ground. The fox grabbed the meat and said, "If you had brains as well as a voice, you would make a very good King."

— AESOP

A crow, perched in a tree with a piece of cheese in his beak, attracted the eye and nose of a fox. "If you can sing as prettily as you sit," said the fox, "then you are the prettiest singer within my scent and sight." The fox had read somewhere, and somewhere, and somewhere else, that praising the voice of a crow with a cheese in his beak would make him drop the cheese and sing. But this is not what happened to this particular crow in this particular case.

"They say you are sly and they say you are crazy," said the crow, having carefully removed the cheese from his beak with the claws of one foot, "but you must be nearsighted as well. Warblers wear gay hats and colored jackets and bright vests, and they are a dollar a hundred. I wear black and I am unique." He began nibbling the cheese, dropping not a single crumb.

"I am sure you are," said the fox, who was neither crazy nor nearsighted, but sly. "I recognize you, now that I look more closely, as the most famed and talented of all birds, and I fain would hear you tell about yourself, but I am hungry and must go."

"Tarry awhile," said the crow quickly, "and share my lunch with me." Whereupon he tossed the cunning fox the lion's share of the cheese and began to tell about himself. "A ship that sails without a crow's nest sails to doom," he said. "Bars may come and bars may go, but crow bars last forever. I am the pioneer of flight, I am the map maker. Last, but never least, my flight is known to scientists and engineers, geometrists and scholars, as the shortest distance between two points. Any two points," he concluded arrogantly.

"Oh, every two points, I am sure," said the fox. "And thank you for the lion's share of what I know you could not spare." And with this he trotted away into the woods, his appetite appeased, leaving the hungry crow perched forlornly in the tree.

MORAL: *'Twas true in Aesop's time, and La Fontaine's, and now, no one else can praise thee quite so well as thou.*

— JAMES THURBER

A crow, perched debonairly on a branch,
    Was holding a cheese he'd found — by chance.
Along came a fox. He sniffed that cheese,
    And he spoke to its owner in words like these:

"Good morning, good morning, dear Brother Crow!
    My, you look fine! I've never seen you so —
So — *handsome.* Yes! I mean every word of it!
    And your lovely voice! Won't you sing a bit?"

The crow was enchanted — he could see no choice
    But give the fox a sample of his voice.
He opened his beak, and — cheese, good-by!
    The fox grabbed it up without batting an eye.

Said the fox: "As a payment for what you've lost
    I'll give you a lesson worth twice the cost:
Flattery's a game for two, my dear,
    One to talk — and another to hear."

— LA FONTAINE

A writer often reaches back into the past and uses the work of an earlier writer for his own purpose. So Shakespeare drew upon the lives of Brutus, Caesar, and Antony written by Plutarch for the tragedy Julius Caesar. George Bernard Shaw used the Greek myth of Pygmalion and Galatea for the pattern of his play Pygmalion, the source of My Fair Lady.

In the following short story a sophisticated Englishman draws a parallel between a famous animal fable and an incident from modern life. Such older forms of literature as the myth or the animal fable are not merely relics of the past; they form living truths which writers continue to draw upon.

The Ant and the Grasshopper

SOMERSET MAUGHAM

When I was a very small boy, I was made to learn by heart certain of the fables of La Fontaine, and the moral of each was carefully explained to me. Among those learned was "The Ant and the Grasshopper," which is devised to bring home to the young the useful lesson that in an imperfect world industry is rewarded and giddiness punished. In this admirable fable (I apologize for telling something which everyone is politely, but inexactly, supposed to know) the ant spends a laborious summer gathering its winter store, while the grasshopper sits on a blade of grass singing to the sun. Winter comes and the ant is comfortably provided for, but the grasshopper has an empty larder: he goes to the ant and begs for a little food. Then the ant gives him her classic answer:

"What were you doing in the summertime?"

"Saving your presence, I sang. I sang all day, all night."

"You sang. Why, then go and dance."

I do not ascribe it to perversity on my part but rather to the inconsequence of childhood, which is deficient in moral sense, that I could never quite reconcile myself to the lesson. My sympathies were with the grasshopper, and for some time I never saw an ant

119

without putting my foot on it. In this summary (and as I have discovered since, entirely human) fashion I sought to express my disapproval of prudence and common sense.

I could not help thinking of this fable when the other day I saw George Ramsay lunching by himself in a restaurant. I never saw anyone wear an expression of such deep gloom. He was staring into space. He looked as though the burden of the whole world sat upon his shoulders. I was sorry for him: I suspected at once that his unfortunate brother had been causing trouble again. I went up to him and held out my hand.

"How are you?" I asked.

"I'm not in hilarious spirits," he answered.

"Is it Tom again?"

He sighed.

"Yes, it's Tom again."

"Why don't you chuck him? You've done everything in the world for him. You must know by now that he's quite hopeless."

I suppose every family has a black sheep. Tom had been a sore trial to his for twenty years. He had begun life decently enough: he went into business, married, and had two children. The Ramsays were perfectly respectable people, and there was every reason to suppose that Tom Ramsay would have a useful and honorable career. But one day, without warning, he announced that he didn't like work and that he wasn't suited for marriage. He wanted to enjoy himself. He would listen to no expostulations.[1] He left his wife and his office. He had a little money, and he spent two happy years in various capitals of Europe. Rumors of his doings reached his relations from time to time, and they were profoundly shocked. He certainly had a very good time. They shook their heads and asked what would happen when his money was spent. They soon found out: he borrowed. He was charming and unscrupulous. I have never met anyone to whom it was more difficult to refuse a loan. He made a steady income from his friends, and he made friends easily. But he always said that the money you spent on necessities was boring; the money that was amusing to spend was the money you spent on luxuries. For this he depended on his brother George. He did not waste his charm on him. George was respectable. Once or twice he fell to Tom's promises of amendment and gave him considerable

---

[1] *expostulations*: earnest arguments.

sums in order that he might make a fresh start. On these Tom bought a motorcar and some very nice jewelry. But when circumstances forced George to realize that his brother would never settle down and he washed his hands of him, Tom, without a qualm, began to blackmail him. It was not very nice for a respectable lawyer to find his brother shaking cocktails behind the bar of his favorite restaurant or to see him waiting on the box seat of a taxi outside his club. Tom said that to serve in a bar or to drive a taxi was a perfectly decent occupation, but if George could oblige him with a couple of hundred pounds, he didn't mind for the honor of the family giving it up. George paid.

Once Tom nearly went to prison. George was terribly upset. He went into the whole discreditable affair. Really Tom had gone too far. He had been wild, thoughtless, and selfish, but he had never before done anything dishonest, by which George meant illegal; and if he were prosecuted, he would assuredly be convicted. But you cannot allow your only brother to go to jail. The man Tom had cheated, a man called Cronshaw, was vindictive. He was determined to take the matter into court; he said Tom was a scoundrel and should be punished. It cost George an infinite deal of trouble and five hundred pounds to settle the affair. I have never seen him in such a rage as when he heard that Tom and Cronshaw had gone off together to Monte Carlo the moment they cashed the check. They spent a happy month there.

For twenty years Tom raced and gambled, philandered [2] with the prettiest girls, danced, ate in the most expensive restaurants, and dressed beautifully. He always looked as if he had just stepped out of a bandbox. Though he was forty-six, you would never have taken him for more than thirty-five. He was a most amusing companion, and though you knew he was perfectly worthless, you could not but enjoy his society. He had high spirits, and unfailing gaiety, and incredible charm. I never grudged the contributions he regularly levied on me for the necessities of his existence. I never lent him fifty pounds without feeling that I was in his debt. Tom Ramsay knew everyone, and everyone knew Tom Ramsay. You could not approve of him, but you could not help liking him.

Poor George, only a year older than his scapegrace [3] brother,

---

[2] *philandered:* to flirt without serious intentions.
[3] *scapegrace:* "good-for-nothing."

looked sixty. He had never taken more than a fortnight's holiday in the year for a quarter of a century. He was in his office every morning at nine-thirty and never left it till six. He was honest, industrious, and worthy. He had a good wife, to whom he had never been unfaithful even in thought, and four daughters to whom he was the best of fathers. He made a point of saving a third of his income, and his plan was to retire at fifty-five to a little house in the country, where he proposed to cultivate his garden and play golf. His life was blameless. He was glad that he was growing old because Tom was growing old too. He rubbed his hands and said:

"It was all very well when Tom was young and good-looking, but he's only a year younger than I am. In four years he'll be fifty. He won't find life too easy then. I shall have thirty thousand pounds by the time I'm fifty. For twenty-five years I've said that Tom would end in the gutter. And we shall see how he likes that. We shall see if it really pays best to work or be idle."

Poor George! I sympathized with him. I wondered now as I sat down beside him what infamous thing Tom had done. George was evidently very much upset.

"Do you know what's happened now?" he asked me.

I was prepared for the worst. I wondered if Tom had got into the hands of the police at last. George could hardly bring himself to speak.

"You're not going to deny that all my life I've been hard-working, decent, respectable, and straightforward. After a life of industry and thrift I can look forward to retiring on a small income in gilt-edged securities. I've always done my duty in that state of life in which it has pleased Providence to place me."

"True."

"And you can't deny that Tom has been an idle, worthless, dissolute, and dishonorable rogue. If there were any justice, he'd be in the workhouse."

"True."

George grew red in the face.

"A few weeks ago he became engaged to a woman old enough to be his mother. And now she's died and left him everything she had. Half a million pounds, a yacht, a house in London, and a house in the country."

George Ramsay beat his clenched fist on the table.

"It's not fair, I tell you, it's not fair."

I could not help it. I burst into a shout of laughter as I looked at George's wrathful face. I rolled in my chair, I very nearly fell on the floor. George never forgave me. But Tom often asks me to excellent dinners in his charming house in Mayfair, and if he occasionally borrows a trifle from me, that is merely from force of habit. It is never more than a sovereign.[4]

The concept of freedom of speech is a relatively new idea for mankind. The animal fable is one way for writers to get around censorship and to discuss the relation of master and servant, slavery and freedom, the ruler and the ruled. In this fable, La Fontaine asks whether a change of government makes any real difference to the individual.

The Old Man and His Donkey

JEAN DE LA FONTAINE

An old man riding on his donkey
Came by a field full of grass and flowers.
He dismounted and allowed his beast
To rest and graze for a couple of hours.

The donkey kicked his heels and brayed
And stuffed himself with good green grass.
Just then an enemy soldier appeared.
"Run!" cried the man. "Fly! Alas!!!"

"Why?" said the donkey. "Will the enemy
Make me carry more weight on my back?"
"No," said the man, as he ran out of sight.
"So what?" said the donkey. "The enemy's pack

Is no heavier than yours. I don't care
Who owns me. Save yourself! Run faster!
I'll stay here eating. Because to me,
The enemy's just another master."

---

[4] *sovereign:* a British coin worth about five dollars at the time this story was written.

"You said a moment ago that everybody you look at seems to be a rabbit. Now just what do you mean by that, Mrs. Sprague?"

"What have you done with Dr. Millmoss?"

Two cartoons by James Thurber.

THE POWER OF LAUGHTER

*"Philosophers and sages have stayed up
many and many a night, seeking an
explanation, trying out a definition of
comedy, but have gone to bed no wiser,
and dead tired, while man kept on
laughing."*
    SEAN O'CASEY, "The Power of Laughter"

"Comedy is a very serious business." This remark, or a similar one, is often made by humorists. In one sense, the humorist or comedian means that he has to work very hard to be funny. He also means that comedy, no matter how funny, is about serious things.

At first glance, some comedy appears to be only amusement. But, in fact, even the silliest piece of slapstick — one man throwing a custard pie in another man's face — is a comment on human behavior. Think back to Animal Farm. As we read it, we are amused. Orwell is laughing at certain aspects of human nature through the means of an animal fable. But what is Animal Farm about? It's about human greed and cruelty, about the way in which dictators crush freedom and kill citizens who are no longer "useful." It's about the helplessness of the decent individual in the face of the police state. It's about the way leaders can manipulate language to deceive the common man. It all sounds pretty grim. Yet, as you know, Animal Farm has its comic aspects.

So comedy is one way of looking at life. George Orwell could have treated his subject in a grim or tragic manner. As a matter of fact, he wrote another novel about life under a dictatorship, Nineteen Eighty-Four, which is not at all comic. But in Animal Farm, Orwell chose to attack certain aspects of modern life in terms of comedy.

Laughter has a universal power. It can serve as a weapon of defense or as a means of attack. As a defense, it can help us keep our balance when life begins to look too grim. As an offensive weapon, laughter can be aimed at something that annoys us. Laughter can — and has — actually changed men and society. Literature which uses laughter or ridicule as a corrective weapon is called satire.

Mark Twain, one of the greatest writers of satire, said: "Humor must not professedly teach and it must not professedly preach, but it must do both if it would live forever. By forever, I mean thirty years." Twain's undercutting of the pompous forever in his own remark is typical of the way in which laughter brings us back to a sense of balance. Anything which takes itself too seriously or swells up with smug satisfaction is ripe and ready to be punctured by the simple, satiric power of laughter.

*Sean O'Casey is best known as a great Irish playwright, but in this
essay he speaks directly and personally to the reader. His subject is
laughter, but he does not attempt to "cover the topic" with a
systematic criticism. He speaks of laughter as a poet might, in lyrical,
figurative language, trying to show how he feels. With wit and gusto,
O'Casey reminds us of the function of laughter in our lives.*

from The Power of Laughter: Weapon Against Evil

SEAN O'CASEY

Laughter is wine for the soul — laughter soft, or loud and deep,
tinged through with seriousness. Comedy and tragedy step through
life together, arm in arm, all along, out along, down along lea.[1] A
laugh is a great natural stimulator, a pushful entry into life; and
once we can laugh, we can live. It is the hilarious declaration made
by man that life is worth living. Man is always hopeful of, always
pushing toward, better things; and to bring this about, a change
must be made in the actual way of life, so laughter is brought in to
mock at things as they are so that they may topple down and make
room for better things to come.

People are somewhat afraid of laughing. Many times, when
laughter abounded, I have heard the warning remark, "Oh, give it a
rest, or it'll end in a cry." It is odd how many seem to be curiously
envious of laughter, never of grief. You can have more than your
fill of grief, and nobody minds: they never grudge your grief to you.
You are given the world to grieve in; laughter is more often confined
to a corner. We are more afraid of laughter than we are of grief.
The saying is all wrong — it should be "Grieve, and the world grieves
with you; laugh, and you laugh alone." Laughter may be a bad thing;
grief is invariably a good or a harmless one.

---

[1] *lea:* a grassy field.

Nothing could kill or stay laughter, or hold it fast in one place. It spread itself out all over the world, for though men show their thoughts in many different manners and modes, they all laugh the same way.

Nothing seems too high or low for the humorist; he is above honor, above faith, preserving sense in religion and sanity in life. The minstrels thought (as we should think, too) that "The most completely lost of all days is that on which one hasn't laughed." So, if you get a chance in the hurry and complexity of life, laugh when the sun shines, when the rain falls, or even when the frost bites the skin or touches the heart with a chill.

Laughter has always been a puzzle to the thinker, a kind of a monkey puzzle,[2] a tree that doesn't look like a tree at all but is as much a tree as any other one. Philosophers and sages have stayed up many and many a night, seeking an explanation, trying out a definition of comedy, but have gone to bed no wiser, and dead tired, while man kept on laughing, content to enjoy it, and never bothering his head as to what it was. Crowds of thinkers have set down big theories about laughter and comedy, among them the great Aristotle, Plato, Socrates, and Kant;[3] but though all of them were often blue in the face thinking it out, none of them got to the bottom of its mystery.

The conscious humorist, said Vico,[4] is a very low fellow. We're all very low fellows, for all of us, some time or another, are conscious humorists. And well we are, for our souls' sake, and for the sake of man's sanity. We couldn't live without comedy. Let us pray: Oh, Lord, give us a sense of humor with courage to manifest it forth, so that we may laugh to shame the pomps, the vanities, the sense of self-importance of the Big Fellows that the world sometimes sends among us and who try to take our peace away. Amen.

---

[2] *monkey puzzle:* Chilean tree.
[3] *Aristotle . . . Kant:* The first three were great Greek philosophers, the fourth a German philosopher.
[4] *Vico:* an Italian philosopher of the eighteenth century.

*Anton Chekhov, one of <u>Russia's greatest writers</u>, is known for both
his stories and his <u>plays</u>, which are studies of human frustration,
loneliness, and self-deception. Many people think that Chekhov's plays
are gloomy, but he insisted that they are comedies because they
show the foolishness of mankind's self-deception. Humorists have
always poked fun at the kind of gossip that runs wild in a small
town. The following story is in this tradition.*

A Slander

ANTON CHEKHOV

[handwritten: Slander - a rumor that degrades a reputation.]

[handwritten: status - standings]

[handwritten: setting - 12 midnight]

The penmanship teacher Sergei Kapitonich Ahineyev was marry-
ing his daughter Natalia to the history and geography teacher. The
wedding gaiety was at its height. People sang, played, and danced in
the ballroom. Hired waiters, dressed in black tails and dirty white
ties, scurried back and forth like madmen. Noise filled the air. The
mathematics teacher, the French teacher, and the tax assessor, sitting
side by side on the sofa, talked hurriedly, interrupting each other
to tell the guests about cases of people buried alive and expressing
their opinions of spiritualism.[1] None of the three believed in spiritualism, but all admitted that there are many things in this world
which a human mind will never understand. In the next room the
literature teacher was explaining the cases in which a sentry has the
right to shoot at passers-by. As you can see, the conversations were
terrifying but highly pleasant. From the yard, people whose social
standing did not give them the right to enter looked through the
windows.

Exactly at midnight, Ahineyev, the host, walked into the kitchen
to see whether everything was ready for supper. The kitchen was full
of fumes from the goose and duck, mixed with many other smells.
Appetizers and drinks were spread in artistic disorder on two tables.
Marfa, <u>the cook</u>, a red-faced woman <u>whose figure was like a balloon
with a belt around it,</u> bustled near the tables.

[1] *spiritualism*: the belief that dead spirits communicate with the living.

"Show me the sturgeon,[2] Marfa," said Ahineyev, rubbing his hands and licking his lips. "What an aroma! I could eat up the whole kitchen. Now then, show me the sturgeon!"

Marfa went to a bench and carefully lifted a greasy newspaper. Under the paper, on an enormous platter, rested a big jellied sturgeon, dazzling with olives and carrots. Ahineyev looked at the sturgeon and gasped. His face beamed, his eyes rolled up. He bent over and made a sound like an ungreased wheel. After a while he snapped his fingers with pleasure and smacked his lips once more.

"Oh, the sound of a passionate kiss! . . . Who are you kissing in there, little Marfa?" asked a voice from the next room, and Vankin, an assistant teacher, stuck his cropped head through the door. "Who are you with? Ah, ah, ah . . . very nice! With Sergei Kapitonich! You're a fine grandfather, alone here with a woman!"

"Not at all, I am not kissing her," said Ahineyev with embarrassment. "Who told you that, you fool? I just . . . smacked my lips because of . . . my pleasure . . . at the sight of the fish."

"Tell me another one!" Vankin's head smiled broadly and disappeared behind the door. Ahineyev blushed.

"What now?" he thought. "The scoundrel will go now and gossip. He will put me to shame before the whole town, the beast . . ."

Ahineyev timidly entered the ballroom and looked around: where was Vankin? Vankin was standing at the piano and dashingly bent over to whisper something to the laughing sister-in-law of the inspector.

"It is about me," thought Ahineyev, "about me. He should be torn apart! And she believes . . . believes! She's laughing. I can't let this go on . . . no . . . I must arrange it so that no one will believe him . . . I will talk to everybody and show what a fool and gossip he is."

Ahineyev scratched himself and, still embarrassed, approached the French teacher.

"I was just in the kitchen, arranging the supper," he told the Frenchman. "I know you love fish and I have a sturgeon, old chap. Two yards long. Ha, ha, ha . . . oh, yes, I almost forgot . . . in the kitchen now, with the sturgeon . . . it was a real joke! I went to the kitchen and wanted to examine the food . . . I looked at the sturgeon and from the pleasure, the aroma of it, I smacked my lips!

---

[2] *sturgeon:* a large fresh-water fish.

But at this moment suddenly this fool Vankin came in and said . . . ha, ha, ha . . . and said . . . 'Ah, are you kissing in here?' Kissing Marfa, the cook! He made it all up, the fool. The woman looks like a beast, such a face, such skin . . . and he . . . kissing! Funny man!"

"Who is funny?" asked the mathematics teacher, coming over.

"That one there, Vankin! I came into the kitchen . . ." and he told the story of Vankin. "He made me laugh, he's so funny! I think I'd rather kiss a stray dog than Marfa," added Ahineyev, turning around and seeing the tax assessor behind him.

"We are talking about Vankin," said he. "Such a funny man! He came in the kitchen, saw me near Marfa . . . well, he started to invent all kinds of stories. 'Why,' he says, 'are you kissing?' He was drunk and made it up. And I said, 'I would rather kiss a turkey than Marfa. I have a wife,' I told him, 'you are such a fool.' He made me laugh."

"Who made you laugh?" asked the priest, who taught Scripture in the school, coming to Ahineyev.

"Vankin. I was, you know, standing in the kitchen and looking at the sturgeon . . ."

And so forth. In half an hour all the guests knew the story of the sturgeon and Vankin.

"Let him tell the stories now!" thought Ahineyev, rubbing his hands. "Let him! He'll start telling stories, and everyone will say right away: 'Stop talking nonsense, you fool! We know all about it.'"

And Ahineyev was so reassured that he drank four glasses too much from joy. After supper he saw the newlyweds to their room, went home, and slept like an innocent child, and the next day he had already forgotten the story of the sturgeon. But, alas! Man supposes, but God disposes. Wicked tongues will wag, and Ahineyev's cunning did not help him. Exactly a week later, after the third lesson on Wednesday, when Ahineyev was standing in the staff room discussing the evil ways of one of his students, the principal came to him and called him aside.

"Well, Sergei Kapitonich," said the principal, "excuse me . . . it is not my business, but still I must explain . . . my duty . . . you see, there is talk that you have kissed this . . . cook. It is not my business, but . . . kiss her . . . anything you want but, please, not so publicly. Please! Don't forget, you are a teacher."

Ahineyev got chilly and faint. He felt as if he had been stung by a swarm of bees and scalded with boiling water. As he walked home, it seemed to him that the whole town was looking at him as if he were smeared with tar. New trouble awaited him at home.

"Why don't you eat anything?" his wife asked him during dinner. "What are you thinking about? Your love life? Lonesome without little Marfa? I know all about it, Mohammedan![3] Good people opened my eyes! O-o-oh, barbarian!"

And she slapped him on the cheek. He left the table in a daze, without his hat and coat, and wandered to Vankin. Vankin was home.

"You scoundrel!" Ahineyev addressed Vankin. "Why did you smear me with mud before the entire world? Why did you slander me?"

"What slander? What are you inventing?"

"Who gossiped that I kissed Marfa? Not you? Not you, robber?"

Vankin blinked and winked with all his worn face, raised his eyes to the icon,[4] and said, "Let God punish me! Let my eyes burst, let me die, if I ever said one word about you! Bad luck to me! Cholera is not enough!"

The sincerity of Vankin could not be doubted. Evidently he had not gossiped.

"But who? Who?" thought Ahineyev, turning over in his mind all his acquaintances and beating his breast. "Who else?"

"Who else?" we will also ask the reader . . .

---

[3] *Mohammedan:* Members of this religion may take more than one wife.
[4] *icon:* religious picture.

*Like George Orwell, <u>Saki</u> (H. H. Munro), a Scot, was born
in the Far East. The name Saki was taken from a famous Persian
poem, The Rubáiyát of Omar Khayyám, where Saki is a cupbearer
of tempting wine. Like Orwell, Saki was educated in England, but
unlike Orwell, he had the misfortune to be brought up almost entirely
by strict and stuffy maiden aunts. His dislike for stuffy people in
general and strict aunts in particular is clear in many of his stories,
including this one, which takes place in a British railroad carriage.*

pen name

The Storyteller

SAKI

It was a hot afternoon, and the railway carriage was correspond-
ingly sultry, and the next stop was at Templecombe, nearly an hour
ahead. The occupants of the carriage were a small girl and a smaller
girl and a small boy. An aunt belonging to the children occupied
one corner seat, and the further corner seat on the opposite side was
occupied by a bachelor who was a stranger to their party, but the
small girls and the small boy emphatically occupied the compart-
ment. Both the aunt and the children were conversational in a limited, persistent way, reminding one of the attentions of a housefly
that refused to be discouraged. Most of the aunt's remarks seemed
to begin with "Don't," and nearly all of the children's remarks began with "Why?" The bachelor said nothing out loud.

"Don't, Cyril, don't," exclaimed the aunt, as the small boy began
smacking the cushions of the seat, producing a cloud of dust at each
blow.

"Come and look out of the window," she added.

The child moved reluctantly to the window. "Why are those
sheep being driven out of that field?" he asked.

"I expect they are being driven to another field where there is
more grass," said the aunt weakly.

"But there is lots of grass in that field," protested the boy;

"there's nothing else but grass there. Aunt, there's lots of grass in that field."

"Perhaps the grass in the other field is better," suggested the aunt fatuously.

"Why is it better?" came the swift, inevitable question.

"Oh, look at those cows!" exclaimed the aunt. Nearly every field along the line had contained cows or bullocks, but she spoke as though she were drawing attention to a rarity.

"Why is the grass in the other field better?" persisted Cyril.

The frown on the bachelor's face was deepening to a scowl. He was a hard, unsympathetic man, the aunt decided in her mind. She was utterly unable to come to any satisfactory decision about the grass in the other field.

The smaller girl created a diversion by beginning to recite "On the Road to Mandalay." She only knew the first line, but she put her limited knowledge to the fullest possible use. She repeated the line over and over again in a dreamy but resolute and very audible voice; it seemed to the bachelor as though someone had had a bet with her that she could not repeat the line aloud two thousand times without stopping. Whoever it was who had made the wager was likely to lose his bet.

"Come over here and listen to a story," said the aunt, when the bachelor had looked twice at her and once at the communication cord.

The children moved listlessly toward the aunt's end of the carriage. Evidently her reputation as a storyteller did not rank high in their estimation.

In a low, confidential voice, interrupted at frequent intervals by loud, petulant questions from her listeners, she began an unenterprising and deplorably uninteresting story about a little girl who was good and made friends with everyone on account of her goodness and was finally saved from a mad bull by a number of rescuers who admired her moral character.

"Wouldn't they have saved her if she hadn't been good?" demanded the bigger of the small girls. It was exactly the question that the bachelor had wanted to ask.

"Well, yes," admitted the aunt lamely, "but I don't think they would have run quite so fast to her help if they had not liked her so much."

"It's the stupidest story I've ever heard," said the bigger of the small girls, with immense conviction.

"I didn't listen after the first bit, it was so stupid," said Cyril.

The smaller girl made no actual comment on the story, but she had long ago recommenced a murmured repetition of her favorite line.

"You don't seem to be a success as a storyteller," said the bachelor suddenly from his corner.

The aunt bristled in instant defense at this unexpected attack.

"It's a very difficult thing to tell stories that children can both understand and appreciate," she said stiffly.

"I don't agree with you," said the bachelor.

"Perhaps *you* would like to tell them a story," was the aunt's retort.

"Tell us a story," demanded the bigger of the small girls.

"Once upon a time," began the bachelor, "there was a little girl called Bertha, who was extraordinarily good."

The children's momentarily aroused interest began at once to flicker; all stories seemed dreadfully alike, no matter who told them.

"She did all that she was told, she was always truthful, she kept her clothes clean, ate milk puddings as though they were jam tarts, learned her lessons perfectly, and was polite in her manners."

"Was she pretty?" asked the bigger of the small girls.

"Not as pretty as any of you," said the bachelor, "but she was horribly good."

There was a wave of reaction in favor of the story; the word horrible in connection with goodness was a novelty that commended itself. It seemed to introduce a ring of truth that was absent from the aunt's tales of infant life.

"She was so good," continued the bachelor, "that she won several medals for goodness, which she always wore, pinned on to her dress. There was a medal for obedience, another medal for punctuality, and a third for good behavior. They were large metal medals, and they clinked against one another as she walked. No other child in the town where she lived had as many as three medals, so everybody knew that she must be an extra good child."

"Horribly good," quoted Cyril.

"Everybody talked about her goodness, and the Prince of the country got to hear about it, and he said that as she was so very good she might be allowed once a week to walk in his park, which was just outside the town. It was a beautiful park, and no children were ever allowed in it, so it was a great honor for Bertha to be allowed to go there."

"Were there any sheep in the park?" demanded Cyril.

"No," said the bachelor, "there were no sheep."

"Why weren't there any sheep?" came the inevitable question arising out of that answer.

The aunt permitted herself a smile, which might almost have been described as a grin.

"There were no sheep in the park," said the bachelor, "because the Prince's mother had once had a dream that her son would either be killed by a sheep or else by a clock falling on him. For that reason the Prince never kept a sheep in his park or a clock in his palace."

The aunt suppressed a gasp of admiration.

"Was the Prince killed by a sheep or by a clock?" asked Cyril.

"He is still alive, so we can't tell whether the dream will come true," said the bachelor unconcernedly. "Anyway, there were no sheep in the park, but there were lots of little pigs running all over the place."

"What color were they?"

"Black with white faces, white with black spots, black all over, gray with white patches, and some were white all over."

The storyteller paused to let a full idea of the park's treasures sink into the children's imaginations; then he resumed:

"Bertha was rather sorry to find that there were no flowers in the park. She had promised her aunts, with tears in her eyes, that she would not pick any of the kind Prince's flowers, and she had meant to keep her promise, so of course it made her feel silly to find that there were no flowers to pick."

"Why weren't there any flowers?"

"Because the pigs had eaten them all," said the bachelor promptly. "The gardeners had told the Prince that you couldn't have pigs and flowers, so he decided to have pigs and no flowers."

There was a murmur of approval at the excellence of the Prince's decision; so many people would have decided the other way.

"There were lots of other delightful things in the park. There were ponds with gold and blue and green fish in them, and trees with beautiful parrots that said clever things at a moment's notice, and hummingbirds that hummed all the popular tunes of the day. Bertha walked up and down and enjoyed herself immensely, and thought to herself: 'If I were not so extraordinarily good, I should not have been allowed to come into this beautiful park and enjoy all that there is to be seen in it,' and her three medals clinked against one another as she walked and helped to remind her how very good she really was. Just then an enormous wolf came prowling into the park to see if it could catch a fat little pig for its supper."

"What color was it?" asked the children, amid an immediate quickening of interest.

"Mud color all over, with a black tongue and pale gray eyes that gleamed with unspeakable ferocity. The first thing that it saw in the park was Bertha; her pinafore was so spotlessly white and clean that it could be seen from a great distance. Bertha saw the wolf and saw that it was stealing toward her, and she began to wish that she had never been allowed to come into the park. She ran as hard as she could, and the wolf came after her with huge leaps and bounds. She managed to reach a shrubbery of myrtle bushes, and she hid herself in one of the thickest of the bushes. The wolf came sniffing among the branches, its black tongue lolling out of its mouth and its pale gray eyes glaring with rage. Bertha was terribly frightened and thought to herself: 'If I had not been so extraordinarily good, I should have been safe in the town at this moment.' However, the scent of the myrtle was so strong that the wolf could not sniff out where Bertha was hiding, and the bushes were so thick that he might have hunted about in them for a long time without catching sight of her, so he thought he might as well go off and catch a little pig instead. Bertha was trembling very much at having the wolf prowling and sniffing so near her, and as she trembled, the medal for obedience clinked against the medals for good conduct and punctuality. The wolf was just moving away when he heard the sound of the medals clinking and stopped to listen; they clinked again in a bush quite near him. He dashed into the bush, his pale gray eyes gleaming with ferocity and triumph, and dragged Bertha out and devoured her to the last morsel. All that was left of her were her shoes, bits of clothing, and the three medals for goodness."

"Were any of the little pigs killed?"

"No, they all escaped."

"The story began badly," said the smaller of the small girls, "but it had a beautiful ending."

"It is the most beautiful story that I ever heard," said the bigger of the small girls, with immense decision.

"It is the *only* beautiful story I have ever heard," said Cyril.

A dissentient opinion came from the aunt.

"A most improper story to tell to young children! You have undermined the effect of years of careful teaching."

"At any rate," said the bachelor, collecting his belongings preparatory to leaving the carriage, "I kept them quiet for ten minutes, which was more than you were able to do."

"Unhappy woman!" he observed to himself as he walked down the platform of Templecombe station. "For the next six months or so those children will assail her in public with demands for an improper story!"

Parody is a special form of satire which makes fun of the weaknesses and peculiarities of an author or of some kind of writing. Parody usually works by exaggerating some of the characteristic features of the writing it is aimed at. These two parodies by Robert Benchley give a new perspective on the "gay little legends" people often think of as good reading for children.

Happy Childhood Tales

ROBERT BENCHLEY

We have had so many stories lately dealing with the sordid facts of life, about kitchen sinks and young girls thrown out into the streets by mean old farmers who live in horsehair trunks, to say nothing of incidental subjects, such as gin and cold oatmeal and unfortunate people who have only one glove apiece, that a reaction is taking place in the mind of the reading public and a demand is going up for some of the fanciful happy tales of our youth.

"Enough of these stories of crime and unhappiness!" the people are crying. "Tell us again some of the ancient myths of an older day, the gay little legends on which we were brought up before the world grew grim and sordid."

And so, my little readers, I am going to try to recall to you some of the charming fairy tales or, at any rate, to make up some like them, and I hope that after this little trip back into the Never-Never Land of our youth, those little cheeks of yours will be blooming again and that you will shut your traps. For, after all, there must be some good in the world, else why were erasers put on the ends of lead pencils?

ENDREMIA AND LIASON

(FROM THE GREEK MYTHOLOGY)

Endremia was the daughter of Polygaminous, the God of Ensilage, and Reba, the Goddess of Licorice. She was the child of a most unhappy union, it later turned out, for when she was a tiny

child her father struck her mother with an anvil and turned himsel:
into a lily pad to avoid the vengeance of Jove. But Jove was too sly
for Polygaminous and struck him with a bolt of lightning the size
of the Merchants Bank Building, which threw him completely off
his balance so that he toppled over into a chasm and was dashed to
death.

In the meantime, Little Endremia found herself alone in the
world with nobody but Endrocine, the Goddess of Lettuce, and her
son Bilax, the God of Gum Arabic, to look after her. But, as Polygaminous (her father; have you forgotten so soon, you dope?) had
turned Endremia into a mushroom before he turned himself into a
lily pad, neither of her guardians knew who she was, so their protection did her no good.

But Jove had not so soon forgotten the daughter of his favorite
(Reba) and appeared to her one night in the shape of a mushroom-
gatherer. He asked her how she would like to get off that tree (she
was one of those mushrooms that grow on trees) and get into his
basket. Endremia, not knowing that it was Jove who was asking her,
said not much. Whereupon Jove unloosed his mighty wrath and
struck down the whole tree with a bolt of lightning which he had
brought with him in case Endremia wouldn't listen to reason.

This is why it is never safe to eat the mushrooms which grow on
trees or to refuse to get into Jove's basket.

MILGRIG AND THE TREE WILFS

(SOMETHING LIKE HANS CHRISTIAN ANDERSEN)

Once upon a time there was a little girl named Milgrig, believe it
or not. She lived in the middle of a deep dark forest with her three
ugly sisters and their husbands, who were charcoal burners. Every
night the three ugly sisters used to take little Milgrig and pull out
a strand of her golden hair, so that by the time she was thirteen
years old she looked something awful. And after the three sisters
had pulled out her hair, their three husbands (I forgot to tell you
that the three husbands were even uglier than the three sisters and
much nastier) would stick pins into little Milgrig until she looked
like a war map.

One night, when little Milgrig was so full of pins that she couldn't see straight, a fairy prince came riding up to the door of the charcoal burners' hut and asked if he had lost his way.

"How should I know?" replied the oldest sister, who was uglier than all the rest. "What was your way?"

"My way was to the king's castle," replied the prince, "and I must get there before midnight, for my father is torturing my mother with red-hot irons."

"Your father sounds like a good egg," replied the oldest husband, who was uglier than all the rest. "We must ask him down some night."

The prince, however, did not think that this was very funny and asked if little Milgrig might not be allowed to show him the way to the castle.

The ugly husbands and sisters, thinking that Milgrig would not know the way and would get the prince lost in the forest, agreed heartily to this suggestion, and the pins were pulled out of Milgrig to make it possible for her to walk.

"Good luck and a happy landing!" they all called out after the two young people as they set forth on their perilous journey.

But the prince was no fool and knew his way through the forest as well as you or I do (better, I'll wager), and he took little Milgrig to the palace just as fast as his palfrey [1] would carry him.

She wasn't particularly crazy about going, but a prince is a prince, and she knew enough to keep her mouth shut.

When they reached the palace and the prince found that his father had already killed his mother, he turned to little Milgrig and said:

"Now you are queen."

At this, little Milgrig was very pleased and immediately dispatched messengers to the charcoal burners' hut, where her three ugly sisters and three still uglier brothers-in-law were burned alive in a slow fire. Little Milgrig and the prince, happy in this termination to their little affair, lived happily ever after.

And so now, my readers, you must toddle off to bed, for we have had an evening with the happy, happy storytellers of an earlier day and have had a vacation, for one night at least, from the drab, unpleasant sordidness of present-day writing.

---

[1] *palfrey:* a saddle horse.

Laughter can be used as a satiric weapon against ideas as well as human weaknesses. Everyone who has taken a course in English in which papers are returned with red circles around misspelled words might become enthusiastic about a plan to simplify the English alphabet. One prominent advocate of simplified spelling was the English playwright George Bernard Shaw. In the following essay, Dolton Edwards pursues the idea of such simplification to its logical conclusion.

Meihem in ce Klasrum

DOLTON EDWARDS

Because we are still bearing some of the scars of our brief skirmish with II-B English, it is natural that we should be enchanted by Mr. George Bernard Shaw's current campaign for a simplified alphabet.

Obviously, as Mr. Shaw points out, English spelling is in much need of a general overhauling and streamlining. However, our own resistance to any changes requiring a large expenditure of mental effort in the near future would cause us to view with some apprehension the possibility of some day receiving a morning paper printed in — to us — Greek.

Our own plan would achieve the same end as the legislation proposed by Mr. Shaw but in a less shocking manner, as it consists merely of an acceleration of the normal processes by which the language is continually modernized.

As a catalytic agent,[1] we would suggest that a "National Easy Language Week" be proclaimed, which the President would inaugurate, outlining some short cut to concentrate on during the week and to be adopted during the ensuing year. All school children would be given a holiday, the lost time being the equivalent of that gained by the spelling short cut.

In 1976, for example, we would urge the elimination of the soft *c*, for which we would substitute *s*. Sertainly, such an improvement

---

[1] *catalytic* (kat'ə·lit'ik) *agent*: in chemistry, a substance that begins a reaction.

would be selebrated in all sivic-minded sircles as being suffisiently worth the trouble, and students in all sities in the land would be reseptive toward any shange eliminating the nesessity of learning the differense between the two letters.

In 1977, sinse only the hard c would be left, it would be possible to substitute k for it, both letters being pronounsed identikally. Imagine how greatly only two years of this prosess would klarify the konfusion in the minds of students. Already we would have eliminated an entire letter from the alphabet. Typewriters and linotypes kould all be built with one less letter, and all the manpower and materials previously devoted to making c's kould be turned toward raising the national standard of living.

In the fase of so many notable improvements, it is easy to foresee that by 1978, "National Easy Language Week" would be a pronounsed sukses. All skholl shildren would be looking forward with konsiderable exsitement to the holiday, and in a blaze of national publisity it would be announsed that the double konsonant ph no longer existed, and that the sound would henseforth be written f in all words. This would make sutsh words as fonograf twenty persent shorter in print.

By 1979, publik interest in a fonetik alfabet kan be expekted to have inkreased to the point where a more radikal step forward kan be taken without fear of undue kritisism. We would therefore urge the elimination, at that time of al unesesary double leters, whitsh, although quite harmles, have always ben a nuisanse in the language and a desided deterent to akurate speling. Try it yourself in the next leter you write, and se if both writing and reading are not fasilitated.

With so mutsh progres already made, it might be posible in 1980 to delve further into the posibilities of fonetik speling. After due konsideration of the reseption aforded the previous steps, it should be expedient by this time to spel al difthongs fonetikaly. Most students do not realize that the long i and y, as in time and by, are aktualy the difthong ai, as it is writen in aisle, and that the long a in fate is in reality the difthong ei as in rein. Although perhaps not imediately aparent, the saving in taime and efort wil be tremendous when we leiter elimineite the sailent e, as meide posible bai this last tsheinge.

For, as is wel known, the horible mes of e's apearing in our writen language is kaused prinsipaly bai the present nesesity of indikeiting whether a vowel is long or short. Therefore, in 1981 we kould simply elimineit al sailent *e*'s and kontinu to read and wrait merily along as though we wer in an atomik ag of edukation.

In 1981 we would urg a greit step forward. Sins bai this taim it would have ben four years sins anywun had used the leter *c*, we would sugest that the "National Easy Languag Wek" for 1981 be devoted to substitution of *c* for *th*. To be sur, it would be som taim befor peopl would bekom akustomd to reading ceir newspapers and buks wic sutsh sentenses in cem as "Ceodor caught he had cre cousand cistls crust crough ce cik of his cumb."

In ce seim maner, bai meiking eatsh leter hav its own sound and cat sound only, we kould shorten ce languag stil mor. In 1982 we would elimineit ce *y*; cen in 1983 we kould us ce leter to indikeit ce *sh* sound, cerbai klarifaiing words laik *yugar* and *yur*, as wel as redusing bai wun mor leter al words laik *yut*, *yor*, and so forc. Cink, cen, of al ce benefits to be gaind bai ce distinktion whitsh wil cen be meid between words laik:

ocean now writen *oyean*
machine now writen *mayin*
racial now writen *reiyial*

Al sutsh divers weis of wraiting wun sound would no longer exist, and whenever wun keim akros a *y* sound, he would know exaktli what to wrait.

Kontinuing cis proses, year after year, we would eventuali hav a reli sensibl writen languag. By 1985, wi ventyur tu sei, cer wud bi no mor uv ces teribli trublsum difikultis, wic no tu leters usd to indikeit ce seim nois, and laikwais no tu noises riten wic ce seim leter. Even Mr. Yaw, wi beliv, wud be hapi in ce noleg cat his drims fainali keim tru.

In the poem that follows, the author appears to be writing about animals but really has his eyes on human imperfections. Armour's attitude seems to be that human folly will always be with us, so we might as well enjoy it.

The Ant

RICHARD ARMOUR

The ant, a prodigy of strength,
Lifts objects twice his weight and length
And never stops or sighs or glowers
Because it's after working hours.
Though underground, he bears the onus
And peril without thought of bonus,
And never once is heard to mention
Retiring on a tax-free pension.
Nor does he frown or look askance
At other, lighter-burdened ants.
Not one to bicker, blame, or sob,
Not angling for a better job,
The ant has but one flaw I see,
To wit, he doesn't work for me.

The Termite

OGDEN NASH

Some primal termite knocked on wood,
And tasted it, and found it good,
And that is why your Cousin May
Fell through the parlor floor today.

Humor can come in very conventional wrappings, as it does in the poem that follows. But often a matter-of-fact approach "sets up" the reader for an ironic twist at the end of the story. Compare the theme of this verse with that of "The Ant and the Grasshopper" by Somerset Maugham on page 119.

Those Two Boys

FRANKLIN P. ADAMS

When Bill was a lad he was terribly bad.
 He worried his parents a lot;
He'd lie and he'd swear and pull little girls' hair;
 His boyhood was naught but a blot.

At play and in school he would fracture each rule —
 In mischief from autumn to spring;
And the villagers knew when to manhood he grew
 He would never amount to a thing.

When Jim was a child he was not very wild;
 He was known as a good little boy;
He was honest and bright and the teachers' delight —
 To his father and mother a joy.

All the neighbors were sure that his virtue'd endure,
 That his life would be free of a spot;
They were certain that Jim had a great head on him
 And that Jim would amount to a lot.

And Jim grew to manhood and honor and fame
 And bears a good name;
While Bill is shut up in a dark prison cell —
 You never can tell.

Here is a poem only two words longer than its title, and eleven words shorter than this introduction.

Little Lyric

(Of Great Importance)

LANGSTON HUGHES

I wish the rent
Was heaven sent.

The Purist

OGDEN NASH

I give you now Professor Twist,
A conscientious scientist.
Trustees exclaimed, "He never bungles!"
And sent him off to distant jungles.
Camped on a tropic riverside,
One day he missed his loving bride.
She had, the guide informed him later,
Been eaten by an alligator.
Professor Twist could not but smile.
"You mean," he said, "a crocodile."

The modern American painter Stuart Davis
often incorporated words and letters into his
pictures as in "Owh! in San Pao."

Collection of Whitney Museum of American Art, New York.

LANGUAGE
IN ACTION

"When I sit down to write a book, I do
not say to myself, 'I am going to produce
a work of art.' I write it because there is
some lie I want to expose, some fact to
which I want to draw attention, and my
initial concern is to get a hearing."
GEORGE ORWELL, "Why I Write"

Every time we pick up a newspaper or turn on the television, we
are in a semantic jungle where men are shouting slogans. If they
shout loud enough and long enough, we begin to think a slogan
means something. But more often than not, neither the speaker nor
the listener knows what it means at all.

In Animal Farm, in the tradition of the animal fable, the animals could use language. They talked to each other, gathered to
hear a speech by Old Major, even learned a song, the words of which
excited and inspired them. After the revolution, the intelligent pigs
learned to read and write. When they mastered those skills, the pigs
gradually lost interest in teaching the other animals to read and
write, partly because the task was difficult but mainly because they
did not wish to share the ability to manipulate words. Snowball
painted the Seven Commandments on the barn, but it was not long
before the pigs found it necessary to change the text to suit their
own purposes. Their control of language was a key element in their
rise to power and domination of the other animals:

Once again all rations were reduced, except those of the pigs and the
dogs. . . . For the time being, certainly, it had been found necessary

to make a readjustment of rations (Squealer always spoke of it as a "readjustment," never as a "reduction").

Most people take their language for granted. Words are used simply as a matter of habit to carry on business and to make appropriate noises at the right times. But, for all the habit involved, our use of language is what sets us apart from animals, who may communicate very well but who do not use language. Any language is a complex system, no matter how "simple" or primitive the people may be who use it. Given this complexity, it is not surprising that everyone has some difficulty with language.

SEMANTICS

Language can be studied in terms of syntax, history, sounds, or the meanings of words. Semantics, the study of meanings in language, is of much concern in an age of rapid, global communication. Today it is technologically possible to communicate with anyone in the world, but semantically it is still difficult for any man to make even a simple message clear to another man. Yet there are those who understand how to manipulate other people by controlling language. Among the most successful are those who write advertisements and political propaganda. Among the most dangerous are those who cover their political ambitions with propaganda while they enslave whole nations.

The stories and essays in this section are all about problems of human communication through language. One of the essays is written by S. I. Hayakawa, who has brought the study of semantics to a wide audience. His best-known book, Language in Action, was first published in 1941, when Adolf Hitler had achieved great power through the use of propaganda. Hayakawa later wrote: "Hitler is gone, but if the majority of our fellow-citizens are more susceptible to the slogans of fear and race hatred than to those of peaceful accommodation and mutual respect among human beings, our political liberties remain at the mercy of any eloquent and unscrupulous demagogue." George Orwell looks at this same problem in his essay "Politics and the English Language."

To take a language from a people is to take away their identity and their culture. Wars and revolutions have been waged partly over the attempts of one group to impose its language on another. In recent times we have seen a bitter rivalry between the French- and English-speaking peoples of Canada, involving the French Canadians' efforts to preserve their own language. In India, too, there have been riots over the government's attempts to establish official languages.

"The Last Lesson" is set in the territory of Alsace-Lorraine, a part of France on the German border. The time is the Franco-Prussian War, 1870 to 1871.

Freedom- surrendered . Climax - At noon- trumpets.

The Last Lesson

ALPHONSE DAUDET

I started for school very late that morning and was in great dread of a scolding, especially because M. Hamel had said that he would question us on participles, and I did not know the first word about them. For a moment I thought of running away and spending the day out of doors. It was so warm, so bright! The birds were chirping at the edge of the woods, and in the open field back of the sawmill the Prussian soldiers were drilling. It was all much more tempting than the rule for participles, but I had the strength to resist and hurried off to school.

When I passed the town hall, there was a crowd in front of the bulletin board. For the last two years all our bad news had come from there — the lost battles, the draft, the orders of the commanding officer — and I thought to myself, without stopping:

"What can be the matter now?"

Usually, when school began, there was a great bustle, which could be heard out in the street, the opening and closing of desks, lessons repeated in unison, very loud, with our hands over our ears to understand better, and the teacher's great ruler rapping on the table. But now it was all so still! I had counted on the commotion to get to my desk without being seen, but, of course, that day everything had to be as quiet as Sunday morning. Through the window I saw my classmates, already in their places, and M. Hamel walking up and down with his terrible iron ruler under his arm. I had to open the door and go in before everybody. You can imagine how I blushed and how frightened I was.

But nothing happened. M. Hamel saw me and said very kindly: "Go to your place quickly, little Franz."

I jumped over the bench and sat down at my desk. Not till then, when I had got a little over my fright, did I see that our teacher had on his beautiful green coat, his frilled shirt, and the little black silk cap, all embroidered, that he never wore except on inspection and prize days. Besides, the whole school seemed so strange and solemn. But the thing that surprised me most was to see, on the back benches that were always empty, the village people sitting quietly like ourselves; old Hauser, with his three-cornered hat, the former mayor, the former postmaster, and several others besides. Everybody looked sad, and Hauser had brought an old primer, thumbed at the edges, and he held it open on his knees with his great spectacles lying across the pages.

While I was wondering about it all, M. Hamel mounted his chair and, in the same grave and gentle tone said:

"My children, this is the last lesson I shall give you. The order has come from Berlin to teach only German in the schools of Alsace and Lorraine. The new master comes tomorrow. This is your last French lesson. I want you to be very attentive."

What a thunderclap these words were to me!

Oh, the wretches; that was what they had put up at the town hall!

My last French lesson! Why, I hardly knew how to write! I should never learn any more! I must stop there, then! Oh, how sorry I was for not learning my lessons, for seeking birds' eggs, or going sliding on the Saar! My books, that had seemed such a nuisance a while ago, so heavy to carry, my grammar, and my history of the saints, were old friends now that I couldn't give up. And M. Hamel, too; the idea that he was going away, that I should never see him again, made me forget all about his ruler and how cranky he was.

Poor man! It was in honor of this last lesson that he had put on his fine Sunday clothes, and now I understood why the old men of the village were sitting there in the back of the room. It was because they were sorry, too, that they had not gone to school more. It was their way of thanking our master for his forty years of faithful service and of showing their respect for the country that was theirs no more.

While I was thinking of all this, I heard my name called. It was my turn to recite. What would I not have given to be able to say that dreadful rule for the participle all through, very loud and clear, and without one mistake? But I got mixed up on the first words and stood there, holding on to my desk, my heart beating, and not daring to look up. I heard M. Hamel say to me:

"I won't scold you, little Franz; you must feel bad enough. See how it is! Every day we have said to ourselves: 'Bah! I've plenty of time. I'll learn it tomorrow.' And now you see where we've come out. Ah, that's the great trouble with Alsace; she puts off learning till tomorrow. Now those fellows out there will have the right to say to you: 'How is it; you pretend to be Frenchmen, and yet you can neither speak nor write your own language?' But you are not the worst, poor little Franz. We've all a great deal to reproach ourselves with.

"Your parents were not anxious enough to have you learn. They preferred to put you to work on a farm or at the mills, so as to have a little more money. And I? I've been to blame also. Have I not often sent you to water my flowers instead of learning your lessons? And when I wanted to go fishing, did I not just give you a holiday?"

Then, from one thing to another, M. Hamel went on to talk of the French language, saying that it was the most beautiful language in the world — the clearest, the most logical; that we must guard it among us and never forget it, because when a people are enslaved, as long as they hold fast to their language, it is as if they had the key to their prison. Then he opened a grammar and read us our lesson. I was amazed to see how well I understood it. All he said seemed so easy, so easy! I think, too, that I had never listened so carefully and that he had never explained everything with so much patience. It seemed almost as if the poor man wanted to give us all he knew before going away and to put it all into our heads at one stroke.

After the grammar, we had a lesson in writing. That day M. Hamel had new copies for us, written in a beautiful round hand: France, Alsace, France, Alsace. They looked like little flags floating everywhere in the schoolroom, hung from the rod at the top of our desks. You ought to have seen how every one set to work and how quiet it was! The only sound was the scratching of the pens over the paper. Once some beetles flew in, but nobody paid any attention to them, not even the littlest ones, who worked right on tracing their fishhooks,[1] as if that was French too. On the roof the pigeons cooed very low, and I thought to myself:

"Will they make them sing in German, even the pigeons?"

Whenever I looked up from my writing, I saw M. Hamel sitting motionless in his chair and gazing first at one thing, then at another, as if he wanted to fix in his mind just how everything looked in that little schoolroom. Fancy! For forty years he had been there in the same place, with his garden outside the window and his class in front of him, just like that. Only the desks and benches had been worn smooth; the walnut trees in the garden were taller, and the hop vine that he had planted himself twined about the windows to the roof. How it must have broken his heart to leave it all, poor man; to hear his sister moving about in the room above, packing their trunks! For they must leave the country next day.

But he had the courage to hear every lesson to the very last. After the writing, we had a lesson in history, and then the babies chanted their *ba, be, bi, bo, bu*. Down there at the back of the room old Hauser had put on his spectacles and, holding his primer in both hands, spelled the letters with them. You could see that he, too, was crying; his voice trembled with emotion, and it was so funny to hear him that we all wanted to laugh and cry. Ah, how well I remember it, that last lesson!

All at once the church clock struck twelve. Then the Angelus.[2] At the same moment, the trumpets of the Prussians, returning from drill, sounded under our windows. M. Hamel stood up, very pale, in his chair. I never saw him look so tall. PROUD

"My friends," said he, "I — I — " But something choked him. He could not go on.

Then he turned to the blackboard, took a piece of chalk, and, bearing on with all his might, he wrote as large as he could:

"Vive La France!" [3]

Then he stopped and leaned his head against the wall, and, without a word, he made a gesture to us with his hand: - actions

"School is dismissed — you may go."

---

[1] *fishhooks:* penmanship exercises.
[2] *Angelus:* a prayer said morning, noon, and night.
[3] *Vive La France!:* Long live France!

Often a great deal depends on the meaning of a single word. When two persons interpret that word differently, the results can be comic or serious — or both.

A Day's Wait

ERNEST HEMINGWAY

He came into the room to shut the windows while we were still in bed, and I saw he looked ill. He was shivering, his face was white, and he walked slowly as though it ached to move.

"What's the matter, Schatz?" [1]

"I've got a headache."

"You better go back to bed."

"No. I'm all right."

"You go to bed. I'll see you when I'm dressed."

But when I came downstairs he was dressed, sitting by the fire, looking a very sick and miserable boy of nine years. When I put my hand on his forehead I knew he had a fever.

"You go up to bed," I said, "you're sick."

"I'm all right," he said.

When the doctor came he took the boy's temperature.

"What is it?" I asked him.

"One hundred and two."

Downstairs, the doctor left three different medicines in different colored capsules with instructions for giving them. One was to bring down the fever, another a purgative, the third to overcome an acid condition. The germs of influenza can only exist in an acid condition, he explained. He seemed to know all about influenza and said there was nothing to worry about if the fever did not go above one hundred and four degrees. This was a light epidemic of flu and there was no danger if you avoided pneumonia.

Back in the room I wrote the boy's temperature down and made

---

[1] *Schatz:* German term of endearment.

a note of the time to give the various capsules.

"Do you want me to read to you?"

"All right. If you want to," said the boy. His face was very white and there were dark areas under his eyes. He lay still in the bed and seemed very detached from what was going on.

I read aloud from Howard Pyle's *Book of Pirates*; but I could see he was not following what I was reading.

"How do you feel, Schatz?" I asked him.

"Just the same, so far," he said.

I sat at the foot of the bed and read to myself while I waited for it to be time to give another capsule. It would have been natural for him to go to sleep, but when I looked up he was looking at the foot of the bed, looking very strangely.

"Why don't you try to go to sleep? I'll wake you up for the medicine."

"I'd rather stay awake."

After a while he said to me, "You don't have to stay in here with me, Papa, if it bothers you."

"It doesn't bother me."

"No, I mean you don't have to stay if it's going to bother you."

I thought perhaps he was a little lightheaded and after giving him the prescribed capsules at eleven o'clock I went out for a while.

It was a bright, cold day, the ground covered with a sleet that had frozen so that it seemed as if all the bare trees, the bushes, the cut brush and all the grass and the bare ground had been varnished with ice. I took the young Irish setter for a little walk up the road and along a frozen creek, but it was difficult to stand or walk on the glassy surface, and the red dog slipped and slithered and I fell twice, hard, once dropping my gun and having it slide away over the ice.

We flushed a covey of quail under a high clay bank with overhanging brush and I killed two as they went out of sight over the top of the bank. Some of the covey lit in trees, but most of them scattered into brush piles and it was necessary to jump on the ice-coated mounds of brush several times before they would flush. Coming out while you were poised unsteadily on the icy, springy brush they made difficult shooting, and I killed two, missed five, and started back pleased to have found a covey close to the house and happy there were so many left to find on another day.

At the house they said the boy had refused to let any one come into the room.

"You can't come in," he said. "You mustn't get what I have."

I went up to him and found him in exactly the position I had left him, white-faced, but with the tops of his cheeks flushed by the fever, staring still, as he had stared, at the foot of the bed.

I took his temperature.

"What is it?"

"Something like a hundred," I said. It was one hundred and two and four tenths.

"It was a hundred and two," he said.

"Who said so?"

"The doctor."

"Your temperature is all right," I said. "It's nothing to worry about."

"I don't worry," he said, "but I can't keep from thinking."

"Don't think," I said. "Just take it easy."

"I'm taking it easy," he said and looked straight ahead. He was evidently holding tight onto himself about something.

"Take this with water."

"Do you think it will do any good?"

"Of course it will."

I sat down and opened the *Pirate* book and commenced to read, but I could see he was not following, so I stopped.

"About what time do you think I'm going to die?" he asked.

"What?"

"About how long will it be before I die?"

"You aren't going to die. What's the matter with you?"

"Oh, yes, I am. I heard him say a hundred and two."

"People don't die with a fever of one hundred and two. That's a silly way to talk."

"I know they do. At school in France the boys told me you can't live with forty-four degrees. I've got a hundred and two."

He had been waiting to die all day, ever since nine o'clock in the morning.

"You poor Schatz," I said. "Poor old Schatz. It's like miles and kilometers. You aren't going to die. That's a different thermometer. On that thermometer thirty-seven is normal. On this kind it's ninety-eight."

"Are you sure?"

"Absolutely," I said. "It's like miles and kilometers. You know, like how many kilometers we make when we do seventy miles in the car?"

"Oh," he said.

But his gaze at the foot of the bed relaxed slowly. The hold over himself relaxed too, finally, and the next day it was very slack and he cried very easily at little things that were of no importance.

*S. I. Hayakawa frequently writes about the need for people to
understand the consequences of their use or misuse of language. He
suggests that language should be used with an awareness of its effects
on ourselves and others. Here he suggests that starting a discussion
on "the level of description" can help us to communicate better.*

What Are You
Talking About?

S. I. HAYAKAWA

A friend of mine who had had no previous experience in labor
activity recently found himself elected to the grievance committee
of the union to which he belongs. There were a number of small
grievances around the plant in which he worked, so he found himself sent, along with two experienced committee members, to present the workers' complaints to the manager.

A curious thing happened, my friend relates, as soon as they got
into the manager's office. His two fellow delegates immediately
started talking to the manager in a sullen and aggressive way, as
if they were acting in a play the role of Militant-Workers-Demand-
ing-Their-Rights.

The manager didn't know what it was all about. To start with,
the delegates hadn't explained to him what the grievances were.
Yet he found himself being pushed around and denounced as a
pitiless exploiter of the working people. He looked so miserable that
my friend, sizing up the situation, took over.

My friend approached the manager in a different way. "Look,
Mr. Manager," he began — and he went on to explain the grievances step by step, beginning at the beginning and stating everything clearly, without indignation.

The manager quickly became greatly interested in the grievances.
"Is that so?" he would interject. "Why, I didn't know that was happening! . . . Of course, that isn't right. . . . Why hasn't Mr. Pea-

body brought this to my attention before? . . . Well, well, well
. . . I'll take care of things right away."

"There was nothing to it," my friend explained later. "We had
everything settled in ten minutes. But what interested me most was
what the manager said to me afterward. He said that I was the first
representative of my union who ever took the trouble to describe the
grievances accurately before jumping down his throat."

Now, all workers don't adopt an aggressive attitude in discussing
grievances with management. And sometimes it is management that
is sullen and aggressive. But the incident, it appeared to me, is an
excellent illustration of a semantic principle. It has to do with what
semanticists call "levels of abstraction."

In talking about any situation, there are several levels at which
it can be discussed. First, there is the *descriptive* level, where you try
to state accurately, without getting yourself worked up into a lather,
what the situation is. For example, "Six employees in the shipping
department were not paid for the overtime work they did last
month."

Secondly, there is the *inferential* level, where you make some guess
as to the reasons for the situation. These guesses may be accurate or
not, but they are still guesses — inferences. For example, "The employer is trying to defraud his employees." Other guesses are possible, such as "There was an error in the timekeeper's office" or
"There exist differences between the employer's and the employees'
definitions of what constitutes overtime."

Thirdly, there is the *judgment* level, where you pass some kind of
favorable or unfavorable judgment on the situation. For example,
"The employer is a pitiless exploiter of the working class." Where
both parties to a dispute discuss their differences with each other
only at the levels of inference and judgment, so that in reply to the
charge, "The boss is a mean old skinflint," the employer replies,
"The workers are shiftless goldbrickers," *there is no possibility of
arriving at agreement.*

The point, then, if you want to save your blood pressure and arrive at agreement with people, is to begin discussion at the *descriptive* level. People have a right to know *what* you are talking about
before hearing your inferences and judgments on the subject.

It isn't always easy, however, to separate descriptions from inferences and judgments. When, for example, we see a car weaving

dangerously on the highway, how careful are we about reacting to our inferences? Usually, we make an inference that the driver is drunk and grow angry about it without being aware that what we are angry about is only an inference — possibly correct, but possibly not.

The science of semantics shows many ways in which untrained habits of thought and speech lead to unnecessary conflict and bitterness. One of the major techniques of clarification and agreement is this matter of starting discussion at the descriptive level and continuing *often* to check your inferences and judgments against this level.

If more people were to ask now and then, in the course of heated discussions and arguments, "Just what exactly are we talking about?" and if enough people knew how to answer the question, the world would be a quieter place. And easier to live in, too.

An American poet once said, "Good writers are those who keep the language efficient. That is to say, keep it accurate, keep it clear." George Orwell might have added, "keep it honest."

The following selection is taken from an essay Orwell wrote in 1946, after the collapse of Hitler's Third Reich and Mussolini's Fascist government in Italy. Both these governments, along with Stalin's Russia, were particularly frightening to an artist like Orwell because they were totalitarian states, where a dictator ruled the people by suppressing their voices and strictly regulating all that they might read, or see, or hear. Orwell saw that these governments perverted language in the same way that the pigs in Animal Farm made the Seven Commandments meaningless by constantly rewriting them.

Orwell felt that such political systems encouraged the misuse of language and thereby weakened it. He found much writing of his time to be stale and lacking in precision because writers deliberately chose to be vague and to use twenty words where one would do. The selection here begins with Orwell's "translation" of a passage from the Old Testament.

from Politics and the English Language

GEORGE ORWELL

I am going to translate a passage of good English into modern English of the worst sort. Here is a well-known verse from *Ecclesiastes*:

"I returned and saw under the sun, that the race is not to the swift, nor the battle to the strong, neither yet bread to the wise, nor yet riches to men of understanding, nor yet favor to men of skill; but time and chance happeneth to them all."

Here it is in modern English:

"Objective consideration of contemporary phenomena compels the conclusion that success or failure in competitive activities exhibits no tendency to be commensurate with innate capacity but that a considerable element of the unpredictable must invariably be taken into account."

This is a parody but not a very gross one. It will be seen that I have not made a full translation. The beginning and ending of the sentence follow the original meaning fairly closely, but in the middle the concrete illustrations — race, battle, bread — dissolve into the vague phrase "success or failure in competitive activities." This had to be so, because no modern writer of the kind I am discussing — no one capable of using phrases like "objective consideration of contemporary phenomena" — would ever tabulate his thoughts in that precise and detailed way. The whole tendency of modern prose is away from concreteness. Now analyze these two sentences a little more closely. The first contains forty-nine words but only sixty syllables, and all its words are those of everyday life. The second contains thirty-eight words of ninety syllables: eighteen of its words are from Latin roots and one from Greek. The first sentence contains six vivid images and only one phrase ("time and chance") that could be called vague. The second contains not a single fresh, arresting phrase, and in spite of its ninety syllables it gives only a shortened version of the meaning contained in the first. Yet without a doubt it is the second kind of sentence that is gaining ground in modern English. I do not want to exaggerate. This kind of writing is not yet universal, and outcrops of simplicity will occur here and there in the worst-written page. Still, if you or I were told to write a few lines on the uncertainty of human fortunes, we should probably come much nearer to my imaginary sentence than to the one from *Ecclesiastes*.

In our time it is broadly true that political writing is bad writing. Where it is not true, it will generally be found that the writer is some kind of rebel, expressing his private opinions and not a "party line." Orthodoxy,[1] of whatever color, seems to demand a lifeless, imitative style. The political dialects to be found in pamphlets, leading articles, manifestoes, White Papers and the speeches of under secretaries do, of course, vary from party to party, but they are all alike in that one almost never finds in them a fresh, vivid, home-made turn of speech. When one watches some tired hack on the platform mechanically repeating the familiar phrases — *bestial atrocities, iron heel, bloodstained tyranny, free peoples of the world,*

[1] *Orthodoxy:* adhering to a traditional style or belief.

stands shoulder to shoulder — one often has a curious feeling that one is not watching a live human being but some kind of dummy, a feeling which suddenly becomes stronger at moments when the light catches the speaker's spectacles and turns them into blank disks which seem to have no eyes behind them. And this is not altogether fanciful. A speaker who uses that kind of phraseology has gone some distance toward turning himself into a machine. The appropriate noises are coming out of his larynx, but his brain is not involved as it would be if he were choosing his words for himself. If the speech he is making is one that he is accustomed to make over and over again, he may be almost unconscious of what he is saying, as one is when one utters the responses in church. And this reduced state of consciousness, if not indispensable, is at any rate favorable to political conformity.

In our time, political speech and writing are largely the defense of the indefensible. Things like the continuance of British rule in India, the Russian purges and deportations, the dropping of the atom bombs on Japan can indeed be defended but only by arguments which are too brutal for most people to face and which do not square with the professed aims of political parties. Thus, political language has to consist largely of euphemism,[2] question-begging,[3] and sheer cloudy vagueness. Defenseless villages are bombarded from the air, the inhabitants driven out into the countryside, the cattle machine-gunned, the huts set on fire with incendiary bullets: this is called *pacification*.[4] Millions of peasants are robbed of their farms and sent trudging along the roads with no more than they can carry: this is called *transfer of population* or *rectification of frontiers*. People are imprisoned for years without trial, or shot in the back of the neck, or sent to die of scurvy in Arctic lumber camps: this is called *elimination of unreliable elements*. Such phraseology is needed if one wants to name things without calling up mental pictures of them. Consider, for instance, some comfortable English professor defending Russian totalitarianism. He cannot say outright, "I believe in killing off your opponents when you can get good re-

---

[2] *euphemism*: substituting a roundabout word or expression for another felt to be too blunt.

[3] *question-begging*: the fallacy of making a conclusion based on an assumption that needs to be proved as much as the conclusion itself.

[4] *pacification*: Orwell may have in mind Mussolini's invasion of Ethiopia in 1936.

sults by doing so." Probably, therefore, he will say something like this:

"While freely conceding that the Soviet régime exhibits certain features which the humanitarian may be inclined to deplore, we must, I think, agree that a certain curtailment of the right to political opposition is an unavoidable concomitant of transitional periods and that the rigors which the Russian people have been called upon to undergo have been amply justified in the sphere of concrete achievement."

The inflated style is itself a kind of euphemism. A mass of Latin words falls upon the facts like soft snow, blurring the outlines and covering up all the details. The great enemy of clear language is insincerity. When there is a gap between one's real and one's declared aims, one turns as it were instinctively to long words and exhausted idioms, like a cuttlefish squirting out ink. In our age there is no such thing as "keeping out of politics." All issues are political issues, and politics itself is a mass of lies, evasions, folly, hatred, and schizophrenia. When the general atmosphere is bad, language must suffer. I should expect to find — this is a guess which I have not sufficient knowledge to verify — that the German, Russian, and Italian languages have all deteriorated in the last ten or fifteen years, as a result of dictatorship.

"Robert Frost," portrait by Gardner Cox. (Detail)

THE POETRY OF ROBERT FROST

More people looked at Robert Frost than at any other American poet. In his old age — he lived to be almost eighty-nine — he went up and down and across the land, "saying" his poems at schools and colleges, being photographed and applauded, even holding press conferences. Everywhere he went he was surrounded by crowds of delighted admirers, as though he were a movie star or famous ballplayer. But his fame, after years of neglect, was more lasting and more deserved than that of most celebrities.

People accepted Frost as the American poet, not only because his poems were interesting (as of course they are), but also because of his striking appearance. They felt that Frost radiated both friendliness and self-confidence, liked to be near him, and wanted to please him. He was not tall, but he walked like a very tall man. When he spoke, he enjoyed surprising people; of the atomic bomb, for instance, he said, "If we all die together, we'll be in good company." If asked why he wrote poems, he would sometimes reply, "I write them to see if I can make them sound different from each other." After a night out in Moscow — he once went to Russia on a special mission — he remarked, "We painted the town red, didn't we?"

Often Frost seemed to say whatever had just come into his head — a large, square head covered with handsome white hair in old age. He gave so great an impression of rugged strength in both mind and body that he almost seemed to be an American symbol, like the flag or the Washington Monument. Nobody, therefore, was surprised when John F. Kennedy invited Frost to read a poem at his inauguration as President. "It would give the American public as much pleasure as it would my family and me," wrote Mr. Kennedy. And so Frost was the first poet ever to take part in the ceremony of inauguration of a President. In that year, 1961, Frost could look back on four decades of fame and honor, a Congressional medal, four Pulitzer prizes, and over forty honorary degrees from universities and colleges.

But Robert Frost was nobody at all for almost half of his long life. It is fortunate that he lived to be old because his career started so late. Except for a privately published book of verses, only two copies of which were printed, and some poems that appeared in out-of-the-way places, Frost was unknown as a poet until, at the age of forty-one, he returned to America from a long stay in England. While in England, Frost had published the two books of poems that launched his career: A Boy's Will, 1913, and North of Boston, 1914.

Frost's genius was first recognized by the English. This fact is not very important, except that it shows the wide appeal of his poetry. Frost is a "New England poet" only in the sense that he lived most of his life in that region and wrote about it in many of his poems. But he always rejected the label. "I am not a regionalist," he once remarked. "I am a realmist." While he was in the U.S.S.R., a poem in a Russian newspaper asserted that "Robert Frost is the President of the real America." This bold statement undoubtedly refers to the values of individualism and freedom that are so strongly emphasized in his poems.

In geographical ways, too, Frost is more representative than many other great American writers. He lived in several states outside New England — Florida, Michigan, Iowa, Texas — and he was born far from New England, in San Francisco. Frost early learned the habit of mobility, which is often regarded as an American characteristic. His family had eight different addresses in San Francisco during the first eleven years of his life.

Although he came from a long line of New Englanders, Frost's father was so sympathetic toward the Southern cause in the Civil War that he named his son after General Robert E. Lee. When he grew up, the poet never used his full name. Yet this is what is inscribed on his gravestone, followed by a quotation adapted from one of his poems:

Robert Lee Frost
"He had a lover's quarrel with the world."

Frost as a Poet of Nature

Frost is an out-of-doors poet; nearly every page of his books reflects his interest in the natural world: the ants and the apple orchard, birches and brooks, hornets and hillsides, woodchucks and weather — the list could go on and on. His poems record an older and a more rural America, before housing developments, before the cities started to spread over the countryside. They help us to know what life was like before superhighways, jetliners, and television. They also help make us aware of the natural world that is still all around us. A snow-covered field or a sky full of stars will not seem the same as it did before, after one has read Frost. Like all good poets, Frost helps us to see what we would otherwise only look at.

In Frost's poems nature is not merely pretty things like flowers and sunsets; it is the whole creation, the universe and everything in it not built by men and women. Nature is space, the air, the weather, the rivers, the mountains. Looked at in this way, nature is too important for the poet to gush about it or make it seem prettier and nicer than it actually is. Nature just is, Frost seems to tell us, and if we are to love nature, let us be sure that we love it for what it is and not for something else. Frost had only contempt for what he called "sunset raving."

Frost once said that the incident in this poem was "similar to good news in the morning paper."

Dust of Snow

The way a crow
Shook down on me
The dust of snow
From a hemlock tree

Has given my heart
A change of mood
And saved some part
Of a day I had rued.

The first three stanzas of this poem describe a scene that is common in country places; the last stanzas describe what the birds are doing about it.

The Need of Being Versed in Country Things

The house had gone to bring again
To the midnight sky a sunset glow.
Now the chimney was all of the house that stood,
Like a pistil after the petals go.

The barn opposed across the way,
That would have joined the house in flame
Had it been the will of the wind, was left
To bear forsaken the place's name.

No more it opened with all one end
For teams that came by the stony road   10
To drum on the floor with scurrying hoofs
And brush the mow with the summer load.

The birds that came to it through the air
At broken windows flew out and in,
Their murmur more like the sigh we sigh
From too much dwelling on what has been.

Yet for them the lilac renewed its leaf,
And the aged elm, though touched with fire;
And the dry pump flung up an awkward arm;
And the fence post carried a strand of wire.   20

For them there was really nothing sad.
But though they rejoiced in the nest they kept,
One had to be versed in country things
Not to believe the phoebes wept.

Each of the two preceding poems has shown a contrast between man and nature. The final lines of this poem make a similar comparison.

Tree at My Window

Tree at my window, window tree,
My sash is lowered when night comes on;
But let there never be curtain drawn
Between you and me.

Vague dream-head lifted out of the ground,
And things next most diffuse to cloud,
Not all you light tongues talking aloud
Could be profound.

But, tree, I have seen you taken and tossed,
And if you have seen me when I slept,
You have seen me when I was taken and swept
And all but lost.

The day she put our heads together,
Fate had her imagination about her,
Your head so much concerned with outer,
Mine with inner, weather.

Once by the Pacific

The scattered water made a misty din.
Great waves looked over others coming in,
And thought of doing something to the shore
That water never did to land before.
The clouds were low and hairy in the skies,
Like locks blown forward in the gleam of eyes.
You could not tell, and yet it looked as if
The shore was lucky in being backed by cliff,
The cliff in being backed by continent;
It looked as if a night of dark intent
Was coming, and not only a night, an age.
Someone had better be prepared for rage.
There would be more than ocean-water broken
Before God's last *Put out the Light* was spoken.

To the Thawing Wind

Come with rain, O loud Southwester!
Bring the singer, bring the nester;
Give the buried flower a dream;
Make the settled snowbank steam;
Find the brown beneath the white;
But whate'er you do tonight,
Bathe my window, make it flow,
Melt it as the ice will go;
Melt the glass and leave the sticks
Like a hermit's crucifix;
Burst into my narrow stall;
Swing the picture on the wall;
Run the rattling pages o'er;
Scatter poems on the floor;
Turn the poet out of door.

*A heal-all is a small plant with a flower that is ordinarily violet or blue
and is said to have healing properties.*

Design

I found a dimpled spider, fat and white,
On a white heal-all, holding up a moth
Like a white piece of rigid satin cloth —
Assorted characters of death and blight
Mixed ready to begin the morning right,
Like the ingredients of a witches' broth —
A snow-drop spider, a flower like a froth,
And dead wings carried like a paper kite.

What had that flower to do with being white,
The wayside blue and innocent heal-all?
What brought the kindred spider to that height,
Then steered the white moth thither in the night?
What but design of darkness to appall? —
If design govern in a thing so small.

Frost's Individualism

Individualism is the quality in a person that enables him to be himself rather than another person. It is a quality that Robert Frost admired very much in other people and strove to develop in himself.

The characters in Frost's poems are independent; they think and act for themselves. Many of them share their creator's attitude toward freedom: freedom is humanity's greatest good. All his life Frost tried to be a free spirit, a man who was free to be himself, to make his own discoveries, to be limited only by his own strength, conscience, and intellect. Early in life he apparently decided to be his own man, and he never reversed his decision. It helped him to write poems like nobody else's. It also influenced his behavior. As a schoolteacher, he sabotaged the rules; as a farmer, he did his farm work in his own way; as a poet, he developed his own style. Frost was neither a do-gooder nor a joiner. His advice was this:

> Don't join too many gangs. Join few if any.
> Join the United States and join the family —
> But not much in between unless a college.

Frost disliked fashions. In a letter he once remarked that "Some people save themselves a lot of trouble by not hearing of new things too soon." He distrusted labels and resisted classification. When asked whether he was an optimist or a pessimist, he would say, "Please — no labels." He would reject and ridicule a label by coining a new label. "I'm a pursuitist," he once said, "not an escapist."

Once in an interview he explained in a way that was partly humorous and partly serious why he was no reformer: "I am not much interested in movements. I am not a person of that kind . . . I am too irregular. I keep bad hours. I do not try to reform. I have no quarrel with life, and I do not try to 'run' life."

With a point of view of this kind, Frost naturally felt sympathetic toward a great variety of people and different ways of life. Among the characters in his poems are a census-taker, a plowman, an astronomer, an aviator, a professor, a letter-carrier, and a man who gathers gum from spruce trees. Not all of these characters are "respectable." Frost liked to write about untypical people, good or bad. He has a

man who burns down his house and spends the insurance money on
a telescope and another man who hates a locomotive so much that
he plans to throw a turtle egg at it. Some of Frost's characters are
disturbed and neurotic, others are self-reliant and self-sufficient;
none of them complains or pities himself.

*Frost was seated in a railroad dining car, riding through the Ozarks,
when he glimpsed this figure.*

The Figure in the Doorway

The grade surmounted, we were riding high
Through level mountains nothing to the eye
But scrub oak, scrub oak and the lack of earth
That kept the oaks from getting any girth.
But as through the monotony we ran,
We came to where there was a living man.
His great gaunt figure filled his cabin door,
And had he fallen inward on the floor,
He must have measured to the further wall.
But we who passed were not to see him fall.   10
The miles and miles he lived from anywhere
Were evidently something he could bear.
He stood unshaken, and if grim and gaunt,
It was not necessarily from want.
He had the oaks for heating and for light.
He had a hen, he had a pig in sight.
He had a well, he had the rain to catch.
He had a ten-by-twenty garden patch.
Nor did he lack for common entertainment.
That I assume was what our passing train meant.   20
He could look at us in our diner eating,
And if so moved uncurl a hand in greeting.

*Among the characteristics of New England are the old walls of piled
stones that separate one person's field from another's.*

Mending Wall

Something there is that doesn't love a wall,
That sends the frozen-ground-swell under it,
And spills the upper boulders in the sun;
And makes gaps even two can pass abreast.
The work of hunters is another thing:
I have come after them and made repair
Where they have left not one stone on a stone,
But they would have the rabbit out of hiding,
To please the yelping dogs. The gaps I mean,
No one has seen them made or heard them made,   10
But at spring mending-time we find them there.
I let my neighbor know beyond the hill;
And on a day we meet to walk the line
And set the wall between us once again.
We keep the wall between us as we go.
To each the boulders that have fallen to each.
And some are loaves and some so nearly balls
We have to use a spell to make them balance:
"Stay where you are until our backs are turned!"
We wear our fingers rough with handling them.   20
Oh, just another kind of outdoor game,
One on a side. It comes to little more:
There where it is we do not need the wall:
He is all pine and I am apple orchard.
My apple trees will never get across
And eat the cones under his pines, I tell him.
He only says, "Good fences make good neighbors."
Spring is the mischief in me, and I wonder
If I could put a notion in his head:
"*Why* do they make good neighbors? Isn't it   30
Where there are cows? But here there are no cows.
Before I built a wall I'd ask to know
What I was walling in or walling out,
And to whom I was like to give offense.

Something there is that doesn't love a wall,
That wants it down." I could say "Elves" to him,
But it's not elves exactly, and I'd rather
He said it for himself. I see him there
Bringing a stone grasped firmly by the top
In each hand, like an old-stone savage armed.   40
He moves in darkness as it seems to me,
Not of woods only and the shade of trees.
He will not go behind his father's saying,
And he likes having thought of it so well
He says again, "Good fences make good neighbors."

Of all the forces of nature, a blizzard can be one of the most unpleasant, frightening, and confusing. Finding your way home through a blizzard can be a real test of will.

Willful Homing

It is getting dark and time he drew to a house,
But the blizzard blinds him to any house ahead.
The storm gets down his neck in an icy souse
That sucks his breath like a wicked cat in bed.

The snow blows on him and off him, exerting force
Downward to make him sit astride a drift,
Imprint a saddle and calmly consider a course.
He peers out shrewdly into the thick and swift.

Since he means to come to a door he will come to a door,
Although so compromised of aim and rate
He may fumble wide of the knob a yard or more,
And to those concerned he may seem a little late.

Like the speaker of the poem which follows, Frost also enjoyed splitting firewood. Besides the exercise involved, always striking in the same spot for a clean split is a real test of skill.

Two Tramps in Mud Time

Out of the mud two strangers came
And caught me splitting wood in the yard.
And one of them put me off my aim
By hailing cheerily "Hit them hard!"
I knew pretty well why he dropped behind
And let the other go on a way.
I knew pretty well what he had in mind:
He wanted to take my job for pay.

Good blocks of oak it was I split,
As large around as the chopping block;   10
And every piece I squarely hit
Fell splinterless as a cloven rock.
The blows that a life of self-control
Spares to strike for the common good
That day, giving a loose to my soul,
I spent on an unimportant wood.

The sun was warm but the wind was chill.
You know how it is with an April day
When the sun is out and the wind is still,
You're one month on in the middle of May.   20
But if you so much as dare to speak,
A cloud comes over the sunlit arch,
A wind comes off a frozen peak,
And you're two months back in the middle of March.

A bluebird comes tenderly up to alight
And turns to the wind to unruffle a plume
His song so pitched as not to excite
A single flower as yet to bloom.
It is snowing a flake: and he half knew
Winter was only playing possum.   30
Except in color he isn't blue,
But he wouldn't advise a thing to blossom.

The water for which we may have to look
In summertime with a witching-wand,

In every wheelrut's now a brook,
In every print of a hoof a pond.
Be glad of water, but don't forget
The lurking frost in the earth beneath
That will steal forth after the sun is set
And show on the water its crystal teeth.   40

The time when most I loved my task
These two must make me love it more
By coming with what they came to ask.
You'd think I never had felt before
The weight of an ax-head poised aloft,
The grip on earth of outspread feet,
The life of muscles rocking soft
And smooth and moist in vernal heat.

Out of the woods two hulking tramps
(From sleeping God knows where last night,   50
But not long since in the lumber camps).
They thought all chopping was theirs of right.
Men of the woods and lumberjacks,
They judged me by their appropriate tool.
Except as a fellow handled an ax,
They had no way of knowing a fool.

Nothing on either side was said.
They knew they had but to stay their stay
And all their logic would fill my head:
As that I had no right to play   60
With what was another man's work for gain.
My right might be love but theirs was need.
And where the two exist in twain
Theirs was the better right — agreed.

But yield who will to their separation,
My object in living is to unite
My avocation and my vocation
As my two eyes make one in sight.
Only where love and need are one,
And the work is play for mortal stakes,   70
Is the deed ever really done
For Heaven and the future's sakes.

This poem alludes in the final stanza to a famous remark by the French philosopher Pascal about the space between galaxies and stars: "The eternal silence of those infinite spaces strikes me with terror."

Desert Places

Snow falling and night falling fast, oh, fast
In a field I looked into going past,
And the ground almost covered smooth in snow,
But a few weeds and stubble showing last.

The woods around it have it — it is theirs.
All animals are smothered in their lairs.
I am too absent-spirited to count;
The loneliness includes me unawares.

And lonely as it is that loneliness
Will be more lonely ere it will be less —
A blanker whiteness of benighted snow
With no expression, nothing to express.

They cannot scare me with their empty spaces
Between stars — on stars where no human race is.
I have it in me so much nearer home
To scare myself with my own desert places.

Three Famous Frost Poems

In a public lecture Frost once called three of his poems — "The Road Not Taken," "Stopping by Woods on a Snowy Evening," and "Come In" — his "triple theme song." Each of these poems combines Frost's themes of individualism and nature in an incident involving character, choice, and temptation.

The Road Not Taken

[handwritten: early morning he took the road most people didnt take.]

Two roads diverged in a yellow wood,
And sorry I could not travel both
And be one traveler, long I stood
And looked down one as far as I could
To where it bent in the undergrowth;

Then took the other, as just as fair,
And having perhaps the better claim,
Because it was grassy and wanted wear;
Though as for that the passing there
Had worn them really about the same,   10

And both that morning equally lay
In leaves no step had trodden black.
Oh, I kept the first for another day!
Yet knowing how way leads on to way,
I doubted if I should ever come back.

I shall be telling this with a sigh
Somewhere ages and ages hence:
Two roads diverged in a wood, and I —
I took the one less traveled by,
And that has made all the difference.   20

Frost once said that he would like to print "forty pages of footnotes"
after this, the most famous of all his poems.

Stopping by Woods on a Snowy Evening

Whose woods these are I think I know.
His house is in the village though;
He will not see me stopping here
To watch his woods fill up with snow.

My little horse must think it queer
To stop without a farmhouse near
Between the woods and frozen lake
The darkest evening of the year.

He gives his harness bells a shake
To ask if there is some mistake.
The only other sound's the sweep
Of easy wind and downy flake.

The woods are lovely, dark and deep,
But I have promises to keep,
And miles to go before I sleep,
And miles to go before I sleep.

Come In

As I came to the edge of the woods,
Thrush music — hark!
Now if it was dusk outside,
Inside it was dark.

Too dark in the woods for a bird
By sleight of wing
To better its perch for the night,
Though it still could sing.

The last of the light of the sun
That had died in the west   10
Still lived for one song more
In a thrush's breast.

Far in the pillared dark
Thrush music went —
Almost like a call to come in
To the dark and lament.

But no, I was out for stars:
I would not come in.
I meant not even if asked,
And I hadn't been.   20

On October 26, 1963, President Kennedy took part in a ceremony at Amherst College in Massachusetts, dedicating a library to the memory of Robert Frost. The following tribute is the second half of his speech; the omitted parts contained praise of Amherst and general remarks about the nation. This was one of President Kennedy's last speeches.

In Tribute
to Robert Frost

JOHN F. KENNEDY

This day devoted to the memory of Robert Frost offers an opportunity for reflection which is prized by politicians as well as by others, and even by poets, for Robert Frost was one of the granite figures of our time in America. He was supremely two things: an artist and an American. A nation reveals itself not only by the men it produces but also by the men it honors, the men it remembers. In America, our heroes have customarily run to men of large accomplishments. But today this college and country honors a man whose contribution was not to our size but to our spirit, not to our political beliefs but to our insight, not to our self-esteem but to our self-comprehension. In honoring Robert Frost, we therefore can pay honor to the deepest sources of our national strength. That strength takes many forms, and the most obvious forms are not always the most significant. The men who create power make an indispensable contribution to the nation's greatness, but the men who question power make a contribution just as indispensable, especially when that questioning is disinterested, for they determine whether we use power or power uses us. Our national strength matters, but the spirit which informs and controls our strength matters just as much. This was the special significance of Robert Frost. He brought an unsparing instinct for reality to bear on the platitudes and pieties of society. His sense of the human tragedy fortified him against self-deception and easy consolation. I have been, he wrote, one acquainted with the night. And because he knew the midnight as well as the high noon, because he understood the ordeal as well as the triumph of the human spirit, he gave his age strength with which to overcome despair. At bottom, he held a deep faith in the spirit of man, and it is hardly an accident that Robert Frost coupled poetry and power, for he saw poetry as the means of saving power from itself. When power leads man towards arrogance, poetry reminds him of his limitations. When power narrows the areas of man's concern, poetry reminds him of the richness and diversity of his existence. When power corrupts, poetry cleanses. For art establishes the basic human truth which must serve as the touchstone of our judgment. The artist, however faithful to his personal vision of reality, becomes the last champion of the individual mind and sensibility against an intrusive society and an officious state. The great artist is thus a solitary figure. He has, as Frost said, a lover's quarrel with the world. In pursuing his perceptions of reality, he must often sail against the currents of his time. This is not a popular role. If Robert Frost was much honored during his lifetime, it was because a good many preferred to ignore his darker truths. Yet in retrospect, we see how the artist's fidelity has strengthened the fiber of our national life.

I look forward to an America which will reward achievement in the arts as we reward achievement in business or statecraft. I look forward to an America which will steadily raise the standards of artistic accomplishment and which will steadily enlarge cultural opportunities for all of our citizens. And I look forward to an America which commands respect throughout the world not only for its strength but for its civilization as well. And I look forward to a world which will be safe not only for democracy and diversity but also for personal distinction. Robert Frost was often skeptical about projects for human improvement, yet I do not think he would disdain this hope. As he wrote during the uncertain days of the Second World War, take human nature altogether since time began, and it must be a little more in favor of man, say a fraction of one percent at the very least, or our hold on the planet wouldn't have so increased.

Because of Mr. Frost's life and work, because of the life and work of this college, our hold on this planet has increased.

"Interlude" by James Wells.

EIGHT WAYS OF THINKING ABOUT POETRY

*"The figure a poem makes. It begins
in delight and ends in wisdom."*
ROBERT FROST

The following pages attempt a fresh look at poetry — eight ways of looking at it, in fact. But there is no point in looking at poetry at all (or at any kind of literature, for that matter) unless there is a possibility that it will give you delight, surprise, pleasure. Obviously, all poems cannot give the same amount of pleasure, or the same kind of pleasure, to all readers. Sometimes a poet may start out with a high, serious purpose: he wants to do nothing less than change the reader's life. At other times, in other poems, he may wish to do no more than be light and amusing. The word poetry, in fact, is used to describe such a wide variety of writing that no single definition of poetry includes all the things we call "poems."

Here are a few remarks that people have made about poetry and poets. Notice that some of these writers more or less agree, while others take very different points of view. "What is poetry?" someone once asked Samuel Johnson. "Why, Sir," Dr. Johnson answered, "it is much easier to say what it is not. We all know what light is, but it is not easy to tell what it is."

A man is a poet who lives . . . by watching his moods. An old poet comes at last to watching his moods as narrowly as a cat does a mouse.

— HENRY DAVID THOREAU

Moon talk by a poet who has not been in the moon is likely to be dull.

— MARK TWAIN

I never had the least thought or inclination of turning poet till I got once heartily in love.

— ROBERT BURNS

A poet is the most unpoetical of anything in existence, because he has no identity; he is continually filling some other body.

— JOHN KEATS

You must have rules in poetry, if it is only for the pleasure of breaking them.

— GEORGE MOORE

Poetry is saying something that cannot be said.

— ANONYMOUS

Poetry gives most pleasure when only generally and not perfectly understood.

— WILLIAM WORDSWORTH

Poetry is certainly something more than good sense, but it must be good sense, at all events; just as a palace is more than a house, but it must be a house, at least.

— SAMUEL TAYLOR COLERIDGE

One: A Poem Is a Surprise

One of the reasons people read poems is to be surprised.

A poem may surprise in the sense that it does not necessarily say what the reader expects it to say when he reads the title or first line. It may even say just the opposite of what he expects. A good reader, therefore, needs an open mind and needs to be on the lookout for surprises: he must not expect the poem to say what it would say if he were writing it himself. The better a poem, the more unpredictable it is likely to be.

A poem may be surprising in so many different ways that it would be impossible to name them all. Three of the most common ways are these:

1. The feelings or ideas expressed in the poem may be unusual or unexpected.
2. The order of the words may be different from the order in which words are usually found in prose or in common speech.
3. The words may be used in original and unique ways, stretching their ordinary meanings.

Even the appearance of a poem on the page may be a little surprising. Unlike a writer of prose, whose writing fills the space between set margins, a poet breaks off his lines, in order to achieve emphasis or rhythm, so that the right-hand margin is uneven. There is usually much more blank space in a page of poetry than in other kinds of writing. Some readers are bothered at first by this unusual arrangement of words on the page, but it has its purposes, as we shall see. Like other surprises, the surprises of poetry may be upsetting at first, but once you are used to them, you begin to enjoy them.

In reading a poem, remember that a line of poetry is not the same as a sentence. Often several lines of poetry are needed to contain one sentence, and the sentence may even stop in the middle of a line. Therefore, when you read a poem you cannot stop at the end of each line as if it contains a complete thought: you must go on until the thought is complete.

Read the following three poems with an eye for the surprises in each.

I Counsel You Beware

A. E. HOUSMAN

Good creatures, do you love your lives
   And have your ears for sense?
Here is a knife like other knives,
   That cost me eighteen pence.

I need but stick it in my heart
   And down will come the sky,
And earth's foundations will depart
   And all you folk will die.

Who Knows If the Moon's a Balloon

E. E. CUMMINGS

who knows if the moon's
a balloon,coming out of a keen city
in the sky—filled with pretty people?
(and if you and i should

get into it,if they
should take me and take you into their balloon,
why then
we'd go up higher with all the pretty people

than houses and steeples and clouds:
go sailing
away and away sailing into a keen
city which nobody's ever visited,where

always
    it's
       Spring)and everyone's
in love and flowers pick themselves

Emily Dickinson probably never intended her poetry to be published.
This poem is printed as closely as possible to the way in which she
wrote it, using her unusual system of capitalization and punctuation.

The Wind Begun to Rock

EMILY DICKINSON

The wind begun to rock the Grass *SWAY*
With threatening Tunes and low *—sounds*
He threw a Menace at the Earth —
A Menace at the Sky.

The Leaves unhooked themselves from Trees — *fell*
And started all abroad
The Dust did scoop itself like Hands
And threw away the Road. *cover*

The Wagons quickened on the Streets
The Thunder hurried slow —   10
The Lightning showed a Yellow Beak
And then a livid Claw.

The Birds put up the Bars to Nests —
The Cattle fled to Barns —
There came one drop of Giant Rain
And then as if the Hands

That held the Dams had parted hold
The Waters Wrecked the Sky,
But overlooked my Father's House —
Just quartering a Tree —   20

Two: A Poem Makes a Sound

A poem should be heard as well as seen.

Most people enjoy hearing music although they would find it hard to explain why. Likewise, it is hard to say just why we find pleasure in the rhymes and other sound devices in poetry. Rhyme is the recurrence of similar sounds, usually (but not always!) at the ends of lines in poetry. The rhyme scheme of a poem is described by a string of small letters. For instance, the rhyme scheme of the following poem is *aabb*:

Infant Innocence

A. E. HOUSMAN

> Reader, behold! this monster wild
> Has gobbled up the infant child.
> The infant child is not aware
> It has been eaten by the bear.

Here *wild* rhymes with *child* — the *a* rhyme — and *aware* rhymes with *bear* — the *b* rhyme. Without the rhyme and without the rhythm, the poem becomes foolish rather than amusing:

> There once was a grizzly bear.
> He was huge and wild.
> He devoured an infant.
> The infant did not know it had been eaten.

Look back at "The Moon's a Balloon" on page 190. Note that this poem has no rhymes at the ends of the lines; however, it does have two strong *internal* rhymes — *balloon* and *moon*, and *people* and *steeple*. Although rhyme is probably the best-known sound effect in poetry, there are many successful poems in which there is no rhyme at all.

All good poems, rhymed and unrhymed, profit from being read aloud. Often a poem that seems difficult or pointless on the printed page may become clear and interesting when read aloud. As you read the next three poems, give special attention to the sound effects in them.

Here the poet has tried to capture some feature of the sound of the wind.

The Wind

JAMES STEPHENS

The wind stood up and gave a shout
He whistled on his fingers and

Kicked the withered leaves about
And thumped the branches with his hand

And said he'd kill and kill and kill,
And so he will and so he will.

A player piano is a piano in which the notes are struck mechanically rather than by a human hand. For each song there is a roll of paper with holes in it, like an IBM card, causing the keys to be struck in the right order.

Player Piano

JOHN UPDIKE

My stick fingers click with a snicker
And, chuckling, they knuckle the keys;   *internal rhyming*
Light-footed, my steel feelers flicker
And pluck from these keys melodies.

My paper can caper; abandon
In broadcast by dint of my din,   *aliteration*
And no man or band has a hand in   *assonance; I.R.*
The tones I turn on from within.

At times I'm a jumble of rumbles,   *I.R*
At others I'm light like the moon,
But never my numb plunker fumbles,
Misstrums me, or tries a new tune.

*Here is a poem in which sound is used for a very playful effect. The
poet claims that he "took particular pleasure in putting it together."
The name of one of the ladies, Lalage, is unusual. In order to fit
the rhythm, it must have three syllables. Pronounce it lä′lə′jə.*

The Private Dining Room

OGDEN NASH

Miss Rafferty wore taffeta,
Miss Cavendish wore lavender.
We ate pickerel and mackerel
And other lavish provender,
Miss Cavendish was Lalage,
Miss Rafferty was Barbara.
We gobbled pickled mackerel
And broke the candelabara,
Miss Cavendish in lavender,
In taffeta, Miss Rafferty,   10
The girls in taffeta lavender,
And we, of course, in mufti.°

Miss Rafferty wore taffeta,
The taffeta was lavender,
Was lavend, lavender, lavenderest,
As the wine improved the provender.
Miss Cavendish wore lavender,
The lavender was taffeta.
We boggled mackled pickerel,
And bumpers° did we quaffeta.   20
And Lalage wore lavender,
And lavender wore Barbara,
Rafferta taffeta Cavender lavender
Barbara abracadabra.

Miss Rafferty in taffeta
Grew definitely raffisher.
Miss Cavendish in lavender
Grew less and less stand-offisher.
With Lalage and Barbara

---

12. *mufti:* civilian dress, plain clothes.   20. *bumpers:* full glasses.

We grew a little pickereled,   30
We ordered Mumm and Roederer°
Because the bubbles tickereled.
But lavender and taffeta
Were gone when we were soberer.
I haven't thought for thirty years
Of Lalage and Barbara.

Three: A Poem Is Silent

A poem always suggests more than it says.

In suggesting rather than stating, a poem is very different from a recipe or a set of instructions. If you were telling somebody how to repair a flat tire or how to make vanilla ice cream, you would be careful not to leave any gaps in the instructions. But a poet will leave gaps — we might call them "silent places" — on purpose, because he wants the reader to participate in the poem. That is, he expects the reader to use his own imagination to fill in the blanks and supply necessary thoughts and feelings.

A poem can be silent in many ways. If it tells a story, it may leave certain parts of the story to the reader's imagination. If it describes a scene or an emotion, it may do so in a very few words — but words carefully chosen to suggest a great deal. In a good poem the words work overtime; every single word is intended to contribute something to the reader's experience.

Suppose a poet wants to write about selfishness. He will probably not come out flatly saying, "Selfishness is bad! Down with selfishness!" He does not make the same direct attack that a moralist or preacher would. He will go about his purpose indirectly. Without expressing any direct opinion on the subject, he may just describe a selfish person or a person who acts selfishly on a certain occasion. He expects the reader to be alert, to supply the comment or opinion where the poem itself is silent.

The next four poems all have gaps in them — of time or thought — which the poet expects the reader to fill.

---

31. *Mumm and Roederer:* brands of champagne.

In this poem, notice the gap between the second and third lines.

Bad News

JOEL SLOMAN

The messenger was hanged
because he brought bad news.
No more messengers.

In the following poem there is a gap for the reader to fill between each of the stanzas.

John and Jane

THOMAS HARDY

He sees the world as a boisterous place
Where all things bear a laughing face,
And humorous scenes go hourly on,   *met Jane*
    Does John.   → *got married*

They find the world a pleasant place
Where all is ecstasy and grace,
Where a light has risen that cannot wane,
    Do John and Jane.   → *married*

They see as a palace their cottage-place,
Containing a pearl of the human race,
A hero, maybe, hereafter styled,
    Do John and Jane with a baby-child. → *baby*

They rate the world as a gruesome place,
Where fair looks fade to a skull's grimace —
As a pilgrimage they would fain get done —
    Do John and Jane with their worthless son.
                son born.

*Napoleon led his troops in an attack on Russia, where he said he
was defeated by "General Winter." A complete life of Napoleon might
fill hundreds of pages. Here, the poet has selected only a moment
from Napoleon's life; the rest is suggestion.*

Napoleon

WALTER DE LA MARE

"What is this world, O soldiers?
          It is I;
I this incessant snow,
          This northern sky;
Soldiers, this solitude
          Through which we go
               Is I."

White Was the Sheet

ANONYMOUS

White was the sheet that she spread for her lover,
White was the sheet and embroidered the cover.
But whiter the sheet and the canopy grander
When he lay down to sleep where the hill-foxes wander.

Four: A Poem Has a Speaker

The "I" in a poem is almost never exactly the same as the poet
himself.

Emily Dickinson put it plainly in a letter to a friend: "When I
state myself as the representative of the verse it does not mean me
but a supposed person."

In this way, poems are like plays. When an author writes a play,
he puts words into the mouths of characters he has imagined, and
each of these characters refers to himself as "I." A poet often does
the same thing. Even if he is writing about himself, his "I" will not
be the person he really is so much as the person he thinks himself
to be or wants himself to be. A poet is like a playwright because
both invent characters who speak.

It has become the custom to refer to the "I" in a poem as "the speaker." The speaker in a poem written by a woman may be a man, and vice versa. The speaker may even be an animal or a dead person. We have seen an example of the latter in "Napoleon" on page 197. A poet is free to imagine anyone or anything as the speaker of his poem.

The speakers of the following poems include a dog and a fly.

Bee!

EMILY DICKINSON

Bee! I'm expecting you!
Was saying Yesterday
To Somebody you know
That you were due —

The Frogs got Home last Week —
Are settled, and at work —
Birds, mostly back —
The Clover warm and thick —

You'll get my Letter by
The seventeenth; Reply
Or better, be with me —
Yours, Fly.

This — for the Moon — Yes?

CARL SANDBURG

This is a good book? Yes?
Throw it at the moon.
Stand on the ball of your right foot
And come to the lunge of a center fielder
Straddling in a throw for the home plate,
Let her go — spang — this book for the moon — yes?
And then — other books, good books, even the best books — shoot
    'em with a long twist at the moon, yes?

Epitaph for a Dog

ANONYMOUS

Stranger, as you pass by this road, do not smile
When you see that this grave is only a dog's.
When I died, my Master wept, dug my grave
With his own hands, and wrote these lines for this stone.

boy; bike; bike owner

Fifteen

WILLIAM STAFFORD

characteristics of speaker
fifteen; admiring
ready; friendly
honest; imaginative
ambitious;

South of the bridge on Seventeenth
I found back of the willows one summer
day a motorcycle with engine running
as it lay on its side, ticking over
slowly in the high grass. I was fifteen.

I admired all that pulsing gleam, the
shiny flanks, the demure headlights
fringed where it lay; I led it gently
to the road and stood with that
companion, ready and friendly. I was fifteen.   10

man owns bike
he can ride it.

We could find the end of a road, meet
the sky on out Seventeenth. I thought about
hills, and patting the handle got back a
confident opinion. On the bridge we indulged
a forward feeling, a tremble. I was fifteen.

Thinking, back further in the grass I found
the owner, just coming to, where he had flipped
over the rail. He had blood on his hand, was pale —
I helped him walk to his machine. He ran his hand
over it, called me good man, roared away.   20

I stood there, fifteen.

Five: A Poem Is a Game

People are interested in poems for some of the same reasons that they are interested in games.

Like a game, a poem has rules; without rules, there would be no poems and no games. But there is one important difference between the rules of games and the rules of poetry. All games of baseball follow the same rules, as do all games of Monopoly, field hockey, and so on. But all poems do not follow the same rules. Each poem has its own set of rules, which may differ greatly or slightly from the rules that govern other poems. An unoriginal poem may follow the rules set down by another poem, but every good poem has some unique rules of its own. Often these rules are not even known to the poet as he starts to write his poem. He discovers them as he goes along.

In order to enjoy the game of reading a poem, the reader must be aware of the poem's rules. Not that he has to think about them all the time! It would be a very boring game — both for the players and the spectators — if everybody had to keep every single regulation in mind every minute. Yet the rules of the game are always there, and without them there would be no game — only chaos.

Also, if you don't read and think about the whole poem before you make up your mind what it is saying, you are like someone who leaves the stadium during the third quarter of a football game or like someone who sits in the stands with his eyes covered during the last minutes of play.

Look in the next four poems for the rules which each poet has set for himself.

Interior

DOROTHY PARKER

Her mind lives in a quiet room,
A narrow room, and tall,
With pretty lamps to quench the gloom
And mottoes on the wall.

There all the things are waxen neat
    And set in decorous lines;
And there are posies, round and sweet,
    And little, straightened vines.

Her mind lives tidily, apart
    From cold and noise and pain,
And bolts the door against her heart,
    Out wailing in the rain.

*If you heard this poem read aloud before you saw it printed, would
you know that it was a poem containing rhymes? Would you know
that the rhymes come at the ends of lines?*

Sky Diving

RICHMOND LATTIMORE

They step from the high plane and begin to tumble
down. Below is the painted ground, above
is bare sky. They do not fumble
with the catch, but only fall; drop sheer; begin to move

in the breakless void; stretch and turn, freed
from pressure; stand in weightless air
and softly walk across their own speed;
gather and group, these dropping bundles, where

the neighbor in the sky stands, reach touch
and clasp hands, separate and swim
back to the station (did swimmer ever shear such
thin water?) falling still. Now at last pull the slim

cord. Parasols bloom in the air, slow
the swift sky-fall. Collapsed tents cover
the ground. They rise up, plain people now.
Their little sky-time is over.

Poem

WILLIAM CARLOS WILLIAMS

As the cat
climbed over
the top of

the jamcloset
first the right
forefoot

carefully
then the hind
stepped down

into the pit of
the empty
flowerpot

Mother Goose

KENNETH REXROTH

Jeanette Brunette
Had a wooden leg.
Her mother beat her,
And set her to beg.
She begged for meat,
She begged for bread.
They gave her swine's feet
And spoiled cabbage head.
She begged for gold.
They gave her a nail.
The nail made her bold.
She hid it in a pail.
When her mother was asleep
She drove it in her head.
She didn't cry a bit
When her mother lay dead.

Six: A Poem Is Untrue

In almost any poem you can find statements that are literally not true, statements that cannot be proved or verified, statements that cannot be taken at their face value — in short, statements that are lies, although they are told with no intent of deceiving anyone.

In the Field Forever

ROBERT WALLACE

> Sun's a roaring dandelion, hour by hour.
> Sometimes the moon's a scythe, sometimes a silver flower.
> But the stars! All night long the stars are clover.
> Over, and over, and over!

The sun, of course, is not really a dandelion, and dandelions are not the kind of lions that roar. These are interesting and surprising fictions. There is no more "truth" in what the poem says about the moon and stars. The title, also, which refers to the sky as a field, is untrue.

"Lies" of the kind found in the poem are called *metaphors*. Metaphor occurs whenever a speaker or writer — who has no intention of deceiving anyone — says that something *is* what it *isn't*. Metaphor is very common in everyday conversation and in any kind of writing that tries to be interesting and entertaining. Almost all slang consists of metaphor. "Get a load of that creep in the stovepipe hat" contains at least three metaphors. Imaginative people who invent slang expressions are a lot like poets.

Metaphor, then, is a way of saying something in a concise, striking, and original way. It is also a way of saying one thing and meaning another. When Robert Wallace, in the poem above, says *field*, he means *sky*. He calls the sky a field because he wants us to see it in a new way.

In the same way many proverbs say one thing and mean something else. When we say "A new broom sweeps clean" we aren't really talking about brooms and sweeping. We are talking about how people (the same as brooms) work very well (sweep very clean) when they first start a job (when they are new), and we are silently suggesting that later they slow down and become less eager and efficient (just as a broom wears out). Notice that the proverb is much shorter than the explanation, because the proverb uses a few concrete, specific words, while the explanation runs to generalities and abstractions. The proverb is memorable; our explanation forgettable.

Many proverbs, then, can be regarded as short poems. It is a useful exercise to compare what a proverb "says" with what it "means." Try these, and think of some others:

> You can lead a horse to water, but you can't make him drink.
> The devil can cite Scripture for his purpose.
> A stitch in time saves nine.
> A rolling stone gathers no moss.
> A leopard cannot change his spots.
> When the cat's away, the mice will play.

Finally, let us look back at "In the Field Forever" and ask why the poet called the sky a field, the moon a scythe, the stars clover. This is a hard question, to which there are many kinds of answers. For now, it is enough to say that the poet used these metaphors because he was writing this poem. If you take them away from the poem, you will find that the poem itself has vanished. The same thing will happen with the other poems in this section. Try removing the metaphors and see what happens.

This poem — by an English teacher, of course — uses metaphors to pass judgment on other English teachers.

figurative - meaning
literal - what is says.

Spare Fast

SIDNEY L. EATON

> The teacher of English
> Though lofty his goal
> Can seldom distinguish
> Twixt doughnut and hole.
>
> But his underfed pupils
> Look shriveled and gray;
> When they've feasted on hole,
> He throws doughnut away.

Here the poet makes a metaphor out of a swimming lesson.

First Lesson

PHILIP BOOTH

Lie back, daughter, let your head
be tipped back in the cup of my hand.
Gently, and I will hold you. Spread
your arms wide, lie out on the stream
and look high at the gulls. A dead-
man's float is face down. You will dive
and swim soon enough where this tidewater
ebbs to the sea. Daughter, believe
me, when you tire on the long thrash
to your island, lie up, and survive.
As you float now, where I held you
and let you go, remember when fear
cramps your heart, what I told you:
lie gently and wide to the light-year
stars, lie back, and the sea will hold you.

[handwritten annotations: "— look to the future. 1 thing at a time."; "— Don't give up"; "— learning to be independence, have confidence"]

This poem is not about waves, or drowning, or an island.

[handwritten: "Jesse B. Semple — man he used in poems." "BLAck poet:"]

Island

LANGSTON HUGHES

[handwritten: "Island - desolate   Island = Future"]

[handwritten: "Prejudice"] — Wave of sorrow,
— Do not drown me now: *[handwritten: "reject"]*

I see the island *[handwritten: "— end of prejudice"]*
Still ahead somehow.

I see the island
And its sands are fair: *[handwritten: "people"]*

Wave of sorrow,
Take me there.

Stop All the Clocks

W. H. AUDEN

Stop all the clocks, cut off the telephone,
Prevent the dog from barking with a juicy bone,
Silence the pianos and with muffled drum
Bring out the coffin, let the mourners come.

Let aeroplanes circle moaning overhead
Scribbling on the sky the message He Is Dead,— not there
Put crepe bows round the white necks of the public doves,
Let the traffic policemen wear black cotton gloves.

He was my North, my South, my East and West,
My working week and my Sunday rest,
My noon, my midnight, my talk, my song:
I thought that love would last for ever: I was wrong.

The stars are not wanted now; put out every one:
Pack up the moon and dismantle the sun;
Pour away the ocean and sweep up the woods;
For nothing now can ever come to any good.

Seven: A Poem Is an Experience

It is not enough just to read a poem. Poetry is to be experienced,
by the feelings as well as the mind.

If you feel nothing when you read a particular poem, maybe it is
because you are not fully exposing yourself to the poem. Remember
that even the most popular songs often need several hearings before
you come to understand or enjoy them. You have to give a poem
the same chance you would to a new song, a chance to break through

your lack of interest and your habits of thought in order to reward
you with a pleasurable experience.

Poetry communicates experience largely by means of images —
words or phrases that make an impression on the reader's senses:
on his sight and on his sense of hearing, touch, taste, smell and even
on the sense of motion. In the poem that follows, for instance, the
word *yell* is an image. If when you are reading the poem you do not
experience this yell with all its force — if you do not actually hear
it within your mind's ear, then you are not letting the poem communicate its full experience to you.

On the High Upland Plain

JOSEPHINE MILES

On the high upland plain, the boys yell in their cars,
They drive from east to west, still they are on
The high upland plain, they drive from Mac's to Barbecue,
Still they are on the high upland plain.

They yell through the small towns, finally they fall
Under the steering wheel and sleep, high
Over them drives the wheel of sky,
Still they are on the upland plain.

The Dark House

GERALD BULLETT

Coming home from the fields
Where with other brave ones
I had sailed stormy seas
And won new horizons,
I found the house dark,
The door shut against me,
No answer to my knock.

The day had been friendly:
Now it was departed

And night not yet come.   10
I wondered, I waited,
My only companion
A beetle in a matchbox,
Beautiful but dumb.

Desolated, homeless,
I wondered, I waited.
While aeons went by,
Five minutes of the clock,
I grew old and gray,
Learning by foretaste   20
The ultimate aloneness.

Old Man Traveling

WILLIAM WORDSWORTH

The little hedge-row birds
That peck along the road regard him not.
He travels on, and in his face, his step,
His gait, is one expression; every limb,
His look and bending figure, all bespeak
A man who does not move with pain, but moves
With thought. He is insensibly subdued
To settled quiet. He is one by whom
All effort seems forgotten, one to whom
Long patience has such mild composure given   10
That patience now doth seem a thing of which
He hath no need. He is by nature led
To peace so perfect that the young behold
With envy what the old man hardly feels.
I asked him whither he was bound, and what
The object of his journey. He replied,
"Sir, I am going many miles to take
A last leave of my son, a mariner,
Who from a sea fight has been brought to Falmouth,
And there is dying in a hospital."   20

Eight: A Poem Is True

A good poem may be described as a collection of untruths that add up to some kind of truth.

Of course, there are other kinds of truth that poetry is little concerned with, scientific facts, for instance. Poetry, like novels, plays, and stories, is not written to communicate factual knowledge but another kind of truth. Poetry shows us people, and their feelings, and their thoughts, good and bad. It tries to represent humanity and the real world in a way that is honest and truthful, and it also creates imaginary worlds that seem to be true while we read about them. Poetry expresses all the sorrow, delight, indignation, cheerfulness, love, rage, and other emotions that people feel.

A few poems — a rather small percentage of the total amount of good poetry — have as their aim the teaching of a moral or a useful lesson. These are called *didactic* poems. The message or moral usually comes at the end of a didactic poem, and it is usually clearly stated. You read several such poems in the section on Animal Fables beginning on page 111. But it is important to remember that there are relatively few didactic poems and that poems do not necessarily teach morality or proper behavior. Since most poems exist for their own sake, not in order to convey a message, it is futile to search them for lessons or advice.

Instead of telling us what to do, poems tell us what we are. We read poetry to learn what it truly means to be a human being. In that way, each of the following poems is true.

Meditatio

EZRA POUND

When I carefully consider the curious habits of dogs
I am compelled to conclude
That man is the superior animal.

When I consider the curious habits of man
I confess, my friend, I am puzzled.

Elegy for J.F.K.
(November 22, 1963)

W. H. AUDEN

Why *then*, why *there*,
Why *thus*, we cry, did he die?
The heavens are silent.

What he was, he was:
What he is fated to become
Depends on us.

Remembering his death,
How we choose to live
Will decide its meaning.

When a just man dies,
Lamentation and praise,
Sorrow and joy, are one.

Compare this poem with Sandburg's "This — for the Moon — Yes?" on page 198.

When I Heard the Learn'd Astronomer

WALT WHITMAN

When I heard the learn'd astronomer
When the proofs, the figures, were ranged in columns before me,
When I was shown the charts and diagrams, to add, divide, and
    measure them,
When I was sitting heard the astronomer where he lectured with
    much applause in the lecture-room,
How soon unaccountable I became tired and sick,
Till rising and gliding out I wandered off by myself,
In the mystical moist night-air, and from time to time,
Looked up in perfect silence at the stars.

Loveliest of Trees

A. E. HOUSMAN

Loveliest of trees, the cherry now
Is hung with bloom along the bough,
And stands about the woodland ride
Wearing white for Eastertide.

Now, of my threescore years and ten,
Twenty will not come again,
And take from seventy springs a score,
It only leaves me fifty more.

And since to look at things in bloom
Fifty springs are little room
About the woodlands I will go
To see the cherry hung with snow.

The Bat

THEODORE ROETHKE

By day the bat is cousin to the mouse.
He likes the attic of an aging house.

His fingers make a hat about his head.
His pulse beat is so slow we think him dead.

He loops in crazy figures half the night
Among the trees that face the corner light.

But when he brushes up against a screen,
We are afraid of what our eyes have seen:

For something is amiss or out of place
When mice with wings can wear a human face.

*The author of this poem writes about herself: "When I was thirteen
I got spinal meningitis and at the time it seemed to be a mean, cruel
thing. It was during my convalescence, however, that I began to
write, as a result of searching myself."*

*Once we happen to know this kind of biographical information
about Miss Cuestas, we can see that her poem is very personal. But the
poem itself would be just as true if she had never been seriously ill
or if we knew nothing about her at all.*

Soil

KATHERINE CUESTAS

One day, a long time ago,
I planted my soul
and found that the soil changed very often.

Once it was love (that proved to be harmful)
once it was nature (that proved to be excellent, but not
steady enough for so important a task)
once it was myself (that proved to be the rockiest and
driest soil; I don't know myself well enough)
one content time it was God (it was really him all along,
but I knew it not).   10

One time a strong wind or something knocked my pot
and all my soil over
with my soul still in it.
I was spread over a vast area and I was griefstricken.
Some kind being (probably God again) came and
replanted my soul for me;
now I am growing, because as he replanted me,
with every pat of the soil and every drop of water
he uttered the words:

STAY ALIVE   20

and I did.

A Poetic Tradition:

The Sonnet

A sonnet is a poem of fourteen lines which operates according to certain long-established rules. Usually each line of a sonnet contains a total of ten syllables. In a successful sonnet what is said exactly fills the fourteen lines without being padded out or cut short abruptly. It is this strict requirement that makes really good sonnets both rare and surprising.

Sonnets were first made in Italy, and they were brought to an early perfection by two great writers, Dante and Petrarch. The Italian sonnet has a rhyme scheme that links together the first eight lines in this pattern: *abbaabba*. This part of the sonnet is called the *octave*. The last six lines of the sonnet are called the *sestet*, and they are linked by a rhyme pattern, but it is not as strict as the pattern for the octave. A common pattern for the sestet is *cdcdcd*; another is *cdecde*.

It is not as important to remember the names *octave* and *sestet* and the rhyme schemes that go with them as it is to be aware that the Italian sonnet is a thing with two unequal parts which balance against each other. For instance, the octave may ask a question or state a problem, and the sestet may provide an answer or a solution. An Italian sonnet has a turning point. Robert Frost once remarked: "A sonnet is supposed to go for eight lines, then take a turn for better or worse and go six more."

In the sixteenth century the sonnet was imported into England, and from there it spread to other English-speaking countries. Among some of the best sonneteers are Wyatt, Sidney, Shakespeare, Donne, Milton, Wordsworth, Keats, Hopkins, Frost, and Auden. Some writers of sonnets in English have followed the Italian form. Others have adopted the English form, which Shakespeare made popular.

The English sonnet consists of three groups of four lines followed
by one group of two lines. A diagram of an English sonnet might be:

a
b   first quatrain (four lines linked by end rhymes)
a
b

c
d   second quatrain (four lines linked by end rhymes)
c
d

e
f   third quatrain (four lines linked by end rhymes)
e
f

(Turn. Notice how late this comes in the English sonnet.)

g   final couplet (two lines linked by end rhyme)
g

There are other variations. Getting the details of these variations
straight is not very important. More important is to grasp the spirit
of the sonnet as a form. Like the Italian sonnet, the English sonnet
has two main parts, and a turn. The three quatrains correspond to
the octave; the final couplet corresponds to the sestet.

In reading the following four sonnets, keep in mind all you have
learned about poems in the sections above. Watch for surprises,
sounds, silences, the speaker, the rules by which it is written, and the
metaphors. Most important, leave yourself open to whatever experience the poem has to give you.

No Longer Mourn for Me When I Am Dead

WILLIAM SHAKESPEARE

No longer mourn for me when I am dead
Than you shall hear the surly sullen bell
Give the warning to the world that I am fled
From this vile world, with vilest worms to dwell.
Nay, if you read this line, remember not
The hand that writ it, for I love you so
That I in your sweet thoughts would be forgot
If thinking on me then should make you woe.
O, if, I say, you look upon this verse
When I perhaps compounded am with clay,
Do not so much as my poor name rehearse,
But let your love even with my life decay,
    Lest the wise world should look into your moan,
    And mock you with me after I am gone.

Westminster Bridge crosses the river Thames near the central part of London.

Composed upon Westminster Bridge

WILLIAM WORDSWORTH

Earth has not anything to show more fair:
Dull would he be of soul who could pass by
A sight so touching in its majesty:
The city now doth, like a garment, wear
The beauty of the morning; silent, bare,
Ships, towers, domes, theaters, and temples lie
Open unto the fields, and to the sky;
All bright and glittering in the smokeless air.
Never did sun more beautifully steep
In his first splendor, valley, rock, or hill;
Ne'er saw I, never felt, a calm so deep!
The river glideth at his own sweet will:
Dear God, the very houses seem asleep;
And all that mighty heart is lying still.

Spoils

ROBERT GRAVES

When all is over and you march for home,
The spoils of war are easily disposed of:
Standards, weapons of combat, helmets, drums
May decorate a staircase or a study,
While lesser gleanings of the battlefield —
Coins, watches, wedding-rings, gold teeth, and such —
Are sold anonymously for solid cash.

The spoils of love present a different case,
When all is over and you march for home:
That lock of hair, these letters and the portrait
May not be publicly displayed; nor sold;
Nor burned; nor returned (the heart being obstinate) —
Yet never dare entrust them to a safe
For fear they burn a hole through two-foot steel.

Village Spa

PHYLLIS MC GINLEY

By scribbled names on walls, by telephone number,
    Cleft heart, bold slogan, carved in every booth,
This sanctum shall be known. This holy lumber
    Proclaims a temple dedicate to Youth.
Daily in garments lawful to their tribe,
    In moccasins and sweaters, come the Exalted
To lean on spotty counters and imbibe
    Their ritual Cokes or drink a chocolate malted.

This refuge is their own. Here the cracked voice,
    Giving the secret passwords, does not falter.
And here the monstrous deity of their choice
    Sits bellowing from his fantastic altar,
A juke-box god, enshrined and well at home,
    Dreadful with neon, shuddering with chrome.

A Poet of Today: Gwendolyn Brooks

Gwendolyn Brooks was born with a talent for writing poetry. At thirteen she wrote her first poems, at twenty-six she started winning prizes for her work, and at thirty-three she earned one of the nation's most important awards, the Pulitzer prize for poetry. Miss Brooks makes her poems out of everyday materials — poor people, lively children, lovers separated by war — city people mainly, because she is a city dweller and a poet of the city.

Born in Topeka, Kansas, and long a resident of Chicago, Miss Brooks worked as a secretary until her marriage. Now she keeps house for her family, teaches college classes in poetry writing, and writes poems and novels.

In an interview, she once remarked, "The poems that I write are generally about people and what happens to them." She could have added that her characters are mainly poor and unimportant and what happens to them is mostly bad. Yet Gwendolyn Brooks does not write depressing, tearful poems; her talents, courage, and sense of humor save her from such faults.

The Bean Eaters

They eat beans mostly, this old yellow pair.
Dinner is a casual affair.
Plain chipware on a plain and creaking wood,
Tin flatware.

Two who are Mostly Good.
Two who have lived their day,
But keep on putting on their clothes
And putting things away.

And remembering . . .
Remembering, with twinklings and twinges,   10
As they lean over the beans in their rented back room that is full of
  beads and receipts and dolls and cloths, tobacco crumbs, vases
  and fringes.

This poem is modeled on the folk ballad. In an old folk ballad, a woman's bedroom might be called a bower.

the ballad of late Annie

Late Annie in her bower lay,
Though sun was up and spinning.
The blush-brown shoulder was so bare,
Blush-brown lip was winning.

Out then shrieked the mother-dear,
"Be I to fetch and carry?
Get a broom to whish the doors
Or get a man to marry."

"Men there were and men there be
But never men so many
Chief enough to marry me,"
Thought the proud late Annie.

"Whom I raise my shades before
Must be gist and lacquer.
With melted opals for my milk,
Pearl-leaf for my cracker."

Old Mary

My last defense
Is the present tense.

It little hurts me now to know
I shall not go

Cathedral-hunting in Spain
Nor cherrying in Michigan or Maine.

Of Robert Frost

There is a little lightning in his eyes.
Iron at the mouth.
His brows ride neither too far up nor down.

He is splendid. With a place to stand.

Some glowing in the common blood.
Some specialness within.

*The following is a portion of an interview with Gwendolyn Brooks
conducted by Robert Glauber, editor of* The Beloit Poetry Journal.

An Interview with Gwendolyn Brooks

MR. GLAUBER: How do you think people feel about poetry today?

MISS BROOKS: I believe that the Beats brought back an interest
to the young. They began to see that poetry could pertain to themselves. I play records of Beat poets in my workshop. Those who are
afraid to say what *they* mean — not what Shelley meant or what
Wordsworth meant — seem to loosen up when they hear the Beats.
I keep hearing that young people in colleges are reading the very
obscure poets and claiming that they find much to enjoy there.

MR. GLAUBER: How about in high school?

MISS BROOKS: Oh! I still think we have trouble there — although
they seem to be waking a bit.

MR. GLAUBER: What do you mean?

MISS BROOKS: Too much attention has been paid to the mechan-
ics of poetry in high school. A poem is assigned, and the student is
supposed to break it up — to parse it. The poem is looked upon as a
mechanical thing instead of something that's living and breathing.
I think this is unfortunate.

MR. GLAUBER: They say that the dislike many people feel for
Shakespeare is because Julius Caesar was murdered every day for a
month in their high school classrooms. How would you change that?

MISS BROOKS: Give poems to children and just let them enjoy
them. Don't force them to memorize anything just so they can recite
it. That can be a terrible influence. Let me give you some examples

of what happened to me in high school. We were given the poem by Emily Dickinson that begins: "I never saw a moor, I never saw the sea." Perhaps if it had not been treated so medicinally, I would have liked it. But, though I like most of Emily Dickinson now, that is one poem by her I still hold out against. The treatment we had of Carl Sandburg's "Fog" convinced me that I wouldn't like Sandburg. We had "Miniver Cheevy" by Edwin Arlington Robinson, and I couldn't stand it until I came upon it again much later on. All this happened because I was not allowed just to enjoy the poems as poems. This is just terrible when you think that certainly I was someone who always loved poetry.

MR. GLAUBER: Say a student comes to love poetry in high school — what should he do?

MISS BROOKS: He should read and read and read. Of course, if he wants to be a poet, he already will be writing — but reading never should be neglected. A poet can't read too widely among other poets.

MR. GLAUBER: Must a person become a poetry lover early in life? Can he come to it later?

MISS BROOKS: You can come to it later. Some of the people in my class came just out of curiosity. They really had no interest in writing poetry. They came to see what was going on. Now they've become very fond of poetry. You can come to it later — but it's always nicer to grow up with it. You know, it seems so strange for me to be saying this to you, the editor of a poetry magazine!

MR. GLAUBER: Well, as an editor, I've talked to a great many people about poetry over the years, and many feel that liking poetry requires some special sensitivity and that they just don't have the time to cultivate it.

MISS BROOKS: I quarrel with that business about not having time. No matter what you're doing — whether you're engaged in building a business or laying bricks or running a grocery store — suddenly in your twenties or thirties, or even forties, you can come upon a particular poem that will touch you. But you must be willing to let it touch you! From that time you can go on to others. Reading doesn't take much time really. It's more a matter of willingness . . . willingness to try something new . . . to experience the special thing that poetry is. It is up to us [poets] to make ourselves and our work more appetizing. I think that bringing back a narrative interest in poetry will help. People always love stories. When I read poems to groups, those they are chiefly interested in are about people. Abstract ideas seem to make them uneasy.

MR. GLAUBER: In Japan, everybody writes poetry — from the Emperor right down the line. Poetry writing actually rivals sports as a national pastime. Do you think such a thing could ever happen in the United States?

MISS BROOKS: Looking at the United States right now, I wouldn't think so.

MR. GLAUBER: Would you want to see it happen?

MISS BROOKS: Well, it's a beautiful thing to beautify your life with poetry — but whether everyone should actually write some, I don't know. Too many people might want to publish books!

MR. GLAUBER: I was wondering if, as a writer, you are committed only to your way of doing things?

MISS BROOKS: I hope not. I hope I'm changing. My poems are imperfect. I have a long way to go.

MR. GLAUBER: In what directions?

MISS BROOKS: Generally, I want to say what I have to say in a way that will reach people more effectively. I want to work with narrative to make interesting stories and yet not lose the poetic style.

MR. GLAUBER: What advice can you offer to someone who wants to write?

MISS BROOKS: You tell him very simply to live . . . and to write . . . and to read. That might seem like a very plain thing to say, but there isn't very much else that you can or need say. After all, with these three you don't have to worry about anything else. A poet writes because he has to. His poetry is his expression of his experience. It doesn't matter if he's ever published when he really gets going. The poem itself takes over from the writer.

MR. GLAUBER: It becomes compulsive?

MISS BROOKS: Yes, I think so. I would have gone on writing if I never had been published. Being published was Mount Olympus. But I wrote and wrote and wrote. I didn't mind what people said about what I was doing. I guess I just realized that it is creditable to be different. All people don't have to be alike. As a matter of fact, it's part of a poet's job to see that they are not.

"José Herrera" by Peter Hurd.

INDIVIDUALISM

Two roads diverged in a wood, and I —
I took the one less traveled by,
And that has made all the difference.
ROBERT FROST

In his poem "The Road Not Taken," Robert Frost uses as a metaphor the fork in a road that leads through the woods. Frost's traveler understands that it is impossible to follow more than one path "and be one traveler." He is an individualist.

It is difficult for most people to take the road less traveled by. They fear the loneliness, the danger, the creative challenge that faces the individualist. But for each new achievement of mankind, someone had to step out from the crowd, to think a new thought, to risk being laughed at and scorned. Nothing new has ever come into the world without meeting resistance. Someone had to have the courage to "be himself."

"I would rather sit on a pumpkin and have it all to myself than be crowded on a velvet cushion," said Henry David Thoreau in his book Walden. Thoreau was probably one of the most self-reliant individualists ever born. He rebelled against conformity and materialism in society by living alone near Walden Pond in a house he built with his own hands. There he grew most of his own food and tried to depend upon his own resources as much as possible. Of course, his short stay at Walden was more of a symbolic gesture than a practical way of life, for Thoreau knew that "almost all men feel an attraction drawing them to society."

We are all part of society. We draw from it and give ourselves to it in return. Individualism is one response to the challenge of society. For some it is costly; it often means breaking with one's family, losing one's friends, becoming an "outsider." The individualist may find that his only reward is the personal satisfaction of knowing that he has followed his conscience.

"Style is the man himself," wrote a seventeenth-century Frenchman, Georges de Buffon. William Saroyan's exuberant style of writing suggests that he is as much of a free-wheeling individualist as the characters he writes about. The style of "Where I Come From People Are Polite" reflects the personality of its narrator, too, as he breezes through situations that might overwhelm a less confident man.

Where I Come From People Are Polite

WILLIAM SAROYAN

One morning I walked into the office and the bookkeeper was putting on her hat and coat and tears were coming out of her eyes. It was April and what did I care if I was only a fifteen-dollar-a-week clerk in a lousy cemetery company? Didn't I have a new hat and a new pair of shoes and wasn't the Southern Pacific sending special trains at special low rates down to Monterey every weekend and wasn't I going down to Monterey tomorrow? Wasn't I going to take a train ride down the peninsula tomorrow?

I was going to work until noon Saturday and then I was going to get a de luxe hamburger for fifteen cents at Charley's and then I was going to hurry down to the Southern Pacific depot at Third and Townsend and buy me a special weekend round-trip ticket to Monterey and get on the train and be free in the world from Saturday afternoon till Monday morning. I was going to buy a copy of the *Saturday Evening Post* and read stories all the way down to Monterey.

When I walked into the office, though, Mrs. Gilpley, the bookkeeper, was putting on her hat and coat and tears were coming out of her eyes.

I stopped whistling and looked around. It was very quiet. The door of Mr. Wylie's office was just a little open, so I figured he was at his desk. Nobody else was around, though. It was twenty minutes past eight, and the clock was making a lot of noise for a clock you could hardly hear ordinarily.

Good morning, Mrs. Gilpley, I said.

Good morning, Joe, she said.

I didn't go straight to the locker and hang up my hat and go to my desk because I knew something was wrong and I figured it wouldn't be polite to just go and hang up my hat and sit at my desk and not try to understand what was wrong and why Mrs. Gilpley was putting on her hat and coat and crying. Mrs. Gilpley was an old lady and she had a mustache and she was stoop-shouldered and her hands were dry and full of wrinkles and nobody liked Mrs. Gilpley, but it was April in the world and I had a new hat and a new pair of shoes and I had worked in the same office with Mrs. Gilpley from September till April, right straight through winter, and maybe I didn't exactly love her, maybe I wasn't exactly crazy about her, but she was a good-hearted old lady, and I couldn't just go and hang up my hat and start another day. I had to talk to her.

Mrs. Gilpley, I said, is something the matter?

She pointed at the partly open door of Mr. Wylie's private office and made a sign that told me not to talk and just hang up my hat and go to work.

I see, I thought. He's fired her.

After all these years.

Mrs. Gilpley, I said, you haven't lost your job, have you?

I've resigned, she said.

No, you haven't, I said. I wasn't born yesterday. You can't fool me.

Mrs. Gilpley's salary was twenty-seven-fifty per week. It was eight a week when she first started to work for the cemetery company. They taught me to do Mrs. Gilpley's work. My salary was fifteen a week, so they were giving the old lady the gate. Well, I was pretty lucky to have a job and I wanted to go down to Monterey and I felt fine in a new pair of three-dollar shoes and a new hat, but I didn't like the idea of making Mrs. Gilpley cry at her age.

Mrs. Gilpley, I said, I came in this morning to quit my job and I'm *going* to quit. I got an uncle in Portland who's opening a grocery store and I'm going up there to handle his accounts for him. I ain't going to work for any cemetery company all my life. I'm quitting.

Joe, Mrs. Gilpley said, you know you ain't got no uncle in Portland.

Is that so? I said. You'd be surprised where I got uncles. I'm through with this job. Keeping track of dead people's addresses. That's no career for a young man.

Joe, Mrs. Gilpley said, if you quit your job, I'll never speak to you again as long as I live.

I don't need no job in a cemetery company, I said. What do I want to be keeping track of dead people for?

You got no friends in this town, Joe, Mrs. Gilpley said. You told me all about where you're from and what you're doing out here in Frisco, and I know how it is. You need this job, and if you quit it, I'll be deeply hurt.

Mrs. Gilpley, I said, how do you think I feel? Coming in here and taking your job? It ain't right. You been doing this work twenty years or more.

Joe, Mrs. Gilpley said, you go on now and hang up your hat and go to work.

I won't, I said. I'm quitting right now.

I walked straight into Mr. Wylie's office. Mr. Wylie was the vice president. He was an old man with a nose that was squeezed down at the end. He was tall and absent-minded and he wore a derby. And he was mean.

I walked straight into his office. Mr. Wylie, I said, I'm quitting my job beginning this morning.

What's that? he said.

Quitting, I said.

What for? he said.

I ain't getting enough money, I said.

How much do you want? he said.

Boy, was I surprised. I thought he'd throw me out. I figured I'd have to ask for plenty to make him throw me out, so I did.

I want thirty dollars a week, I said.

But you're only eighteen, he said. Such a salary would be a little premature, but perhaps we can arrange it.

If I had tried to put over a thing like that, if I had wanted to put over something like that, and get more money, it never would have worked. Thirty dollars a week was enough to buy me all the stuff I always wanted, in less than six months. Why, I'd be able to buy a Harley-Davidson in no time at thirty a week.

No, I said. I'm quitting.

Why are you quitting? he said. I thought you liked your work?

I used to, I said. But I don't any more. Mr. Wylie, I said, did you fire Mrs. Gilpley?

Mr. Wylie leaned back in his chair and looked at me. He looked sore. Who was I to ask *him* a question like that?

Young man, he said, a check for you will be made out in full this morning. You can come back for it in an hour.

I was sore too.

I want my check *now*, I said.

Then wait in the outer office, he said. Behind the rail.

I went out behind the rail and leaned on the counter.

Mrs. Gilpley looked excited.

I quit, I said.

She couldn't talk.

He wanted to give me thirty dollars a week, I said, but I quit.

She gulped a couple of times.

Mrs. Gilpley, I said, they'll have to give you your job back because they ain't got anybody else to do your work.

Joe, she said, you've hurt me very deeply.

That's all right, I said. Where I come from a young man doesn't take a lady's job. I come from Chicago and I guess I can always go back.

Go back to Chicago? Not me. I liked California. I always liked California. But that's what I said.

Joe, said Mrs. Gilpley, suppose you can't find another job?

I snapped my fingers.

I can get another job just like that, I said.

Mr. Wylie stood in the doorway of his private office and nodded at Mrs. Gilpley and she went into his office and he closed the door. She didn't come out till it was a quarter to nine. She took off her hat and coat and got out the checkbook and wrote a check and took it to Mr. Wylie.

The check was for me. It was a check for thirteen dollars.

Here's your check, Joe, Mrs. Gilpley said. I tried to get him to give you fifteen, but he said you were insolent.

Did he give you your job back? I said.

Yes, she said.

Mrs. Gilpley, I said, I'm very glad you've got your job back. What did he say I was?

Insolent, said Mrs. Gilpley.

What's that mean? I said.

Impolite, Mrs. Gilpley said.

I ain't impolite, I said. Where I come from people are courteous. Who does he think he's calling impolite?

I went into Mr. Wylie's office and asked him.

Mr. Wylie, I said, who do you think you're calling impolite?

What are you talking about? he said.

You can't call me impolite, I said. Where I come from people are courteous. People in Chicago aren't really courteous; not in every part of Chicago, but most of the people in the neighborhood where I lived were pretty polite. Most of the time anyway. I guess I was just sore.

You can't say I ain't got good manners, I said.

Where do you come from? Mr. Wylie said.

Chicago, I said. Didn't you know that?

No, he said.

I used to work on South Water Market Street, I said.

Well, said Mr. Wylie, you've got a lot to learn. You're going to learn it doesn't pay to bite the hand that feeds you.

I didn't bite no hand that fed me, I said.

You quit, didn't you? he said.

Yes, sir, I said. I quit all right, but I didn't bite nobody.

Well, what do you want now? he said.

I just want to say good-by, I said. I just want you to know I've got good manners.

All right, said Mr. Wylie. Good-by.

Good-by, I said.

I went out of the office and said good-by to Mrs. Gilpley. Mr. Wylie came out of his private office while I was saying good-by to Mrs. Gilpley. She got all excited when he came out of his office, but I wouldn't stop talking.

Mrs. Gilpley, I said, all my life I've wanted to buy a Harley-Davidson and ride around and see a lot of small towns and I guess I could have done it if I had wanted to keep my job here, but where I come from a man don't keep a job and buy a Harley-David-son and get somebody else who needs a job worse fired.

What's a Harley-Davidson? Mr. Wylie said.

It's a motorcycle, I said.

Oh, he said.

And don't think I won't get along all right, Mrs. Gilpley, I said, because I will.

What do you want with a motorcycle? Mr. Wylie said.

I want to ride it, I said.

What for? he said.

To get somewhere, I said. Travel.

That's no way to travel, Mr. Wylie said.

It's one of the best ways in the world, I said. Mr. Wylie, I don't suppose you've ever driven a motorcycle.

No, I haven't, he said.

There ain't nothing like it, I said. A good motorcycle can go eighty miles an hour, easy.

Mrs. Gilpley, I said, if I ever get a motorcycle with a sidecar, I'd be very happy to take you for a little ride through Golden Gate Park, just to give you an idea how pleasant motorcycle riding can be.

Thank you very much, Joe, Mrs. Gilpley said.

Good-by, I said.

Good-by, said Mrs. Gilpley.

Good-by, said Mr. Wylie.

I went out and rang for the elevator. It was the Greek, George.

Where you going? he said.

Portland, I said.

Portland? he said. What are you going to do in Portland?

I don't know, I said.

What's the matter? he said.

I just quit my job, I said.

What do you want to quit your job for? he said.

I didn't like it, I said. I don't like keeping track of dead people.

You're crazy, he said.

I ain't crazy at all, I said.

I walked out of the elevator, out of the building, and up Market Street. I don't know how it happened, but I went straight to the Harley-Davidson agency, and they showed me the new model. I asked the salesman if I could try one out for a little while, and he talked it over with somebody in an inside office and then he said I could try one out if I would leave some money. In case, he said.

Well, I had the check, so I gave him the check.

It was a beautiful machine. I tore down Market Street and stopped at the building where I used to work and went upstairs and walked into Mr. Wylie's office.

He looked dumbfounded.

Mr. Wylie, I said, I got a beautiful Harley-Davidson downstairs and if you'd like to go for a ride, I'd be more than glad to let you sit behind me. It's a big seat and if I move up toward the front, you'll be comfortable.

I don't want to ride no motorcycle, he said.

I thought maybe you would, I said.

I went out of the office, and then I went back.

Well, would you care to *see* it? I said.

No, he said.

All right, I said, and I went on downstairs and got on the motorcycle and drove away. It was a beautiful job. The motor was great. I got out on the Great Highway at the beach and then I remembered Monterey and I figured maybe I ought to let her out and tear down to Monterey and then tear back, and then give them back their motorcycle and start looking for another job. They'd maybe give me back some of the money, and maybe not, but even if they didn't, I figured it would be worth it, so I let her out. It was the real thing. April. And the Harley-Davidson under me, and the Pacific Ocean beside me. And the world. And the towns. And the people. And the trees. And I roared down to Monterey in no time.

It was a fine town. There were some old buildings in the town, and ships. Fishing ships. There was a fine smell of fish down there, and a lot of sunlight. The fishermen talked very loud in Italian. I drove the Harley-Davidson all around town and right out onto the wet sand of the beach and along the beach for quite a way. I scared a lot of sea gulls and then I stopped at a place and had three hamburgers and two cups of coffee.

Then I started back to Frisco.

It was a great trip, going and coming. It was the most beautiful machine I ever saw. I could do anything with it. I could make it go anywhere, and I did. And I could make it go slower than a man walking, and faster than any expensive car on the highway. I'll bet I passed at least sixty millionaires on the highway. I could make it roar too. I could drive it zig-zag. I could ride it leaning away over on one side. I guess I scared a lot of people on the highway. I drove it a mile no hands. I stood on the seat a long time, holding the handlebars. People think that's dangerous, but it isn't if you know how to do it.

I had a great time with the Harley-Davidson. Then I took it back and turned it in. The salesman said, Where did you go?

I went down to Monterey, I said.

Monterey? he said. We didn't know you wanted to go that far. We just thought you wanted to find out how it worked.

Well, I said, I always wanted to go down there. Can I have my money back?

Are you going to buy the motorcycle? he said.

How much is it? I said.

It's two hundred and seventy-five dollars, he said.

No, I said. I ain't got that much.

How much have you got? he said.

I got that check, that's all, I said. Them thirteen dollars.

We thought you were going to buy the motorcycle, he said.

I would have bought it if I hadn't quit my job, I said. Can I have my money back?

I don't think so, the salesman said. I'll talk to the manager.

He went into an office and talked, and then he came out and another man was with him. The other man looked important and sore.

What do you mean by taking a new bike and riding it to Monterey and back? he said.

What? I said.

I didn't know what to say. What did *he* mean, *what did I mean?* I didn't mean anything.

You can't do that, he said. We thought you just wanted to ride the motorcycle around the block or show it to somebody.

I showed it to a few people, I said. Can I have my money back?

I'm afraid *you* owe *us* money, said the manager. That machine's a new machine. It's for sale. It's secondhand now.

Can't I have *some* of my money back? I said.

No, said the manager.

It's a swell motorcycle, I said.

I walked out of the place and walked up to my room and I didn't even stop to think where I'd ever be able to find a job. I was feeling too happy about the ride to Monterey and back.

Individualism requires courage, a fact that is at no time more apparent than when political pressure is brought to bear on a man in public office. No one can lose prestige or public favor so quickly as a politician who makes an unpopular decision. Edmund G. Ross was at the beginning of a promising political career in the United States Senate when he was confronted with disgrace and ruin. His story is taken from President Kennedy's book Profiles in Courage.

Edmund G. Ross

JOHN F. KENNEDY

In a lonely grave, forgotten and unknown, lies "the man who saved a President" and who as a result may well have preserved for ourselves and posterity constitutional government in the United States — the man who performed in 1868 what one historian has called "the most heroic act in American history, incomparably more difficult than any deed of valor upon the field of battle" — but a United States Senator whose name no one recalls: Edmund G. Ross of Kansas.

The impeachment[1] of President Andrew Johnson, the event in which the obscure Ross was to play such a dramatic role, was the sensational climax to the bitter struggle between the President, determined to carry out Abraham Lincoln's policies of reconciliation with the defeated South, and the more radical Republican leaders in Congress, who sought to administer the downtrodden Southern states as conquered provinces which had forfeited their rights under the Constitution. It was, moreover, a struggle between Executive and Legislative authority. Andrew Johnson, the courageous if untactful Tennessean who had been the only Southern Member of Congress to refuse to secede with his state, had committed himself to the policies of the Great Emancipator to whose high station he had succeeded only by the course of an assassin's bullet. He knew

---

[1] *impeachment*: bringing a high official of the federal government to trial before the Senate.

that Lincoln prior to his death had already clashed with the ex-
tremists in Congress, who had opposed his approach to reconstruction in a constitutional and charitable manner and sought to make
the Legislative Branch of the government supreme. And his own
belligerent temperament soon destroyed any hope that Congress
might now join hands in carrying out Lincoln's policies of permitting the South to resume its place in the Union with as little delay
and controversy as possible.

By 1866, when Edmund Ross first came to the Senate, the two
branches of the government were already at each other's throats,
snarling and bristling with anger. Bill after bill was vetoed by the
President on the grounds that they were unconstitutional, too harsh
in their treatment of the South, an unnecessary prolongation of
military rule in peacetime or undue interference with the authority
of the Executive Branch. And for the first time in our nation's history, important public measures were passed over a President's veto
and became law without his support.

But not all of Andrew Johnson's vetoes were overturned; and the
"Radical" [2] Republicans of the Congress promptly realized that one
final step was necessary before they could crush their despised foe
(and in the heat of political battle their vengeance was turned upon
their President far more than their former military enemies of the
South). That one remaining step was the assurance of a two-thirds
majority in the Senate — for under the Constitution, such a majority was necessary to override a Presidential veto. And more important, such a majority was constitutionally required to accomplish
their major ambition, now an ill-kept secret, conviction of the President under an impeachment and his dismissal from office!

The temporary and unstable two-thirds majority which had enabled the Senate Radical Republicans on several occasions to enact
legislation over the President's veto was, they knew, insufficiently
reliable for an impeachment conviction. To solidify this block became the paramount goal of Congress, expressly or impliedly gov-
erning its decisions on other issues — particularly the admission of
new states, the readmission of Southern states, and the determination
of senatorial credentials. By extremely dubious methods a pro-John-
son Senator was denied his seat. Over the President's veto Nebraska

---

[2] *Radical:* the extremist branch of the party that wanted strong, repressive measures against the South.

was admitted to the Union, seating two more anti-administration Senators. Although last-minute maneuvers failed to admit Colorado over the President's veto (sparsely populated Colorado had rejected statehood in a referendum), an unexpected tragedy brought false tears and fresh hopes for a new vote, in Kansas.

Senator Jim Lane of Kansas had been a "conservative" Republican sympathetic to Johnson's plans to carry out Lincoln's reconstruction policies. But his frontier state was one of the most "radical" in the Union. When Lane voted to uphold Johnson's veto of the Civil Rights Bill of 1866 and introduced the administration's bill for recognition of the new state government of Arkansas, Kansas had arisen in outraged heat. A mass meeting at Lawrence had vilified the Senator and speedily reported resolutions sharply condemning his position. Humiliated, mentally ailing, broken in health, and laboring under charges of financial irregularities, Jim Lane took his own life on July 1, 1866.

With this thorn in their side removed, the Radical Republicans in Washington looked anxiously toward Kansas and the selection of Lane's successor. Their fondest hopes were realized, for the new Senator from Kansas turned out to be Edmund G. Ross, the very man who had introduced the resolutions attacking Lane at Lawrence.

There could be no doubt as to where Ross's sympathies lay, for his entire career was one of determined opposition to the slave states of the South, their practices, and their friends. In 1854, when only twenty-eight, he had taken part in the mob rescue of a fugitive slave in Milwaukee. In 1856 he had joined that flood of antislavery immigrants to "bleeding" Kansas who intended to keep it a free territory. Disgusted with the Democratic party of his youth, he had left that party and volunteered in the Kansas Free State Army to drive back a force of proslavery men invading the territory. In 1862 he had given up his newspaper work to enlist in the Union Army, from which he emerged a major. His leading role in the condemnation of Lane at Lawrence convinced the Radical Republican leaders in Congress that in Edmund G. Ross they had a solid member of that vital two thirds.

The stage was now set for the final scene — the removal of Johnson. Early in 1867, Congress enacted over the President's veto the Tenure-of-Office Bill, which prevented the President from removing without the consent of the Senate all new officeholders whose appointment required confirmation by that body. At the time nothing more than the cry for more patronage [3] was involved, Cabinet Members having originally been specifically exempt.

On August 5, 1867, President Johnson — convinced that the Secretary of War, whom he had inherited from Lincoln, Edwin M. Stanton, was the surreptitious tool of the Radical Republicans and was seeking to become the almighty dictator of the conquered South — asked for his immediate resignation; and Stanton arrogantly fired back the reply that he declined to resign before the next meeting of Congress. Not one to cower before this kind of effrontery, the President one week later suspended Stanton and appointed in his place the one man whom Stanton did not dare resist, General Grant. On January 13, 1868, an angry Senate notified the President and Grant that it did not concur in the suspension of Stanton, and Grant vacated the office upon Stanton's return. But the situation was intolerable. The Secretary of War was unable to attend Cabinet meetings or associate with his colleagues in the administration; and on February 21, President Johnson, anxious to obtain a court test of the act he believed obviously unconstitutional, again notified Stanton that he had been summarily removed from the office of Secretary of War.

While Stanton, refusing to yield possession, barricaded himself in his office, public opinion in the nation ran heavily against the President. He had intentionally broken the law and dictatorially thwarted the will of Congress! Although previous resolutions of impeachment had been defeated in the House, both in committee and on the floor, a new resolution was swiftly reported and adopted on February 24 by a tremendous vote. Every single Republican voted in the affirmative, and Thaddeus Stevens of Pennsylvania — the crippled, fanatical personification of the extremes of the Radical Republican movement, master of the House of Representatives, with a mouth like the thin edge of an ax — warned both Houses of the Congress coldly: "Let me see the recreant who would vote to let such a criminal escape. Point me to one who will dare do it and I will show you one who will dare the infamy of posterity."

With the President impeached — in effect, indicted [4] — by the

---

[3] *patronage:* power to distribute political offices.
[4] *indicted* (in·dīt′əd): formally charged with an offense or crime.

House, the frenzied trial for his conviction or acquittal under the Articles of Impeachment began on March 5 in the Senate, presided over by the Chief Justice. It was a trial to rank with all the great trials in history — Charles I before the High Court of Justice, Louis XVI before the French Convention, and Warren Hastings before the House of Lords.[5] Two great elements of drama were missing: the actual cause for which the President was being tried was not fundamental to the welfare of the nation, and the defendant himself was at all times absent.

But every other element of the highest courtroom drama was present. To each Senator the Chief Justice administered an oath "to do impartial justice" (including even the hot-headed Radical Senator from Ohio, Benjamin Wade, who as President *pro tempore* of the Senate was next in line for the Presidency). The chief prosecutor for the House was General Benjamin F. Butler, the "butcher of New Orleans," a talented but coarse and demagogic Congressman from Massachusetts. (When he lost his seat in 1874, he was so hated by his own party as well as his opponents that one Republican wired concerning the Democratic sweep, "Butler defeated, everything else lost.") Some one thousand tickets were printed for admission to the Senate galleries during the trial, and every conceivable device was used to obtain one of the four tickets allotted each Senator.

From the fifth of March to the sixteenth of May, the drama continued. Of the eleven Articles of Impeachment adopted by the House, the first eight were based upon the removal of Stanton and the appointment of a new Secretary of War in violation of the Tenure-of-Office Act; the ninth related to Johnson's conversation with a general which was said to induce violations of the Army Appropriations Act; the tenth recited that Johnson had delivered "intemperate, inflammatory and scandalous harangues . . . as well against Congress as the laws of the United States"; and the eleventh was a deliberately obscure conglomeration of all the charges in the preceding articles, which had been designed by Thaddeus Stevens to

---

[5] *Charles I before the High Court of Justice:* The king of Great Britain who was tried for treason and executed. *Louis XVI before the French Convention:* King of France who was tried for treason during the French Revolution and sent to the guillotine in 1793. *Warren Hastings before the House of Lords:* A British soldier and statesman, who was charged with cruelty and dishonesty in his post as the first governor-general of India, brought to trial in 1788, and, after seven years, found "Not guilty" by the House of Lords.

furnish a common ground for those who favored conviction but were unwilling to identify themselves on basic issues. In opposition to Butler's inflammatory arguments in support of this hastily drawn indictment, Johnson's able and learned counsel replied with considerable effectiveness. They insisted that the Tenure-of-Office Act was null and void as a clear violation of the Constitution; that even if it were valid, it would not apply to Stanton, for the reasons previously mentioned; and that the only way that a judicial test of the law could be obtained was for Stanton to be dismissed and sue for his rights in the courts.

But as the trial progressed, it became increasingly apparent that the impatient Republicans did not intend to give the President a fair trial on the formal issues upon which the impeachment was drawn but intended instead to depose him from the White House on any grounds, real or imagined, for refusing to accept their policies. Telling evidence in the President's favor was arbitrarily excluded. Prejudgment on the part of most Senators was brazenly announced. Attempted bribery and other forms of pressure were rampant. The chief interest was not in the trial or the evidence but in the tallying of votes necessary for conviction.

Twenty-seven states (excluding the unrecognized Southern states) in the Union meant fifty-four members of the Senate, and thirty-six votes were required to constitute the two-thirds majority necessary for conviction. All twelve Democratic votes were obviously lost, and the forty-two Republicans knew that they could afford to lose only six of their own members if Johnson were to be ousted. To their dismay, at a preliminary Republican caucus, six courageous Republicans indicated that the evidence so far introduced was not in their opinion sufficient to convict Johnson under the Articles of Impeachment. "Infamy!" cried the Philadelphia *Press*. The Republic has "been betrayed in the house of its friends!"

But if the remaining thirty-six Republicans would hold, there would be no doubt as to the outcome. All must stand together! But one Republican Senator would not announce his verdict in the preliminary poll — Edmund G. Ross of Kansas. The Radicals were outraged that a Senator from such an anti-Johnson stronghold as Kansas could be doubtful. "It was a very clear case," Senator Sumner of Massachusetts fumed, "especially for a Kansas man. I did not think that a Kansas man could quibble against his country."

From the very time Ross had taken his seat, the Radical leaders had been confident of his vote. His entire background, as already indicated, was one of firm support of their cause. One of his first acts in the Senate had been to read a declaration of his adherence to Radical Republican policy, and he had silently voted for all of their measures. He had made it clear that he was not in sympathy with Andrew Johnson personally or politically; and after the removal of Stanton, he had voted with the majority in adopting a resolution declaring such removal unlawful. His colleague from Kansas, Senator Pomeroy, was one of the most Radical leaders of the anti-Johnson group. The Republicans insisted that Ross's crucial vote was rightfully theirs, and they were determined to get it by whatever means available. As stated by DeWitt in his memorable *Impeachment of Andrew Johnson,* "The full brunt of the struggle turned at last on the one remaining doubtful Senator, Edmund G. Ross."

When the impeachment resolution had passed the House, Senator Ross had casually remarked to Senator Sprague of Rhode Island, "Well, Sprague, the thing is here; and, so far as I am concerned, though a Republican and opposed to Mr. Johnson and his policy, he shall have as fair a trial as an accused man ever had on this earth." Immediately the word spread that "Ross was shaky." From that hour," he later wrote, "not a day passed that did not bring me, by mail and telegraph and in personal intercourse, appeals to stand fast for impeachment, and not a few were the admonitions of condign visitations upon any indication even of lukewarmness."

Throughout the country, and in all walks of life, as indicated by the correspondence of members of the Senate, the condition of the public mind was not unlike that preceding a great battle. The dominant party of the nation seemed to occupy the position of public prosecutor, and it was scarcely in the mood to brook delay for trial or to hear defense. Washington had become during the trial the central point of the politically dissatisfied and swarmed with representatives of every state of the Union, demanding in a practically united voice the deposition of the President. The footsteps of the anti-impeaching Republicans were dogged from the day's beginning to its end and far into the night with entreaties, considerations, and threats. The newspapers came daily filled with not a few threats of violence upon their return to their constituents.

Ross and his fellow doubtful Republicans were daily pestered, spied upon and subjected to every form of pressure. Their residences were carefully watched, their social circles suspiciously scrutinized, and their every move and companions secretly marked in special notebooks. They were warned in the party press, harangued by their constituents, and sent dire warnings threatening political ostracism and even assassination. Stanton himself, from his barricaded head-quarters in the War Department, worked day and night to bring to bear upon the doubtful Senators all the weight of his impressive military associations. The Philadelphia *Press* reported "a fearful avalanche of telegrams from every section of the country," a great surge of public opinion from the "common people" who had given their money and lives to the country and would not "willingly or unavenged see their great sacrifice made naught."

The New York *Tribune* reported that Edmund Ross in particular was "mercilessly dragged this way and that by both sides, hunted like a fox night and day and badgered by his own colleagues, like the bridge at Arcola now trod upon by one Army and now trampled by the other." His background and life were investigated from top to bottom, and his constituents and colleagues pursued him through-out Washington to gain some inkling of his opinion. He was the target of every eye, his name was on every mouth, and his intentions were discussed in every newspaper. Although there is evidence that he gave some hint of agreement to each side, and each attempted to claim him publicly, he actually kept both sides in a state of complete suspense by his judicial silence.

But with no experience in political turmoil, no reputation in the Senate, no independent income, and the most radical state in the Union to deal with, Ross was judged to be the most sensitive to criticism and the most certain to be swayed by expert tactics. A committee of Congressmen and Senators sent to Kansas, and to the states of the other doubtful Republicans, this telegram: "Great danger to the peace of the country and the Republican cause if impeachment fails. Send to your Senators public opinion by resolutions, letters, and delegations." A member of the Kansas Legislature called upon Ross at the Capitol. A general urged on by Stanton remained at his lodge until four o'clock in the morning determined to see him. His brother received a letter offering $20,000 for revelation of the Senator's intentions. Gruff Ben Butler exclaimed of

Ross, "There is a bushel of money! How much does the damned scoundrel want?"

The night before the Senate was to take its first vote for the conviction or acquittal of Johnson, Ross received this telegram from home:

Kansas has heard the evidence and demands the conviction of the President.

[signed] D. R. ANTHONY AND 1,000 OTHERS

And on that fateful morning of May 16 Ross replied:

To. D. R. Anthony and 1,000 Others: I do not recognize your right to demand that I vote either for or against conviction. I have taken an oath to do impartial justice according to the Constitution and laws, and trust that I shall have the courage to vote according to the dictates of my judgment and for the highest good of the country.

[signed] E. G. Ross

That morning spies traced Ross to his breakfast, and ten minutes before the vote was taken his Kansas colleague warned him in the presence of Thaddeus Stevens that a vote for acquittal would mean trumped up charges and his political death.

But now the fateful hour was at hand. Neither escape, delay, nor indecision was possible. As Ross himself later described it, "The galleries were packed. Tickets of admission were at an enormous premium. The House had adjourned and all of its members were in the Senate chamber. Every chair on the Senate floor was filled with a Senator, a Cabinet Officer, a member of the President's counsel or a member of the House." Every Senator was in his seat, the desperately ill Grimes of Iowa being literally carried in.

It had been decided to take the first vote under that broad Eleventh Article of Impeachment, believed to command the widest support. As the Chief Justice announced the voting would begin, he reminded "the citizens and strangers in the galleries that absolute silence and perfect order are required." But already a deathlike stillness enveloped the Senate chamber. A Congressman later recalled that "Some of the members of the House near me grew pale and sick under the burden of "suspense"; and Ross noted that there was even "a subsidence of the shuffling of feet, the rustling of silks, the fluttering of fans, and of conversation."

The voting tensely commenced. By the time the Chief Justice reached the name of Edmund Ross, twenty-four "guilties" had been pronounced. Ten more were certain and one other practically certain. Only Ross's vote was needed to obtain the thirty-six votes necessary to convict the President. But not a single person in the room knew how this young Kansan would vote. Unable to conceal the suspense and emotion in his voice, the Chief Justice put the question to him: "Mr. Senator Ross, how say you? Is the respondent Andrew Johnson guilty or not guilty of a high misdemeanor as charged in this Article?" Every voice was still; every eye was upon the freshman Senator from Kansas. The hopes and fears, the hatred and bitterness of past decades were centered upon this one man.

As Ross himself later described it, his "powers of hearing and seeing seemed developed in an abnormal degree."

Every individual in that great audience seemed distinctly visible, some with lips apart and bending forward in anxious expectancy, others with hand uplifted as if to ward off an apprehended blow . . . and each peering with an intensity that was almost tragic upon the face of him who was about to cast the fateful vote. . . . Every fan was folded, not a foot moved, not the rustle of a garment, not a whisper was heard. . . . Hope and fear seemed blended in every face, instantaneously alternating, some with revengeful hate . . . others lighted with hope. . . . The Senators in their seats leaned over their desks, many with hand to ear. . . . It was a tremendous responsibility, and it was not strange that he upon whom it had been imposed by a fateful combination of conditions should have sought to avoid it, to put it away from him as one shuns, or tries to fight off, a nightmare. . . . I almost literally looked down into my open grave. Friendships, position, fortune, everything that makes life desirable to an ambitious man were about to be swept away by the breath of my mouth, perhaps forever. It is not strange that my answer was carried waveringly over the air and failed to reach the limits of the audience, or that repetition was called for by distant Senators on the opposite side of the Chamber.

Then came the answer again in a voice that could not be misunderstood — full, final, definite, unhesitating, and unmistakable: "Not guilty." The deed was done, the President saved, the trial as good as over, and the conviction lost. The remainder of the roll call was unimportant; conviction had failed by the margin of a single vote, and a general rumbling filled the chamber until the Chief Justice proclaimed that "on this Article thirty-five Senators having voted guilty and nineteen not guilty, a two-thirds majority not having voted for conviction, the President is, therefore, acquitted under this Article."

A ten-day recess followed, ten turbulent days to change votes on the remaining Articles. An attempt was made to rush through bills to readmit six Southern states, whose twelve Senators were guaranteed to vote for conviction. But this could not be accomplished in time. Again Ross was the only one uncommitted on the other Articles, the only one whose vote could not be predicted in advance. And again he was subjected to terrible pressure. From "D. R. Anthony and others," he received a wire informing him that "Kansas repudiates you as she does all perjurers and skunks." Every incident of his life was examined and distorted. Professional witnesses were found by Senator Pomeroy to testify before a special House committee that Ross had indicated a willingness to change his vote for a consideration. (Unfortunately this witness was so delighted in his exciting role that he also swore that Senator Pomeroy had made an offer to produce three votes for acquittal for $40,000.) When Ross, in his capacity as a Committee Chairman, took several bills to the President, James G. Blaine remarked: "There goes the rascal to get his pay."

Again the wild rumors spread that Ross had been won over on the remaining Articles of Impeachment. As the Senate reassembled, he was the only one of the seven "renegade" Republicans to vote with the majority on preliminary procedural matters. But when the second and third Articles of Impeachment were read, and the name of Ross was reached again with the same intense suspense of ten days earlier, again came the calm answer "Not guilty."

Neither Ross nor any other Republican who had voted for the acquittal of Johnson was ever re-elected to the Senate, not a one of them retaining the support of their party's organization. When he returned to Kansas in 1871, he and his family suffered social ostracism, physical attack, and near poverty.

Who was Edmund G. Ross? Practically nobody. Not a single public law bears his name, not a single history book includes his picture, not a single list of Senate "greats" mentions his service. His one heroic deed has been all but forgotten. But who might Edmund G. Ross have been? That is the question — for Ross, a man with an excellent command of words, an excellent background for politics and an excellent future in the Senate, might well have outstripped his colleagues in prestige and power throughout a long Senate career. Instead, he chose to throw all of this away for one act of conscience.

*As Edmund G. Ross learned, persecution is often the price that must
be paid for individualism. Unpopular habits seldom go unnoticed or
unrebuked. Joseph Palmer was mocked and laughed at simply because
he refused to go along with fashion.*

The Beard of
Joseph Palmer

STEWART H. HOLBROOK

One of the unsung but really great individualists who helped to
make the United States a better and a safer place to live in was
Joseph Palmer of Fitchburg and Harvard, Massachusetts, a man to
be reckoned with in any discussion of the Bill of Rights. He is forgotten now, and this is bad forgetting, for Palmer was of a race of
men that is now all but extinct. And his story, I think, is as heart-
warming as it is improbable.

Palmer came to national attention because he was the victim of
one of the strangest persecutions in history. Neither race nor religion
played a part in Palmer's case, which with some reason might otherwise be termed *l'affaire Dreyfus* [1] of Fitchburg. It was brought about
by the fact that Joe Palmer liked to wear a beard, one of the most
magnificent growths ever seen in New England or, for that matter,
in the United States; and what made this beard particularly heinous
was that it was almost, if not quite, the only beard east of the Rocky
Mountains, and possibly beyond.

One lone set of whiskers amid millions of smooth-shaven faces is
something to contemplate, and Palmer paid dearly for his eccen-

---

[1] *l'affaire Dreyfus:* "The Dreyfus Affair." Alfred Dreyfus was a French army
officer who, in 1895, was unjustly convicted of treason and imprisoned. It was
claimed that some of the army and court officials were prejudiced against
Dreyfus because of his Jewish religion. When the French government failed
to take action, the case attracted international attention, with protests pouring
in from many countries. Finally, after some five years' delay and a change of
government, Dreyfus was released and declared innocent.

tricity. Indeed, one might say, with but little stretch of imagination and metaphor, that it was Joe Palmer who carried the Knowledge of Whiskers through the dark ages of beardless America. He was born almost a century too late and seventy-five years too soon to wear whiskers with impunity. He was forty-two years old in 1830, when he moved from his nearby farm into the hustling village of Fitchburg. He came of sturdy old Yankee stock. His father had served in the Revolution, and Joe himself had carried a musket in 1812. He was married and had one son, Thomas.

When the beard first made its appearance isn't of record, but Joe was wearing it when he came to Fitchburg, and here, because of it, he immediately became the butt of cruel jokes and derision and, in time, the victim of downright persecution. But before relating the violence caused by Palmer's famous beard, it is imperative — if one is to comprehend the proceedings at all — to trace briefly the history of whiskers in America up to the time of the Palmer beard.

This continent was explored by men of many nationalities, almost all of them wearing whiskers. About Columbus and Amerigo Vespucci we are uncertain, since there are no authenticated contemporary portraits of them. But after them came a host of beards. Cortés, Ponce de León, Cartier, Champlain, Drake, Raleigh, Captain John Smith, De Soto — all sported whiskers of varying length and style. Little wonder the Indians thought them gods.

Then came the Pilgrims and the Puritans, bearded almost to a man when they arrived at the Rock and elsewhere. But the beards of the first settlers didn't last. American whiskers were reduced gradually in size until they were scarcely more than mild goatees, and soon disappeared entirely. By 1720 at the latest, American colonists were wholly free of facial hair. Try to find a Copley portrait, or a Ralph Earle [2] with a whisker in it. And the fighting men of the Revolution were beardless. Not a mustache or a suspicion of a mutton chop appeared on the faces of Washington, Gates, Greene, Knox. Even old John Stark and Israel Putnam were smooth-shaven, and so was the backwoods general Ethan Allen. It was the same with the other Patriots, and with the British also — Cornwallis, the Howes,

---

[2] *Copley . . . Earle:* John Singleton Copley (1738–1815) and Ralph Earle (1751–1801) were famous American portrait painters of the late eighteenth century.

Burgoyne. No signer of the Declaration had either beard or mustache.

And so it continued down the years. No President before Lincoln had any hair on his face. Until 1858 the cartoonists' conception of their own creature, Uncle Sam — otherwise much as he is today — was of a tall and lanky but smooth-shaven man. America did not really go hairy until the War Between the States was well under way.

Thus, when Joe Palmer came to town wearing a beard in 1830, whiskers had been virtually nonexistent for at least a hundred years. In spite of his hirsute oddity, Palmer was an honest, kindly man and a good citizen, deeply religious but tolerant, and a man of many intellectual interests. He was also quite immovable when it came to principles, which in his case included the right to wear a full, flowing beard.

Everywhere he went, small boys threw stones and shouted at him and made life miserable for his son, Tom. Women sniffed and crossed to the other side of the street when they saw him coming. Often the windows of his modest home were broken by unknown rowdies. Grown men jeered at him openly. The Reverend George Trask, local pastor, took him to task for his eccentricity, but Joe replied with exact Scriptural reasons — nay, commands — for beard-wearing. Old Doctor Williams told Joe to his face that he should "be prosecuted for wearing such a monstrosity." And when Joe went to Boston to attend literary and reform meetings, huge crowds "followed him the length of Tremont Street, jeering." He was present at the celebrated Chardon Street Convention in 1840, and one has no difficulty locating him in Emerson's [3] comment on that gathering:

If the assembly was disorderly, it was picturesque. Madmen, madwomen, men with beards, Dunkers, Muggletonians, Come-outers, Groaners, Agrarians, Seventh-Day Baptists, Quakers, Abolitionists, Calvinists, Unitarians, and Philosophers — all came successively to the top, and seized their moment, if not their hour, wherein to chide, or pray, or preach, or protest.

By the time of this convention, Joe Palmer was a national character, made so by two events that had happened in quick succession in his home town of Fitchburg. In spite of the snubs of the congregation, Joe never missed a church service, but one Sunday he quite

---

[3] *Ralph Waldo Emerson:* American philosopher and poet.

justifiably lost his usually serene temper. It was a Communion Sunday in 1830. Joe knelt with the rest, only to be publicly humiliated when the officiating clergyman ignored him, "passed him by with the communion bread and wine." Joe was cut to the quick. He rose up and strode to the communion table. He lifted the cup to his lips and took a mighty swig. Then: "I love my Jesus," he shouted in a voice loud with hurt and anger, "as well, and better, than any of you!" Then he went home.

A few days later, as he was coming out of the Fitchburg Hotel, he was seized by four men armed with shears, brush, soap, and razor. They told him that the sentiment of the town was that his beard should come off and they were going to do the job there and then. When Joe started to struggle, the four men threw him violently to the ground, seriously injuring his back and head. But Joe had just begun to fight. When they were about to apply the shears, he managed to get an old jackknife out of his pocket. He laid about him wildly, cutting two of his assailants in their legs, not seriously but sufficiently to discourage any barber work. When Joe stood up, hurt and bleeding, his gorgeous beard was intact.

Presently he was arrested, charged with "an unprovoked assault." Fined by Justice Brigham he refused to pay. Matter of principle, he said. He was put in the city jail at Worcester, and there he remained for more than a year, part of the time in solitary confinement. Even here he had to fight for his whiskers, for once Jailor Bellows came with several men with the idea of removing the now-famous beard. Joe threw himself at them and fought so furiously that the mob retreated without a hair. He also successfully repulsed at least two attempts by prisoners to shave him.

In the jail Joe wrote letters which he smuggled out a window to his son, who took them to the Worcester *Spy*. They were published and soon were being widely copied by other newspapers. In his letters the bearded prisoner stated that he was in jail not for assault but because he chose to wear whiskers — which was unquestionably the case. He complained of the food, of the quarters, and of the lack of any religious life behind the bars. People all over Massachusetts read these letters. They began to talk, and even to reflect. It wasn't long before the sheriff came to realize that he had a Tartar[4] and possibly a martyr on his hands. He went to Joe and told him to run

---

[4] *Tartar*: a person of savage temper; an unexpectedly strong opponent.

along home and forget it — the fine and everything. No, said Joe. The jailor urged him to leave. His aged mother wrote him to come home. All in vain. Nothing could move the man who was now known as the Bearded Prisoner of Worcester.

Day after day he sat in his limbo, keeping an elaborate and pathetic journal of his persecutions. And time after time he told officers and worried magistrates that they had put him there, and they would have to take him out. "I won't walk one single step toward freedom!" he roared through the bar. Nor did he. He sat there in a chair like a whiskered Buddha until the desperate sheriff and jailors picked him up in his chair and carried him to the street.

Never again was violence attempted on Joe Palmer's beard, which by the time of his release, or rather his eviction, from jail, was a beard famous as far away as New York and Philadelphia. Free now, he soon became a minor figure in New England's intellectual ferment. A hater of slavery, he went to Boston often for the meetings of Parker and Garrison,[5] contributing both time and money to the movement for abolition. He met Emerson, Thoreau, Alcott, Channing, and these men found him an odd but staunch character, the possessor of much good sense. He loathed liquor as much as he did slavery and was active at Temperance meetings. He visited the communities at Brook Farm and Hopedale.

When Bronson Alcott and family, with Charles Lane and a few others, bought a farm in Harvard, near Fitchburg, named it Fruitlands, and attempted to found the Con-Sociate Family,[6] Joe Palmer was vastly interested. He donated a lot of fine old furniture and up-to-date farm implements to the colony. When he saw that Alcott's idiotic ideas about farming were going to bring famine to the group, he brought his own team and plow and turned up the soil. He was, in fact, the only sensible male in that wondrous experiment. (Joe Palmer appears in Louisa May Alcott's *Transcendental Wild Oats* as Moses White.)

Fruitlands had the distinction of being the worst-managed and shortest-lived of all American colonies. When the half-starved Alcotts and the others had moved away, Joe Palmer bought the farm and moved there with his wife and family. Here, for more than

---

[5] *Theodore Parker and William Lloyd Garrison:* leading figures in the movement for abolition of slavery.

[6] *Con-Sociate Family:* unsuccessful experiment in communal living

twenty years, he carried on a strange sort of community life of his own devising. He was widely known now and never lacked for company. Emerson and Thoreau visited him, and so did every reformer who passed through or operated in New England. The merely curious came to see the famous beard. The Palmers always had a pot of beans on the stove, plenty of bread in the butt'ry. All were welcome to come and to stay, so long as they had no trace of liquor about them.

In place of persecution, Joe now found himself something of a hero. The years crept on, and with them his great beard grew even more famously, spreading like a willow. A photograph taken at about this time shows a growth that makes Walt Whitman seem a beardless youth in comparison. And at last, many years before he died, the whiskers of all America came into their fullest glory. This second coming of the beard was sudden, an almost instantaneous wilderness of hair that covered the face of male America.

One cannot know with certainty the reason for this sudden era of whiskers; it can only be recorded. Lincoln, when elected, was smooth-shaven, but, when inaugurated, wore a beard. Grant, the lieutenant, had worn a tiny mustache; Grant, the general, had a full beard. Robert E. Lee went smooth of face to war and was presently full-bearded. In 1860 Jeff Davis was clean of chin. He was soon wearing whiskers longer than Lincoln's. Nearly all of the generals of the War Between the States, on both sides, were peering out of whiskers by 1862, and so were their men. Stonewall Jackson grew a mighty beard. Custer grew a unique combination beard and mustache, but it was General Ambrose E. Burnside who gave his name to a special type of whiskers.

The baseball players of the sixties and seventies, as depicted by the careful Currier & Ives,[7] had whiskers. Bankers grew a style all their own. Razors went into the discard, and vendors of quack beard-growers swarmed into the new market. The proper gift to a male was an elegant mustache cup. Manufacturers of soap, patent medicines, and cough drops — notably cough drops — came out with one or more bearded faces on their labels. Whiskers, through some odd turn of the folkways, now were a sign of solid worth, a badge of integrity in every line of endeavor. If the poor barbers thought the

---

[7] *Currier & Ives:* an American printing firm noted for detailed and realistic lithographs of American scenes.

end of things had arrived, it is easy to understand why.

As for old Joe Palmer, he was immensely happy, a true prophet who had lived to see his justification. Few prophets have been so fortunate. All over America, Joe Palmer knew, were now full beards, Van Dykes, goatees, galways, dundrearys, mutton chops, burnsides, fringe beards, and millions of stupendous mustaches of the over-Niagara type. Aye, the prophet had come into his own. Yet Joe was no gloater. He seems to have remarked only once on the greatly changed styles of what men wore on their faces. That was when he met the same Reverend Trask who had so churlishly upbraided him many years before for wearing his beard. Trask himself was now wearing a luxuriant growth. Meeting him on a Fitchburg street one day, Joe stroked his own beard and remarked: "Knowest thou that thy redeemer liveth?"

Joe Palmer died in 1875, when beards were at their fullest, and was thus spared the dreadful sight of their withering and final disappearance. What happened during the thirty-five years following Joe's death would certainly have saddened him.

The whisker debacle of the last quarter of the nineteenth century has engrossed only a few of us minor social historians, but Mr. Lewis Gannett has charted the decline so graphically that little more research needs to be done. He used his alma mater, Harvard University, to demonstrate the mysterious rises and falls of male American hair; and his studies show that graduating classes of the 1860's were hairy as goats. The Class of 1870 had four beards. Two years later a good majority were wearing not beards but mustaches and burnsides. By 1890 beards and burnsides (sideburns are the same thing, only there isn't quite so much to them) were distinctly obsolete, and the mustache was at or nearing its peak.

Decline now followed with tragic speed. The Class of 1900 was without one beard, the first such crowd of sissies since the Mexican War. The last Harvard football mustache appeared in 1901, Mr. Gannett's chart shows, and the last Harvard baseball mustache in 1905. Since then Harvard men — except for a few professors — have been mostly smooth of chin and lip.

The White House witnessed a similar decline of hair. From Lincoln to Wilson, only one man without at least a mustache was elected to the Presidency. Grant had a beard, Hayes was positively hairy. Garfield fairly burgeoned with whiskers. Cleveland had a sizable mustache, Harrison a flowing beard, and both Theodore Roosevelt and Taft had mustaches. The lone smooth-shaven President during this entire period was McKinley.

Beginning with Wilson in 1912 and continuing to the present, no President has worn hair on his face. Many thought it was his beard that defeated Hughes,[8] and his was for years the only honest beard to wag on the once heavily whiskered Supreme Court.

Old Joe Palmer, then, died at exactly the right time, and he took some pains to make certain, no matter what styles frivolous men might adopt, that he was not wholly forgotten. In the old cemetery in North Leominster, not far from Fitchburg, is his monument, a rugged square stone as tall as a man; and on its front is an excellent medallion carving of Joe's head, with its noble beard flowing and rippling in white marble. Below the head appears a simple legend: "Persecuted for Wearing the Beard."

Joe Palmer's last home, the celebrated Fruitlands in nearby Harvard, has been restored with loving care as a historical showplace by Clara Endicott Sears — not so much in memory of Palmer as of the Alcotts. In this charming house, however, one may see old Joe's beautiful furniture, and a good photograph of the kindly yet determined old gentleman who wished to be remembered only as the Redeemer of the Beard.

---

[8] *Charles Evans Hughes:* Chief Justice of the United States (1930–41) and candidate for President in 1916.

The increasing use of machines in the nineteenth century was motivated by the idea of efficiency in producing goods. At the same time it was a threat to individualism: workers seemed to become dehumanized slaves of machinery. The goods produced were cheap but at the same time shoddy. A bowl no longer bore the individual touch of a potter — it was exactly like ten thousand others. Craftsmanship was displaced by mass production, which in turn was promoted by techniques of advertising through mass communications. In the story which follows, a German shoemaker noted for his workmanship is confronted by the "pressure" techniques of his competitors.

Quality

JOHN GALSWORTHY

I knew him from the days of my extreme youth because he made my father's boots, inhabiting with his elder brother two little shops let into one, in a small by-street — now no more but then most fashionably placed in the West End.

That tenement had a certain quiet distinction; there was no sign upon its face that he made for any of the Royal Family — merely his own German name of Gessler Brothers and in the window a few pairs of boots. I remember that it always troubled me to account for those unvarying boots in the window, for he made only what was ordered, reaching nothing down, and it seemed so inconceivable that what he made could ever have failed to fit. Had he bought them to put there? That, too, seemed inconceivable. He would never have tolerated in his house leather on which he had not worked himself. Besides, they were too beautiful — the pair of pumps, so inexpressibly slim, the patent leathers with cloth tops, making water come into one's mouth, the tall brown riding-boots with marvelous sooty glow, as if, though new, they had been worn a hundred years. Those pairs could only have been made by one who saw before him the Soul of Boot — so truly were they prototypes, incarnating the very spirit of all footwear. These thoughts, of course, came to me later, though even when I was promoted to him, at the age of perhaps fourteen, some inkling haunted me of the dignity of himself and brother. For to make boots — such boots as he made — seemed to me then, and still seems to me, mysterious and wonderful.

I remember well my shy remark, one day, while stretching out to him my youthful foot:

"Isn't it awfully hard to do, Mr. Gessler?"

And his answer, given with a sudden smile from out of the sardonic redness of his beard: "Id is an Ardt!"

Himself, he was a little as if made of leather, with his yellow crinkly face, and crinkly reddish hair and beard, and neat folds slanting down his cheeks to the corners of his mouth, and his guttural [1] and one-toned voice, for leather is a sardonic substance, and stiff and slow of purpose. And that was the character of his face, save that his eyes, which were gray-blue, had in them the simple gravity of one secretly possessed by the Ideal. His elder brother was so very like him — though watery, paler in every way, with a great industry — that sometimes in early days I was not quite sure of him until the interview was over. Then I knew that it was he, if the words, "I will ask my brudder," had not been spoken and that if they had, it was the elder brother.

When one grew old and wild and ran up bills, one somehow never ran them up with Gessler Brothers. It would not have seemed becoming to go in there and stretch out one's foot to that blue iron-spectacled face, owing him for more than — say two pairs — just the comfortable reassurance that one was still his client.

For it was not possible to go to him very often — his boots lasted terribly, having something beyond the temporary — some, as it were, essence of boot stitched into them.

One went in, not as into most shops, in the mood of: "Please serve me, and let me go!" but restfully, as one enters a church and, sitting on the single wooden chair, waited — for there was never anybody there. Soon — over the top edge of that sort of well — rather dark and smelling soothingly of leather — which formed the shop, there would be seen his face, or that of his elder brother, peering down. A guttural sound, and the tip-tap of bast slippers beating the

---

[1] *guttural:* sounds produced in the throat. Gessler's native tongue, German, has many guttural sounds.

narrow wooden stairs, and he would stand before one without coat, a little bent, in leather apron, with sleeves turned back, blinking — as if awakened from some dream of boots, or like an owl surprised in daylight and annoyed at this interruption.

And I would say: "How do you do, Mr. Gessler? Could you make me a pair of Russia leather boots?"

Without a word he would leave me, retiring whence he came, or into the other portion of the shop, and I would continue to rest in the wooden chair, inhaling the incense of his trade. Soon he would come back, holding in his thin, veined hand a piece of gold-brown leather. With eyes fixed on it, he would remark: "What a beaudiful biece!" When I, too, had admired it, he would speak again. "When do you wand dem?" And I would answer: "Oh! As soon as you conveniently can." And he would say: "Tomorrow fordnighd?"[2] Or if he were his elder brother: "I will ask my brudder!"

Then I would murmur: "Thank you! Good-morning, Mr. Gessler." "Goot-morning!" he would reply, still looking at the leather in his hand. And as I moved to the door, I would hear the tip-tap of his bast slippers restoring him, up the stairs, to his dream of boots. But if it were some new kind of footgear that he had not yet made me, then indeed he would observe ceremony — divesting me of my boot and holding it long in his hand, looking at it with eyes at once critical and loving, as if recalling the glow with which he had created it, and rebuking the way in which one had disorganized this masterpiece. Then, placing my foot on a piece of paper, he would two or three times tickle the outer edges with a pencil and pass his nervous fingers over my toes, feeling himself into the heart of my requirements.

I cannot forget that day on which I had occasion to say to him: "Mr. Gessler, that last pair of town walking-boots creaked, you know."

He looked at me for a time without replying, as if expecting me to withdraw or qualify the statement, then said:

"Id shouldn't 'ave greaked."

"It did, I'm afraid."

"You god dem wed before dey found demselves?"

"I don't think so."

At that he lowered his eyes, as if hunting for memory of those

---

[2] *fordnighd:* fortnight, two weeks.

QUALITY

255

boots, and I felt sorry I had mentioned this grave thing.

"Zend dem back!" he said; "I will look at dem."

A feeling of compassion for my creaking boots surged up in me, so well could I imagine the sorrowful long curiosity of regard which he would bend on them.

"Zome boods," he said slowly, "are bad from birdt. If I can do noding wid dem, I dake dem off your bill."

Once (once only) I went absent-mindedly into his shop in a pair of boots bought in an emergency at some large firm. He took my order without showing me any leather, and I could feel his eyes penetrating the inferior integument of my foot. At last he said:

"Dose are nod my boods."

The tone was not one of anger, nor of sorrow, not even of contempt, but there was in it something quiet that froze the blood. He put his hand down and pressed a finger on the place where the left boot, endeavoring to be fashionable, was not quite comfortable.

"Id 'urds you dere," he said. "Dose big virms 'ave no self-respect. Drash!" And then, as if something had given way within him, he spoke long and bitterly. It was the only time I ever heard him discuss the conditions and hardships of his trade.

"Dey get id all," he said, "dey get id by adverdisement, nod by work. Dey dake it away from us, who lofe our boods. Id gomes to this — bresently I haf no work. Every year id gets less — you will see." And looking at his lined face I saw things I had never noticed before, bitter things and bitter struggle — and what a lot of gray hairs there seemed suddenly in his red beard!

As best I could, I explained the circumstances of the purchase of those ill-omened boots. But his face and voice made a so deep impression that during the next few minutes I ordered many pairs! Nemesis [3] fell! They lasted more terribly than ever. And I was not able conscientiously to go to him for nearly two years.

When at last I went I was surprised that outside one of the two little windows of his shop another name was painted, also that of a bootmaker — making, of course, for the Royal Family. The old familiar boots, no longer in dignified isolation, were huddled in the single window. Inside, the now contracted well of the one little shop was more scented and darker than ever. And it was longer than usual, too, before a face peered down, and the tip-tap of the bast

---

[3] *Nemesis*: vengeance.

slippers began. At last he stood before me, and, gazing through those rusty iron spectacles, said:

"Mr. ——, isn'd it?"

"Ah! Mr. Gessler," I stammered, "but your boots are really *too* good, you know! See, these are quite decent still!" And I stretched out to him my foot. He looked at it.

"Yes," he said, "beople do nod wand good boods, id seems."

To get away from his reproachful eyes and voice I hastily remarked: "What have you done to your shop?"

He answered quietly: "Id was to exbensif. Do you wand some boods?"

I ordered three pairs, though I had only wanted two, and quickly left. I had, I know not quite what feeling of being part, in his mind, of a conspiracy against him, or not perhaps so much against him as against his idea of boot. One does not, I suppose, care to feel like that, for it was again many months before my next visit to his shop, paid, I remember, with the feeling: "Oh! well, I can't leave the old boy — so here goes! Perhaps it'll be his elder brother!"

For his elder brother, I knew, had not character enough to reproach me, even dumbly.

And, to my relief, in the shop there did appear to be his elder brother, handling a piece of leather.

"Well, Mr. Gessler," I said, "how are you?"

He came close, and peered at me.

"I am breddy well," he said slowly, "but my elder brudder is dead."

And I saw that it was indeed himself — but how aged and wan! And never before had I heard him mention his brother. Much shocked, I murmured: "Oh! I am sorry!"

"Yes," he answered, "he was a good man, he made a good bood, but he is dead." And he touched the top of his head, where the hair had suddenly gone as thin as it had been on that of his poor brother, to indicate, I suppose, the cause of death. "He could nod ged over losing de oder shop. Do you wand any boods?" And he held up the leather in his hand: "Id's a beaudiful biece."

I ordered several pairs. It was very long before they came — but they were better than ever. One simply could not wear them out. And soon after that I went abroad.

It was over a year before I was again in London. And the first shop

I went to was my old friend's. I had left a man of sixty, I came back to find one of seventy-five, pinched and worn and tremulous, who genuinely, this time, did not at first know me.

"Oh! Mr. Gessler," I said, sick at heart, "how splendid your boots are! See, I've been wearing this pair nearly all the time I've been abroad, and they're not half worn out, are they?"

He looked long at my boots — a pair of Russia leather — and his face seemed to regain its steadiness. Putting his hand on my instep, he said:

"Do dey vid you here? I 'ad drouble wid dat bair, I remember."

I assured him that they had fitted beautifully.

"Do you wand any boods?" he said. "I can make dem quickly; id is a slack dime."

I answered: "Please, please! I want boots all round — every kind!"

"I vill make a vresh model. Your food must be bigger." And with utter slowness, he traced around my foot, and felt my toes, only once looking up to say:

"Did I dell you my brudder was dead?"

To watch him was quite painful, so feeble had he grown; I was glad to get away.

I had given those boots up, when one evening they came. Opening the parcel, I set the four pairs out in a row. Then one by one I tried them on. There was no doubt about it. In shape and fit, in finish and quality of leather, they were the best he had ever made me. And in the mouth of one of the town walking-boots I found his bill. The amount was the same as usual, but it gave me quite a shock. He had never before sent it in until quarter day. I flew downstairs and wrote a check and posted it at once with my own hand.

A week later, passing the little street, I thought I would go in and tell him how splendidly the new boots fitted. But when I came to where his shop had been, his name was gone. Still there, in the window, were the slim pumps, the patent leathers with cloth tops, the sooty riding-boots.

I went in, very much disturbed. In the two little shops — again made into one — was a young man with an English face.

"Mr. Gessler in?" I said.

He gave me a strange, ingratiating look.

"No, sir," he said, "no. But we can attend to anything with pleasure. We've taken the shop over. You've seen our name, no doubt, next door. We make for some very good people."

"Yes, yes," I said, "but Mr. Gessler?"

"Oh!" he answered, "dead."

"Dead! But I only received these boots from him last Wednesday week."

"Ah!" he said, "a shockin' go. Poor old man starved 'imself."

"Good God!"

"Slow starvation, the doctor called it! You see he went to work in such a way! Would keep the shop on; wouldn't have a soul touch his boots except himself. When he got an order, it took him such a time. People won't wait. He lost everybody. And there he'd sit, goin' on and on — I will say that for him — not a man in London made a better boot! But look at the competition! He never advertised! Would 'ave the best leather, too, and do it all 'imself. Well, there it is. What could you expect with his ideas?"

"But starvation — !"

"That may be a bit flowery, as the sayin' is — but I know myself he was sittin' over his boots day and night, to the very last. You see, I used to watch him. Never gave 'imself time to eat, never had a penny in the house. All went in rent and leather. How he lived so long I don't know. He regular let his fire go out. He was a character. But he made good boots."

"Yes," I said, "he made good boots."

*The common theme of the stories in this section has been the value
of individualism. Shoemaker and senator alike have struggled with the
problems of being an individual in the face of overwhelming
pressures. By contrast, here is the story of a man whose life seems
diminished by remaining too much apart from his neighbors.*

Bill Trapp's Silence

from Beetlecreek

characters – Bill Trapp
Johnny Johnson
Uncle David

WILLIAM DEMBY

Always when he looked in the mirror, his eyes were different.
Sometimes they peered from out of the broken glass asking an unanswerable question, sometimes they were angry and damning,
sometimes they were sullen and brooding — too often they were the
eyes of a dead man, jellied and blank. This ritual of looking at
himself went on every day as soon as he got out of bed. His thick,
blunt fingers would clutch at each other, moving back and forth
slowly like the antennae of insects. His long, fleshy nose with its
countless red pin pricks would expand and contract in time to his
breathing, and the gray-striped lips that refused to open over the
severe outward slant of the front teeth would strain themselves
into the subtlest kind of smile. There were deep vertical wrinkles
along his cheek and at the corners of his eyes which gave an impression of kindliness. These wrinkles moved up and down, restlessly
recording the changing climates of his emotions. Thus he would
stand, sometimes for over an hour, a silent ugly man who could
no longer tell whether he was inside the mirror or inside himself.

Bill Trapp had not long been at the mirror that afternoon when
he heard a rustling in the bushes near the stone wall. Quickly he
ran his hand through his matted hair and put on a huge felt hat.
He walked very slowly, half on tiptoes, until he arrived at a bush.
There, he kneeled down on the cold mud and parted the branches.
He waited until he heard the rustling again and then rose high

enough to see the intruders. His heart beat fast as it always did. Always when they came he would look into their faces. He would be filled with uncontrollable excitement, knowing that he was seeing them while they couldn't see him. Faster and faster his heart would beat until, filled with shame and rage, he would rush out at them waving his arms wildly, shouting, almost screaming, long after they had disappeared down the road.

In fifteen years he had had only one visitor, a tramp who came to his door to beg because he was too proud to beg from the Negroes down by the bridge. He gave coffee and sandwiches to this tramp, who, as soon as he had finished eating, went away. Once some colored ladies started to come into the yard, and he chased them away with his shotgun. Sometimes, out of a furious impulse to break the clammy silence, he would begin singing songs he had heard in the towns along the river. Once a week, when he went to town to fetch the provisions he needed to live on or to sell the fruits and vegetables he grew, he found himself still talking in whispers, and people who spoke with him then would whisper too.

This time there were four boy Negroes under the tree. Three of them, wild-eyed and grinning, were signaling frantically to the boy in the tree to hurry and throw down to them some of the waxy red apples.

The face of the boy in the tree held Bill Trapp's attention. He had never seen this boy before, although the faces of the others were all familiar. All the boys were between the ages of thirteen and fifteen, but the face of this boy seemed at once younger and older. It was a gentle, pear-shaped face; the eyes were clever and slanted, and there was a serious monkey expression on it as the boy tried to concentrate on reaching for the apples.

For almost ten minutes the white man watched. Soon he felt the familiar itchy nervousness coming. But instead of rage this time, he was filled with curiosity. Very careful not to rustle the leaves, he rose to his feet; then, slowly and silently, he walked toward where the boys were crouching.

As soon as they saw him, the boys on the ground fled shrieking, but he paid no attention to them. His eyes were on the boy in the tree, and toward him he walked. Even as he came nearer and nearer the tree and saw that the boy made no move to escape, he felt that it was he himself who should be fleeing. Closer and closer he came to the tree, and slower and slower became his footsteps. Then, as he realized there was no backing away, that he would have to speak to the boy, he was filled with complete panic.

The boy's eyes swept back and forth like the eyes of a movable valentine. His pouting lips were parted, and he breathed with difficulty.

"Come down," Bill Trapp said, and while the words were still forming on his lips, he realized that by an act of his own will he was ending his fifteen years of silence and solitude.

He bade the boy Negro sit down on the porch while he went into the shack, mumbling incoherently that he had something to do. The moment he was inside, he peeped out the window and was surprised that the boy seemed not to be frightened but was relaxed against the two-by-four support of the roof. Realizing that the boy was not going to run away as he had at first hoped and feared, he experienced a strange feeling — a feeling of tenderness toward the boy and indeed, to all people. With no more preparation than that — in one instant — the fifteen-year-old desire to be alone was wiped away.

He ran to the mirror and looked at himself. He tried to smile. For years and years he hadn't washed his teeth. He found a broken piece of comb and tried to do something with his hair. He found two cracked cups and filled them with cider he had bought recently from the A&P. These he carried out to the boy on the porch, who turned with wide-eyed surprise to face him. Still trembling, he offered one of the cups to the boy. They drank nervously and silently. Neither would look at the other.

"I didn' mean nothing by it," the boy said finally, holding the empty cup close to his ear as if he were listening to a seashell.

The sound of the boy's voice came as a shock to him, came as a clap of thunder, and he didn't know what he should say.

"You kids should ask for the fruit . . . all you had to do was ask, and you coulda had all you wanted."

The cider was all gone — they each had had three cups — and there was no longer any excuse for the boy to stay. Once the boy turned toward him and looked straight into his eyes. Bill Trapp blushed and tried desperately to pry his mouth open in some kind of smile. He felt dizzy, tingling all over with thoughts that appeared and disappeared in his consciousness like so many fireflies. He kept saying to himself: Chase the kid away, give him a bawling out and chase him away. Instead, he asked the boy his name. And then asked him where he lived, realizing after a few moments that he was having a conversation with him. The boy's name was Johnny Johnson. He was from Pittsburgh and had come to stay with his aunt and uncle while his mother was in the hospital. He wanted to look at the boy's face again to see if he was scared. He found himself rooting in his nostril, wiping his thick finger on his pants. But the boy didn't see this, and he was relieved. He coughed and began to fidget.

"I could tell you something, Johnny, about being here all by yourself. I never would of chased nobody away 'cept they don't ask. I come from respectable folks and I respect people's property." But he saw that the boy wasn't listening.

When he looked toward where the boy was looking, he saw the gate burst open and a tall, distracted-looking Negro run into the yard. He looked questioning at Johnny and even moved closer to the boy as if to protect himself.

"That's my uncle," Johnny said.

"What's he want?" Bill Trapp asked. "I've got my rights and I repect people's property. . . ."

"What're you doing with that boy?" the man demanded, grasping hold of Johnny's hand as if to pull him away.

Bill Trapp couldn't open his mouth to speak. He was deaf. There was too much sound about him. He could hear the clock on the table inside the house. What did it mean, having these people on his porch? He was afraid, but he had gone this far, there was no turning back.

"He wasn't hurting me, Uncle David," the boy said. "We was just talking."

"I respect people's property, Mister. I'm a law-abidin' citizen. I'm an old man now. But I don't hurt nobody. See all this place here. I built it up. We come from respectable folks." He got up and went into the house. When he came out he brought a bottle of dandelion wine. The Negro man and boy became very quiet.

They drank; their breaths and sighs were in unison. They stole looks at each other from out of the corner of their eyes. And then the Negro man laughed.

"So you're Mister Bill Trapp?" he said. "Well, sir, it's a pleasure to be here with you. A real pleasure."

"I don't have many visitors," Bill Trapp said. "I'm what you call a retired man. I've done my share. But I could tell you a thing or two about being here all alone, no one to talk to. Gets so you forget a lot of things. But we come from respectable folks. I don't mean nobody no harm."

The light faded to near darkness, and the three of them were still sitting there. To Bill Trapp it was like something out of his fantastic dreams to have the Negro man and boy on his porch. There was a lot of talk. The Negro man talked continuously with a nervous, jerky flow of words that Bill Trapp finally gave up trying to follow. He had been too long alone. He remembered a warning feeling which came to him, a feeling which as soon as it came he hastened to brush away. He felt vaguely that he was in danger. But dominating all that he was feeling was the tremendous resolution not to go back to the lonely ways of before. He was conscious of a change of life in him, a change that seemed to have come suddenly but which he knew was prepared for years before.

Before his visitors left, he recklessly promised to meet the man that night, promised to go with him to Telrico's Café.

Alone once more, still trembling, he went to the mirror and looked at his eyes. They were milky damp. His eyelids were sweating. This time he stayed at the mirror until it was so dark he could see only the slightest reflection on the whites of his eyes. What kind of mad thing had he let himself in for? He stayed up just long enough to warm himself a can of beans. By six o'clock he was undressed and in bed speculating on whether or not he would get up to meet the Negro man. He was hot and sweating. He kept the lamp lit so that he could watch the clock.

"*Distant Thunder*" by Andrew Wyeth.

MAN
AND NATURE

"Turn the poet out of door."
ROBERT FROST

Man finds both beauty and terror in his natural surroundings, a conflict Robert Frost saw as "the drama of man in nature." Frost understood that man yearns to be a part of nature and yet fears that it will be hostile or indifferent to him. As a poet, he defined nature in terms of man's feelings about it.

Nature is defined as often by poets as by scientists. Many of our attitudes about nature were shaped in the nineteenth century by the Romantic poets of England. The Romantics found nature beautiful and harmonious. To them, cities seemed artificial, man-made places where evil and tension overwhelmed the spirit. Only by direct contact with nature, they suggested, could man find "spontaneous wisdom." The most powerful spokesman for the Romantic view of nature, William Wordsworth, wrote:

> One impulse from a vernal wood
> May teach you more of man,
> Of moral evil and of good,
> Than all the sages can.

This Romantic attitude remains as an important influence on American life today. On weekends and vacations, millions of Americans do everything they can to flee from the cities and suburbs to get "back to nature."

Our ancestors saw the wilderness as an enemy to overcome. Nature was an unknown area stretching endlessly ahead — a wilderness to be mapped, conquered, cleared, and planted. The pioneer had little time to contemplate nature as a Romantic poet might have done. He learned the lessons of nature the hard way as he struggled for survival. Some men were destroyed by nature, as the writers in this book testify. To the hero of Jack London's "To Build a Fire," untamed nature is the enemy.

In America today, nature has been domesticated and subdued for the most part. Wild land has been farmed or cleared away for towns and cities. Yet reminders of the wilderness still persist in our lives. A blade of grass will push its way through a concrete sidewalk. Flowers bloom on fire escapes. For man does not seek to subdue nature completely, and we view with alarm industrial "progress," which threatens to destroy our air and water, animals, and perhaps even ourselves.

The writers of the stories and essays which follow have varying ideas about nature. They discuss both nature's treatment of man and man's treatment of nature.

Antaeus, in the Greek myth, was a powerful wrestler who was the son of Mother Earth (Gaia) and who drew his strength from the earth. The mighty hero Hercules was able to defeat Antaeus in a wrestling match only by lifting him and holding him off the ground until his strength drained from him. The Antaeus in this modern story is also a "son of Mother Earth" who draws his strength of soul and spirit from the soil.

Antaeus

BORDEN DEAL

This was during the wartime, when lots of people were coming North for jobs in factories and war industries, when people moved around a lot more than they do now and sometimes kids were thrown into new groups and new lives that were completely different from anything they had ever known before. I remember this one kid, T.J. his name was, from somewhere down South, whose family moved into our building during that time. They'd come North with everything they owned piled into the back seat of an old-model sedan that you wouldn't expect could make the trip, with T.J. and his three younger sisters riding shakily on top of the load of junk.

Our building was just like all the others there, with families crowded into a few rooms, and I guess there were twenty-five or thirty kids about my age in that one building. Of course, there were a few of us who formed a gang and ran together all the time after school, and I was the one who brought T.J. in and started the whole thing.

The building right next door to us was a factory where they made walking dolls. It was a low building with a flat, tarred roof that had a parapet [1] all around it about head-high, and we'd found out a long time before that no one, not even the watchman, paid any attention to the roof because it was higher than any of the other buildings around. So my gang used the roof as a headquarters. We could

---

[1] *parapet:* low wall around the edge of a roof.

get up there by crossing over to the fire escape from our own roof on a plank and then going on up. It was a secret place for us, where nobody else could go without our permission.

I remember the day I first took T.J. up there to meet the gang. He was a stocky, robust kid with a shock of white hair, nothing sissy about him except his voice — he talked in this slow, gentle voice like you never heard before. He talked different from any of us and you noticed it right away. But I liked him anyway, so I told him to come on up.

We climbed up over the parapet and dropped down on the roof. The rest of the gang were already there.

"Hi," I said. I jerked my thumb at T.J. "He just moved into the building yesterday."

He just stood there, not scared or anything, just looking, like the first time you see somebody you're not sure you're going to like.

"Hi," Blackie said. "Where are you from?"

"Marion County," T.J. said.

We laughed. "Marion County?" I said. "Where's that?"

He looked at me for a moment like I was a stranger, too. "It's in Alabama," he said, like I ought to know where it was.

"What's your name?" Charley said.

"T.J.," he said, looking back at him. He had pale blue eyes that looked washed-out but he looked directly at Charley, waiting for his reaction. He'll be all right, I thought. No sissy in him . . . except that voice. Who ever talked like that?

"T.J.," Blackie said. "That's just initials. What's your real name? Nobody in the world has just initials."

"I do," he said. "And they're T.J. That's all the name I got."

His voice was resolute with the knowledge of his rightness, and for a moment no one had anything to say. T.J. looked around at the rooftop and down at the black tar under his feet. "Down yonder where I come from," he said, "we played out in the woods. Don't you-all have no woods around here?"

"Naw," Blackie said. "There's the park a few blocks over, but it's full of kids and cops and old women. You can't do a thing."

T.J. kept looking at the tar under his feet. "You mean you ain't got no fields to raise nothing in? . . . no watermelons or nothing?"

"Naw," I said scornfully. "What do you want to grow something for? The folks can buy everything they need at the store."

He looked at me again with that strange, unknowing look. "In Marion County," he said, "I had my own acre of cotton and my own acre of corn. It was mine to plant and make ever' year."

He sounded like it was something to be proud of, and in some obscure way it made the rest of us angry. Blackie said, "Who'd want to have their own acre of cotton and corn? That's just work. What can you do with an acre of cotton and corn?"

T.J. looked at him. "Well, you get part of the bale offen your acre," he said seriously. "And I fed my acre of corn to my calf."

We didn't really know what he was talking about, so we were more puzzled than angry; otherwise, I guess, we'd have chased him off the roof and wouldn't let him be part of our gang. But he was strange and different, and we were all attracted by his stolid sense of rightness and belonging, maybe by the strange softness of his voice contrasting our own tones of speech into harshness.

He moved his foot against the black tar. "We could make our own field right here," he said softly, thoughtfully. "Come spring we could raise us what we want to . . . watermelons and garden truck and no telling what all."

"You'd have to be a good farmer to make these tar roofs grow any watermelons," I said. We all laughed.

But T.J. looked serious. "We could haul us some dirt up here," he said. "And spread it out even and water it and before you know it we'd have us a crop in here." He looked at us intently. "Wouldn't that be fun?"

"They wouldn't let us," Blackie said quickly.

"I thought you said this was you-all's roof," T.J. said to me. "That you-all could do anything you wanted to up here."

"They've never bothered us," I said. I felt the idea beginning to catch fire in me. It was a big idea, and it took a while for it to sink in, but the more I thought about it, the better I liked it. "Say," I said to the gang. "He might have something there. Just make us a regular roof garden, with flowers and grass and trees and everything. And all ours, too," I said. "We wouldn't let anybody up here except the ones we wanted to."

"It'd take a while to grow trees," T.J. said quickly, but we weren't paying any attention to him. They were all talking about it suddenly, all excited with the idea after I'd put it in a way they could catch hold of it. Only rich people had roof gardens, we knew, and the idea of our own private domain excited them.

"We could bring it up in sacks and boxes," Blackie said. "We'd have to do it while the folks weren't paying any attention to us, for we'd have to come up to the roof of our building and then cross over with it."

"Where could we get the dirt?" somebody said worriedly.

"Out of those vacant lots over close to school," Blackie said. "Nobody'd notice if we scraped it up."

I slapped T.J. on the shoulder. "Man, you had a wonderful idea," I said, and everybody grinned at him, remembering that he had started it. "Our own private roof garden."

He grinned back. "It'll be ourn," he said. "All ourn." Then he looked thoughtful again. "Maybe I can lay my hands on some cottonseed, too. You think we could raise us some cotton?"

We'd started big projects before at one time or another, like any gang of kids, but they'd always petered out for lack of organization and direction. But this one didn't . . . somehow or other T.J. kept it going all through the winter months. He kept talking about the watermelons and the cotton we'd raise, come spring, and when even that wouldn't work he'd switch around to my idea of flowers and grass and trees, though he was always honest enough to add that it'd take a while to get any trees started. He always had it on his mind, and he'd mention it in school, getting them lined up to carry dirt that afternoon, saying in a casual way that he reckoned a few more weeks ought to see the job through.

Our little area of private earth grew slowly. T.J. was smart enough to start in one corner of the building, heaping up the carried earth two or three feet thick, so that we had an immediate result to look at, to contemplate with awe. Some of the evenings T.J. alone was carrying earth up to the building, the rest of the gang distracted by other enterprises or interests, but T.J. kept plugging along on his own, and eventually we'd all come back to him again and then our own little acre would grow more rapidly.

He was careful about the kind of dirt he'd let us carry up there and more than once he dumped a sandy load over the parapet into the areaway below because it wasn't good enough. He found out the kinds of earth in all the vacant lots for blocks around. He'd pick it up and feel it and smell it, frozen though it was sometimes, and then he'd say it was good growing soil or it wasn't worth anything, and we'd have to go on somewhere else.

Thinking about it now, I don't see how he kept us at it. It was hard work, lugging paper sacks and boxes of dirt all the way up the stairs of our own building, keeping out of the way of the grownups so they wouldn't catch on to what we were doing. They probably wouldn't have cared, for they didn't pay much attention to us, but we wanted to keep it secret anyway. Then we had to go through the trap door to our roof, teeter over a plank to the fire escape, then climb two or three stories to the parapet and drop down onto the roof. All that for a small pile of earth that sometimes didn't seem worth the effort. But T.J. kept the vision bright within us, his words shrewd and calculated toward the fulfillment of his dream; and he worked harder than any of us. He seemed driven toward a goal that we couldn't see, a particular point in time that would be definitely marked by signs and wonders that only he could see.

The laborious earth just lay there during the cold months, inert and lifeless, the clods lumpy and cold under our feet when we walked over it. But one day it rained and afterward there was a softness in the air and the earth was live and giving again with moisture and warmth. That evening T.J. smelled the air, his nostrils dilating with the odor of the earth under his feet.

"It's spring," he said, and there was a gladness rising in his voice that filled us all with the same feeling. "It's mighty late for it, but it's spring. I'd just about decided it wasn't never gonna get here at all."

We were all sniffing at the air, too, trying to smell it the way that T.J. did, and I can still remember the sweet odor of the earth under our feet. It was the first time in my life that spring and spring earth had meant anything to me. I looked at T.J. then, knowing in a faint way the hunger within him through the toilsome winter months, knowing the dream that lay behind his plan. He was a new Antaeus, preparing his own bed of strength.

"Planting time," he said. "We'll have to find us some seed."

"What do we do?" Blackie said. "How do we do it?"

"First we'll have to break up the clods," T.J. said. "That won't be hard to do. Then we plant the seed and after a while they come up. Then you got you a crop." He frowned. "But you ain't got it raised yet. You got to tend it and hoe it and take care of it, and all the time it's growing and growing, while you're awake and while you're asleep. Then you lay it by when it's growed and let it ripen and then you got you a crop."

"There's those wholesale seed houses over on Sixth," I said. "We could probably swipe some grass seed over there."

T.J. looked at the earth. "You-all seem mighty set on raising some grass," he said. "I ain't never put no effort into that. I spent all my life trying not to raise grass."

"But it's pretty," Blackie said. "We could play on it and take sunbaths on it. Like having our own lawn. Lots of people got lawns."

"Well," T.J. said. He looked at the rest of us, hesitant for the first time. He kept on looking at us for a moment. "I did have it in mind to raise some corn and vegetables. But we'll plant grass."

He was smart. He knew where to give in. And I don't suppose it made any difference to him, really. He just wanted to grow something, even if it was grass.

"Of course," he said, "I do think we ought to plant a row of watermelons. They'd be mighty nice to eat while we was a-laying on that grass."

We all laughed. "All right," I said. "We'll plant us a row of watermelons."

Things went very quickly then. Perhaps half the roof was covered with the earth, the half that wasn't broken by ventilators, and we swiped pocketfuls of grass seed from the open bins in the wholesale seed house, mingling among the buyers on Saturdays and during the school lunch hour. T.J. showed us how to prepare the earth, breaking up the clods and smoothing it and sowing the grass seed. It looked rich and black now with moisture, receiving of the seed, and it seemed that the grass sprang up overnight, pale green in the early spring.

We couldn't keep from looking at it, unable to believe that we had created this delicate growth. We looked at T.J. with understanding now, knowing the fulfillment of the plan he had carried alone within his mind. We had worked without full understanding of the task, but he had known all the time.

We found that we couldn't walk or play on the delicate blades, as we had expected to, but we didn't mind. It was enough just to look at it, to realize that it was the work of our own hands, and each evening the whole gang was there, trying to measure the growth that had been achieved that day.

One time a foot was placed on the plot of ground . . . one time only, Blackie stepping onto it with sudden bravado.[2] Then he looked at the crushed blades, and there was shame in his face. He did not do it again. This was his grass, too, and not to be desecrated. No one said anything, for it was not necessary.

T.J. had reserved a small section for watermelons, and he was still trying to find some seed for it. The wholesale house didn't have any watermelon seed and we didn't know where we could lay our hands on them. T.J. shaped the earth into mounds, ready to receive them, three mounds lying in a straight line along the edge of the grass plot.

We had just about decided that we'd have to buy the seed if we were to get them. It was a violation of our principles, but we were anxious to get the watermelons started. Somewhere or other, T.J. got his hands on a seed catalogue and brought it one evening to our roof garden.

"We can order them now," he said, showing us the catalogue. "Look!"

We all crowded around, looking at the fat, green watermelons pictured in full color on the pages. Some of them were split open, showing the red, tempting meat, making our mouths water.

"Now we got to scrape up some seed money," T.J. said, looking at us. "I got a quarter. How much you-all got?"

We made up a couple of dollars between us, and T.J. nodded his head. "That'll be more than enough. Now we got to decide what kind to get. I think them Kleckley Sweets. What do you-all think?"

He was going into esoteric matters beyond our reach. We hadn't even known there were different kinds of melons. So we just nodded our heads and agreed that Yes, we thought the Kleckley Sweets too.

"I'll order them tonight," T.J. said. "We ought to have them in a few days."

"What are you boys doing up here?" an adult voice said behind us.

It startled us, for no one had ever come up here before in all the time we had been using the roof of the factory. We jerked around and saw three men standing near the trap door at the other end of

---

[2] *bravado* (brə·vä′dō): boastful defiance; pretended bravery.

the roof. They weren't policemen or nightwatchmen, but three men in plump business suits, looking at us. They walked toward us.

"What are you boys doing up here?" the one in the middle said again.

We stood still, guilt heavy among us, levied by the tone of voice, and looked at the three strangers.

The men stared at the grass flourishing behind us. "What's this?" the man said. "How did this get up here?"

"Sure is growing good, ain't it?" T.J. said conversationally. "We planted it."

The men kept looking at the grass as if they didn't believe it. It was a thick carpet over the earth now, a patch of deep greenness startling in the sterile industrial surroundings.

"Yes sir," T.J. said proudly. "We toted that earth up here and planted that grass." He fluttered the seed catalogue. "And we're just fixing to plant us some watermelon."

The man looked at him then, his eyes strange and faraway. "What do you mean, putting this on the roof of my building?" he said. "Do you want to go to jail?"

T.J. looked shaken. The rest of us were silent, frightened by the authority of his voice. We had grown up aware of adult authority, of policemen and night watchmen and teachers, and this man sounded like all the others. But it was a new thing to T.J.

"Well, you wan't using the roof," T.J. said. He paused a moment and added shrewdly, "So we just thought to pretty it up a little bit."

"And sag it so I'd have to rebuild it," the man said sharply. He started turning away, saying to another man beside him, "See that all that junk is shoveled off by tomorrow."

"Yes sir," the man said.

T.J. started forward. "You can't do that," he said. "We toted it up here, and it's our earth. We planted it and raised it and toted it up here."

The man stared at him coldly. "But it's my building," he said. "It's to be shoveled off tomorrow."

"It's our earth," T.J. said desperately. "You ain't got no right!"

The men walked on without listening and descended clumsily through the trap door. T.J. stood looking after them, his body tense with anger, until they had disappeared. They wouldn't even argue with him, wouldn't let him defend his earth-rights.

He turned to us. "We won't let 'em do it," he said fiercely. "We'll stay up here all day tomorrow and the day after that, and we won't let 'em do it."

We just looked at him. We knew that there was no stopping it. He saw it in our faces and his face wavered for a moment before he gripped it into determination.

"They ain't got no right," he said. "It's our earth. It's our land. Can't nobody touch a man's own land."

We kept on looking at him, listening to the words but knowing that it was no use. The adult world had descended on us even in our richest dream, and we knew there was no calculating the adult world, no fighting it, no winning against it.

We started moving slowly toward the parapet and the fire escape, avoiding a last look at the green beauty of the earth that T.J. had planted for us . . . had planted deeply in our minds as well as in our experience. We filed slowly over the edge and down the steps to the plank, T.J. coming last, and all of us could feel the weight of his grief behind us.

"Wait a minute," he said suddenly, his voice harsh with the effort of calling. We stopped and turned, held by the tone of his voice, and looked up at him standing above us on the fire escape.

"We can't stop them?" he said, looking down at us, his face strange in the dusky light. "There ain't no way to stop 'em?"

"No," Blackie said with finality. "They own the building."

We stood still for a moment, looking up at T.J., caught into in-action by the decision working in his face. He stared back at us and his face was pale and mean in the poor light, with a bald nakedness in his skin like cripples have sometimes.

"They ain't gonna touch my earth," he said fiercely. "They ain't gonna lay a hand on it! Come on."

He turned around and started up the fire escape again, almost running against the effort of climbing. We followed more slowly, not knowing what he intended. By the time we reached him, he had seized a board and thrust it into the soil, scooping it up and flinging it over the parapet into the areaway below. He straightened and looked at us.

"They can't touch it," he said. "I won't let 'em lay a dirty hand on it!"

We saw it then. He stooped to his labor again and we followed, the gusts of his anger moving in frenzied labor among us as we scattered along the edge of earth, scooping it and throwing it over the parapet, destroying with anger the growth we had nurtured with such tender care. The soil carried so laboriously upward to the light and the sun cascaded swiftly into the dark areaway, the green blades of grass crumpled and twisted in the falling.

It took less time than you would think . . . the task of destruction is infinitely easier than that of creation. We stopped at the end, leaving only a scattering of loose soil, and when it was finally over a stillness stood among the group and over the factory building. We looked down at the bare sterility of black tar, felt the harsh texture of it under the soles of our shoes, and the anger had gone out of us, leaving only a sore aching in our minds like overstretched muscles.

T.J. stood for a moment, his breathing slowing from anger and effort, caught into the same contemplation of destruction as all of us. He stooped slowly, finally, and picked up a lonely blade of grass left trampled under our feet and put it between his teeth, tasting it, sucking the greenness out of it into his mouth. Then he started walking toward the fire escape, moving before any of us were ready to move, and disappeared over the edge.

We followed him but he was already halfway down to the ground, going on past the board where we crossed over, climbing down into the areaway. We saw the last section swing down with his weight, and then he stood on the concrete below us, looking at the small pile of anonymous earth scattered by our throwing. Then he walked across the place where we could see him and disappeared toward the street without glancing back, without looking up to see us watching him.

They did not find him for two weeks. Then the Nashville police caught him just outside the Nashville freight yards. He was walking along the railroad track, still heading south, still heading home.

As for us, who had no remembered home to call us . . . none of us ever again climbed the escape-way to the roof.

Few writers have had more adventurous lives than Jack London, who was a sailor at the age of seventeen, a hobo, and a prospector for gold in the Yukon. His experiences in the Klondike form the background for this classic story about man's relationship to nature and the qualities required for his survival.

respect nature
We have no control
much more powerful

To Build a Fire

JACK LONDON *- he went to Alaska - for gold*
didn't get gold - ideas.

negative outlook

Day had broken <u>cold</u> and <u>gray</u>, exceedingly <u>cold</u> and <u>gray</u>, when the man turned aside from the main Yukon trail and climbed the high earth bank, where a <u>dim</u> and <u>little-traveled trail</u> led eastward through the fat spruce timberland. It was a <u>steep</u> bank, and he paused for breath at the top, excusing the act to himself by looking at his watch. It was nine o'clock. There was no sun or hint of sun, though there was not a cloud in the sky. It was a clear day, and yet there seemed an intangible <u>pall</u> over the face of things, a <u>subtle gloom</u> that made the day <u>dark</u>, and that was due to the absence of sun. This fact did not worry the man. He was used to the lack of sun. It had been days since he had seen the sun, and he knew that a few more days must pass before that cheerful orb, due south, would just peep above the sky line and dip immediately from view.

The man flung a look back along the way he had come. The Yukon lay a mile wide and hidden under three feet of ice. On top of this ice were as many feet of snow. It was all pure white, rolling in gentle undulations where the ice jams of the freeze-up had formed. North and south, as far as his eye could see, it was unbroken white, save for a dark hairline that curved and twisted from around the spruce-covered island to the south and that curved and twisted away into the north, where it disappeared behind another spruce-covered island. This dark hairline was the trail — the main trail — that led south five hundred miles to the Chilkoot Pass, Dyea, and salt water and that led north seventy miles to Dawson, and still on to the north a thousand miles to Nulato, and finally to St. Michael on Bering Sea, a thousand miles and half a thousand more.

But all this — the mysterious, far-reaching hairline trail, the absence of sun from the sky, the tremendous cold, and the strangeness and weirdness of it all — made no impression on the man. It was not because he was long used to it. He was a newcomer in the land, a cheechako,[1] and this was his first winter. The trouble with him was that he was without imagination. He was quick and alert in the things of life but only in the things and not in the significances. Fifty degrees below zero meant eighty-odd degrees of frost. Such fact impressed him as being cold and uncomfortable, and that was all. It did not lead him to meditate upon his frailty as a creature of temperature and upon man's frailty in general, able only to live within certain narrow limits of heat and cold, and from there on it did not lead him to the conjectural field of immortality and man's place in the universe. Fifty degrees below zero stood for a bite of frost that hurt and that must be guarded against by the use of mittens, ear flaps, warm moccasins, and thick socks. Fifty degrees below zero was to him just precisely fifty degrees below zero. That there should be anything more to it than that was a thought that never entered his head.

As he turned to go on, he spat speculatively. There was a sharp, explosive crackle that startled him. He spat again. And again, in the air, before it could fall to the snow, the spittle crackled. He knew that at fifty below, spittle crackled on the snow, but his spittle had crackled in the air. Undoubtedly it was colder than fifty below — how much colder he did not know. But the temperature did not matter. He was bound for the old claim on the left fork of Henderson Creek, where the boys were already. They had come over across the divide from the Indian Creek country, while he had come the roundabout way to take a look at the possibilities of getting out logs in the spring from the islands in the Yukon. He would be into camp by six o'clock, a bit after dark, it was true, but the boys would be there, a fire would be going, and a hot supper would be ready. As for lunch, he pressed his hand against the protruding bundle under his jacket. It was also under his shirt, wrapped up in a handkerchief and lying against the naked skin. It was the only way to keep the biscuits

---

[1] *cheechako*: A newcomer to Alaska or the Yukon.

from freezing. He smiled agreeably to himself as he thought of those biscuits, each cut open and sopped in bacon grease, and each enclosing a generous slice of fried bacon.

He plunged in among the big spruce trees. The trail was faint. A foot of snow had fallen since the last sled had passed over, and he was glad he was without a sled, traveling light. In fact, he carried nothing but the lunch wrapped in the handkerchief. He was surprised, however, at the cold. It certainly was cold, he concluded, as he rubbed his numb nose and cheekbones with his mittened hand. He was a warm-whiskered man, but the hair on his face did not protect the high cheekbones and the eager nose that thrust itself aggressively into the frosty air.

At the man's heels trotted a dog, a big native husky, the proper wolf dog, gray-coated and without any visible or temperamental difference from its brother, the wild wolf. The animal was depressed by the tremendous cold. It knew that it was no time for traveling. Its instinct told it a truer tale than was told to the man by the man's judgment. In reality, it was not merely colder than fifty below zero; it was colder than sixty below, than seventy below. It was seventy-five below zero. Since the freezing point is thirty-two above zero, it meant that one hundred and seven degrees of frost obtained. The dog did not know anything about thermometers. Possibly in its brain there was no sharp consciousness of a condition of very cold such as was in the man's brain. But the brute had its instinct. It experienced a vague but menacing apprehension that subdued it and made it slink along at the man's heels and that made it question eagerly every unwonted movement of the man, as if expecting him to go into camp or to seek shelter somewhere and build a fire. The dog had learned fire, and it wanted fire, or else to burrow under the snow and cuddle its warmth away from the air.

The frozen moisture of its breathing had settled on its fur in a fine powder of frost, and especially were its jowls, muzzle, and eyelashes whitened by its crystaled breath. The man's red beard and mustache were likewise frosted, but more solidly, the deposit taking the form of ice and increasing with every warm, moist breath he exhaled. Also, the man was chewing tobacco, and the muzzle of ice held his lips so rigidly that he was unable to clear his chin when he expelled the juice. The result was that a crystal beard of the color and solidity of amber was increasing its length on his chin. If he fell down, it would shatter itself, like glass, into brittle fragments. But he did not mind the appendage. It was the penalty all tobacco chewers paid in that country, and he had been out before in two cold snaps. They had not been so cold as this, he knew, but by the spirit thermometer at Sixty Mile he knew they had been registered at fifty below and at fifty-five.

He held on through the level stretch of woods for several miles, crossed a wide flat, and dropped down a bank to the frozen bed of a small stream. This was Henderson Creek, and he knew he was ten miles from the forks. He looked at his watch. It was ten o'clock. He was making four miles an hour, and he calculated that he would arrive at the forks at half-past twelve. He decided to celebrate that event by eating his lunch there.

The dog dropped in again at his heels, with a tail drooping discouragement, as the man swung along the creek bed. The furrow of the old sled trail was plainly visible, but a dozen inches of snow covered the marks of the last runners. In a month no man had come up or down that silent creek. The man held steadily on. He was not much given to thinking, and just then particularly he had nothing to think about save that he would eat lunch at the forks and that at six o'clock he would be in camp with the boys. There was nobody to talk to; and, had there been, speech would have been impossible because of the ice muzzle on his mouth. So he continued monotonously to chew tobacco and to increase the length of his amber beard.

Once in a while the thought reiterated itself that it was very cold and that he had never experienced such cold. As he walked along, he rubbed his cheekbones and nose with the back of his mittened hand. He did this automatically, now and again changing hands. But rub as he would, the instant he stopped his cheekbones went numb, and the following instant the end of his nose went numb. He was sure to frost his cheeks; he knew that and experienced a pang of regret that he had not devised a nose strap of the sort Bud wore in cold snaps. Such a strap passed across the cheeks, as well, and saved them. But it didn't matter much, after all. What were frosted cheeks? A bit painful, that was all; they were never serious.

Empty as the man's mind was of thought, he was keenly observant, and he noticed the changes in the creek, the curves and bends and timber jams, and always he sharply noted where he placed his feet. Once, coming around a bend, he shied abruptly, like a startled horse, curved away from the place where he had been walking, and retreated several paces back along the trail. The creek, he knew, was frozen clear to the bottom — no creek could contain water in that arctic winter — but he knew also that there were springs that bubbled out from the hillsides and ran along under the snow and on top of the ice of the creek. He knew that the coldest snaps never froze these springs, and he knew likewise their danger. They were traps. They hid pools of water under the snow that might be three inches deep, or three feet. Sometimes a skin of ice half an inch thick covered them, and in turn was covered by the snow. Sometimes there were alternate layers of water and ice skin, so that when one broke through, he kept on breaking through for a while, sometimes wetting himself to the waist.

That was why he had shied in such panic. He had felt the give under his feet and heard the crackle of a snow-hidden ice skin. And to get his feet wet in such a temperature meant trouble and danger. At the very least it meant delay, for he would be forced to stop and build a fire and under its protection to bare his feet while he dried his socks and moccasins. He stood and studied the creek bed and its banks and decided that the flow of water came from the right. He reflected a while, rubbing his nose and cheeks, then skirted to the left, stepping gingerly and testing the footing for each step. Once clear of the danger, he took a fresh chew of tobacco and swung along at his four-mile gait.

In the course of the next two hours he came upon several similar traps. Usually the snow above the hidden pools had a sunken, candied appearance that advertised the danger. Once again, however, he had a close call; and once, suspecting danger, he compelled the dog to go on in front. The dog did not want to go. It hung back until the man shoved it forward, and then it went quickly across the white, unbroken surface. Suddenly it broke through, floundered to one side, and got away to firmer footing. It had wet its forefeet and legs, and almost immediately the water that clung to it turned to ice. It made quick efforts to lick the ice off its legs, then dropped down in the snow and began to bite out the ice that had formed between the toes. This was a matter of instinct. To permit the ice to remain would mean sore feet. It did not know this. It merely obeyed the mysterious prompting that arose from the deep crypts of its being. But the man knew, having achieved a judgment on the subject, and he removed the mitten from his right hand and helped tear out the ice particles. He did not expose his fingers more than a minute and was astonished at the swift numbness that smote them. It certainly was cold. He pulled on the mitten hastily and beat the hand savagely across his chest.

At twelve o'clock the day was at its brightest. Yet the sun was too far south on its winter journey to clear the horizon. The bulge of the earth intervened between it and Henderson Creek, where the man walked under a clear sky at noon and cast no shadow. At half-past twelve, to the minute, he arrived at the forks of the creek. He was pleased at the speed he had made. If he kept it up, he would certainly be with the boys by six. He unbuttoned his jacket and shirt and drew forth his lunch. The action consumed no more than a quarter of a minute, yet in that brief moment the numbness laid hold of the exposed fingers. He did not put the mitten on but, instead, struck the fingers a dozen sharp smashes against his leg. Then he sat down on a snow-covered log to eat. The sting that followed upon the striking of his fingers against his leg ceased so quickly that he was startled. He had had no chance to take a bite of biscuit. He struck the fingers repeatedly and returned them to the mitten, baring the other hand for the purpose of eating. He tried to take a mouthful, but the ice muzzle prevented. He had forgotten to build a fire and thaw out. He chuckled at his foolishness, and as he chuckled, he noted the numbness creeping into the exposed fingers. Also he noted that the stinging which had first come to his toes when he sat down was already passing away. He wondered whether the toes were warm or numb. He moved them inside the moccasins and decided that they were numb.

He pulled the mitten on hurriedly and stood up. He was a bit frightened. He stamped up and down until the stinging returned into the feet. It certainly was cold, was his thought. That man from Sulphur Creek had spoken the truth when telling how cold it sometimes got in the country. And he had laughed at him at the time! That showed one must not be too sure of things. There was no mistake about it, it *was* cold. He strode up and down, stamping his feet and threshing his arms, until reassured by the returning warmth. Then he got out matches and proceeded to make a fire. From the undergrowth, where high water of the previous spring had lodged a supply of seasoned twigs, he got his firewood. Working carefully from a small beginning, he soon had a roaring fire, over which he thawed the ice from his face and in the protection of which he ate his biscuits. For the moment the cold of space was outwitted. The dog took satisfaction in the fire, stretching out close enough for warmth and far enough away to escape being singed.

When the man had finished, he filled his pipe and took his comfortable time over a smoke. Then he pulled on his mittens, settled the ear flaps of his cap firmly about his ears, and took the creek trail up the left fork. The dog was disappointed and yearned back toward the fire. This man did not know cold. Possibly all the generations of his ancestry had been ignorant of cold, of real cold, of cold one hundred and seven degrees below freezing point. But the dog knew; all its ancestry knew, and it had inherited the knowledge. And it knew that it was not good to walk abroad in such fearful cold. It was the time to lie snug in a hole in the snow and wait for a curtain of cloud to be drawn across the face of outer space whence this cold came. On the other hand, there was no keen intimacy between the dog and the man. The one was the toil-slave of the other, and the only caresses it had ever received were the caresses of the whiplash and of harsh and menacing throat sounds that threatened the whiplash. So the dog made no effort to communicate its apprehension to the man. It was not concerned in the welfare of the man; it was for its own sake that it yearned back toward the fire. But the man whistled, and spoke to it with the sound of whiplashes, and the dog swung in at the man's heels and followed after.

The man took a chew of tobacco and proceeded to start a new amber beard. Also, his moist breath quickly powdered with white his mustache, eyebrows, and lashes. There did not seem to be so many springs on the left fork of the Henderson, and for half an hour the man saw no signs of any. And then it happened. At a place where there were no signs, where the soft, unbroken snow seemed to advertise solidity beneath, the man broke through. It was not deep. He wet himself halfway to the knees before he floundered out to the firm crust.

He was angry and cursed his luck aloud. He had hoped to get into camp with the boys at six o'clock, and this would delay him an hour, for he would have to build a fire and dry out his footgear. This was imperative at that low temperature — he knew that much; and he turned aside to the bank, which he climbed. On top, tangled in the underbrush about the trunks of several small spruce trees, was a high-water deposit of dry firewood — sticks and twigs, principally, but also larger portions of seasoned branches and fine, dry, last year's grasses. He threw down several large pieces on top of the snow. This served for a foundation and prevented the young flame from drowning itself in the snow it otherwise would melt. The flame he got by touching a match to a small shred of birch bark that he took from his pocket. This burned even more readily than paper. Placing it on the foundation, he fed the young flame with wisps of dry grass and with the tiniest dry twigs.

He worked slowly and carefully, keenly aware of his danger. Gradually, as the flame grew stronger, he increased the size of the twigs with which he fed it. He squatted in the snow, pulling the twigs out from their entanglement in the brush and feeding directly to the flame. He knew there must be no failure. When it is seventy-five below zero, a man must not fail in his first attempt to build a fire — that is, if his feet are wet. If his feet are dry, and he fails, he can run along the trail for half a mile and restore his circulation. But the circulation of wet and freezing feet cannot be restored by running when it is seventy-five below. No matter how fast he runs, the wet feet will freeze the harder.

All this the man knew. The old-timer on Sulphur Creek had told him about it the previous fall, and now he was appreciating the advice. Already all sensation had gone out of his feet. To build the fire, he had been forced to remove his mittens, and the fingers had quickly gone numb. His pace of four miles an hour had kept his heart pumping blood to the surface of his body and to all the extremities. But the instant he stopped, the action of the pump eased down. The cold of space smote the unprotected tip of the planet, and he, being on that unprotected tip, received the full force of the blow. The blood of his body recoiled before it. The blood was alive, like the dog, and like the dog it wanted to hide away and cover itself up from the fearful cold. So long as he walked four miles an hour, he pumped that blood, willy-nilly, to the surface; but now it ebbed away and sank down into the recesses of his body. The extremities were the first to feel its absence. His wet feet froze the faster, and his exposed fingers numbed the faster, though they had not yet begun to freeze. Nose and cheeks were already freezing, while the skin of all his body chilled as it lost its blood.

But he was safe. Toes and nose and cheeks would be only touched by the frost, for the fire was beginning to burn with strength. He was feeding it with twigs the size of his finger. In another minute he would be able to feed it with branches the size of his wrist, and then he could remove his wet footgear, and, while it dried, he could keep his naked feet warm by the fire, rubbing them at first, of course, with snow. The fire was a success. He was safe. He remembered the advice of the old-timer on Sulphur Creek, and smiled. The old-timer had been very serious in laying down the law that no man must travel alone in the Klondike after fifty below. Well, here he was: he had had the accident, he was alone, and he had saved himself. Those old-timers were rather womanish, some of them, he thought. All a man had to do was to keep his head, and he was all right. Any man who was a man could travel alone. But it was surprising the rapidity with which his cheeks and nose were freezing. And he had not thought his fingers could go lifeless in so short a time. Lifeless they were, for he could scarcely make them move together to grip a twig, and they seemed remote from his body and from him. When he touched a twig, he had to look to see whether or not he had hold of it. The wires were pretty well down between him and his finger ends.

All of which counted for little. There was the fire, snapping and crackling and promising life with every dancing flame. He started to untie his moccasins. They were coated with ice, the thick German socks were like sheaths of iron halfway to the knees, and the moccasin strings were like rods of steel all twisted and knotted as by some conflagration.[2] For a moment he tugged with his numb fingers, then, realizing the folly of it, he drew his sheath knife.

But before he could cut the strings, it happened. It was his own fault, or, rather, his mistake. He should not have built the fire under the spruce tree. He should have built it in the open. But it had been easier to pull the twigs from the bush and drop them directly on the fire. Now the tree under which he had done this carried a weight of snow on its boughs. No wind had blow for weeks, and each bough was fully freighted. Each time he had pulled a twig he had communicated a slight agitation to the tree — an imperceptible agitation, so far as he was concerned, but an agitation sufficient to

---

[2] *conflagration* (kon'flə·grā'shən): a great or extensive fire.

bring about the disaster. High up in the tree one bough capsized its load of snow. This fell on the boughs beneath, capsizing them. This process continued, spreading out and involving the whole tree. It grew like an avalanche, and it descended without warning upon the man and the fire, and the fire was blotted out! Where it had burned was a mantle of fresh and disordered snow.

The man was shocked. It was as though he had just heard his own sentence of death. For a moment he sat and stared at the spot where the fire had been. Then he grew very calm. Perhaps the old-timer on Sulphur Creek was right. If he had only had a trailmate, he would have been in no danger now. The trailmate could have built the fire. Well, it was up to him to build the fire over again, and this second time there must be no failure. Even if he succeeded, he would most likely lose some toes. His feet must be badly frozen by now, and there would be some time before the second fire was ready.

Such were his thoughts, but he did not sit and think them. He was busy all the time they were passing through his mind. He made a new foundation for a fire, this time in the open, where no treacherous tree could blot it out. Next he gathered dry grasses and tiny twigs from the high-water flotsam.[3] He could not bring his fingers together to pull them out, but he was able to gather them by the handful. In this way he got many rotten twigs and bits of green moss that were undesirable, but it was the best he could do. He worked methodically, even collecting an armful of the larger branches to be used later when the fire gathered strength. And all the while the dog sat and watched him, a certain yearning wistfulness in its eyes, for it looked upon him as the fire provider, and the fire was slow in coming.

When all was ready, the man reached in his pocket for a second piece of birch bark. He knew the bark was there, and, though he could not feel it with his fingers, he could hear its crisp rustling as he fumbled for it. Try as he would, he could not clutch hold of it. And all the time, in his consciousness, was the knowledge that each instant his feet were freezing. This thought tended to put him in a panic, but he fought against it and kept calm. He pulled on his mittens with his teeth and threshed his arms back and forth, beating his hands with all his might against his sides. He did this sitting down, and he stood up to do it; and all the while the dog sat in the

---

[3] *flotsam* (flŏt′səm): objects floating on a body of water.

snow, its wolf brush of a tail curled around warmly over its fore-feet, its sharp wolf ears pricked forward intently as it watched the man. And the man, as he beat and threshed with his arms and hands, felt a great surge of envy as he regarded the creature that was warm and secure in its natural covering.

After a time he was aware of the first faraway signals of sensation in his beaten fingers. The faint tingling grew stronger till it evolved into a stinging ache that was excruciating but which the man hailed with satisfaction. He stripped the mitten from his right hand and fetched forth the birch bark. The exposed fingers were quickly going numb again. Next he brought out his bunch of sulfur matches. But the tremendous cold had already driven the life out of his fingers. In his effort to separate one match from the others, the whole bunch fell in the snow. He tried to pick it out of the snow, but failed. The dead fingers could neither touch nor clutch. He was very careful. He drove the thought of his freezing feet, and nose, and cheeks, out of his mind, devoting his whole soul to the matches. He watched, using the sense of vision in place of that of touch, and when he saw his fingers on each side of the bunch, he closed them — that is, he willed to close them, but the wires were down, and the fingers did not obey. He pulled the mitten on the right hand and beat it fiercely against his knee. Then, with both mittened hands, he scooped the bunch of matches, along with much snow, into his lap. Yet he was no better off.

After some manipulation he managed to get the bunch between the heels of his mittened hands. In this fashion he carried it to his mouth. The ice crackled and snapped when by a violent effort he opened his mouth. He drew the lower jaw in, curled the upper lip out of the way, and scraped the bunch with his upper teeth in order to separate a match. He succeeded in getting one, which he dropped on his lap. He was no better off. He could not pick it up. Then he devised a way. He picked it up in his teeth and scratched it on his leg. Twenty times he scratched before he succeeded in lighting it. As it flamed, he held it with his teeth to the birch bark. But the burning brimstone went up his nostrils and into his lungs, causing him to cough spasmodically. The match fell into the snow and went out.

The old-timer on Sulphur Creek was right, he thought in the moment of controlled despair that ensued: after fifty below, a man should travel with a partner. He beat his hands but failed in exciting any sensation. Suddenly he bared both hands, removing the mittens with his teeth. He caught the whole bunch between the heels of his hands. His arm muscles, not being frozen, enabled him to press the hand heels tightly against the matches. Then he scratched the bunch along his leg. It flared into flame, seventy sulfur matches at once! There was no wind to blow them out. He kept his head to one side to escape the strangling fumes and held the blazing bunch to the birch bark. As he so held it, he became aware of sensation in his hand. His flesh was burning. He could smell it. Deep down below the surface he could feel it. The sensation developed into pain that grew acute. And still he endured it, holding the flame of the matches clumsily to the bark that would not light readily because his own burning hands were in the way, absorbing most of the flame.

At last, when he could endure no more, he jerked his hands apart. The blazing matches fell sizzling into the snow, but the birch bark was alight. He began laying dry grasses and the tiniest twigs on the flame. He could not pick and choose, for he had to lift the fuel between the heels of his hands. Small pieces of rotten wood and green moss clung to the twigs, and he bit them off as well as he could with his teeth. He cherished the flame carefully and awkwardly. It meant life, and it must not perish. The withdrawal of blood from the surface of his body now made him begin to shiver, and he grew more awkward. A large piece of green moss fell squarely on the little fire. He tried to poke it out with his fingers, but his shivering frame made him poke too far, and he disrupted the nucleus of the little fire, the burning grasses and tiny twigs separating and scattering. He tried to poke them together again, but, in spite of the tenseness of the effort, his shivering got away with him, and the twigs were hopelessly scattered. Each twig gushed a puff of smoke and went out. The fire provider had failed. As he looked apathetically about him, his eyes chanced on the dog, sitting across the ruins of the fire from him, in the snow, making restless, hunching movements, slightly lifting one forefoot and then the other, shifting its weight back and forth on them with wistful eagerness.

The sight of the dog put a wild idea into his head. He remembered the tale of the man, caught in a blizzard, who killed a steer and crawled inside the carcass, and so was saved. He would kill the dog and bury his hands in the warm body until the numbness went out of them. Then he could build another fire. He spoke to the dog, calling it to him; but in his voice was a strange note of fear that frightened the animal, who had never known the man to speak in such way before. Something was the matter, and its suspicious nature sensed danger — it knew not what danger, but somewhere, somehow, in its brain arose an apprehension of the man. It flattened its ears down at the sound of the man's voice, and its restless, hunching movements and the lifting and shiftings of its forefeet became more pronounced, but it would not come to the man. He got on his hands and knees and crawled toward the dog. This unusual posture again excited suspicion, and the animal sidled mincingly away.

The man sat up in the snow for a moment and struggled for calmness. Then he pulled on his mittens, by means of his teeth, and got upon his feet. He glanced down at first in order to assure himself that he was really standing up, for the absence of sensation in his feet left him unrelated to the earth. His erect position in itself started to drive the webs of suspicion from the dog's mind; and when he spoke peremptorily with the sound of whiplashes in his voice, the dog rendered its customary allegiance and came to him. As it came within reaching distance, the man lost his control. His arms flashed out to the dog, and he experienced genuine surprise when he discovered that his hands could not clutch, that there was neither bend nor feeling in the fingers. He had forgotten for the moment that they were frozen and that they were freezing more and more. All this happened quickly, and before the animal could get away, he encircled its body with his arms. He sat down in the snow, and in this fashion held the dog, while it snarled and whined and struggled.

But it was all he could do, hold its body encircled in his arms and sit there. He realized that he could not kill the dog. There was no way to do it. With his helpless hands he could neither draw nor hold his sheath knife nor throttle the animal. He released it, and it plunged wildly away, with tail between its legs, and still snarling. It halted forty feet away and surveyed him curiously, with ears sharply pricked forward. The man looked down at his hands in order to locate them, and found them hanging on the ends of his arms. It struck him as curious that one should have to use his eyes in order to find out where his hands were. He began threshing his arms back and forth, beating the mittened hands against his sides. He did this for five minutes, violently, and his heart pumped enough blood up to the surface to put a stop to his shivering. But no sensation was aroused in the hands. He had an impression that they hung like weights on the ends of his arms, but when he tried to run the impression down, he could not find it.

A certain fear of death, dull and oppressive, came to him. This fear quickly became poignant [4] as he realized that it was no longer a mere matter of freezing his fingers and toes, or of losing his hands and feet, but that it was a matter of life and death, with the chances against him. This threw him into a panic, and he turned and ran up the creek bed along the old dim trail. The dog joined in behind and kept up with him. He ran blindly, without intention, in fear such as he had never known in his life. Slowly, as he plowed and floundered through the snow, he began to see things again — the banks of the creek, the old timber jams, the leafless aspens, and the sky. The running made him feel better. He did not shiver. Maybe, if he ran on, his feet would thaw out; and, anyway, if he ran far enough, he would reach the camp and the boys. Without doubt he would lose some fingers and toes and some of his face; but the boys would take care of him and save the rest of him when he got there. And at the same time there was another thought in his mind that said he would never get to the camp and the boys, that it was too many miles away, that the freezing had too great a start on him, and that he would soon be stiff and dead. This thought he kept in the background and refused to consider. Sometimes it pushed itself forward and demanded to be heard, but he thrust it back and strove to think of other things.

It struck him as curious that he could run at all on feet so frozen that he could not feel them when they struck the earth and took the weight of his body. He seemed to himself to skim along above the surface and to have no connection with the earth. Somewhere he had once seen a winged Mercury,[5] and he wondered if Mercury felt as he felt when skimming over the earth.

His theory of running until he reached camp and the boys had one flaw in it: he lacked the endurance. Several times he stumbled, and finally he tottered, crumpled up, and fell. When he tried to rise, he failed. He must sit and rest, he decided, and next time he would merely walk and keep on going. As he sat and regained his breath, he

---

[4] *poignant:* (poin′yənt): painful to feelings.
[5] *Mercury:* messenger of the gods who had wings on his ankles for quick travel.

noted that he was feeling quite warm and comfortable. He was not shivering, and it even seemed that a warm glow had come to his chest and trunk. And yet, when he touched his nose or cheeks, there was no sensation. Running would not thaw them out. Nor would it thaw out his hands and feet. Then the thought came to him that the frozen portions of his body must be extending. He tried to keep this thought down, to forget it, to think of something else; he was aware of the panicky feeling that it caused, and he was afraid of the panic. But the thought asserted itself, and persisted, until it produced a vision of his body totally frozen. This was too much, and he made another wild run along the trail. Once he slowed down to a walk, but the thought of the freezing extending itself made him run again.

And all the time the dog ran with him, at his heels. When he fell down a second time, it curled its tail over its forefeet and sat in front of him, facing him, curiously eager and intent. The warmth and security of the animal angered him, and he cursed it till it flattened down its ears appeasingly. This time the shivering came more quickly upon the man. He was losing in his battle with the frost. It was creeping into his body from all sides. The thought of it drove him on, but he ran no more than a hundred feet, when he staggered and pitched headlong. It was his last panic. When he had recovered his breath and control, he sat up and entertained in his mind the conception of meeting death with dignity. However, the conception did not come to him in such terms. His idea of it was that he had been making a fool of himself, running around like a chicken with its head cut off — such was the simile that occurred to him. Well, he was bound to freeze anyway, and he might as well take it decently. With this new-found peace of mind came the first glimmerings of drowsiness. A good idea, he thought, to sleep off to death. It was like taking an anesthetic. Freezing was not so bad as people thought. There were lots worse ways to die.

He pictured the boys finding his body next day. Suddenly he found himself with them, coming along the trail and looking for himself. And, still with them, he came around a turn in the trail and found himself lying in the snow. He did not belong with himself any more, for even then he was out of himself standing with the boys and looking at himself in the snow. It certainly was cold, was his thought. When he got back to the States, he could tell the folks what real cold was. He drifted on from this to a vision of the old-timer on Sulphur Creek. He could see him quite clearly, warm and comfortable, and smoking a pipe.

"You were right, old hoss; you were right," the man mumbled to the old-timer of Sulphur Creek.

Then the man drowsed off into what seemed to him the most comfortable and satisfying sleep he had ever known. The dog sat facing him and waiting. The brief day drew to a close in a long, slow twilight. There were no signs of a fire to be made, and, besides, never in the dog's experience had it known a man to sit like that in the snow and make no fire. As the twilight drew on, its eager yearning for the fire mastered it, and with a great lifting and shifting of forefeet, it whined softly, then flattened its ears down in anticipation of being chidden by the man. But the man remained silent. Later, the dog whined loudly. And still later it crept close to the man and caught the scent of death. This made the animal bristle and back away. A little longer it delayed, howling under the stars that leaped and danced and shone brightly in the cold sky. Then it turned and trotted up the trail in the direction of the camp it knew, where were the other food providers and fire providers.

*The sea is perhaps the last of nature's great frontiers, with waves as
high as fifty feet in storms and depths alive with unimagined forms of
life. In this true story, a modern-day explorer, Thor Heyerdahl,
writes of his attempt with five others to float four thousand miles
across the Pacific Ocean on a raft of balsa wood. Most people predicted
that their raft, Kon-Tiki, would not carry the explorers to their
objective, the Polynesian Islands.*

Kon-Tiki

THOR HEYERDAHL

Usually men who have embarked on an ocean raft in modern
times have been shipwrecked sailors whose sole desire was to escape
the perils of the open sea and reach the nearest coast. But this was
not the case in April of last year,[1] when the tugboat *Guardian Rio*
towed a clumsy raft away from the sheltered docks of the Peruvian
port of Callao and left it adrift well outside the harbor entrance.
The six of us that were left aboard the raft were filled with one
single hope — that the wind and current would push our primitive
craft far away from the South American mainland and right into the
wide-open span of the vast Pacific Ocean.

Our purpose was not to flee the Republic of Peru. Leading officials of many nations had bidden us hearty farewell at the dock as
the Peruvian Navy tugged us to our point of departure. Nor did we
possess any desire to establish a world record in hazardous ocean
drift. Yet the betting went high at the docks when we left.

Some claimed that we would be picked up off the coast in a few
days or would never be seen again. The nine logs of porous balsa
wood upon which we floated were too fragile and would break
asunder in the heavy coastal swells, or they would at least be waterlogged and sink underneath us far short of the halfway mark to
Polynesia, whose nearest islands lay some four thousand miles from

---

[1] *last year:* 1947.

Peru. With a foot and a half of freeboard [2] at the highest section of the bamboo deck and with an open bamboo hut with thatched roof as our only shelter, we would be at the constant mercy of the waves and the weather and be lost in the first storm.

Others claimed that ropes were no good in the tropic sun and in the sea water and that the complete absence of nails, pegs, and wire in our raft would allow it to tear to pieces as soon as the constant movements of the logs started to chafe the hemp-rope lashings. And if a balsa-wood raft, against all the warnings of the experts, should prove to be seaworthy, it would still not be navigable with its clumsy, square sail and primitive steering oar. How, then, could we possibly expect to hit one of the tiny, far-flung islands? The distance ahead was twice the journey of Columbus, and the clumsy raft not even comparable.

All these sinister but well-meant warnings were haunting my mind the first night after the last smoke of the tugboat had dissolved behind the horizon. When I was relieved from watch and tried to sleep, I realized how everything was in motion, not so much the pitching and rolling, as the restlessly undulating movement of the bamboo matting on which we lay on top of the great logs. Each time the stern was lifted by the seas, I saw dancing black hills of water, silhouetted against the stars as they chased along both sides of our raft, with whitecaps hissing at us as they passed. I listened to the squeaking and gnawing of a hundred ropes and the splashing and hammering of water everywhere. At regular intervals heavy seas thundered on board astern, but I noticed with comfort how the water, after whirling up to the waists of the two steersmen, instantly dwindled by falling between the open logs or over the sides of the raft. The seas fell in a pit before they could reach the unprotected bamboo hut lashed on deck a few feet from the stern. Therefore, we struggled to hold the stern to the weather and never let the seas in from the sides.

Gradually I felt happy and proud of our peculiar craft. But I could not quite get away from the complaining music of all the light and heavy ropes as everything aboard moved slowly up and down and even sideways as far as the ropes would permit.

What would the future bring us? How would the raft behave after a week, a month, or perhaps a year at sea?

---

[2] *freeboard:* the side of a vessel between water and the main deck.

I was not a sailor, and only one of my companions was experienced in handling an ordinary boat at sea. I had not been able, word by word, to answer the pessimistic warnings of naval authorities and other experts before we put out to sea. I was, nevertheless, firmly convinced that our raft could float across the ocean and bring us safely to some distant Polynesian shore. The secret of my stubborn confidence was that I felt certain that this same ocean route had been covered before by prehistoric men on the very same type of craft.

Already in 1937, after leaving the University of Oslo, I had made a zoological-ethnological survey [3] on the lonely Marquesas Islands in the southeast Pacific. What I found led me to suspect that an influence from early Central or South America had somehow preceded the present Polynesian culture in this area. It is well known that a number of striking similarities in the culture of South America and Polynesia have been noted. These include two of the important cultivated plants — the sweet potato and the bottle gourd — and many cultural features. The theory has therefore frequently been advanced — and again as frequently rejected — that there must have been a prehistoric contact between these two areas.

There can be no possibility of any land bridge having existed in human times, for a comparative study of the animal life of Polynesia proves its hoary isolation. The island people, when first discovered by Europeans, possessed good sea-going canoes, whereas the natives of Peru had only clumsy balsa rafts for their coastal navigation. Because of this, it has usually been assumed by the few who believe there was a cultural transfer that the South American cultures were influenced by the island people rather than vice versa. This view has never been fully accepted and is even doubted by competent scholars of the present day. It is too obvious that some of the Peruvian constructions, artifacts, and food plants in question date from an earlier period in America than A.D. 500, which is commonly accepted, through comparative genealogy, as the approximate date when the first Polynesians spread into the East Pacific.

Thus I had found myself inescapably drawn toward the alternative theory to explain the striking parallels between Peru and Polynesia — namely, that an offshoot from the amazing cultures of early Peru drifted, intentionally or otherwise, into the Pacific.

---

[3] *zoological-ethnological survey:* study of biological environments.

I was instantly met by one killing argument: How could the Peruvians have covered the thousands of miles of intermediate ocean when their only means of navigation in prehistoric times was an open balsa raft?

To me, there was only one satisfactory answer, and that was to build such a balsa raft and see if it could survive this journey.

I selected five dependable men who volunteered to join me on the experimental voyage. One of them, Herman Watzinger, was a technical engineer, and he directed the building of the balsa raft, guided by detailed accounts and sketches left in the earliest records after the conquest of Peru. First we had to get into the heart of the Ecuadorian jungle to find present-day balsa trees that would match the dimensions of the prehistoric rafts. We cut down nine giant trees and floated on them down a jungle river to the Pacific coast. With the blessings of the President of Peru and his Naval Minister, the prehistoric type of craft was built in the main naval harbor of Callao under our own supervision.

The nine balsa logs were lashed together side by side with many separate pieces of hemp rope. The bow of the raft took an organ-pipe design, with the longest log in the middle measuring forty-five feet and projecting beyond the others both in the front and in the stern. In the stern it supported a big chunk of balsa holding thole pins [4] for the steering oar. Of the two-foot cross section of these logs, more than half was submerged in the water, but nine smaller cross beams of light balsa covered with bamboo lifted the highest portion of the deck (including the floor of the open hut upon which we slept) eighteen inches above the sea. The little plaited bamboo hut with thatched roof, two hardwood masts side by side, with a square sail, five centerboards two feet wide and six feet deep, inserted at irregular intervals between the logs, and a long wooden steering oar astern completed our replica of the colorful prehistoric craft.

We named our raft *Kon-Tiki* in honor of the mythical sun king who the Incas claim built the enormous stone constructions near Lake Titicaca [5] before he was defeated in war by local tribes. After the defeat, according to legend, he fled with his light-colored people down to the coast and then westward into the Pacific Ocean, never

---

[4] *thole pins:* a pair of pegs to hold the oar in position.
[5] *Lake Titicaca:* a lake on the boundaries of Peru and Bolivia.

again to return to Peru. Throughout the Polynesian islands, Tiki is remembered as the mythical hero who was first in the line of aboriginal chiefs to settle the islands and to claim direct descent from the sun. The Peruvian prefix "Kon" means Sun.

The six of us went aboard on April 28 and were left at the mercy of the elements in the old Inca fishing grounds outside the port of Callao. Our ages ranged from twenty-five to thirty-two. Herman Watzinger, second-in-command, was in charge of testing and hydrographic and meteorologic [6] measurements. Erik Hesselberg, an artist, was responsible for plotting our drift. Our radio operators were Knut Haugland and Torstein Raaby, both famous for their sabotage activities during World War II (instrumental, respectively, in the important sabotage of the German Heavy-Water Plant and the battleship *Tirpitz*). Bengt Danielsson, lonely Swede on our Norwegian expedition, was an ethnologist from the University of Uppsala who joined us in South America after an expedition in the jungles of Brazil.

Our voyage would carry us through a vast span of ocean that was very little known, since it was outside all the usual shipping lanes. We had therefore been requested to make continuous observations and transfer them via the amateur radio network to the United States Weather Bureau. But unless we should use the radio for calling help, it would not alter the primitive conditions of our experiment in any way.

The first weeks at sea were hard. One man was seasick for several days and confined to the hut; consequently, with the ocean breaking over us, two of us at a time constantly had to battle with the clumsy steering oar, trying to hold our stern against the short, racing seas of the Humboldt Current. We were soon caught by the offshore trade winds and were then only able to sail before the wind. We now realized that we had cut all our bridges and that there was no road back to the coast.

We had been at sea only a couple of days when an airplane flew out to bring us a last farewell. We never saw the plane (our horizons were narrowly fenced in with watery hills on all sides), nor did they see us, but we spoke to them for several hours with our little radio.

After the first weeks we came into calmer seas with long, rolling

---

[6] *hydrographic and meteorologic:* surveying and mapping seas and recording weather conditions.

swells. The great blue ocean was dotted with whitecaps, and trade-wind clouds drifted across the blue sky. We had soft days with swimming and rest, and we traveled along in comfort. Our drift turned from northwest to west as we left the green and cold Humboldt Current and entered the blue and increasingly warm South Equatorial Current. We made as much progress as seventy-two miles in one day, with a daily average of forty-two miles for the entire voyage. The surface drift exceeded the current drift and occasionally blew us out of the main sweep of the central current.

We found little wearing on the ropes and learned the reason why. The balsa was too soft to chafe them. In case of friction, a rope would soon work itself into the waterlogged surface of the balsa logs and thus remain protected. It was more discomforting to observe that splinters cut from the surface of the logs had become waterlogged and sank when thrown overboard. It had been common opinion in Peru that the logs would be completely submerged before we sighted the islands.

Archeologists no longer doubt that the prehistoric Peruvians used sails. Not only are there good historical descriptions of rafts equipped with sails, but centerboards of late pre-European date have been found. Our testings with centerboards clearly proved that they are useless on a raft if it is merely paddled or carried along by the current.

The first real excitement we ran into after entering the South Equatorial Current was the largest monster of the seas — the rare but famous whale shark. Accompanied by a shoal of pilot fish, this giant among all fishes slowly caught up with us from astern, and the water splashed around its enormous, white-speckled back as though on a small reef. The fish bumped into the steering oar and placed its huge, froglike head, with tiny eyes and a five-foot mouth, right up against the raft. The whale shark has been measured to a length of forty-five feet and undoubtedly grows larger. We would never have dared such an estimate, but while the head appeared on one side of the raft, the tail simultaneously appeared on the other.

The whale shark kept us company for several hours, and the excitement on board was great, with everybody prepared with spears, hand harpoons, and motion picture camera. The peaceful visit ended when the excited navigator ran his harpoon with all his strength down between his legs and into the cartilaginous head of the monter. During the terrific commotion the whale shark dived, broke he harpoon, snapped the rope, and disappeared.

Only at one other time were we visited by what we suspected to be whale sharks. It was during a fairly calm night when three immensely large and phosphorescent bodies swam in circles under us. But occasionally we ran into schools of whales. The huge, snorting animals rolled right up beside us without the slightest fear. They could have splintered our raft with a single blow of their mighty tails, but after an exhibition of their swimming ability, they left us behind.

Some six hundred miles southwest of the Galápagos we were twice visited by giant sea turtles. One was under constant attack by a dozen furious dolphins which tried to snap at the turtle's neck and fins. After sighting the raft, the turtle made its way right up to our side but swam away as soon as it saw us. Three of our men, equipped with rope, pursued the turtle in a tiny, inflatable rubber float, but our visitor escaped while the bewildered dolphins concentrated all their attention on the bouncing little float.

Weather permitting, we often got into our rubber float, two or three at a time, and took a "vacation" from our sturdy log raft to study our craft from a distance. We could imagine the sight that early Peruvian seafarers must have had when they sailed their flotillas [7] of rafts side by side along the coast — or into the ocean like Inca Tupac Yupanqui, who according to legend discovered some east Pacific islands before the Spanish Conquest. Particularly at night, we experienced an unforgettable sight. Night-black seas, billowing on all sides, and twinkling stars formed our entire world.

The year 1947 — A.D. or B.C. — what did it mean? We were at least alive. Time had little meaning; we were lost in the endless dark. Ahead of us *Kon-Tiki* rose and then sank between the seas. In moonlight there was an unbelievable atmosphere around the raft. The huge wet logs fringed with seaweed, the square contour of the sail, the bushy jungle hut with a petrol lamp astern looked like something cut from a fairy tale rather than from reality. . . . Now and then the raft would disappear entirely behind the black sea; then, with water pouring from the logs, it would rise high to be silhouetted against the stars.

Although we spent 101 days and nights drifting on our raft, we never sighted a ship or any floating debris left by mankind. If a ship

---

[7] *flotillas:* fleets of small vessels.

had crossed our path during an average day at sea, it would have found us slowly dancing up and down over great rolling swells dotted with minor waves that were stirred up by the trade winds, which constantly blow from the New World into the island domain. A tanned and bearded man, devoid of clothing, would have been sighted at the stern of the raft, either desperately struggling with the ropes of a long steering oar or, if the wind were steady, sitting and dozing in the sun. Bengt would be found on his stomach in the doorway of the hut reading one of his seventy-three sociological books. Herman would be seen busily occupied anywhere, at the top of the mast, underneath the logs, or running around with instruments to measure wind and water. Knut and Torstein were always struggling with the weather-beaten radio sets, repairing damage and sending out reports at night to the amateur stations that could hear our signals. Erik was always mending sail and splicing rope and sketching fishes and bearded men alike. And each noon he grabbed his sextant and gazed at the sun to determine how far we had moved since the day before. As to myself, I was writing logs, collecting plankton for food experimentation, and fishing or filming.

The day started with a glorious sunrise over the sea, the cook being relieved by the last night watchman to collect the flying fish that had flown on board during the night. These were fried on a small primus stove and devoured at the edge of the raft after a quick morning dip in the sea. Extra flying fish were used as bait for the great colorful dolphin fish that followed the raft day in and day out across the ocean. Dolphins that we did not eat were used as bait for the great sharks that calmly swam around us day and night. When the sea was high, we could see them sideways as though through a perpendicular glass wall raised high above the level of the raft. Then the raft tipped up and let the water and the slowly moving sharks pass beneath us. They never seemed treacherous except when we cleaned fish, and they scented blood. Then they would wake up in a fury. Yet we never quite trusted them, and in one day we pulled aboard nine six- to ten-foot sharks just to dispose of their intimate company.

When we slid the sharks up onto our shallow and slippery logs, the remoras, clinging to the sharks' skin by suction, would jump off and attach themselves to the side of the raft; and the pilot fish, having lost their king and master, would find a substitute in *Kon-*

Tiki, joining us in nice formation before the bow or between the centerboards. If a big blue shark passed, they would occasionally follow him away, but more than forty of them tailed us right across the ocean until our raft was shattered on the reef.

Although we carried our rations lashed to the logs beneath the bamboo deck, it was still of great importance to me to find out whether primitive man, accustomed to hardship as he was, would have been able to renew his supply of food and water on such a long-lasting drift. The answer was affirmative. After the fourth day at sea, there was not a single day throughout the journey when we were not accompanied by numbers of dolphin fish. They kept to the side of the raft or beneath us and could be fished, speared, or hooked whenever we desired. Edible barnacles and seaweeds grew all over the huge logs and could be picked like garden greens. And they often housed tiny, edible pelagic crabs or very small fishes. A dozen or more flying fish, often accompanied by baby squids, came aboard almost every night, sailing through the air in schools right above the surface if pursued by dolphins or sharks. Twice in mid-ocean on dark nights, a long snakelike fish with huge eyes and carnivorous jaws jumped right into our sleeping bags inside the bamboo hut and caused a great commotion. It was probably the *Gempylus,* which was seen this way by man for the first time, only a couple of skeletons having previously been found on South American shores. Soaked shark meat, delicious bonito, and yellow-fin tuna completed our seafood menu and made it clear enough that early, hardy raftsmen were not menaced by hunger.

We carried two hundred coconuts and samples of the Peruvian sweet potato and gourd, which were important food plants that the aborigines of Peru shared with those of Polynesia. Those not eaten en route were successfully planted upon our arrival on the islands, to prove that they could be carried on a raft without loss of germinating power. These prehistoric food plants could never have drifted across the ocean without the aid and care of human hands, and the aboriginal name for sweet potato was *Kumara* — both in Peru and on the Polynesian islands.

The early raftsmen along the dry South American coast carried their water supply in gourds or pottery containers and in huge canes of bamboo with the joints pierced out. Left in the shade underneath the bamboo deck, where they were constantly washed by the seas, we found that our plain Peruvian spring water was preserved for more than two months before the first samples began to rot. At that time we had already entered a part of the ocean where drizzles were frequent and rains occasional, and we were able to collect sufficient rainwater for our daily needs. We consumed a ton of water on the journey, along with more than ample rations, and the buoyancy of the balsa logs would have permitted us to double our water supply in easily stored bamboo canes under the deck. With the warm climate creating a demand for salt, we could mix up to 40 percent of sea water with our drinking water without evil effects. Like our early predecessors and many sailors shipwrecked during the war, we found several simple methods of abstracting the thirst-quenching juice from raw fish, a supply that never ran short.

In this way, with the days full of testings and practical experiments, we found ourselves carried across the ocean bit by bit. By the forty-fifth day we had drifted from the seventy-eighth meridian to the one hundred-eighth and were exactly halfway to the first islands. During those days we were more than two thousand miles away from the nearest shore in any direction. When the ocean was smoothly rolling, we could leave our raft in the little float and row away into the blue space between eternal sea and sky. As we watched our grotesque craft growing smaller and smaller in the distance, an oppressive sense of loneliness came over us. It was as though we were suspended in space, like disembodied spirits. When we rowed back to our distant raft, we felt a strange feeling of relief and were happy to crawl on board our precious, weather-beaten logs and find shade from the glaring sun inside the bamboo hut. The now familiar scent of bamboo and thatched roof made us feel that we were back in our earthly home again, inside a jungle dwelling that was far away from the limitless sea.

We enjoyed our evening meals as the glorious sun sank into the sea before our bow, while sky and water became a dream of colors. Small, striped pilot fish would rush to the surface to snap at our crumbs, and they were occasionally followed by a lazy shark, like kittens by a bulldog.

As darkness came we would light our petrol lamp, and Erik would fetch his guitar. Then merry song and music from the raft spread with the dim light over the nearest waves of a trackless, endless ocean. We would soon roll up on the bamboo matting inside the hut, leaving the watchman alone with the stars and the steering oar.

We hit two storms when we approached the end of the journey. The first lasted one day and the second five. With sail down and ropes shrieking, Kon-Tiki rode the breaking ocean like a duck. A raft in high seas with wet and slippery logs and no railing requires careful stepping. The second storm had just begun when Herman went overboard. When visible again, he was seen struggling behind the stern. He struck for the blade of the steering oar, but a strong wind pushed us ahead, and he missed. We could not turn our raft around to go back a single inch. There was no possibility of even stopping our stubborn craft in its reckless trek to the west. The airy float would blow like a feather ahead of the raft if put to sea in such a wind. We threw out a life belt, once, twice, but it blew right back on board. We became desperate as Herman, our best swimmer, was left farther and farther behind. With a line in one hand, Knut leaped into the sea, and slowly the two friends worked their way toward each other. Thirty yards behind the raft they joined hands, and the four of us on board pulled them in.

We had a green parrot as ship's pet. It was a perfect sailor and a joyous companion, until a big sea stole it on the sixtieth day.

At the end of the third month, we were constantly visited by Polynesian frigate birds and boobies in increasing numbers. Then we sighted a rising cumulo-nimbus cloud, revealing the existence of some hidden, sun-baked isle beneath the western horizon. We steered for the cloud as best we could, and as the golden sun rose from the sea on the ninety-third day, the blue haze of land was outlined against a reddish sky. We were passing the tiny atoll of Puka-puka, but wind and current would not permit us to turn around. We had covered four thousand miles of ocean heading west, and yet we could not force ourselves four miles to the east to reach the island. More than ever was this a plain and unmistakable lesson, stressing the fact that in this ocean a drifting craft and a natural migration would inevitably be pushed to the west. And it was with strange feelings that we sat quietly down on our raft and saw the little, solid speck of land — the first and only for twelve weeks — slide away on our port stern. For a moment the wind carried a mild whiff of verdant tropical foliage and smoky native household odors, and we filled our salty lungs before the *fata morgana* [8] — the mirage of our hopes — sank into the sea.

On the ninety-seventh day another island grew up out of the ocean, straight ahead of us in line with the bow. As we approached, we saw from the top of the mast that a roaring reef was twisted like a submerged snake all around the island, blocking the approach to the palm-clad beaches behind. All day long we struggled in the current alongside the island to keep clear of the boiling reef and yet be close enough to attempt a landfall wherever an opening might be seen.

Late in the afternoon we sighted the first natives on a beach, and we hoisted all our flags in joy. A great commotion was seen on the beach, and shortly after, the first Polynesians in small outrigger canoes slid through a passage in the reef and swarmed aboard the *Kon-Tiki*. A strong wind blew up, and our ocean raft struggled away from land as the sun went down in the sea. There was a desperate fight against the elements, in which we were assisted by all the friendly natives who were able to get out and join us in the open sea. As the dark night engulfed the island and the sea, a great campfire was lit on shore to show us the direction of the entrance through the reef. But the wind increased its grip and won another battle. When the glare of the great fire dwindled like a spark in the distance and the roar of the reef was no longer heard, our excited native friends jumped into their canoes to return to their homes on Angatau for fear of drifting with some crazy strangers into the open sea. And we drifted farther into the heart of the Tuamotu, or Dangerous Archipelago.

One night an unusual motion of the raft awakened me, and I suspected land ahead. Next morning, our one hundred-first at sea, we were alarmed by the watchman on the top of the mast, who had sighted an enormous reef that spanned the entire horizon ahead of us. It was the treacherous twenty-mile reef of Raroia Atoll. With white spray shooting high into the air, the surf battered the endless reef in fury.

As we rode directly into this boiling inferno, we had three hours to prepare for all eventualities. We lowered the sail and threw out an improvised anchor on a long rope that kept sliding along the bottom. We carried valuable cargo into the hut and lashed it fast

---

[8] *fata morgana:* a mirage appearing over water.

in watertight bags. We cut off all ropes holding the centerboards in position and pulled them up to get a shallow draft. With shoes on for the first time in one hundred days, we concentrated on the last order: Hang on — hang onto the raft whatever happens!

The first walls of thundering water broke down upon us from above as soon as our logs ran against the solid coral reef. Tons of crashing water tore up the deck, flattened the hut, broke the hardwood mast like a match, and splintered the steering oar and stern cross-beam, while we were thrown in and dragged out, thrown in and dragged out, by the furious ocean. During these minutes, when we cramped every existing muscle to withhold the deadly grasp of the passing seas, we made up for all the leisure of the average ocean day. I felt the last of my strength giving way when a wave larger than the others lifted Kon-Tiki free of the water and tossed us high up on the reef. Other waves pushed us closer to shore, until we could jump off the raft and wade the shallow coral reef to a tiny, uninhabited coconut island. Never did any tiny piece of land embody paradise so perfectly to me as this verdant, palm-clad isle with its white and shiny beach facing a crystal-clear lagoon, calm as green glass.

A week later we were found by natives who had detected from another island six miles across the lagoon the drift wreckage and the light from our campfire. And about the same time Kon-Tiki was carried by high seas right across the solid reef and left becalmed inside the lagoon. The nine main logs that had carried us 4,300 miles across the ocean in 101 days were still intact, and after an unforgettable two-week Polynesian welcome party on lonely Raroia, our battered raft was towed to Tahiti by the French government schooner Tamara, which was sent expressly to pick us up.

We shall never forget the welcome on these Polynesian islands.

From Tahiti the Kon-Tiki was carried as deck cargo back to the Norwegian Museum of Navigation in Oslo.

What is the difference between a mechanical and a living thing? In the following essay, Loren Eiseley, a noted naturalist and writer, contrasts today's mechanical world with the more innocent world of his youth, when he was assigned "to lay hands on the present" — to bring back alive birds and reptiles to restock a zoo. His first captive was a fine, young sparrow hawk. But a man like Eiseley was never meant to work for a zoo.

The Bird
and the Machine

LOREN EISELEY

I suppose their little bones have years ago been lost among the stones and winds of those high glacial pastures. I suppose their feathers blew eventually into the piles of tumbleweed beneath the straggling cattle fences and rotted there in the mountain snows, along with dead steers and all the other things that drift to an end in the corners of the wire. I do not quite know why I should be thinking of birds over *The New York Times* at breakfast, particularly the birds of my youth half a continent away. It is a funny thing what the brain will do with memories and how it will treasure them and finally bring them into odd juxtapositions with other things, as though it wanted to make a design, or get some meaning out of them, whether you want it or not, or even see it.

It used to seem marvelous to me, but I read now that there are machines that can do these things in a small way, machines that can crawl about like animals, and that it may not be long now until they do more things — maybe even make themselves — I saw that piece in the *Times* just now. And then they will, maybe — well, who knows — but you read about it more and more with no one making any protest, and already they can add better than we and reach up and hear things through the dark and finger the guns over the night sky.

This is the new world that I read about at breakfast. This is the world that confronts me in my biological books and journals, until there are times when I sit quietly in my chair and try to hear the little purr of the cogs in my head and the tubes flaring and dying as the messages go through them and the circuits snap shut or open. This is the great age, make no mistake about it; the robot has been born somewhat appropriately along with the atom bomb, and the brain they say now is just another type of more complicated feedback system. The engineers have its basic principles worked out: it's mechanical, you know, nothing to get superstitious about, and man can always improve on nature once he gets the idea. Well, he's got it all right, and that's why, I guess, that I sit here in my chair, with the article crunched in my hand, remembering those two birds and that blue mountain sunlight. There is another magazine article on my desk that reads "Machines Are Getting Smarter Every Day." I don't deny it, but I'll still stick with the birds. It's life I believe in, not machines.

Maybe you don't believe there is any difference. A skeleton is all joints and pulleys, I'll admit. And when man was in his simpler stages of machine building in the eighteenth century, he quickly saw the resemblances. "What," wrote Hobbes, "is the heart but a spring, and the nerves but so many strings, and the joints but so many wheels, giving motion to the whole body?" Tinkering about in their shops, it was inevitable in the end that men would see the world as a huge machine "subdivided into an infinite number of lesser machines."

The idea took on with a vengeance. Little automatons toured the country — dolls controlled by clockwork. Clocks described as little worlds were taken on tours by their designers. They were made up of moving figures, shifting scenes, and other remarkable devices. The life of the cell was unknown. Man, whether he was conceived as possessing a soul or not, moved and jerked about like these tiny puppets. A human being thought of himself in terms of his own tools and implements. He had been fashioned like the puppets he produced and was only a more clever model made by a greater designer.

Then in the nineteenth century, the cell was discovered, and the single machine in its turn was found to be the product of millions of infinitesimal machines — the cells. Now, finally, the cell itself dissolves away into an abstract chemical machine — and that into some intangible, inexpressible flow of energy. The secret seems to lurk all about, the wheels get smaller and smaller, and they turn more rapidly, but when you try to seize it, the life is gone — and so, by popular definition, some would say that life was never there in the first place. The wheels and the cogs are the secret, and we can make them better in time — machines that will run faster and more accurately than real mice to real cheese.

I have no doubt it can be done, though a mouse harvesting seeds on an autumn thistle is to me a fine sight and more complicated, I think, in his multiform activity, than a machine "mouse" running a maze. Also, I like to think of the possible shape of the future brooding in mice, just as it brooded once in a rather ordinary mousy insectivore who became a man. It leaves a nice fine indeterminate sense of wonder that even an electronic brain hasn't got, because you know perfectly well that if the electronic brain changes, it will be because of something man has done to it. But what man will do to himself he doesn't really know. A certain scale of time and a ghostly intangible thing called change are ticking in him. Powers and potentialities like the oak in the seed, or a red and awful ruin. Either way, it's impressive; and the mouse has it, too. Or those birds, I'll never forget those birds — yet before I measured their significance, I learned the lesson of time first of all. I was young then and left alone in a great desert — part of an expedition that had scattered its men over several hundred miles in order to carry on research more effectively. I learned there that time is a series of planes existing superficially in the same universe. The tempo is a human illusion, a subjective clock ticking in our own kind of protoplasm.

As the long months passed, I began to live on the slower planes and to observe more readily what passed for life there. I sauntered, I passed more and more slowly up and down the canyons in the dry, baking heat of midsummer. I slumbered for long hours in the shade of huge brown boulders that had gathered in tilted companies out on the flats. I had forgotten the world of men and the world had forgotten me. Now and then I found a skull in the canyons, and these justified my remaining there. I took a serene cold interest in these discoveries. I had come, like many a naturalist before me, to view life with a wary and subdued attention. I had grown to take pleasure in the divested bone.

I sat once in a high ridge that fell away before me into a waste of sand dunes. I sat through hours of a long afternoon. Finally, as I glanced beside my boot, an indistinct configuration caught my eye. It was a coiled rattlesnake, a big one. How long he had sat with me I do not know. I had not frightened him. We were both locked in the sleep-walking tempo of the earlier world, baking in the same high air and sunshine. Perhaps he had been there when I came. He slept on as I left, his coils, so ill-discerned by me, dissolving once more among the stones and gravel from which I had barely made him out.

Another time I got on a higher ridge, among some tough little wind-warped pines half covered over with sand in a basin-like depression that caught everything carried by the air up to those heights. There were a few thin bones of birds, some cracked shells of indeterminable age, and the knotty fingers of pine roots bulged out of shape from their long and agonizing grasp upon the crevices of the rock. I lay under the pines in the sparse shade and went to sleep once more.

It grew cold finally, for autumn was in the air by then, and the few things that lived thereabouts were sinking down into an even chillier scale of time. In the moments between sleeping and waking I saw the roots about me and slowly, slowly, a foot in what seemed many centuries, I moved my sleep-stiffened hands over the scaling bark and lifted my numbed face after the vanishing sun. I was a great awkward thing of knots and aching limbs, trapped up there in some long, patient endurance that involved the necessity of putting living fingers into rock and by slow, aching expansion bursting those rocks asunder. I suppose, so thin and slow was the time of my pulse by then, that I might have stayed on to drift still deeper into the lower cadences of the frost, or the crystalline life that glistens pebbles or shines in a snowflake or dreams in the meteoric iron between the worlds.

It was a dim descent, but time was present in it. Somewhere far down in that scale the notion struck me that one might come the other way. Not many months thereafter I joined some colleagues heading higher into a remote, windy tableland where huge bones were reputed to protrude like boulders from the turf. I had drowsed with reptiles and moved with the century-long pulse of trees; now, lethargically, I was climbing back up some invisible ladder of quickening hours. There had been talk of birds in connection with my duties. Birds are intense, fast-living creatures — reptiles, I suppose one might say, that have escaped out of the heavy sleep of time, transformed fairy creatures dancing over sunlit meadows. It is a youthful fancy, no doubt, but because of something that happened up there among the escarpments of that range, it remains with me a lifelong impression. I can never bear to see a bird imprisoned.

We came into that valley through the trailing mists of a spring night. It was a place that looked as though it might never have known the foot of man, but our scouts had been ahead of us, and we knew all about the abandoned cabin of stone that lay far up on one hillside. It had been built in the land rush of the last century and then lost to the cattlemen again as the marginal soils failed to take to the plow.

There were spots like this all over that country. Lost graves marked by unlettered stones and old corroding rim-fire cartridge cases lying where somebody had made a stand among the boulders that rimmed the valley. They are all that remain of the range wars; the men are under the stones now. I could see our cavalcade winding in and out through the mist below us: torches, the reflection of the truck lights on our collecting tins, and the far-off bumping of a loose dinosaur thigh bone in the bottom of a trailer. I stood on a rock a moment looking down and thinking what it cost in money and equipment to capture the past.

We had, in addition, instructions to lay hands on the present. The word had come through to get them alive — birds, reptiles, anything. A zoo somewhere abroad needed restocking. It was one of those reciprocal matters in which science involves itself. Maybe our museum needed a stray ostrich egg, and this was the pay-off. Anyhow, my job was to help capture some birds, and that was why I was there before the trucks.

The cabin had not been occupied for years. We intended to clean it out and live in it, but there were holes in the roof, and the birds had come in and were roosting in the rafters. You could depend on it in a place like this where everything blew away, and even a bird needed some place out of the weather and away from coyotes. A cabin going back to nature in a wild place draws them till they come in, listening at the eaves, I imagine, pecking softly among the shingles till they find a hole, and then suddenly the place is theirs and man is forgotten.

Sometimes of late years I find myself thinking the most beautiful sight in the world might be the birds taking over New York after the last man has run away to the hills. I will never live to see it, of course, but I know just how it will sound because I've lived up high and I know the sort of watch birds keep on us. I've listened to sparrows tapping tentatively on the outside of air conditioners when they thought no one was listening, and I know how other birds test the vibrations that come up to them through the television aerials.

"Is he gone?" they ask, and the vibrations come up from below, "Not yet, not yet."

Well, to come back, I got the door open softly, and I had the spotlight all ready to turn on and blind whatever birds there were so they couldn't see to get out through the roof. I had a short piece of ladder to put against the far wall, where there was a shelf on which I expected to make the biggest haul. I had all the information I needed just like any skilled assassin. I pushed the door open, the hinges squeaking only a little. A bird or two stirred — I could hear them — but nothing flew and there was a faint starlight through the holes in the roof.

I padded across the floor, got the ladder up and the light ready, and slithered up the ladder till my head and arms were over the shelf. Everything was dark as pitch except for the starlight at the little place back of the shelf near the eaves. With the light to blind them, they'd never make it. I had them. I reached my arm carefully over in order to be ready to seize whatever was there, and I put the flash on the edge of the shelf where it would stand by itself when I turned it on. That way I'd be able to use both hands.

Everything worked perfectly except for one detail — I didn't know what kind of birds were there. I never thought about it at all, and it wouldn't have mattered if I had. My orders were to get something interesting. I snapped on the flash and sure enough there was a great beating and feathers flying, but instead of my having them, they, or rather he, had me. He had my hand, that is, and for a small hawk not much bigger than my fist, he was doing all right. I heard him give one short metallic cry when the light went on and my hand descended on the bird beside him; after that he was busy with his claws, and his beak was sunk in my thumb. In the struggle I knocked the lamp over on the shelf, and his mate got her sight back and whisked neatly through the hole in the roof and off among the stars outside. It all happened in fifteen seconds, and you might think I would have fallen down the ladder, but no, I had a professional assassin's reputation to keep up, and the bird, of course, made the mistake of thinking the hand was the enemy and not the eyes behind it. He chewed my thumb up pretty effectively and lacerated my hand with his claws, but in the end I got him, having two hands to work with.

He was a sparrow hawk and a fine young male in the prime of life. I was sorry not to catch the pair of them, but as I dripped blood and folded his wings carefully, holding him by the back so that he couldn't strike again, I had to admit the two of them might have been more than I could have handled under the circumstances. The little fellow had saved his mate by diverting me, and that was that. He was born to it and made no outcry now, resting in my hand hopelessly but peering toward me in the shadows behind the lamp with a fierce, almost indifferent glance. He neither gave nor expected mercy, and something out of the high air passed from him to me, stirring a faint embarrassment.

I quit looking into that eye and managed to get my huge carcass with its fist full of prey back down the ladder. I put the bird in a box too small to allow him to injure himself by struggle and walked out to welcome the arriving trucks. It had been a long day and camp still to make in the darkness. In the morning that bird would be just another episode. He would go back with the bones in the truck to a small cage in a city where he would spend the rest of his life. And a good thing, too. I sucked my aching thumb and spat out some blood. An assassin has to get used to these things. I had a professional reputation to keep up.

In the morning, with the change that comes on suddenly in that high country, the mist that had hovered below us in the valley was gone. The sky was a deep blue, and one could see for miles over the high outcroppings of stone. I was up early and brought the box in which the little hawk was imprisoned out onto the grass where I was building a cage. A wind as cool as a mountain spring ran over the grass and stirred my hair. It was a fine day to be alive. I looked up and all around and at the hole in the cabin roof out of which the other little hawk had fled. There was no sign of her anywhere that I could see.

"Probably in the next county by now," I thought cynically, but before beginning work I decided I'd have a look at my last night's capture.

Secretively, I looked again all around the camp and up and down and opened the box. I got him right out in my hand with his wings folded properly, and I was careful not to startle him. He lay limp in my grasp and I could feel his heart pound under the feathers, but he only looked beyond me and up.

I saw him look that last look away beyond me into a sky so full of light that I could not follow his gaze. The little breeze flowed over me again, and nearby a mountain aspen shook all its tiny leaves. I suppose I must have had an idea then of what I was going to do, but I never let it come up into consciousness. I just reached over and laid the hawk on the grass.

He lay there a long minute without hope, unmoving, his eyes still fixed on that blue vault above him. It must have been that he was already so far away in heart that he never felt the release from my hand. He never even stood. He just lay with his breast against the grass.

In the next second after that long minute he was gone. Like a flicker of light, he had vanished with my eyes full on him but without actually seeing even a premonitory wing beat. He was gone straight into that towering emptiness of light and crystal that my eyes could scarcely bear to penetrate. For another long moment there was silence. I could not see him. The light was too intense. Then from far up somewhere a cry came ringing down.

I was young then and had seen little of the world, but when I heard that cry my heart turned over. It was not the cry of the hawk I had captured; for, by shifting my position against the sun, I was now seeing further up. Straight out of the sun's eye, where she must have been soaring restlessly above us for untold hours, hurtled his mate. And from far up, ringing from peak to peak of the summits over us, came a cry of such unutterable and ecstatic joy that it sounds down across the years and tingles among the cups on my quiet breakfast table.

I saw them both now. He was rising fast to meet her. They met in a great soaring gyre [1] that turned to a whirling circle and a dance of wings. Once more, just once, their two voices, joined in a harsh wild medley of question and response, struck and echoed against the pinnacles of the valley. Then they were gone forever somewhere into those upper regions beyond the eyes of men.

I am older now, and sleep less, and have seen most of what there is to see and am not very much impressed any more, I suppose, by anything. "What Next in the Attributes of Machines?" my morning headline runs. "It Might Be the Power to Reproduce Themselves."

I lay the paper down and across my mind a phrase floats insinuatingly: "It does not seem that there is anything in the construction, constituents, or behavior of the human being which it is essentially impossible for science to duplicate and synthesize. On the other hand . . ."

All over the city the cogs in the hard, bright mechanisms have begun to turn. Figures move through computers, names are spelled out, a thoughtful machine selects the fingerprints of a wanted criminal from an array of thousands. In the laboratory an electronic mouse runs swiftly through a maze toward the cheese it can neither taste nor enjoy. On the second run it does better than a living mouse.

"On the other hand . . ." Ah, my mind takes up, on the other hand the machine does not bleed, ache, hang for hours in the empty sky in a torment of hope to learn the fate of another machine, nor does it cry out with joy nor dance in the air with the fierce passion of a bird. Far off, over a distance greater than space, that remote cry from the heart of heaven makes a faint buzzing among my breakfast dishes and passes on and away.

---

[1] *gyre:* a spiral path.

Like everything important to the human spirit, nature has its
desecraters, *those who destroy something awesome and beautiful. In*
the following essay, written in 1961, Vance Packard describes the
American landscape he has observed in his wide travels.

America the Beautiful— and Its Desecraters

VANCE PACKARD

A friend relates that while he was driving through a lovely stretch
of forest in Maine recently, he saw the car ahead, full of people,
slow down and a half-open cardboard box sail out its right rear window. Eggshells, beer cans, and scraps of sandwiches and paper were
spewed out along the roadside.

Another friend, a minister, became offended by the sight of dis-
carded liquor bottles while he was driving along the otherwise beautiful beach road leading into Edgartown, Massachusetts. He began
to pick up the bottles nearest the road. By the time he had reached
the edge of town he had piled so many bottles into the back of his
sedan that they rose above the level of the seat. People in this area
who own homes along the seashore report they must, as a fairly
frequent chore, scoop up and bury the oil-soaked remains of sea
gulls drowned and immobilized by waste oil dumped just offshore
by commercial boats.

These evidences of rampant slobbism, I must confess, do not surprise me. I live near a stretch of lonely road in Connecticut that
edges the Silvermine River. A two-hundred-year-old waterfall attracts
many motorcars. Every few weeks I, or one of my children, as a regular task, go along this road with a bushel basket picking up the sacks
of beer cans and other refuse that have been tossed into the bushes.

Last summer, to cite another case, I went strolling barefoot on a
magnificent beach on Martha's Vineyard and found myself watching

a father and his ten-year-old son amuse themselves. Father was photographing the terns; the son was hurling stones at bottles which he had set up in the sand. When I protested the bottle smashing, the father seemed surprised by my vehemence but suggested that his son find other amusement. I cleaned up the broken glass as best I could.

These instances are thoughtless manifestations of a spreading desecration of the American landscape today which threatens to make a cruel jest of the phrase "America the Beautiful." Refuse, even broken glass, can be cleaned up. And I suppose that the careless boobs who toss it about are so fixed in their habit patterns that we can do little to reform them. But some of the more serious man-made desecration being committed upon the U.S. landscape, often for profit, is beyond retrieval.

I have just completed a journey which took me into seventeen states. In the West my wife, Virginia, an artist, accompanied me, and we traveled by car because we were eager to get our first close look at many areas which have in years past been acclaimed for their spectacular natural beauty. Most of our excursions left us feeling frustrated and depressed. It was evident that, just in the past decade, many of these places had become so scarified by man that the natural beauty of the landscape, once breath-taking, was largely lost.

Our drive up the California coastline from Los Angeles to San Francisco was a case in point. Some of the stretches are still delightful. The lovely rolling countryside north of Buellton gives one a sense of the original West at its best. Then you approach Santa Maria. The setting is spectacular, with wildly upheaved mountains in the background. But they are difficult to see through the maze of billboards. The first mile or so of Santa Maria — the new part — is a jungle of neon signs, trailer parks, used-car lots, and look-alike development houses packed tightly together. Farther north, the once-famed El Camino Real approaching San Francisco has now become just another aisle through a gaudy, seemingly endless mart. It is lined with vendors of seat covers, ice cream, gasoline, and gifts. To the visitor, it is indistinguishable from New Jersey's Route 17, Florida's Route 1 above Fort Lauderdale, or southern California's Long Beach Boulevard. There is one short stretch of this once-royal road north of Palo Alto where beautiful eucalyptus trees line an uncommercialized section. A friend who pointed this out to me said wistfully: "This will give you an idea of how it used to be."

Each perceptive American probably has his favorite candidates for the worst desecraters of our landscape. I would like to advance here five of my own. I will cite first those whose desecrations could be most readily corrected by an aroused citizenry, since the scars they have created are temporary or removable.

First I would nominate those who clutter up the areas along scenic routes with the remains of castoff motorcars or blocked-up trailers or parking lots. The state of New York spent many millions of dollars on a scenic thruway up into the Catskills. A visitor there now sees three motorcar junkyards while traveling one five-mile stretch of the road. If you take an excursion to the world-famed falls of Watkins Glen at the foot of Lake Seneca, New York, you cannot avoid seeing an auto junkyard within a few dozen yards of one of the falls. Or if you motor up the Penobscot River into rural Maine, you will find a titanic auto graveyard, covering many acres, near Old Town.

Perhaps the worst squalor created by motorcars that I have ever seen is along the supposedly scenic Route 10 crossing northern Idaho. There, near a lovely lake outside Coeur d'Alene, one passes within a few hundred feet of a junkyard containing at least a thousand carcasses of motorcars, piled four and five high. As you continue east into the mountainous mining communities, the junked motorcars are no longer gathered together systematically into yards. They simply lie abandoned, often upside-down, beside the road.

The gaudy blocked-up metallic trailers, which are starting to appear in the United States in phenomenal numbers, qualify as desecrations, I believe, when they are mass-packed in scenic areas, as they are along the shore of Lake Keuka, New York, or when they are installed singly in shocking juxtaposition on empty lots beside fine Early American homes, as is happening in a number of otherwise delightful New England communities. Some trailer owners who decide to expand their homes create startling appendages. The owner of a blocked-up trailer near New Bedford, Massachusetts, has added a two-car garage.

Outdoor advertisers who shrewdly decide that their billboards will have maximum impact in lovely rustic settings are the second group of desecraters I would nominate. Thousands of miles of rural scenery in the United States have been ruined by the jarring presence of commercial signs. The signs, of course, can be taken down if enough citizens make their anger felt.

A few of the nation's great scenic highways have been preserved from the billboard desecraters. The Merritt Parkway in Connecticut is an excellent example. On the other hand, some types of billboards have started appearing in open country along the costly Massachusetts Turnpike. In New York, the new thruway into the Catskill Mountains is in some sections virtually lined with billboards. I counted fifty-one billboards in one seven-mile stretch above Middletown. New York's advertising lobbyists were even able to prevail upon the Borough of Manhattan to trim the tops of trees planted in Duffy Square so that, as author Edward Higbee put it, the "towering billboards could be seen in their four-story splendor." In Louisiana a beer advertiser employing billboards sought to ease the hostility of local drys by adding to the sign a message urging viewers to attend the church of their choice.

The new interstate highway network which the federal government is helping the states construct threatens to become a billboard slum unless many more state legislatures act to prevent it. This past spring, legislators in many states found themselves caught between the pressures of the massive and affluent billboard lobby and a moderately tempting offer of free booty from the federal government. The U.S. Congress, after it was advised of a general tendency for new and expensive scenic highways to become quickly lined with commercial billboards, offered states a $\frac{1}{2}$ percent bonus in federal funds for highway building if the states would agree to control billboards on the highways to be built. For New York State, for example, the bonus would amount to $2 million. It is a grim commentary on our political life that state governments must be offered cash bounties to protect their own historic and scenic attractions from desecration.

As the deadline for qualifying approached, a handful of state legislatures — in Maryland, Connecticut, Kentucky, New York, North Dakota, West Virginia, Wisconsin, and Washington, among others — managed to enact presumably acceptable legislation.

One advertising firm has developed a titanic new kind of billboard for use in states that do enact restrictive legislation. Called the Land-Mark Hi-Sign, it is twenty-four times as big as a conventional twenty-four-sheet billboard. The sign itself, a hundred feet wide by eighty feet high, hangs from a suspension bridge built between two great aluminum towers and can be read by motorists a third of a mile away. One such sign structure is standing at Romulus, Michigan, outside Detroit.

Roadside desecration takes forms other than billboards. In the attractive rolling country near Vacaville, California, motorists are confronted with the question "WHERE'S HARVEY'S?" spelled out in thirty-foot-high letters on a grassy hillside. Cows graze among the letters. A few hundred yards further down the road you learn the answer from another great sign blocked out on a verdant hillside: Harvey's is on Highway 50, near Lake Tahoe. It apparently has not dawned upon those responsible that these signs are atrocities in an otherwise beautiful region.

It is becoming difficult to escape commercial placards in one form or another. If you journey for vacation purposes to the great public beach in Fort Lauderdale, Florida, you find that hundreds of the benches facing the ocean have small billboards attached to their backs. And just offshore you will frequently see an old airplane roar by, flying low, towing a fluttering advertisement.

Meanwhile, the Unexcelled Chemical Corporation has been demonstrating to interested marketers in various parts of the country a marvelous magic lantern called the Skyjector that can project messages hundreds of yards long against mountaintops and clouds. And, worse, two advertising journals have headlined the news that Lockheed engineers are now reasonably confident that a space-writing satellite can be developed which can spell out messages hundreds of miles long in orange letters against the evening sky.

Since the U.S. outdoor advertising industry seems incapable of more than token restraint, legislation appears to be the only hope. The federal government should flatly ban all billboards from new scenic highways built with the help of federal funds. And the states that hope to save themselves from being overwhelmed by billboards everywhere should start requiring that all persons seeking to erect billboards, in nonurban areas at least, be required to present a convincing justification to a citizens' commission attached to the state highway commissioner's office or to a special outdoor advertising board.

Another group of desecraters I want to cite are the people who plant utility towers or television towers or a jungle of large television aerials in settings that have been cherished for their beauty or charm. Such mechanical obstacles intruding upon scenic panoramas were a fairly constant source of frustration during our drive up the California coastline. Usually there was a utility line — and often two of them — between the highway and the nearby ocean. If the utility lines had to follow the highway, why couldn't they at least be placed on the interior side?

Let us grant that our modern way of life demands the existence of such technological accessories. But usually a little thought, and little, if any, extra cost, could produce a disposition of such accessories that would make them a less dominant part of the landscape. One frequently gets the impression that the officials locating their poles and towers are totally oblivious to, if not hostile to, aesthetic considerations.

As we approached Lake Mead from Nevada, our first sight of the lake midst brilliantly colored, starkly barren mountains was through the wires of a giant power line. This line and its towers, in fact, blocked the view for more than a mile. The pylons supporting cross-country power lines scarify an otherwise lovely landscape. They are massive. And they slash straight across the countryside instead of following natural contours. At this writing, a power company is pressing a proposal to erect a series of high towers across the lovely countryside in the Sudbury-Wayland area of Massachusetts, once dear to Thoreau.

In Santa Barbara, California, one of the historic landmarks is the Santa Barbara Mission, located high up on the hillside behind the town. Monks work about the grounds. Their view of the bay and the Santa Cruz Island beyond was once awe-inspiring. Now monks and visitors alike must see this vista through a maze of four-tiered television aerials — many of them twenty-five feet high and each with at least a half a dozen guy wires — which jut up from recently built houses on the hillside just below the mission. Santa Barbara has its own television station (which would require only a very small aerial), but most of the residents build tremendous aerials upon their rooftops in order to try to coax in telecasts from Los Angeles, nearly a hundred miles away. These thousands of aerials give a harsh look to what has long been considered to be one of the nation's loveliest cities. Let us hope that soon our electronic wonder-workers will apply some of their vaunted ingenuity to finding less intrusive ways of bringing in television signals.

Community planners surely must be held responsible for much of the ugliness being created in our towns and cities. They have been dodging their responsibility to guide growth in a way that will make a community fully satisfying and stimulating rather than merely habitable. These planners often seem more interested in any scheme that will give the town treasury or the town's business community quick added revenue.

The planners, in approving subdivision plans of the big developers, allow them to impose their hardly objective views on the shape the new mass-produced community is to take. The result has usually been a layout containing the maximum number of housing units that the zoning laws permit, grouped around a shopping center (which the developer leases out on stiff terms, since he can offer merchants a virtually captive clientele). The amenities of good living that ordinarily have gone with a community in times past, such as parks, playgrounds, libraries, schools, churches, and museums, are included, if at all, only grudgingly and in spots that will interfere least with the revenue-producing objectives of the developer.

In recent decades, planners have rarely given much thought to creating a psychologically satisfying focal point or heart for their city, town, or neighborhood. One night recently, I thought back over eighteen European towns and cities I visited three years ago. In every instance, the European metropolis remained vivid in my mind because it was built around a square or a monument or a fine boulevard or a park, with public buildings usually prominent in the concept.

Americans in earlier centuries built their communities around a focal point. Witness Boston, with its Common and its Public Garden. Most New England towns and cities still have a clearly perceived heart, and many of the smaller, older-fashioned midwestern towns such as Woodstock, Illinois, still do, too (and so do a few larger cities, such as Indianapolis). But in the majority of American cities, the heart of downtown typically is the street intersection where the largest bank faces the largest department store. Downtown Dallas, Oklahoma City, Los Angeles, Sioux City, Des Moines, Milwaukee, Birmingham, and Winston-Salem seem a blur of almost indistinguishable commercial buildings.

One also misses in the typical U.S. city a sense of graciousness or greenness. Acquisition of new parkland has not kept pace with population growth, and in many cities the planners have been stealing land from existing parks for projects with higher priority, such as superhighways and parking lots. The newer the metropolitan area, the more likely it is to be short of a decent minimum of greenery. I suppose Los Angeles has a park somewhere, but I have never seen it.

Much of Denver's beauty comes from trees that were planted and parks that were established more than forty years ago. I would say, on the basis of having very recently viewed some of the jam-packed, look-alike houses now springing up on the north side of Denver, that not much is being done to make the city beautiful forty years hence.

The most damaging desecrater of all is the polluter. Raw sewage floats in the Potomac right past the monuments to Lincoln, Washington, and Jefferson. More than five thousand U.S. communities dump raw or inadequately treated wastes into the nation's waterways and are utterly indifferent to the needs and sensibilities of their downstream neighbors. Thousands of industrial plants, with equal indifference, dump their foul-smelling and often poisonous wastes into rivers. Oil is dumped into the Great Lakes, and radioactive material has been discharged into the Tennessee River. Rivers in the Idaho mining country often have a milkish appearance from pollution.

Perhaps the most befouled of all U.S. rivers is the mighty Missouri, which has aptly been called a thousand-mile-sewer. Cities and packing houses alike have been discharging their untreated wastes into the river. According to one report, Public Health Service engineers have told of seeing floating excrement and other sewage solids. And they noted that the juncture of the Floyd and Missouri rivers "appeared almost clogged with untreated packing plant wastes. Where the water was not red with bloody wastes, it was gray with decomposing organic wastes."

The nation's aquatic wildlife has been finding our inland waters increasingly unbearable. Some months ago, ten thousand scarce canvasback and redhead ducks were destroyed on the Detroit River by the release of untreated sewage. Thousands of dead fish have turned up in the Passaic River, from which several northern New

Jersey communities had been drawing their drinking water. Fish can no longer survive in parts of New Hampshire's Merrimack, once famed for its fishing. Many of the salmon runs of the Northwest are being disrupted by the fact that the fish, in their relentless migrations up to the headwaters of streams, perish in badly polluted stretches of these streams. The Public Health Service reports finding in many parts of the country that fish taken alive from waters downstream from sewer outfalls have been sickly or dwarfed. And it reports finding hundreds of cases of complete fish kills. By "complete," it means that every fish, in stretches of water up to nineteen miles long, has perished.

Drinking water in many areas is not escaping the impact of all the waste in rivers, despite massive chlorination. Oklahoma Senator Robert Kerr states that U.S. cities now tolerate twice as much sewage in their drinking water as was considered safe only a half-dozen years ago. One specific problem which is causing concern is the widespread appearance in drinking water of a sewage-born microscopic worm called the nematode. It appears often to be able to survive ordinary chlorination and gives tap water an earthy, musty odor. U.S. health officials found in one sampling that nematodes turned up in drinking water drawn from thirteen out of fourteen rivers.

Many cities have been indifferent to pleas from downstream neighbors to clean up water before they discharge it back into the river. Selfishly, many have seen no gain to themselves in building expensive sewage treatment plants that only benefit downstream neighbors. When St. Joseph, Missouri, residents turned down a bond issue referendum for a proposed sewage treatment plant, a newspaper hailed the voters for their "pioneering independence" of Washington "bureaucrats" who had been demanding that Saint Joseph stop befouling the Missouri. The U.S. government has since brought suit against the city.

Industrial pollution discharged into the nation's waterways has increased 1,000 percent in this century. Many industrialists maintain that use of rivers for dumping waste is a part of their American heritage and that they should be expected to clean up their discharged water only when it is "economically feasible." The National Association of Manufacturers has often opposed proposals that would permit the federal government to act against pollution of the nation's waterways. It wants decisions left to state and local governments, which tend to be far more responsive to the wishes of local industries.

With the great growth in leisure-time activities, millions of Americans are turning to water sports: fishing, swimming, water skiing, and skin diving. Clean water exhilarates and relaxes. The relentless disappearance of safe beaches and inviting water may well bring about a greatly increased demand for pollution control.

For one thing, there is urgent need to develop more effective treatment techniques, especially in view of the many new, persistent chemicals draining into our waterways. Experts insist we actually have not progressed very much from the water purification methods used by the ancient Romans.

With the fantastic increase in demand for water that is projected for the future, we must keep pollution in check. It seems obvious that all users of public water — municipal and industrial users alike — should be required to return the water they have borrowed in as clean a condition as it was when they diverted it, or at least as clean as technically possible.

A society as prosperous and ambitious as ours should certainly act against the desecraters. Let us start in the schools, if not the homes, to bring up youngsters who will have a decent respect for this land of ours. Let us look to the eyesores in our communities, states, and nation and by our protests to elected officials make a start toward reducing the desecration.

Certainly we can get the junkyards off our scenic highways, especially along the new highways being built. We can oppose the outdoor-billboard lobbyists in the many state capitals which must still take action to protect the new interstate highways from desecration by billboard. The Mexican government, in a burst of political courage, has flatly outlawed billboards as distractions from the picturesque countryside.

Let us also act firmly to protect our beauty spots from the building developers and parking lot entrepreneurs. And let us demand that power lines through scenic areas go underground.

Let us work to bring back a real love for our neighborhoods by seeing that they have the variety of centers for work, play, and contemplation that make them really inviting and distinctive.

And, finally, let us cherish and protect our few remaining areas of unspoiled wilderness, if only as reminders of how we are changing our land. Historian Frederick Jackson Turner made an observation many years ago that might well be pondered today. He said: "The Western wilds, from the Alleghenies to the Pacific, constituted the richest free gift that was ever spread out before civilized man. . . . Never again can such an opportunity come to the sons of men."

Let us not further abuse this opportunity.

The arch of Titus and the ruins of the Coliseum in Rome.

BOOK THREE | PART 1

JULIUS CAESAR

William Shakespeare

About 500 B.C., Rome ceased to be governed by a king and became a republic. Tarquin, a cruel ruler, was forced from his throne by wealthy families of Rome called patricians, who elected from their own class two chief magistrates, or consuls, and a Senate, which made the laws. After a time, the common people, the plebeians, won certain rights in the government and were permitted to select tribunes, representatives to the Senate who had the power to protect the lives and property of the plebeians and to speak for them. Four hundred years later — the time of Julius Caesar — the Senate passed a law permitting the appointment of a dictator during times of crisis.

Julius Caesar was born a patrician, but his early political moves were designed to win the support of the plebeians. In public office he spent money freely on games and amusements for the people and exempted farm workers and tradesmen from heavy taxes. His popularity gave him the power to become one of the ruling triumvirate, a group of three men who governed all of Rome and its provinces. This triumvirate included Crassus, a wealthy patrician, and Pompey, a popular general.

In 62 B.C., Caesar was made governor of the Roman part of Gaul (France), and he soon conquered the rest of Gaul, sending home great sums of money for his soldiers and the people. Soon thereafter, the triumvirate ran into trouble. Crassus was killed in battle, and Pompey, jealous of Caesar's success and popularity, formed an alliance with the senators against Caesar. The Senate ordered Caesar to disband his army, but he defied the order and marched his army across the Rubicon River from Gaul toward Rome. Pompey tried to raise an army, but failed and had to flee to the east with many of the ruling class.

Caesar continued his military conquests, building the great Roman Empire. He returned to Rome in 45 B.C. to receive all the awards a grateful Senate could bestow upon him. He was then absolute dictator with command of all armies, sole control of all public money, and total immunity from the vetoes of the tribunes, who thus became his enemies. On March 15, 44 B.C., Julius Caesar was assassinated by a group of senators.

SHAKESPEARE AND CAESAR

William Shakespeare's tragedy Julius Caesar is the best-known account of the conspiracy against Caesar, his assassination, and its bloody aftermath. Written sixteen centuries after the death of Caesar, the play is not a purely historical account of what happened. It is one of several tragedies Shakespeare wrote which dramatize the inner conflicts of men during times of great calamity. For these plays, Shakespeare borrowed stories from history and retold them with great dramatic skill.

We probably know more about Julius Caesar than we do about William Shakespeare. Shakespeare was born in Stratford, England, in 1564 and must have been educated in the local grammar school, receiving the equivalent of a good high school education. He left

Stratford for London and began to write plays that were popular and highly successful: between 1589 and 1613 he wrote more than thirty tragedies, comedies, and histories. He died on April 23, 1616, and was buried in Stratford.

SHAKESPEAREAN TRAGEDY

In all Shakespeare's tragedies, there is a central figure, a hero who is usually a leader of men. The plays often show the hero at the pinnacle of success, but there are signs that success will not last. The hero is a man of exceptional nature who is accustomed to exercising power; not only is he a leader of men, but he is also a man of great stature and nobility who deserves his power and acclaim. But there is, in his greatness of character, a fundamental flaw or weakness, perhaps a virtue carried to excess.

The struggles of Shakespeare's tragic heroes are often highlighted by supernatural happenings (dreams, visions, ghosts, witches), and almost all his plays involve some crucial chance or accident. Yet in every play the main course of action grows out of the hero's inner struggle. His tragic flaw brings about a widespread calamity that finally engulfs him and results in his downfall and death.

Caesar fulfills many of the requirements of a tragic hero. But, although the play is called Julius Caesar, it is really Brutus, one of the senators who killed Caesar, who is the central figure. He is one of the purest idealists in English literature. The play recounts the inner struggles which spring from Brutus's character and which in the end bring him to both the heights and depths of tragedy.

The death mask of Julius Caesar.

CHARACTERS

JULIUS CAESAR, Rome's greatest general, now dictator

BRUTUS	LIGARIUS	
CASSIUS	DECIUS	conspirators against
CASCA	METELLUS CIMBER	Julius Caesar
TREBONIUS	CINNA	

[handwritten: stab Caesar]

CICERO *[handwritten: Dead]*
PUBLIUS } senators
POPILIUS LENA

[handwritten: – Power structure]

ANTONY, a young general, Caesar's friend
OCTAVIUS CAESAR, Caesar's grandnephew and heir
LEPIDUS, a Roman general
} the triumvirate that ruled Rome after Caesar's death

FLAVIUS
MARULLUS } tribunes of the people

[handwritten: tribun – repr. the people.]

CALPURNIA, Caesar's wife
PORTIA, Brutus's wife *[handwritten: Dead]*

A SOOTHSAYER *[handwritten: – predicts future]*
ARTEMIDORUS, citizen friendly to Caesar
CINNA, a poet *[handwritten: Dead]*
ANOTHER POET

LUCIUS *[CAPTURED]*	VARRO	*[Dead]*
TITINIUS *[△]*	CLITUS	*[Dead]*
MESSALA *[CAPTURED]*	CLAUDIUS	soldiers in Brutus's army
YOUNG CATO *[△]*	STRATO	*[CAP]*
VOLUMNIUS *[CAP]*	DARDANIUS	*[CAP]*

PINDARUS, soldier in Cassius's army *[handwritten: ESCAPED]*
LUCIUS, a boy, Brutus's servant

SENATORS, CITIZENS, GUARDS, ATTENDANTS, etc.

Julius Caesar

ACT I

SCENE I

A street in Rome. It is the Lupercalia, a Roman holiday. JULIUS
CAESAR, *the most powerful Roman general, has recently returned to
Rome in triumph. A group of* COMMONERS *enter, celebrating Caesar's
victories. They are met by* FLAVIUS *and* MARULLUS, *tribunes of the
people, who fear Caesar's popularity.*

FLAVIUS. Hence! Home, you idle creatures, get you home.
  Is this a holiday? What! Know you not,
  Being mechanical,° you ought not walk
  Upon a laboring day without the sign
  Of your profession°? Speak, what trade art thou?   5
FIRST COMMONER. Why, sir, a carpenter.
MARULLUS. Where is thy leather apron and thy rule?
  What dost thou with thy best apparel on?
  You, sir, what trade are you?
SECOND COMMONER. Truly, sir, in respect of a fine workman, I   10
  am but, as you would say, a cobbler.°
MARULLUS. But what trade art thou? Answer me directly.
SECOND COMMONER. A trade, sir, that I hope I may use with a safe
  conscience, which is indeed, sir, a mender of bad soles.
MARULLUS. What trade, thou knave? Thou naughty knave,   15
  what trade?
SECOND COMMONER. Nay, I beseech you, sir, be not out° with me. Yet
  if you be out, sir, I can mend you.
MARULLUS. What mean'st thou by that? Mend me, thou saucy
  fellow!   20
SECOND COMMONER. Why, sir, cobble you.
FLAVIUS. Thou art a cobbler, art thou?

SCENE I. 3. *mechanical:* workmen. 4–5. *sign of your profession:* tools and work
clothes. 11. *cobbler:* a shoemaker (also a bungler, which makes Marullus repeat
his question). Notice the other puns in this scene: *all-awl* and *sole-soul.* 17. *out:*
angry.

SECOND COMMONER. Truly, sir, all that I live by is with the awl. I
  meddle with no tradesman's matters, nor women's matters, but
  with awl. I am indeed, sir, a surgeon to old shoes. When they   25
  are in great danger, I re-cover them. As proper men as ever trod
  upon neat's leather° have gone upon my handiwork.

FLAVIUS. But wherefore art not in thy shop today? Why dost thou
  lead these men about the streets?

SECOND COMMONER. Truly, sir, to wear out their shoes, to get   30
  myself into more work. But indeed, sir, we make holidays, to see
  Caesar and to rejoice his triumph.°

MARULLUS. Wherefore rejoice? What conquest brings he home?
  What tributaries° follow him to Rome,
  To grace in captive bonds his chariot wheels?   35
  You blocks, you stones, you worse than senseless things!
  O you hard hearts, you cruel men of Rome,
  Knew you not Pompey?° Many a time and oft
  Have you climbed up to walls and battlements,
  To towers and windows, yea, to chimney tops,   40
  Your infants in your arms, and there have sat
  The livelong day with patient expectation
  To see great Pompey pass the streets of Rome.
  And when you saw his chariot but appear,
  Have you not made a universal shout,   45
  That Tiber° trembled underneath her banks
  To hear the replication° of your sounds
  Made in her concave shores?
  And do you now put on your best attire?
  And do you now cull out° a holiday?   50
  And do you now strew flowers in his way
  That comes in triumph over Pompey's blood?
  Be gone!
  Run to your houses, fall upon your knees,
  Pray to the gods to intermit° the plague   55
  That needs must light on this ingratitude.

---

27. *neat's leather:* oxhide. 32. *triumph:* over his defeat of Pompey. 34. *tribu-taries:* captives. 38. *Pompey:* another Roman general who had been Caesar's co-ruler and rival. After his death Caesar conquered Pompey's sons, which is why Marullus says that (line 52) Caesar "comes in triumph over Pompey's blood." 46. *Tiber:* the river that flows through Rome. 47. *replication:* echo. 50. *cull out:* choose to take. 55. *intermit:* prevent.

FLAVIUS. Go, go, good countrymen, and for this fault
    Assemble all the poor men of your sort.
    Draw them to Tiber banks and weep your tears
    Into the channel till the lowest stream   60
    Do kiss the most exalted shores of all.

                     [*Exeunt all the* COMMONERS.]
    See whether their basest metal° be not moved.
    They vanish tongue-tied in their guiltiness.
    Go you down that way toward the Capitol,
    This way will I. Disrobe the images°   65
    If you do find them decked with ceremonies.°
MARULLUS. May we do so?
    You know it is the feast of Lupercal.
FLAVIUS. It is no matter. Let no images
    Be hung with Caesar's trophies. I'll about,
    And drive away the vulgar° from the streets.   70
    So do you too, where you perceive them thick.
    These growing feathers plucked from Caesar's wing
    Will make him fly an ordinary pitch,°
    Who else would soar above the view of men   75
    And keep us all in servile fearfulness.   [*Exeunt.*]

SCENE II

A public square. A crowd has gathered to watch the race that takes place on the feast of the Lupercal. Among the crowd is a SOOTH-SAYER. *Flourish of trumpets. Enter* CAESAR, *his wife* CALPURNIA, POR-TIA, DECIUS, CICERO, BRUTUS, CASSIUS, *and* CASCA. ANTONY *is with them "for the course," that is, dressed like an athlete ready to run in the race.*

CAESAR. Calpurnia!
CASCA.   Peace, ho! Caesar speaks.
CAESAR.   [*Music ceases.*]   Calpurnia!
CALPURNIA. Here, my lord.
CAESAR. Stand you directly in Antonius' way

---

62. *metal:* spirit (pun on mettle). 65. *images:* statues of Caesar. 66. *ceremonies:* garlands or wreaths. 71. *vulgar:* the common people. 74. *pitch:* height.

When he doth run his course.° Antonius!

ANTONY. Caesar, my lord?   5

CAESAR. Forget not, in your speed, Antonius,
To touch Calpurnia, for our elders say
The barren, touchèd in this holy chase,
Shake off their sterile curse.°

ANTONY.   I shall remember:
When Caesar says "Do this," it is performed.   10

CAESAR. Set on, and leave no ceremony out.   [*Flourish of trumpets.*]

SOOTHSAYER.° Caesar!

CAESAR. Ha! Who calls?

CASCA. Bid every noise be still — peace yet again!

CAESAR. Who is it in the press° that calls on me?   15
I hear a tongue, shriller than all the music,
Cry "Caesar." Speak. Caesar is turned to hear.

SOOTHSAYER. Beware the ides of March.°

CAESAR.   What man is that?

BRUTUS. A soothsayer bids you beware the ides of March.

CAESAR. Set him before me. Let me see his face.   20

CASSIUS. Fellow, come from the throng. Look upon Caesar.

CAESAR. What say'st thou to me now? Speak once again.

SOOTHSAYER. Beware the ides of March.

CAESAR. He is a dreamer. Let us leave him — pass.

               [*Trumpets sound. Exeunt all but* BRUTUS *and* CASSIUS.]

CASSIUS. Will you go see the order of the course?   25

BRUTUS. Not I.

CASSIUS. I pray you, do.

BRUTUS. I am not gamesome.° I do lack some part
Of that quick spirit that is in Antony.
Let me not hinder, Cassius, your desires.   30
I'll leave you.

CASSIUS. Brutus, I do observe you now of late.
I have not from your eyes that gentleness
And show of love as I was wont to° have.

SCENE II. 4. *course:* race. 7–9. *Calpurnia . . . curse:* The Romans believed that women without children, like Calpurnia, could bear children if touched by a whip of goat's hide carried by a racer during the Lupercalia. 12. *Soothsayer:* one who predicts the future; literally, a truth-sayer. 15. *press:* crowd. 18. *ides of March:* March 15, one month away. 28. *gamesome:* interested in sports. 34. *was wont to:* used to.

You bear° too stubborn and too strange a hand   35
Over your friend that loves you.

BRUTUS.   Cassius,
Be not deceived. If I have veiled my look,
I turn the trouble of my countenance
Merely upon myself. Vexèd I am
Of late with passions of some difference,°   40
Conceptions only proper to myself,
Which give some soil° perhaps to my behaviors.
But let not therefore my good friends be grieved —
Among which number, Cassius, be you one —
Nor construe° any further my neglect   45
Than that poor Brutus, with himself at war,
Forgets the shows of love to other men.

CASSIUS. Then, Brutus, I have much mistook your passion,
By means whereof this breast of mine hath buried
Thoughts of great value, worthy cogitations.   50
Tell me, good Brutus, can you see your face?

BRUTUS. No, Cassius, for the eye sees not itself
But by reflection, by some other things.

CASSIUS. 'Tis just.°
And it is very much lamented, Brutus,   55
That you have no such mirrors as will turn
Your hidden worthiness into your eye,
That you might see your shadow.° I have heard
Where many of the best respect in Rome,
Except immortal° Caesar, speaking of Brutus,   60
And groaning underneath this age's yoke,
Have wished that noble Brutus had his eyes.

BRUTUS. Into what dangers would you lead me, Cassius,
That you would have me seek into myself
For that which is not in me?   65

CASSIUS. Therefore, good Brutus, be prepared to hear.
And since you know you cannot see yourself
So well as by reflection, I your glass°
Will modestly discover to yourself

---

35. *bear:* hold (like reins). 40. *passions of some difference:* conflicting emotions. 42. *soil:* blemish. 45. *construe:* interpret, guess at. 54. *just:* true. 58. *shadow:* reflection. 60. *immortal:* Cassius is sarcastic. 68. *I your glass:* I will be a mirror for you.

That of yourself which you yet know not of.   70
And be not jealous on° me, gentle Brutus.
Were I a common laugher, or did use
To stale° with ordinary oaths my love
To every new protester;° if you know
That I do fawn on men and hug them hard,   75
And after scandal° them; or if you know
That I profess myself in banqueting
To all the rout° — then hold me dangerous.

                        [*Flourish of trumpets and a shout.*]

BRUTUS. What means this shouting? I do fear the people
  Choose Caesar for their king.

CASSIUS.   Aye, do you fear it?   80
  Then must I think you would not have it so.

BRUTUS. I would not, Cassius, yet I love him well.
  But wherefore do you hold me here so long?
  What is it that you would impart to me?
  If it be aught toward the general good,   85
  Set honor in one eye and death i' the other,
  And I will look on both indifferently;
  For let the gods so speed° me as I love
  The name of honor more than I fear death.

CASSIUS. I know that virtue to be in you, Brutus,   90
  As well as I do know your outward favor.°
  Well, honor is the subject of my story.
  I cannot tell what you and other men
  Think of this life, but for my single self
  I had as lief° not be as live to be   95
  In awe of such a thing as I myself.°
  I was born free as Caesar; so were you.
  We both have fed as well, and we can both
  Endure the winter's cold as well as he.
  For once, upon a raw and gusty day,   100
  The troubled Tiber chafing with her shores,
  Caesar said to me "Darest thou, Cassius, now

---

71. *jealous on:* suspicious of. 73. *stale:* make common. 74. *protester:* every newcomer declaring friendship. 76. *scandal:* slander. 77–78. *profess . . . rout:* claim
to be the friend of all the common people at a banquet. 78. *rout:* rabble, crowd.
88. *so speed:* assist. 91. *favor:* appearance. 95. *I had as lief:* I would prefer.
96. *as I myself:* as another mere man.

Leap in with me into this angry flood
And swim to yonder point?" Upon the word,
Accoutered° as I was, I plungèd in   105
And bade him follow. So indeed he did.
The torrent roared, and we did buffet it
With lusty sinews, throwing it aside
And stemming it with hearts of controversy.°
But ere we could arrive the point proposed,   110
Caesar cried, "Help me, Cassius, or I sink!"
I, as Aeneas° our great ancestor
Did from the flames of Troy upon his shoulder
The old Anchises bear, so from the waves of Tiber
Did I the tired Caesar — and this man   115
Is now become a god, and Cassius is
A wretched creature, and must bend his body
If Caesar carelessly but nod on him.
He had a fever when he was in Spain,
And when the fit was on him, I did mark   120
How he did shake. 'Tis true, this god did shake.
His coward lips did from their color fly,
And that same eye whose bend doth awe the world
Did lose his° luster. I did hear him groan.
Aye, and that tongue of his that bade the Romans   125
Mark him and write his speeches in their books,
Alas, it cried, "Give me some drink, Titinius,"
As a sick girl. Yet gods! It doth amaze me
A man of such a feeble temper should
So get the start° of the majestic world   130
And bear the palm° alone.   [Shout. Trumpets.]
BRUTUS. Another general shout!
    I do believe that these applauses are
    For some new honors that are heaped on Caesar.
CASSIUS. Why, man, he doth bestride the narrow world   135
    Like a Colossus,° and we petty men

---

105. *Accoutered:* dressed in armor. 109. *hearts of controversy:* in rivalry.
112. *Aeneas:* the legendary founder of Rome who carried his father, Anchises,
on his back from Troy. 124. *his:* its. 130. *get the start:* become the leader.
131. *palm:* prize. 136. *Colossus:* a gigantic statue. The Colossus of Rhodes, one
of the seven wonders of the ancient world, was so large that ships could sail
between the legs of the statue.

Walk under his huge legs and peep about
To find ourselves dishonorable graves.
Men at some time are masters of their fates.
The fault, dear Brutus, is not in our stars   140
But in ourselves, that we are underlings.
Brutus and Caesar. What should be in that Caesar?
Why should that name be sounded more than yours?
Write them together, yours is as fair a name.
Sound them, it doth become the mouth as well.   145
Weigh them, it is as heavy. Conjure° with 'em,
Brutus will start° a spirit as soon as Caesar.
Now, in the names of all the gods at once,
Upon what meat doth this our Caesar feed
That he is grown so great? Age, thou art shamed!   150
Rome, thou hast lost the breed of noble bloods!
When went there by an age, since the great flood,
But it was famed with more than with one man?
When could they say till now that talked of Rome
That her wide walls encompassed but one man?   155
Now is it Rome indeed, and room° enough,
When there is in it but one only man.
Oh, you and I have heard our fathers say
There was a Brutus° once that would have brooked°
The eternal Devil to keep his state in Rome   160
As easily as a king.
BRUTUS. That you do love me, I am nothing jealous.°
What you would work me to, I have some aim.°
How I have thought of this and of these times,
I shall recount hereafter; for this present,   165
I would not, so with love I might entreat you,
Be any further moved. What you have said
I will consider. What you have to say
I will with patience hear, and find a time
Both meet° to hear and answer such high things.   170
Till then, my noble friend, chew upon this:

---

146. *conjure:* call up spirits. 147. *start:* invoke. 156. *Rome . . . room:* These
words were pronounced alike in Shakespeare's day. 159. *Brutus:* Brutus's ancestor, Lucius Junius Brutus, who helped establish the Republic of Rome by ex-
pelling Tarquin, the last king of Rome. 159. *brooked:* allowed. 162. *jealous:* I
do not doubt. 163. *aim:* idea. 170. *meet:* suitable.

Brutus had rather be a villager
Than to repute himself a son of Rome
Under these hard conditions as this time
Is like to lay upon us.   175

CASSIUS. I am glad that my weak words
   Have struck but thus much show of fire from Brutus.

BRUTUS. The games are done, and Caesar is returning.

CASSIUS. As they pass by, pluck Casca by the sleeve,
   And he will, after his sour fashion, tell you   180
   What hath proceeded worthy note today.

                    [*Enter* CAESAR *and his train.*]

BRUTUS. I will do so. But look you, Cassius,
   The angry spot doth glow on Caesar's brow,
   And all the rest look like a chidden train.°
   Calpurnia's cheek is pale, and Cicero   185
   Looks with such ferret° and such fiery eyes
   As we have seen him in the Capitol,
   Being crossed in conference by some Senators.

CASSIUS. Casca will tell us what the matter is.

CAESAR. Antonius!   190

ANTONY. Caesar?

CAESAR. Let me have men about me that are fat,
   Sleek-headed men, and such as sleep o' nights.
   Yond Cassius has a lean and hungry look.
   He thinks too much. Such men are dangerous.   195

ANTONY. Fear him not, Caesar. He's not dangerous,
   He is a noble Roman, and well given.°

CAESAR. Would he were fatter! But I fear him not.
   Yet if my name were liable to fear,
   I do not know the man I should avoid   200
   So soon as that spare Cassius. He reads much,
   He is a great observer, and he looks
   Quite through the deeds of men. He loves no plays
   As thou dost, Antony; he hears no music.
   Seldom he smiles, and smiles in such a sort   205
   As if he mocked himself, and scorned his spirit
   That could be moved to smile at anything.

---

184. *chidden train:* scolded followers. 186. *ferret:* looks like a ferret, a weasel-like animal with red eyes. 197. *well given:* trustworthy.

Such men as he be never at heart's ease
While they behold a greater than themselves,
And therefore are they very dangerous.   210
I rather tell thee what is to be feared
Than what I fear, for always I am Caesar.
Come on my right hand, for this ear is deaf,
And tell me truly what thou think'st of him.

[*Trumpets. Exeunt* CAESAR *and all his train but* CASCA.]

CASCA. You pulled me by the cloak. Would you speak with me?   215
BRUTUS. Aye, Casca. Tell us what hath chanced today
  That Caesar looks so sad.
CASCA. Why, you were with him, were you not?
BRUTUS. I should not then ask Casca what had chanced.
CASCA. Why, there was a crown offered him; and being offered   220
  him, he put it by with the back of his hand, thus. And then the
  people fell a-shouting.
BRUTUS. What was the second noise for?
CASCA. Why, for that too.
CASSIUS. They shouted thrice. What was the last cry for?   225
CASCA. Why, for that too.
BRUTUS. Was the crown offered him thrice?
CASCA. Aye, marry, was 't,° and he put it by thrice, every time gentler
  than other. And at every putting-by mine honest neighbors
  shouted.   230
CASSIUS. Who offered him the crown?
CASCA. Why, Antony.
BRUTUS. Tell us the manner of it, gentle Casca.
CASCA. I can as well be hanged as tell the manner of it. It was mere
  foolery — I did not mark it. I saw Mark Antony offer him a   235
  crown, yet 'twas not a crown neither, 'twas one of these coronets;°
  and, as I told you, he put it by once. But for all that, to my thinking, he would fain° have had it. Then he offered it to him again,
  then he put it by again. But, to my thinking, he was very loath to
  lay his fingers off it. And then he offered it the third time, he   240
  put it the third time by. And still as he refused it the rabblement
  hooted and clapped their chopped° hands and threw up their
  sweaty nightcaps° and uttered such a deal of stinking breath be-

---

228. *marry, was 't:* indeed it was. 236. *coronets:* small crowns wreathed with
laurel. 238. *fain:* gladly. 242. *chopped:* rough from work. 243. *nightcaps:* caps
that only commoners would wear.

cause Caesar refused the crown that it had almost choked Caesar; for he swounded° and fell down at it. And for mine own   245 part, I durst not laugh, for fear of opening my lips and receiving the bad air.

CASSIUS. But soft, I pray you. What, did Caesar swound?

CASCA. He fell down in the market place and foamed at mouth and was speechless.   250

BRUTUS. 'Tis very like — he hath the falling sickness.°

CASSIUS. No, Caesar hath it not. But you, and I,
And honest Casca, we have the falling sickness.

CASCA. I know not what you mean by that, but I am sure Caesar fell down. If the tagrag people did not clap him and hiss him   255 according as he pleased and displeased them, as they use to do the players in the theater, I am no true man.

BRUTUS. What said he when he came unto himself?

CASCA. Marry, before he fell down, when he perceived the common herd was glad he refused the crown, he plucked me ope° his   260 doublet and offered them his throat to cut. An I had been a man of any occupation,° if I would not have taken him at a word, I would I might go to Hell among the rogues. And so he fell. When he came to himself again, he said if he had done or said anything amiss, he desired their worships° to think it was his infirmity.   265 Three or four wenches where I stood cried, "Alas, good soul!" and forgave him with all their hearts: but there's no heed to be taken of them. If Caesar had stabbed their mothers, they would have done no less.

BRUTUS. And after that, he came, thus sad, away?   270

CASCA. Aye.

CASSIUS. Did Cicero say anything?

CASCA. Aye, he spoke Greek.

CASSIUS. To what effect?

CASCA. Nay, an I tell you that, I'll ne'er look you i' the face   275 again. But those that understood him smiled at one another and shook their heads — but for mine own part, it was Greek to me. I could tell you more news too. Marullus and Flavius, for pulling scarfs° off Caesar's images, are put to silence.° Fare you well.

---

245. *swounded:* fainted. 251. *falling sickness:* epilepsy. 260. *plucked me ope:* opened. 262. *occupation:* enterprise. 265. *their worships:* Casca is making fun of the way in which Caesar kowtows to the common people. 279. *scarfs:* decorations. 279. *put to silence:* imprisoned.

There was more foolery yet, if I could remember it.   280
CASSIUS. Will you sup with me tonight, Casca?
CASCA. No, I am promised forth.
CASSIUS. Will you dine with me tomorrow?
CASCA. Aye, if I be alive, and your mind hold, and your dinner worth
    the eating.   285
CASSIUS. Good. I will expect you.   [*Exit.*]
BRUTUS. What a blunt fellow is this grown to be!
    He was quick mettle° when he went to school.
CASSIUS. So is he now in execution
    Of any bold or noble enterprise,   290
    However he puts on this tardy form.°
    This rudeness is a sauce to his good wit,
    Which gives me stomach to digest his words
    With better appetite.
BRUTUS. And so it is. For this time I will leave you.   295
    Tomorrow, if you please to speak with me,
    I will come home to you, or, if you will,
    Come home to me and I will wait for you,
CASSIUS. I will do so. Till then, think of the world.   [*Exit* BRUTUS.]
    Well, Brutus, thou art noble. Yet I see   300
    Thy honorable mettle may be wrought
    From that it is disposed.° Therefore it is meet
    That noble minds keep ever with their likes,
    For who so firm that cannot be seduced?
    Caesar doth bear me hard,° but he loves Brutus.   305
    If I were Brutus now and he were Cassius,
    He should not humor° me. I will this night,
    In several hands,° in at his windows throw,
    As if they came from several citizens,
    Writings, all tending to the great opinion   310
    That Rome holds of his name, wherein obscurely
    Caesar's ambition shall be glancèd at.
    And after this let Caesar seat him sure,°
    For we will shake him, or worse days endure.   [*Exit.*]

---

288. *quick mettle:* quick spirited, keen. 291. *tardy form:* appearance of slowness. 302. *that it is disposed:* its natural inclination. 305. *bear me hard:* holds a
grudge. 307. *humor:* influence. 308. *in several hands:* in different kinds of handwriting. 313. *seat him sure:* make himself secure.

SCENE III

About a month later, the night before the Ides of March. A street
in Rome. Thunder and lightning. Meeting in the street are CASCA,
with his sword drawn, and CICERO.

CICERO. Good even, Casca. Brought you Caesar home?
    Why are you breathless? And why stare you so?
CASCA. Are not you moved, when all the sway of earth°
    Shakes like a thing unfirm? O Cicero,
    I have seen tempests when the scolding winds   5
    Have rived° the knotty oaks, and I have seen
    The ambitious ocean swell and rage and foam,
    To be exalted with° the threatening clouds.
    But never till tonight, never till now,
    Did I go through a tempest dropping fire.°   10
    Either there is a civil strife in Heaven,
    Or else the world, too saucy with the gods,
    Incenses them to send destruction.
CICERO. Why, saw you anything more wonderful?
CASCA. A common slave — you know him well by sight —   15
    Held up his left hand, which did flame and burn
    Like twenty torches joined, and yet his hand,
    Not sensible of° fire, remained unscorched.
    Besides — I ha' not since put up my sword —
    Against the Capitol I met a lion,   20
    Who glazed° upon me and went surly by
    Without annoying me. And there were drawn
    Upon a heap° a hundred ghastly women
    Transformèd with their fear, who swore they saw
    Men all in fire walk up and down the streets.   25
    And yesterday the bird of night° did sit
    Even at noonday upon the market place,
    Hooting and shrieking. When these prodigies°
    Do so conjointly meet, let not men say
    "These are their reasons, they are natural."   30

SCENE III. 3. *sway of earth:* the world. 6. *rived:* split. 8. *exalted with:* raised as
high as. 10. *fire:* the fiery skies and the other unnatural events Casca describes
are omens of the chaos about to erupt in Rome. 18. *not sensible of:* did not
feel. 21. *glazed:* glared. 22–23. *drawn upon a heap:* huddled together. 26. *bird
of night:* the owl, a bird of ill omen. 28. *prodigies:* extraordinary events.

For I believe they are portentous things
Unto the climate that they point upon.°
CICERO. Indeed, it is a strange-disposèd time.
But men may construe things after their fashion,
Clean from the purpose° of the things themselves.   35
Comes Caesar to the Capitol tomorrow?
CASCA. He doth, for he did bid Antonius
Send word to you he would be there tomorrow.
CICERO. Good night then, Casca. This disturbèd sky
Is not to walk in.
CASCA.   Farewell, Cicero. [*Exit* CICERO. *Enter* CASSIUS.]   40
CASSIUS. Who's there?
CASCA.   A Roman.
CASSIUS.   Casca, by your voice.
CASCA. Your ear is good. Cassius, what night is this!
CASSIUS. A very pleasing night to honest men.
CASCA. Who ever knew the heavens menace so?
CASSIUS. Those that have known the earth so full of faults.   45
For my part, I have walked about the streets,
Submitting me unto the perilous night,
And thus unbraced,° Casca, as you see,
Have bared my bosom to the thunder stone.°
And when the cross° blue lightning seemed to open   50
The breast of Heaven, I did present myself
Even in the aim and very flash of it.
CASCA. But wherefore did you so much tempt the heavens?
It is the part of men to fear and tremble
When the most mighty gods by tokens send   55
Such dreadful heralds to astonish us.
CASSIUS. You are dull, Casca, and those sparks of life
That should be in a Roman you do want,°
Or else you use not. You look pale and gaze
And put on fear and cast yourself in wonder,   60
To see the strange impatience of the heavens.
But if you would consider the true cause
Why all these fires, why all these gliding ghosts,

31–32. *portentous . . . upon:* these are omens of disaster. 35. *Clean from the purpose:* opposite to the real meaning. 48. *unbraced:* with his doublet untied and opened. 49. *thunder stone:* thunderbolt. 50. *cross:* zig-zag. 58. *want:* lack.

Why birds and beasts from quality and kind,°
Why old men fool and children calculate,°   65
Why all these things change from their ordinance,°
Their natures and preformèd faculties,
To monstrous quality, why, you shall find
That Heaven hath infused them with these spirits
To make them instruments of fear and warning   70
Unto some monstrous state.
Now could I, Casca, name to thee a man
Most like this dreadful night
That thunders, lightens, opens graves, and roars
As doth the lion in the Capitol —   75
A man no mightier than thyself or me
In personal action, yet prodigious grown°
And fearful, as these strange eruptions are.

CASCA. 'Tis Caesar that you mean, is it not, Cassius?

CASSIUS. Let it be who it is. For Romans now   80
Have thews° and limbs like to their ancestors.
But, woe the while!° our fathers' minds are dead,
And we are governed with our mothers' spirits,
Our yoke and sufferance° show us womanish.

CASCA. Indeed they say the Senators tomorrow   85
Mean to establish Caesar as a king,
And he shall wear his crown by sea and land
In every place save here in Italy.

CASSIUS. I know where I will wear this dagger then;
Cassius from bondage will deliver Cassius.   90
Therein, ye gods, you make the weak most strong.
Therein, ye gods, you tyrants do defeat.
Nor stony tower, nor walls of beaten brass,
Nor airless dungeon, nor strong links of iron,
Can be retentive to the strength of spirit;   95
But life, being weary of these worldly bars,
Never lacks power to dismiss itself.
If I know this, know all the world besides,
That part of tyranny that I do bear

---

64. *from quality and kind:* acting contrary to their natures. 65. *calculate:* make
prophecies. 66. *ordinance:* natural order. 77. *prodigious grown:* alarming in his
growth. 81. *thews:* sinews (strength). 82. *woe the while:* alas for these times.
84. *yoke and sufferance:* meek submission.

I can shake off at pleasure.°   [*Thunder still.*]

CASCA.   So can I.   100

So every bondman° in his own hand bears
The power to cancel his captivity.

CASSIUS. And why should Caesar be a tyrant, then?
Poor man! I know he would not be a wolf
But that he sees the Romans are but sheep.   105
He were no lion were not Romans hinds.°
Those that with haste will make a mighty fire
Begin it with weak straws. What trash is Rome,
What rubbish and what offal,° when it serves
For the base matter to illuminate   110
So vile a thing as Caesar! But, O Grief,
Where hast thou led me? I perhaps speak this
Before a willing bondman; then I know
My answer must be made. But I am armed,
And dangers are to me indifferent.   115

CASCA. You speak to Casca, and to such a man
That is no fleering° telltale. Hold, my hand
Be factious for redress° of all these griefs,
And I will set this foot of mine as far
As who goes farthest.

CASSIUS.   There's a bargain made.   120
Now know you, Casca, I have moved already
Some certain of the noblest-minded Romans
To undergo with me an enterprise
Of honorable-dangerous consequence.
And I do know, by this they stay for me   125
In Pompey's porch;° for now, this fearful night,
There is no stir or walking in the streets,
And the complexion of the element°
Is favored like° the work we have in hand,
Most bloody, fiery, and most terrible.   [*Enter* CINNA.]   130

CASCA. Stand close° awhile, for here comes one in haste.

---

100. In this speech, Cassius boasts that as long as he has the freedom to kill himself he will never submit to a tyrant. 101. *bondman:* slave. 106. *hinds:* female deer. 109. *offal:* garbage. 117. *fleering:* sneering. 118. *factious for redress:* active in setting things right. 126. *Pompey's porch:* the covered entrance to the theater built by Pompey. 128. *complexion of the element:* appearance of the sky. 129. *Is favored like:* looks like. 131. *close:* concealed.

CASSIUS. 'Tis Cinna, I do know him by his gait —
　He is a friend. Cinna, where haste you so?
CINNA. To find out you. Who's that? Metellus Cimber?
CASSIUS. No, it is Casca, one incorporate   135
　To our attempts.° Am I not stayed for,° Cinna?
CINNA. I am glad on 't. What a fearful night is this!
　There's two or three of us have seen strange sights.
CASSIUS. Am I not stayed for? Tell me.
CINNA.   Yes, you are.
　O Cassius, if you could   140
　But win the noble Brutus to our party ——
CASSIUS. Be you content. Good Cinna, take this paper,
　And look you lay it in the praetor's chair,°
　Where Brutus may but find it, and throw this
　In at his window; set this up with wax   145
　Upon old Brutus'° statue. All this done,
　Repair to Pompey's porch, where you shall find us.
　Is Decius Brutus and Trebonius there?
CINNA. All but Metellus Cimber, and he's gone
　To seek you at your house. Well, I will hie,°   150
　And so bestow these papers as you bade me.
CASSIUS. That done, repair to Pompey's theater.   [Exit CINNA.]
　Come, Casca, you and I will yet ere day
　See Brutus at his house. Three parts of him
　Is ours already, and the man entire   155
　Upon the next encounter yields him ours.
CASCA. Oh, he sits high in all the people's hearts,
　And that which would appear offense in us,
　His countenance, like richest alchemy,°
　Will change to virtue and to worthiness.°   160
CASSIUS. Him and his worth and our great need of him
　You have right well conceited.° Let us go,
　For it is after midnight, and ere day
　We will awake him and be sure of him.   [Exeunt.]

135–36. *incorporate to our attempts*: part of our conspiracy. 136. *stayed for*:
waited for. 143. *praetor's chair*: the official chair of the praetor, the high office
Brutus held. 146. *old Brutus*: Brutus's ancestor, founder of the Republic.
150. *hie*: hurry. 159. *alchemy*: ancient pseudo-science which tried to change
common metal to gold. 160. *worthiness*: Casca says that without Brutus the
conspirators will look like villains; with him, like patriots. 162. *conceited*: understood.

ACT II

SCENE I

BRUTUS's *house.* BRUTUS *is discovered in his orchard.*

BRUTUS. What, Lucius, ho!
  I cannot, by the progress of the stars,
  Give guess how near to day. Lucius, I say!
  I would it were my fault to sleep so soundly.
  When, Lucius, when? Awake, I say! What, Lucius!   5
                          [*Enter* LUCIUS.]

LUCIUS. Called you, my lord?
BRUTUS. Get me a taper° in my study, Lucius.
  When it is lighted, come and call me here.
LUCIUS. I will, my lord.   [*Exit.*]
BRUTUS. It must be by his° death and for my part   10
  I know no personal cause to spurn at him,
  But for the general.° He would be crowned.
  How that might change his nature, there's the question.
  It is the bright day that brings forth the adder,
  And that craves wary walking. Crown him? — That —   15
  And then, I grant, we put a sting in him,
  That at his will he may do danger with.
  The abuse of greatness is when it disjoins
  Remorse from power; and to speak truth of Caesar,
  I have not known when his affections swayed   20
  More than his reason.° But 'tis a common proof°
  That lowliness is young ambition's ladder,
  Whereto the climber-upward turns his face.
  But when he once attains the upmost round,°
  He then unto the ladder turns his back,   25
  Looks in the clouds, scorning the base degrees
  By which he did ascend. So Caesar may.
  Then, lest he may, prevent. And since the quarrel

SCENE I. 7. *taper:* candle. 10. *his:* Caesar's. 12. *general:* public good. 20–21. *I have . . . reason:* I have not known him to act from emotion rather than reason. 21. *proof:* truth. 24. *round:* rung.

Will bear no color for the thing he is,°
Fashion it thus: that what he is, augmented,°   30
Would run to these and these extremities.
And therefore think him as a serpent's egg
Which hatched would as his kind grow mischievous,
And kill him in the shell.   [*Enter* LUCIUS.]
LUCIUS. The taper burneth in your closet,° sir.   35
Searching the window for a flint, I found
This paper thus sealed up, and I am sure
It did not lie there when I went to bed.   [*Gives him the letter.*]
BRUTUS. Get you to bed again. It is not day.
Is not tomorrow, boy, the ides of March?   40
LUCIUS. I know not, sir.
BRUTUS. Look in the calendar and bring me word.
LUCIUS. I will, sir.   [*Exit.*]
BRUTUS. The exhalations° whizzing in the air
Give so much light that I may read by them.   45
          [*Reads the letter.*]
Brutus, thou sleep'st. Awake and see thyself.
Shall Rome, etc. Speak, strike, redress.
Brutus, thou sleep'st. Awake.
Such instigations° have been often dropped
Where I have took them up.   50
Shall Rome, etc. Thus must I piece it out:
Shall Rome stand under one man's awe? What, Rome?
My ancestors did from the streets of Rome
The Tarquin drive, when he was called a king.
Speak, strike, redress. Am I entreated   55
To speak and strike? O Rome, I make thee promise,
If the redress will follow, thou receivest
Thy full petition at the hand of Brutus!   [*Enter* LUCIUS.]
LUCIUS. Sir, March is wasted fifteen days.   [*Knocking within.*°]
BRUTUS. 'Tis good. Go to the gate. Somebody knocks.   60
          [*Exit* LUCIUS.]
Since Cassius first did whet me against Caesar
I have not slept.

28–29. *since the quarrel . . . thing he is:* the reason for killing Caesar will not
seem justified measured by what he is *now.* 30. *augmented:* made greater.
35. *closet:* room. 44. *exhalations:* meteors. 49. *instigations:* urgings. 59. *within:*
backstage (a direction for the stage manager).

Between the acting of a dreadful thing
And the first motion,° all the interim is
Like a phantasma° or a hideous dream.   65
The Genius and the mortal instruments
Are then in council, and the state of man,
Like to a little kingdom, suffers then
The nature of an insurrection.°   [Enter LUCIUS.]

LUCIUS. Sir, 'tis your brother° Cassius at the door,   70
  Who doth desire to see you.

BRUTUS.   Is he alone?

LUCIUS. No, sir, there are moe° with him.

BRUTUS.   Do you know them?

LUCIUS. No, sir. Their hats are plucked about their ears,
  And half their faces buried in their cloaks,
  That by no means I may discover them   75
  By any mark of favor.°

BRUTUS.   Let 'em enter.   [Exit LUCIUS.]
  They are the faction. O Conspiracy,
  Shamest thou to show thy dangerous brow by night,
  When evils are most free? Oh, then by day
  Where wilt thou find a cavern dark enough   80
  To mask thy monstrous visage? Seek none, Conspiracy —
  Hide it in smiles and affability.
  For if thou put thy native semblance° on,
  Not Erebus° itself were dim enough
  To hide thee from prevention.°   85

[Enter CASSIUS, CASCA, DECIUS, CINNA, METELLUS CIMBER, and
  TREBONIUS.]

CASSIUS. I think we are too bold upon your rest.
  Good morrow, Brutus. Do we trouble you?

BRUTUS. I have been up this hour, awake all night.
  Know I these men that come along with you?

CASSIUS. Yes, every man of them, and no man here   90
  But honors you, and every one doth wish
  You had but that opinion of yourself

---

64. *motion:* thought. 65. *phantasma:* horrible illusion. 66–69. *Genius . . . in-*
surrection: the mind and body are like a kingdom in civil war. 70. *brother:*
brother-in-law. Cassius married Brutus's sister. 73. *moe:* more. 76. *mark of*
favor: feature. 83. *native semblance:* natural appearance. 84. *Erebus:* the dark
path to Hades, the underworld. 85. *prevention:* being discovered and stopped.

Which every noble Roman bears of you.
This is Trebonius.

BRUTUS.   He is welcome hither.

CASSIUS. This, Decius Brutus.

BRUTUS.   He is welcome too.   95

CASSIUS. This, Casca, this, Cinna, and this, Metellus Cimber.

BRUTUS. They are all welcome.
What watchful cares do interpose themselves
Betwixt your eyes and night?°

CASSIUS. Shall I entreat a word?   100

                       [CASSIUS *and* BRUTUS *whisper together.*]

DECIUS. Here lies the east. Doth not the day break here?

CASCA. No.

CINNA. Oh, pardon, sir, it doth, and yon gray lines
That fret° the clouds are messengers of day.

CASCA. You shall confess that you are both deceived.   105
Here, as I point my sword, the sun arises,
Which is a great way growing on the south,
Weighing the youthful season of the year.
Some two months hence up higher toward the north
He first presents his fire, and the high east   110
Stands as the Capitol, directly here.

                     [BRUTUS *and* CASSIUS *rejoin the others.*]

BRUTUS. Give me your hands all over, one by one.°

CASSIUS. And let us swear our resolution.

BRUTUS. No, not an oath. If not the face of men,
The sufferance of our souls, the time's abuse —   115
If these be motives weak, break off betimes,°
And every man hence to his idle bed.
So let high-sighted° tyranny range on
Till each man drop by lottery.° But if these,
As I am sure they do, bear fire enough   120
To kindle cowards and to steel with valor
The melting spirits of women, then, countrymen,
What need we any spur but our own cause
To prick us to redress? What other bond

98–99. *interpose . . . night:* keep you up. 104. *fret:* lace. 112. Brutus has been told of the conspiracy and now offers his hand to pledge his support. 116. *betimes:* right now. 118. *high-sighted:* with proud looks. 119. *lottery:* random chance.

Than secret Romans that have spoke the word, 125
And will not palter?° And what other oath
Than honesty to honesty engaged
That this shall be or we will fall for it?
Swear priests and cowards and men cautelous,°
Old feeble carrions° and such suffering souls 130
That welcome wrongs; unto bad causes swear
Such creatures as men doubt; but do not stain
The even virtue of our enterprise,
Nor the insuppressive mettle of our spirits,
To think that or° our cause or our performance 135
Did need an oath when every drop of blood
That every Roman bears, and nobly bears,
Is guilty of a several bastardy°
If he do break the smallest particle
Of any promise that hath passed from him. 140

CASSIUS. But what of Cicero? Shall we sound him?
I think he will stand very strong with us.

CASCA. Let us not leave him out.

CINNA.   No, by no means.

METELLUS. Oh, let us have him, for his silver hairs
Will purchase us a good opinion, 145
And buy men's voices to commend our deeds.
It shall be said his judgment ruled our hands.
Our youths and wildness shall no whit appear,
But all be buried in his gravity.

BRUTUS. Oh, name him not. Let us not break with him, 150
For he will never follow anything
That other men begin.

CASSIUS.   Then leave him out.

CASCA. Indeed he is not fit.

DECIUS. Shall no man else be touched but only Caesar?

CASSIUS. Decius, well urged. I think it is not meet° 155
Mark Antony, so well beloved of Caesar,
Should outlive Caesar. We shall find of him
A shrewd contriver;° and you know his means,

---

126. *palter:* play false, cheat. 129. *cautelous:* crafty. 130. *carrions:* dead bodies, those of men without spirits. 135. *or:* either. 138. *several bastardy:* separate betrayal. 155. *meet:* right. 158. *contriver:* plotter.

If he improve them, may well stretch so far
As to annoy° us all. Which to prevent,   160
Let Antony and Caesar fall together.

BRUTUS. Our course will seem too bloody, Caius Cassius,
To cut the head off and then hack the limbs,
Like wrath in death and envy° afterward.
For Antony is but a limb of Caesar.   165
Let us be sacrificers, but not butchers, Caius.
We all stand up against the spirit of Caesar,
And in the spirit of men there is no blood.
Oh, that we then could come by Caesar's spirit,
And not dismember Caesar! But, alas,   170
Caesar must bleed for it! And, gentle friends,
Let's kill him boldly, but not wrathfully.
Let's carve him as a dish fit for the gods,
Not hew him as a carcass fit for hounds.
And let our hearts, as subtle masters do,   175
Stir up their servants to an act of rage
And after seem to chide 'em. This shall make
Our purpose necessary and not envious,
Which so appearing to the common eyes,
We shall be called purgers,° not murderers.   180
And for Mark Antony, think not of him,
For he can do no more than Caesar's arm
When Caesar's head is off.

CASSIUS.   Yet I fear him,
For in the ingrafted° love he bears to Caesar——

BRUTUS. Alas, good Cassius, do not think of him.   185
If he love Caesar, all that he can do
Is to himself, take thought and die for Caesar.
And that were much he should, for he is given
To sports, to wildness and much company.

TREBONIUS. There is no fear° in him. Let him not die,   190
For he will live and laugh at this hereafter.   [Clock strikes.]

BRUTUS. Peace! Count the clock.

CASSIUS.   The clock hath stricken three.

TREBONIUS. 'Tis time to part.

---

160. *annoy:* harm. 164. *envy:* hatred. 180. *purgers:* removers of evil. 184. *ingrafted:* deeply rooted. 190. *no fear:* nothing to fear.

CASSIUS.   But it is doubtful yet
   Whether Caesar will come forth today or no,
   For he is superstitious grown of late,   195
   Quite from the main opinion he held once
   Of fantasy, of dreams and ceremonies.°
   It may be these apparent prodigies,
   The unaccustomed terror of this night
   And the persuasion of his augurers,°   200
   May hold him from the Capitol today.
DECIUS. Never fear that. If he be so resolved,
   I can o'ersway him. For he loves to hear
   That unicorns may be betrayed with trees
   And bears with glasses, elephants with holes,   205
   Lions with toils° and men with flatterers —
   But when I tell him he hates flatterers,
   He says he does, being then most flattered.
   Let me work,
   For I can give his humor the true bent,°   210
   And I will bring him to the Capitol.
CASSIUS. Nay, we will all of us be there to fetch him.
BRUTUS. By the eighth hour. Is that the uttermost?°
CINNA. Be that the uttermost, and fail not then.
METELLUS. Caius Ligarius doth bear Caesar hard,   215
   Who rated° him for speaking well of Pompey.
   I wonder none of you have thought of him.
BRUTUS. Now, good Metellus, go along by him.
   He loves me well, and I have given him reasons.
   Send him but hither and I'll fashion him.   220
CASSIUS. The morning comes upon 's. We'll leave you, Brutus.
   And friends, disperse yourselves, but all remember
   What you have said, and show yourselves true Romans.
BRUTUS. Good gentlemen, look fresh and merrily.
   Let not our looks put on our purposes,   225
   But bear it as our Roman actors do,
   With untired spirits and formal constancy.°

---

197. *ceremonies:* signs. 200. *augurers:* priests who make prophecies.
204–06. *unicorns . . . toils:* various methods of trapping animals. 210. *can
. . . bent:* control his mood. 213. *uttermost:* latest. 216. *rated:* rebuked.
227. *constancy:* calm appearance.

And so, good morrow to you every one.   [*Exeunt all but* BRUTUS.]
Boy! Lucius! Fast asleep! It is no matter.
Enjoy the honey-heavy dew of slumber.   230
Thou hast no figures nor no fantasies°
Which busy care draws in the brains of men,
Therefore thou sleep'st so sound.   [*Enter* PORTIA.]
PORTIA.   Brutus, my lord!
BRUTUS. Portia, what mean you? Wherefore rise you now?
It is not for your health thus to commit   235
Your weak condition to the raw cold morning.
PORTIA. Nor for yours neither. You've ungently, Brutus,
Stole from my bed. And yesternight at supper
You suddenly arose and walked about,
Musing and sighing, with your arms across.   240
And when I asked you what the matter was,
You stared upon me with ungentle looks.
I urged you further, then you scratched your head,
And too impatiently stamped with your foot.
Yet I insisted, yet you answered not,   245
But with an angry wafture° of your hand
Gave sign for me to leave you. So I did,
Fearing to strengthen that impatience
Which seemed too much enkindled, and withal°
Hoping it was but an effect of humor,°   250
Which sometime hath his hour with every man.
It will not let you eat, nor talk, nor sleep,
And, could it work so much upon your shape
As it hath much prevailed on your condition,
I should not know you, Brutus. Dear my lord,   255
Make me acquainted with your cause of grief.
BRUTUS. I am not well in health, and that is all.
PORTIA. Brutus is wise, and were he not in health,
He would embrace the means to come by it.
BRUTUS. Why, so I do. Good Portia, go to bed.   260
PORTIA. Is Brutus sick, and is it physical°
To walk unbraced and suck up the humors°

---

231. *figures nor no fantasies:* visions or dreams. 246. *wafture:* wave. 249. *withal:*
moreover. 250. *humor:* mood. 261. *physical:* healthy. 262. *humors:* vapors of
the night, believed to be unhealthy.

Of the dank morning? What, is Brutus sick,
And will he steal out of his wholesome bed
To dare the vile contagion of the night,   265
And tempt the rheumy° and upurgèd air
To add unto his sickness? No, my Brutus;
You have some sick offense within your mind,
Which by the right and virtue of my place
I ought to know of. And, upon my knees,   270
I charm you, by my once commended beauty,
By all your vows of love and that great vow
Which did incorporate and make us one,
That you unfold to me, yourself, your half,
Why you are heavy, and what men tonight   275
Have had resort to you; for here have been
Some six or seven who did hide their faces
Even from darkness.

BRUTUS.   Kneel not, gentle Portia.

PORTIA. I should not need if you were gentle Brutus.
Within the bond of marriage, tell me, Brutus,   280
Is it excepted I should know no secrets
That appertain to you? Am I yourself°
But, as it were, in sort or limitation,
To keep with you at meals, comfort your bed,
And talk to you sometimes? Dwell I but in the suburbs   285
Of your good pleasure? If it be no more,
Portia is Brutus' harlot, not his wife.

BRUTUS. You are my true and honorable wife,
As dear to me as are the ruddy drops°
That visit my sad heart.   290

PORTIA. If this were true, then should I know this secret.
I grant I am a woman, but withal
A woman that Lord Brutus took to wife.
I grant I am a woman, but withal
A woman well reputed, Cato's daughter.°   295
Think you I am no stronger than my sex,
Being so fathered and so husbanded?

---

266. *rheumy:* moist. 282. *yourself:* your other half through marriage.
289. *drops:* blood. 295. *Cato's daughter:* Cato opposed Caesar and sided with
Pompey; he killed himself after Pompey was defeated.

Tell me your counsels, I will not disclose 'em.
I have made strong proof of my constancy,
Giving myself a voluntary wound   300
Here in the thigh.° Can I bear that with patience
And not my husband's secrets?

BRUTUS.   O ye gods,
Render me worthy of this noble wife!   [*Knocking within.*]
Hark, hark! One knocks. Portia, go in a while,
And by and by thy bosom shall partake   305
The secrets of my heart.
All my engagements I will construe° to thee,
All the charactery of my sad brows.°
Leave me with haste. [*Exit* PORTIA.] Lucius, who's that knocks?

                        [*Enter* LUCIUS *with* LIGARIUS.]

LUCIUS. Here is a sick man that would speak with you.   310
BRUTUS. Caius Ligarius, that Metellus spake of.
   Boy, stand aside. Caius Ligarius! How?
LIGARIUS. Vouchsafe° good morrow from a feeble tongue.
BRUTUS. Oh, what a time have you chose out, brave Caius,
   To wear a kerchief!° Would you were not sick!   315
LIGARIUS. I am not sick if Brutus have in hand
   Any exploit worthy the name of honor.
BRUTUS. Such an exploit have I in hand, Ligarius,
   Had you a healthful ear to hear of it.
LIGARIUS. By all the gods that Romans bow before,   320
   I here discard my sickness! Soul of Rome!
   Brave son, derived from honorable loins!
   Thou, like an exorcist,° has conjured up
   My mortified° spirit. Now bid me run,
   And I will strive with things impossible,   325
   Yea, get the better of them. What's to do?
BRUTUS. A piece of work that will make sick men whole.
LIGARIUS. But are not some whole that we must make sick?
BRUTUS. That must we also. What it is, my Caius,
   I shall unfold to thee as we are going   330

─────────────

299–301. *proof . . . thigh:* Plutarch describes how Portia tested her own courage by deeply slashing her thigh. 307. *construe:* explain. 308. *charactery of my
sad brows:* lines written in my face. 313. *Vouchsafe:* please accept. 315. *kerchief:*
muffler worn by the sick. 323. *exorcist:* one who drives out the spirits of the
dead. 324. *mortified:* dead.

To whom it must be done.

LIGARIUS.   Set on your foot,
And with a heart new-fired I follow you,
To do I know not what, but it sufficeth
That Brutus leads me on.

BRUTUS.   Follow me, then.   [*Exeunt.*]

SCENE II

CAESAR's *house in* Rome. *Thunder and lightning. Enter* CAESAR *in his nightgown.*

CAESAR. Nor Heaven nor earth have been at peace tonight.
    Thrice hath Calpurnia in her sleep cried out,
    "Help, ho! They murder Caesar!" Who's within?
                                        [*Enter a* SERVANT.]

SERVANT. My lord?
CAESAR. Go bid the priests do present° sacrifice,   5
    And bring me their opinions of success.

SERVANT. I will, my lord.   [*Exit. Enter* CALPURNIA.]

CALPURNIA. What mean you, Caesar? Think you to walk forth?
    You shall not stir out of your house today.

CAESAR. Caesar shall forth. The things that threatened me   10
    Ne'er looked but on my back. When they shall see
    The face of Caesar, they are vanishèd.

CALPURNIA. Caesar, I never stood on ceremonies,°
    Yet now they fright me. There is one within,
    Besides the things that we have heard and seen,   15
    Recounts most horrid sights seen by the watch.°
    A lioness hath whelpèd° in the streets.
    And graves have yawned and yielded up their dead.
    Fierce fiery warriors fight upon the clouds,
    In ranks and squadrons and right form of war,   20
    Which drizzled blood upon the Capitol.
    The noise of battle hurtled in the air,
    Horses did neigh and dying men did groan,
    And ghosts did shriek and squeal about the streets.

SCENE II. 5. *present:* now. 13. *stood on ceremonies:* put faith in omens.
16. *watch:* watchmen. 17. *whelpèd:* given birth.

O Caesar! these things are beyond all use,°   25
And I do fear them.

CAESAR.   What can be avoided
Whose end is purposed by the mighty gods?
Yet Caesar shall go forth, for these predictions
Are to the world in general as to Caesar.

CALPURNIA. When beggars die, there are no comets seen.   30
The heavens themselves blaze forth the death of princes.

CAESAR. Cowards die many times before their deaths,
The valiant never taste of death but once.
Of all the wonders that I yet have heard,
It seems to me most strange that men should fear,   35
Seeing that death, a necessary end,
Will come when it will come.   [*Enter* SERVANT.]
                What say the augurers?

SERVANT. They would not have you to stir forth today.
Plucking the entrails of an offering forth,
They could not find a heart within the beast.°   40

CAESAR. The gods do this in shame of cowardice.
Caesar should be a beast without a heart
If he should stay at home today for fear.
No, Caesar shall not. Danger knows full well
That Caesar is more dangerous than he,   45
We are two lions littered in one day,
And I the elder and more terrible.
And Caesar shall go forth.

CALPURNIA.   Alas, my lord,
Your wisdom is consumed in confidence.°
Do not go forth today. Call it my fear   50
That keeps you in the house, and not your own.
We'll send Mark Antony to the Senate House,
And he shall say you are not well today.
Let me, upon my knee, prevail in this.

CAESAR. Mark Antony shall say I am not well,   55
And, for thy humor,° I will stay at home.   [*Enter* DECIUS.]
Here's Decius Brutus. He shall tell them so.

---

25. *use:* usual conditions. 39–40. *plucking . . . beast:* the priests, or augurers,
have found no heart in the animal they sacrificed. This would be interpreted as
a bad omen. 49. *confidence:* that is, you are overconfident. 56. *for thy humor:*
to humor you.

DECIUS. Caesar, all hail! Good morrow, worthy Caesar.
    I come to fetch you to the Senate House.
CAESAR. And you are come in very happy time,   60
    To bear my greeting to the Senators
    And tell them that I will not come today. *his decision*
    Cannot is false, and that I dare not, falser —
    I will not come today. Tell them so, Decius.
CALPURNIA. Say he is sick.
CAESAR.   Shall Caesar send a lie?   65
    Have I in conquest stretched mine arm so far,
    To be afeared to tell graybeards the truth?
    Decius, go tell them Caesar will not come.
DECIUS. Most mighty Caesar, let me know some cause,
    Lest I be laughed at when I tell them so.   70
CAESAR. The cause is in my will — I will not come.
    That is enough to satisfy the Senate.
    But, for your private satisfaction,
    Because I love you, I will let you know.
    Calpurnia here, my wife, stays me at home.   75
    She dreamt tonight she saw my statue,
    Which like a fountain with a hundred spouts
    Did run pure blood, and many lusty Romans
    Came smiling and did bathe their hands in it.
    And these does she apply for warnings and portents   80
    And evils imminent, and on her knee
    Hath begged that I will stay at home today.
DECIUS. This dream is all amiss interpreted.
    It was a vision fair and fortunate.
    Your statue spouting blood in many pipes,   85
    In which so many smiling Romans bathed,
    Signifies that from you great Rome shall suck
    Reviving blood, and that great men shall press
    For tinctures, stains, relics, and cognizance.°
    This by Calpurnia's dream is signified.   90
CAESAR. And this way have you well expounded° it. *explained*
DECIUS. I have, when you have heard what I can say.
    And know it now — the Senate have concluded

Decius's version

---

89. *tinctures . . . cognizances:* all mementoes of great men. 91. *expounded:* explained.

To give this day a crown to mighty Caesar.
If you shall send them word you will not come, 95
Their minds may change. Besides, it were a mock
Apt to be rendered, for someone to say
"Break up the Senate till another time,
When Caesar's wife shall meet with better dreams,"
If Caesar hide himself, shall they not whisper 100
"Lo, Caesar is afraid"?
Pardon me, Caesar, for my dear dear love
To your proceeding bids me tell you this,
And reason to my love is liable.°

CAESAR. How foolish do your fears seem now, Calpurnia! 105
I am ashamèd I did yield to them.
Give me my robe, for I will go.

[*Enter* PUBLIUS, BRUTUS, LIGARIUS, METELLUS, CASCA, TREBONIUS, *and*
CINNA.]

And look where Publius is come to fetch me.
PUBLIUS. Good morrow, Caesar.
CAESAR.   Welcome, Publius.
What, Brutus, are you stirred so early too? 110
Good morrow, Casca. Caius Ligarius,
Caesar was ne'er so much your enemy
As that same ague° which hath made you lean.
What is 't o'clock?
BRUTUS.   Caesar, 'tis strucken eight.
CAESAR. I thank you for your pains and courtesy. 115

[*Enter* ANTONY.]

See! Antony, that revels long o' nights,°
Is notwithstanding up. Good morrow, Antony.
ANTONY. So to most noble Caesar.
CAESAR.   Bid them prepare within.
I am to blame to be thus waited for.
Now, Cinna, now, Metellus. What, Trebonius! 120
I have an hour's talk in store for you.
Remember that you call on me today.
Be near me, that I may remember you.

---

104. *reason to my love is liable:* because I love you, I owe you reasonable advice.
113. *ague:* sickness. 116. *revels long o' nights:* stays up late, merrymaking.

TREBONIUS. Caesar, I will. [*Aside.*] And so near will I be
    That your best friends shall wish I had been further.   125
CAESAR. Good friends, go in and taste some wine with me,
    And we like friends will straightway go together.
BRUTUS. [*Aside*] That every like° is not the same, O Caesar,
    The heart of Brutus yearns° to think upon!   [*Exeunt.*]

SCENE III

A street near the Capitol. Enter ARTEMIDORUS, *reading a paper.*

ARTEMIDORUS. *Caesar, beware of Brutus; take heed of Cassius; come
not near Casca; have an eye to Cinna; trust not Trebonius; mark
well Metellus Cimber; Decius Brutus loves thee not; thou hast
wronged Caius Ligarius. There is but one mind in all these men,
and it is bent against Caesar. If thou beest not immortal, look   5
about you. Security gives way to conspiracy. The mighty gods defend thee!*
                             Thy lover, Artemidorus.
Here will I stand till Caesar pass along,
And as a suitor° will I give him this.
My heart laments that virtue cannot live   10
Out of the teeth of emulation.°
If thou read this, O Caesar, thou mayst live;
If not, the Fates with traitors do contrive.°   [*Exit.*]

SCENE IV

Before the house of BRUTUS. *Enter* PORTIA *and* LUCIUS.

PORTIA. I prithee,° boy, run to the Senate House.
    Stay not to answer me, but get thee gone.
    Why dost thou stay?
LUCIUS.   To know my errand, madam.
PORTIA. I would have had thee there, and here again,
    Ere I can tell thee what thou shouldst do there.   5

---

128. *like:* Brutus refers to Caesar's "like friends" in the preceding line.
129. *yearns:* grieves.
SCENE III. 10. *suitor:* one seeking a favor. 12. *emulation:* envy. 14. *contrive:*
plot.
SCENE IV. 1. *prithee:* I pray thee.

O Constancy, be strong upon my side!
Set a huge mountain 'tween my heart and tongue!
I have a man's mind, but a woman's might.
How hard it is for women to keep counsel! (secret)
Art thou here yet?

LUCIUS.   Madam, what should I do?   10
Run to the Capitol, and nothing else?
And so return to you, nothing else?

PORTIA. Yes, bring me word, boy, if thy lord look well,
For he went sickly forth. And take good note
What Caesar doth, what suitors press to him.   15
Hark, boy! What noise is that?

LUCIUS. I hear none, madam.

PORTIA.   Prithee, listen well.
I heard a bustling rumor like a fray,°
And the wind brings it from the Capitol.

LUCIUS. Sooth,° madam, I hear nothing.   [*Enter* SOOTHSAYER.]

PORTIA.   Come hither, fellow.   20
Which way hast thou been?

SOOTHSAYER.   At mine own house, good lady.

PORTIA. What is 't o'clock?

SOOTHSAYER.   About the ninth hour, lady.

PORTIA. Is Caesar yet gone to the Capitol?

SOOTHSAYER. Madam, not yet. I go to take my stand
To see him pass on to the Capitol.   25

PORTIA. Thou hast some suit to Caesar, hast thou not?

SOOTHSAYER. That I have, lady. If it will please Caesar
To be so good to Caesar as to hear me,
I shall beseech him to befriend himself.

PORTIA. Why, know'st thou any harm's intended toward him?   30

SOOTHSAYER. None that I know will be, much that I fear may chance.
Good morrow to you. Here the street is narrow,
The throng that follows Caesar at the heels
Of Senators, of praetors, common suitors,
Will crowd a feeble man almost to death.   35
I'll get me to a place more void,° and there
Speak to great Caesar as he comes along.   [*Exit.*]

PORTIA. I must go in. Aye me, how weak a thing

---

18. *rumor like a fray:* noise like a fight. 20. *sooth:* truly. 36. *void:* empty.

The heart of woman is! O Brutus,
The heavens speed thee in thine enterprise!   40
Sure, the boy heard me. Brutus hath a suit
That Caesar will not grant. Oh, I grow faint.
Run, Lucìus, and commend me to my lord.
Say I am merry. Come to me again,
And bring me word what he doth say to thee.   45

[*Exeunt separately.*]

ACT III

SCENE I

Rome. Before the Capitol, the Senate seated above. Enter CITIZENS, *including* ARTEMIDORUS *and* SOOTHSAYER.

Trumpets. Enter CAESAR, BRUTUS, CASSIUS, CASCA, DECIUS, METELLUS, TREBONIUS, CINNA, ANTONY, LEPIDUS, POPILIUS, *and* PUBLIUS.

CAESAR. The ides of March are come.
SOOTHSAYER. Aye, Caesar, but not gone.
ARTEMIDORUS. Hail, Caesar! Read this schedule.°
DECIUS. Trebonius doth desire you to o'erread,
    At your best leisure, this his humble suit.   5
ARTEMIDORUS. O Caesar, read mine first, for mine's a suit
    That touches Caesar nearer. Read it, great Caesar.
CAESAR. What touches us ourself shall be last served.
ARTEMIDORUS. Delay not, Caesar. Read it instantly.
CAESAR. What, is the fellow mad?
PUBLIUS.   Sirrah,° give place.°   10
CASSIUS. What, urge you your petitions in the street?
    Come to the Capitol.
POPILIUS. I wish your enterprise today may thrive.
CASSIUS. What enterprise, Popilius?
POPILIUS.   Fare you well.
BRUTUS. What said Popilius Lena?   15

SCENE I. 3. *schedule:* scroll. This is the warning that Artemidorus read in Act II, Scene III. 10. *Sirrah:* insulting way to address an inferior. 10. *give place:* move.

CASSIUS. He wished today our enterprise might thrive.

    I fear our purpose is discovered.

BRUTUS. Look how he makes to Caesar. Mark him.

CASSIUS.   Casca,

    Be sudden, for we fear prevention.° *discovery*

    Brutus, what shall be done? If this be known,   20

    Cassius or Caesar never shall turn back,

    For I will slay myself.

BRUTUS.   Cassius, be constant.

    Popilius Lena speaks not of our purposes,

    For look he smiles and Caesar doth not change.

CASSIUS. Trebonius knows his time, for look you, Brutus,   25

    He draws Mark Antony out of the way.

                        [*Exeunt* ANTONY *and* TREBONIUS.]

DECIUS. Where is Metellus Cimber? Let him go,

    And presently prefer his suit to Caesar.

BRUTUS. He is addressed. Press near and second him.

CINNA. Casca, you are the first that rears your hand.   30

CAESAR. Are we all ready? What is now amiss

    That Caesar and his Senate must redress?

METELLUS. Most high, most mighty, and most puissant° *powerful* Caesar,

    Metellus Cimber throws before thy seat

    A humble heart——

CAESAR.   I must prevent thee, Cimber.   35

    These couchings and these lowly courtesies°

    Might fire the blood of ordinary men,

    And turn preordinance and first decree

    Into the law of children.° Be not fond, *foolish*

    To think that Caesar bears such rebel blood   40

    That will be thawed from the true quality

    With that which melteth fools — I mean sweet words,

    Low-crookèd curtsies,° and base spaniel fawning.

    Thy brother by decree is banished.

    If thou dost bend and pray and fawn for him,   45

    I spurn thee like a cur out of my way.

    Know, Caesar doth not wrong, nor without cause

---

19. *prevention:* discovery. 33. *puissant:* powerful. 36. *couchings . . . courtesies:* grovelings and bowings. 38–39. *turn . . . children:* turn old laws and decrees into childish whims. 39. *fond:* foolish. 43. *low-crooked curtsies:* deep bows.

Will he be satisfied.

METELLUS. Is there no voice more worthy than my own,
To sound more sweetly in great Caesar's ear 50
For the repealing of my banished brother?

BRUTUS. I kiss thy hand, but not in flattery, Caesar,
Desiring thee that Publius Cimber may
Have an immediate freedom of repeal.

CAESAR. What, Brutus!

CASSIUS.   Pardon, Caesar, Caesar, pardon. 55
As low as to thy foot doth Cassius fall,
To beg enfranchisement° for Publius Cimber.

CAESAR. I could be well moved, if I were as you.
If I could pray to move, prayers would move me;
But I am constant as the Northern Star, 60
Of whose true-fixed and resting quality
There is no fellow° in the firmament.°
The skies are painted with unnumbered sparks,
They are all fire, and every one doth shine,
But there's but one in all doth hold his place. 65
So in the world. 'Tis furnished well with men,
And men are flesh and blood, and apprehensive;°
Yet in the number I do know but one
That unassailable holds on his rank,
Unshaked of motion. And that I am he, 70
Let me a little show it, even in this,
That I was constant Cimber should be banished,
And constant do remain to keep him so.

CINNA. O Caesar ——

CAESAR.   Hence! Wilt thou lift up Olympus?°

DECIUS. Great Caesar ——

CAESAR.   Doth not Brutus bootless° kneel? 75

CASCA. Speak, hands, for me!

[CASCA *first, then the other conspirators, and finally BRUTUS stab*
    CAESAR.]

CAESAR. *Et tu, Brute?*° Then fall, Caesar!   [*Dies.*]

---

57. *enfranchisement:* freedom. 62. *no fellow:* no other. 63. *firmament:* heavens.
67. *apprehensive:* capable of understanding, of thinking and feeling. 74. *Olympus:* mountain in Greece where the gods were thought to reside. 75. *bootless:* uselessly. 77. *Et tu, Brute?:* Latin for "And you, Brutus?" These were Caesar's last words, according to popular tradition.

CINNA. Liberty! Freedom! Tyranny is dead!
Run hence, proclaim, cry it about the streets.

CASSIUS. Some to the common pulpits, and cry out   80
"Liberty, freedom, and enfranchisement!"

BRUTUS. People, and Senators, be not affrighted.
Fly not, stand still. Ambition's debt is paid.

CASCA. Go to the pulpit, Brutus.

DECIUS.   And Cassius too.

BRUTUS. Where's Publius?   85

CINNA. Here, quite confounded° with this mutiny.

METELLUS. Stand fast together, lest some friend of Caesar's
Should chance ——

BRUTUS. Talk not of standing. Publius, good cheer.
There is no harm intended to your person,   90
Nor to no Roman else. So tell them, Publius.

CASSIUS. And leave us, Publius, lest that the people
Rushing on us should do your age some mischief.

BRUTUS. Do so, and let no man abide° this deed
But we the doers.   [*Enter* TREBONIUS.]

CASSIUS.   Where is Antony?   95

TREBONIUS. Fled to his house amazed.
Men, wives, and children stare, cry out, and run
As it were Doomsday.

BRUTUS.   Fates, we will know your pleasures.
That we shall die, we know; 'tis but the time,
And drawing days out, that men stand upon.°   100

CASCA. Why, he that cuts off twenty years of life
Cuts off so many years of fearing death.

BRUTUS. Grant that, and then is death a benefit.
So are we Caesar's friends that have abridged°
His time of fearing death. Stoop, Romans, stoop,   105
And let us bathe our hands in Caesar's blood
Up to the elbows, and besmear our swords.
Then walk we forth, even to the market place,
And waving our red weapons o'er our heads,
Let's all cry "Peace, freedom, and liberty!"   110

CASSIUS. Stoop then, and wash. How many ages hence

---

86. *confounded:* confused. 94. *abide:* be responsible for. 100. *stand upon:* worry about. 104. *abridged:* shortened.

[handwritten margin note: Think of People of Rome owe them]

Shall this our lofty scene be acted over
In states unborn and accents° yet unknown!

BRUTUS. How many times shall Caesar bleed in sport,°
That now on Pompey's basis° lies along°
No worthier than the dust!

CASSIUS.   So oft as that shall be,
So often shall the knot of us be called
The men that gave their country liberty.

[handwritten margin note: Servant sent by Antony]

DECIUS. What, shall we forth?

CASSIUS.   Aye, every man away.
Brutus shall lead, and we will grace his heels   120
With the most boldest and best hearts of Rome.

                                        [*Enter a* SERVANT.]

BRUTUS. Soft! Who comes here? A friend of Antony's.

SERVANT. Thus, Brutus, did my master bid me kneel;
Thus did Mark Antony bid me fall down,
And, being prostrate, thus he bade me say: 125
Brutus is noble, wise, valiant, and honest,
Caesar was mighty, bold, royal, and loving.
Say I love Brutus and I honor him,
Say I feared Caesar, honored him, and loved him.
If Brutus will vouchsafe that Antony   130
May safely come to him and be resolved°
How Caesar hath deserved to lie in death,
Mark Antony shall not love Caesar dead
So well as Brutus living, but will follow
The fortunes and affairs of noble Brutus   135
Thorough the hazards of this untrod state
With all true faith. So says my master Antony.

BRUTUS. Thy master is a wise and valiant Roman —
I never thought him worse.
Tell him, so please him come unto this place,   140
He shall be satisfied and, by my honor,
Depart untouched.

SERVANT.   I'll fetch him presently.   [*Exit.*]

BRUTUS. I know that we shall have him well to friend.°

---

113. *accents:* languages. 114. *in sport:* in the theater. 115. *Pompey's basis:* the
base of Pompey's statue. 115. *along:* stretched out. 131. *resolved:* convinced.
143. *well to friend:* as a good friend.

CASSIUS. I wish we may, but yet have I a mind
  That fears him much, and my misgiving still   145
  Falls shrewdly to the purpose.°   [*Enter* ANTONY.]
BRUTUS. But here comes Antony. Welcome, Mark Antony.
ANTONY. O mighty Caesar, dost thou lie so low?
  Are all thy conquests, glories, triumphs, spoils,
  Shrunk to this little measure? Fare thee well.   150
  I know not, gentlemen, what you intend,
  Who else must be let blood, who else is rank.°
  If I myself, there is no hour so fit
  As Caesar's death's hour, nor no instrument
  Of half that worth as those your swords, made rich   155
  With the most noble blood of all this world.
  I do beseech ye, if you bear me hard,
  Now, whilst your purpled hands do reek and smoke,
  Fulfill your pleasure. Live a thousand years,
  I shall not find myself so apt to die.   160
  No place will please me so, no mean° of death,
  As here by Caesar, and by you cut off,
  The choice and master spirits of this age.
BRUTUS. O Antony, beg not your death of us.
  Though now we must appear bloody and cruel,   165
  As by our hands and this our present act
  You see we do. Yet see you but° our hands
  And this the bleeding business they have done.
  Our hearts you see not. They are pitiful,
  And pity to the general wrong of Rome —   170
  As fire drives out fire, so pity pity —
  Hath done this deed on Caesar. For your part,
  To you our swords have leaden° points, Mark Antony.
  Our arms in strength of malice,° and our hearts
  Of brothers' temper, do receive you in   175
  With all kind love, good thoughts, and reverence.
CASSIUS. Your voice shall be as strong as any man's

---

146. *falls shrewdly to the purpose:* hints at trouble ahead. 152. *rank:* sick. One
of the ways doctors treated illness was to open a vein and let the patient bleed.
Antony is being ironic in comparing the conspirators to doctors and Caesar to a
patient. 161. *mean:* means. 167. *but:* only. 173. *leaden:* blunt, not intended
for Antony. 174. *in strength of malice:* strong against enemies.

Antony- wants revenge

In the disposing of new dignities.°

BRUTUS. Only be patient till we have appeased
  The multitude, beside themselves with fear,   180
  And then we will deliver you the cause
  Why I, that did love Caesar when I struck him,
  Have thus proceeded.

ANTONY.   I doubt not of your wisdom.
  Let each man render me his bloody hand.
  First, Marcus Brutus, will I shake with you.   185
  Next, Caius Cassius, do I take your hand.
  Now, Decius Brutus, yours, now yours, Metellus;
  Yours, Cinna, and, my valiant Casca, yours —
  Though last not least in love, yours, good Trebonius.
  Gentlemen all — alas, what shall I say?
  My credit° now stands on such slippery ground   *c- begging for life*
  That one of two bad ways you must conceit° me,   *Flatterer- get into*   190
  Either a coward or a flatterer.   *Power with them*
  That I did love thee, Caesar, oh, 'tis true.
  If then thy spirit look upon us now,   195
  Shall it not grieve thee dearer than thy death
  To see thy Antony making his peace,
  Shaking the bloody fingers of thy foes,
  Most noble! in the presence of thy corse?°
  Had I as many eyes as thou hast wounds,   200
  Weeping as fast as they stream forth thy blood,
  It would become me better than to close
  In terms of friendship with thine enemies.
  Pardon me, Julius! Here wast thou bayed,° brave hart,°
  Here didst thou fall, and here thy hunters stand,   205
  Signed in thy spoil° and crimsoned in thy lethe.°
  O world, thou wast the forest to this hart,
  And this, indeed, O world, the heart of thee.
  How like a deer strucken by many princes
  Dost thou here lie!   210

CASSIUS. Mark Antony ——

---

178. *disposing . . . dignities:* distribution of political posts. 191. *credit:* reputation. 192. *conceit:* think of. 199. *corse:* corpse. 204. *bayed:* brought to bay (cornered by hounds). 204. *hart:* deer. Later in this speech, Antony puns upon hart-heart. 206. *Signed in thy spoil:* smeared with blood of slaughter. 206. *lethe:* blood (flowing like the Lethe, river of the dead).

ANTONY.   Pardon me, Caius Cassius.
　　The enemies of Caesar shall say this;
　　Then, in a friend, it is cold modesty.
CASSIUS. I blame you not for praising Caesar so,
　　But what compact mean you to have with us?   215
　　Will you be pricked in number° of our friends,
　　Or shall we on, and not depend on you?
ANTONY. Therefore I took your hands, but was indeed
　　Swayed from the point by looking down on Caesar.
　　Friends am I with you all and love you all,   220
　　Upon this hope that you shall give me reasons
　　Why and wherein Caesar was dangerous.
BRUTUS. Or else were this a savage spectacle.
　　Our reasons are so full of good regard
　　That were you, Antony, the son of Caesar,   225
　　You should be satisfied.
ANTONY.   That's all I seek.
　　And am moreover suitor° that I may
　　Produce his body to the market place,
　　And in the pulpit, as becomes a friend,
　　Speak in the order of his funeral.   230
BRUTUS. You shall, Mark Antony.
CASSIUS.   Brutus, a word with you.
　　[Aside to BRUTUS.] You know not what you do. Do not consent
　　That Antony speak in his funeral.
　　Know you how much the people may be moved
　　By that which he will utter?
BRUTUS.   By your pardon,   235
　　I will myself into the pulpit first,
　　And show the reason of our Caesar's death.
　　What Antony shall speak, I will protest
　　He speaks by leave and by permission,
　　And that we are contented Caesar shall   240
　　Have all true rites and lawful ceremonies.
　　It shall advantage more than do us wrong.
CASSIUS. I know not what may fall. I like it not.
BRUTUS. Mark Antony, here, take you Caesar's body.
　　You shall not in your funeral speech blame us,   245

---
216. *pricked in number*: marked in the roll. 227. *am moreover suitor*: ask.

But speak all good you can devise of Caesar,
And say you do 't by our permission.
Else shall you not have any hand at all
About his funeral. And you shall speak
In the same pulpit whereto I am going —   250
After my speech is ended.

ANTONY.   Be it so.
I do desire no more.

BRUTUS. Prepare the body then, and follow us.

                    [*Exeunt all but* ANTONY.]

ANTONY. O, pardon me, thou bleeding piece of earth,   *Soliloquy*
That I am meek and gentle with these butchers!   255
Thou art the ruins of the noblest man
That ever livèd in the tide of times.
Woe to the hand that shed this costly blood!
Over thy wounds now do I prophesy,
Which like dumb mouths do ope their ruby lips   260
To beg the voice and utterance of my tongue,
A curse shall light upon the limbs of men.
Domestic fury and fierce civil strife
Shall cumber° all the parts of Italy.
Blood and destruction shall be so in use,   265
And dreadful objects so familiar,
That mothers shall but smile when they behold
Their infants quartered° with the hands of war,
All pity choked with custom of fell° deeds.
And Caesar's spirit ranging for revenge,   270
With Até° by his side come hot from Hell,
Shall in these confines with a monarch's voice
Cry havoc,° and let slip the dogs of war,
That this foul deed shall smell above the earth
With carrion men, groaning for burial.   [*Enter a* SERVANT.]   275
You serve Octavius Caesar,° do you not?

SERVANT. I do, Mark Antony.

ANTONY. Caesar did write for him to come to Rome.

SERVANT. He did receive his letters, and is coming,

---

264. *cumber:* encumber, burden. 268. *quartered:* torn apart. 269. *fell:* frightful.
271. *Até:* the goddess of discord. 273. *Cry havoc:* in war, "havoc" meant "spare
no one." 276. *Octavius Caesar:* Caesar's grandnephew and heir.

And bid me say to you by word of mouth —   280
    [*Seeing the body.*] O Caesar!
ANTONY. Thy heart is big. Get thee apart and weep.
    Passion, I see, is catching, for mine eyes,
    Seeing those beads of sorrow stand in thine,
    Began to water. Is thy master coming?   285
SERVANT. He lies tonight within seven leagues of Rome.
ANTONY. Post° back with speed, and tell him what hath chanced.
    Here is a mourning Rome, a dangerous Rome,
    No Rome of safety for Octavius yet.
    Hie hence,° and tell him so. Yet stay awhile.   290
    Thou shalt not back till I have borne this corse
    Into the market place. There shall I try,°
    In my oration, how the people take
    The cruel issue° of these bloody men,
    According to the which, thou shalt discourse   295
    To young Octavius of the state of things.
    Lend me your hand.   [*Exeunt with* CAESAR's *body.*]

SCENE II

The Forum. Enter BRUTUS, CASSIUS, *and* CITIZENS.

CITIZENS. We will be satisfied. Let us be satisfied.
BRUTUS. Then follow me, and give me audience, friends.
    Cassius, go you into the other street,
    And part the numbers.
    Those that will hear me speak, let 'em stay here,   5
    Those that will follow Cassius, go with him,
    And public reasons shall be rendered
    Of Caesar's death.
FIRST CITIZEN.   I will hear Brutus speak.
SECOND CITIZEN. I will hear Cassius, and compare their reasons
    When severally° we hear them rendered.   10
[*Exit* CASSIUS, *with some of the* CITIZENS. BRUTUS *goes into the
    pulpit.*]
THIRD CITIZEN. The noble Brutus is ascended. Silence!

---

287. *Post:* ride. 290. *Hie hence:* hurry away. 292. *try:* test. 294. *issue:* act.
SCENE II. 10. *severally:* separately.

BRUTUS. Be patient till the last.

Romans, countrymen, and lovers! Hear me for my cause, and be
silent, that you may hear. Believe me for mine honor, and have
respect to mine honor, that you may believe. Censure° me in   15
your wisdom, and awake your senses, that you may the better
judge. If there be any in this assembly, any dear friend of Caesar's,
to him I say that Brutus' love to Caesar was no less than his. If
then that friend demand why Brutus rose against Caesar, this is
my answer — not that I loved Caesar less, but that I loved   20
Rome more. Had you rather Caesar were living, and die all slaves,
than that Caesar were dead, to live all free men? As Caesar loved
me, I weep for him; as he was fortunate, I rejoice at it; as he was
valiant, I honor him. But as he was ambitious, I slew him. There
is tears for his love, joy for his fortune, honor for his valor,   25
and death for his ambition. Who is here so base that would be a
bondman? If any, speak, for him have I offended. Who is here
so rude° that would not be a Roman? If any, speak, for him have
I offended. Who is here so vile that will not love his country?
If any, speak, for him have I offended. I pause for a reply.   30

ALL. None, Brutus, none.

BRUTUS. Then none have I offended. I have done no more to Caesar
than you shall do to Brutus. The question of his death is en-
rolled in the Capitol, his glory not extenuated,° wherein he was
worthy, nor his offenses enforced,° for which he suffered   35
death.   [Enter ANTONY with CAESAR's body.]
Here comes his body, mourned by Mark Antony, who, though he
had no hand in his death, shall receive the benefit of his dying,
a place in the commonwealth — as which of you shall not? With
this I depart — that, as I slew my best lover for the good of   40
Rome, I have the same dagger for myself when it shall please my
country to need my death.

ALL. Live, Brutus! Live, live!

FIRST CITIZEN. Bring him with triumph home unto his house.

SECOND CITIZEN. Give him a statue with his ancestors.   45

THIRD CITIZEN. Let him be Caesar.

FOURTH CITIZEN.   Caesar's better parts
Shall be crowned in Brutus.

---

15. Censure: judge. 28. rude: uncivilized. 34. extenuated: minimized. 35. enforced: exaggerated.

FIRST CITIZEN. We'll bring him to his house with shouts and clamors.

BRUTUS. My countrymen ——

SECOND CITIZEN.   Peace! Silence! Brutus speaks.

FIRST CITIZEN. Peace, ho!   50

BRUTUS. Good countrymen, let me depart alone,
    And, for my sake, stay here with Antony.
    Do grace to Caesar's corpse, and grace his speech
    Tending to Caesar's glories, which Mark Antony
    By our permission is allowed to make.   55
    I do entreat you, not a man depart,
    Save I alone, till Antony have spoke.   [*Exit.*]

FIRST CITIZEN. Stay, ho, and let us hear Mark Antony!

THIRD CITIZEN. Let him go up into the public chair.
    We'll hear him. Noble Antony, go up.   60

ANTONY. For Brutus' sake, I am beholding° to you.
                                    [*Goes up to the pulpit.*]

FOURTH CITIZEN. What does he say of Brutus?

THIRD CITIZEN.   He says, for Brutus' sake,
    He finds himself beholding to us all.

FOURTH CITIZEN. 'Twere best he speak no harm of Brutus here.

FIRST CITIZEN. This Caesar was a tyrant.

THIRD CITIZEN.   Nay, that's certain.   65
    We are blest that Rome is rid of him.

SECOND CITIZEN. Peace! Let us hear what Antony can say.

ANTONY. You gentle Romans ——

ALL.   Peace, ho! Let us hear him.

ANTONY. Friends, Romans, countrymen, lend me your ears.
    I come to bury Caesar, not to praise him.   70
    The evil that men do lives after them,
    The good is oft interrèd° with their bones.
    So let it be with Caesar. The noble Brutus
    Hath told you Caesar was ambitious.
    If it were so, it was a grievous fault.   75
    And grievously hath Caesar answered it.
    Here, under leave of Brutus and the rest —
    For Brutus is an honorable man,
    So are they all, all honorable men —
    Come I to speak in Caesar's funeral.   80

---

61. *beholding:* indebted. 72. *interrèd:* buried.

He was my friend, faithful and just to me.
But Brutus says he was ambitious,
And Brutus is an honorable man.
He hath brought many captives home to Rome,
Whose ransoms did the general coffers° fill.   85
Did this in Caesar seem ambitious?
When that the poor have cried, Caesar hath wept
Ambition should be made of sterner stuff.
Yet Brutus says he was ambitious,
And Brutus is an honorable man.   90
You all did see that on the Lupercal
I thrice presented him a kingly crown,
Which he did thrice refuse.° Was this ambition?
Yet Brutus says he was ambitious,
And, sure, he is an honorable man.   95
I speak not to disprove what Brutus spoke,
But here I am to speak what I do know.
You all did love him once, not without cause.
What cause withholds you then to mourn for him?
O judgment, thou art fled to brutish beasts,   100
And men have lost their reason! Bear with me,
My heart is in the coffin there with Caesar,
And I must pause till it come back to me.

FIRST CITIZEN. Methinks there is much reason in his sayings.
SECOND CITIZEN. If thou consider rightly of the matter,   105
   Caesar has had great wrong.
THIRD CITIZEN.   Has he, masters?
   I fear there will a worse come in his place.
FOURTH CITIZEN. Mark ye his words? He would not take the crown,
   Therefore 'tis certain he was not ambitious.
FIRST CITIZEN. If it be found so, some will dear abide it.°   110
SECOND CITIZEN. Poor soul! His eyes are red as fire with weeping.
THIRD CITIZEN. There's not a nobler man in Rome than Antony.
FOURTH CITIZEN. Now mark him, he begins again to speak.
ANTONY. But yesterday the word of Caesar might
   Have stood against the world. Now lies he there,   115
   And none so poor to do him reverence.

---

85. *general coffers:* public treasury. 93. *thrice refuse:* Casca described this action in Act I, Scene II. 110. *dear abide it:* pay dearly for it.

O masters, if I were disposed to stir
Your hearts and minds to mutiny and rage,
I should do Brutus wrong and Cassius wrong,
Who, you all know, are honorable men.   120
I will not do them wrong; I rather choose
To wrong the dead, to wrong myself and you,
Than I will wrong such honorable men.
But here's a parchment with the seal of Caesar —
I found it in his closet — 'tis his will.   125
Let but the commons° hear this testament —
Which, pardon me, I do not mean to read —
And they would go and kiss dead Caesar's wounds
And dip their napkins in his sacred blood,
Yea, beg a hair of him for memory,   130
And, dying, mention it within their wills,
Bequeathing it as a rich legacy
Unto their issue.°

FOURTH CITIZEN. We'll hear the will. Read it, Mark Antony.
ALL. The will, the will! We will hear Caesar's will   135
ANTONY. Have patience, gentle friends. I must not read it.
It is not meet° you know how Caesar loved you.
You are not wood, you are not stones, but men;
And, being men, hearing the will of Caesar,
It will inflame you, it will make you mad.   140
'Tis good you know not that you are his heirs,
For if you should, oh, what would come of it!

FOURTH CITIZEN. Read the will. We'll hear it, Antony.
You shall read us the will, Caesar's will.

ANTONY. Will you be patient? Will you stay awhile?   145
I have o'ershot° myself to tell you of it.
I fear I wrong the honorable men
Whose daggers have stabbed Caesar. I do fear it.

FOURTH CITIZEN. They were traitors — honorable men!
ALL. The will! The testament!   150
SECOND CITIZEN. They were villains, murderers. The will! Read the
will.

ANTONY. You will compel me then to read the will?

---

126. *commons:* common people. 133. *issue:* children. 137. *meet:* fit. 146. *o'er-
shot:* gone too far.

Then make a ring about the corpse of Caesar,
And let me show you him that made the will. 155
Shall I descend? And will you give me leave?

ALL. Come down.

SECOND CITIZEN. Descend.   [ANTONY *comes down from the pulpit.*]

THIRD CITIZEN. You shall have leave.

FOURTH CITIZEN. A ring. Stand round. 160

FIRST CITIZEN. Stand from the hearse, stand from the body.

SECOND CITIZEN. Room for Antony, most noble Antony.

ANTONY. Nay, press not so upon me. Stand far off.

ALL. Stand back. Room! Bear back.

ANTONY. If you have tears, prepare to shed them now. 165
   You all do know this mantle. I remember
   The first time ever Caesar put it on.
   'Twas on a summer's evening, in his tent,
   That day he overcame the Nervii.°
   Look, in this place ran Cassius' dagger through. 170
   See what a rent the envious Casca made.
   Through this the well-belovèd Brutus stabbed,
   And as he plucked his cursèd steel away,
   Mark how the blood of Caesar followed it,
   As rushing out of doors, to be resolved 175
   If Brutus so unkindly knocked, or no.
   For Brutus, as you know, was Caesar's angel.
   Judge, O you gods, how dearly Caesar loved him!
   This was the most unkindest cut of all,
   For when the noble Caesar saw him stab, 180
   Ingratitude, more strong than traitors' arms,
   Quite vanquished him. Then burst his mighty heart,
   And, in his mantle muffling up his face,
   Even at the base of Pompey's statue,
   Which all the while ran blood, great Caesar fell. 185
   Oh, what a fall was there, my countrymen!
   Then I, and you, and all of us fell down,
   Whilst bloody treason flourished over us.
   Oh, now you weep, and I perceive you feel
   The dint° of pity. These are gracious drops. 190
   Kind souls, what weep you when you but behold

---

169. *Nervii:* a tribe defeated by Caesar in the Gallic Wars. 190. *dint:* blow.

Our Caesar's vesture° wounded? Look you here —
Here is himself, marred, as you see, with traitors.

[*He pulls the cloak off* CAESAR's *body.*]

FIRST CITIZEN. Oh, piteous spectacle!

SECOND CITIZEN. Oh, noble Caesar!   195

THIRD CITIZEN. Oh, woeful day!

FOURTH CITIZEN. Oh, traitors, villains!

FIRST CITIZEN. Oh, most bloody sight!

SECOND CITIZEN. We will be revenged.

ALL. Revenge! About! Seek! Burn! Fire! Kill! Slay!   200
Let not a traitor live!

ANTONY. Stay, countrymen.

FIRST CITIZEN. Peace there! Hear the noble Antony.

SECOND CITIZEN. We'll hear him, we'll follow him, we'll die with
him.   205

ANTONY. Good friends, sweet friends, let me not stir you up
To such a sudden flood of mutiny.
They that have done this deed are honorable.
What private griefs they have, alas, I know not,
That made them do it. They are wise and honorable,   210
And will, no doubt, with reasons answer you.
I come not, friends, to steal away your hearts.
I am no orator, as Brutus is,
But, as you know me all, a plain blunt man
That love my friend; and that they know full well   215
That gave me public leave to speak of him.
For I have neither wit, nor words, nor worth,
Action, nor utterance, nor the power of speech,
To stir men's blood. I only speak right on,°
I tell you that which you yourselves do know,   220
Show you sweet Caesar's wounds, poor poor dumb mouths,
And bid them speak for me. But were I Brutus,
And Brutus Antony, there were an Antony
Would ruffle up your spirits, and put a tongue
In every wound of Caesar that should move   225
The stones of Rome to rise and mutiny.

ALL. We'll mutiny.

FIRST CITIZEN. We'll burn the house of Brutus.

---

192. *vesture:* garment. 219. *right on:* directly.

THIRD CITIZEN. Away, then! Come, seek the conspirators.

ANTONY. Yet hear me, countrymen, yet hear me speak. 230

ALL. Peace, ho! Hear Antony. Most noble Antony!

ANTONY. Why, friends, you go to do you know not what.
Wherein hath Caesar thus deserved your loves?
Alas, you know not. I must tell you, then —
You have forgot the will I told you of. 235

ALL. Most true, the will! Let's stay and hear the will.

ANTONY. Here is the will, and under Caesar's seal.
To every Roman citizen he gives,
To every several° man, seventy-five drachmas.°

SECOND CITIZEN. Most noble Caesar! We'll revenge his death. 240

THIRD CITIZEN. Oh, royal Caesar!

ANTONY. Hear me with patience.

ALL. Peace, ho!

ANTONY. Moreover, he hath left you all his walks,
His private arbors and new-planted orchards, 245
On this side Tiber. He hath left them you,
And to your heirs forever — common pleasures,
To walk abroad and recreate yourselves.
Here was a Caesar! When comes such another?

FIRST CITIZEN. Never, never. Come, away, away! 250
We'll burn his body in the holy place,
And with the brands fire the traitors' houses.
Take up the body.

SECOND CITIZEN. Go fetch fire.

THIRD CITIZEN. Pluck down benches. 255

FOURTH CITIZEN. Pluck down forms,° windows, anything.

[*Exeunt* CITIZENS *with the body.*]

ANTONY. Now let it work. Mischief, thou art afoot,
Take thou what course thou wilt. [*Enter a* SERVANT.]
How now, fellow?

SERVANT. Sir, Octavius is already come to Rome.

ANTONY. Where is he? 260

SERVANT. He and Lepidus° are at Caesar's house.

ANTONY. And thither will I straight to visit him.

---

239. *every several:* each. 239. *drachmas:* coins. 256. *forms:* benches. 261.
idus: the general who will join Antony and Octavius in a new triumvirat/

382 WILLIAM SHAKESPEARE

He comes upon a wish.° Fortune is merry,
And in this mood will give us anything.

SERVANT. I heard him say Brutus and Cassius   265
Are rid like madmen through the gates of Rome.

ANTONY. Belike° they had some notice of the people,
How I had moved them. Bring me to Octavius.   [*Exeunt.*]

SCENE III

A street in Rome. Enter CINNA *the poet, and* CITIZENS *after him.*

CINNA. I dreamt tonight that I did feast with Caesar,
And things unluckily charge my fantasy.°
I have no will to wander forth of doors,
Yet something leads me forth.

FIRST CITIZEN. What is your name?   5

SECOND CITIZEN. Whither are you going?

THIRD CITIZEN. Where do you dwell?

FOURTH CITIZEN. Are you a married man or a bachelor?

SECOND CITIZEN. Answer every man directly.

FIRST CITIZEN. Aye, and briefly.   10

FOURTH CITIZEN. Aye, and wisely.

THIRD CITIZEN. Aye, and truly, you were best.

CINNA. What is my name? Whither am I going? Where do I dwell?
Am I a married man or a bachelor? Then, to answer every man
directly and briefly, wisely and truly, wisely I say I am a   15
bachelor.

SECOND CITIZEN. That's as much as to say they are fools that marry.
You'll bear me a bang° for that, I fear. Proceed, directly.

CINNA. Directly, I am going to Caesar's funeral.

FIRST CITIZEN. As a friend or an enemy?   20

CINNA. As a friend.

SECOND CITIZEN. That matter is answered directly.

FOURTH CITIZEN. For your dwelling, briefly.

CINNA. Briefly, I dwell by the Capitol.

THIRD CITIZEN. Your name, sir, truly.   25

---

263. *upon a wish:* just when I want him. 267. *Belike:* probably.
SCENE II. 2. *unluckily charge my fantasy:* the dream seems a bad omen.
18. *bear me a bang:* get struck by me.

CINNA. Truly, my name is Cinna.

FIRST CITIZEN. Tear him to pieces. He's a conspirator.

CINNA. I am Cinna the poet, I am Cinna the poet.

FOURTH CITIZEN. Tear him for his bad verses, tear him for his bad
  verses.   30

CINNA. I am not Cinna the conspirator.

FOURTH CITIZEN. It is no matter, his name's Cinna. Pluck but his
  name out of his heart, and turn him going.

THIRD CITIZEN. Tear him, tear him! Come, brands. Ho, firebrands —
  to Brutus', to Cassius'! Burn all. Some to Decius' house, and   35
  some to Casca's, some to Ligarius'. Away, go!   [*Exeunt.*]

ACT IV

SCENE I

ANTONY's *house in Rome.* ANTONY, OCTAVIUS, *and* LEPIDUS.

ANTONY. These many then shall die, their names are pricked.°

OCTAVIUS. Your brother too must die. Consent you, Lepidus?

LEPIDUS. I do consent.

OCTAVIUS.   Prick him down, Antony.

LEPIDUS. Upon condition Publius shall not live,
  Who is your sister's son, Mark Antony.   5

ANTONY. He shall not live. Look, with a spot I damn him.
  But, Lepidus, go you to Caesar's house.
  Fetch the will hither, and we shall determine
  How to cut off some charge in legacies.°

LEPIDUS. What, shall I find you here?   10

OCTAVIUS. Or here or at the Capitol.   [*Exit* LEPIDUS.]

ANTONY. This° is a slight unmeritable man,
  Meet to be sent on errands. Is it fit,
  The threefold world divided, he should stand
  One of the three to share it?

OCTAVIUS.   So you thought him.   15

SCENE I. 1. *pricked:* listed. 9. *cut . . . legacies:* avoid paying some of Caesar's
bequests. Note that Antony is now trying to avoid carrying out the same will he
used to excite the crowd in his oration after Caesar's death. 12. *This:* Lepidus.

And took his voice who should be pricked to die
In our black sentence and proscription.°

ANTONY. Octavius, I have seen more days than you.
And though we lay these honors on this man,
To ease ourselves of divers slanderous loads,   *—get out of trub*   20
He shall but bear them as the ass bears gold,   *—take on problem*
To groan and sweat under the business,
Either led or driven, as we point the way.
And having brought our treasure where we will,
Then take we down his load and turn him off,   25
Like to the empty ass, to shake his ears
And gaze in commons.

OCTAVIUS.   You may do your will.
But he's a tried and valiant soldier.

ANTONY. So is my horse, Octavius, and for that
I do appoint him store of provender.°   30
It is a creature that I teach to fight,
To wind,° to stop, to run directly on,
His corporal° motion governed by my spirit.
And, in some taste,° is Lepidus but so.
He must be taught, and trained, and bid go forth, 35
A barren-spirited fellow, one that feeds
On abjects, orts,° and imitations,
Which, out of use and staled by other men,
Begin his fashion. Do not talk of him   *use Lepidus*
But as a property.° And now, Octavius,   40
Listen great things. Brutus and Cassius
Are levying powers.° We must straight make head.°
Therefore let our alliance be combined,
Our best friends made, our means stretched,
And let us presently go sit in council   45
How covert matters may be best disclosed,
And open perils surest answered.

OCTAVIUS. Let us do so, for we are at the stake,°

---

17. *sentence and proscription:* list of those to be killed. 30. *provender:* food.
32. *wind:* turn. 33. *corporal:* bodily. 34. *in some taste:* to some extent. 37. *abjects, orts:* worthless things, scraps. 40. *property:* a useful tool. 42. *levying powers:* raising an army. 42. *head:* headway. 48. *at the stake:* like a bear tied to a stake and "bayed about" by barking dogs.

And bayed about with many enemies.
And some that smile have in their hearts, I fear,   50
Millions of mischiefs.   [*Exeunt.*]

SCENE II

A camp near Sardis, in Greece. Some time has passed since the action of Scene I. Brutus and Cassius have been forced to flee from Rome. They are pursued by the armies of the Triumvirate, led by ANTONY *and* OCTAVIUS. *In front of* BRUTUS's *tent. Drums. Enter* BRUTUS, LUCILIUS, LUCIUS, *and* SOLDIERS. TITINIUS *and* PINDARUS *meet them.*

BRUTUS. Stand, ho!
LUCILIUS. Give the word, ho! and stand.
BRUTUS. What now, Lucilius! Is Cassius near?
LUCILIUS. He is at hand, and Pindarus is come
    To do you salutation from his master.   5
BRUTUS. He greets me well. Your master, Pindarus,
    In his own change, or by ill officers,°
    Hath given me some worthy cause to wish
    Things done undone. But if he be at hand,
    I shall be satisfied.
PINDARUS.   I do not doubt   10
    But that my noble master will appear
    Such as he is, full of regard and honor.
BRUTUS. He is not doubted. A word, Lucilius,
    How he received you. Let me be resolved.
LUCILIUS. With courtesy and with respect enough,   15
    But not with such familiar instances,°
    Nor with such free and friendly conference,
    As he hath used of old.
BRUTUS.   Thou hast described
    A hot friend cooling. Ever note, Lucilius,
    When love begins to sicken and decay,   20
    It useth an enforcèd ceremony.
    There are no tricks in plain and simple faith.

[handwritten margin notes: "Cassius' servant" and "Criticizing Cassius"]

SCENE II. 7. *change . . . officers:* by his change in attitude or because his subordinates have represented him badly. 16. *familiar instances:* friendly behavior.

But hollow men, like horses hot at hand,°
Make gallant show and promise of their mettle,
But when they should endure the bloody spur,   25
They fall their crests° and like deceitful jades°
Sink in the trial. Comes his army on?
LUCILIUS. They mean this night in Sardis to be quartered.
    The greater part, the horse in general,°
    Are come with Cassius.   [*Low march within.*]
BRUTUS.   Hark! He is arrived.   30
    March gently on to meet him. [*Enter* CASSIUS *and his* SOLDIERS.]
CASSIUS. Stand, ho!
BRUTUS. Stand, ho! Speak the word along.
FIRST SOLDIER. Stand!
SECOND SOLDIER. Stand!   35
THIRD SOLDIER. Stand!
CASSIUS. Most noble brother, you have done me wrong.
BRUTUS. Judge me, you gods; wrong I mine enemies?
    And if not so, how should I wrong a brother?
CASSIUS. Brutus, this sober form° of yours hides wrongs,   40
    And when you do them ——
BRUTUS.   Cassius, be content,
    Speak your griefs softly. I do know you well.
    Before the eyes of both our armies here,
    Which should perceive nothing but love from us,
    Let us not wrangle. Bid them move away,   45
    Then in my tent, Cassius, enlarge your griefs,
    And I will give you audience.
CASSIUS.   Pindarus,
    Bid our commanders lead their charges off
    A little from this ground.
BRUTUS. Lucilius, do you the like, and let no man   50
    Come to our tent till we have done our conference.
    Let Lucius and Titinius guard our door.   [*Exeunt.*]

---

23. *hot at hand:* restless, as horses eager to run. 26. *fall their crests:* lower their
manes. 26. *jades:* nags. 29. *the horse in general:* the cavalry. 40. *form:* appearance.

SCENE III

Inside BRUTUS's *tent.*

CASSIUS. That you have wronged me doth appear in this:
    You have condemned and noted° Lucius Pella
    For taking bribes here of the Sardians,
    Wherein my letters, praying on his side,
    Because I knew the man, were slighted off.   5
BRUTUS. You wronged yourself to write in such a case.
CASSIUS. In such a time as this it is not meet
    That every nice offense should bear his comment.°

[handwritten: —admit breaking the law.]

BRUTUS. Let me tell you, Cassius, you yourself
    Are much condemned to have an itching palm,   10
    To sell and mart° your offices for gold
    To undeservers.
CASSIUS.   I an itching palm!
    You know that you are Brutus that speaks this,
    Or, by the gods, this speech were else your last.
BRUTUS. The name of Cassius honors this corruption,   15
    And chastisement doth therefore hide his head.
CASSIUS. Chastisement!
BRUTUS. Remember March, the ides of March remember.

[handwritten: going against original plan]

    Did not great Julius bleed for justice' sake?
    What villain touched his body that did stab,   20
    And not for justice? What, shall one of us,
    That struck the foremost man of all this world
    But for supporting robbers, shall we now
    Contaminate our fingers with base bribes,
    And sell the mighty space of our large honors   25
    For so much trash as may be graspèd thus?
    I had rather be a dog and bay the moon
    Than such a Roman.
CASSIUS.   Brutus, bait not me,
    I'll not endure it. You forget yourself,
    To hedge me in. I am a soldier, I,   30
    Older in practice, abler than yourself— *[handwritten: doesn't say "I am better]*

SCENE III. 2. *noted:* publicly written. 7–8. *not meet . . . comment:* not fit that
Brutus should carefully note every small offense. 11. *mart:* market, trade.

To make conditions.°

BRUTUS.   Go to. You are not, Cassius.

CASSIUS. I am.

BRUTUS. I say you are not.

CASSIUS. Urge me no more, I shall forget myself.   35

Have mind upon your health, tempt me no farther.

BRUTUS. Away, slight man!

CASSIUS. Is 't possible?

BRUTUS   Hear me, for I will speak.

Must I give way and room to your rash choler? *anger*

Shall I be frighted when a madman stares?   40

CASSIUS. O ye gods, ye gods! Must I endure all this?

BRUTUS. All this! Aye, more. Fret till your proud heart break.

Go show your slaves how choleric you are,

And make your bondmen tremble. Must I budge?

Must I observe you? Must I stand and crouch   45

Under your testy° humor? By the gods,

You shall digest the venom of your spleen,°

Though it do split you; for, from this day forth,

I'll use you for my mirth, yea, for my laughter,

When you are waspish.°

CASSIUS.   Is it come to this?   50

BRUTUS. You say you are a better soldier.

Let it appear so, make your vaunting° true

And it shall please me well. For mine own part,

I shall be glad to learn of noble men.

CASSIUS. You wrong me every way, you wrong me, Brutus.   55

I said an elder soldier, not a better.

Did I say better?

BRUTUS.   If you did, I care not.

CASSIUS. When Caesar lived, he durst not thus have moved me.

BRUTUS. Peace, peace! You durst not so have tempted him.

CASSIUS. I durst not!   60

BRUTUS. No.

CASSIUS. What, durst not tempt him!

BRUTUS.   For your life you durst not.

---

32. *make conditions*: decide matters. 39. *choler*: anger. 46. *testy*: quarrelsome.
47. *digest . . . spleen*: swallow the poison of your bad temper. 50. *waspish*:
irritable. 52. *vaunting*: boasting.

CASSIUS. Do not presume too much upon my love.
　　I may do that I shall be sorry for.

BRUTUS. You have done that you should be sorry for.   65
　　There is no terror, Cassius, in your threats,
　　For I am armed so strong in honesty
　　That they pass by me as the idle wind,
　　Which I respect not. I did send to you
　　For certain sums of gold, which you denied me;   70
　　For I can raise no money by vile means —
　　By heaven, I had rather coin my heart,
　　And drop my blood for drachmas, than to wring
　　From the hard hands of peasants their vile trash
　　By any indirection.° I did send   75
　　To you for gold to pay my legions,
　　Which you denied me. Was that done like Cassius?
　　Should I have answered Caius Cassius so?
　　When Marcus Brutus grows so covetous,
　　To lock such rascal counters° from his friends,   80
　　Be ready, gods, with all your thunderbolts,
　　Dash him to pieces!

CASSIUS.　　　　　　　　　I denied you not.

BRUTUS. You did.

CASSIUS.　　　　　I did not. He was but a fool
　　That brought my answer back. Brutus hath rived° my heart.
　　A friend should bear his friend's infirmities.   85
　　But Brutus makes mine greater than they are.

BRUTUS. I do not, till you practice them on me.

CASSIUS. You love me not.

BRUTUS.　　　　　　　　I do not like your faults.

CASSIUS. A friendly eye could never see such faults.

BRUTUS. A flatterer's would not, though they do appear   90
　　As huge as high Olympus.

CASSIUS. Come, Antony, and young Octavius, come,
　　Revenge yourselves alone on Cassius,
　　For Cassius is aweary of the world —
　　Hated by one he loves, braved° by his brother,   95
　　Checked like a bondman, all his faults observed,

----

75. *indirection:* crooked ways. 80. *rascal counters:* wretched coins. 84. *rived:* broken. 95. *braved:* taunted.

Set in a notebook, learned and conned by rote,°
To cast into my teeth. Oh, I could weep
My spirit from mine eyes! There is my dagger,
And here my naked breast; within, a heart   100
Dearer than Plutus'° mine, richer than gold.
If that thou be'st a Roman, take it forth,
I, that denied thee gold, will give my heart.
Strike, as thou didst at Caesar; for I know
When thou didst hate him worst, thou lovedst him better   105
Than ever thou lovedst Cassius.

BRUTUS.   Sheathe your dagger.
Be angry when you will, it shall have scope;°
Do what you will, dishonor shall be humor.°
O Cassius, you are yokèd° with a lamb
That carries anger as the flint bears fire,   110
Who, much enforcèd, shows a hasty spark
And straight is cold again.

CASSIUS.   Hath Cassius lived
To be but mirth and laughter to his Brutus,
When grief and blood ill-tempered vexeth him?

BRUTUS. When I spoke that, I was ill-tempered too.   115

CASSIUS. Do you confess so much? Give me your hand.

BRUTUS. And my heart too.

CASSIUS.   O Brutus!

BRUTUS.   What's the matter?

CASSIUS. Have not you love enough to bear with me
When that rash humor which my mother gave me
Makes me forgetful?

BRUTUS.   Yes, Cassius, and from henceforth,   120
When you are overearnest with your Brutus,
He'll think your mother chides, and leave you so.

POET. [Within] Let me go in to see the generals.
There is some grudge between 'em, 'tis not meet
They be alone.   125

LUCILIUS. [Within] You shall not come to them.

POET. [Within] Nothing but death shall stay me.

---

97. *conned by rote:* memorized. 101. *Plutus':* Plutus was the god of wealth.
107. *scope:* free play. 108. *dishonor shall be humor:* I shall regard any insult as
a result of your mood. 109. *yokèd:* harnessed.

[*Enter* POET, *followed by* LUCILIUS, TITINIUS, *and* LUCIUS.]

CASSIUS. How now! What's the matter?

POET. For shame, you generals! What do you mean?
  Love and be friends, as two such men should be,   130
  For I have seen more years, I'm sure, than ye.

CASSIUS. Ha, ha! How vilely doth this cynic° rhyme!

BRUTUS. Get you hence, sirrah. Saucy fellow, hence!

CASSIUS. Bear with him, Brutus. 'Tis his fashion.

BRUTUS. I'll know his humor when he knows his time.°   135
  What should the wars do with these jigging fools?
  Companion,° hence!

CASSIUS.   Away, away, be gone!   [*Exit* POET.]

BRUTUS. Lucilius and Titinius, bid the commanders
  Prepare to lodge their companies tonight.

CASSIUS. And come yourselves, and bring Messala with you   140
  Immediately to us.   [*Exeunt* LUCILIUS *and* TITINIUS.]

BRUTUS.   Lucius, a bowl of wine!   [*Exit* LUCIUS.]

CASSIUS. I did not think you could have been so angry.

BRUTUS. O Cassius, I am sick of many griefs.

CASSIUS. Of your philosophy you make no use
  If you give place to accidental evils.   145

BRUTUS. No man bears sorrow better. Portia is dead.

CASSIUS. Ha! Portia!

BRUTUS. She is dead.

CASSIUS. How 'scaped I killing when I crossed you so?
  Oh, insupportable and touching loss!   150
  Upon what sickness?

BRUTUS.   Impatient of my absence,
  And grief that young Octavius with Mark Antony
  Have made themselves so strong — for with her death
  That tidings came — with this she fell distract,
  And, her attendants absent, swallowed fire.   155

CASSIUS. And died so?

BRUTUS.   Even so.

CASSIUS.   O ye immortal gods!
              [*Enter* LUCIUS, *with wine and a taper.*]

BRUTUS. Speak no more of her. Give me a bowl of wine.

---

132. *cynic:* uncouth fellow. 135. *his time:* the proper time to speak. 137. *Companion:* fellow, here used scornfully.

In this I bury all unkindness, Cassius.

CASSIUS. My heart is thirsty for that noble pledge.

Fill, Lucius, till the wine o'erswell the cup.   160

I cannot drink too much of Brutus' love.

BRUTUS. Come in, Titinius!

[*Exit* LUCIUS. *Enter* TITINIUS, *with* MESSALA.]

Welcome, good Messala.

Now sit we close about this taper here,

And call in question our necessities.

CASSIUS. Portia, art thou gone?

BRUTUS.   No more, I pray you.   165

Messala, I have here receivèd letters

That young Octavius and Mark Antony

Come down upon us with a mighty power,

Bending their expedition toward Philippi.

MESSALA. Myself have letters of the selfsame tenor.   170

BRUTUS. With what addition?

MESSALA. That by proscription and bills of outlawry

Octavius, Antony, and Lepidus

Have put to death a hundred Senators.

BRUTUS. Therein our letters do not well agree.   175

Mine speak of seventy Senators that died

By their proscriptions, Cicero being one.

CASSIUS. Cicero one!

MESSALA.   Cicero is dead,

And by that order of proscription.

BRUTUS. Well, to our work alive. What do you think   180

Of marching to Philippi presently?

CASSIUS. I do not think it good.

BRUTUS.   Your reason?

CASSIUS.   This it is:

'Tis better that the enemy seek us.

So shall he waste his means, weary his soldiers,

Doing himself offense, whilst we lying still   185

Are full of rest, defense, and nimbleness.

BRUTUS. Good reasons must of force give place to better.

The people 'twixt Philippi and this ground

Do stand in a forced affection,

For they have grudged us contribution.   190

The enemy, marching along by them,
By them shall make a fuller number up,
Come on refreshed, new-added, and encouraged.
From which advantage shall we cut him off
If at Philippi we do face him there,   195
These people at our back.
CASSIUS.   Hear me, good brother ——
BRUTUS. Under your pardon. You must note beside
    That we have tried the utmost of our friends,
    Our legions are brimful, our cause is ripe.
    The enemy increaseth every day,   200
    We, at the height, are ready to decline.
    There is a tide in the affairs of men
    Which taken at the flood leads on to fortune;
    Omitted, all the voyage of their life
    Is bound in shallows and in miseries.   205
    On such a full sea are we now afloat,
    And we must take the current when it serves,
    Or lose our ventures.
CASSIUS.   Then, with your will, go on.
    We'll along ourselves and meet them at Philippi.
BRUTUS. The deep of night is crept upon our talk,   210
    And nature must obey necessity,
    Which we will niggard with° a little rest.
    There is no more to say?
CASSIUS.   No more. Good night.
    Early tomorrow will we rise and hence.   214
BRUTUS. Lucius! [*Enter* LUCIUS.] My gown.   [*Exit* LUCIUS.]
                                    Farewell, good Messala.
    Good night, Titinius. Noble, noble Cassius,
    Good night, and good repose.
CASSIUS.   O my dear brother!
    This was an ill beginning of the night.
    Never come such division 'tween our souls!
    Let it not, Brutus.
BRUTUS.   Everything is well.   220
CASSIUS. Good night, my lord.

---

212. *niggard with:* satisfy cheaply. The meaning of lines 211–12 is: We have to
sleep, but let us take only the bare necessity of rest.

BRUTUS.   Good night, good brother.

TITINIUS *and* MESSALA. Good night, Lord Brutus.

BRUTUS.   Farewell, everyone.

   [*Exeunt all but* BRUTUS. *Enter* LUCIUS, *with the gown.*]

   Give me the gown. Where is thy instrument?

LUCIUS. Here in the tent.

BRUTUS.   What, thou speak'st drowsily?

   Poor knave, I blame thee not, thou art o'erwatched.°   225

   Call Claudius and some other of my men.

   I'll have them sleep on cushions in my tent.

LUCIUS. Varro and Claudius!   [*Enter* VARRO *and* CLAUDIUS.]

VARRO. Calls my lord?

BRUTUS. I pray you, sirs, lie in my tent and sleep.   230

   It may be I shall raise you by and by

   On business to my brother Cassius.

VARRO. So please you, we will stand and watch your pleasure.

BRUTUS. I will not have it so. Lie down, good sirs.

   It may be I shall otherwise bethink me.   235

   Look, Lucius, here's the book I sought for so,

   I put it in the pocket of my gown.

LUCIUS. I was sure your lordship did not give it me.

BRUTUS. Bear with me, good boy, I am much forgetful.

   Canst thou hold up thy heavy eyes awhile,   240

   And touch thy instrument a strain or two?

LUCIUS. Aye, my lord, an 't please you.

BRUTUS.   It does, my boy.

   I trouble thee too much, but thou art willing.

LUCIUS. It is my duty, sir.

BRUTUS. I should not urge thy duty past thy might —   245

   I know young bloods look for a time of rest.

LUCIUS. I have slept, my lord, already.

BRUTUS. It was well done, and thou shalt sleep again,

   I will not hold thee long. If I do live,

   I will be good to thee.   250

      [*Music, and a song.* LUCIUS *falls asleep as he sings.*]

   This is a sleepy tune. O murderous slumber,

   Lay'st thou thy leaden mace° upon my boy,

   That plays thee music? Gentle knave, good night.

---

225. *o'erwatched:* weary with too much watching. 252. *mace:* club.

I will not do thee so much wrong to wake thee.
If thou dost nod, thou break'st thy instrument,   255
I'll take it from thee, and, good boy, good night.
Let me see, let me see, is not the leaf turned down
Where I left reading? Here it is, I think.

                             [*Enter the* GHOST OF CAESAR.]

How ill this taper burns! Ha! Who comes here?
I think it is the weakness of mine eyes   260
That shapes this monstrous apparition.
It comes upon me. Art thou anything?
Art thou some god, some angel, or some devil,
That makest my blood cold, and my hair to stare?
Speak to me what thou art.   265

GHOST. Thy evil spirit, Brutus.
BRUTUS.   Why comest thou?
GHOST. To tell thee thou shalt see me at Philippi.
BRUTUS. Well, then I shall see thee again?
GHOST. Ay, at Philippi.
BRUTUS. Why, I will see thee at Philippi then.   [*Exit* GHOST.] 270
  Now I have taken heart, thou vanishest.
  Ill spirit, I would hold more talk with thee.
  Boy, Lucius! Varro! Claudius! Sirs, awake!
  Claudius!
LUCIUS.   The strings, my lord, are false.°   275
BRUTUS. He thinks he still is at his instrument.
  Lucius, awake!
LUCIUS. My lord?
BRUTUS. Didst thou dream, Lucius, that thou so criedst out?
LUCIUS. My lord, I do not know that I did cry.   280
BRUTUS. Yes, that thou didst. Didst thou see anything?
LUCIUS. Nothing, my lord.
BRUTUS. Sleep again, Lucius. Sirrah Claudius!
  [*To* VARRO.] Fellow thou, awake!
VARRO. My lord?   285
CLAUDIUS. My lord?
BRUTUS. Why did you so cry out, sirs, in your sleep?
VARRO *and* CLAUDIUS. Did we, my lord?
BRUTUS.   Aye. Saw you anything?

---

275. *false:* out of tune.

VARRO. No, my lord, I saw nothing.

CLAUDIUS.   Nor I, my lord.

BRUTUS. Go and commend me to my brother Cassius.   290
Bid him set on his powers betimes before,°
And we will follow.

VARRO *and* CLAUDIUS. It shall be done, my lord.   [*Exeunt.*]

ACT V

SCENE I

The plains of Philippi. Enter OCTAVIUS, ANTONY, *and their* SOLDIERS.

OCTAVIUS. Now, Antony, our hopes are answerèd.
You said the enemy would not come down,
But keep the hills and upper regions.
It proves not so, their battles° are at hand,
They mean to warn us at Philippi here,   5
Answering before we do demand of them.

ANTONY. Tut, I am in their bosoms,° and I know
Wherefore they do it. They could be content
To visit other places, and come down
With fearful bravery, thinking by this face   10
To fasten in our thoughts that they have courage.
But 'tis not so.   [*Enter a* MESSENGER.]

MESSENGER.   Prepare you, generals.
The enemy comes on in gallant show.
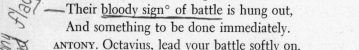
Their bloody sign° of battle is hung out,
And something to be done immediately.   15

ANTONY. Octavius, lead your battle softly on,
Upon the left hand of the even field.

OCTAVIUS. Upon the right hand I. Keep thou the left.

ANTONY. Why do you cross me in this exigent?°

OCTAVIUS. I do not cross you, but I will do so.   20

Mark Antony / changed flag

---

291. *Bid . . . before:* tell him to send his army ahead of me.
SCENE I. 4. *battles:* armies. 7. *I am in their bosoms:* I can read their thoughts.
14. *bloody sign:* red flag. 19. *exigent:* emergency.

[*March. Drum. Enter* BRUTUS, CASSIUS, *and their* ARMY, LUCILIUS,
  TITINIUS, MESSALA, *and others.*]

BRUTUS. They stand, and would have parley.°

CASSIUS. Stand fast, Titinius. We must out and talk.

OCTAVIUS. Mark Antony, shall we give sign of battle?

ANTONY. No, Caesar, we will answer on their charge.

    Make forth, the generals would have some words.   25

OCTAVIUS. Stir not until the signal.

BRUTUS. Words before blows: is it so, countrymen?

OCTAVIUS. Not that we love words better, as you do.

BRUTUS. Good words are better than bad strokes, Octavius.

ANTONY. In your bad strokes, Brutus, you give good words.   30

    Witness the hole you made in Caesar's heart,

    Crying "Long live! Hail, Caesar!"

CASSIUS.   Antony,

    The posture of your blows are yet unknown,

    But for your words, they rob the Hybla° bees,

    And leave them honeyless.

ANTONY.   Not stingless too.   35

BRUTUS. Oh, yes, and soundless too,

    For you have stol'n their buzzing, Antony,

    And very wisely threat before you sting.

ANTONY. Villains, you did not so when your vile daggers

    Hacked one another in the sides of Caesar.   40

    You showed your teeth like apes, and fawned like hounds,

    And bowed like bondmen, kissing Caesar's feet,

    Whilst damnèd Casca, like a cur, behind

    Struck Caesar on the neck. O you flatterers!

CASSIUS. Flatterers! Now, Brutus, thank yourself.   45

    This tongue had not offended so today

    If Cassius might have ruled.°

OCTAVIUS. Come, come, the cause. If arguing make us sweat,

    The proof of it will turn to redder drops.

    Look,   50

    I draw a sword against conspirators.

    When think you that the sword goes up° again?

---

21. *would have parley:* are willing to talk. 34. *Hybla:* the bees of Mt. Hybla
were famous for their honey. 46–47. *This tongue . . . ruled:* I warned you not
to let Antony live to achieve power. 52. *goes up:* will be put back in its scab-
bard.

*Octavius—
revenge for Caesar's
death*

Never, till Caesar's three and thirty wounds
Be well avenged, or till another Caesar°
Have added slaughter to the sword of traitors.   55
BRUTUS. Caesar, thou canst not die by traitors' hands,
Unless thou bring'st them with thee.
OCTAVIUS.   So I hope.
I was not born to die on Brutus' sword.
BRUTUS. Oh, if thou wert the noblest of thy strain,
Young man, thou couldst not die more honorable.   60
CASSIUS. A peevish schoolboy, worthless of such honor,
Joined with a masquer° and a reveler!
ANTONY. Old Cassius still!
OCTAVIUS.   Come, Antony, away!
Defiance, traitors, hurl we in your teeth.
If you dare fight today, come to the field;   65
If not, when you have stomachs.°
                    [*Exeunt* OCTAVIUS, ANTONY, *and their* ARMY.]
CASSIUS. Why, now, blow wind, swell billow, and swim bark!°
The storm is up, and all is on the hazard.
BRUTUS. Ho, Lucilius! Hark, a word with you.
LUCILIUS. My lord?   [*They speak apart.*]
CASSIUS. Messala!   70
MESSALA. What says my general?
CASSIUS.   Messala,
This is my birthday, as this very day
Was Cassius born. Give me thy hand, Messala.
Be thou my witness that, against my will,
As Pompey was, am I compelled to set   75
Upon one battle all our liberties.
You know that I held Epicurus° strong,
And his opinion. Now I change my mind,
And partly credit things that do presage.°
Coming from Sardis, on our former ensign°   80
Two mighty eagles fell, and there they perched,
Gorging and feeding from our soldiers' hands,

---

54. *another Caesar:* Octavius is talking about himself. 62. *masquer:* one who
attended "masques," Elizabethan court dramas. 66. *stomachs:* appetite for battle. 67. *bark:* a ship. 77. *Epicurus:* a philosopher who told his followers that
omens were only superstitions. 79. *presage:* foretell. 80. *former ensign:* foremost
battle flag.

Who to Philippi here consorted° us.
This morning are they fled away and gone,
And in their steads do ravens, crows, and kites°   85
Fly o'er our heads and downward look on us,
As we were sickly prey. Their shadows seem
A canopy most fatal, under which
Our army lies, ready to give up the ghost.

MESSALA. Believe not so.

CASSIUS.   I but believe it partly,   90
For I am fresh of spirit and resolved
To meet all perils very constantly.

BRUTUS. Even so, Lucilius.

CASSIUS.   Now, most noble Brutus,
The gods today stand friendly, that we may,
Lovers in peace, lead on our days to age!   95
But since the affairs of men rest still incertain,
Let's reason with the worst that may befall.
If we do lose this battle, then is this
The very last time we shall speak together.
What are you then determinèd to do?   100

BRUTUS. Even by the rule of that philosophy°
By which I did blame Cato for the death
Which he did give himself — I know not how,
But I do find it cowardly and vile,
For fear of what might fall, so to prevent   105
The time of life° — arming myself with patience
To stay° the providence of some high powers
That govern us below.

CASSIUS.   Then, if we lose this battle,
You are contented to be led in triumph
Thorough the streets of Rome?   110

BRUTUS. No, Cassius, no. Think not, thou noble Roman,
That ever Brutus will go bound to Rome.
He bears too great a mind. But this same day

---

83. *consorted:* accompanied. 85. *ravens, crows, and kites:* birds associated with death. 101. *that philosophy:* stoicism. Brutus says that even if he is defeated, he will continue to live and trust to providence. Cato, Brutus's father-in-law, committed suicide in defeat. Brutus does not approve of his action. Compare Cassius' speech on suicide (Act I, Scene III), in which he takes the opposite side of the argument. 106. *time of life:* natural end of life. 107. *stay:* await.

Say goodbye to each other [handwritten note in left margin]

Must end that work the ides of March begun,
And whether we shall meet again I know not.   115
Therefore our everlasting farewell take.
Forever and forever, farewell, Cassius!
If we do meet again, why, we shall smile;
If not, why then this parting was well made.

CASSIUS. Forever and forever farewell, Brutus!   120
If we do meet again, we'll smile indeed;
If not, 'tis true this parting was well made.

BRUTUS. Why then, lead on. Oh, that a man might know
The end of this day's business ere it come!
But it sufficeth that the day will end,   125
And then the end is known. Come, ho! Away!   [*Exeunt.*]

SCENE II

*The field of battle. Alarums.** Enter* BRUTUS *and* MESSALA.

winning his battle [handwritten note in left margin]

BRUTUS. Ride, ride, Messala, ride, and give these bills°
Unto the legions on the other side.   [*Loud alarum.*]
Let them set on at once, for I perceive
But cold demeanor° in Octavius' wing,
And sudden push gives them the overthrow.   5
Ride, ride, Messala. Let them all come down.   [*Exeunt.*]

SCENE III

Another part of the field. Alarums. Enter CASSIUS *and* TITINIUS.

CASSIUS. Oh, look, Titinius, look, the villains fly!
    [handwritten note above: *his men*]
Myself have to mine own turned enemy.°
This ensign° here of mine was turning back.
I slew the coward, and did take it from him.

TITINIUS. O Cassius, Brutus gave the word too early,   5
Who, having some advantage on Octavius,

SCENE II. **Alarums:* bugle calls, cries, battle noises. 1. *bills:* orders. 4. *cold
demeanor:* lack of spirit.
SCENE III. 2. *Myself . . . enemy:* Cassius is fighting his own men, who are
fleeing. 3. *ensign:* flag bearer.

[handwritten: Brutus men don't aid Cassius—take stuff of Bodies.]

Took it too eagerly. His soldiers fell to spoil°
Whilst we by Antony are all enclosed.   [*Enter* PINDARUS.]

[handwritten: Brutus gave battle to early.]

PINDARUS. Fly further off, my lord, fly further off.
Mark Antony is in your tents, my lord.   10
Fly, therefore, noble Cassius, fly far off.

CASSIUS. This hill is far enough. Look, look, Titinius,
Are those my tents where I perceive the fire?

[handwritten: Cassius tents Signal burning]

TITINIUS. They are, my lord.

CASSIUS.   Titinius, if thou lovest me,
Mount thou my horse and hide thy spurs in him   15
Till he have brought thee up to yonder troops
And here again, that I may rest assured
Whether yond troops are friend or enemy.

[handwritten: to go see whose tents, & whats happening]

TITINIUS. I will be here again, even with a thought.   [*Exit.*]

CASSIUS. Go, Pindarus, get higher on that hill —   20
My sight was ever thick.° Regard Titinius,
And tell me what thou notest about the field.

                            [PINDARUS *ascends the hill.*]

This day I breathèd first. Time is come round,
And where I did begin, there shall I end,

[handwritten: — foreshadow his death]

My life is run his compass. Sirrah, what news?   25

PINDARUS. [*Above.*] O my lord!

CASSIUS. What news?

[handwritten: mis interpretation]

PINDARUS. [*Above.*] Titinius is enclosèd round about
With horsemen that make to him on the spur,
Yet he spurs on. Now they are almost on him.   30
Now, Titinius! Now some light.° Oh, he lights too.
He's ta'en. [*Shout.*] And, hark! They shout for joy.

CASSIUS. Come down, behold no more.
Oh, coward that I am, to live so long,
To see my best friend ta'en before my face!   35

                            [PINDARUS *descends.*]

Come hither, sirrah.
In Parthia did I take thee prisoner,
And then I swore thee, saving of thy life.
That whatsoever I did bid thee do
Thou shouldst attempt it. Come now, keep thine oath.   40
Now be a free man, and with this good sword,

---

7. *fell to spoil*: started looting. 21. *thick*: weak. 31. *light*: descend.

That ran through Caesar's bowels, search this bosom.
Stand not to answer. Here, take thou the hilts,
And when my face is covered, as 'tis now,
Guide thou the sword.   [PINDARUS *stabs him.*]
                              Caesar, thou art revenged,   45
Even with the sword that killed thee.   [*Dies.*]
PINDARUS. So, I am free, yet would not so have been,
    Durst I have done my will. O Cassius!
    Far from this country Pindarus shall run,
    Where never Roman shall take note of him.   50
                    [*Exit. Enter* TITINIUS *with* MESSALA.]
MESSALA. It is but change,° Titinius, for Octavius
    Is overthrown by noble Brutus' power,
    As Cassius' legions are by Antony.
TITINIUS. These tidings will well comfort Cassius.
MESSALA. Where did you leave him?
TITINIUS.   All disconsolate,   55
    With Pindarus his bondman, on this hill.
MESSALA. Is not that he that lies upon the ground?
TITINIUS. He lies not like the living. Oh, my heart!
MESSALA. Is not that he?
TITINIUS.   No, this was he, Messala,
    But Cassius is no more. O setting sun,   60
    As in thy red rays thou dost sink to night,
    So in his red blood Cassius' day is set,
    The sun of Rome is set! Our day is gone,
    Clouds, dews, and dangers come. Our deeds are done!
    Mistrust of my success hath done this deed.   65
MESSALA. Mistrust of good success hath done this deed.
    O hateful error, melancholy's child,
    Why dost thou show to the apt° thoughts of men
    The things that are not? O error, soon conceived,
    Thou never comest unto a happy birth,   70
    But kill'st the mother that engendered thee!
TITINIUS. What, Pindarus! Where art thou, Pindarus?
MESSALA. Seek him, Titinius, whilst I go to meet
    The noble Brutus, thrusting this report
    Into his ears. I may say "thrusting" it,   75

---

51. *change*: exchange (a see-saw battle). 68. *apt*: quick.

For piercing steel and darts envenomèd
Shall be as welcome to the ears of Brutus
As tidings of this sight.

TITINIUS.   Hie you, Messala,
  And I will seek for Pindarus the while.   [*Exit* MESSALA.]
  Why didst thou send me forth, brave Cassius?   80
  Did I not meet thy friends? And did not they
  Put on my brows this wreath of victory,
  And bid me give it thee? Didst thou not hear their shouts?
  Alas, thou has misconstrued everything!
  But hold thee, take this garland on thy brow.   85
  Thy Brutus bid me give it thee, and I
  Will do his bidding. Brutus, come apace,°
  And see how I regarded Caius Cassius.
  By your leave, gods, this is a Roman's part.
  Come, Cassius' sword, and find Titinius' heart.   [*Dies.*]   90
[*Alarum. Enter* MESSALA, *with* BRUTUS, *young* CATO, *and others.*]
BRUTUS. Where, where, Messala, doth his body lie?
MESSALA. Lo, yonder, and Titinius mourning it.
BRUTUS. Titinius' face is upward.
CATO.   He is slain.
BRUTUS. O Julius Caesar, thou art mighty yet!
  Thy spirit walks abroad, and turns our swords   95
  In our own proper entrails.   [*Low alarums.*]
CATO.   Brave Titinius!
  Look whether he have not crowned dead Cassius!
BRUTUS. Are yet two Romans living such as these?
  The last of all the Romans, fare thee well!
  It is impossible that ever Rome   100
  Should breed thy fellow. Friends, I owe moe tears
  To this dead man than you shall see me pay.
  I shall find time, Cassius, I shall find time.
  Come therefore, and to Thasos send his body.
  His funerals shall not be in our camp,   105
  Lest it discomfort° us. Lucilius, come,
  And come, young Cato. Let us to the field.
  Labeo and Flavius,° set our battles on.

---

87. *apace:* quickly. 106. *discomfort:* depress. 108. *Labeo and Flavius:* two soldiers in Brutus's army.

'Tis three o'clock, and, Romans, yet ere night
We shall try fortune in a second fight.   [*Exeunt.*]   110

SCENE IV

Another part of the field. Alarum. Enter BRUTUS, MESSALA, YOUNG
CATO, LUCILIUS, FLAVIUS, *and* SOLDIERS, *fighting.*

BRUTUS. Yet, countrymen, oh, yet hold up your heads!
CATO. What fellow doth not? Who will go with me?
     I will proclaim my name about the field.
     I am the son of Marcus Cato, ho! —
     A foe of tyrants, and my country's friend.   5
     I am the son of Marcus Cato, ho!
BRUTUS. And I am Brutus, Marcus Brutus, I —
     Brutus, my country's friend. Know me for Brutus!   [*Exit.*]
LUCILIUS. O young and noble Cato, art thou down?
     Why, now thou diest as bravely as Titinius,   10
     And mayst be honored, being Cato's son.
FIRST SOLDIER. Yield, or thou diest.
LUCILIUS.   Only I yield to die.
     [*Offering money.*] There is so much that thou wilt kill me straight.
     Kill Brutus,° and be honored in his death.
FIRST SOLDIER. We must not. A noble prisoner!   15
SECOND SOLDIER. Room, ho! Tell Antony, Brutus is ta'en.
FIRST SOLDIER. I'll tell the news. Here comes the general.
                                             [*Enter* ANTONY.]
     Brutus is ta'en, Brutus is ta'en, my lord.
ANTONY. Where is he?
LUCILIUS. Safe, Antony, Brutus is safe enough.   20
     I dare assure thee that no enemy
     Shall ever take alive the noble Brutus.
     The gods defend him from so great a shame!
     When you do find him, or alive or dead,
     He will be found like Brutus, like himself.   25
ANTONY. This is not Brutus, friend, but, I assure you,
     A prize no less in worth. Keep this man safe,

---

14. *kill Brutus:* Lucilius pretends he is Brutus so that the real Brutus might escape.

Give him all kindness. I had rather have
Such men my friends than enemies. Go on,
And see whether Brutus be alive or dead,   30
And bring us word unto Octavius' tent
How everything is chanced.   [*Exeunt.*]

SCENE V

Another part of the field. Enter BRUTUS, DARDANIUS, CLITUS, STRATO,
and VOLUMNIUS.

BRUTUS. Come, poor remains of friends, rest on this rock.

CLITUS. Statilius showed the torchlight, but, my lord,
He came not back. He is or ta'en or slain.

BRUTUS. Sit thee down, Clitus. Slaying is the word,
It is a deed in fashion. Hark thee, Clitus.   5
[*Whispering.*]

CLITUS. What, I, my lord? No, not for all the world.

BRUTUS. Peace then, no words.

CLITUS.   I'll rather kill myself.

BRUTUS. [*Whispering.*] Hark thee, Dardanius.

DARDANIUS.   Shall I do such a deed?

CLITUS. O Dardanius!

DARDANIUS. O Clitus!   10

CLITUS. What ill request did Brutus make to thee?

DARDANIUS. To kill him, Clitus. Look, he meditates.

CLITUS. Now is that noble vessel full of grief,
That it runs over even at his eyes.

BRUTUS. Come hither, good Volumnius, list° a word.   15

VOLUMNIUS. What says my lord?

BRUTUS.   Why, this, Volumnius.
The ghost of Caesar hath appeared to me
To several° times by night — at Sardis once,
And this last night here in Philippi fields.
I know my hour is come.

VOLUMNIUS.   Not so, my lord.   20

BRUTUS. Nay, I am sure it is, Volumnius.
Thou seest the world, Volumnius, how it goes,
Our enemies have beat us to the pit.   [*Low alarums.*]

SCENE V. 15. *list:* listen to. 18. *several:* different.

It is more worthy to leap in ourselves
Than tarry till they push us. Good Volumnius,   25
Thou know'st that we two went to school together.
Even for that our love of old, I prithee
Hold thou my sword hilts whilst I run on it.
VOLUMNIUS. That's not an office for a friend, my lord. [*Alarum still.*]
CLITUS. Fly, fly, my lord, there is no tarrying here.   30
BRUTUS. Farewell to you, and you, and you, Volumnius.
  Strato, thou hast been all this while asleep —
  Farewell to thee too, Strato. Countrymen,
  My heart doth joy that yet in all my life
  I found no man but he was true to me.   35
  I shall have glory by this losing day,
  More than Octavius and Mark Antony
  By this vile conquest shall attain unto.
  So, fare you well at once, for Brutus' tongue
  Hath almost ended his life's history.   40
  Night hangs upon mine eyes, my bones would rest
  That have but labored to attain this hour.
                        [*Alarum. Cry within,* Fly, fly, fly!]
CLITUS. Fly, my lord, fly!
BRUTUS.   Hence! I will follow.
                 [*Exeunt* CLITUS, DARDANIUS, *and* VOLUMNIUS.]
  I prithee, Strato, stay thou by thy lord.
  Thou art a fellow of a good respect,   45
  Thy life hath had some smatch° of honor in it.
  Hold then my sword, and turn away thy face
  While I do run upon it. Wilt thou, Strato?
STRATO. Give me your hand first. Fare you well, my lord.
BRUTUS. Farewell, good Strato. [*Runs on his sword.*] Caesar, now be
  still.   50
  I killed not thee with half so good a will.   [*Dies.*]
[*Alarum. Retreat. Enter* OCTAVIUS, ANTONY, MESSALA, LUCILIUS, *and
  the army.*]
OCTAVIUS. What man is that?
MESSALA. My master's man. Strato, where is thy master?
STRATO. Free from the bondage you are in, Messala.
  The conquerors can but make a fire of him,   55

---
46. *smatch:* taste.

For Brutus only overcame himself,
And no man else hath honor by his death.

LUCILIUS. So Brutus should be found. I thank thee, Brutus,
That thou hast proved Lucilius' saying true.

OCTAVIUS. All that served Brutus, I will entertain them.°   60
Fellow, wilt thou bestow thy time with me?

STRATO. Aye, if Messala will prefer° me to you.

OCTAVIUS. Do so, good Messala.

MESSALA. How died my master, Strato?

STRATO. I held the sword, and he did run on it.

MESSALA. Octavius, then take him to follow thee
That did the latest° service to my master.

ANTONY. This was the noblest Roman of them all.
All the conspirators, save only he,
Did that they did in envy of great Caesar.   70
He only, in a general honest thought
And common good to all, made one of them.
His life was gentle, and the elements
So mixed in him that Nature might stand up
And say to all the world, "This was a man."   75

OCTAVIUS. According to his virtue let us use him,
With all respect and rites of burial.
Within my tent his bones tonight shall lie,
Most like a soldier, ordered honorably.
So call the field to rest, and let's away,   80
To part° the glories of this happy day.   [*Exeunt.*]

---

60. *entertain them*: take into my service. 62. *prefer*: recommend. 67. *latest*: last.
81. *part*: divide up.

[Handwritten annotations: "Brutus more noble than himself," "B didn't envy Caesar — defending Brutus' enrollment in conspiracy," "Biggest complement," "Biggest compliment."]

"Figure with Clasped Hands" by the
Mexican artist José Clemente Orozco.

PROBLEMS OF CONSCIENCE

*"Conscience doth make cowards
of us all."*

SHAKESPEARE

Literature is often the record of struggle. On a heroic scale, struggle involves armies engaged in mortal combat. Such a struggle takes place at the end of Julius Caesar. But struggle is also an individual matter, an internal problem of conscience. Even on the battlefield, the heroes of literature, like Brutus, must confront their consciences. The struggle of a man and his conscience is the real theme of most literature, for we are ultimately concerned with individuals, not armies. The eternal problems are moral, not political.

The central figure in Julius Caesar is not Caesar, although he is a great conqueror about to receive the crown of the Empire. It is Brutus, whom we come to understand best because we know so much more about how he thinks and feels. We do not know whether Caesar listens to his conscience or not: it is ambition that keeps him awake nights. Brutus cannot sleep because he feels so much anguish. In a brief soliloquy, he ponders:

Since Cassius first did whet me against Caesar,
I have not slept.
Between the acting of a dreadful thing
And the first motion, all the interim is
Like a phantasma, or a hideous dream:
The Genius and the mortal instruments

> Are then in council; and the state of man
> Like to a little kingdom, suffers then
> The nature of an insurrection.

The "insurrection" within Brutus is his struggle with his conscience. Should he act for the "good of the State" by murdering Caesar or should he listen to his conscience, which tells him murder is a grievous moral offense? Shakespeare describes the problem of conscience as the conflict between "the Genius and the mortal instruments," between the spirit and body of man.

Is conscience an instinct? Thomas Jefferson thought so: "The moral sense," he wrote, "is as much a part of a man as his leg or arm." And the French philosopher Rousseau said, "Where do I get my rules of conduct? I find them in my heart. Whatever I feel to be good is good. Whatever I feel to be evil is evil."

Others have claimed that conscience is a product of culture, formed by social pressures. Historian Henry Taylor said, a bit cynically, "Conscience is, in most men, an anticipation of the opinion of others."

Benjamin, the donkey in Animal Farm, kept silent when his conscience told him that the revolution had produced greater tyranny than the rule of Mr. Jones. Only when his friend Boxer was carted off to the slaughterhouse did Benjamin find his voice, too late then to save Boxer or to turn back the rule of the pigs. Too often, people have kept silent while horrendous wrongs were committed. Thousands of "decent" people kept silent as Hitler and Stalin carried out their barbaric purges.

The German poet Goethe wrote, "No one knows what he is doing, so long as he is acting rightly, but one is always conscious of what is wrong." The knowledge of doing what is wrong plagues characters in each of the selections which follow. For those characters, the powerful forces of conscience at work create the same internal insurrection that gave Brutus sleepless nights.

Sometimes the pangs of conscience are felt immediately. But sometimes they wait, to return later, like Caesar's ghost.

Sherrel

WHIT BURNETT

I do not know whether I can do this thing or not. Maybe it is just a thought, maybe I just think it is necessary to do it. I mean about the name. I have thought about it a lot though and it keeps urging at me. It is not easy to understand. But I must try to understand and explain it.

You see, I actually did have a brother. People sometimes asked me, Are you the only boy in the family? And I've said, Yes. This wasn't a lie wholly. I was the first born in my family. But there were others, two others. One died in long clothes.[1] We have his picture at home. The other was named Sherrel.

It is easy to remember him. My mother had us photographed together, for instance. And one especial print was transferred onto little smooth disks the size of a saucer. The disks fit into small twisted wire easels, and my brother and I used to sit on the easel like that on my mother's bureau in the bedroom.

He was, as I said, younger than I. This is important. The neighbors used to say, It's the difference in their ages. They tried to explain in that way why I was so mean. And you can see the difference clearly enough on the picture disks. We both stood by the photographer's chair, a plush chair. But I was up to the top of it. My brother's hand rested on the arm. It looks pretty small to me now because I'm twice as old as I was then. We both wore black velvet tam-o'-shanters and dark red velvet coats and pants. My mouth was a little open, too, looking at the photographer. I did not touch my brother. He had one hand, which was very small, on the chair, and the other one had hold of me. His hair was lighter than mine and

---

[1] *in long clothes:* as an infant.

softer, and his eyes wider and bluer. He had a small mouth like a flower, and it was smiling. He was a beautiful child. This was the brother I killed.

I am not telling you about a melodrama. I won't be arrested and hanged. I did not kill him yesterday. It was a long time ago, in fact, and I do not remember it all the time, only sometimes when something suggests the way I was then or when someone asks, Have you any other brothers? And I say, No. And here too in this other town at this school except for a girl I know I am quite alone in certain ways, and in the winter as now I have seen any number of things to remind me. There is, for example, an epidemic of smallpox here, and instead of smooth fast automobile hearses they still have funeral carriages that drag along slowly through the streets. Only once have I ridden in such a carriage. And that was then.

There are some things difficult to remember out of childhood. I do not remember when my brother was born. There was not so much difference then. Only four years before, I had been born. But I remember clearly when I was nine. My brother then was five. And we were two in the family. But I was the first.

Do you know how this is? Nine and five? Well, nine is somebody. Five is still curls. At nine I have seen something of the world. What have you seen at five? Go on, you can't come with us! Go on back to the house! We're going down to the store. You'll get run over. Go on, you can't play with us. You ain't big enough. Go on, grow up some before you come tagging around after us. Who asked you along? Beat it! I know how that is. I said all that, more brutally even. He didn't say anything. He didn't cry or whine or crab. I probably would have. He stopped following simply, and stood there. And then we ran off. He stood alone. Sometimes I found him other places alone, sitting still in a corner thinking quietly about something. I am always a little puzzled now I am older. I have talked it over with others. He would have been important. . . . But at nine one is a weed, growing wild. Five is still in the hothouse.

We lived near the sand hills. It wasn't until several years later that I really got into the hills exploring them with a cousin of my own age. Sherrel never did get there. And there was a great liking in both of us for the hills, his maybe different from mine. I often found him sitting dreaming looking at them. But one day late in the spring the hills in a way came down to our house. A cloudburst drenched them, rolling down soft sand, cutting great ditches in the road in front of our place. We weren't long in discovering that, I'll tell you. When Sherrel wandered out of the kitchen, the ditch was full of us kids. It was a peach of a ditch, as high as our head, gnawed with caves and dangers.

I started the discoveries. There's some hole, I yelled. And down I had gone, doing what the others wanted to do, the first to absorb their wishes. Then they followed, yelling too. Sherrel, I suppose, could hear my voice coming up out of the ground. He came over to the ditch and looked down, standing alone above us. Go on back, I shouted, you'll fall in. He moved away. I paid no more attention then to him, and the rest of us ran racing, hiding, searching, together in the wash.

And then, separated from the others for a moment or so, I noticed something odd about my hands. Hey, kids, I cried, lookee! Look at my hands! They looked. They stood back in wonderment. They looked at their own hands. No, they couldn't, they said. It was something funny. Look what Martin can do! Lookee, he can peel off his hands! It was true, something had happened to my hands. I took hold and pulled off long shreds of skin. I amazed them all. They stood astounded.

Let me see, said somebody. It was Sherrel.

Say, I yelled, didn't I say not to come down here? You ain't big enough to be in this here ditch. Let me see your hands, he said. The kids were all looking at me. I'll let you see, all right! I said. He stood his ground and didn't go. That makes me mad, I felt. No, I said. I took him by the shoulder and talked straight in his face, hard. How many times do I have to tell you to get out of this ditch! He turned around and walked up the gorge to a shallower spot and climbed slowly out.

A day or so later Sherrel stayed in bed. There's something the matter with him, my mother said. She didn't know what. Then he took a high fever, they said, and was delirious. I thought it was strange about delirious. Sherrel's eyes were shut and he looked as if he was sleeping, but he was talking without any sense. We'll have to have a doctor, my mother said. And that afternoon the doctor came to our house, wiping his feet at the door and entering with a serious look. Let's see the other young fellow, he said. Anything wrong with him? He had a little sore throat, my mother said, but he's all right. He looked down my throat. Look at my hands, I said, ain't they funny?

What I thought, he said.

The same afternoon a man from downtown came and nailed up a yellow flag. It was a cloth sign saying, black on orange, Scarlet Fever. I couldn't go out of the yard. That's sure tough, the kids said, peering through the pickets. I even had to keep back from the fence, too. It was catching.

I sat on the steps fronting north from our bare two-room brick house and looked at the hills. I had had the Scarlet Fever and hadn't even known it. Why, my mother said, he was playing around all the time. Why, he was out there playing in the ditch with all those children. That's bad, said the doctor. But my brother was worse. He had it good.

I remember the windows in the front room were darkened and my mother never went to bed. She never took her clothes off. And my father didn't go to work. My aunt came to the fence with a bag of oranges and bananas. How is he? she asked. If he isn't any better, Dr. Anderson says he'd better have a consultation, said my mother. How is Dr. Anderson? asked my aunt. He is the best doctor in town, my mother said.

I sat in the sun all tired now and weak. But I wasn't sick. I was big and nine.

I remember the consultation. There were four doctors in the kitchen standing around and talking low and sitting down and getting up. I could see in from outside. My mother was nervous and walking around, and my father, who was a big heavy man, stood around too and sat down and then got up. They were waiting for something definite they spoke of that I could not understand. It was the Crisis. I asked what it was, and my mother had said, Sherrel will get better then. I didn't know what a Crisis would be like, and I opened the door slowly and got into the house quietly, past the doctors.

My father and mother were in the front room by the bed where Sherrel lay. He was still and wasn't talking deliriously. And then my mother, who was standing by him with my father waiting, suddenly cried terribly for a minute or so, and then she took hold of my father and pulled him down by the bed to the floor. I didn't know what was happening. I was frightened, too. Pray, she sobbed. Pray, if you never prayed before. O God, she began . . . and she was crying more and more. My father was kneeling heavily and strangely in a big dark bulk. He put his arm around my mother. There, there, he said. I never saw them like that before. My father is English, my mother is German. I did not think about that though then. I thought, I am scared; this is all different, and dark. I stood in the doorway, too frightened to move.

Come in, Martin, my mother suddenly cried out to me. Come in to your brother. Come here with us. I came over, and there we were all kneeling down together.

Do you want your brother to die? she asked. No, I said. I was frightened at her, at the strange heavy silence on my father, at my brother even. Go and look at him, she told me.

I got up and looked at my brother's white face. It was like a face of ivory with pale lips. I looked hard. He was different too. What do I do? I thought. I am rough, not like that. My mother is looking at me terribly. Kiss him. I bent over and touched his face. His lips opened with a quiet breath, like a little flower bursting on my cheek.

The crisis came and passed. It came while we were in the room there. My mother could not wait. She went to the bed, trying to wake up my brother. Look, Sherrel, she whispered, we are going to get you the nice pearl-handled pocketknife tomorrow. You won't have to wait till Christmas. Tomorrow. You just get well, now. Sherrel! Do you hear me, Sherrel?

Or, he can have mine, I thought.

But he didn't hear us. He didn't hear anybody. Then my mother went to sleep suddenly, it seemed, and drooped down by the bed and they put her in the other room on a couch.

I stood in the dark by a curtain when the doctors came in. Too bad, said Dr. Anderson. He leaned over my brother. Remarkable head, said one of the others. Isn't it! spoke up another one. Artist's head, said the one with the beard. Yes. . . . Then the doctors walked out together into the room where my mother was, and in a little while they all left the house.

A few days later there were the strange preparations for the funeral. I don't want to dwell on the funeral. That is not the point. But we rode in a carriage shut in by ourselves, still quarantined, the others following slowly behind us. I remember we passed the Wat-

sons' place. They were standing at the gate, the family staring stu-
pidly at the procession as the horse carriages jogged down the hilly
street rolling off to the cemetery.

This is all strange, I thought, riding along past the Watsons'
house in a carriage like this. My mother and my father and myself.
I was taken up with the thought and looked back out of the carriage window now and then at the carriages behind me. My mother
pulled me back to sit up straight. My mother's face was drawn and
tired, and she was crying. My father's eyes had tears in them too.
I could not cry. I thought, I ought to cry. How can I cry? I am not
hurt any place where I can feel. I squeezed into the corner of the
carriage opposite them, pressing up against one hand hard to make
it hurt. It turned numb and pained but not in a crying way. You
cry easy differently, I thought. Onions, for instance, make you cry.
Would it have been a trick, I thought, or right and honest if I had
put an onion in my handkerchief, no one seeing me, and then
smelled it now and then in the curtained shadows of the carriage? I
would have cried then. I wanted to cry. But all I could think was,
Sherrel was a queer kid. Were we brothers sure enough? Am I anybody's brother? Why don't I cry? . . .

You see, he would sit in a corner quiet and frailly beautiful. I
was nine and active. It's the difference in their ages. Maybe so.
There were the Elwell brothers, now. They were twins. They had a
carpenter's shop. It was a peach of a shop, down in a cellar, and
they worked together great, making book ends and rabbit hutches
and things like that.

I gave him that sickness. I knew that. That killed him. That is
why my brother is dead. But I am trying to remember, to clear
things up. I am trying to remember if I thought that then. I remember I thought, It's funny just he got it. Why not Leona Eads,
Ed or Billy Simons? They touched my hands. I wondered if I hadn't
forced my sickness on my brother out of hatred for him, out of my
own peculiar older-brother hatred. Did I slap him, maybe strike him
in the face with my peeling hand? Perhaps I did. I wondered over
this for many weeks now and then.

I'm not even sure now. I might have. It's funny how mean, you
see, a person can be. I've thought of that. I've got a girl. I've talked
things over with her, not everything, but generally, you know. She
doesn't like meanness either. I remember when I was about twelve,

my sister was just coming along then. She was about two, and I had
to tend her occasionally. I didn't like it. Once my mother said to
me, Do you want your little sister to die too? Well, no, I said. She
might even have said, Do you want to kill your little sister too?
Maybe this was it, because I asked myself that a lot later, trying to
be better. I said, Do you want to kill your sister too? No, I said.

I didn't, either. But I remembered what I'd said when she was
born. I said, There's enough in this family already. But I didn't
want to kill her. Still I had killed my brother. I had killed Sherrel.
Not only by giving him sickness. But by meanness.

This is how I figure it now. I killed my brother by meanness. And
it is too bad. I wouldn't do it now. I am not that way. I could have
got him a job here in this other town where I am now after he got
out of school. I'll be out of school here pretty soon. I'm eighteen
next week. Then I'll go on a paper where I've got a stand-in. I'd
have said, Now you keep on at school and read a lot of good things,
good books you know, poetry and good things and learn how to
write. You've got good stuff in you, I can tell. You're going to be
an artist. So am I. We'll be two artists, brothers, maybe different,
but we can help each other. You've got a poetic style, and I've got
a stronger style. I see things more as they are. I'm a little tougher.
I can digest more. But that's all right. When I get going, I'll help
you. You've got fine things in you. I'll help you bring them out.

That's the kind of a person he would have been. He would have
been an artist. There's nothing any bigger than that. Nothing finer.
It's the best, in a holy way. It has to be in you first. It hides sometimes and doesn't get a chance to come out where people are.

I've talked that over with people, with that girl I spoke of. I want
to be an artist. A writer. I can see back from where I am, though.
I've been pretty mean, pretty contemptible. It's funny to look back
like that and see yourself in old pictures and things. It's hard to
think you had the same name, even.

And that's what I'm puzzling over now. There's nothing wrong
with my name, actually. Mark. Mark Stowe. It was first Martin. It
was even Martin Tilton Stowe. I didn't like it. All that, I mean. I
cut it down to Mark Stowe. It made me feel surer, quicker, stronger.

But even that doesn't quite go. It doesn't all fit. I'm not all blunt,
like that. Mark. Mark Stowe. I've got other things. I've written poems, even, and I wouldn't kiss a girl hard. I know how my brother

was. He would have been like that too, only a lot more.

And, you know, about the name. . . . My folks are getting along now. Sisters don't count, the way I mean, that is. I'm the only boy in the family. And I've been thinking, what if I should write a poem, a long, good one — here I am, alive and everything — and sign it not Mark Stowe but, well, Sherrel Stowe? Do you see what I mean? And then by and by there would be another poem, and after a while I would just go ahead and use it right along. Can you understand that? How I would be more him too, then — Sherrel?

When a friendship or love affair goes awry, conscience often makes us try to heal the breach. But some wounds will not be healed.

Friendship

B. TRAVEN

One early afternoon the French owner of a restaurant located on Bolivar Street in Mexico City noticed a medium-sized black dog sitting on the sidewalk near the open door of his establishment. Looking in at the Frenchman with soft brown eyes which sparkled with a suggestion of making friends, the dog put on that good-natured, innocent, somewhat tragicomic expression found on some old tramps, who, no matter what happens to them, always have a humorous answer in store, even if they are kicked down the porch steps and a bucket of water is thrown into their face.

For a moment the Frenchman glanced at the dog. Interpreting that look in his own way, the dog wagged his tail, cocked his head, and gave his open mouth such a quizzical twist that he appeared to be grinning at the Frenchman.

So he couldn't help but smile back, and for an instant he had the strange sensation that a little spark of the golden sun had crept into his heart as if to touch it and warm it.

His tail wagging faster now, the dog rose slightly, sat down again and, remaining in this sitting position, moved a few inches closer to the door, yet did not enter.

Considering this a very decent attitude for a hungry street dog, the Frenchman could resist no longer. From a half-empty plate, just taken from a table by a waitress walking past him toward the kitchen, he picked up a steak which the customer, obviously not hungry, had only nibbled.

Lifting that juicy steak with two fingers, holding it high for a few seconds, his eyes fixed on the dog, he waved it invitingly and, by a move of his head, hinted at the dog to come inside and get it. The

419

dog, wagging not only his tail but his whole hindquarters, closed and opened his mouth quickly, licking his lips with a rosy tongue. Still, he would not enter.

The Frenchman, becoming more interested in the dog than in his patrons, left his place behind the counter and took the steak to the door, playing it before the dog's nose for a few moments before he let it go to its final destination.

The dog caught it more gently than hastily, gave the donor a grateful look, stepped back from the door and lay down on the sidewalk close to the cafe. There he ate that big steak in the undisturbed manner that comes only from a clear conscience.

Done with his meal, the dog stood up, approached the cafe door, sat down and waited patiently until the Frenchman would once again notice him. As soon as the Frenchman granted him that hoped-for look, the dog rose, wagged his tail, put on his comical grin, shook his head as if in fun so that his ears fairly shook, turned, and went on his way.

The Frenchman, naturally, thought that the dog had returned to face him hoping for another helping. But when he came to the door, holding between his fingers a chicken leg with lots of meat on it, the dog was gone. So he concluded that the dog had appeared a second time for no other reason than to say, "Thanks a lot, monsieur"; otherwise he would have waited until given another mouthful.

The Frenchman quickly forgot the incident, believing the animal to be only another street dog that visited café doors, searching for food, begging diners for a roll or a bone, until driven away by the waitresses.

Next day, however, about the same time, at half past three, the dog was sitting again at the same place by the open door. The Frenchman, seeing him seated there, smiled at him as if he were an old acquaintance. The dog smiled back, with a very funny expression of silent laughter. When he caught the Frenchman's friendly smile of welcome, he got halfway up, just as he had done the day before, wagged his tail in greeting, and widened his grin with his pink tongue dangling over his lower jaw.

With a backward jerk of his head, the Frenchman invited the dog to come inside and have his free lunch close to the counter. The dog, however, who clearly had grasped the meaning of that gesture, came only one short step nearer the door — but enter he would not. The Frenchman realized that the dog refrained from coming inside not so much out of fear as from the apparently inborn decency of intelligent dogs who sense that a room in which humans dwell is not the proper place for dogs living on and by the street.

The Frenchman raised his hand to the countertop, drummed his fingers, and looked at the dog, trying to make him understand that he should wait a few minutes for a plate with a tasty bone on it to come back from one of the tables. To the man's great surprise, the dog understood this finger language perfectly. He stepped back a little from the door, as if not to molest patrons coming in or going out. He lay down on the sidewalk, his head between his forepaws, and, with eyes half closed, he watched the Frenchman attending customers at the counter and collecting money brought by the waitresses to the cash register.

Five minutes later, when a waitress carried a tray of dishes from the tables, the owner winked at her, picked up a huge leftover sirloin T-bone, took it out to the dog, played it before his nose, and let go.

The dog took it from the man's hand as gently as if it had been offered by a child. And as he had done the day before, he lay down on the sidewalk close to the café and there enjoyed his lunch without hurry.

Now, remembering the dog's peculiar attitude of yesterday, the Frenchman was anxious to learn what the dog would do today, once he had finished his bone. He wished to know whether yesterday the dog had acted in that particular way only because of an occasional impulse or because of natural good manners or by some sort of training.

He was just about to bet a patron that the dog would come to the door to say "Thank you," when he noticed a shadow on the floor near the entrance. He watched the dog from one corner of his eye, purposely avoiding a full look at the animal now sitting by the door and patiently waiting to be noticed by the owner. But the Frenchman busied himself behind the counter and at the cash register, all the while watching the dog by stealth just to see how long he would remain sitting there hoping to get his chance to say, "Thank you very much, until tomorrow."

Three or four minutes had passed before the Frenchman decided to look up and gaze straight at the dog's face. Right away, and as if the dog had been ordered to do just that, he rose, wagged his tail, put on his quizzical grin, turned around, and disappeared.

From that day on, the Frenchman always had a juicy piece of leftover meat ready for the dog. And he came every day, appearing at the door so punctually that one could set one's watch by his arrival. Always at half past three the Frenchman would direct a glance toward the door and see the dog sitting there greeting the owner with his drollish grin.

And so it went for six or seven weeks without the slightest change in pattern. In fact, the Frenchman came to regard the black street dog as his most faithful customer, and he considered him a sort of mascot.

In spite of the fact that the dog now felt positively assured of the Frenchman's sincere friendship, he did not relax his formal manners. Never once had he come inside, no matter how often or how insistently the friendly owner invited him to enter.

The Frenchman grew very fond of the dog. He wanted him to hang around for good, make himself useful by chasing less decent dogs away, and guard the premises night and day — or just wait around and have a good time. He, of course, didn't know whether the dog had a master or lived on his own. Lately he had begun to caress the dog for a few moments when he gave him his lunch. It seemed the dog had never in his life known what love was, so he liked that sign of true affection. Yes, he relished the caresses. While he was stroked and patted, he would wait patiently, a steak in his mouth, until the Frenchman ceased petting him and returned to his counter. Only then, and not before, would the dog step back from the door, lie down in his accustomed place on the sidewalk, and eat his meal. When finished, he would come back to the door to wag his tail, grin at the Frenchman, thereby telling him in his own way, "Merci beaucoup,[1] monsieur, same time tomorrow, bye-bye," and then turn and trot away.

Came a certain day when the Frenchman had a terrific argument with a patron who had been served a hard roll and who, setting his teeth into that roll for a hearty bite, had broken a tooth.

The Frenchman was angry with the waitress who, poor girl, was

---

[1] *Merci beaucoup:* Thank you very much.

fired immediately and now crouched in a dark corner weeping bitterly. It hadn't been her fault, entirely. Of course she ought to have noticed that the roll was hard like wood, but so should the customer have noticed it. Anyway, it wouldn't be hygienic or mannerly for a waitress to take each roll into her hand and squeeze it to test its freshness before serving it. But she had served that roll, and so she was blamed for what happened.

The real culprit, though, was the baker who had intentionally or carelessly thrown that hard old roll among the hot fresh ones. Anyhow, the damage was done.

The Frenchman, in a thundering rage, rang up the baker and told him that he was on his way, loaded gun in hand, to kill that careless dough-kneader like the rat that he was, for he never was anything else but a stinking sewer rat, whereupon the baker told the Frenchman a few of those little mind-openers which, if uttered inside a church, would make its whitewashed walls turn deep red and stay red for keeps. This lively exchange of personal opinions ended with the Frenchman's hanging up the receiver with such force that — had telephone engineers not foreseen attacks of this kind and calculated almost perfectly the force which a maddened telephone-user might employ — nothing of the apparatus would have been left intact. As it was, only the hook was bent and the wall plaster nicked.

His face red as a ripe tomato, two bluish veins protruding from his hot forehead, the Frenchman returned to the counter and, looking up, saw his friend the black street dog sitting by the door, grinning, amused as ever, patiently waiting for his lunch to be served.

Seeing that dog sitting there so quiet and innocent, apparently unbothered by any of the worries which make café owners appear to be twenty years older than their true age, gazing at the animal as if spying it for the first time in his life, seeing him eagerly wag his tail to greet his benefactor and put on his comical grin to please the friend who liked that doggy face so very much, the Frenchman — practically blinded with madness and driven by a sudden brutal impulse which he, who had no violent temper, later could never explain to himself — took that hard roll from the counter and threw it with all his force at the dog.

The dog had clearly observed the Frenchman's move. He had watched the angry man pick up the roll and had no doubt about the roll being aimed at him. He had seen it shooting through the air toward him. He could easily have dodged that roll had he wished to, for he was a dog that lived entirely on what the street offered him and he was used to the hard life without a master or with a master so poor that he could give little else to his dog but love. Surely the dog had cleverly dodged, perhaps hundreds of times, the sticks and stones thrown at him, and he certainly was an expert at avoiding any sort of missile.

A slight movement of the head would have sufficed to save him from being hit by that hard roll. Yet he did not move. Not an inch did he move. He kept his soft warm eyes fixed straight at the Frenchman's face without a flicker. And without a tremor he most bravely took the shot.

For several seconds he kept sitting in the same place as if stunned, not so much by the blow as by sheer bewilderment caused by a happening which he believed impossible.

The roll lay at the tips of his forepaws where it had dropped after hitting him between the eyes. He gave the roll a short glance, as though he thought it might be a live thing which might jump up and prove to him that he had been mistaken in believing his friend capable of doing such a thoughtless thing.

Now, raising his eyes from the roll, he let them wander across the floor and slowly up the counter until they ultimately came to rest on the Frenchman's frozen face. There they fixed themselves, as if held by magnetic power. No accusation was in the dog's eyes, simply a profound sadness, the sadness of one who infinitely trusts somebody's honest friendship and then unexpectedly finds himself betrayed and cannot tell why it all happened.

The Frenchman, suddenly realizing what he had done, stood aghast as though he, by accident, had killed a human being. An involuntary shiver straightened his whole body, and he came to.

For a few seconds he stared at the dog with astonished eyes, as if seeing an apparition. Now the dog slowly rose, shook his head so that his ears flapped against his jaws, turned around, and went his way.

On seeing the dog disappear from the door, the Frenchman got irritated, looked around vaguely as if to find something very quick, without for a moment knowing exactly what it was; and looking down, his eyes came to rest upon a patron sitting at the counter who was just sticking a fork into a steak that had been placed before him by a waitress. Deftly, the Frenchman snatched that steak from the platter of the astonished diner, who, with an earsplitting yell, jumped from his seat and loudly and energetically protested against the outrageous violation of a citizen's constitutional right to eat his food in peace.

Holding that steak between his fingers, the Frenchman darted out of the door and ran along the street. He saw the dog already trotting along in the next block, and he started running after him, whistling and calling, not in the least minding the people on the street who stopped to watch a lunatic with a steak dangling from his fingers whistling for a street dog to come and get it. When he reached the third block and could no longer see the dog or make out where he had gone, he let the steak drop and walked back to his restaurant.

"Perdone me, señor, siento mucho," [2] he said to the patron, who in the meantime had returned to the counter, where he had been given another steak in order to calm him. "Excuse me, friend, the steak wasn't good anyway, you see . . . besides I just wanted to give it to somebody who might need it more than you! Please forget it, amigo.[3] Order anything special, and whatever it may be, it'll be on the house."

"Caramba,[4] such things don't happen in an ordinary day's work, so it's okay by me. Don't mention it. I got another steak, thanks to the elegant service you give in this here joint. And say, señor, as to that special order on the house, make mine a double-sized pie à la mode, see. Okay?"

"Right, mister, and a double-sized à la mode it'll be, and you're welcome to it."

Restlessly walking about the place, moving in a daze, here pushing a chair there a table into another position, pulling a tablecloth straight, he presently reached that dark corner where the waitress was crouched, still crying.

"It's all right, Bertha, you can stay on. It wasn't all your fault. I'll murder that baker some day even if I get shot for it. Well, anyhow, I'll change that baker instead of you. That's all. I just got upset with

---

[2] *"Perdone me, señor, siento mucho"*: "Pardon me, sir, I'm very sorry."

[3] *amigo*: friend.

[4] *Caramba*: a Spanish expression for which there is no direct translation. It is used to give emphasis to a statement, but is stronger than such English expressions as "Gosh!" or "Gee!"

that guy hollering about his cracked false tooth like a monkey gone mad."

"Thanks, boss," Bertha sniffled. "I'm really grateful, really I am, 'n sure thing I'll make it up to you by being a real help around here. See, boss, I got a mother and two brats to care for, and I tell you it ain't so easy to land another job as good as the one I got here, tips and all . . ."

"Stop talking and get to work. I told you it's okay, so what are you kicking about?"

"I'm not kicking, not at all. I only meant to say thanks, boss." Turning to an impatient patron, she said, "Yeah, yeah, mister, I heard you the first time. Just keep your shirt on and wait a second, okay?"

The Frenchman consoled himself that the dog would come again next day. He wouldn't miss his lunch for a little misunderstanding like that. Why, things like that can happen every day in a dozen places, most anywhere. Every dog is whipped by his master now and then if he deserve it, and the dog stays on, forgetting all about it in an hour or so, perhaps. Dogs are faithful, they stick to the one who feeds them.

Yet, despite reassuring himself, he couldn't feel at ease. For the rest of the day his conscience kept reminding him of the dog's habitual and quizzical grin which had amused him so much whenever he saw it, and he thought how it had died on the dog's face and changed into a desolate sadness, as though in that bad moment something had broken within the dog. The more he tried to forget the dog, the more frequently did he shoot a glance at the door, expecting to see him sitting there. Over and over he told himself that this dog was just a common mongrel, an ordinary street dog, living off the garbage cans, with no character or personality in particular. Yes, hand him a bone and you're his eternal friend. "Gosh," he finally muttered, "can I never concentrate on anything else but that stray dog which is not even mine? Why, I don't even know his name. Well, well. Let's forget it. He isn't worth the trouble, anyhow."

Next day, however, by three in the afternoon, the Frenchman had a good piece of steak ready, juicy and rare, with which to welcome the dog and to apologize at the same time for the insult he had given, and so renew the old friendship.

Half past three. And as if materialized by the striking of the nearest clock, there was the dog sitting at his usual place near the door.

The Frenchman's heart leaped with joy. "I knew it, I knew he'd be there," he said to himself with a satisfied smile.

Yet while saying so, he felt slightly disappointed that this dog should prove to be exactly like any other dog. As he had come to like the dog, if not to love him, he had expected him to be different from other dogs, more proud or distinguished. Anyhow, he was pleased that the dog had come again and had given him a chance to make the animal feel that only by mistake had he been ill-treated and that he, Monsieur Leblanc, had never meant to hurt him at all. Generously he forgave the dog his apparent lack of pride, telling himself that man must accept dogs as they are made, since man has no power whatever to change either their physical make-up or their canine nature.

There the dog sat, almost motionless, looking at the Frenchman with its velvety warm eyes as though searching that man's mind.

Greeting the animal with a wide-open smile of welcome, the Frenchman expected the dog to wag his tail and put on his clown-ish grin as a sign that no bad feelings existed between them. Yet the dog kept his mouth closed and made not the slightest move, either with his head or with his tail, even when he saw the Frenchman pick up the steak and wave it at him from behind the counter. The Frenchman jerked his head to indicate to the dog that he might come in and eat his lunch close to the counter and thus feel more at home.

The dog, however, remained quietly sitting at his usual place outside the door, looking in at the Frenchman without a flicker of the eye, staring him straight in the face as if he meant to hypnotize the man.

Once more the Frenchman beckoned, with the steak swinging from between his fingers. He smacked his lips at the dog and clucked struuush-struuush to arouse the dog's appetite and to make his mouth water. This time the dog answered by slightly moving his tail but stopped abruptly when, so it seemed, he realized what he was doing.

Presently, the Frenchman, carrying the steak between his fingers, went out to the dog. Going close to him, he played the meat be-

fore the dog's nose, as he often used to do when he was in a mood
to tease the dog a bit before letting him have the meal.

The dog, on seeing the Frenchman step up to him, raised his eyes
but otherwise did not move. When the dog refused the offered gift
even as it dangled before his nose, the Frenchman, not losing his
patience, laid the steak down on the pavement in front of the dog's
forepaws. He stroked the animal, pulled one ear gently and patted
him on the back while the dog wagged his tail now — but so slightly
that the move was barely noticeable. Yet, no matter what the
Frenchman did, the dog never let his eyes waver from the man's.

Nodding at the dog with a big smile on his face, the Frenchman
returned to his place behind the counter and watched the dog from
there, expecting that he would now pick up the steak and eat it as
usual out on the sidewalk.

However, the dog didn't. He lowered his head, sniffed without interest the meat before him on the ground, raised his eyes again to
the man's face, stood up, turned around, and left.

The Frenchman rushed out onto the sidewalk and saw the dog
ambling alongside the buildings, with not one look back at the man
staring after him. Soon he disappeared amid the people walking
along the street.

Next day, punctual as ever, the dog again was sitting by the door,
gazing at the face of his lost friend. And again, just as on the previous day, when the Frenchman approached, with a huge calf's bone
this time, the dog only stared at him without taking the slightest interest in the man's gift laid before him on the sidewalk.

The dog, not for a moment ceasing to stare into the man's eyes,
now wagged his tail when the Frenchman stroked and caressed the
animal's head and fondled his ears.

Then the dog rose, pushed the man's caressing hand from his
head with his nose, licked that hand over and over again for a full
minute, once more looked up into the man's eyes — and, without
picking up the meaty bone or even sniffing at it, turned around,
walked from the doorway, and left.

This was the last time the Frenchman ever saw that dog. He
never came back to the café, and never again was he seen anywhere
in the neighborhood.

*Does conscience tell us that we should deal the same with all men?
Or do we have one set of values for "our own people" and different
values for "others"?*

You Can't
Do That

JOHN P. MARQUAND

Since the year 1806 a cloak of red-and-yellow feathers has hung in
the hallway of the March house on the Ridge, with a helmet made
from the same plumage suspended above it. These two articles have
always held the same position on the wall, except for such times as
they have been put away in camphor to protect them from the
moths. The cloak was brought there by John March and indicates
very accurately the first venture of the March ships in the fur-and-
sandalwood trade with China. It was hung there by John March
when he returned as supercargo [1] on the brig *Polly*, Moses March,
owner, and Elihu Griggs, master. A single glance at that cloak in
the shady, spacious hallway of that square Federalist [2] house is startling to anyone who is even remotely familiar with the curiosities of
the South Seas.

It hangs there, an alien object, and yet, through association, somehow strangely suitable to a house like the old March house in a
New England seaport town. Granted that its presence there is
known to many scholars, familiarity cannot avert a shock of surprise
at a sight of that vivid garment, for it is one of the most beautiful
objects ever conceived by the mind or executed by the hand of man.
It is strange, too, to realize that if that cloak and the helmet above
it were sold today, their price would probably equal the March prof-
its in their precarious trade of another century. It is a long, fine

---

[1] *supercargo:* ship's agent in charge of cargo.
[2] *Federalist:* from the early years of the American Republic.

cloak — and the Marches have always been careful of everything they have laid their hands on — one of the best of the hundred-and-some-odd feather garments which are known to be extant today, and there will never be another made. The o-o which supplied those yellow feathers, only one beneath each wing, a shy bird which once fluttered through the crimson-blossomed ohia and the tree-fern forest of the Hawaiian mountains, is virtually extinct, and the bird that wore the red plumage is in hardly a better case. He is vanishing from the face of this earth like the genial race whose ancestors collected and attached those feathers to their delicate base of fiber netting in a manner so admired by Captain Cook.[3] Granted that the labor which went into the making of that garment is beyond all accurate calculation, the result was worth it. The reds and yellows are nearly as vivid as when the coat was new. They glisten there in the hallway, jewellike, with a depth of luster and lacy velvet texture that is more vital than inanimate. On an evening when the lights are lit, John March's cloak glows like flame and there is an element of awe in its splendor.

This is not odd, for it was intended to indicate greatness. The red lozenge [4] pattern upon the yellow marks it as belonging not alone to one of the *alii* [5] but to a Hawaiian chief of a royal lineage that was very near to kingship. Its size and the amount of yellow are a sufficient indication of its former owner's greatness. If the shadow of a commoner were to touch the shadow of the man who wore it, that commoner would suffer death, for the man who wore it was sublimated in the complicated feudal ritual of his islands into a being more than human. The feather kahili [6] was carried behind him; an attendant bore his calabash [7] of koa wood to preserve his spittle, his nail pairings, and his fallen hair, so that they might not fall into the hands of enemies whose kahunas, or witch doctors, might use them in fatal incantations. When the man who wore that cloak walked abroad, the populace assumed a prone position on pain of death. Some trace of the majesty of its first owner's presence still seems to linger about that feather cloak, incongruously, in a New England town.

---

[3] *Captain Cook:* James Cook (1728–1779), English South Seas explorer.
[4] *lozenge:* diamond-shaped.
[5] *alii:* chief or noble.
[6] *kahili:* long decorated pole used in ceremonies.
[7] *calabash:* a bowl.

The cloak was owned by the chieftain Kualai, as his name is spelled, probably incorrectly, in the March letter books and the log of the brig *Polly*, since there were no missionaries then to bring order to the Hawaiian phonetics — no missionaries, no mosquitoes, no red ants to kill the kou trees, no colds, and no disease. Kualai ruled his share of the Kona coast, on what is now known as the Big Island, under the protection of the great king Kamehameha in the days when John March was young. In Kualai's youth he had been one of the king's best warriors; in the war exercises he could evade six spears thrown at him simultaneously from varying directions; and he could trace his descent from one of the gods who had sailed with his attendants from the south.

Kualai gave his cloak and helmet to young John March when the *Polly* anchored in a bay on the Kona coast to exchange Yankee notions for sandalwood before proceeding to Canton. There is no doubt that John March valued the gift, for it is mentioned in his will. The clause reads:

"Item, the Feather Cloak that was given me by my friend Kualai on my first voyage to the Sandwich Islands, and the feather hat that goes with it, I leave to my daughter, Polly March, and I ask her to guard it carefully."

John March sailed other seas before he died and brought back other curious things, but there is every reason why the cloak should have had a value to him which was more than intrinsic; and his descendants have never sold that cloak because of the reason why it was given him, a reason that is closely connected with honor and integrity. John March was a shrewd trader, but he was an honest man.

In the New England harbor town which was the home port for the March ships, a voyage around the world was not an unusual matter when John March was young. As long as John March could remember, his town had been a port of travelers, although a part of it was cast in the narrow mold of puritanical tradition. When John March was young, no music was allowed in the white church with the rooster on its spire where merchants and clerks and shipwrights and returned mariners listened for three hours each Sunday to discourses on original sin. Not even the note of a pipe was allowed, to indicate the pitch for the singing of the psalms. Yet in such surroundings of a Sunday one could see from the square box of the

March pew a distinctly cosmopolitan congregation, for the world across the seas was closer to the town in those days than it has ever been since. Nearly every man and boy and most of the women in the pews and the Reverend Thomas himself, who thundered forth his nasal sermon while the sands ran from his hourglass on the pulpit, knew their geography as well as they knew the intricacies of their catechism. They could talk familiarly of the Baltic ports and of St. Eustatius and St. Kitts. There were plenty who knew the ivory factories and the slave pens on the Grain Coast and the anchorages along Fernando Po. There were plenty who had seen the sand upon the lead from soundings off Madagascar. The weather off Cape Hope was common talk. A restless, burning energy that made the town a lively place, except on Saturday nights and Sunday, had driven others to the factories at Canton. The townspeople were familiar with nearly every world port where money could be gained, for the town lived from shipping. One had to go, of necessity, a long way to make money then, what with European wars and privateers and orders in council and blockades. It was a time for gambling with lives and ships, a time of huge losses and huge gains, and no one could judge which until the ships came in.

It seemed hardly more than a piece of everyday business to John March when his father called him into the square parlor of the March house on the Ridge. It was an evening in April; a bright, fresh fire was burning in the parlor, and the candles were lighted on the mahogany table in the center of the room. Moses March and a man whom John March had never seen before were seated somewhat stiffly by the table with a punch bowl between them. When John March saw the punch, he knew that they were discussing important business, for his father, particularly in his later years, was abstemious with liquor. Moses March had not changed much since John March could remember him. His brown hair, done in a queue,[8] was heavily streaked with gray, and the shrewd lines around his eyes and mouth were deeper and more pronounced. There was an added stoop to his lanky shoulders, but his eyes were as bright as ever and his voice was vibrant, without any quaver of age.

"John," said Moses March, nodding at his guest, "this here is Captain Griggs from Boston. Captain Griggs, he's been sailing for the Perkinses in the fur trade."

---

[8] *queue* (kyōō): a braid of hair, a pigtail.

In many ways it seemed to John March that Captain Griggs was a younger replica of his father. The captain had the same bony facial contours and the same slouch to his shoulders. When he spoke he had the same flat voice, but his eyes were different — more mobile and less steady. The captain raised a hand before his tight-lipped mouth and coughed, then he rose from his chair with a creaking of his joints, a tall, somber man who might have been a deacon in a church. His eyes met John's and looked away toward some invisible object on the floor, then darted back and looked away again.

"Pleased to meet you," he said. . . . "I compliment you, Mr. March; he's handy looking, that's a fact."

"He's kind of peaked," said Moses March, "but John here's almighty quick at figures."

There was a silence. Captain Griggs ladled himself a fresh tumbler of punch, drank it at a gulp, and said, "He needs to be. It pays to be sharp, don't it, Mr. March?"

Moses March smiled in faint embarrassment. He had never been able to acquire a manner with his captains, nor to stop undue familiarity.

"Yes," he said, "I guess so. . . . John, Captain Griggs is taking out the *Polly*. You're sailing with him, supercargo."

John March looked at Captain Griggs again. The captain was staring intently at a lemon peel in the bottom of his glass. The news was entirely unexpected.

"Where to, Father?" he asked.

"Where you haven't been, son," said Moses March, "but you've heard the talk, I guess. Up along the Northwest Coast for sea otter, trading with the savages, then to these new islands you've heard Enoch Mayo talk about, to put aboard sandalwood, then the whole cargo sold at Canton for tea. The *Polly*, she's sailing the end of the month. You'll start in working over the cargo tomorrow. Your mother, she'll get your things packed."

John March nodded without speaking, and he showed no emotion. It was not the first time that his father had surprised him, because it was one of his father's maxims never to talk about what he proposed to do until he was ready. His father was always reaching for something new; his mind was always working. Probably he had been pondering over the matter all winter, and now, as though he were speaking about arrangements for hauling firewood, he was making plans to send one of his vessels where a March ship had never gone before.

It was strange to think that while he sat there, a homely, uncouth man, his mind could reach around the world and back. His life had never seemed so plain or matter-of-fact. The order of the March house, each piece of furniture exactly in its place, had never seemed so perfect as when he spoke of that voyage. That literal order of the letter books and the columns in the ledger were all a part of the business. There was no expression of doubt, because they all knew by then that a ship could go wherever there was water.

Captain Griggs ladled himself another tumbler of punch and blew his nose on a long blue handkerchief which seemed to have imparted some of its own color to his nose. Not having been asked to sit down, John March stood examining his new captain, comparing him with other seafaring men whom he had met. The captain was evidently a heavy and competent drinker and no doubt a capable master, but behind his lantern jaws and his high, narrow forehead there were hidden convolutions of character beyond John March's grasp. He only knew that by the time the voyage ended he would know the captain like a book. At the present time all John March could do was to stand staring at the pictures of his own imagination, striving to conjure up the sights which he and Captain Griggs would see. Captain Griggs was staring at him moodily across the brim of his glass.

"He'll do. He'll fill out," he said. "He'll be aft with the mate and me, of course. Does he know navigation, sir?"

"Yes," said Moses March, "he ain't a fool, but I hadn't aimed to make him a sailor. He'll handle this business ashore when I get through."

Captain Griggs nodded in a melancholy way. "I hope he ain't squeamish," he said. "He'll see some rough sights, like as not. We have a saying on the coast: 'You hang your conscience on the Horn.'"

"Yes," said Moses March, "I've heard it, but you, Captain, I'd like for you to keep your conscience on your ship."

"God bless you, sir," Captain Griggs said quickly, "no owner's ever complained of me. I'm always in my owner's interest. It's just dealing with these here savages, I mean. They've killed crews on the coast and they're murdering thieves on the islands." He rose stiffly. "You'll be satisfied, Mr. March. You'll be pleased as punch with me. There ain't no tricks in the trade that I don't know thereabouts. Four four-pounders and a bow chaser will be enough, and the grape-shot and plenty of small arms, and thanking you, I'll pick my own mate, and now I'll be under way, and I'll wish you a very good evening, and you, mister." He nodded to John March.

When the captain was gone, Moses March called to John March again.

"John," he said, "set down. You've been to the Baltic, you've been to the Indies, and I'd proposed keeping you ashore, but I want for you to learn this trade when it's still new." Moses March paused and rubbed his jaw. "I hear tell there's money in it, and we're going where there's money."

"Yes, sir," said John March.

"It seems," his father continued, staring at the fire, "as how these savages put aboard furs, and these other savages put aboard sandal-wood, for nothing more than notions and novelties in trading goods. Well, I got 'em for you; you and Griggs can get the rest. He'll try hard. He has his money and more than the usual prerequisites."

"Yes, sir," said John March.

"And sandalwood and furs are worth a mint of money in Canton."

"Yes, sir," said John March.

"You know about it, do you?"

"Yes, sir," said John March, "I've heard 'em talking."

His father smiled. "That's right," he said, "listen to 'em talk, but keep your own mouth shut. Have you anything to say?"

John March thought a moment. He had a number of things to say, but he kept them to himself. "No," he said. "I can obey orders, I guess. You know what you're doing, I guess, Father."

Moses March stroked his chin slowly, and then he asked a sudden question: "How did you like Griggs?"

"He looks too sharp to me," John March said, "but I guess we'll get along."

"Yes," said Moses March, "he's sharp, but maybe that's all right. But mind you watch him, John. I'm sharp, but I guess I'm honest. Mind you watch him."

Even when he was three thousand miles away from town and farther than that by water, something of the town was always with him. The *Polly* was a part of the town because she had been built in the yards by the river, a good tight brig of two hundred and fifty tons. The crew was a part of the town, because most of the men before the mast had been born within its limits. The sense of the nearness of things he knew gave John March a certain peace when everything else was strange. The emptiness of the Pacific Coast, the incredible size of its fir trees, the frowning menace of its mountains, would have oppressed him if it had not been for that sense of home. As it was, everyone stood together and behaved, in order to keep reputations intact when they got home.

John March was used to work. He was satisfactory to Captain Griggs, and he was treated well because he was the owner's son. Once they began bartering for furs off the Northwest Coast, there was no doubt that the captain knew his business, and John March admired in silence the way the captain worked. Martin Sprague, the mate, knew his business, too, in caring for the ship. The men were armed; there was a sharp lookout day and night. The four-pounders were loaded with grapeshot, and the matches were kept burning. Only a definite number of the painted dugout canoes of the Indians were allowed alongside, and only a certain number of savages were permitted on deck to trade. There were very few ships off the coast that year, so that the selection of pelts was particularly fine. Sea-otter pelts came aboard in great quantity in exchange for powder, shot, nails, muskets, beads, and blankets. It was a pretty sight to see the captain read faces and weigh the desire to sell. He seemed to have an intuitive sense of when to bargain and when to buy immediately.

"If there's any trade goods left after the islands," he said, "we'll stand back here again and use 'em up. It's a pity to see this fine fur wasting here. I wish we had six ships."

John March could feel the excitement as small goods turned suddenly into a valuable cargo. It was better than any figuring in the countinghouse to see the fur pelts come aboard and to estimate their probable value in a Chinese port.

"Yes, sir," said Captain Griggs, "it seems a pity to haul off and leave this. We ought to buy the villages out and to the devil with the islands and the wood."

They were in the cabin at the time, the captain and Sprague, the mate, a heavy muscular man, and John March, a thin blond boy.

"Mr. Sprague," said the captain, "pass the rum. What do you think, mister? Shall we do all the trading here and simply water at the islands?"

Martin Sprague rubbed the palm of his left hand over the knuckles of his right. "I never seen trading so easy," he said. "Yes, sir, I think I should."

Then John March spoke up; it was the first time on the voyage that he'd made a positive statement. "We can't," he said.

Captain Griggs set down his glass and scowled. "Young man," he said, "I'm surprised at you. You ought to know better. You do know better. You've behaved yourself fine up till now, my boy. You've done your duty, and more, and I shall be pleased to report favorably to your father if you continue, but there's two things for you to get inside your head. The first is, you were sent here to learn to trade. You don't know this business, and don't you forget it. The second is, I'm captain, and this brig goes where I tell it to. I'm sorry to be obliged to tell you straight."

John March did not shift his position at the table. He knew that he was young and that he was green. He had interrupted solely from a conscientious sense inherited from his race. It had come over him that he was a representative of the March family and of the March cargo. Now that the eyes of the older men were upon him, he found himself stammering, because he was shy in those days, but his hesitation only made him the more determined to speak out.

"Captain," he said, "I understand what you say. This is your ship, of course, but you are under owner's orders, just as I am. A portion of these trade goods was allotted for furs and the rest for sandalwood. The owner's orders are to stop and trade at the Sandwich Islands. There may be more profit here, but we are to establish relations there. We may send out another ship."

Captain Griggs leaned half across the table. "Young man," he inquired, "are you insinuating I'm not looking after owner's interest? Because if you are, I will not tolerate it. I'm thinking of my owner all the time, and a sight better than you are, maybe. We'll make for the islands tomorrow, and there's an end to that, but if there's any trade goods left when we're through there, why, then, with your kind permission, we'll come back here. I hope that satisfies you."

"Yes," said John March, "it does, and I ask your pardon, Captain."

Mr. Sprague rose. "I must be up with the watch," he said, "if you'll excuse me, sir. . . . Will you come with me, Mr. March?"

It was a fine night on deck, clear, with bright stars and a faint, quivering circle of the northern lights. The night was cool, without a breath of wind. The ship, with her own small lights, was like an insignificant fragment of a distant world anchored there in space. The mate took out his pipe and tinderbox. There was a flash of spark as he expertly hit the flint against the steel, and then the tinder glowed.

"Johnny March," he said, "I've kind of got to like you. Now you listen to what I say. This kind of spark's all right, but not the kind that you were striking in the cabin. You leave the old man be. He's as good a master as there is, and he's honest with the owners, and that's all we have to care for. I've sailed with Griggs before. I don't need to tell you that a master's king aboard his ship, and you know it makes 'em queer. I've never seen a skipper yet who liked to be crossed. You better leave him be."

"Yes, sir," said John March.

"And listen, Johnny," the mate said, "the islands are a fine place. You'll like the islands. The islands are like heaven, pretty near. The captain will take you ashore, of course, to make the bargain. You'll see plenty of funny sights, but keep your mouth shut, Johnny, except to say 'Yes, sir' to the captain. We've got a long way yet to go."

"Yes, sir," said John March.

"That's right," said Sprague, "that's right. I like a tight-lipped boy."

It was said in the forecastle of the *Polly*, just as it was said aft, that Johnny March was taciturn. As a supercargo he had no fixed duties in working the ship, and few knew much about him except that he was March's son. They only saw him as a thin, brown-faced, gray-eyed boy with yellow hair who made no trouble or complaint. They did not know the impression which strange sights made upon him, because he was studiously silent on that voyage to the islands, hardly ever venturing a remark, only answering courteously when addressed. No one on the *Polly* knew — and perhaps it was just as well — that his thoughts were poetic, because there was no room for poetry on a Yankee trading brig.

The evening before they sighted land, he had a sense of the land's nearness. The banks of clouds off the port bow as the sun went down were pink and gold and were more like land clouds than sea clouds. The *Polly* was moving in the steady breath of the trades, and the setting sun struck the bellying sails forward, making their colors soft and golden. The only sounds were the creaking of wood, the straining of ropes, and the splash of waves on the bow. He had seen many evenings like that one, but subtly this was different. There was a mystery in the warmth of the air, an intangible unreality in the cloud banks. Captain Griggs came and stood beside him, smelling strongly of rum.

"Mr. Sprague," he said, "you've got everything locked up, I hope. Tomorrow we'll be overrun by island thieves and their women. Clew [9] up the courses and continue under topsails. Set a watch up in the crosstree and keep an eye out for breakers. We must not get in too close tonight. . . . And, Mr. March — "

"Yes, sir," said John.

"You and I will go ashore."

"Yes, sir," said Johnny March, and then he cleared his throat: "How will we speak to them, sir?"

"You'll soon learn, boy," said Captain Griggs. "You've got a lot to learn. These islands have kings, or chiefs, and the chiefs will have someone who can speak trading English. The sandalwood is up in the mountains. It will be the property of the king, or chief. We will agree to purchase so many piculs,[10] and he'll send his people to cut it. The chief will come aboard to see our goods, and we will make a bargain for the cargo, payable when the wood is safe aboard, you understand. There's no need to make our crew work when the chief will make his people load it. The islanders are handy men on ships. We'll go to see the chief, and we'll make the chief a present. Break out that clock that strikes the hour, and two cutlasses. That will be enough, and maybe" — Captain Griggs paused and hesitated — "three yards of bright print calico; he ought to like it — paper's all they dress in."

"Yes, sir," said Johnny March. "Did you say that they dressed in paper?"

---

[9] *Clew*: furl.
[10] *picul*: a measure of weight.

The hard lines of the captain's face wrinkled into an indulgent smile.

"Young man," he said, "it's a fact they dress in paper, when they dress at all, which isn't often. The women, they pound it out of the bark of a tree. They have nothing else on the islands, or almost nothing. Time was when they'd sell a pig for three tenpenny nails. Will you come below for a glass of rum?"

"No, thank you, sir," said Johnny March. "I'll stay on deck — that is, if you don't mind."

The sun had dipped out of sight behind a bank of clouds, and then suddenly the light was gone. Without a prelude of dusk, the dark came over them like a warm black garment. It seemed only a second before that the sky had been red and gold. Then, in another second, the sky was a void of darkness, filled with the trade wind and with stars. He stood for a while listening to the wind singing through the ropes, and then he went below. It was still dark when John March was awakened by a long-drawn-out call and by Mr. Sprague's voice shouting, "Where away?" and he knew that they had come in sight of land. Once he was up on deck, the topsails were slatting sleepily, and off the starboard bow there was a glow in the sky like fire.

"We've hit it to a second, sir," the mate was saying to Captain Griggs. "Yonder's the volcano; we're in the lee of the mountains."

Captain Griggs was a shadow in the starlight. It was too dark to see his face, but his voice was satisfied. "A pretty piece of navigating," he said, "if I do say so, mister. There'll be an inshore breeze by dawn, and then we'll make the bay." He sniffed the air. "We can't be far from land," he said, "but there's no use heaving lead.[11] It shelves off here as deep as hell. There'll be an inshore breeze with dawn."

"Is that a light yonder, sir?" asked Johnny March.

Near the horizon there was a twinkling, glimmering point.

"Your eyesight's good," the captain said. "Yes, that will be a fire. We're close to land."

The dawn came as suddenly as the dark, in a swift rush of light, as though a hand had snatched away a veil, and John March saw the land. It was a solemn sight to see land which seemed to have risen out of nowhere. Off the bows of the *Polly* was a mountain,

---

[11] *heaving lead:* taking a sounding.

black and green, that rose in a gradual slope up into snow and clouds. The coast was dark from volcanic rock which made ugly black gashes between green forests. Close to the water's edge there was a fringe of palms and beeches between black lava headlands. The sea was smooth and calm and streaked with violet; the air was as soft as the air of spring at home and was subtly laden with the smells of land. All the colors were soft in a faint, early-morning haze. The black rocks merged into reds and purples. The greens of the upland forest blended subtly from shades of silver to emerald, and Captain Griggs was right — a soft breeze was filling the sails, moving the *Polly* gently along the coast.

"That's where the sandalwood comes from," Mr. Sprague was saying, "up yonder in the mountains. The coast hereabouts is the favorite place of the kings. Do you see the stone walls and the yellow thatch of the houses of the villages? The chiefs own straight from the tops of the mountains to the sea. How do you like it, son?"

The question made John March tongue-tied. "I think it's very handsome, sir," he said, "a very pleasant island."

The *Polly* was moving under topsails into a small bay. It opened out before them, a smooth amphitheater of water, surrounded by high cliffs. "Yonder's where the kings are buried," the mate said. "They scrape the flesh off their bones and tie them up in paper cloth and put them there in caves with their canoes."

At the head of the bay John March could see a beach fringed with tall palm trees, the leaves of which moved idly in the breeze, and he could see the thatch of houses beneath them. There was a dark crowd of people on the beach, pushing canoes into the water, log dugouts, balanced by an outrigger and manned by naked paddlers. Captain Griggs was wearing clean linen and a black broadcloth coat, although the day was hot.

"Mister," he said, "we'll anchor. Let go falls and clew up lower topsails and order the stern boat cleared."

By the time the anchor struck the water, the *Polly* was surrounded by canoes and the water was full of swimmers who were pulling themselves up the anchor chain, smiling and laughing; men and women as beautiful as statues, their straight dark hair glistening with the water. Captain Griggs stared at his visitors sourly from the quarter-deck.

"They've got the minds of children," he said. "The chief's man should be here. Look at those shameless hussies, will you? There's no decency on these islands. They don't care for decency; no, they don't care."

As Captain Griggs finished speaking, a native pushed his way through the crowd at the waist and walked aft; evidently a man of importance, because the crowd gave way respectfully. He wore a pair of sailor's castoff trousers, and his skin was lighter than the others'. His voice rose above the babel of strange words in English.

"Mr. Captain," he called out, "I am Kualai's man."

"Who's he?" asked Captain Griggs. "The chief?"

The other nodded, bobbing his head up and down, still smiling. "Yes," he said, "yes, yes. And he sends me because I speak English good. I've been a sailor on a Boston boat. I speak English very good. Kualai sends me to say *aloha*. He is glad to see you. He asks you will you trade for wood?"

"Yes," said Captain Griggs, "we're here for wood. What's your name?"

"Moku," said the native. "Billy Adams Moku. Kualai ask what name."

The captain nodded condescendingly. "Captain Griggs," he said, "brig *Polly*. Moses March, owner. We're carrying very fine calicoes, ironware, tinware, lead and copper, and even a few muskets. Has your chief got wood?"

Moku nodded. "The wood is coming down. Kualai, he will see you." He pointed to a laden canoe. "Kualai sends you food."

Captain Griggs looked at the canoe carefully as it drew alongside. "Very good," he said. "When will he see me?"

"Mister," said Moku. "He waits on the shore."

"Mister," the captain called, "have the stern boat lowered. Mr. March and I will go ashore, and, Mr. March, give that man a pocketknife and bring along the presents."

The dark sand of the beach at the head of the bay seemed insecure under John March's feet, since he had been so long on the water. In the sunshine like a warm June day at home, every sight and sound was new. The crowd of natives standing on the beach drew back from them shyly and smiled, but their tongues kept chattering busily, commenting, probably, on the way these strangers looked. The chief's man walked first, then Captain Griggs, nonchalant and cool, and then John March behind him. They walked along a path beneath a grove of coconut palms and beneath large broad-leafed trees such as he had never seen. They were threading their way through a settlement of houses made of dried grass, past small gardens enclosed between walls of black volcanic rock. His memory of that day always brought back living green against dark rock and dark smiling faces and red hibiscus flowers. In his memory of the place a soft breeze was always blowing and there was always a strange dry rattle from the leaves of the coconut palms. There was a group of larger houses not far back from the beach which evidently belonged to a man of importance. Natives were busying themselves about a fire in a pit; women and children were staring from open doorways. There was an open pavilion near the center of this group of buildings, and the chief's man led them toward it. Seated in a Cantonese armchair under the pavilion was one of the largest men that John March had ever seen. He was middle-aged and so corpulent that the chair seemed to creak beneath his weight. A single look at his face was enough to indicate that he was the ruler, Kualai, of whom the man had spoken. The face was set in benign lines that could only have come upon it through suave and complete authority. It was all that was necessary to indicate his rank, but he also had the exterior show of office. He was wearing a yellow-and-red cloak of feathers, dazzlingly bright, which fell below his waist, and an attendant stood behind him holding a large stick which bore a tuft of colored feathers on the end. Moku stopped dead still at the entrance of the pavilion, and the great man rose from his chair and stepped slowly forward, gracefully, in spite of his heavy paunch. It was plain that he had seen other white men and knew something of their manners, because he smiled graciously and held out his right hand. At the same time he spoke melodiously in a language that was all vowels, so that his words sounded like rippling water.

"What's he saying?" asked Captain Griggs.

"Kualai," Moku translated, "he say he's, oh, very glad to see you."

"Well, I guess we're glad to see him too," said Captain Griggs as he shook hands. Then John March saw that Kualai was looking at him.

"He wants to know," said Moko, "who is the other man?"

"Tell him he's the son of the man who owns the vessel," said Captain Griggs.

"He wants to know," said Moku, "is he a chief's son?"

"Tell him yes," said Captain Griggs.

"He would like," said Moku, "to feel his hair. He would like to know if it is real."

"Take off your hat," said Captain Griggs, "and let him feel your hair. Don't be afraid of him. He won't hurt you."

"All right," said Johnny March. He felt very much like a child as he walked toward Kualai, for the man, now that he was standing, must have been close to seven feet in height. His skin was glistening with coconut oil. He was stretching out his arm. He touched Johnny March's hair gently and then he pulled it softly. Johnny March looked up at him and smiled, and Kualai smiled back.

"Break out the presents," said Captain Griggs, "bow to him, and put 'em on the ground."

Kualai's face lighted up at the sight of the clock when John March held it toward him. It was evident that he had never seen such a mechanism — a battered ship's chronometer whose useful days were over. He touched it gingerly and imitated its sound.

"Tick-tick," he said, and John March nodded and repeated after him "Tick-tick." That interchange of words always seemed to him ridiculous, but somehow there was an exchange of thought with the words which made them friends.

"He asks you to stay and eat," said Moku. "He will come on the ship tomorrow and see the goods, and he asks the young man to stay with him until the trade is over, to sleep inside his house."

Captain Griggs muttered something beneath his breath, and then he said, "March, you'd better stay."

"Yes, sir," said John March, "I'd be very glad to stay." He turned to Moko. "Tell him I'll be glad."

Then Moku spoke again: "Kualai says he will trade with the young man."

"All right," said Captain Griggs, "as long as I'm there too. And tell him" — Captain Griggs's eyes shifted toward the bay and back — "you tell him I want the wood measured on the beach and put aboard by his people. Tell him my men are tired." And then he drew a bottle of rum from his pocket and added plaintively: "Ain't we had enough of this? Let's everybody have a drink, and bring on the dancing girls."

Some half-perceptible change in Captain Griggs's voice made

John March turn to watch him. The captain's face was bleak and impassive, but his eyes were shifting from point to point, from the chief to John March, then away to the matting on the ground, then to the houses of the settlement. John March knew him well enough by then to know that the captain was turning over in his mind some thought which he wished entirely to conceal.

"Ah," he said suddenly, "here comes some wood," and he nodded toward a path which led upward to the mountains.

A dozen men and women were staggering down the path in single file, each bearing a burden of long sticks, and John March knew from hearsay that these were the chief's people, who had been sent to the upland forests where the sandalwood grew. The chief called out an order, which Moku ran to obey, and a few moments later a pile of the sandalwood lay on the matting before his chair, a heap of sticks which varied in size from a few inches to a foot in diameter. The bark had been stripped off, leaving a heavy wood of deep yellow which verged on orange. Captain Griggs ripped out his clasp knife, whittled at the sticks, and sniffed the shavings.

"It ain't bad," he said. "In fact, it's prime."

He was right that the wood was fine, since sandalwood was plentiful in the islands then, when the trade was new, and John March did not suspect that he would live to see the time when hardly a stick would be left standing on the entire island group. Captain Griggs stood there, staring at the pile of wood, apparently lost in thought.

"Tell him we'll pay him well for it," he said, and his voice was soft and almost kindly, "once he lands it on the deck."

But all the while John March was sure that Captain Griggs was concealing some other thought.

It took nearly two weeks to collect the wood and measure it, a space of time which moved in a peculiar series of days and nights, but it was strange to John March how soon the life there grew familiar. Though he could hardly understand a word which was spoken, though nearly every sight and sound in those two weeks was new, he became aware immediately of certain human values. Kualai, in his way, was a cultivated man of gentle breeding, who had developed his own taste for the arts and qualities of understanding which were the same on that isolated island as they were elsewhere. He would sit for hours of an evening watching interpretive dances and listening to his minstrels sing of the exploits of his ancestors. He had a good eye for patterns in the tapa cloth and a nice skill in various games of chance, which he played daily with his choice companions, but, above all, he had a sense of hospitality. He lost no occasion to make John March feel politely that he was a welcome guest. He took him fishing in his war canoe, he took him to the caves and the lava rocks, he took him to watch the young men perform feats of strength; he was even careful that John March's privacy should not be disturbed unduly. When he came aboard the *Polly*, he kept John March beside him. He was greatly pleased with the calico and nails and lead and copper in the trading cargo, but he went through the intricacies of the bargain in a detached way, like a gentleman. In those days trading was easy on the islands, before the chiefs were glutted with material possessions.

"He say he want you to be happy," Moku said the last time Kualai came aboard, "he want you to come again."

"Tell him we're happy," said Captain Griggs. "He understands when all the wood's aboard that we'll give out the goods."

Moku nodded. "He understands," he said. "He knows you're good men."

Captain Griggs coughed slightly. "I shall want Mr. March back with me," he said, "tomorrow morning. . . . Mr. March, you come here; I want to speak with you in the cabin."

It occurred to John March, when they were in the cabin, that it was the first time since they had been on the islands that he and Captain Griggs had been alone. Captain Griggs rubbed his long hands together and poured himself a glass of rum.

"Young man," he said, "you've done fine. You've kept that old heathen happy, and that's all we needed — to keep him happy — and now we're all finished shipshape. We'll get the wood stowed tonight" — Captain Griggs smiled happily — "and tomorrow they can come aboard and take off their goods, but I want you aboard first, understand?"

"Yes, sir," said John March, "but there's one thing I don't see. I don't see why you haven't put the goods ashore before this, sir."

Captain Griggs poured himself a second tumbler of rum.

"Young man," he said, "when you take a few more voyages, you'll understand you can't trust natives. How do you know we'd get the wood if we put the goods ashore?"

"Because Kualai's honest," John March said.

Captain Griggs looked thoughtfully at the ceiling. "Maybe," he said, "and maybe not. Anyways, we've got the wood. You come aboard tomorrow." And Captain Griggs smiled genially, but even when he smiled, John March had a suspicion that something had been left unsaid, that there was some thought in the captain's mind of which he had not spoken.

Mr. Sprague came up to get him the next morning, carrying a bundle of small presents and perspiring in the heat of the early sun.

"Say good-by to the chief," he said. "The captain's orders are to leave right now. You're to stay aboard until we sail. The quarter boat's [12] waiting at the beach."

John March was sorry, now that it was time to go. He walked to Kualai and held out his hand. "Thank you very much," he said, and the interpreter, Moku, gave him back the chief's answer:

"He say for you to come back soon."

The canoes were gathering about the *Polly* already, by the time he reached the beach. He and Mr. Sprague sat in the stern sheets of the quarter boat while two men rowed, helped by a light breeze offshore.

It was only when they were halfway out that John March was aware of something disturbing.

"Look," he said, "they're setting the lower topsails!"

"Yes," said Mr. Sprague shortly, "so they are. We've got a fair breeze, haven't we?"

"But it'll take a good six hours to put off those goods," said Johnny March.

Mr. Sprague put a heavy hand on his knee and smiled. "Don't you worry, boy," he said. "Captain Griggs will see about those goods."

They were beside the companion ladder by that time, and even John March was puzzled, but nothing more. He was not aware of Captain Griggs's idea until he was on the poop, then he saw that the tarpaulins were off the guns and that men were beside them with matches, and then he saw that the decks were clear and that

---

[12] *quarter boat:* a small boat hung to the side of a ship.

the sandalwood and the trade goods were all back in the hold. Captain Griggs grinned at him.

"Safe and sound," he said. "You've done very well, Mr. March; your father will be very pleased, I think. . . . Mister, you can man the capstan now."

John March found himself stammering: "But what about the goods, Captain? We haven't put the goods ashore."

"No, boy," said Captain Griggs, "we ain't, and we ain't going to. What's the use when we've got the wood aboard? Those goods are going to go for skins."

Even then John March did not entirely understand him. "But you can't do that," he said. "We owe the chief the goods."

"Listen, boy," said Captain Griggs, "this ain't like home. There're plenty of other chiefs, and plenty of other islands. Let 'em come and get the goods, and I'll blow 'em out of the water. There ain't no law out here. Now you be quiet, boy."

For a moment John March found it impossible to speak. Now that the whole matter was completely clear, he knew that he should have suspected long ago what must have been in the back of the captain's mind. Captain Griggs proposed sheer robbery, but he would not have called it that. He would have called it a clever piece of business in a place where there was no law.

"You see," Captain Griggs was saying, "it isn't as though they were civilized people, Mr. March. More fools they, that's all."

Then John March found his voice. "Captain," he said, "this is a March ship. You don't leave until you've set those goods on shore. We don't do things that way, Captain. You can't — "

Captain Griggs turned toward him quickly.

"That'll be enough from you," he said. "Who says I can't? I'm trying to make a profit on this voyage. I can, and I will, and I'm taking full responsibility. If you don't like it, get below."

John March's tongue felt dry and parched as he tried to speak. Even in that short while a hundred things were happening. The fore and aft staysails and the lower topsails were set by then, and the call came from forward, "Hawser short!" A glance toward the beach was enough to show him that the islanders were aware of the captain's trick. Men were running toward the water. He could hear the beating of a drum. Men in canoes were gesticulating and shouting. Men with spears and clubs and slings were hurrying to the beach.

"Break out anchor, mister," shouted Captain Griggs, "and stand by them guns! Forward there, pass out the small arms! By God, we'll show 'em!"

"Captain," said John March suddenly. He knew there was only one thing to do as he spoke. "If you go, you'll leave me here. I'm going back ashore."

Captain Griggs looked at him and laughed. "They'll kill you back ashore," he said. "Look at 'em on the beach."

John March spoke with difficulty. "You and I are different sorts of men," he said. "You can either set those goods ashore or I'm going."

"May I inquire," said Captain Griggs, "how you're going to go? Keep your mouth shut, boy!"

In the haste of getting under way, the quarter boat was still drifting alongside, and the captain must have perceived John March's intention from his glance.

He made a lunge at John March, but John March broke away, and then he went on the bulwarks.

"Get ahold of that fool!" shouted Captain Griggs. "Lay ahold of him!"

Two of the crew ran toward him, and he jumped crashing into the quarter boat. "Get in there after him!" Captain Griggs was shouting. "Don't let him go!"

And then John March cut the painter, and the quarter boat was drifting from the side.

"You fool!" shouted Captain Griggs. "You hear my orders! Come back here or they'll kill you, March!"

Once the boat was drifting from the side, John March was amazed at himself. His anger and his lack of fear amazed him. He was standing amidships in the quarter boat, shouting back at Captain Griggs.

"I'd rather be killed ashore," he shouted, "than stay aboard with you!" Then he picked up the oars and began to row ashore, slowly, because the boat was heavy for a single man to handle.

John March saw that the anchor was aweigh and the *Polly* was standing slowly out to the open sea. His back was to the beach as he pulled toward it, but he heard the shouting and the beating of the drums. It must have been his anger at Captain Griggs that did not make him afraid or an assurance within himself that he was right and Captain Griggs was wrong. A glance astern of the quarter boat as he strained at the oars showed him the *Polly* standing out to sea, but he did not look over his shoulder toward the beach. He did not look until the bottom of the quarter boat grated on the sand, then he shipped his oars carefully and stepped ashore. He found himself surrounded by shouting men who waved their spears and their fists in his face, but somehow they were not so real to him as the reality which lay inside himself. He only realized later that a single gesture of fear might have meant his death, but then he was so involved in his own preoccupation and with the single desire which was in him that he walked calmly enough across the beach toward the palm trees and the thatched houses; the crowd in front of him gave way as he walked and then followed on his heels. He was taking the path to Kualai's house, and the shouting around him died away as he drew near it.

Then he saw Kualai walking toward him in the feather cloak which he had worn the first day they had met, carrying a light throwing spear in his right hand. Kualai was shouting something to him — obviously a question which he could not understand — and Moku was standing near him.

"Tell Kualai," John March said, "that I come from honest people. Tell him that I have come here to stay until he is paid for his wood." He saw Kualai listening intently to his answer, and then Kualai raised his right arm and drove his spear into the earth.

"He says you are his son," Moku said. "He asks you: Will you please to shake his hand?"

The reaction from what he had done came over him when Kualai grasped his hand. He knew the harsh and accurate consequences of his action then, as the smells and sounds of that Polynesian village came over him like a wave. Captain Griggs had left him, and every vestige of home was gone. He was a stranger among savages, and he might be there forever, for anything he knew, yet even then he knew that he had done the only proper thing. Suddenly he found that he was homesick, because the chief was kind.

"Ask him if I can be alone," he said. "Tell him I want to be alone."

He was given a house of his own that night, next to where the chief slept. He was given a pile of woven mats for his bed and a piece of tapa cloth to cover him. He was given baked pig and sweet potatoes and the gray paste made from the taro root, called poi, for his evening meal, and mullet from Kualai's fishpond. He was as comfortable as he could have hoped to be that night. For a moment, when he was awakened early the next morning, he thought he was at home, until he saw the rafters and the thatch above him. Moku was standing near him in his ragged sailor breeches, and Kualai himself was bending his head, just entering the door.

"Wake up!" Moku was saying. "The ship is back!"

John March sat up on his bed of mats and rubbed his arm across his face. Although he spoke to Moku, his eyes were on Kualai.

"The ship?" he asked. "What ship?"

"Your ship," said Moku. "She come back, and now the captain, he unloads the goods."

John March stood up. He had no great capacity for showing emotion.

"Ask Kualai if he is satisfied," he said.

Moku nodded. "He says, 'Yes, very much,' " he said, and Kualai nodded back. "He asks for you to stay a long time — always."

"Thank him, please," said John March, "but tell him it's my ship. Tell him I must go to see that the goods are right."

"Kualai," Moku answered, "says he will go with you to the beach."

Mr. Sprague had landed in the longboat by the time they had reached the shore, and the beach was already covered with bolts of calico and small goods and ironware and lead and copper. Mr. Sprague nodded to John March formally, as though nothing had happened. "The captain sends his compliments," he said, "and asks you to come aboard, so that he can resume the voyage." And then Sprague grinned and added, "It's lucky for you, John March, that you're the owner's son."

John March looked at the goods upon the shore. "You can thank the captain for me for coming back," he answered. "You can tell him that I hope we both can forget what has happened, but the complete consignment is not landed yet. I'll stay here until the list is checked."

"You're an accurate man," said Sprague.

John March nodded. "I've been taught to be," he said, and he stayed there on the beach until every item was verified. Then he turned to Kualai and his interpreter.

"Tell the chief," he said, "that I believe that everything is right. Ask his pardon for the delay, but tell him our house will make any mistakes correct. Thank him, and tell him that I am going."

Moku spoke quickly in the musical language of the islands while Kualai stood, looking first at John March and then at the ship that brought him. After Kualai had listened, he stood silently for a moment. Then he smiled and spoke swiftly. He raised a hand and took off his feather helmet, and one of his men very carefully removed his feather cloak from his shoulders.

"He says there will always be wood for you," said Moku. "He asks you to take his coat."

A pawnshop is a museum of broken dreams. Everything brought to a pawnshop represents human need, a lost job, illness, bad luck. The proprietor lends his customers small sums of money in exchange for their possessions. If the borrower cannot repay the loan and the often high interest, the pawnbroker can sell the pledged item. So the job of a valuer is to get the customer to accept as little money as possible for the item he is pawning.

The Dream

ANTON CHEKHOV

Sometimes the winter weather, perhaps angry with man's weakness, calls on the severe autumn for help and works together with it. Snow and rain whirl in the black, foggy air. Damp, cold, piercing wind knocks at the windows and roofs with violent anger. It howls in the pipes and weeps in the ventilators. Anguish hangs in the air like soot. . . . Nature is sick. . . . It is damp, cold, sinister.

It was just this kind of weather on Christmas Eve, 1882, before I was in the convict labor gang, when I was serving as an appraiser in the pawnshop of the retired captain Tupaev.

It was midnight. The storeroom, where my employer wanted me to stay nights like a watchdog, was dimly lit by the blue flame of a candle. It was a large, square room filled with bundles, trunks, shelves. . . . Rabbit-fur coats, men's coats, rifles, paintings, wall lamps, a guitar were hanging on the gray wooden walls. Tattered straw stuck out of the chinks in the walls. . . . Obliged to watch nights over these goods, I was lying on a large red trunk behind a showcase filled with jewels. I stared thoughtfully at the candle. . . .

For some reason I was afraid. Things kept in the storeroom of a pawnshop are terrifying. . . . In the night they seem alive in dim candlelight. . . . And now, as the rain murmured behind the window and the wind wailed plaintively in the stove and over the ceiling, it seemed to me that the pawned things were making wailing sounds. They all had to pass through the hands of the appraiser —

my hands — before coming here, and therefore I knew all about every one of them. . . . I knew, for instance, that the money received for this guitar had bought medicine for a sick person. . . . I knew that a drunkard had killed himself with this gun; his wife had concealed the gun from the police, pawned it, and bought the coffin. The bracelet looking at me from the showcase had been pawned by the man who had stolen it. . . . Two lace dresses, marked No. 178, had been pawned by a girl who needed money. . . . In short, I read in everything a desperate sorrow, sickness, crime, depravity. . . .

These things were especially eloquent on Christmas Eve.

"Let us go home," it seemed to me they wept with the wind. "Let us go!"

But not only these things made me afraid. When I thrust out my head from behind the showcase and looked timidly at the dark, misty window, it seemed to me that human faces looked into the storeroom from the street.

"What nonsense!" I cheered myself. "What a stupid feeling!"

The fact is that a man endowed by nature with an appraiser's nerves was tortured by his conscience on the night before Christmas — an incredible and even fantastic event. Conscience is something else you pawn at a pawnshop. Here conscience is understood as an object to be bought and sold; no other functions for it are accepted. It was amazing — how could I have a conscience? I turned from side to side on my hard trunk and blinked my eyes from the candlelight as I tried with all my strength to suppress the new, unbidden feeling. But my efforts were in vain . . .

Of course, it was partly the fault of physical and moral fatigue after working hard all day. On the day before Christmas, crowds of poor people would fill the pawnshop. During a great holiday and especially in bad weather, poverty is not a vice but a terrible misfortune! At this time the drowning fellow looks at the pawnshop for a straw and receives a stone instead. . . . On Christmas Eve we had so many people that we had to put three fourths of the pawned objects in the barn; there was no place for them in the storeroom. From early morning until late in the evening, not stopping for a minute, I haggled with ragged fellows, squeezed pennies from them, saw tears, heard futile begging. . . . I could barely stand at the end of the day. Body and soul were exhausted. No wonder I couldn't sleep now as I lay turning from side to side, feeling terrible. . . .

Somebody cautiously knocked at my door. After the knocks I heard my employer's voice:

"Are you asleep, Peter Demianovitch?"

"Not yet. What is it?"

"You know, I think maybe we should open the door early tomorrow morning. It is a great holiday, and the weather is terrible. The poor people will rush to us like flies to honey. So please do not go to church tomorrow morning but stay behind the counter. Good night."

"I am so afraid," I decided after my employer left, "because my candle is blinking . . . I must put it out. . . ."

I got up from the bed and went to the corner where the candle was hanging. The blue flame, faintly blazing, was dying. Each gleam briefly illuminated the icon,[1] the walls, the bundles, the dark window. . . . Two pale faces in the window pressed against the glass and looked into the storeroom.

"There is nobody," I decided. "I imagined it."

And when I put out the candle and gropingly made my way to the bed, something happened that had a considerable influence on my mood. . . . A loud, violently screeching noise suddenly rang out over my head, continuing for no more than a second. Something cracked and, as if in terrible pain, screamed loudly. A guitar string had snapped, but I, terror-stricken, closed my ears and ran madly to my bed, stumbling over trunks and bundles. . . . I buried my head under the pillow and, barely breathing, dying from terror, started to listen.

"Let us go," wailed the wind, together with the pawned things. "It's Christmas. Let us go! You are poor yourself, you understand! You yourself suffered from cold and hunger! Let us go!"

Yes, I myself was poor and knew what hunger and cold meant. Poverty pushed me into this accursed appraiser's job. Poverty forced me to despise sorrow and tears for a piece of bread. If it weren't for poverty, would I have the courage to appraise in pennies what is worth health, warmth, holiday cheer? So why was the wind blaming me? Why was my conscience tormenting me?

But although my heart was throbbing with fear and remorse, exhaustion overcame me. I fell asleep. My sleep was light . . . once

---

[1] *icon* (ī'kon): a religious picture.

more I heard my employer knock, the bells ring at midnight. . . . I heard the wailing of the wind and the noise of the rain on the roof. My eyes were closed, but I saw the pawned things, the show-case, the dark window, the icon. The pawned things were crowding around me and asking me to let them go home. The strings of the guitar were snapping with a screech, one after another, snapping all the time. . . . Beggars and old women were looking into the win-dow, waiting for me to open the door and return their things to them.

In my dream I heard something scratch like a mouse, scratching for a long time, monotonously. I turned over and pulled myself tight because of the cold and dampness which blew on me. Covering my-self with the blanket, I heard a rustle and a human whisper.

"What a bad dream!" I thought. "How frightening! If only I could wake up."

Some glass fell and broke. A light flashed behind the showcase and played on the ceiling.

"Don't make noise," I heard a whisper. "You will wake up that tyrant. . . . Take off your boots."

Somebody came to the showcase, looked at me, and touched the padlock. It was an old, bearded man with a pale, haggard face, in a torn soldier's coat and ragged shoes. A tall, skinny fellow with tre-mendously long arms, wearing an overshirt and a short, torn jacket, approached him. Both whispered and were tinkering around the showcase.

"Robbers!" flashed through my mind.

Although I was asleep, I remembered that there was always a gun under my pillow. Quietly I found it and squeezed it in my hand. Glass tinkled in the showcase.

"Be quiet, you'll wake him. Then we'll have to bump him off."

I dreamed further that I screamed wildly and, frightened by my own voice, jumped up. The old man and the young fellow pounced on me, spreading their arms, but seeing the gun, they moved back. I remember that a moment later they were standing before me, pale and tearfully blinking their eyes, imploring me to let them go. The wind burst strongly through the broken window and played with the flame of the candle lighted by the thieves.

"Your excellency!" said somebody in the window with a whining voice. "Our benefactor! Mercy!"

I looked at the window and saw an old woman's face, pale, thin, drenched in the rain.

"Don't touch them! Let them go!" she cried, looking at me with imploring eyes. "Such poverty!"

"Poverty!" confirmed the old man.

"Poverty!" sang the wind.

The pain wrung my heart, and I pinched myself trying to wake up. . . . But instead of waking up, I was standing at the showcase taking out the jewels and convulsively shoving them into the pockets of the old man and the young fellow.

"Take them fast," I choked. "Tomorrow is Christmas, and you are beggars! Take!"

After stuffing the beggars' pockets, I put the remaining jewels in a bundle and tossed them to the old woman. I gave the old woman a fur coat, a bundle with the black suit, the lace dresses, and also the guitar. Such strange dreams happen! After this, I remember, the door opened. My employer, a police officer, and other policemen appeared before me as if they had sprung from the earth. My employer stood near me, but I kept making bundles as if I did not see him.

"What are you doing, you scoundrel?"

"Tomorrow is Christmas," I answered. "They must eat."

Here the curtain goes down, then goes up again, and I see a new scene. I am no longer in the storeroom but in some other place. A policeman is walking near me, gives me a jug of water, and mutters, "See! See! Now how do you like what you did for the holiday!" When I woke up, it was daylight. The rain was no longer knocking at the window, the wind was not wailing. The holiday sun was playing gaily on the wall. The first to give me holiday greetings was the police chief.

"And with a new home . . ." he added.

A month later I was on trial. Why? I assured the judges that it was a dream, that it is unfair to judge a man for a nightmare. Judge for yourselves: Could I give somebody else's things to thieves for no reason? And how could I give things back without receiving payment? But the court decided that the dream was a reality and condemned me. As you see, I am in the convict labor gang. Could you speak for me somewhere? I am not guilty.

Where Brutus had to struggle with his conscience to make a decision for the good of Rome, the leading character in this play is forced to make a decision for the safety of his family.

Rod Serling was one of the first playwrights to make his reputation as a writer for television rather than the stage or the movies. Many of the camera directions from the original shooting script have been retained in the following version.

The Shelter

ROD SERLING

ACT ONE

EXTERIOR SHOT OF RESIDENTIAL STREET. NIGHT. LONG ANGLE SHOT LOOKING DOWN A TREE–LINED SMALL–TOWN STREET.

On a summer evening. The lights from the big, old, stately houses that flank on either side cast warm, orange glows, intermingled with the moonlight that is streaming through the broad-leafed trees. The camera pans down them across toward one house in particular. A sign in the front yard announces that this is the home of DR. WILLIAM STOCKTON. And from inside we can hear the sound of laughter and merry-making.

DISSOLVE THRU TO:

INTERIOR OF DINING ROOM. NIGHT.

There are four couples there gathered around the table. The HENDER-SONS, the WEISSES, DR. STOCKTON and his WIFE, and MARTHA and JERRY HARLOWE. The last is standing at his place at the table and knocking a glass with a spoon, calling for quiet. We see the remnant of a dinner and also one half of a large cake with candles. HARLOWE holds up his hand and throws the glass down.

HARLOWE. Ladies and gentlemen . . . may I have your attention, please! [*The laughter and talk subside, and they all stare up smiling at* HARLOWE.] No birthday celebration is complete without an after-dinner speech! [*More laughter and applause at this, then* HARLOWE *looks toward the guest of honor,* DR. STOCKTON.] And to get to the business at hand and the honoring of one Dr. William Stockton who's grown one year older and will admit to being over twenty-one! [*More laughter, and the doctor's wife leans over to hug him.*] And who in the short space of twenty years has taken care of us, our kids . . . even our grandkids! And I doubt if there's a single person in this room who still doesn't owe the good doctor for a visit or two! [*Again laughter, humorous protests, et al.*]

A VOICE (*shouts out*). What about this hammering at all hours of the night? That's another thing we owe him for. [*There's laughter at this.*]

HARLOWE (*joins in the laughter then holds up his hand*). Oh, yes, the good doctor's bomb shelter. I think we might as well forgive him for this. Despite the fact that what he thinks of as far-sightedness on his part is a pain in the neck to all the rest of us with the concrete trucks and the nocturnal hammering and all the rest of it. [*There's some joshing and more good-natured cat-calls at this.*] Anyway . . . when Grace — (*he points toward the woman sitting next to Stockton*) mentioned that it was your birthday — we took it on ourselves to handle the proceedings. And just as a little personal aside let me conclude this way. [HARLOWE'S *smile fades.*] You're a very beloved fellah . . . and rightfully so. And you may not have the biggest practice in the history of medicine . . . but there isn't a sawbones in any one of the fifty states whose patients have such a regard . . . an affection . . . a respect for the man with the black bag . . . as we do for ours!

[*There's applause and laughter.* GRACE STOCKTON *leans over to kiss her husband, who returns the kiss, then stands and holds out his hand to* HARLOWE, *who grips it with both of his.*]

STOCKTON (*with a grin*). You dirty dog, you! First a surprise party — which I abhor. And then that sloppy sentimental speech! [*But the two men continue to stand there and grip their hands together.*]

CUT TO:

ENTRANCE TO THE DINING ROOM.

[*As the Stockton's twelve-year-old boy enters.*]

BOY. Hey, Pop . . . Pop?

[STOCKTON *looks over toward the youngster.*]

STOCKTON. What is it, Paul?

PAUL. The picture went out on the television set. Then there was some kind of goofy announcement. Something about —

[*The boy continues to speak, but he's drowned out by one of the women laughing.* WEISS's *face suddenly looks serious. He rises and crosses the room and then in a loud voice —*]

WEISS. Hold it, everybody. [*There's a gradual silence.*] What did you say, Paul?

PAUL. The announcer said something about turning to the Conelrad station on the radio.

PAN SHOT. AROUND THE ROOM.

[*The people suddenly become deadly still and faces take on a sudden tight, grim cast.*]

STOCKTON. You must have heard it wrong, Paul —

PAUL. I didn't hear it wrong, Pop. That's what he said. Turn on your Conelrad station, then everything went blank completely.

[STOCKTON *comes out on the run over to a small table radio. He flicks it on then whirls the dials around. After a moment we hear an announcer's voice.*]

ANNOUNCER'S VOICE. . . . . direct from Washington, D.C. Repeating that. Four minutes ago the President of the United States made the following announcement. I quote: "At 11:04 P.M. Eastern Standard Time both our Distant Early Warning line and Ballistics Early Warning line reported radar evidence of unidentified flying objects due southeast. As of this moment we have been unable to determine the nature of these objects, but for the time being in the interest of national safety we are declaring a state of Yellow Alert. [*A pause.*] The Civil Defense authorities request that if you have a shelter already prepared, go there at once. If you do not have a shelter, use your time to move supplies of food, water, medicine, and other supplies to a central place. Keep all windows and doors closed. We repeat: if you're in your home, go to your prepared shelters or to your basement . . .

[*His voice fades. As after a stunned moment of sheer inarticulate horror, the people in the room start toward the front door and outside.*]

CUT TO:

EXTERIOR OF THE HOUSE. NIGHT.

As they come out, cross the porch, and then start down the steps in a mad, frenetic exodus toward each of their houses. As they arrive outside, a siren starts to blare out its dissonant, shrieking scream, and the sound of it stops them in their tracks.

SERIES OF CLOSE SHOTS. FACES OF THE MEN AND WOMEN.

As they stare toward the sky. The voice of the Conelrad radio announcer continues underneath from the house. Then they each break off and head in different directions toward their homes.

NARRATOR. What you're about to watch is a nightmare. It is not meant to be prophetic. It need not happen. It is the fervent and urgent prayer of all men of good will that it shall never happen. [*A pause*] But in this place . . . in this moment . . . it does happen.

FADE IN ON:

INTERIOR OF A CELLAR. STOCKTON'S HOUSE. NIGHT.

At the far end of the room is a concrete wall with a heavy steel door, now open, revealing a small, perhaps ten-by-ten, shelter encased by reinforced concrete walls. Three cots, a shelf full of canned goods, and a portable radio, which is on.

ANNOUNCER'S VOICE. This is Conelrad, your emergency broadcasting station. You will find Conelrad at either 640 or 1240 on your dial. Remain tuned to this frequency. We repeat our previous announcement. We are in a state of Yellow Alert. If you have a shelter already prepared, go there at once. If you do not have a shelter, use your time to move supplies of food, water, medicine, and other supplies to a central place. Keep all windows and doors closed. We repeat: If you're in your home, go to your prepared shelters or to your basement . . .

CUT TO:

STOCKTON KITCHEN. NIGHT.

The water is just dribbling out of the tap. GRACE STOCKTON *has collected several jugs and vases and is filling them.* PAUL *hurries through the kitchen carrying a box full of canned goods, followed by his father, who goes over toward the sink and hoists up two of the jugs.*

STOCKTON. Fill up as many as you can, Grace. I'm going to start the generator up in the shelter in case the power goes off. [*Looking up toward dimming lights.*] And that may happen any moment now.

GRACE. And there's hardly any water coming through the tap —

STOCKTON. That's because everybody and his brother are doing the same thing we are. Keep it on full force until it stops.

[GRACE *picks up a jug that's partially filled, shoves another one under the tap in its place. But in the process of moving the filled one onto the sink counter, it slips and smashes on the floor. She lets out a gasp and puts her hands to the sides of her head.*]

STOCKTON (*gentle, but firm*). Easy, honey, easy. Make believe it's perfume and it costs a hundred bucks an ounce. Maybe in an hour or so it'll be worth even more than that —

PAUL (*enters from the basement*). What else, Pop?

STOCKTON. All the canned goods down?

PAUL. All that I could find.

GRACE. How about the fruit cellar?

PAUL. I put all those in too.

STOCKTON. Get my bag from the bedroom. Put that in there too.

PAUL. What about books and stuff?

GRACE (*close to hysteria*). Your father told you to get his bag — !

STOCKTON (*reaches out and holds* GRACE's *arm*). There's time, Grace. There's plenty of time. And we'll need books and things. Who knows how long we'll have to stay down there.

PAUL (*crossing the room and heading out into the dining room*). I'll get your bag, Pop.

STOCKTON. What about light bulbs? Where do you keep the light bulbs?

GRACE (*points*). Top shelf in that cupboard there. (*then closes her eyes tightly and clenches her fists*) We don't have any. I ran out yesterday. I was going to buy some at the store. There was a sale on — (*she lets out one sob*) Oh, my dear God, I'm talking like an idiot. (*then even more frightened*) How much time do we have?

STOCKTON. There's no telling. Seems to me I remember reading some-place from the first alarm we might have anywhere from fifteen minutes to half an hour.

GRACE (*her eyes going wide*). Fifteen minutes!

STOCKTON. I'm winging it, Grace. I don't know for sure. I don't think anyone does. (*he heads toward the door to dining room*) Keep pouring the water.

CUT TO:

INTERIOR OF DINING ROOM.

[STOCKTON *enters, goes through and then into the front hall. He calls.*]

STOCKTON. Paul? You get my bag?

[PAUL *comes down the steps carrying a bag and an armful of books and magazines.*]

PAUL. I got everything, Pop.

[STOCKTON *takes the things from his arms at the foot of the steps.*]

STOCKTON. Lemmee give you a hand.

CUT TO:

KITCHEN.

[*As the water in the tap drips . . . drips . . . and finally stops altogether.* GRACE *whirls around from the sink and shouts.*]

GRACE. Bill, there's no more water.

[STOCKTON *and* PAUL *enter the kitchen and head toward the base-ment door.*]

STOCKTON. It doesn't make any difference. I think we've got enough now anyway. Bring a jug with you, Grace. Paul and I'll get the rest in a minute.

[*All three head down basement steps.*]

CUT TO:

INTERIOR OF SHELTER.

Now loaded down with boxes, jugs, et al., as the three of them enter and deposit their loads.

STOCKTON. You two stay here. I'll get the rest of the water. (*he suddenly snaps his fingers*) There's a five-gallon can of gasoline in the garage. Paul, you run out and get that. We'll need it for the generator.

PAUL. Right, Pop. [*He goes out past his father.* GRACE *sits down on the cot, her fist clenched, staring out at nothing.*]

STOCKTON. I'll get the rest of the water. [GRACE *nods. He makes a move to leave, then looks at her intently, crosses over to her and kneels down in front of her. He takes both her hands in his.*] If it's a bomb, there's no assurance that it'll land near us. And if it doesn't —

GRACE (*interrupting, pulling her hands away*). But if it does . . . we're forty miles from New York. And New York's going to get it. We know that. And then we'll get it too. All of it. The poison, the radiation, the whole thing. We'll get it too.

STOCKTON. We'll be in a shelter, Grace. And with any luck at all, we'll survive. We've got enough food and water to last us at least two weeks. Maybe even longer if we use it wisely.

GRACE. And then what? Then what, Bill? We crawl out of here like gophers to tiptoe through all the rubble up above. The rubble and the ruins and the bodies of our friends — (*she gives him a long, queer look, composite of horror and a building panic*) Why is it so necessary that we survive? What's the good of it, Bill? (*she suddenly breaks, grabbing him, her voice a long drawn-out sob*) Bill, wouldn't it be better . . . wouldn't it be quicker and easier if we just —

[*At this moment there's the sound of* PAUL's *voice from up above calling down to them.*]

PAUL'S VOICE. I got the gasoline, Pop. Is that all you need from out there?

STOCKTON (*turns toward his wife, evenly*). That's why we have to survive. *That's* the reason. He may inherit just rubble now, but he's twelve years old. (*he turns away thoughtfully*) He's twelve years old, Grace . . . (*then he rises and calls out*) Paul!

PAUL'S VOICE (*nearer*). I got the gas, Pop. [*The boy appears at the door to the shelter.*]

STOCKTON. Lay it down there next to the generator. I'll go up and get the rest of the water. [*He walks through the basement and starts up the steps toward the kitchen.*]

CUT TO:

INTERIOR OF KITCHEN.

As he goes over to the sink, starts to collect the last of the jugs. There's a sudden knock on the back door and through the window and the semi-parted curtains we see the face of JERRY HARLOWE. STOCKTON crosses over, unlocks the door and opens it.

HARLOWE. How you doing, Bill?

STOCKTON. Collecting water, which is what you should be doing.

HARLOWE. We got about thirty gallons, and the water stopped. Did yours stop too?

STOCKTON (*nods*). You better get on home, Jerry. Get into your shel — (*he stops abruptly, wets his lips*) Into your basement. I'd board up the windows if I were you. And if you've got any wood putty or anything, I'd seal the corners.

HARLOWE (*his voice is very gentle*). We don't have a cellar, Bill. Remember? (*then a lopsided grin*) The benefits of modern architecture. We've got the one brand-new house on the street. Everything at your beck and call. Everything at your fingertips. And a nice electrical laundry room right off the kitchen. (*his voice shakes slightly*) Every wonder of modern science taken into account except the one that's heading for us now. (*there's a silence, and* HARLOWE *tries to keep the supplication out of his voice*) Bill, can I bring Martha and the kids over here?

STOCKTON. Over *here*?

HARLOWE. We're sitting ducks over there. Sitting ducks. We don't have any protection at all.

STOCKTON (*after a moment's hesitation*). You can use our basement.

HARLOWE. Your basement? What about your shelter? That's the only place anyone can survive! We've got to get into a shelter.

STOCKTON (*after a pause*). I don't have any room, Jerry. I don't have near enough room. Or supplies or anything. It's designed for three people.

HARLOWE. We'll bring our own water and our own food. We'll sleep on top of one another if necessary. Please . . . Bill. We've got to use your shelter. I've got to keep my family alive. We won't use any of your stuff.

STOCKTON. What about your own air? Will you bring your own air? That's a ten-by-ten room, Jerry.

HARLOWE (*momentarily taken aback and having to recover*). Just let us stay in there the first forty-eight hours or so, then we'll get out. Just so we can have a chance during the rough time.

STOCKTON. When that door gets closed and locked — it *stays* closed and locked. There'll be radiation and heaven knows what else. (*and now his face torn by anguish*) I'm sorry, Jerry. As God is my witness, I'm sorry. But I built that for *my* family.

HARLOWE (*grabbing him, his voice high, shrill and unsteady*). And what about *mine*? What do *we* do? Just rock on the front porch until we get burned into cinders?

STOCKTON (*breaks away from him*). That's not my concern. Right at this given moment it's my family I have to worry about. [*He picks up the water jugs and starts toward the basement door.* HARLOWE *runs toward him, whirls him around, grabs him.*]

HARLOWE. I am not going to sit by and watch my wife and children die in agony. I'm not going to do that. Do you understand me, Bill? (*he shakes* STOCKTON) I am not going to do — [*In the process and as* STOCKTON *tries to pull away, he trips and falls through the cellar-door opening. One of the jugs rolls down one step at a time, miraculously not breaking.* STOCKTON *slowly rises to his feet.*]

CLOSE SHOT. THE TWO MEN.

HARLOWE (*closes his eyes and lowers his head*). I'm sorry, Bill. Please forgive me.

STOCKTON (*guiltily averts his eyes then looks up, in a very soft and gentle voice*). I kept telling you. All of you. Build a shelter. Get ready. Forget the card parties and the barbecues for maybe two hours a week. And make an admission to yourself that the worst is possible. (*he shakes his head*) But you didn't want to listen, Jerry. None of you wanted to listen. To build a shelter was admitting the kind of age we lived in, and none of you had the guts to face that. So now, Jerry, now you've got to find some guts to face something far worse. Not just the possibility . . . that was easy to live with. Now you've got to face the reality. God protect you, Jerry. It's out of my hands now. It's simply out of my hands. It's got to be God. [*He turns and starts down the basement steps.*]

CUT TO;

FRONT DOOR.

It's flung open, and in walks MARTY WEISS, *his* WIFE, *a tiny sleepy little boy in a pair of Dr. Dentons, rubbing his eyes, and an infant in his arms. He barges into the dining room, calling.*

WEISS. Bill? Bill, where are you?

MRS. WEISS (*coming up close to him, her face pale with terror*). They're already in the shelter. I told you they'd be in the shelter. They've locked themselves in. [*At this moment* HARLOWE *comes out from the kitchen. He looks at them briefly.*]

HARLOWE. It's no use, Marty. He won't let anyone in.

WEISS (*close to hysteria*). He's got to let us in. We don't even have any windows in half the basement. I don't have anything to plug them up either. And a basement wouldn't be any help anyway. [*He starts to push his way past* HARLOWE.] Where is he? Is he downstairs? Is he in the shelter?

CUT TO:

ANGLE SHOT. LOOKING UP THE STEPS AT WEISS.

[*As he appears at top of stairs, shouting down.*]

WEISS. Bill? Bill, it's Marty. We've got the kids with us. (*he frantically stumbles halfway down the cellar steps*) Bill? Bill?

[*He goes down the rest of the steps, turns and starts across the basement toward the shelter which has now been closed and locked. Halfway across the room the lights suddenly go out and once again the sirens can be heard.*]

SHELTER DOOR.

[*As* WEISS *gropes his way over to it, stumbles, reaches out to clutch at it for support.*]

WEISS. Bill? Bill, please. Please —

[*Above him we hear the sound of his little boy suddenly screaming in fear, then his wife's voice.*]

MRS. WEISS'S VOICE. Marty? Marty, where are you? The light are out. Marty, please . . . come back and get us —

[WEISS *presses his cheek against the shelter door.*]

WEISS. Bill. Please, Bill, please let us in. Please.

CUT TO:

EXTREMELY TIGHT CLOSE SHOT. STOCKTON.

On the other side of the door. WEISS'S *voice can be heard, muffled.*

WEISS'S VOICE. Please, Bill. Please let us in.

EXTREMELY TIGHT CLOSE SHOT. GRACE.

As she closes her eyes as if by this act she could blot out the voices. STOCKTON *crosses over, manipulates a few buttons, then pulls a small starter knob attached to the tiny generator. It starts up after a few preliminary coughs and then hums into action. At this moment the lights go on in the shelter.* STOCKTON's *face is suddenly illuminated by the lights. It's creased, lined, furrowed with the results of this massive attack on first his conscience, his beliefs, the habit pattern of a lifetime, which he must suddenly simply turn aside. He takes a hesitant step toward the door, facing it. His lips move for a moment and finally speech comes.*

STOCKTON. Marty, I would if I could. Do you understand? I swear to you, I would.

WEISS'S VOICE. Bill, please. Please. You've got to. You've got to let us in.

[STOCKTON *drops to his knees and presses his face against the side of the door. His lips tremble.*]

STOCKTON. I can't, Marty. Don't stay there asking me. Because I can't. I can't and I won't.

CUT TO:

CLOSE SHOT. WEISS.

WEISS (*his voice breaking perceptibly*). I feel sorry for you then, Bill. I really do. You probably will survive — but you're going to have blood on your hands. Do you hear me, Bill? You'll have blood on your hands!

CUT TO:

CLOSE SHOT. PAUL.

His young face white with the terror of it, of the sudden exposure to naked emotions of adults set against a background of terror that he cannot even assimilate.

CLOSE SHOT. GRACE.

As she closes her eyes tightly and leans her head against her fists.

CLOSE SHOT. STOCKTON.

As he slowly turns away from the door. At this moment he can hear the sound of the child crying again and MRS. WEISS's *forlorn, lost cry for her husband.*

STOCKTON (*very softly*). That was a million years ago. A million years ago. (*he whirls around, slams himself against the door*) Marty, get out of here! Do you hear me? *Get out of here.* [*Then he closes his eyes tightly and lets his head sink forward as the sound of the radio intermingles with the cry of a small child.*]

FADE TO BLACK:

ACT TWO

INTERIOR OF DINING ROOM. STOCKTON HOUSE. NIGHT.

MARTY WEISS, HIS WIFE, and CHILDREN *feel their way through the kitchen toward the dining table, where the burned-down candles of the birthday banquet give them some light.* MARTY *takes the candles* and assists HIS WIFE *through the dining room toward the living room as we hear and see* MRS. HARLOWE *and* CHILDREN.

MRS. HARLOWE. Well, go back!

[HARLOWE, *standing in front doorway.*]

HARLOWE. Wouldn't help.
MRS. HARLOWE. Jerry, ask again.

[*By the time* WEISS *and his* WIFE *reach the front door beside* HARLOWE.]

CUT TO:

STREET OUTSIDE STOCKTON HOME.

[HENDERSON *and* MRS. HENDERSON *enter front door of* STOCKTON *house.*]

HENDERSON. It'll land any minute. I just know it. It's going to land any minute —
MRS. HENDERSON (*grabs hold of him*). What are we going to do, Frank? What are we going to do?

[*Throughout above and following dialogue, a portable radio carried by one of the children carries the following dialogue:*]

ANNOUNCER'S VOICE. This is Conelrad. This is Conelrad. We are still in a state of Yellow Alert. If you are a public official or government employee with an emergency assignment, or a civil defense worker, you should report to your post immediately. If you are a public official or government employee . . .
HARLOWE. Don't waste your time. He won't let anyone in.
MRS. HENDERSON. What'll we do?
HARLOWE. Maybe we ought to pick out just one basement and go to work on it. Pool all our stuff. Food, water, everything.
MARTHA HARLOWE. It isn't fair. (*she points toward Stockton house*) He's down there in a bomb shelter completely safe. And *our* kids have to just wait around for a bomb to drop and —
HENDERSON. Let's just go down into his basement and break down the door?

[*A chorus of voices greet this with assent.*]

CUT TO:

INTERIOR OF DINING ROOM.

[As HENDERSON *streaks through toward the basement entrance.*
HARLOWE *overtakes him, saying:*]

HARLOWE. Wait a minute, wait a minute. All of us couldn't fit in
there. That would be crazy to even try.

WEISS. Why don't we draw lots? Pick out *one* family?

HARLOWE. What difference would it make? He won't let us in.

HENDERSON. We can all march down there and tell him he's got the
whole street against him. We could do that.

HARLOWE. What good would that do? I keep telling you. Even if
we were to break down the door, it couldn't accommodate all of
us. We'd just be killing everybody and for no reason.

MRS. HENDERSON. If it saves even one of these kids out here — I call
that a reason.

[*The voice comes up again.*]

WEISS. Jerry, you know him better than any of us. You're his best
friend. Why don't you go down again? Try to talk to him. Plead
with him. Tell him to pick out one family — draw lots or something —

HENDERSON. One family meaning yours, Weiss, huh?

WEISS (*whirls around to him*). Why not? I've got a three-month-old
infant —

MRS. HENDERSON. What difference does that make? Is your baby's
life any more precious than our kids?

WEISS (*shouting at her*). I never said that. If you're going to start
trying to argue about who deserves to live more than the next
one —

HENDERSON. Why don't you shut your mouth, Weiss? (*with a wild,
illogical anger*) That's the way it is when the foreigners come over
here. Pushy, grabby, semi-Americans —

CLOSE SHOT. WEISS.

[*His face goes white.*]

WEISS. Why, you garbage-brained idiot, you —

MRS. HENDERSON. It still goes, Weiss! For my dough you're at the
bottom of the list —

[WEISS *suddenly flings himself through the crowd toward* HENDER-SON, *and there's a brief, inexpert grappling between them broken up by* HARLOWE, *who stands between them breathless.*]

HARLOWE. Keep it up, both of you. Just keep it up. We won't need a bomb. We can slaughter each other.

MRS. WEISS (*pleading*). Marty, go down to Bill's shelter again. Ask him —

WEISS. I've already asked him. It wouldn't do any good.

[*Once again the siren sounds, and the people seem to move closer together, staring up toward the night sky. Off in the distance we see searchlights.*]

HARLOWE. Searchlights. It must be coming closer. (*then to the man with the portable*) Anything *new* on the radio?

MAN #1 (*listens for a moment*). No . . .

HENDERSON (*as he suddenly pushes* HARLOWE *aside and heads for the steps*). I'm going down there and get him to open up that door. I don't care what the rest of you think. That's the only thing left to do.

MAN #1. He's right. Come on, let's do it.

CUT TO:

INTERIOR OF SHELTER.

GRACE *is holding tight to* PAUL. STOCKTON *stands close to the door listening to the noises from outside as they approach. There's a pounding on the shelter door that reverberates. We hear voice of* HENDERSON.

HENDERSON. Bill? Bill Stockton? You've got a bunch of your neighbors out here who want to stay alive. Now you can open the door and talk to us and figure out with us how many can come in there. Or else you can just keep doing what you're doing — and we'll bust our way in there.

CUT TO:

INTERIOR OF BASEMENT. THE OTHER SIDE OF THE SHELTER DOOR.

[HARLOWE *appears and pushes his way through the group and goes over to the shelter door.*]

HARLOWE. Bill. This is Jerry. They mean business out here.

STOCKTON'S VOICE. And I mean business in *here*. I've already told you, Jerry. You're wasting your time. You're wasting precious time that could be used for something else . . . like figuring out how you can survive.

MAN #1. Why don't we get some kind of battering ram?

HENDERSON. We could go over to Bennett Avenue. Phil Kline has a bunch of two-by-fours in his basement. I've seen them.

MAN #1. That would get him into the act then and who cares about saving *him?* The minute we do that, then we let all those people know that there's a shelter on this street. We'd have a whole mob to contend with. A whole bunch of outsiders.

MRS. HENDERSON. Sure, and what right have they got to come over here? This isn't *their* street. This isn't *their* shelter.

[HARLOWE's *been listening to all of this, and he slowly shakes his head, clenching and unclenching his fists. He suddenly pushes himself through to the shelter door and turns with his back against it.*]

HARLOWE. This is *our* shelter, huh? And on the next street — that's a different country. Patronize home industries. You idiots. You fools. You're insane now, all of you.

MRS. WEISS. Maybe you don't want to live, Jerry. Maybe you don't care.

HARLOWE. I care. Believe me, I care. I'd like to see the morning come too. But you're becoming a mob now. And a mob doesn't have any brains, and that's what you're proving.

HENDERSON. I say let's get the battering ram. And we'll just tell Kline to keep his mouth shut as to why we want it.

WEISS. I agree with Jerry. Let's get hold of ourselves. Let's stop and think for a minute —

HENDERSON (*turning to face* WEISS). Nobody cares what you think. You or your kind. I thought I made that clear upstairs. I think the first order of business is to get you out of here.

[*With this he lashes out, smashing his fist into* WEISS's *face in a blow so unexpected and so wild that* WEISS, *totally unprepared, is battered against the wall.* HIS WIFE *screams and, still holding the baby, rushes to him. There's a commotion as several men try to grab the neighbor, and* HARLOWE *is immediately at* WEISS's *side trying to help him to his feet. Once again the sirens blast, and it's almost as if it were some kind of a signal re-igniting the panic.*]

HENDERSON (*shouts over the noise and commotion*). Come on, let's get something to smash this door down. [*They start out of the cellar toward the steps.* HENDERSON *shouts over his shoulder.*] You had your chance, Stockton. Just remember that. You had your chance —

CUT TO:

INTERIOR OF SHELTER.

As STOCKTON *slowly turns to face his wife. The angry screaming cries of the people ring in their ears even as they depart. Grace looks up.*

GRACE. Bill? Who were those people?

[STOCKTON *turns to stare toward the door.*]

STOCKTON. "Those people"? Those are our neighbors, Grace. Our friends. The people we've lived with and alongside for twenty years. (*then in a different fixed expression and in a different tone*) Come on, Paul. Let's put stuff up against this door. Everything we can.

[*The man and boy then start to pile up a barricade, using furniture, the generator, books, any movable object they can get their hands on.*]

DISSOLVE TO:

THE STREET.

As *the mob marches down the street carrying a giant two-by-four that is perhaps fifteen feet long. Their own shouts mix with the sound of the intermittent siren and with the voice of the announcer on the Conelrad station.*

ANNOUNCER'S VOICE. We've been asked to once again remind the population that they are to remain calm, stay off the streets. This is urgent. *Please remain off the streets.* Everything possible is being done in the way of protection. But the military and important civil defense vehicles must have the streets clear. So you're once again reminded to remain off the streets. *Remain off the streets!*

THE STOCKTON HOUSE.

The mob converges on it.

CUT TO:

INTERIOR OF THE HOUSE.

As they smash into it, carrying the battering ram. They move down the cellar steps.

CUT TO:

SHELTER DOOR.

As the board smashes into it. The siren goes up louder and more piercing, and it is at this moment that we see both WEISS *and* HARLOWE *join the men on the battering ram to lend their support to it.*

CUT TO:

INTERIOR OF SHELTER.

As STOCKTON *and* PAUL *lean against it as it starts to give under the weight, under the pressure. The air is filled with angry shouts, the intermittent siren, the cries of women and children.*

INSIDE AND OUTSIDE OF THE SHELTER.

And it all reaches one vast pitch just as the door buckles and is forced open. PAUL *and* STOCKTON *are pushed back into the shelter, and just at this moment the lights go on in the basement. The siren also reaches its pinnacle and then suddenly goes off, and there is absolute dead silence for a long moment. The camera pans past the faces of the people, including the occupants of the shelter to the portable radio in the corner.*

ANNOUNCER'S VOICE. This is Conelrad. This is Conelrad. Remain tuned for an important message. Remain tuned for an important message. (*a pause*) The President of the United States has just announced that the previously unidentified objects have now been definitely ascertained as being satellites. Repeat. There are no enemy missiles approaching. Repeat. There are no enemy missiles approaching. The objects have been identified as satellites. They are harmless, and we are in no danger. Repeat. We are in no danger. The state of emergency has officially been called off. We are in no danger. Repeat. There is no enemy attack. There is no enemy attack.

[*This news registers on the faces of the people and sinks in.*]

MRS. WEISS (*her eyes closed and crying softly*). Thank God. Oh, thank God.

[WEISS's *face is bruised and blood-clotted.*]

WEISS (*in a whisper*). Amen to that.

[MAN #1 *doesn't seem to know whether to smile or cry or what. Finally he turns to* WEISS, *cups his face in his hands.*]

HENDERSON. Hey, Marty . . . Marty . . . I went off my rocker. You understand that, don't you? I just went off my rocker. I didn't mean all the things I said. [*He wets his lips, his voice shaking.*] We were all of us . . . we were so scared . . . so confused. [*He holds out his hands in a gesture.*] Well, it's no wonder really, is it? I mean . . . well you can understand why we blew our tops a little —

[*There's a murmur of voices, a few perfunctory, half-hearted nods, but they're all still in a state of shock.*]

HARLOWE. I don't think Marty's going to hold it against you. (*then turning to* STOCKTON) I just hope Bill won't hold *this* — (*he points to the wreckage and rubble around him*) against us. We'll pay for the damage, Bill. We'll take up a collection right away.

[STOCKTON *walks past them across the cellar and up toward the stairs. All eyes are on him, and there's an absolute dead silence.*]

WEISS (*his voice shaky and nervous*). We could . . . we could have a block party or something tomorrow night. A big celebration. I think we rate one now.

[*He looks around smiling at the others, a nervous smile born of a carryover of fear and the realization that something has taken hold of all of them now. Something deadening in its effect and dis-*

quieting beyond words. STOCKTON *takes a step up on the stairs, then stops and turns back toward them. His face is impassive — more thoughtful than anything.*]

HARLOWE (*with phony laughter desperately trying to relieve situation*). Block party's not a bad idea. (*looking around at the others*) Anything to get back to normal.

CLOSE SHOT. STOCKTON.

[*As he looks from face to face and slowly shakes his head.*]

STOCKTON. Normal? (*a pause*) I don't know. I don't know what "normal" is. I thought I did, but I don't any more.

GROUP SHOT.

HARLOWE. I told you we'd pay for the damages —
STOCKTON (*stares at him*). The damages? (*he nods*) I wonder if we realize just what those damages are? (*he looks from face to face again*) Maybe the worst of them was finding out just what we're like when we're normal. The kind of people we are. Just underneath the surface. I mean all of us. A lot of naked animals who put such a premium on staying alive that they claw their neighbors to death just for the privilege. (*he leans against the stairway wall, suddenly desperately tired, very softly as he turns away from them*) We were spared a bomb tonight . . . but I wonder if we weren't destroyed even without it. [*He continues up the steps.*]

DISSOLVE TO:

EXTERIOR OF STOCKTON HOUSE.

As the people come out quietly in twos and threes and disappear in all directions, back to their houses. Over this shot we hear NARRATOR'*s voice.*

NARRATOR. No moral . . . no message . . . no prophetic tract. Just a simple statement of fact. For civilization to survive . . . the human race has to remain civilized.

FADE TO BLACK:

THE END

"Trooper Meditating Beside a Grave"
by Winslow Homer.

BOOK THREE | PART 3

CONFLICTS

*"The true satisfaction of life lies in
imaginative conflict. Whatever their
ultimate purpose, men are alive only when
they struggle. When they grow aware of
the futility of their effort, and yet strive
to fashion something from it, they
become noble and tragic."*

SIEGFRIED SASSOON

Brutus against Caesar, Brutus against Antony, Caesar against the
Republic, idealist against politician — Julius Caesar is a play of many
conflicts. All Rome is caught in the conflict that leads to the assassination of Caesar and erupts into a civil war after his death. Friend
turns against friend, senator against senator, even the elements suggest conflict when meteors turn night into day.

Conflict is an important theme in most literature, whether between men or ideas or nations, or between man and his environ-
ment. The most obvious conflicts are physical and external battles
of men and nations. But much literature is built around inner struggles: a tension between ideas (the most important conflict in Animal
Farm) or within the conscience of an individual. Even the simplest
little comic poem contains conflicts. Look at Langston Hughes's
"Little Lyric (Of Great Importance)" on page 147. In only two
lines there are at least three conflicts: between the speaker's wish
and the facts of life, between his empty pocket and his economic
needs, and between the words "little" and "great" in the title.

In Julius Caesar, the conflict of Brutus and his conscience leads
to the political conflicts of Caesar's successors. Conflict brings chaos

to the State. Caesar is destroyed by his ambition. Brutus is destroyed by his misguided idealism. Reason is destroyed by the angry voice of the mob.

In Animal Farm, conflict first serves to unite the animals against Mr. Jones to bring about the revolution. Then conflict between the individual animals destroys the ideals of equality and freedom for which the animals originally fought.

The following selections show many, but not all, of the kinds of conflict reflected in literature. In some ("The Fight") the emphasis is on external conflict; in others ("Through the Tunnel") the internal conflict is more important. Most of the selections are a mixture of both.

Conflict is a part of growing up, a process that is often painful. In all ages, young people have had to prove themselves to their schoolmates. Here, a boy from the South is fatalistic about his first day at a new school. The selection is from Richard Wright's autobiography, Black Boy.

[handwritten: Black]

[handwritten: external conflict]

The Fight

[handwritten: internal conflict - If he would be accepted]

RICHARD WRIGHT

After breakfast, Uncle Clark took me to school, introduced me to the principal. The first half of the school day passed without incident. I sat looking at the strange reading book, following the lessons. The subjects seemed simple, and I felt that I could keep up. My anxiety was still in me; I was wondering how I would get on with the boys. Each new school meant a new area of life to be conquered. Were the boys tough? How hard did they fight? I took it for granted that they fought.

At noon recess I went into the school grounds, and a group of boys sauntered up to me, looked at me from my head to my feet, whispering among themselves. I leaned against a wall, trying to conceal my uneasiness.

"Where you from?" a boy asked abruptly.

"Jackson," I answered.

"How come they make you people so ugly in Jackson?" he demanded.

There was loud laughter.

"You're not any too good-looking yourself," I countered instantly.

"Oh!"

"Aw!"

"You hear what he told 'im?"

"You think you're smart, don't you?" the boy asked, sneering.

"Listen, I ain't picking a fight," I said. "But if you want to fight, I'll fight."

"Hunh, hard guy, ain't you?"

"As hard as you."

"Do you know who you can tell that to?" he asked me.

"And you know who you can tell it back to?" I asked.

"Are you talking about my mama?" he asked, edging forward.

"If you want it that way," I said.

This was my test. If I failed now, I would have failed at school, for the first trial came not in books but in how one's fellows took one, what value they placed upon one's willingness to fight.

"Take back what you said," the boy challenged me.

"Make me," I said.

The crowd howled, sensing a fight. The boy hesitated, weighing his chances of beating me.

"You ain't gonna take what that new boy said, is you?" someone taunted the boy.

The boy came close. I stood my ground. Our faces were four inches apart.

"You think I'm scared of you, don't you?" he asked.

"I told you what I think," I said.

Somebody, eager and afraid that we would not fight, pushed the boy, and he bumped into me. I shoved him away violently.

"Don't push me!" the boy said.

"Then keep off me!" I said.

He was pushed again, and I struck out with my right and caught him in the mouth. The crowd yelled, milled, surging so close that I could barely lift my arm to land a blow. When either of us tried to strike the other, we would be thrown off balance by the screaming boys. Every blow landed elicited shouts of delight. Knowing that if I did not win or make a good showing, I would have to fight a new boy each day, I fought tigerishly, trying to leave a scar, seeking to draw blood as proof that I was not a coward, that I could take care of myself. The bell rang, and the crowd pulled us apart. The fight seemed a draw.

"I ain't through with you!" the boy shouted.

In the classroom the boys asked me questions about myself; I was someone worth knowing. When the bell rang for school to be dismissed, I was set to fight again, but the boy was not in sight.

On my way home I found a cheap ring in the streets, and at once I knew what I was going to do with it. The ring had a red stone held by tiny prongs which I loosened, took the stone out, leaving the sharp tiny prongs jutting up. I slid the ring on to my finger and shadow-boxed. Now let a bully come, and I would show him how to fight; I would leave a crimson streak on his face with every blow.

But I never had to use the ring. After I had exhibited my new weapon at school, a description of it spread among the boys. I challenged my enemy to another fight, but he would not respond. Fighting was now not necessary. I had been accepted.

"The Fight" was about the most elemental kind of conflict between two individuals. The following story has more subtle conflicts in it. At first it may appear to be a struggle of man and nature as a swimmer tests himself against the sea. But the real conflict is an inner one.

Through the Tunnel

DORIS LESSING

Going to the shore on the first morning of the holiday, the young English boy stopped at a turning of the path and looked down at a wild and rocky bay and then over to the crowded beach he knew so well from other years. His mother walked on in front of him, carrying a bright striped bag in one hand. Her other arm, swinging loose, was very white in the sun.

The boy watched that white, naked arm and turned his eyes, which had a frown behind them, toward the bay and back again to his mother. When she felt he was not with her, she swung around.

"Oh, there you are, Jerry!" she said. She looked impatient, then smiled. "Why, darling, would you rather not come with me? Would you rather — " she frowned, conscientiously worrying over what amusements he might secretly be longing for which she had been too busy to imagine.

He was very familiar with that anxious, apologetic smile. Contrition sent him running after her. And yet, as he ran, he looked back over his shoulder at the wild bay; and all morning, as he played on the safe beach, he was thinking of it.

Next morning, when it was time for the routine of swimming and sunbathing, his mother said, "Are you tired of the usual beach, Jerry? Would you like to go somewhere else?"

"Oh, no!" he said quickly, smiling at her out of that unfailing impulse of contrition — a sort of chivalry. Yet, walking down the path with her, he blurted out, "I'd like to go and have a look at those rocks down there."

She gave the idea her attention. It was a wild-looking place, and there was no one there, but she said, "Of course, Jerry. When you've had enough, come to the big beach. Or just go straight back to the villa, if you like."

She walked away, that bare arm, now slightly reddened from yesterday's sun, swinging. And he almost ran after her again, feeling it unbearable that she should go by herself, but he did not.

She was thinking. Of course he's old enough to be safe without me. Have I been keeping him too close? He mustn't feel he ought to be with me. I must be careful.

He was an only child. She was a widow. She was determined to be neither possessive nor lacking in devotion. She went worrying off to her beach.

As for Jerry, once he saw that his mother had gained her beach, he began the steep descent to the bay. From where he was, high up among red-brown rocks, it was a scoop of moving bluish green fringed with white.

As he went lower, he saw that it spread among small promontories [1] and inlets of rough, sharp rock, and the crisping, lapping surface showed stains of purple and darker blue. Finally, as he ran sliding and scraping down the last few yards, he saw an edge of white surf, and the shallow, luminous movement of water over white sand, and, beyond that, a solid, heavy blue.

He ran straight into the water and began swimming. He was a good swimmer. He went out fast over the gleaming sand, over a middle region where rocks lay like discolored monsters under the surface, and then he was in the real sea — a warm sea where irregular cold currents from the deep water shocked his limbs.

When he was so far out that he could look back not only on the little bay but past the promontory that was between it and the big beach, he floated on the buoyant surface and looked for his mother. There she was, a speck of yellow under an umbrella that looked like a slice of orange peel. He swam back to shore, relieved at being sure she was there, but all at once very lonely.

On the edge of a small cape that marked the side of the bay away from the promontory was a loose scatter of rocks. Above them,

---

[1] *promontories*: high points of land extending into the sea.

some boys were stripping off their clothes. They came running, down to the rocks.

The English boy swam toward them and kept his distance at a stone's throw. They were of that coast, all of them burned smooth dark brown and speaking a language he did not understand. To be with them, of them, was a craving that filled his whole body. He swam a little closer; they turned and watched him with narrowed, alert dark eyes.

Then one smiled and waved. It was enough. In a minute, he had swum in and was on the rocks beside them, smiling with a desperate, nervous supplication. They shouted cheerful greetings at him, and then, as he preserved his nervous, uncomprehending smile, they understood that he was a foreigner strayed from his own beach, and they proceeded to forget him. But he was happy. He was with them.

They began diving again and again from a high point into a well of blue sea between rough, pointed rocks. After they had dived and come up, they swam around, hauled themselves up, and waited their turn to dive again.

They were big boys — men to Jerry. He dived, and they watched him, and when he swam around to take his place, they made way for him. He felt he was accepted, and he dived again carefully, proud of himself.

Soon the biggest of the boys poised himself, shot down into the water, and did not come up. The others stood about watching. Jerry, after waiting for the sleek brown head to appear, let out a yell of warning; they looked at him idly and turned their eyes back toward the water.

After a long time, the boy came up on the other side of a big dark rock, letting the air out of his lungs in a sputtering gasp and a shout of triumph. Immediately, the rest of them dived in. One moment, the morning seemed full of chattering boys; the next, the air and the surface of the water were empty. But through the heavy blue, dark shapes could be seen moving and groping.

Jerry dived, shot past the school of underwater swimmers, saw a black wall of rock looming at him, touched it, and bobbed up at once to the surface, where the wall was a low barrier he could see across. There was no one visible; under him, in the water, the dim shapes of the swimmers had disappeared. Then one, and then another of the boys came up on the far side of the barrier of rock, and he understood that they had swum through some gap or hole in it. He plunged down again.

He could see nothing through the stinging salt water but the blank rock. When he came up, the boys were all on the diving rock, preparing to attempt the feat again. And now, in a panic of failure, he yelled up, in English, "Look at me! Look!" and he began splashing and kicking in the water like a foolish dog.

They looked down gravely, frowning. He knew the frown. At moments of failure, when he clowned to claim his mother's attention, it was with just this grave embarrassed inspection that she rewarded him.

Through his hot shame, feeling the pleading grin on his face like a scar that he could never remove, he looked up at the group of big brown boys on the rock and shouted, *"Bonjour! Merci! Au revoir! Monsieur, monsieur!"* [2] while he hooked his fingers round his ears and waggled them.

Water surged into his mouth; he choked, sank, came up. The rock, lately weighted with the boys, seemed to rear up out of the water as their weight was removed. They were flying down past him, now, into the water; the air was full of falling bodies. Then the rock was empty in the hot sunlight. He counted one, two, three. . . .

At fifty, he was terrified. They must all be drowning beneath him, in the watery caves of the rock! At a hundred, he stared around him at the empty hillside, wondering if he should yell for help.

He counted faster, faster, to hurry them up, to bring them to the surface quickly, to drown them quickly — anything rather than the terror of counting on and on into the blue emptiness of the morning. And then, at a hundred and sixty, the water beyond the rock was full of boys blowing like brown whales. They swam back to the shore without a look at him.

He climbed back to the diving rock and sat down, feeling the hot roughness of it under his thighs. The boys were gathering up their bits of clothing and running off along the shore to another promontory.

They were leaving to get away from him. He cried openly, fists

---

[2] *"Bonjour . . . monsieur!"*: French for "Good morning! Thank you! Good-bye! Mister, mister!"

in his eyes. There was no one to see him, and he cried himself out.

It seemed to him that a long time had passed and he swam out to where he could see his mother. Yes, she was still there, a yellow spot under an orange umbrella. He swam back to the big rock, climbed up, and dived into the blue pool among the fanged and angry boulders. Down he went, until he touched the wall of rock again. But the salt was so painful in his eyes that he could not see.

He came to the surface, swam to shore, and went back to the villa to wait for his mother. Soon she walked slowly up the path, swinging her striped bag, the flushed, naked arm dangling beside her. "I want some swimming goggles," he panted, defiant and beseeching.

She gave him a patient, inquisitive look as she said casually, "Well, of course, darling."

But now, now, now! He must have them this minute, and no other time. He nagged and pestered until she went with him to a shop. As soon as she had bought the goggles, he grabbed them from her hand as if she were going to claim them for herself and was off, running down the steep path to the bay.

Jerry swam out to the big barrier rock, adjusted the goggles, and dived. The impact of the water broke the rubber-enclosed vacuum, and the goggles came loose.

He understood that he must swim down to the base of the rock from the surface of the water. He fixed the goggles tight and firm, filled his lungs, and floated, face down on the water.

Now he could see. It was as if he had eyes of a different kind — fish-eyes that showed everything clear and delicate and wavering in the bright water.

Under him, six or seven feet down, was a floor of perfectly clean, shining white sand, rippled firm and hard by the tides. Two grayish shapes steered there, like long, rounded pieces of wood or slate.

They were fish. He saw them nose toward each other, poise motionless, make a dart forward, swerve off, and come around again. It was like a water dance.

A few inches above them, the water sparkled as if sequins were dropping through it. Fish again — myriads of minute fish, the length of his fingernail, were drifting through the water, and in a moment he could feel the innumerable tiny touches of them, against his limbs. It was like swimming in flaked silver.

The great rock the big boys had swum through rose sheer out of the white sand, black, tufted lightly with greenish weed. He could see no gap in it. He swam down to its base.

Again and again he rose, took a big chestful of air, and went down. Again and again he groped over the surface of the rock, feeling it, almost hugging it in the desperate need to find the entrance.

And then, once, while he was clinging to the black wall, his knees came up and he shot his feet out forward and they met no obstacle. He had found the hole.

He gained the surface, clambered about the stones that littered the barrier rock until he found a big one, and, with this in his arms, let himself down over the side of the rock. He dropped, with the weight, to the sandy floor.

Clinging tight to the anchor of the stone, he lay on his side and looked in under the dark shelf at the place where his feet had gone. He could see the hole.

It was an irregular, dark gap, but he could not see deep into it. He let go of his anchor, clung with his hands to the edges of the hole, and tried to push himself in.

He got his head in, found his shoulders jammed, moved them in sidewise, and was inside as far as his waist. He could see nothing ahead.

Something soft and clammy touched his mouth. He saw a dark frond moving against the grayish rock, and panic filled him. He thought of octopuses, or clinging weed.

He pushed himself out backward and caught a glimpse, as he retreated, of a harmless tentacle of seaweed drifting in the mouth of the tunnel. But it was enough.

He reached the sunlight, swam to shore, and lay on the diving rock. He looked down into the blue well of water. He knew he must find his way through that cave, or hole, or tunnel, and out the other side.

First, he thought, he must learn to control his breathing. He let himself down into the water with another big stone in his arms, so that he could lie effortlessly on the bottom.

One, two, three. He counted steadily. He could hear the movement of blood in his head. Fifty-one, fifty-two . . .

His chest was hurting. He let go of the rock and went up into the air. He saw that the sun was low. He rushed to the villa and found his mother at her supper. She said only, "Did you enjoy yourself?" and he said, "Yes."

All night, the boy dreamed of the water-filled cave in the rock and as soon as breakfast was over, he went to the bay.

That night, his nose bled badly. For hours he had been underwater, learning to hold his breath, and now he felt weak and dizzy. His mother said, "I shouldn't overdo things, darling, if I were you."

That day and the next, Jerry exercised his lungs as if everything, the whole of his life, all that he would become, depended upon it. Again his nose bled at night, and his mother insisted on his coming with her the next day.

It was a torment to him to waste a day of his careful self-training, but he stayed with her on that other beach, which now seemed a place for small children, a place where his mother might lie safe in the sun. It was not his beach.

He did not ask for permission, on the following day, to go to his beach. He went, before his mother could consider the complicated rights and wrongs of the matter.

A day's rest, he discovered, had improved his count by ten. The big boys had made the passage while he counted a hundred and sixty. He had been counting fast, in his fright. Probably now, if he tried, he could get through that long tunnel, but he was not going to try yet.

A curious, most unchildlike persistence, a controlled impatience, made him wait. In the meantime, he lay underwater on the white sand, littered now by stones he had brought down from the upper air, and studied the entrance to the tunnel. He knew every jut and corner of it, as far as it was possible to see. It was as if he already felt its sharpness about his shoulders.

He sat by the clock in the villa, when his mother was not near, and checked his time. He was incredulous and then proud to find he could hold his breath without strain for two minutes. The words "two minutes," authorized by the clock, brought the adventure that was so necessary to him close.

In another four days, his mother said casually one morning, they must go home. On the day before they left, he would do it. He would do it if it killed him, he said defiantly to himself. But two days before they were to leave—a day of triumph when he increased his count by fifteen—his nose bled so badly that he turned dizzy and had to lie limply over the big rock like a bit of seaweed, watching the thick red blood flow onto the rock and trickle slowly down to the sea. He was frightened.

Supposing he turned dizzy in the tunnel? Supposing he died there, trapped? Supposing—His head went around in the hot sun, and he almost gave up. He thought he would return to the house and lie down, and next summer, perhaps, when he had another year's growth in him—then he would go through the hole.

But even after he had made the decision, or thought he had, he found himself sitting up on the rock and looking down into the water, and he knew that now, this moment, when his nose had only just stopped bleeding, when his head was still sore and throbbing—this was the moment when he would try. If he did not do it now, he never would.

He was trembling with fear that he would not go, and he was trembling with horror at that long, long tunnel under the rock, under the sea. Even in the open sunlight, the barrier rock seemed very wide and very heavy; tons of rock pressed down on where he would go. If he died there, he would lie until one day—perhaps not before next year—those big boys would swim into it and find it blocked.

He put on his goggles, fitted them tight, tested the vacuum. His hands were shaking. Then he chose the biggest stone he could carry and slipped over the edge of the rock until half of him was in the cool, enclosing water and half in the hot sun.

He looked up once at the empty sky, filled his lungs once, twice, and then sank fast to the bottom with the stone. He let it go and began to count. He took the edges of the hole in his hands and drew himself into it, wriggling his shoulders in sidewise as he remembered he must.

Soon he was clear inside. He was in a small rock-bound hole filled with yellowish-gray water. The water was pushing him up against the roof. The roof was sharp and pained his back. He pulled himself along with his hands—fast, fast—and used his legs as levers.

His head knocked against something; a sharp pain dizzied him. Fifty, fifty-one, fifty-two. . . . He was without light, and the water seemed to press upon him with the weight of rock. Seventy-one, seventy-two. . . . There was no strain on his lungs. He felt like an inflated balloon, his lungs were so light and easy, but his head was pulsing.

He was being continually pressed against the sharp roof, which felt slimy as well as sharp. Again he thought of octopuses and wondered if the tunnel might be filled with weed that could tangle him. He gave himself a panicky, convulsive kick forward, ducked his head, and swam.

His feet and hands moved freely, as if in open water. The hole must have widened out. He thought he must be swimming fast, and he was frightened of banging his head if the tunnel narrowed.

A hundred, a hundred and one. . . . The water paled. Victory filled him. His lungs were beginning to hurt. A few more strokes and he would be out. He was counting wildly; he said a hundred and fifteen, and then, a long time later, a hundred and fifteen again. The water was a clear jewel-green all around him. Then he saw, above his head, a crack running up through the rock. Sunlight was falling through it, showing the clean dark rock of the tunnel, a single mussel shell, and darkness ahead.

He was at the end of what he could do. He looked up at the crack as if it were filled with air and not water, as if he could put his mouth to it to draw in air. A hundred and fifteen, he heard himself say inside his head — but he had said that long ago.

He must go on into the blackness ahead, or he would drown. His head was welling, his lungs cracking. A hundred and fifteen, a hundred and fifteen pounded through his head, and he feebly clutched at rocks in the dark, pulling himself forward, leaving the brief space of sunlit water behind.

He felt he was dying. He was no longer quite conscious. He struggled on in the darkness between lapses into unconsciousness. An immense, swelling pain filled his head, and then the darkness cracked with an explosion of green light. His hands, groping forward, met nothing, and his feet, kicking back, propelled him out into the open sea.

He drifted to the surface, his face turned up to the air. He was gasping like a fish. He felt he would sink now and drown; he could not swim the few feet back to the rock. Then he was clutching it and pulling himself up onto it.

He lay face down, gasping. He could see nothing but a red-veined, clotted dark. His eyes must have burst, he thought; they were full of blood. He tore off his goggles and a gout [3] of blood went into the sea. His nose was bleeding, and the blood had filled the goggles.

He scooped up handfuls of water from the cool, salty sea, to splash on his face, and did not know whether it was blood or salt water he tasted. After a time, his heart quieted, his eyes cleared, and he sat up.

He could see the local boys diving and playing half a mile away. He did not want them. He wanted nothing but to get back home and lie down.

In a short while, Jerry swam to shore and climbed slowly up the path to the villa. He flung himself on his bed and slept, waking at the sound of feet on the path outside. His mother was coming back. He rushed to the bathroom, thinking she must not see his face with bloodstains, or tearstains, on it. He came out of the bathroom and met her as she walked into the villa.

"Have a nice morning?" she asked, laying her hand on his warm brown shoulder a moment.

"Oh, yes, thank you," he said.

"You look a bit pale." And then, sharp and anxious, "How did you bang your head?"

"Oh, just banged it," he told her.

She looked at him closely. He was strained. His eyes were glazed-looking. She was worried. And then she said to herself, "Oh, don't fuss! Nothing can happen. He can swim like a fish."

They sat down to lunch together.

"Mummy," he said. "I can stay under water for two minutes — three minutes, at least." It came bursting out of him.

"Can you, darling?" she said. "Well, I shouldn't overdo it. I don't think you ought to swim any more today."

She was ready for a battle of wills, but he gave in at once. It was no longer of the least importance to go to the bay.

---

[3] *gout:* drop.

Flight

JOHN STEINBECK

About fifteen miles below Monterey, on the wild coast, the Torres family had their farm, a few sloping acres above a cliff that dropped to the brown reefs and to the hissing white waters of the ocean. Behind the farm the stone mountains stood up against the sky. The farm buildings huddled like the clinging aphids [1] on the mountain skirts, crouched low to the ground as though the wind might blow them into the sea. The little shack, the rattling, rotting barn were gray-bitten with sea salt, beaten by the damp wind until they had taken on the color of the granite hills. Two horses, a red cow and a red calf, half a dozen pigs and a flock of lean, multicolored chickens stocked the place. A little corn was raised on the sterile slope, and it grew short and thick under the wind, and all the cobs formed on the landward sides of the stalks.

Mamma Torres, a lean, dry woman with ancient eyes, had ruled the farm for ten years, ever since her husband tripped over a stone in the field one day and fell full length on a rattlesnake. When one is bitten on the chest, there is not much that can be done.

Mamma Torres had three children, two undersized ones of twelve and fourteen, Emilio and Rosy, whom Mamma kept fishing on the rocks below the farm when the sea was kind and when the truant officer was in some distant part of Monterey County. And there was Pepé, the tall smiling son of nineteen, a gentle, affectionate boy but very lazy. Pepé had a tall head, pointed at the top, and from its peak coarse black hair grew down like a thatch all around. Over his smiling little eyes Mama cut a straight bang so he could see. Pepé had sharp Indian cheekbones and an eagle nose, but his mouth was as sweet and shapely as a girl's mouth, and his chin was fragile and chiseled. He was loose and gangling, all legs and feet and wrists, and he was very lazy. Mama thought him fine and brave, but she never told him so. She said, "Some lazy cow must have got into thy fa-

[1] *aphids:* small insects which live on plants.

ther's family, else how could I have a son like thee?" And she said, "When I carried thee, a sneaking lazy coyote came out of the brush and looked at me one day. That must have made thee so."

Pepé smiled sheepishly and stabbed at the ground with his knife to keep the blade sharp and free from rust. It was his inheritance, that knife, his father's knife. The long, heavy blade folded back into the black handle. There was a button on the handle. When Pepé pressed the button, the blade leaped out ready for use. The knife was with Pepé always, for it had been his father's knife.

One sunny morning when the sea below the cliff was glinting and blue and the white surf creamed on the reef, when even the stone mountains looked kindly, Mamma Torres called out the door of the shack, "Pepé, I have a labor for thee."

There was no answer. Mama listened. From behind the barn she heard a burst of laughter. She lifted her full long skirt and walked in the direction of the noise.

Pepé was sitting on the ground with his back against a box. His white teeth glistened. On either side of him stood the two little ones, tense and expectant. Fifteen feet away a redwood post was set in the ground. Pepé's right hand lay limply in his lap, and in the palm the big, black knife rested. The blade was closed back into the handle. Pepé looked smiling at the sky.

Suddenly Emilio cried, "Ya!"

Pepé's wrist flicked like the head of a snake. The blade seemed to fly open in mid-air, and with a thump the point dug into the redwood post, and the black handle quivered. The three burst into excited laughter. Rosy ran to the post and pulled out the knife and brought it back to Pepé. He closed the blade and settled the knife carefully in his listless palm again. He grinned self-consciously at the sky.

"Ya!"

The heavy knife lanced out and sunk into the post again. Mama moved forward like a ship and scattered the play.

"All day you do foolish things with the knife, like a toy baby," she stormed. "Get up on thy huge feet that eat up shoes. Get up!" She took him by one loose shoulder and hoisted at him. Pepé grinned sheepishly and came half-heartedly to his feet. "Look!" Mama cried. "Big lazy, you must catch the horse and put on him thy father's saddle. You must ride to Monterey. The medicine bottle is empty.

There is no salt. Go thou now, Peanut! Catch the horse."

A revolution took place in the relaxed figure of Pepé. "To Monterey, me? Alone? *Sí*, Mama."

She scowled at him. "Do not think, big sheep, that you will buy candy. No, I will give you only enough for the medicine and the salt."

Pepé smiled. "Mama, you will put the hatband on the hat?"

She relented then. "Yes, Pepé. You may wear the hatband."

His voice grew insinuating. "And the green handkerchief, Mama?"

"Yes, if you go quickly and return with no trouble, the silk green handkerchief will go. If you make sure to take off the handkerchief when you eat so no spot may fall on it."

"*Sí*, Mama. I will be careful. I am a man."

"Thou? A man? Thou art a peanut."

He went into the rickety barn and brought out a rope, and he walked agilely enough up the hill to catch the horse.

When he was ready and mounted before the door, mounted on his father's saddle that was so old that the oaken frame showed through torn leather in many places, then Mama brought out the round black hat with the tooled leather band, and she reached up and knotted the green silk handkerchief about his neck. Pepé's blue denim coat was much darker than his jeans, for it had been washed much less often.

Mama handed up the big medicine bottle and the silver coins. "That for the medicine," she said, "and that for the salt. That for a candle to burn for the papa. That for *dulces* [2] for the little ones. Our friend Mrs. Rodriguez will give you dinner and maybe a bed for the night. When you go to the church, say only ten paternosters and only twenty-five Ave Marias.[3] Oh! I know, big coyote. You would sit there flapping your mouth over Aves all day while you looked at the candles and the holy pictures. That is not good devotion to stare at the pretty things."

The black hat, covering the high pointed head and black thatched hair of Pepé, gave him dignity and age. He sat the rangy horse well. Mama thought how handsome he was, dark and lean and tall. "I

---

[2] *dulces* (do͞ol'sāz): candy.
[3] *paternosters, Ave Marias*: "Our Fathers" and "Hail Marys."

would not send thee now alone, thou little one, except for the medicine," she said softly. "It is not good to have no medicine, for who knows when the toothache will come, or the sadness of the stomach? These things are."

"Adiós, Mama," Pepé cried. "I will come back soon. You may send me often alone. I am a man."

"Thou art a foolish chicken."

He straightened his shoulders, flipped the reins against the horse's shoulder, and rode away. He turned once and saw that they still watched him, Emilio and Rosy and Mama. Pepé grinned with pride and gladness and lifted the tough buckskin horse to a trot.

When he had dropped out of sight over a little dip in the road, Mama turned to the little ones, but she spoke to herself. "He is nearly a man now," she said. "It will be a nice thing to have a man in the house again." Her eyes sharpened on the children. "Go to the rocks now. The tide is going out. There will be abalones [4] to be found." She put the iron hooks into their hands and saw them down the steep trail to the reefs. She brought the smooth stone metate [5] to the doorway and sat grinding her corn to flour and looking occasionally at the road over which Pepé had gone. The noonday came and then the afternoon, when the little ones beat the abalones on a rock to make them tender and Mama patted the *tortillas* to make them thin. They ate their dinner as the red sun was plunging down toward the ocean. They sat on the doorsteps and watched a big white moon come over the mountaintops.

Mama said, "He is now at the house of our friend Mrs. Rodriguez. She will give him nice things to eat and maybe a present."

Emilio said, "Some day I, too, will ride to Monterey for medicine. Did Pepé come to be a man today?"

Mama said wisely, "A boy gets to be a man when a man is needed. Remember this thing. I have known boys forty years old because there was no need for a man."

Soon afterward they retired, Mama in her big oak bed on one side of the room, Emilio and Rosy in their boxes full of straw and sheepskins on the other side of the room.

The moon went over the sky and the surf roared on the rocks.

---

[4] *abalones* (ab'ə·lō'nēz): edible shellfish.
[5] *metate* (mā·tä'tä): a stone used for grinding grain.

The roosters crowed the first call. The surf subsided to a whispering surge against the reef. The moon dropped toward the sea. The roosters crowed again.

The moon was near down to the water when Pepé rode on a winded horse to his home flat. His dog bounced out and circled the horse, yelping with pleasure. Pepé slid off the saddle to the ground. The weathered little shack was silver in the moonlight and the square shadow of it was black to the north and east. Against the east the piling mountains were misty with light; their tops melted into the sky.

Pepé walked wearily up the three steps and into the house. It was dark inside. There was a rustle in the corner.

Mama cried out from her bed. "Who comes? Pepé, is it thou?"

"Sí, Mama."

"Did you get the medicine?"

"Sí, Mama."

"Well, go to sleep, then. I thought you would be sleeping at the house of Mrs. Rodriguez." Pepé stood silently in the dark room. "Why do you stand there, Pepé? Did you drink wine?"

"Sí, Mama."

"Well, go to bed then and sleep out the wine."

His voice was tired and patient, but very firm. "Light the candle, Mama. I must go away into the mountains."

"What is this, Pepé? You are crazy." Mama struck a sulfur match and held the little blue burr until the flame spread up the stick. She set light to the candle on the floor beside her bed. "Now, Pepé, what is this you say?" She looked anxiously into his face.

He was changed. The fragile quality seemed to have gone from his chin. His mouth was less full than it had been, the lines of the lips were straighter, but in his eyes the greatest change had taken place. There was no laughter in them any more, nor any bashfulness. They were sharp and bright and purposeful.

He told her in a tired monotone, told her everything just as it had happened. A few people came into the kitchen of Mrs. Rodriguez. There was wine to drink. Pepé drank wine. The little quarrel — the man started toward Pepé and then the knife — it went almost by itself. It flew, it darted before Pepé knew it. As he talked,

Mama's face grew stern, and it seemed to grow more lean. Pepé finished. "I am a man now, Mama. The man said names to me I could not allow."

Mama nodded. "Yes, thou art a man, my poor little Pepé. Thou art a man. I have seen it coming on thee. I have watched you throwing the knife into the post, and I have been afraid." For a moment her face had softened, but now it grew stern again. "Come! We must get you ready. Go. Awaken Emilio and Rosy. Go quickly."

Pepé stepped over to the corner where his brother and sister slept among the sheepskins. He leaned down and shook them gently. "Come, Rosy! Come, Emilio! The Mama says you must arise."

The little ones sat up and rubbed their eyes in the candlelight. Mama was out of bed now, her long black skirt over her nightgown. "Emilio," she cried. "Go up and catch the other horse for Pepé. Quickly, now! Quickly." Emilio put his legs in his overalls and stumbled sleepily out the door.

"You heard no one behind you on the road?" Mama demanded.

"No, Mama. I listened carefully. No one was on the road."

Mama darted like a bird about the room. From a nail on the wall she took a canvas water bag and threw it on the floor. She stripped a blanket from her bed and rolled it into a tight tube and tied the ends with string. From a box beside the stove she lifted a flour sack half full of black, stringy jerky.[6] "Your father's black coat, Pepé. Here, put it on."

Pepé stood in the middle of the floor watching her activity. She reached behind the door and brought out the rifle, a long 38–56, worn shiny the whole length of the barrel. Pepé took it from her and held it in the crook of his elbow. Mama brought a little leather bag and counted the cartridges into his hand. "Only ten left," she warned. "You must not waste them."

Emilio put his head in the door. " '*Qui 'st 'l caballo,*[7] Mama."

"Put on the saddle from the other horse. Tie on the blanket. Here, tie the jerky to the saddle horn."

Still Pepé stood silently watching his mother's frantic activity. His chin looked hard, and his sweet mouth was drawn and thin. His little eyes followed Mama about the room almost suspiciously.

---

[6] *jerky:* strips of dried meat.

[7] *'Qui 'st 'l caballo* (in good Spanish *Aquí está el caballo*): Here is the horse.

Rosy asked softly, "Where goes Pepé?"

Mama's eyes were fierce. "Pepé goes on a journey. Pepé is a man now. He has a man's thing to do."

Pepé straightened his shoulders. His mouth changed until he looked very much like Mama.

At last the preparation was finished. The loaded horse stood outside the door. The water bag dripped a line of moisture down the bay shoulder.

The moonlight was being thinned by the dawn, and the big white moon was near down to the sea. The family stood by the shack. Mama confronted Pepé. "Look, my son! Do not stop until it is dark again. Do not sleep even though you are tired. Take care of the horse in order that he may not stop of weariness. Remember to be careful with the bullets — there are only ten. Do not fill thy stomach with jerky or it will make thee sick. Eat a little jerky and fill thy stomach with grass. When thou comest to the high mountains, if thou seest any of the dark watching men, go not near to them nor try to speak to them. And forget not thy prayers." She put her lean hands on Pepé's shoulders, stood on her toes, and kissed him formally on both cheeks, and Pepé kissed her on both cheeks. Then he went to Emilio and Rosy and kissed both of their cheeks.

Pepé turned back to Mama. He seemed to look for a little softness, a little weakness in her. His eyes were searching, but Mama's face remained fierce. "Go now," she said. "Do not wait to be caught like a chicken."

Pepé pulled himself into the saddle. "I am a man," he said.

It was the first dawn when he rode up the hill toward the little canyon which let a trail into the mountains. Moonlight and daylight fought with each other, and the two warring qualities made it difficult to see. Before Pepé had gone a hundred yards, the outlines of his figure were misty; and long before he entered the canyon, he had become a gray, indefinite shadow.

Mama stood stiffly in front of her doorstep, and on either side of her stood Emilio and Rosy. They cast furtive glances at Mama now and then.

When the gray shape of Pepé melted into the hillside and disappeared, Mama relaxed. She began the high, whining keen of the death wail. "Our beautiful — our brave," she cried. "Our protector, our son is gone." Emilio and Rosy moaned beside her. "Our beautiful — our brave, he is gone." It was the formal wail. It rose to a high, piercing whine and subsided to a moan. Mama raised it three times, and then she turned and went into the house and shut the door.

Emilio and Rosy stood wondering in the dawn. They heard Mama whimpering in the house. They went out to sit on the cliff above the ocean. They touched shoulders. "When did Pepé come to be a man?" Emilio asked.

"Last night," said Rosy. "Last night in Monterey." The ocean clouds turned red with the sun that was behind the mountains.

"We will have no breakfast," said Emilio. "Mama will not want to cook." Rosy did not answer him. "Where is Pepé gone?" he asked.

Rosy looked around at him. She drew her knowledge from the quiet air. "He has gone on a journey. He will never come back."

"Is he dead? Do you think he is dead?"

Rosy looked back at the ocean again. A little steamer, drawing a line of smoke, sat on the edge of the horizon. "He is not dead," Rosy explained. "Not yet."

Pepé rested the big rifle across the saddle in front of him. He let the horse walk up the hill and he didn't look back. The stony slope took on a coat of short brush so that Pepé found the entrance to a trail and entered it.

When he came to the canyon opening, he swung once in his saddle and looked back, but the houses were swallowed in the misty light. Pepé jerked forward again. The high shoulder of the canyon closed in on him. His horse stretched out its neck and sighed and settled to the trail.

It was a well-worn path, dark, soft leaf-mold earth strewn with broken pieces of sandstone. The trail rounded the shoulder of the canyon and dropped steeply into the bed of the stream. In the shallows the water ran smoothly, glinting in the first morning sun. Small round stones on the bottom were as brown as rust with sun moss. In the sand along the edges of the stream the tall, rich wild mint grew, while in the water itself the cress, old and tough, had gone to heavy seed.

The path went into the stream and emerged on the other side. The horse sloshed into the water and stopped. Pepé dropped his bridle and let the beast drink of the running water.

Soon the canyon sides became steep and the first giant sentinel redwoods guarded the trail, great round red trunks bearing foliage as green and lacy as ferns. Once Pepé was among the trees, the sun was lost. A perfumed and purple light lay in the pale green of the underbrush. Gooseberry bushes and blackberries and tall ferns lined the stream, and overhead the branches of the redwoods met and cut off the sky.

Pepé drank from the water bag, and he reached into the flour sack and brought out a black string of jerky. His white teeth gnawed at the string until the tough meat parted. He chewed slowly and drank occasionally from the water bag. His little eyes were slumberous and tired, but the muscles of his face were hard-set. The earth of the trail was black now. It gave up a hollow sound under the walking hoofbeats.

The stream fell more sharply. Little waterfalls splashed on the stones. Five-fingered ferns hung over the water and dripped spray from their finger tips. Pepé rode half over his saddle, dangling one leg loosely. He picked a bay leaf from a tree beside the way and put it into his mouth for a moment to flavor the dry jerky. He held the gun loosely across the pommel.[8]

Suddenly he squared in his saddle, swung the horse from the trail, and kicked it hurriedly up behind a big redwood tree. He pulled up the reins tight against the bit to keep the horse from whinnying. His face was intent and his nostrils quivered a little.

A hollow pounding came down the trail, and a horseman rode by, a fat man with red cheeks and a white stubble beard. His horse put down his head and blubbered at the trail when it came to the place where Pepé had turned off. "Hold up!" said the man, and he pulled up his horse's head.

When the last sound of the hoofs died away, Pepé came back into the trail again. He did not relax in the saddle any more. He lifted the big rifle and swung the lever to throw a shell into the chamber, and then he let down the hammer to half cock.

The trail grew very steep. Now the redwood trees were smaller

---

[8] *pommel:* a knob at the front of a saddle.

and their tops were dead, bitten dead where the wind reached them. The horse plodded on; the sun went slowly overhead and started down toward the afternoon.

Where the stream came out of a side canyon, the trail left it. Pepé dismounted and watered his horse and filled up his water bag. As soon as the trail had parted from the stream, the trees were gone and only the thick brittle sage and manzanita and chaparral [9] edged the trail. And the soft black earth was gone, too, leaving only the light tan broken rock for the trail bed. Lizards scampered away into the brush as the horse rattled over the little stones.

Pepé turned in his saddle and looked back. He was in the open now: he could be seen from a distance. As he ascended the trail, the country grew more rough and terrible and dry. The way wound about the bases of great square rocks. Little gray rabbits skittered in the brush. A bird made a monotonous high creaking. Eastward the bare rock mountaintops were pale and powder-dry under the dropping sun. The horse plodded up and up the trail toward a little V in the ridge which was the pass.

Pepé looked suspiciously back every minute or so, and his eyes sought the tops of the ridges ahead. Once, on a white barren spur, he saw a black figure for a moment; but he looked quickly away, for it was one of the dark watchers. No one knew who the watchers were, nor where they lived, but it was better to ignore them and never to show interest in them. They did not bother one who stayed on the trail and minded his own business.

The air was parched and full of light dust blown by the breeze from the eroding mountains. Pepé drank sparingly from his bag and corked it tightly and hung it on the horn again. The trail moved up the dry shale hillside, avoiding rocks, dropping under clefts, climbing in and out of old water scars. When he arrived at the little pass, he stopped and looked back for a long time. No dark watchers were to be seen now. The trail behind was empty. Only the high tops of the redwoods indicated where the stream flowed.

Pepé rode on through the pass. His little eyes were nearly closed with weariness, but his face was stern, relentless, and manly. The high mountain wind coasted sighing through the pass and whistled on the edges of the big blocks of broken granite. In the air, a red-

---

[9] *manzanita and chaparral:* evergreen shrubs.

tailed hawk sailed over close to the ridge and screamed angrily. Pepé went slowly through the broken, jagged pass and looked down on the other side.

The trail dropped quickly, staggering among broken rock. At the bottom of the slope there was a dark crease, thick with brush, and on the other side of the crease a little flat, in which a grove of oak trees grew. A scar of green grass cut across the flat. And behind the flat another mountain rose, desolate with dead rocks and starving little black bushes. Pepé drank from the bag again, for the air was so dry that it encrusted his nostrils and burned his lips. He put the horse down the trail. The hoofs slipped and struggled on the steep way, starting little stones that rolled off into the brush. The sun was gone behind the westward mountain now, but still it glowed brilliantly on the oaks and on the grassy flat. The rocks and the hillsides still sent up waves of the heat they had gathered from the day's sun.

Pepé looked up to the top of the next dry, withered ridge. He saw a dark form against the sky, a man's figure standing on top of a rock, and he glanced away quickly not to appear curious. When a moment later he looked up again, the figure was gone.

Downward the trail was quickly covered. Sometimes the horse floundered for footing, sometimes set his feet and slid a little way. They came at last to the bottom, where the dark chaparral was higher than Pepé's head. He held up his rifle on one side and his arm on the other to shield his face from the sharp, brittle fingers of the brush.

Up and out of the crease he rode, and up a little cliff. The grassy flat was before him, and the round comfortable oaks. For a moment he studied the trail down which he had come, but there was no movement and no sound from it. Finally he rode out over the flat, to the green streak, and at the upper end of the damp he found a little spring welling out of the earth and dropping into a dug basin before it seeped out over the flat.

Pepé filled his bag first, and then he let the thirsty horse drink out of the pool. He led the horse to the clump of oaks, and in the middle of the grove, fairly protected from sight on all sides, he took off the saddle and the bridle and laid them on the ground. The horse stretched his jaws sideways and yawned. Pepé knotted the lead rope about the horse's neck and tied him to a sapling among the oaks, where he could graze in a fairly large circle.

When the horse was gnawing hungrily at the dry grass, Pepé went to the saddle and took a black string of jerky from the sack and strolled to an oak tree on the edge of the grove, from under which he could watch the trail. He sat down in the crisp dry oak leaves and automatically felt for his big black knife to cut the jerky, but he had no knife. He leaned back on his elbow and gnawed at the tough strong meat. His face was blank, but it was a man's face.

The bright evening light washed the eastern ridge, but the valley was darkening. Doves flew down from the hills to the spring, and the quail came running out of the brush and joined them, calling clearly to one another.

Out of the corner of his eye Pepé saw a shadow grow out of the bushy crease. He turned his head slowly. A big, spotted wildcat was creeping toward the spring, belly to the ground, moving like thought.

Pepé cocked his rifle and edged the muzzle slowly around. Then he looked apprehensively up the trail and dropped the hammer again. From the ground beside him he picked an oak twig and threw it toward the spring. The quail flew up with a roar and the doves whistled away. The big cat stood up; for a long moment he looked at Pepé with cold yellow eyes, and then fearlessly walked back into the gulch.

The dusk gathered quickly in the deep valley. Pepé muttered his prayers, put his head down on his arm and went instantly to sleep.

The moon came up and filled the valley with cold blue light, and the wind swept rustling down from the peaks. The owls worked up and down the slopes looking for rabbits. Down in the brush of the gulch a coyote gabbled. The oak trees whispered softly in the night breeze.

Pepé started up, listening. His horse had whinnied. The moon was just slipping behind the western ridge, leaving the valley in darkness behind it. Pepé sat tensely gripping his rifle. From far up the trail he heard an answering whinny and the crash of shod hoofs on the broken rock. He jumped to his feet, ran to his horse, and led it under the trees. He threw on the saddle and cinched it tight for the steep trail, caught the unwilling head and forced the bit into the mouth. He felt the saddle to make sure the water bag and the sack of jerky were there. Then he mounted and turned up the hill.

It was velvet-dark. The horse found the entrance to the trail where it left the flat, and started up, stumbling and slipping on the rocks. Pepé's hand rose up to his head. His hat was gone. He had left it under the oak tree.

The horse had struggled far up the trail when the first change of dawn came into the air, a steel grayness as light mixed thoroughly with dark. Gradually the sharp snaggled edge of the ridge stood out above them, rotten granite tortured and eaten by the winds of time. Pepé had dropped his reins on the horn, leaving direction to the horse. The brush grabbed at his legs in the dark until one knee of his jeans was ripped.

Gradually the light flowed down over the ridge. The starved brush and rocks stood out in the half-light, strange and lonely in high perspective. Then there came warmth into the light. Pepé drew up and looked back, but he could see nothing in the darker valley below. The sky turned blue over the coming sun. In the waste of the mountainside, the poor dry brush grew only three feet high. Here and there, big outcroppings of unrotted granite stood up like moldering houses. Pepé relaxed a little. He drank from his water bag and bit off a piece of jerky. A single eagle flew over, high in the light.

Without warning Pepé's horse screamed and fell on its side. He was almost down before the rifle crash echoed up from the valley. From a hole behind the struggling shoulder, a stream of bright crimson blood pumped and stopped and pumped and stopped. The hoofs threshed on the ground. Pepé lay half stunned beside the horse. He looked slowly down the hill. A piece of sage clipped off beside his head and another crash echoed up from side to side of the canyon. Pepé flung himself frantically behind a bush.

He crawled up the hill on his knees and one hand. His right hand held the rifle up off the ground and pushed it ahead of him. He moved with the instinctive care of an animal. Rapidly he wormed his way toward one of the big outcroppings of granite on the hill above him. Where the brush was high, he doubled up and ran; but where the cover was slight, he wriggled forward on his stomach, pushing the rifle ahead of him. In the last little distance there was no cover at all. Pepé poised and then he darted across the space and flashed around the corner of the rock.

He leaned panting against the stone. When his breath came

easier, he moved along behind the big rock until he came to a narrow split that offered a thin section of vision down the hill. Pepé lay on his stomach and pushed the rifle barrel through the slit and waited.

The sun reddened the western ridges now. Already the buzzards were settling down toward the place where the horse lay. A small brown bird scratched in the dead sage leaves directly in front of the rifle muzzle. The coasting eagle flew back toward the rising sun.

Pepé saw a little movement in the brush far below. His grip tightened on the gun. A little brown doe stepped daintily out on the trail and crossed it and disappeared into the brush again. For a long time Pepé waited. Far below he could see the little flat and the oak trees and the slash of green. Suddenly his eyes flashed back at the trail again. A quarter of a mile down there had been a quick movement in the chaparral. The rifle swung over. The front sight nestled in the V of the rear sight. Pepé studied for a moment and then raised the rear sight a notch. The little movement in the brush came again. The sight settled on it. Pepé squeezed the trigger. The explosion crashed down the mountain and up the other side and came rattling back. The whole side of the slope grew still. No more movement. And then a white streak cut into the granite of the slit and a bullet whined away and a crash sounded up from below. Pepé felt a sharp pain in his right hand. A sliver of granite was sticking out from between his first and second knuckles and the point protruded from his palm. Carefully he pulled out the sliver of stone. The wound bled evenly and gently. No vein or artery was cut.

Pepé looked into a little dusty cave in the rock and gathered a handful of spider web, and he pressed the mass into the cut, plastering the soft web into the blood. The flow stopped almost at once.

The rifle was on the ground. Pepé picked it up, levered a new shell into the chamber. And then he slid into the brush on his stomach. Far to the right he crawled and then up the hill, moving slowly and carefully, crawling to cover and resting and then crawling again.

In the mountains the sun is high in its arc before it penetrates the gorges. The hot face looked over the hill and brought instant heat with it. The white light beat on the rocks and reflected from them and rose up quivering from the earth again, and the rocks and bushes seemed to quiver behind the air.

Pepé crawled in the general direction of the ridge peak, zigzagging for cover. The deep cut between his knuckles began to throb. He crawled close to a rattlesnake before he saw it, and when it raised its dry head and made a soft beginning whir, he backed up and took another way. The quick gray lizards flashed in front of him, raising a tiny line of dust. He found another mass of spider web and pressed it against his throbbing hand.

Pepé was pushing the rifle with his left hand now. Little drops of sweat ran to the ends of his coarse black hair and rolled down his cheeks. His lips and tongue were growing thick and heavy. His lips writhed to draw saliva into his mouth. His little dark eyes were uneasy and suspicious. Once when a gray lizard paused in front of him on the parched ground and turned its head sideways, he crushed it flat with a stone.

When the sun slid past noon, he had not gone a mile. He crawled exhaustedly a last hundred yards to a patch of high sharp manzanita, crawled desperately, and when the patch was reached he wriggled in among the tough gnarly trunks and dropped his head on his left arm. There was little shade in the meager brush, but there was cover and safety. Pepé went to sleep as he lay and the sun beat on his back. A few little birds hopped close to him and peered and hopped away. Pepé squirmed in his sleep, and he raised and dropped his wounded hand again and again.

The sun went down behind the peaks, and the cool evening came, and then the dark. A coyote yelled from the hillside. Pepé started awake and looked about with misty eyes. His hand was swollen and heavy; a little thread of pain ran up the inside of his arm and settled in a pocket in his armpit. He peered about and then stood up, for the mountains were black and the moon had not yet risen. Pepé stood up in the dark. The coat of his father pressed on his arm. His tongue was swollen until it nearly filled his mouth. He wriggled out of the coat and dropped it in the brush, and then he struggled up the hill, falling over rocks and tearing his way through the brush. The rifle knocked against stones as he went. Little dry avalanches of gravel and shattered stone went whispering down the hill behind him.

After a while the old moon came up and showed the jagged

ridgetop ahead of him. By moonlight Pepé traveled more easily. He bent forward so that his throbbing arm hung away from his body. The journey uphill was made in dashes and rests, a frantic rush up a few yards and then a rest. The wind coasted down the slope, rattling the dry stems of the bushes.

The moon was at meridian [10] when Pepé came at last to the sharp backbone of the ridgetop. On the last hundred yards of the rise no soil had clung under the wearing winds. The way was on solid rock. He clambered to the top and looked down on the other side. There was a draw like the last below him, misty with moonlight, brushed with dry struggling sage and chaparral. On the other side the hill rose up sharply and at the top the jagged rotten teeth of the mountain showed against the sky. At the bottom of the cut the brush was thick and dark.

Pepé stumbled down the hill. His throat was almost closed with thirst. At first he tried to run, but immediately he fell and rolled. After that he went more carefully. The moon was just disappearing behind the mountains when he came to the bottom. He crawled into the heavy brush, feeling with his fingers for water. There was no water in the bed of the stream, only damp earth. Pepé laid his gun down and scooped up a handful of mud and put it in his mouth, and then he spluttered and scraped the earth from his tongue with his finger, for the mud drew at his mouth like a poultice. He dug a hole in the stream bed with his fingers, dug a little basin to catch water; but before it was very deep, his head fell forward on the damp ground and he slept.

The dawn came and the heat of the day fell on the earth, and still Pepé slept. Late in the afternoon his head jerked up. He looked slowly around. His eyes were slits of weariness. Twenty feet away in the heavy brush a big tawny mountain lion stood looking at him. Its long thick tail waved gracefully; its ears were erect with interest, not laid back dangerously. The lion squatted down on its stomach and watched him.

Pepé looked at the hole he had dug in the earth. A half inch of muddy water had collected in the bottom. He tore the sleeve from his hurt arm, with his teeth ripped out a little square, soaked it in the water and put it in his mouth. Over and over he filled the cloth and sucked it.

---

[10] *meridian*: the highest point.

Still the lion sat and watched him. The evening came down, but there was no movement on the hills. No birds visited the dry bottom of the cut. Pepé looked occasionally at the lion. The eyes of the yellow beast drooped as though he were about to sleep. He yawned and his long thin red tongue curled out. Suddenly his head jerked around and his nostrils quivered. His big tail lashed. He stood up and slunk like a tawny shadow into the thick brush.

A moment later Pepé heard the sound, the faint far crash of horses' hoofs on gravel. And he heard something else, a high whining yelp of a dog.

Pepé took his rifle in his left hand, and he glided into the brush almost as quietly as the lion had. In the darkening evening he crouched up the hill toward the next ridge. Only when the dark came did he stand up. His energy was short. Once it was dark, he fell over the rocks and slipped to his knees on the steep slope, but he moved on and on up the hill, climbing and scrambling over the broken hillside.

When he was far up toward the top, he lay down and slept for a little while. The withered moon, shining on his face, awakened him. He stood up and moved up the hill. Fifty yards away he stopped and turned back, for he had forgotten his rifle. He walked heavily down and poked about in the brush, but he could not find his gun. At last he lay down to rest. The pocket of pain in his armpit had grown more sharp. His arm seemed to swell out and fall with every heartbeat. There was no position lying down where the heavy arm did not press against his armpit.

With the effort of a hurt beast, Pepé got up and moved again toward the top of the ridge. He held his swollen arm away from his body with his left hand. Up the steep hill he dragged himself, a few steps and a rest, and a few more steps. At last he was nearing the top. The moon showed the uneven sharp back of it against the sky.

Pepé's brain spun in a big spiral up and away from him. He slumped to the ground and lay still. The rock ridgetop was only a hundred feet above him.

The moon moved over the sky. Pepé half turned on his back. His tongue tried to make words, but only a thick hissing came from between his lips.

When the dawn came, Pepé pulled himself up. His eyes were sane again. He drew his great puffed arm in front of him and looked at the angry wound. The black line ran up from his wrist to his armpit. Automatically he reached in his pocket for the big black knife, but it was not there. His eyes searched the ground. He picked up a sharp blade of stone and scraped at the wound, sawed at the proud flesh and then squeezed the green juice out in big drops. Instantly he threw back his head and whined like a dog. His whole right side shuddered at the pain, but the pain cleared his head.

In the gray light he struggled up the last slope to the ridge and crawled over and lay down behind a line of rocks. Below him lay a deep canyon exactly like the last, waterless and desolate. There was no flat, no oak trees, not even heavy brush in the bottom of it. And on the other side a sharp ridge stood up, thinly brushed with starving sage, littered with broken granite. Strewn over the hill there were giant outcroppings, and on the top the granite teeth stood out against the sky.

The new day was light now. The flame of the sun came over the ridge and fell on Pepé where he lay on the ground. His coarse black hair was littered with twigs and bits of spider web. His eyes had retreated back into his head. Between his lips the tip of his black tongue showed.

He sat up and dragged his great arm into his lap and nursed it, rocking his body and moaning in his throat. He threw back his head and looked up into the pale sky. A big black bird circled nearly out of sight, and far to the left another was sailing near.

He lifted his head to listen, for a familiar sound had come to him from the valley he had climbed out of; it was the crying yelp of hounds, excited and feverish, on a trail.

Pepé bowed his head quickly. He tried to speak rapid words, but only a thick hiss came from his lips. He drew a shaky cross on his breast with his left hand. It was a long struggle to get to his feet. He crawled slowly and mechanically to the top of a big rock on the ridge peak. Once there, he arose slowly, swaying to his feet, and stood erect. Far below he could see the dark brush where he had slept. He braced his feet and stood there, black against the morning sky.

There came a ripping sound at his feet. A piece of stone flew up and a bullet droned off into the next gorge. The hollow crash echoed up from below. Pepé looked down for a moment and then pulled himself straight again.

His body jarred back. His left hand fluttered helplessly toward his breast. The second crash sounded from below. Pepé swung forward and toppled from the rock. His body struck and rolled over and over, starting a little avalanche. And when at last he stopped against a bush, the avalanche slid slowly down and covered up his head.

In the following story social conflict is reflected in the psychological problems of one American family.

A Visit to Grandmother

WILLIAM MELVIN KELLEY

Chig knew something was wrong the instant his father kissed her. He had always known his father to be the warmest of men, a man so kind that when people ventured timidly into his office, it took only a few words from him to make them relax, and even laugh. Doctor Charles Dunford cared about people.

But when he had bent to kiss the old lady's black face, something new and almost ugly had come into his eyes: fear, uncertainty, sadness, and perhaps even hatred.

Ten days before in New York, Chig's father had decided suddenly he wanted to go to Nashville to attend his college class reunion, twenty years out. Both Chig's brother and sister, Peter and Connie, were packing for camp and besides were too young for such an affair. But Chig was seventeen, had nothing to do that summer, and his father asked if he would like to go along. His father had given him additional reasons: "All my running buddies got their diplomas and were snapped up by them crafty young gals and had kids within a year — now all those kids, some of them gals, are your age."

The reunion had lasted a week. As they packed for home, his father, in a far too offhand way, had suggested they visit Chig's grandmother. "We this close. We might as well drop in on her and my brothers."

So, instead of going north, they had gone farther south, had just entered her house. And Chig had a suspicion now that the reunion had been only an excuse to drive south, that his father had been heading to this house all the time.

His father had never talked much about his family, with the exception of his brother, GL, who seemed part con man, part practical joker and part Don Juan; he had spoken of GL with the kind of indulgence he would have shown a cute, but ill-behaved and potentially dangerous five-year-old.

Chig's father had left home when he was fifteen. When asked why, he would answer: "I wanted to go to school. They didn't have a Negro high school at home, so I went up to Knoxville and lived with a cousin and went to school."

They had been met at the door by Aunt Rose, GL's wife, and ushered into the living room. The old lady had looked up from her seat by the window. Aunt Rose stood between the visitors.

The old lady eyed his father. "Rose, who that? Rose?" She squinted. She looked like a doll, made of black straw, the wrinkles in her face running in one direction like the head of a broom. Her hair was white and coarse and grew out straight from her head. Her eyes were brown — the whites, too, seemed light brown — and were hidden behind thick glasses, which remained somehow on a tiny nose. "That Hiram?" That was another of his father's brothers. "No, it ain't Hiram; too big for Hiram." She turned then to Chig. "Now that man, he look like Eleanor, Charles's wife, but Charles wouldn't never send my grandson to see me. I never even hear from Charles." She stopped again.

"It Charles, Mama. That who it is." Aunt Rose, between them, led them closer. "It Charles come all the way from New York to see you, and brung little Charles with him."

The old lady stared up at them. "Charles? Rose, that really Charles?" She turned away, and reached for a handkerchief in the pocket of her clean, ironed, flowered housecoat, and wiped her eyes. "God have mercy. Charles." She spread her arms up to him, and he bent down and kissed her cheek. That was when Chig saw his face, grimacing. She hugged him; Chig watched the muscles in her arms as they tightened around his father's neck. She half rose out of her chair. "How are you, son?"

Chig could not hear his father's answer.

She let him go, and fell back into her chair, grabbing the arms. Her hands were as dark as the wood and seemed to become part of it. "Now, who that standing there? Who that man?"

"That's one of your grandsons, Mama." His father's voice cracked. "Charles Dunford, junior. You saw him once, when he was a baby, in Chicago. He's grown now."

"I can see that, boy!" She looked at Chig squarely. "Come here, son, and kiss me once." He did. "What they call you? Charles too?"

"No, ma'am, they call me Chig."

She smiled. She had all her teeth, but they were too perfect to be her own. "That's good. Can't have two boys answering to Charles in the same house. Won't nobody at all come. So you that little boy. You don't remember me, do you? I used to take you to church in Chicago, and you'd get up and hop in time to the music. You studying to be a preacher?"

"No, ma'am. I don't think so. I might be a lawyer."

"You'll be an honest one, won't you?"

"I'll try."

"Trying ain't enough! You be honest, you hear? Promise me. You be honest like your daddy."

"All right. I promise."

"Good. Rose, where's GL at? Where's that thief? He gone again?"

"I don't know, Mama." Aunt Rose looked embarrassed. "He say he was going by his liquor store. He'll be back."

"Well, then where's Hiram? You call up those boys, and get them over here — now! You got enough to eat? Let me go see." She started to get up. Chig reached out his hand. She shook him off. "What they tell you about me, Chig? They tell you I'm all laid up? Don't believe it. They don't know nothing about old ladies. When I want help, I'll let you know. Only time I'll need help getting any-wheres is when I dies and they lift me into the ground."

She was standing now, her back and shoulders straight. She came only to Chig's chest. She squinted up at him. "You eat much? Your daddy ate like two men."

"Yes, ma'am."

"That's good. That means you ain't nervous. Your mama, she ain't nervous. I remember that. In Chicago, she'd sit down by a window all afternoon and never say nothing, just knit." She smiled. "Let me see what we got to eat."

"I'll do that, Mama." Aunt Rose spoke softly. "You haven't seen

Charles in a long time. You sit and talk."

The old lady squinted at her. "You can do the cooking if you promise it ain't because you think I can't."

Aunt Rose chuckled. "I know you can do it, Mama."

"All right. I'll just sit and talk a spell." She sat again and arranged her skirt around her short legs.

Chig did most of the talking, told all about himself before she asked. His father only spoke when he was spoken to, and then, only one word at a time, as if by coming back home, he had become a small boy again, sitting in the parlor while his mother spoke with her guests.

When Uncle Hiram and Mae, his wife, came they sat down to eat. Chig did not have to ask about Uncle GL's absence; Aunt Rose volunteered an explanation: "Can't never tell where the man is at. One Thursday morning he left here and next thing we knew, he was calling from Chicago, saying he went up to see Joe Louis fight. He'll be here though; he ain't as young and foot-loose as he used to be." Chig's father had mentioned driving down that GL was about five years older than he was, nearly fifty.

Uncle Hiram was somewhat smaller than Chig's father; his short-cropped kinky hair was half gray, half black. One spot, just off his forehead, was totally white. Later, Chig found out it had been that way since he was twenty. Mae (Chig could not bring himself to call her Aunt) was a good deal younger than Hiram, pretty enough so that Chig would have looked at her twice on the street. She was a honey-colored woman, with long eyelashes. She was wearing a white sheath.

At dinner, Chig and his father sat on one side, opposite Uncle Hiram and Mae; his grandmother and Aunt Rose sat at the ends. The food was good; there was a lot and Chig ate a lot. All through the meal, they talked about the family as it had been thirty years before, and particularly about the young GL. Mae and Chig asked questions; the old lady answered; Aunt Rose directed the discussion, steering the old lady onto the best stories; Chig's father laughed from time to time; Uncle Hiram ate.

"Why don't you tell them about the horse, Mama?" Aunt Rose, over Chig's weak protest, was spooning mashed potatoes onto his plate. "There now, Chig."

"I'm trying to think." The old lady was holding her fork half-way to her mouth, looking at them over her glasses. "Oh, you talking about that crazy horse GL brung home that time."

"That's right, Mama." Aunt Rose nodded and slid another slice of white meat on Chig's plate.

Mae started to giggle. "Oh, I've heard this. This is funny, Chig."

The old lady put down her fork and began: Well, GL went out of the house one day with an old, no-good chair I wanted him to take over to the church for a bazaar, and he met up with this man who'd just brung in some horses from out West. Now, I reckon you can expect one swindler to be in every town, but you don't rightly think there'll be two, and God forbid they should ever meet — but they did, GL and his chair, this man and his horses. Well, I wished I'd-a been there; there must-a been some mighty high-powered talking going on. That man with his horses, he told GL them horses was half-Arab, half-Indian, and GL told that man the chair was an antique he'd stole from some rich white folks. So they swapped. Well, I was a-looking out the window and seen GL dragging this animal to the house. It looked pretty gentle and its eyes was most closed and its feet was shuffling.

"GL, where'd you get that thing?" I says.

"I swapped him for that old chair, Mama," he says. "And made myself a bargain. This is even better than Papa's horse."

Well, I'm a-looking at this horse and noticing how he be looking more and more wide awake every minute, sort of warming up like a teakettle until, I swears to you, that horse is blowing steam out its nose.

"Come on, Mama," GL says, "come on and I'll take you for a ride." Now George, my husband, God rest his tired soul, he'd brung home this white folks' buggy which had a busted wheel and fixed it and was to take it back that day and GL says: "Come on, Mama, we'll use this fine buggy and take us a ride."

"GL," I says, "no, we ain't. Them white folks'll burn us alive if we use their buggy. You just take that horse right on back." You see, I was sure that boy'd come by that animal ungainly.

"Mama, I can't take him back," GL says.

"Why not?" I says.

"Because I don't rightly know where that man is at," GL says.

"Oh," I says. "Well, then I reckon we stuck with it." And I turned around to go back into the house because it was getting late, near dinnertime, and I was cooking for ten.

"Mama," GL says to my back. "Mama, ain't you coming for a ride with me?"

"Go on, boy. You ain't getting me inside kicking range of that animal." I was eying that beast and it was boiling hotter all the time. I reckon maybe that man had drugged it. "That horse is wild, GL," I says.

"No, he ain't. He ain't. That man say he is buggy and saddle broke and as sweet as the inside of a apple."

My oldest girl, Essie, had-a come out on the porch and she says: "Go on, Mama. I'll cook. You ain't been out the house in weeks."

"Sure, come on, Mama," GL says. "There ain't nothing to be fidgety about. This horse is gentle as a rose petal." And just then that animal snorts so hard it sets up a little dust storm around its feet.

"Yes, Mama," Essie says, "you can see he gentle." Well, I looked at Essie and then at that horse because I didn't think we could be looking at the same animal. I should-a figured how Essie's eyes ain't never been so good.

"Come on, Mama," GL says.

"All right," I says. So I stood on the porch and watched GL hitching that horse up to the white folks' buggy. For a while there, the animal was pretty quiet, pawing a little, but not much. And I was feeling a little better about riding with GL behind that crazy-looking horse. I could see how GL was happy I was going with him. He was scurrying around that animal buckling buckles and strapping straps, all the time smiling, and that made me feel good.

Then he was finished, and I must say, that horse looked mighty fine hitched to that buggy and I knew anybody what climbed up there would look pretty good too. GL came around and stood at the bottom of the steps, and took off his hat and bowed and said: "Madam," and reached out his hand to me and I was feeling real elegant like a fine lady. He helped me up to the seat and then got up beside me and we moved out down our alley. And I remember how colored folks came out on their porches and shook their heads, saying: "Lord now, will you look at Eva Dunford, the fine lady!

Don't she look good sitting up there!" And I pretended not to hear and sat up straight and proud.

We rode on through the center of town, up Market Street, and all the way out where Hiram is living now, which in them days was all woods, there not being even a farm in sight and that's when that horse must-a first realized he weren't at all broke or tame or maybe thought he was back out West again, and started to gallop.

"GL," I says, "now you ain't joking with your mama, is you? Because if you is, I'll strap you purple if I live through this."

Well, GL was pulling on the reins with all his meager strength, and yelling, "Whoa, you. Say now, whoa!" He turned to me just long enough to say, "I ain't fooling with you, Mama. Honest!"

I reckon that animal weren't too satisfied with the road, because it made a sharp right turn just then, down into a gulley and struck out across a hilly meadow. "Mama," GL yells. "Mama, do something!"

I didn't know what to do, but I figured I had to do something, so I stood up, hopped down onto the horse's back, and pulled it to a stop. Don't ask me how I did that; I reckon it was that I was a mother and my baby asked me to do something, is all.

"Well, we walked that animal all the way home; sometimes I had to club it over the nose with my fist to make it come, but we made it, GL and me. You remember how tired we was, Charles?"

"I wasn't here at the time." Chig turned to his father and found his face completely blank, without even a trace of a smile or a laugh.

"Well, of course you was, son. That happened in . . . in . . . it was a hot summer that year and — "

"I left here in June of that year. You wrote me about it."

The old lady stared past Chig at him. They all turned to him; Uncle Hiram looked up from his plate.

"Then you don't remember how we all laughed?"

"No, I don't, Mama. And I probably wouldn't have laughed. I don't think it was funny." They were staring into each other's eyes.

"Why not, Charles?"

"Because in the first place, the horse was gained by fraud. And in the second place, both of you might have been seriously injured or even killed." He broke off their stare and spoke to himself more than to any of them: "And if I'd done it, you would've beaten me good for it."

"Pardon?" The old lady had not heard him; only Chig had heard.

Chig's father sat up straight as if preparing to debate. "I said that if I had done it, if I had done just exactly what GL did, you would have beaten me good for it, Mama." He was looking at her again.

"Why you say that, son?" She was leaning toward him.

"Don't you know? Tell the truth. It can't hurt me now." His voice cracked, but only once. "If GL and I did something wrong, you'd beat me first and then be too tired to beat him. At dinner, he'd always get seconds and I wouldn't. You'd do things with him, like ride in that buggy, but if I wanted you to do something with me, you were always too busy." He paused and considered whether to say what he finally did say: "I cried when I left here. Nobody loved me, Mama. I cried all the way up to Knoxville. That was the last time I ever cried in my life."

"Oh, Charles." She started to get up, to come around the table to him.

He stopped her. "It's too late."

"But you don't understand."

"What don't I understand? I understood then; I understand now."

Tears now traveled down the lines in her face, but when she spoke, her voice was clear. "I thought you knew. I had ten children. I had to give all of them what they needed most." She nodded. "I paid more mind to GL. I had to. GL could-a ended up swinging if I hadn't. But you was smarter. You was more growed up than GL when you was five and he was ten, and I tried to show you that by letting you do what you wanted to do."

"That's not true, Mama. You know it. GL was light-skinned and had good hair and looked almost white and you loved him for that."

"Charles, no. No, son. I didn't love any one of you more than any other."

"That can't be true." His father was standing now, his fist clenched tight. "Admit it, Mama . . . please!" Chig looked at him, shocked; the man was actually crying.

"It may not-a been right what I done, but I ain't no liar." Chig knew she did not really understand what had happened, what he wanted of her. "I'm not lying to you, Charles."

Chig's father had gone pale. He spoke very softly. "You're about thirty years too late, Mama." He bolted from the table. Silverware and dishes rang and jumped. Chig heard him hurrying up to their room.

They sat in silence for a while and then heard a key in the front door. A man with a new, lacquered straw hat came in. He was wearing brown and white two-tone shoes with very pointed toes and a white summer suit. "Say now! Man! I heard my brother was in town. Where he at? Where that rascal?"

He stood in the doorway, smiling broadly, an engaging, open, friendly smile, the innocent smile of a five-year-old.

FIVE POEMS OF CONFLICT

William Blake was a painter, engraver, and poet who illustrated his own editions of his poems. Much of his poetry deals with the conflicts between good and evil, innocence and guilt.

A Poison Tree

WILLIAM BLAKE

[handwritten notes: man vs. man / friend vs. I / I vs. enemy / man stole apple and died, I is glad he's dead.]

[handwritten notes: Friend, I enemy]

I was angry with my friend:
I told my wrath, my wrath did end.
I was angry with my foe:
I told it not, my wrath did grow.

And I watered it in fears,
Night and morning with my tears:
And I sunned it with smiles,
And with soft deceitful wiles.

And it grew both day and night, *[handwritten: bible]*
Till it bore an apple bright;
And my foe beheld it shine,
And he knew that it was mine,

And into my garden stole
When the night had veiled the pole:
In the morning glad I see
My foe outstretched beneath the tree.

A Man Said to the Universe

STEPHEN CRANE

A man said to the universe:
"Sir, I exist!"
"However," replied the universe,
"The fact has not created in me
A sense of obligation."

522

My Dreams Are of a Field Afar

A. E. HOUSMAN

man vs. himself

My dreams are of a field afar
    And blood and smoke and shot.
There in their graves my comrades are,
    In my grave I am not.

I too was taught the trade of man —war
    And spelt the lesson plain;
But they, when I forgot and ran,
    Remembered and remain.

Success Is Counted Sweetest

EMILY DICKINSON

sucess vs. failure
man vs. man

Success is counted sweetest
By those who ne'er succeed.
To comprehend a nectar—*sucess friend + foe.*
Requires sorest need.—*want it*

Not one of all the purple host
Who took the flag today
Can tell the definition,
So clear, of victory,

As he, defeated, dying,
On whose forbidden ear
The distant strains of triumph
Break, agonized and clear.

Here a modern poet uses the traditional ballad form to describe the conflict that arises between two onlookers as an enemy army patrol advances toward them.

O What Is That Sound

W. H. AUDEN

O what is that sound which so thrills the ear
   Down in the valley drumming, drumming?
Only the scarlet soldiers, dear,
   The soldiers coming.

O what is that light I see flashing so clear
   Over the distance brightly, brightly?
Only the sun on their weapons, dear,
   As they step lightly.

O what are they doing with all that gear;
   What are they doing this morning, this morning?   10
Only the usual maneuvers, dear,
   Or perhaps a warning.

O why have they left the road down there;
   Why are they suddenly wheeling, wheeling?
Perhaps a change in the orders, dear;
   Why are you kneeling?

O haven't they stopped for the doctor's care;
   Haven't they reined their horses, their horses?
Why, they are none of them wounded, dear.
   None of these forces.   20

O is it the parson they want, with white hair;
   Is it the parson, is it, is it?
No, they are passing his gateway, dear,
   Without a visit.

O it must be the farmer who lives so near,
  It must be the farmer, so cunning, cunning;
They have passed the farm already, dear,
  And now they are running.

O where are you going? stay with me here.
  Were the vows you swore me deceiving, deceiving?   30
No, I promised to love you, my dear,
  But I must be leaving.

O it's broken the lock and splintered the door,
  O it's the gate where they're turning, turning;
Their feet are heavy on the floor
  And their eyes are burning.

Late Greek sculpture of Jupiter.

THE HERO
IN LITERATURE

"Show me the man you honor. I know by that symptom better than any other what kind of man you yourself are. For you show me there what your ideal of manhood is, what kind of man you long inexpressibly to be."

THOMAS CARLYLE

The choice of a hero is a personal thing, a projection of the self you want to be. One man's hero may be a great general, another's a pop singer. So too for nations and cultures: heroes change as the values that inspire them change. Today, it is often said that we live in an unheroic age. But every age has said that about itself. The great figures of the past usually appear taller, nobler, stronger than the men of our own time.

In talking about novels or plays, we often use the word "hero" to mean "the leading male character." In this sense, the hero of a modern work of literature may be a child or an ordinary man who works on a farm or in a factory or office. Such a hero would have been unthinkable to the ancient Greeks, or to Shakespeare for that matter. The heroes of Shakespeare's tragedies, as in Julius Caesar, are always kings, generals, princes, men of high birth whose well-being reflects the well-being of their people. The affairs of Brutus, Caesar, and Antony are the affairs of Rome.

The selections that follow trace the changing face of the hero from ancient to modern times. The first, the story of Perseus, is a myth — that is, the story of a god or a demigod (half god, half man). The selections then move through other stages of the hero. King Arthur is human but lives in a world of Romance, filled with magic and mystery. The modern hero (in this case a heroine) is represented by "The Iron Lady," in which the leading character is human and lives in a world much like that of the reader himself. Thurber's "The Greatest Man in the World" is an example of a common theme in modern literature, the ironic hero or anti-hero. The title of the final selection speaks for itself: From Hero to Celebrity.

I. THE HERO OF MYTH

Many of the elements of myth and legend recur again and again in literature. Some of these recurring elements are found in the Perseus story: his origin is mysterious and his true father is unknown to him (like Oedipus); he is rescued from a wild place, in this case from water (like Moses); he goes on a quest and kills a monster (like St. George or King Arthur's knights).

Perseus

EDITH HAMILTON

King Acrisius [1] of Argos [2] had only one child, a daughter, Danaë.[3] She was beautiful above all the other women of the land, but this was small comfort to the king for not having a son. He journeyed to Delphi [4] to ask the god if there was any hope that some day he would be the father of a boy. The priestess told him no and added what was far worse: that his daughter would have a son who would kill him.

The only sure way to escape that fate was for the king to have Danaë instantly put to death — taking no chances but seeing to it himself. This Acrisius would not do. His fatherly affection was not strong, as events proved, but his fear of the gods was. They visited with terrible punishment those who shed the blood of kindred. Acrisius did not dare slay his daughter. Instead, he had a house built all of bronze and sunk underground but with part of the roof open to the sky so that light and air could come through. Here he shut her up and guarded her.

---

[1] *Acrisius* (ə·krēs'ē·əs).
[2] *Argos:* a city in southern Greece.
[3] *Danaë* (dan'i·ē).
[4] *Delphi:* ancient Grecian city where the Oracle of Apollo predicted the future.

> So Danaë endured, the beautiful,
> To change the glad daylight for brass-bound walls,
> And in that chamber secret as the grave
> She lived a prisoner. Yet to her came
> Zeus in the golden rain.

As she sat there through the long days and hours with nothing to do, nothing to see except the clouds moving by overhead, a mysterious thing happened, a shower of gold fell from the sky and filled her chamber. How it was revealed to her that it was Zeus who had visited her in this shape we are not told, but she knew that the child she bore was his son.

For a time she kept his birth secret from her father, but it became increasingly difficult to do so in the narrow limits of that bronze house, and finally one day the little boy — his name was Perseus [5] — was discovered by his grandfather. "Your child!" Acrisius cried in great anger. "Who is his father?" But when Danaë answered proudly, "Zeus," he would not believe her. One thing only he was sure of, that the boy's life was a terrible danger to his own. He was afraid to kill him for the same reason that had kept him from killing her, fear of Zeus and the Furies who pursue such murderers. But if he could not kill them outright, he could put them in the way of tolerably certain death. He had a great chest made and the two placed in it. Then it was taken out to sea and cast into the water.

In that strange boat Danaë sat with her little son. The daylight faded, and she was alone on the sea.

> When in the carven chest the winds and waves
> Struck fear into her heart she put her arms,
> Not without tears, round Perseus tenderly
> She said, "O son, what grief is mine.
> But you sleep softly, little child,
> Sunk deep in rest within your cheerless home,
> Only a box, brass-bound. The night, this darkness visible,
> The scudding waves so near to your soft curls,
> The shrill voice of the wind, you do not heed,
> Nestled in your red cloak, fair little face."

Through the night in the tossing chest she listened to the waters that seemed always about to wash over them. The dawn came but with no comfort to her, for she could not see it. Neither could she

---

[5] *Perseus* (pûr'sē·əs).

see that around them there were islands rising high above the sea, many islands. All she knew was that presently a wave seemed to lift them and carry them swiftly on and then, retreating, leave them on something solid and motionless. They had made land; they were safe from the sea, but they were still in the chest with no way to get out.

Fate willed it — or perhaps Zeus, who up to now had done little for his love and his child — that they should be discovered by a good man, a fisherman named Dictys. He came upon the great box and broke it open and took the pitiful cargo home to his wife, who was as kind as he. They had no children, and they cared for Danaë and Perseus as if they were their own. The two lived there many years, Danaë content to let her son follow the fisherman's humble trade, out of harm's way. But in the end more trouble came. Polydectes, the ruler of the little island, was the brother of Dictys, but he was a cruel and ruthless man. He seems to have taken no notice of the mother and son for a long time, but at last Danaë attracted his attention. She was still radiantly beautiful even though Perseus by now was full grown, and Polydectes fell in love with her. He wanted her, but he did not want her son, and he set himself to think out a way of getting rid of him.

There were some fearsome monsters called Gorgons who lived on an island and were known far and wide because of their deadly power. Polydectes evidently talked to Perseus about them; he probably told him that he would rather have the head of one of them than anything else in the world. This seems practically certain from the plan he devised for killing Perseus. He announced that he was about to be married and he called his friends together for a celebration, including Perseus in the invitation. Each guest, as was customary, brought a gift for the bride-to-be, except Perseus alone. He had nothing he could give. He was young and proud and keenly mortified. He stood up before them all and did exactly what the king had hoped he would do, declared that he would give him a present better than any there. He would go off and kill Medusa [6] and bring back her head as his gift. Nothing could have suited the king better. No one in his senses would have made such a proposal. Medusa was one of the Gorgons,

---

[6] *Medusa* (mə·dōō′sə).

> And they are three, the Gorgons, each with wings
> And snaky hair, most horrible to mortals.
> Whom no man shall behold and draw again
> The breath of life,

for the reason that whoever looked at them was turned instantly into stone. It seemed that Perseus had been led by his angry pride into making an empty boast. No man unaided could kill Medusa.

But Perseus was saved from his folly. Two great gods were watching over him. He took ship as soon as he left the king's hall, not daring to see his mother first and tell her what he intended, and he sailed to Greece to learn where the three monsters were to be found. He went to Delphi, but all the priestess would say was to bid him seek the land where men eat not Demeter's [7] golden grain but only acorns. So he went to Dodona, in the land of oak trees, where the talking oaks were which declared Zeus's will and where the Selli lived who made their bread from acorns. They could tell him, however, no more than this, that he was under the protection of the gods. They did not know where the Gorgons lived.

When and how Hermes [8] and Athena [9] came to his help is not told in any story, but he must have known despair before they did so. At last, however, as he wandered on, he met a strange and beautiful person. We know what he looked like from many a poem, a young man with the first down upon his cheek, when youth is loveliest, carrying, as no other young man ever did, a wand of gold with wings at one end, wearing a winged hat, too, and winged sandals. At sight of him hope must have entered Perseus' heart, for he would know that this could be none other than Hermes, the guide and the giver of good.

This radiant personage told him that before he attacked Medusa, he must first be properly equipped and that what he needed was in the possession of the nymphs of the North. To find the nymphs' abode, they must go to the Gray Women, who alone could tell them the way. These women dwelt in a land where all was dim and shrouded in twilight. No ray of sun looked ever on that country, nor the moon by night. In that gray place the three women lived, all gray themselves and withered as in extreme old age. They were

---

[7] *Demeter* (di·mē′tər): Greek goddess of agriculture.
[8] *Hermes* (hûr′mēz): messenger of the Greek gods.
[9] *Athena* (ə·thē′nə): Greek goddess of wisdom, sometimes called Pallas Athena.

strange creatures, indeed, most of all because they had but one eye for the three, which it was their custom to take turns with, each removing it from her forehead when she had had it for a time and handing it to another.

All this Hermes told Perseus, and then he unfolded his plan. He would himself guide Perseus to them. Once there Perseus must keep hidden until he saw one of them take the eye out of her forehead to pass it on. At that moment, when none of the three could see, he must rush forward and seize the eye and refuse to give it back until they told him how to reach the nymphs of the North.

He himself, Hermes said, would give him a sword to attack Medusa with — which could not be bent or broken by the Gorgon's scales, no matter how hard they were. This was a wonderful gift, no doubt, and yet of what use was a sword when the creature to be struck by it could turn the swordsman into stone before he was within striking distance? But another great deity was at hand to help. Pallas Athena stood beside Perseus. She took off the shield of polished bronze which covered her breast and held it out to him. "Look into this when you attack the Gorgon," she said. "You will be able to see her in it as in a mirror, and so avoid her deadly power."

Now, indeed, Perseus had good reason to hope. The journey to the twilight land was long, over the stream of Ocean and on to the very border of the black country where the Cimmerians [10] dwell, but Hermes was his guide and he could not go astray. They found the Gray Women at last, looking in the wavering light like gray birds, for they had the shape of swans. But their heads were human and beneath their wings they had arms and hands. Perseus did just as Hermes had said, he held back until he saw one of them take the eye out of her forehead. Then before she could give it to her sister, he snatched it out of her hand. It was a moment or two before the three realized they had lost it. Each thought one of the others had it. But Perseus spoke out and told them he had taken it and that it would be theirs again only when they showed him how to find the nymphs of the North. They gave him full directions at once; they would have done anything to get their eye back. He returned it to them and went on the way they had pointed out to him. He was bound, although he did not know it, to the blessed country

---

[10] *Cimmerians:* mythical people who lived in complete darkness.

of the Hyperboreans,[11] at the back of the North Wind, of which it is said: "Neither by ship nor yet by land shall one find the wondrous road to the gathering place of the Hyperboreans." But Perseus had Hermes with him, so that the road lay open to him, and he reached that host of happy people who are always banqueting and holding joyful revelry. They showed him great kindness: they welcomed him to their feast, and the maidens dancing to the sound of flute and lyre paused to get for him the gifts he sought. These were three: winged sandals, a magic wallet [12] which would always become the right size for whatever was to be carried in it, and, most important of all, a cap which made the wearer invisible. With these and Athena's shield and Hermes's sword, Perseus was ready for the Gorgons. Hermes knew where they lived, and leaving the happy land the two flew back across Ocean and over the sea to the Terrible Sisters' island.

By great good fortune they were all asleep when Perseus found them. In the mirror of the bright shield he could see them clearly, creatures with great wings and bodies covered with golden scales and hair a mass of twisting snakes. Athena was beside him now as well as Hermes. They told him which one was Medusa, and that was important, for she alone of the three could be killed; the other two were immortal. Perseus on his winged sandals hovered above them, looking, however, only at the shield. Then he aimed a stroke down at Medusa's throat, and Athena guided his hand. With a single sweep of his sword he cut through her neck, and, his eyes still fixed on the shield with never a glance at her, he swooped low enough to seize the head. He dropped it into the wallet, which closed around it. He had nothing to fear from it now. But the two other Gorgons had awakened and, horrified at the sight of their sister slain, tried to pursue the slayer. Perseus was safe; he had on the cap of darkness, and they could not find him.

> So over the sea rich-haired Danaë's son,
> Perseus, on his winged sandals sped,
> Flying swift as thought.
> In a wallet of silver,
> A wonder to behold,

---

[11] *Hyperboreans* (hī′pər·bar′ē·ənz): mythical people who lived in complete sunshine and peace.

[12] *wallet:* knapsack.

He bore the head of the monster,
While Hermes, the son of Maia,
The messenger of Zeus,
Kept ever at his side.

On his way back he came to Ethiopia [13] and alighted there. By
this time Hermes had left him. Perseus found, as Hercules [14] was
later to find, that a lovely maiden had been given up to be devoured by a horrible sea serpent. Her name was Andromeda,[15] and
she was the daughter of a silly vain woman,

That starred Ethiop queen who strove
To set her beauty's praise above
The sea-nymphs, and their power offended.

She had boasted that she was more beautiful than the daughters of
Nereus,[16] the Sea-god. An absolutely certain way in those days to
draw down on one a wretched fate was to claim superiority in anything over any deity; nevertheless, people were perpetually doing
so. In this case the punishment for the arrogance the gods detested
fell not on Queen Cassiopeia,[17] Andromeda's mother, but on her
daughter. The Ethiopians were being devoured in numbers by the
serpent; and, learning from the oracle that they could be freed from
the pest only if Andromeda were offered up to it, they forced
Cepheus,[18] her father, to consent. When Perseus arrived, the
maiden was on a rocky ledge by the sea, chained there to wait for
the coming of the monster. Perseus saw her and on the instant
loved her. He waited beside her until the great snake came for its
prey; then he cut its head off just as he had the Gorgon's. The
headless body dropped back into the water; Perseus took Andromeda to her parents and asked for her hand, which they gladly gave
him.

With her he sailed back to the island and his mother, but in the
house where he had lived so long he found no one. The fisherman
Dictys's wife was long since dead, and the two others, Danaë and
the man who had been like a father to Perseus, had had to fly and
hide themselves from Polydectes, who was furious at Danaë's re-

---

[13] *Ethiopia* (ē′thē·ō′pē·ə): a real country south of Egypt.
[14] *Hercules* (hûr′kyə·lēz): a demigod of great strength, and another son of Zeus.
[15] *Andromeda* (an·drom′ə·də).
[16] *Nereus* (nir′ōōs).
[17] *Cassiopeia* (kas′ē·ə·pē′ə).
[18] *Cepheus* (sē′fyōōs).

fusal to marry him. They had taken refuge in a temple, Perseus was told. He learned also that the king was holding a banquet in the palace and all the men who favored him were gathered there. Perseus instantly saw his opportunity. He went straight to the palace and entered the hall. As he stood at the entrance, Athena's shining buckler on his breast, the silver wallet at his side, he drew the eyes of every man there. Then before any could look away, he held up the Gorgon's head; and at the sight one and all, the cruel king and his servile courtiers,[19] were turned into stone. There they sat, a row of statues, each, as it were, frozen stiff in the attitude he had struck when he first saw Perseus.

When the islanders knew themselves freed from the tyrant, it was easy for Perseus to find Danaë and Dictys. He made Dictys king of the island, but he and his mother decided that they would go back with Andromeda to Greece and try to be reconciled to Acrisius, to see if the many years that had passed since he had put them in the chest had not softened him so that he would be glad to receive his daughter and grandson. When they reached Argos, however, they found that Acrisius had been driven away from the city, and where he was no one could say. It happened that soon after their arrival Perseus heard that the king of Larissa, in the North, was holding a great athletic contest, and he journeyed there to take part. In the discus-throwing when his turn came and he hurled the heavy missile, it swerved and fell among the spectators. Acrisius was there on a visit to the king, and the discus struck him. The blow was fatal, and he died at once.

So Apollo's oracle was again proved true. If Perseus felt any grief, at least he knew that his grandfather had done his best to kill him and his mother. With his death their troubles came to an end. Perseus and Andromeda lived happily ever after. Their son, Electryon, was the grandfather of Hercules.

Medusa's head was given to Athena, who bore it always upon the aegis, Zeus's shield, which she carried for him.

---

[19] *courtiers* (kôr′tē·ərz): members of a king's court.

II. BETWEEN MYTH AND ROMANCE

Achilleus (also called Achilles) is remembered as the greatest of the
Greek warriors who fought in the Trojan War. He was a mortal and
could die, but his mother was a goddess, a sea-nymph, Thetis. A story
about Achilleus not told in the Iliad is that his mother dipped him
in the magical waters of the river Styx to protect him from any
wounds, but the heel by which she held him was left unprotected.

The story of Achilleus has elements of both myth and romance. In
the following section of the Iliad, we see the hero as a shining,
powerful, almost invincible warrior. The section begins after Patroklos,
Achilleus' best friend, is killed by a Trojan, Hektor, overwhelming
Achilleus with grief. Vowing vengeance, he goes forth to fight and,
in a rage of fury, cuts the Trojan forces in two, driving half back
toward the city and the other half into the river Xanthus. From
the walls of Troy, Priam, the Trojan king, sees that his warriors are
in trouble and orders the gates of the city opened. The Trojans flee
back to the city, and Hektor, left alone to face Achilleus, is chased
three times around the city wall. Then the goddess Athene intervenes
on behalf of Achilleus, and, by disguising herself as Deiphobos,
Hektor's brother, she tricks Hektor into standing fast as Achilleus
approaches.

from The Iliad (Book 22)

HOMER

translated by RICHMOND LATTIMORE

Now as the two in their advance were come close together,
first of the two to speak was tall helm-glittering Hektor:
"Son of Peleus, I will no longer run from you, as before this
I fled three times around the great city of Priam, and dared not
stand to your onfall. But now my spirit in turn has driven me   5
to stand and face you. I must take you now, or I must be taken.

Come then, shall we swear before the gods? For these are the highest
who shall be witnesses and watch over our agreements.
Brutal as you are I will not defile you, if Zeus grants
to me that I can wear you out, and take the life from you.   10
But after I have stripped your glorious armor, Achilleus,
I will give your corpse back to the Achaians.° Do you do likewise."
    Then looking darkly at him swift-footed Achilleus answered:
"Hektor, argue me no agreements. I cannot forgive you.
As there are no trustworthy oaths between men and lions,   15
nor wolves and lambs have spirit that can be brought to agreement
but forever these hold feelings of hate for each other,
so there can be no love between you and me, nor shall there be
oaths between us, but one or the other must fall before then
to glut with his blood Ares° the god who fights under the shield's
    guard.   20
Remember every valor of yours, for now the need comes
hardest upon you to be a spearman and a bold warrior.
There shall be no more escape for you, but Pallas Athene°
will kill you soon by my spear. You will pay in a lump for all those
sorrows of my companions you killed in your spear's fury."   25
    So he spoke, and balanced the spear far shadowed, and threw it;
but glorious Hektor kept his eyes on him, and avoided it,
for he dropped, watchful, to his knee, and the bronze spear flew over
    his shoulder
and stuck in the ground, but Pallas Athene snatched it, and gave it
back to Achilleus, unseen by Hektor shepherd of the people.   30
But now Hektor spoke out to the blameless son of Peleus:
"You missed; and it was not, O Achilleus like the immortals,
from Zeus that you knew my destiny; but you thought so; or rather
you are someone clever in speech and spoke to swindle me,
to make me afraid of you and forget my valor and war strength.   35
You will not stick your spear in my back as I run away from you
but drive it into my chest as I storm straight in against you;
if the god gives you that; and now look out for my brazen
spear. I wish it might be taken full length in your body.
And indeed the war would be a lighter thing for the Trojans   40
if you were dead, seeing that you are their greatest affliction."

---

12. *Achaians* (ə·kā'ənz): Greeks. 20. *Ares:* god of war. 23. *Pallas Athene:*
Zeus's daughter, goddess of wisdom.

So he spoke, and balanced the spear far shadowed, and threw it,
and struck the middle of Peleïdes'° shield, nor missed it,
but the spear was driven far back from the shield, and Hektor was
    angered
because his swift weapon had been loosed from his hand in a vain
    cast.   45
He stood discouraged, and had no other ash spear; but lifting
his voice he called aloud on Deïphobos of the pale shield,
and asked him for a long spear, but Deïphobos was not near him.
And Hektor knew the truth inside his heart, and spoke aloud:
"No use. Here at last the gods have summoned me deathward.   50
I thought Deiphobos the hero was here close beside me,
but he is behind the wall and it was Athene cheating me,
and now evil death is close to me, and no longer far away,
and there is no way out. So it must long since have been pleasing
to Zeus, and Zeus' son who strikes from afar, this way; though before
    this   55
they defended me gladly. But now my death is upon me.
Let me at least not die without a struggle, inglorious,
but do some big thing first, that men to come shall know of it."
    So he spoke, and pulling out the sharp sword that was slung
at the hollow of his side, huge and heavy, and gathering   60
himself together, he made his swoop, like a high-flown eagle
who launches himself out of the murk of the clouds on the flat land
to catch away a tender lamb or a shivering hare; so
Hektor made his swoop, swinging his sharp sword, and Achilleus
charged, the heart within him loaded with savage fury.   65
In front of his chest the beautiful elaborate great shield
covered him, and with the glittering helm with four horns
he nodded; the lovely golden fringes were shaken about it
which Hephaistos° had driven close along the horn of the helmet.
And as a star moves among stars in the night's darkening,   70
Hesper, who is the fairest star who stands in the sky, such
was the shining from the pointed spear Achilleus was shaking
in his right hand with evil intention toward brilliant Hektor.
He was eying Hektor's splendid body, to see where it might best
give way, but all the rest of the skin was held in the armor,   75

---

43. *Peleides:* Achilleus (literally, son of Peleus). 69. *Hephaistos* (hi·fĭs′tos):
Greek god of fire, maker of Achilleus's armor.

brazen and splendid, he stripped when he cut down the strength of
    Patroklos;
yet showed where the collarbones hold the neck from the shoulders,
the throat, where death of the soul comes most swiftly; in this place
brilliant Achilleus drove the spear as he came on in fury,
and clean through the soft part of the neck the spearpoint was
    driven.   80
Yet the ash spear heavy with bronze did not sever the windpipe,
so that Hektor could still make exchange of words spoken.
But he dropped in the dust, and brilliant Achilleus vaunted above
    him:
"Hektor, surely you thought as you killed Patroklos you would be
safe, and since I was far away you thought nothing of me,   85
O fool, for an avenger was left, far greater than he was,
behind him and away by the hollow ships. And it was I;
and I have broken your strength; on you the dogs and the vultures
shall feed and foully rip you; the Achaians will bury Patroklos."
    In his weakness Hektor of the shining helm spoke to him: 90
"I entreat you, by your life, by your knees, by your parents,
do not let the dogs feed on me by the ships of the Achaians,
but take yourself the bronze and gold that are there in abundance,
those gifts that my father and the lady my mother will give you,
and give my body to be taken home again, so that the Trojans   95
and the wives of the Trojans may give me in death my rite of burn-
    ing."
    But looking darkly at him swift-footed Achilleus answered:
"No more entreating of me, you dog, by knees or parents.
I wish only that my spirit and fury would drive me
to hack your meat away and eat it raw for the things that   100
you have done to me. So there is no one who can hold the dogs off
from your head, not if they bring here and set before me ten times
and twenty times the ransom, and promise more in addition,
not if Priam son of Dardanos should offer to weigh out
your bulk in gold; not even so shall the lady your mother   105
who herself bore you lay you on the death-bed and mourn you:
no, but the dogs and the birds will have you all for their feasting."
    Then, dying, Hektor of the shining helmet spoke to him:
"I know you well as I look upon you, I know that I could not
persuade you, since indeed in your breast is a heart of iron.   110

Be careful now; for I might be made into the gods' curse
upon you, on that day when Paris and Phoibos Apollo
destroy you in the Skaian° gates, for all your valor."

   He spoke, and as he spoke the end of death closed in upon him,
and the soul fluttering free of the limbs went down into Death's
      house   115
mourning her destiny, leaving youth and manhood behind her.
Now though he was a dead man brilliant Achilleus spoke to him:
"Die: and I will take my own death at whatever time
Zeus and the rest of the immortals choose to accomplish it."

   He spoke, and pulled the brazen spear from the body, and laid it
on one side, and stripped away from the shoulders the bloody   121
armor. And the other sons of the Achaians came running about him,
and gazed upon the stature and on the imposing beauty
of Hektor; and none stood beside him who did not stab him;
and thus they would speak one to another, each looking at his
      neighbor: 125
"See now, Hektor is much softer to handle than he was
when he set the ships ablaze with the burning firebrand."

   So as they stood beside him they would speak, and stab him.
But now, when he had despoiled the body, swift-footed brilliant
Achilleus stood among the Achaians and addressed them in winged
      words: 130
"Friends, who are leaders of the Argives° and keep their counsel:
since the gods have granted me the killing of this man
who has done us much damage, such as not all the others together
have done, come, let us go in armor about the city
to see if we can find out what purpose is in the Trojans,   135
whether they will abandon their high city, now that this man
has fallen, or are minded to stay, though Hektor lives no longer.
Yet still, why does the heart within me debate on these things?
There is a dead man who lies by the ships, unwept, unburied:
Patroklos: and I will not forget him, never so long as   140
I remain among the living and my knees have their spring beneath
      me.
And though the dead forget the dead in the house of Hades,
even there I shall still remember my beloved companion.
But now, you young men of the Achaians, let us go back, singing

---

113. *Skaian:* western. 131. *Argives:* Greeks.

a victory song, to our hollow ships; and take this with us.   145
We have won ourselves enormous fame; we have killed the great
    Hektor
whom the Trojans glorified as if he were a god in their city."
  He spoke, and now thought of shameful treatment for glorious
    Hektor.
In both of his feet at the back he made holes by the tendons
in the space between ankle and heel, and drew thongs of ox-hide
    through them,   150
and fastened them to the chariot so as to let the head drag,
and mounted the chariot, and lifted the glorious armor inside it,
then whipped the horses to a run, and they winged their way unre-
    luctant.
A cloud of dust rose where Hektor was dragged, his dark hair was
    falling
about him, and all that head that was once so handsome was
    tumbled   155
in the dust; since by this time Zeus had given him over
to his enemies, to be defiled in the land of his fathers.

  So all his head was dragged in the dust; and now his mother
tore out her hair, and threw the shining veil far from her
and raised a great wail as she looked upon her son; and his father
beloved groaned pitifully, and all his people about him   161
were taken with wailing and lamentation all through the city.
It was most like what would have happened, if all lowering
Ilion had been burning top to bottom in fire.
His people could scarcely keep the old man in his impatience   165
from storming out of the Dardanian° gates; he implored them
all, and wallowed in the muck before them calling on each man
and naming him by his name: "Give way, dear friends,
and let me alone though you care for me, leave me to go out
from the city and make my way to the ships of the Achaians.   170
I must be suppliant to this man, who is harsh and violent,
and he might have respect for my age and take pity upon it
since I am old, and his father also is old, as I am,
Peleus, who begot and reared him to be an affliction
on the Trojans. He has given us most sorrow, beyond all others,   175
such is the number of my flowering sons he has cut down.

---

166. *Dardanian:* Trojan.

But for all of these I mourn not so much, in spite of my sorrow,
as for one, Hektor, and the sharp grief for him will carry me down-
    ward
into Death's house. I wish he had died in my arms, for that way
we two, I myself and his mother who bore him unhappy,   180
might so have glutted ourselves with weeping for him and mourn-
    ing."
    So he spoke, in tears, and beside him mourned the citizens.
But for the women of Troy Hekabe° led out the thronging
chant of sorrow: "Child, I am wretched. What shall my life be
in my sorrows, now you are dead, who by day and in the night   185
were my glory in the town, and to all of the Trojans
and the women of Troy a blessing throughout their city. They
    adored you
as if you were a god, since in truth you were their high honor
while you lived. Now death and fate have closed in upon you."
    So she spoke in tears but the wife of Hektor had not yet   190
heard: for no sure messenger had come to her and told her
how her husband had held his ground there outside the gates;
but she was weaving a web in the inner room of the high house,
a red folding robe, and inworking elaborate figures.   194
She called out through the house to her lovely-haired handmaidens
to set a great cauldron over the fire, so that there would be
hot water for Hektor's bath as he came back out of the fighting;
poor innocent, nor knew how, far from waters for bathing,
Pallas Athene had cut him down at the hands of Achilleus.   199
She heard from the great bastion the noise of mourning and sorrow.
Her limbs spun, and the shuttle dropped from her hand to the
    ground. Then
she called aloud to her lovely-haired handmaidens: "Come here.
Two of you come with me, so I can see what has happened.
I heard the voice of Hektor's honored mother; within me
my own heart rising beats in my mouth, my limbs under me   205
are frozen. Surely some evil is near for the children of Priam.
May what I say come never close to my ear; yet dreadfully
I fear that great Achilleus might have cut off bold Hektor
alone, away from the city, and be driving him into the flat land,
might put an end to that bitter pride of courage, that always   210

---

183. *Hekabe* (hek'ə·bə): mother of Hector. Frequently spelled *Hecuba*.

was on him, since he would never stay back where the men were in
    numbers
but break far out in front, and give way in his fury to no man."
    So she spoke, and ran out of the house like a raving woman
with pulsing heart, and her two handmaidens went along with her.
But when she came to the bastion and where the men were gathered
she stopped, staring, on the wall; and she saw him   216
being dragged in front of the city, and the running horses
dragged him at random toward the hollow ships of the Achaians.
The darkness of night misted over the eyes of Andromache.°   219
She fell backward, and gasped the life breath from her, and far off
threw from her head the shining gear that ordered her headdress,
the diadem and the cap, and the holding-band woven together,
and the circlet, which Aphrodite° the golden once had given her
on the day when Hektor of the shining helmet led her forth   224
from the house of Eëtion,° and gave numberless gifts to win her.
And about her stood thronging her husband's sisters and the wives of
    his brothers
and these, in her despair for death, held her up among them.
But she, when she breathed again and the life was gathered back into
    her,
lifted her voice among the women of Troy in mourning:
"Hektor, I grieve for you. You and I were born to a single   230
destiny, you in Troy in the house of Priam, and I
in Thebe, underneath the timbered mountain of Plakos
in the house of Eëtion, who cared for me when I was little,
ill-fated he, I ill-starred. I wish he had never begotten me.
Now you go down to the house of Death in the secret places   235
of the earth, and left me here behind in the sorrow of mourning,
a widow in your house, and the boy is only a baby
who was born to you and me, the unfortunate. You cannot help
    him,
Hektor, any more, since you are dead. Nor can he help you.   239
Though he escape the attack of the Achaians with all its sorrows,
yet all his days for your sake there will be hard work for him
and sorrows, for others will take his lands away from him. The day
of bereavement leaves a child with no agemates to befriend him.

---

219. *Andromache* (an·drom′ə·kē), Hektor's wife. 223. *Aphrodite* (af′rə·dī′tē),
Goddess of love. 225. *Eëtion:* father of Andromache.

He bows his head before every man, his cheeks are bewept, he
goes, needy, a boy among his father's companions,   245
and tugs at this man by the mantle, that man by the tunic,
and they pity him, and one gives him a tiny drink from a goblet,
enough to moisten his lips, not enough to moisten his palate.
But one whose parents are living beats him out of the banquet
hitting him with his fists and in words also abuses him: 250
'Get out, you! Your father is not dining among us.'
And the boy goes away in tears to his widowed mother,
Astyanax,° who in days before on the knees of his father
would eat only the marrow or the flesh of sheep that was fattest.
And when sleep would come upon him and he was done with his
      playing,   255
he would go to sleep in a bed, in the arms of his nurse, in a soft
bed, with his heart given all its fill of luxury.
Now, with his dear father gone, he has much to suffer:
he, whom the Trojans have called Astyanax, lord of the city,   259
since it was you alone who defended the gates and the long walls.
But now, beside the curving ships, far away from your parents,
the writhing worms will feed, when the dogs have had enough of you,
on your naked corpse, though in your house there is clothing laid
      up
that is fine-textured and pleasant, wrought by the hands of women.
But all of these I will burn up in the fire's blazing,   265
no use to you, since you will never be laid away in them;
but in your honor, from the men of Troy and the Trojan women."
    So she spoke, in tears; and the women joined in her mourning.

253. *Astyanax:* Hektor's son.

The hero of Romance is not a god or demigod, but he lives in a world of witches and ogres, enchanted trees and swords, magic spells, prophecies that come true, and other marvelous happenings. One of the great Romances is the legend of King Arthur and his Round Table, which has inspired writers for centuries. From the first appearance of the stories in the twelfth century to the modern musical comedy Camelot, *these tales have captured the imagination of readers.*

As a boy, the English poet Tennyson read the Arthurian legends in a collection by Sir Thomas Malory called Morte d'Arthur. *In later life, Tennyson wrote a long epic poem,* Idylls of the King, *based on Malory's stories. In the* Idylls, *Arthur is born, his birth shrouded in mystery like that of Perseus; he is reared by Merlin the Magician, receives the magical sword Excalibur from the Lady of the Lake, becomes king, and marries Guinevere. In twelve battles, Arthur and his knights drive their enemies out of the kingdom. But for all his victories and all the power and glory of his court, Arthur is betrayed by those nearest him and lives to see his Round Table emptied and his kingdom invaded.*

In the last battle, Arthur, betrayed by Guinevere and Sir Lancelot, goes forth to fight his nephew, Modred. All the knights except Sir Bedivere are killed, and Arthur is mortally wounded. At this point, the last Idyll begins.

Morte d'Arthur

ALFRED, LORD TENNYSON

> So all day long the noise of battle rolled
> Among the mountains by the winter sea,
> Until King Arthur's table, man by man,
> Had fallen in Lyonnesse° about their lord,
> King Arthur; then, because his wound was deep,
> The bold Sir Bedivere uplifted him,
> Sir Bedivere, the last of all his knights,
> And bore him to a chapel nigh the field,
> A broken chancel with a broken cross,

---

4. *Lyonnesse:* legendary country where the battle had been fought and where Arthur had been born.

That stood on a dark strait of barren land. 10
On one side lay the ocean, and on one
Lay a great water, and the moon was full.
   Then spake King Arthur to Sir Bedivere:
"The sequel of today unsolders all
The goodliest fellowship of famous knights
Whereof this world holds record. Such a sleep
They sleep — the men I loved. I think that we
Shall never more, at any future time,
Delight our souls with talk of knightly deeds,
Walking about the gardens and the halls 20
Of Camelot, as in the days that were.
I perish by this people which I made —
Though Merlin sware that I should come again
To rule once more — but let what will be be,
I am so deeply smitten through the helm
That without help I cannot last till morn.
Thou therefore take my brand Excalibur,
Which was my pride, for thou rememberest how
In those old days, one summer noon, an arm
Rose up from out the bosom of the lake, 30
Clothed in white samite,° mystic, wonderful,
Holding the sword — and how I rowed across
And took it, and have worn it, like a king;
And, wheresoever I am sung or told
In aftertime, this also shall be known.
But now delay not; take Excalibur,
And fling him far into the middle mere;°
Watch what thou seest, and lightly bring me word."
   To him replied the bold Sir Bedivere:
"It is not meet, Sir King, to leave thee thus, 40
Aidless, alone, and smitten through the helm.
A little thing may harm a wounded man.
Yet I thy hest° will all perform at full,
Watch what I see, and lightly bring thee word."
   So saying, from the ruined shrine he stepped
And in the moon athwart the place of tombs,
Where lay the mighty bones of ancient men,

---

31. *samite:* a heavy silk fabric. 37. *mere:* lake. 43. *hest:* command.

Old knights, and over them the seawind sang
Shrill, chill, with flakes of foam. He, stepping down
By zigzag paths and juts of pointed rock,   50
Came on the shining levels of the lake.

    There drew he forth the brand Excalibur,
And o'er him, drawing it, the winter moon,
Brightening the skirts of a long cloud, ran forth
And sparkled keen with frost against the hilt;
For all the haft twinkled with diamond sparks,
Myriads of topaz-lights, and jacinth-work°
Of subtlest jewelry. He gazed so long
That both his eyes were dazzled, as he stood,
This way and that dividing the swift mind,   60
In act to throw; but at the last it seemed
Better to leave Excalibur concealed
There in the many-knotted water-flags,°
That whistled stiff and dry about the marge.°
So strode he back slow to the wounded king.

    Then spake King Arthur to Sir Bedivere:
"Hast thou performed my mission which I gave?
What is it thou hast seen, or what hast heard?"

    And answer made the bold Sir Bedivere:
"I heard the ripple washing in the reeds,   70
And the wild water lapping on the crag."

    To whom replied King Arthur, faint and pale:
"Thou hast betrayed thy nature and thy name,
Not rendering true answer, as beseemed
Thy fealty,° nor like a noble knight;
For surer sign had followed, either hand,
Or voice, or else a motion of the mere.
This is a shameful thing for men to lie.
Yet now, I charge thee, quickly go again
As thou art lief° and dear, and do the thing   80
I bade thee, watch, and lightly bring me word."

    Then went Sir Bedivere the second time
Across the ridge, and paced beside the mere,

---

57. *topaz . . . jacinth-work:* semiprecious stones worked into the design.
63. *water-flags:* irislike flowers. 64. *marge:* edge. 75. *fealty:* duty to one's ruler.
80. *lief:* loved.

Counting the dewy pebbles, fixed in thought;
But when he saw the wonder of the hilt,
How curiously and strangely chased,° he smote
His palms together, and he cried aloud:
   "And if indeed I cast the brand away,
Surely a precious thing, one worthy note,
Should thus be lost forever from the earth, 90
Which might have pleased the eyes of many men.
What good should follow this, if this were done?
What harm, undone? deep harm to disobey,
Seeing obedience is the bond of rule.
Were it well to obey then, if a king demand
An act unprofitable, against himself?
The king is sick, and knows not what he does.
What record, or what relic of my lord
Should be to aftertime, but empty breath
And rumors of a doubt? but were this kept, 100
Stored in some treasure house of mighty kings,
Some one might show it at a joust of arms,
Saying, 'King Arthur's sword, Excalibur,
Wrought by the lonely maiden of the lake;
Nine years she wrought it, sitting in the deeps
Upon the hidden bases of the hills.'
So might some old man speak in the aftertime
To all the people, winning reverence;
But now much honor and much fame were lost."
   So spake he, clouded with his own conceit, 110
And hid Excalibur the second time,
And so strode back slow to the wounded king.
   Then spoke King Arthur, breathing heavily:
"What is it thou hast seen, or what hast heard?"
   And answer made the bold Sir Bedivere:
"I heard the water lapping on the crag,
And the long ripple washing in the reeds."
   To whom replied King Arthur, much in wrath:
"Ah, miserable and unkind, untrue,
Unknightly, traitor-hearted! Woe is me! 120
Authority forgets a dying king,

---

86. *chased:* decorated with a raised design.

Laid widowed of the power in his eye
That bowed the will. I see thee what thou art,
For thou, the latest-left of all my knights,
In whom should meet the offices of all,
Thou wouldst betray me for the precious hilt;
Either from lust of gold, or like a girl
Valuing the giddy pleasure of the eyes.
Yet, for a man may fail in duty twice,
And the third time may prosper, get thee hence;   130
But, if thou spare to fling Excalibur,
I will arise and slay thee with my hands."
  Then quickly rose Sir Bedivere, and ran,
And, leaping down the ridges lightly, plunged
Among the bulrush-beds, and clutched the sword,
And strongly wheeled and threw it. The great brand
Made lightnings in the splendor of the moon,
And flashing round and round, and whirled in an arch,
Shot like a streamer of the northern morn,
Seen where the moving isles of winter shock   140
By night, with noises of the northern sea.
So flashed and fell the brand Excalibur;
But ere he dipped the surface, rose an arm
Clothed in white samite, mystic, wonderful,
And caught him by the hilt, and brandished him
Three times, and drew him under in the mere.
And lightly went the other to the king.
  Then spoke King Arthur, drawing thicker breath:
"Now see I by thine eyes that this is done.
Speak out; what is it thou hast heard, or seen?"   150
  And answer made the bold Sir Bedivere:
"Sir King, I closed mine eyelids, lest the gems
Should blind my purpose, for I never saw,
Nor shall see, here, or elsewhere, till I die,
Not though I live three lives of mortal men,
So great a miracle as yonder hilt.
Then with both hands I flung him, wheeling him;
But when I looked again, behold an arm,
Clothed in white samite, mystic, wonderful,
That caught him by the hilt, and brandished him   160

Three times, and drew him under in the mere."
  And answer made King Arthur, breathing hard:
"My end draws nigh; 'tis time that I were gone.
Make broad thy shoulders to receive my weight,
And bear me to the margin; yet I fear
My wound hath taken cold, and I shall die."
  So saying, from the pavement he half rose,
Slowly, with pain, reclining on his arm,
And looking wistfully with wide blue eyes
As in a picture. Him Sir Bedivere   170
Remorsefully regarded through his tears,
And would have spoken, but he found not words,
Then took with care, and kneeling on one knee,
O'er both his shoulders drew the languid hands,
And rising bore him through the place of tombs.
  But, as he walked, King Arthur panted hard,
Like one that feels a nightmare on his bed
When all the house is mute. So sighed the king,
Muttering and murmuring at his ear, "Quick, quick!
I fear it is too late, and I shall die."   180
But the other swiftly strode from ridge to ridge,
Clothed with his breath, and looking, as he walked,
Larger than human on the frozen hills.
He heard the deep behind him, and a cry
Before. His own thought drove him like a goad.
Dry clashed his harness° in the icy caves
And barren chasms, and all to left and right
The bare black cliff clanged round him, as he based
His feet on juts of slippery crag that rang
Sharp-smitten with the dint° of armed heels —   190
And on a sudden, lo! the level lake,
And the long glories of the winter moon.
  Then saw they how there hove a dusky barge,
Dark as a funeral scarf from stem to stern,
Beneath them; and descending they were ware
That all the decks were dense with stately forms
Black-stoled, black-hooded, like a dream — by these
Three queens with crowns of gold — and from them rose

---

186. *harness:* armor and other equipment. 190. *dint:* blow.

A cry that shivered to the tingling stars,
And, as it were one voice, an agony   200
Of lamentation, like a wind that shrills
All night in a waste land, where no one comes,
Or hath come, since the making of the world.
    Then murmured Arthur, "Place me in the barge,"
And to the barge they came. There those three queens
Put forth their hands, and took the king, and wept.
But she that rose the tallest of them all
And fairest laid his head upon her lap,
And loosed the shattered casque,° and chafed his hands,
And called him by his name, complaining loud,   210
And dropping bitter tears against his brow
Striped with dark blood; for all his face was white
And colorless, and like the withered moon
Smote by the fresh beam of the springing east;
And all his greaves° and cuisses° dashed with drops
Of onset; and the light and lustrous curls —
That made his forehead like a rising sun
High from the dais-throne — were parched with dust;
Or, clotted into points and hanging loose,
Mixed with the knightly growth that fringed his lips.   220
So like a shattered column lay the king;
Not like that Arthur who, with lance in rest,
From spur to plume a star of tournament,
Shot through the lists at Camelot, and charged
Before the eyes of ladies and of kings.
    Then loudly cried the bold Sir Bedivere:
"Ah! my Lord Arthur, whither shall I go?
Where shall I hide my forehead and my eyes?
For now I see the true old times are dead,
When every morning brought a noble chance,   230
And every chance brought out a noble knight.
Such times have been not since the light that led
The holy elders° with the gift of myrrh.
But now the whole ROUND TABLE is dissolved

---

209. *casque:* helmet. 215. *greaves:* armor covering shins. 215. *cuisses:* armor covering thighs. 233. *The holy elders:* the Magi who brought gifts to the Christ Child.

Which was an image of the mighty world;
And I, the last, go forth companionless,
And the days darken round me, and the years,
Among new men, strange faces, other minds."
    And slowly answered Arthur from the barge:
"The old order changeth, yielding place to new,   240
And God fulfills himself in many ways,
Lest one good custom should corrupt the world.
Comfort thyself: what comfort is in me?
I have lived my life, and that which I have done
May he within himself make pure! but thou,
If thou shouldst never see my face again,
Pray for my soul. More things are wrought by prayer
Than this world dreams of. Wherefore, let thy voice
Rise like a fountain for me night and day.
For what are men better than sheep or goats   250
That nourish a blind life within the brain,
If, knowing God, they lift not hands of prayer
Both for themselves and those who call them friend?
For so the whole round earth is every way
Bound by gold chains about the feet of God.
But now farewell. I am going a long way
With these thou seest — if indeed I go —
For all my mind is clouded with a doubt —
To the island-valley of Avilion;°
Where falls not hail, or rain, or any snow,   260
Nor ever wind blows loudly, but it lies
Deap-meadowed, happy, fair with orchard lawns
And bowery hollows crowned with summer sea,
Where I will heal me of my grievous wound."
    So said he, and the barge with oar and sail
Moved from the brink, like some full-breasted swan
That, fluting a wild carol ere her death,
Ruffles her pure cold plume, and takes the flood
With swarthy webs. Long stood Sir Bedivere
Revolving many memories, till the hull   270
Looked one black dot against the verge of dawn,
And on the mere the wailing died away.

---

259. *Avilion* (or *Avalon*): in Celtic mythology, the land of Paradise.

IV. THE FOLK HERO

Many American ballads can be traced back to England, Ireland, and Scotland. One ballad that is purely American, however, is "John Henry." Over fifty versions of it have been collected. A true folk ballad, it has no single source, no known author.

Whether or not there was a real John Henry, no one knows. He lives now in this ballad, a folk hero. John Henry was a "steel-driving man"; that is, he hammered steel drills into rock to make holes for dynamite charges. The climax of the ballad is the contest between John Henry and a steam drill, man versus machine. This was supposed to have happened during the construction of the Chesapeake & Ohio Railway in West Virginia.

[handwritten: Ballads 1) repitition-to stress]

John Henry

ANONYMOUS

[handwritten: trochaic trimeter]

[handwritten: command pressure]

When John Henry was a little boy,
Sitting on his father's knee,
His father said, "Look here, my boy,
You <u>must</u> be a steel-driving man like me,
You <u>must</u> be a steel-driving man like me."

[handwritten: wasn't strong enough]

John Henry went upon the mountain,
Just to drive himself some steel.
The rocks was so tall and John Henry so small,
<u>He said lay down hammer and squeal</u>,
He said lay down hammer and squeal.   10

[handwritten: Be true to my work. Pass on story]

John Henry had a little wife,
And the dress she wore was red;
The last thing before he died,
He said, "<u>Be true to me when I'm dead</u>,
Oh, be true to me when I'm dead."

John Henry started on the right-hand side,
And the steam drill started on the left.
He said, "Before I'd let that steam drill beat me down,
I'd hammer my fool self to death,
Oh, I'd hammer my fool self to death."   20

The steam drill started at half past six,
John Henry started the same time.
John Henry struck bottom at half past eight,
And the steam drill didn't bottom till nine,
And the steam drill didn't bottom till nine.

John Henry said to his captain,
"A man, he ain't nothing but a man,
Before I'd let that steam drill beat me down,
I'd die with the hammer in my hand,
Oh, I'd die with the hammer in my hand."   30

John Henry said to his shaker,°
"Shaker, why don't you sing just a few more rounds?
And before the setting sun goes down,
You're gonna hear this hammer of mine sound,
You're gonna hear this hammer of mine sound."

John Henry hammered on the mountain,
He hammmered till half past three,
He said, "This big Bend Tunnel on the C.&O. road
Is going to be the death of me,
Lord! is going to be the death of me."

John Henry had a little baby boy,
You could hold him in the palm of your hand.
The last words before he died,
"Son, you must be a steel-driving man,
Son, you must be a steel-driving man."

John Henry hammering on the mountain,
As the whistle blew for half past two,
The last word I heard him say,
"Captain, I've hammered my insides in two,
Lord, I've hammered my insides in two."   50

---

31. *shaker:* man holding drill.

V. THE COMMON MAN AS HERO

The heroes of the preceding selections, both human and divine, have all been men of outstanding strength. The next stage in the evolution of the hero is that of most modern, realistic fiction. The modern hero is, in the words of the critic Northrop Frye, "one of us: we respond to a sense of his common humanity."

The Iron Lady

CONRAD RICHTER

The old man in the big house heard the carriage stop and the sound of men's voices. He guessed what they wanted. Let them come, he said to himself, and his lip twitched in sardonic humor. Others had come before them, and none had got the secret out of him yet. But they'd better move fast. Wasn't he supposed to be on his deathbed? Any day now his mind might not be clear or he might be gone to that bourn from which no man returneth, or so the parson on his visits to cheer the sick had told him.

Well, it was true he was old and had taken to his bed. But he wasn't laid out yet, not by a long shot. He wasn't even upstairs. He'd ordered his housekeeper, the cook and yard man to fetch his bed down. He told them it would save them running upstairs with trays and downstairs with slops, but all the time he and they knew the real reason. He didn't want to give up being among the living. He didn't want to leave this corner room on the first floor he called his office. Most of his life had been spent here with his high desk and stool, his low desk table and chair with the familiar worn red cushion. Here were his shelves of furnace accounts and records, on the wall a row of wooden pegs with his clothes, including his blue army overcoat, his cocked hat and sword.

Upstairs, the green clutter of leaves shut out everything. Down here he could look out and see his furnace against the hill, built of the same gray-brown stone as the house, everything still intact outside and in, even the ore barrows and charcoal wagons on the upper level. The stack needed only ore, limestone, and charcoal to be fired. But the brown-painted shutters on the furnace were closed tight and the experienced eye saw no heat waves rising against the sky.

He could hear the men now entering the iron gate to the grounds. They would lower their voices presently. The house always sobered people when they got close — the huge solid bulk of it, the tiers of white shutters against the mountain stone, the large windows with their small panes, the big front door with the carved window light above and the long lights on either hand. The furnace men used to say that if the sidelights would swing with the door, you could drive a team through.

The bell on its long rope tinkled. Presently the old man could hear Manda moving through the house to answer it. His lips pursed in ironic anticipation. They were curious lips seen sometimes on the Scotch; not exactly thick, but ropy, as if they got in the way and he had them always to contend with. Ansell Sloan had white hair above, while a ring of the same ran below from his ears like a thin strip of hairy hide pasted around his bare chin. In this frame his face looked like that of a crabbed but lovable saint, so that you forgot the uncompromising lips and wondered how a man with such a gentle, wry face could have had the nickname of Iron Sloan as a soldier before he became an ironmaster.

You could see the strangers relax when they saw him. The house and grounds might be formidable, but this old man would be easy to handle. He didn't look like an iron soldier to them. They were shrewd, sharp-eyed men from Uniontown, with fine clothes and well-fed faces. First they complimented him on the house and grounds. Then they asked about the two paintings.

"This one toward the road was my wife," he said. "The other one, with the flowers under it, was my mother-in-law."

"Isn't that a little unusual, general?" One of them smiled. "Flowers for your mother-in-law?"

"Not for Mary Harris," the old man said quickly. "But that's a long story."

They didn't press him. They were interested in something else, something more valuable than a mother-in-law.

"We understand, general, that not all your iron came from the Cornwall mines." The leader of the group got down to business. "You told some people, I believe, that the best quality iron you ever had came from a secret source of your own."

"Ah!" The ironmaster rubbed a stubbly chin. "So you heard this even as far as Uniontown?"

"It's true then, general, that you owed your success to a secret iron mine?"

"Well, yes, I guess it's true, though I wouldn't call it an iron mine. It's just where my best iron came from. But remember now, I didn't say where I got it."

The men licked their lips and hitched closer.

"Was this source pretty far away? Did it cost you much to freight it here?"

"Didn't cost me hardly nothing."

"You say it was very rich iron?"

"About the best I ever knew."

"Was it worked out?"

"God bless you, no. It gave iron to some others who knew about it and still does to me when I need it."

You could see victory now on their faces.

"Will you, for a consideration, general, draw us a map of the location?"

"No, I couldn't do that."

There was consternation on their faces. "Why not?"

"Because I don't think you could find it."

"That would be our risk. This iron is still in existence?"

"Well, yes, some of it. But the source has moved."

"Moved? How could it move? You said it was never worked out."

"That's true," he agreed.

He could see with enjoyment that they were completely baffled, that they thought him a queer old man. Well, maybe he was. You got queer sometimes in your eighties. Not that they gave up easily. For more than an hour they pestered and cross-examined him. In the end, like the others, they had to go without it, saying they would be back again.

He sat chuckling dryly when they had left. So they wanted to buy his iron mine? Well, they weren't the first and likely wouldn't be the last. But never would he tell them. They wouldn't believe it had been a woman. They wouldn't understand what he was talking about. You had to live back in the 1750's to understand. Today, in the Millburn Valley, you saw mostly fields of grain and corn, with plenty of cattle, grass, fat barns, and peaceful farmhouses. But then all was solid woods and swamps with thick vines running up the big butts in the bottoms, with cabins buried in the wild greenness, with alarms from the savages twice a year and waking up some morning to find your neighbors killed and their cabins burned. You might even wake up and find it done to your own folks.

That's what had happened to him, and him only eight years old. When he fought back and cried, one of the savages gave him a blow, and he remembered nothing till they shook him and threw water on him to get him going. For a week after that, it seemed, they dragged him through the forest, first a large party, then just two, tying him to one or the other of them, jerking him through bogs and runs, driving him over logs and roots. Hardly was he alive when they reached the other Indian party, waiting for them with a captive at a hemlock spring.

Never as long as he lived would he forget the sight of this unknown spot in the wilderness, with the black mountain above, the painted savage faces around the fire below, the ghastly flutter of scalps on stretchers, and sitting on the ground nearby the young white captive, Mary Harris, with her baby at her breast. She wore a gray homespun short gown, muddied and torn by the bush. Her hair was black, her face brown. She was barefoot and her legs badly scratched by roots and briers. Her state looked hopeless, and yet the way she sat there, living for herself, paying no attention to her captors or her fate, gave him the first sensation of life and hope since he was taken. He tried to run to her, but the Indian he was tied to jerked him and he fell to the ground.

He got to his feet, shaken and trembling. Had she sympathized with him a lick by word or look, his tears would have turned into a flood.

"Don't mind them; they don't know no better," she said, matter of fact.

"They killed my ma and pa!" he cried.

She made resigned noises with her tongue, like a grandmother.

"Maybe your ma and pa are lucky. They don't need to go through what me and you do."

"I wish they'd 'a' killed me too."

"Oh, no, you don't," she said dully, almost flatly. "They broke in a young boy's head for cryin' a ways back. You don't wish you was him alyin' back there with his brains on a tree."

What she said sickened him. He pitied himself. To show how bad he felt, he made himself cry noisily. To his surprise, she turned her head away. He bawled and cried, but she acted as if she didn't know he was there. He called out the most pitiful things to make her feel sorry for him, so he could cry with more reason, but she might have been stone-deaf for all the notice of it she took. He found his eyes drying up despite himself. Though he tried to fetch tears again, none would come. Bitterness and hate for her rose in him instead.

"Don't you know me? I'm Ansell Sloan! They call me Andy in Black Run!" he cried at her.

He might as well have been crying to the wind. She sat calm and contained, attending her baby. That puny thing and herself were all that mattered to her. She was like an Indian herself, and next day when they moved through the woods, he watched her carry her pack of savage booty like a squaw. Not once did he hear her rebel or complain. He was only a boy, but twice with spirit he threw off the stolen horns heavy with powder they had hung around his neck. In the end, he had to carry them anyhow, along with the cuts and bruises they gave him.

Now wouldn't you reckon she'd feel for him when his captors beat him so that he would sob for a long time afterward? But hardly a word from her, except to taunt him for bawling. Then hate for her would make him stop quick enough. No sooner would they camp in the evening and the fire at dusk set him crying for home than she would mock him for it until he answered in kind.

The Indians only laughed and egged them on. This was a big joke to them, something that gave the savages pleasure — two white persons who couldn't stand together against their common enemy but fought each other. Most always after a fight between them, the Indians treated her better and slackened her bonds.

"Injun pet! Turncoat!" he scorned her more than once, but she gave him no notice that she had heard.

For days the party had marched through the woods. Once they stopped while two of their men stole away to bring back mysterious news in their own language. Next morning the party split, and the captives were left in camp under the guard of a savage they called Onchedunk. Andy cried when the Indian tied him so tight that it hurt.

"Watch out. Don't cross him," Mary Harris warned. "He's the one that massacred the other boy."

"You care more about that other boy than me!" Andy accused.

"I ought to," Mary Harris said bitterly. "He was my own Billy."

Andy looked at her with a sudden start. He was sober now. His eyes went dry. He stared uneasily at the savage who had done it, his face painted in colors that had run in the rain so that they distorted his features. A large bunch of hair from some former scalping had been dyed bright red and fixed to the top of his head, while a piece of bright metal hung from his nose and covered much of his mouth, so that he looked like a picture of the devil.

Now how could Mary Harris let such a terrifying creature hurt her and never a whimper? He trussed her so that hardly could she hold the babe. He pulled on the knots so it must have cut into her woman's flesh. And all the time he was the one who had killed and scalped her own boy before her eyes. And yet her face hardly changed. Not a complaint did she make. Then Onchedunk took his gun and left.

It wasn't long afterward when a flock of migrating birds, mostly with red-speckled breasts, swarmed into camp, picking up crumbs from around the fire. They must have taken the two bound prisoners for stumps, for they flittered close to both, and especially the young woman, chittering and chirping until finally they flew off into the woods.

"Them birds say anything to you?" Mary Harris asked when they had gone.

"Birds can't talk," the boy told her.

"Oh, they don't talk sniveling and pigeonhearted like you," she said. "Their talk was spunky and cheerful. They said, what was I doin' here? Why didn't I up and go?"

The boy looked at Mary Harris strangely. He had heard that being captured by Indians sometimes affected white minds. Now he saw her begin to inch herself and child toward the fire. When she got there, she struggled to hold her bound bare legs over the low flame. The boy watched. He saw the white ankles grow black with burn, but still she kept them there. Several times her legs tried to burst the bonds, but she had to put herself again to the fire. In the end, the rawhide snapped, but not until a long, painful time had passed. Then she moved quickly to the pile of booty. With her bare toes she pulled out a rusty ax taken from some ravaged white cabin. Holding the blade up between her feet, she bent forward and severed the thongs binding her arms.

Now wasn't it a shame that this was when Onchedunk chose to return. They heard him coming. She tried to get back where she had been, putting the broken strips of hide around her, but before she was settled, he was there. Never in his life would the boy forget the look on the returned Indian's face — a look of fierce rage that she had tried to escape. With the barrel of his gun, he gave her a blow that knocked her over on the ground. The baby screamed.

"Give um!" Onchedunk said, dropping his gun and holding out his hands for the child.

When she refused, he tore at the baby with both hands. Then she let it go sooner than see its tiny arms pulled from their sockets. Twisting his face, Onchedunk lifted it up to dash the small head against a tree. At the sight, Mary Harris sprang like a she-panther. She snatched up the rusty ax and went for him. The Indian saw her coming and quickly laid down the screaming child, motioning for her to do the same with the ax.

"No, you wily snake in the grass!" she answered, and the boy had never seen her eyes so black. "You'd murder us both!"

It was doubtful if the savage understood the words, but he did her face and manner. Jerking at the hatchet in his belt with one hand, he reached for his gun with the other. Before he got hold of it, she was on him with her weapon.

"Now it's either you or us!" she cried.

The boy shut his eyes. He heard a confused series of sounds, but except for the screaming of the baby, he couldn't tell what they were. In his heart he believed that no half-starved, barefooted white woman, not even an outraged mother, could be a match for this Indian. The crying of the baby suddenly ceased. He shuddered, closing his eyes the tighter, waiting for his own end.

"You can look now. It's all over," he heard Mary Harris say.

When he opened his eyes, the Indian lay on his face, and the baby was back in the arms of its mother.

"Did you kill him?" he stammered.

"He'd 'a' took our hair, but we won't take his," she said.

"He looks so — bloody," Andy whimpered.

"How do you expect him to look?" she demanded. "You want your enemies done away with before they do away with you, but you want somebody else to do it someplace where you can't see it. Well, sometimes God Almighty puts you in a place where you got to do it your own self as best you can."

It took only a few moments to cut his thongs.

"I don't know whether to leave you or take you along," she said. "They'll likely kill you if they catch us. But they'll kill you for spite if they find you still here."

She scratched the booty pile, hunting for food. There was nothing save a doeskin bag of spoiled meal, crawling with worms, and a small piece of dried venison, dark and rock-hard. Andy tried to take a captured musket. He lifted its terrible weight.

"It's not for the puny," Mary Harris said. Barefooted, with only the hunk of venison and her child, she started off, taking to the woods instead of the path by which they had come.

"That's not the way," the boy protested.

"They won't look for us so quick in the brush," she said.

Once away from camp, freedom was almost too sweet to bear. They had escaped from the savages at last. Every wild glade looked good. A tiny stream ran across their way, and they lay down on its mossy bank to drink. Before they were on their feet, they heard a savage hallooing far in the leafy reaches behind them.

"They come back and found him," Mary said grimly.

Soon the sound of a musket echoed among the hills. A little later, faintly and from a great distance, came an answer; not one shot, but two. After an interval the nearer rifle sounded again. This time Mary Harris didn't speak. Both of them knew what it meant. Whoever had returned had sounded the alarm. His distant companions had heard and answered, telling him they were on the way back and, whatever the trouble, they would soon be there to help.

The boy hurried on as best he could. He was still free, but only now did he recognize what a terrible freedom it was, a hundred and fifty miles or more in the wilderness, with no roads, just Indian paths and streams that ran as freely in Indian country as in white, and with signs that could be read only by the savages who had the country mapped out in their minds.

They kept going that day until they could no longer see. That night no painful thongs dug into the boy's flesh, but neither was there the comfort of a fire. He lay close to Mary Harris for warmth and for protection against the black unknown. Not for a minute would he have admitted it to her. He had long since learned not to try to enlist her pity. But just being with her made him feel stronger, and the closer the stronger.

At the first glimmer of light through the trees, they were off, stumbling through the fog-choked woods. As a captive he had had little concern of them missing their way. Now their lostness and vast uncertainty in the woods lay on him. But if Mary Harris felt anything, she didn't show it.

"We got sunup to foller in the morning and sunset to keep at our back in the evening. What more do you want?" she said.

Oh, she was a hard taskmaster and let him take no easy way. Once they broke out of the woods into a wild open meadow of coarse grass. It was like coming alive again for the boy, but she plunged him quick as she could into a dense forest of hemlock and pine, where it was dark even by day and the ground lay carpeted with brown needles.

"They won't track us so easy in here," she said.

More than once they came on trails in the forest, not the narrow deer paths that soon petered out. These were wider trails, plainly made by human feet. They looked inviting, a far easier road than over logs and through the brush. The boy would have gladly taken one of them, but Mary Harris would have none of one or the other.

"That's where they'd lay to jump us," she said.

It was late afternoon when they came out on the bushy, bald knob of a hill. This, they could see, was the end of the forest valley they had been traveling since they left camp. Ahead lay two valleys. They couldn't see much, just the wooded openings to each. Now which should they take? Both seemed to lead in an easterly direction. Later they were to learn that only one ran east. The other gradualy turned and led south and back to the western wilderness and the Indians.

For a long time they stood ragged and puzzled, trying to think. Even Mary Harris seemed unable to decide. As they waited, a twittering of birds grew closer in the trees and a flock of red-speckled breasts landed in the bushes about them.

"Why, them look like those same birds that came to our camp," Mary Harris said.

As they watched, the flock, with sudden unity, took wing and flew down the left of the unknown valleys. The boy saw a look of cruel resolve come over his companion's face.

"I listened to them before and I'll listen to them again," she said, and started to follow.

It turned out to be a rough, discouraging valley, filled with obstructions that boded no good for their choice. The second afternoon the boy said he could make it no farther, not till tomorrow anyway. He was plumb worn out. He lay on his face on a drift of last year's leaves. No, he wouldn't get up any more today. Mary Harris had to lay down her child to yank him to his feet. The moment the baby was set on the ground, it started to squall. The squalling must have sounded a long way through the woods. Far off, they heard an Indian halloo, then an answer from the mountain.

At the terrible sound, the boy got to his feet quickly enough. He trembled so much that Marry Harris had to lead him to a fallen hemlock tree. They climbed its prostrate trunk until hidden in the thickest branches. Settled here for only a little while, they heard the unmistakable click of a ramrod in a rifle barrel. Then all was silent, but they knew that an Indian stood nearby, listening for the first sound to give them away.

More than once Andy had complained on the journey that he didn't care if he lived or died, if the savages got him or not. But now that one actually stood only yards away, it terrified him. Every minute he feared the baby would cry again. The smallest sound or gurgle must betray their hiding place. Hour after hour, Mary Harris sat stolidly with the child pressed tightly against her breast. It slept on, and when it awoke she nursed it. What nourishment it could find in its mother's starved body, the boy didn't know. Never had day held on so long. The savage must have gone, he thought. But when dusk fell thick on the woods, they knew he had been there all the time. Still only rods away, he uttered a terrible yell. Then they heard him leave, hallooing to his distant companion.

Before leaving the fallen tree in the morning, they had the last of the carefully treasured hunk of venison. Black, hard, and tasteless as it was, Andy hated to see it go. Now nothing stood between them and starvation. That day they splashed through a swamp where the trees stood gaunt and lifeless above them and the brown, stagnant water smelled of death. They chewed the tendrils of the wild grapevines for food and ate what tiny applelike fruits of the wild thorn trees they could find. Of all the country they went through, the thorn-tree thickets were the worst, whipping them, tearing their clothing to shreds, leaving long, bloody scratches on their bodies.

Wherever darkness overtook them, they spent the night, once in a region of rocks, once in a brake of rhododendrons. Hope each morning was soon succeeded by daze and exhaustion. What day of the week or month it was, neither of them had any notion. The morning after the thorn-thicket passage, the boy fell down and couldn't get up.

"You go on," he told her. "Let the Injuns get me."

"You always got to fight something in this life," she said. "If it ain't Injuns, it's something else."

"I can't fight no more," he told her.

She had to take a stick then to beat him up, like the savages did, and after that she wouldn't let him sit down.

"You're worse'n the Injuns!" he cried at her.

"Go holler and bring 'em on. You'll find out who's the worser," she told him.

"You're a devil!" he sobbed at her another time.

"You ain't seen half of me yet," she promised. "Lay down again and you'll find out."

He called her all the mean names he'd ever heard. Had he known she was like this, never would he have left camp with her. But nothing he said did any good. She kept driving him on. Just the same, he could tell she was weakening. Her gray dress, long whipped by the brush, hung on her in rags. Her arms and legs and face were bleeding. Next morning, through half-closed eyes, he watched her. After nursing her young one, hardly could she draw herself up by a sapling to her feet.

She can't go far any more, he kept telling himself that day. *Then we can both lay down and die together*.

Around noon he thought she was ready to give up. She had turned on him a glazed eye.

"Listen. Did you hear it?" she asked.

"Hear what?" he mumbled. "I didn't hear nothing."

"I thought I heard a hound," she muttered.

They stood for a time, but the only thing that came to their ears was the sound of the wind in the trees. Could it be she was weak and losing her mind already, hearing things like folks did when they got lost in the woods? Many times after that he noticed she stopped; just the way she stood, he could tell she was listening for the hound she thought she heard. But no voice of a dog came, and none during the night. Morning, when he looked at her, she lay like a dead person, the baby like a bundle of skin and bone in her arms. Then he saw her stir and watched as incredibly she pulled herself to her feet.

Never would they get far from this place, the boy told himself. Then they both saw what they had failed to see in the darkness when they lay down last night — what looked like a wall of logs hardly a dozen rods off in the forest. They stumbled nearer. It was an old cabin with a roof of bark and a window such as only a white man would make. The cabin stood black, fallen in and abandoned, but never did any house look so beautiful. Then, as they stood staring at it, they could hear, faint and far away through the morning mist, a sound neither of them could mistake.

"Cowbells!" Mary Harris whispered.

Before noon they reached the river. On the other side they could hear the cowbells more plainly now. To the north, blue pine smoke rose from chimneys among the trees. They took a path under the sycamores till they were across from the settlement. They saw a man fishing on the other side. When they called to him, he dropped his pole and ran. Presently they saw him come back with another man. Both carried guns. They got into a boat. Andy thought they were coming to get them, but the boat moved less than halfway across the water. Here it stopped.

"What do you want?" one of the men called.

"We belong over 'ar. We want to git across."

"You don't look white to us."

"I'm Mary Harris, from Black Run."

The two men conferred.

"You ain't her. She was took by the Indians."

"I know. I'm just agittin' back."

"You ain't Mary Harris. I knowed her. I seed her many a time."

The young woman looked down at herself. As if for the first time, she realized she was half naked, her clothes in shreds, her skin dark with blood and dirt, her hair a tangled mat. She looked forty years old.

"I'm her all right. If you come over, I can prove it."

"No, we ain't comin' nearer. You might have Indian friends in the bushes alayin' for us."

"Well, if you won't come over, I reckon I'll have to wade out to you the best I can," she said.

"No, it's too deep!" both men called, but she paid no attention. She handed the child to the boy. She warned him sternly not to let her fall. Then she stepped into the water and kept on till it reached her shoulders and threatened to engulf her head.

"Wait!" one man called. "We'll come a mite closer!"

Cautiously the boat edged toward her. Bit by bit, it grew nearer, until the boy heard an exclamation, followed by others. The boat came faster now, and he saw both men lift the dripping woman in. After that they paddled for Andy and the baby, left on the bank.

Boys must have run with the news, for the far bank swarmed with folks by the time the boat touched shore. Before they got there, the older boatman had taken off the hunting shirt that came halfway to his knees, and had given it to Mary to hide her nakedness. Now a man on horseback dismounted to let the exhausted woman ride. Against all these well-fed people, she looked little more than a skeleton, and so must he, too, the boy reckoned, for they lifted him up to ride behind her. Over and over, as the people trooped after, he heard them say how never would they have known her.

In the nearest house they put her to bed. Some of the women began pulling thorns from her feet. They counted a hundred and twelve and laid them on a piece of crockery to show. Others of the women had set to cooking. Now it began to smell good. Mary Harris and the young ones had starved a long time, but their empty bellies would get stuffed with rations now.

It was a man they called Major, in smallclothes,[1] his hair in a queue, who put a stop to it. He came stamping into the house with his cane and smelled the cookery.

"What's this?" he thundered. "You'll kill her! And the boy too! The first day you must give them nothing but whey. One spoonful at a time."

The boy hated him. Others would get the venison stew now. But he hated worse the other man who came bursting in the door after dark. All afternoon Andy had been lying on the bed beside Mary, as he had lain beside her so many nights in the woods, but never had he felt such possession and tenderness for her as now when others tried to come between them. She had fetched him out of the woods. If it hadn't been for her, he would not be here. Her face looked almost like a dead woman's on the bolster, but she needn't worry. Never would he leave her. Soon as he was bigger, he would marry and support her.

He felt outraged and affronted when this stranger came and claimed her as his wife. He hadn't even reckoned on a husband. Why couldn't the Indians have got him, like they had so many? But no, here he was putting his rough green-and-blue linsey[2] arm over Mary Harris and her looking up at him like she had never looked at Andy.

"You leave her alone!" the boy said sharply. When some of the onlookers laughed, he turned his face away.

That laugh burned bitter inside of him. He tried to get up and go off by himself, but they wouldn't let him. All night he lay there hating Mary Harris's man. In the woods he had had her all to himself. Now he must share her with this ugly fellow.

Only Mary Harris's babe gave him comfort. The child knew him, had time for him, played with him a little, pulled and fiddled with his long hair. He looked the babe over with lackluster eyes. Anyway, she wasn't married. She wasn't tied up with any man. Should he want to, he might stake first rights to her. She wasn't much as yet, but she was something. If he couldn't have the mother, he might

---

[1] *smallclothes:* close-fitting knee breeches.
[2] *linsey:* a coarse cloth of linen and wool.

have the daughter — some time on ahead when she got old enough to have a man.

The old man came back to the present with a start. Where was he? Oh, yes, here in the mansion office. Well, he did marry the daughter, didn't he? There was her picture hanging on the wall. But it was the woman in the other picture who still stirred him the most. He'd never forget her. She was the one to put iron in a man's soul.

VI. THE IRONIC HERO

A hero is usually thought to be superior in virtue as well as in deed, a model for others to imitate. But many of the heroes of modern literature are really "anti-heroes" — they are absurd or insignificant. In the following story, James Thurber writes about an anti-hero of modern times.

The Greatest Man in the World

JAMES THURBER

Looking back on it now, from the vantage point of 1940, one can only marvel that it hadn't happened long before it did. The United States of America had been, ever since Kitty Hawk,[1] blindly constructing the elaborate petard by which, sooner or later, it must be hoist.[2] It was inevitable that some day there would come roaring out of the skies a national hero of insufficient intelligence, background, and character successfully to endure the mounting orgies of glory prepared by aviators who stayed up a long time or flew a great distance. Both Lindbergh and Byrd,[3] fortunately for national decorum and international amity, had been gentlemen; so had our other famous aviators. They wore their laurels gracefully, withstood the awful weather of publicity, married excellent women, usually of fine family, and quietly retired to private life and the enjoyment of their varying fortunes. No untoward incidents, on a worldwide scale, marred the perfection of their conduct on the perilous heights of fame. The exception to the rule was,

---

[1] *Kitty Hawk:* site of Wright brothers' first airplane flight in 1903.
[2] *petard . . . hoist:* to "hoist with one's own petard" is to be victimized or harmed by one's own plans or actions.
[3] *Admiral Richard E. Byrd* (1888–1957): U.S. aviator and polar explorer.

however, bound to occur, and it did, in July 1937, when Jack ("Pal") Smurch, erstwhile mechanic's helper in a small garage in Westfield, Iowa, flew a second-hand, single-motored Bresthaven Dragon-Fly III monoplane all the way around the world, without stopping.

Never before in the history of aviation had such a flight as Smurch's ever been dreamed of. No one had even taken seriously the weird floating auxiliary gas tanks, invention of the mad New Hampshire professor of astronomy, Dr. Charles Lewis Gresham, upon which Smurch placed full reliance. When the garage worker, a slightly built, surly, unprepossessing young man of twenty-two, appeared at Roosevelt Field in early July 1937, slowly chewing a great quid of scrap tobacco, and announced, "Nobody ain't seen no flyin' yet," the newspapers touched briefly and satirically upon his projected twenty-five-thousand-mile flight. Aeronautical and automotive experts dismissed the idea curtly, implying that it was a hoax, a publicity stunt. The rusty, battered, second-hand plane wouldn't go. The Gresham auxiliary tanks wouldn't work. It was simply a cheap joke.

Smurch, however, after calling on a girl in Brooklyn who worked in the flap-folding department of a large paper-box factory, a girl whom he later described as his "sweet patootie," climbed non-chalantly into his ridiculous plane at dawn of the memorable seventh of July, 1937, spit a curve of tobacco juice into the still air, and took off, carrying with him only a gallon of bootleg gin and six pounds of salami.

When the garage boy thundered out over the ocean, the papers were forced to record, in all seriousness, that a mad, unknown young man — his name was variously misspelled — had actually set out upon a preposterous attempt to span the world in a rickety, one-engined contraption, trusting to the long-distance refueling device of a crazy schoolmaster. When, nine days later, without having stopped once, the tiny plane appeared above San Francisco Bay, headed for New York, spluttering and choking, to be sure, but still magnificently and miraculously aloft, the headlines, which long since had crowded everything else off the front page — even the shooting of the Governor of Illinois by the Vileti gang — swelled to unprecedented size, and the news stories began to run to twenty-five and thirty columns. It was noticeable, however, that the accounts of the epoch-making flight touched rather lightly upon the aviator himself. This was not because facts about the hero as a man were too meager but because they were too complete.

Reporters, who had been rushed out to Iowa when Smurch's plane was first sighted over the little French coast town of Serly-le-Mer, to dig up the story of the great man's life, had promptly discovered that the story of his life could not be printed. His mother, a sullen short-order cook in a shack restaurant on the edge of a tourists' camping ground near Westfield, met all inquiries as to her son with an angry "Ah, I hope he drowns." His father appeared to be in jail somewhere for stealing spotlights and lap robes from tourists' automobiles; his younger brother, a weak-minded lad, had but recently escaped from the Preston, Iowa, Reformatory and was already wanted in several western towns for the theft of money-order blanks from post offices. These alarming discoveries were still piling up at the very time that Pal Smurch, the greatest hero of the twentieth century, blear-eyed, dead for sleep, half-starved, was piloting his crazy junkheap high above the region in which the lamentable story of his private life was being unearthed, headed for New York and a greater glory than any man of his time had ever known.

The necessity for printing some account in the papers of the young man's career and personality had led to a remarkable predicament. It was of course impossible to reveal the facts, for a tremendous popular feeling in favor of the young hero had sprung up, like a grass fire, when he was halfway across Europe on his flight around the globe. He was, therefore, described as a modest chap, taciturn, blond, popular with his friends, popular with girls. The only available snapshot of Smurch, taken at the wheel of a phony automobile in a cheap photo studio at an amusement park, was touched up so that the little vulgarian looked quite handsome. His twisted leer was smoothed into a pleasant smile. The truth was, in this way, kept from the youth's ecstatic compatriots; they did not dream that the Smurch family was despised and feared by its neighbors in the obscure Iowa town, nor that the hero himself, because of numerous unsavory exploits, had come to be regarded in Westfield as a nuisance and a menace. He had, the reporters discovered, once knifed the principal of his high school — not mortally, to be sure, but he had knifed him; and on another occasion, surprised in the act of stealing an altar cloth from a church, he had bashed the sacristan over the head with a pot of Easter lilies; for each of these offenses he had served a sentence in the reformatory.

Inwardly, the authorities, both in New York and in Washington, prayed that an understanding Providence might, however awful such a thing seemed, bring disaster to the rusty, battered plane and its illustrious pilot, whose unheard-of flight had aroused the civilized world to hosannas of hysterical praise. The authorities were convinced that the character of the renowned aviator was such that the limelight of adulation was bound to reveal him, to all the world, as a congenital hooligan mentally and morally unequipped to cope with his own prodigious fame. "I trust," said the Secretary of State, at one of many secret Cabinet meetings called to consider the national dilemma, "I trust that his mother's prayer will be answered," by which he referred to Mrs. Emma Smurch's wish that her might be drowned. It was, however, too late for that — Smurch had leaped the Atlantic and then the Pacific as if they were millponds. At three minutes after two o'clock on the afternoon of July 17, 1937, the garage boy brought his idiotic plane into Roosevelt Field for a perfect three-point landing.

It had, of course, been out of the question to arrange a modest little reception for the greatest flier in the history of the world. He was received at Roosevelt Field with such elaborate and pretentious ceremonies as rocked the world. Fortunately, however, the worn and spent hero promptly swooned, had to be removed bodily from his plane, and was spirited from the field without having opened his mouth once. Thus he did not jeopardize the dignity of this first reception, a reception illumined by the presence of the Secretaries of War and the Navy, Mayor Michael J. Moriarity of New York, the Premier of Canada, Governors Fanniman, Groves, McFeely, and Critchfield, and a brilliant array of European diplomats. Smurch did not, in fact, come to in time to take part in the gigantic hullabaloo arranged at City Hall for the next day. He was rushed to a secluded nursing home and confined in bed. It was nine days before he was able to get up or, to be more exact, before he was permitted to get up. Meanwhile the greatest minds in the country, in solemn assembly, had arranged a secret conference of city, state, and government officials, which Smurch was to attend for the purpose of being instructed in the ethics and behavior of heroism.

On the day that the little mechanic was finally allowed to get up and dress and, for the first time in two weeks, took a great chew of tobacco, he was permitted to receive the newspapermen — this by way of testing him out. Smurch did not wait for questions. "Youse guys," he said — and the *Times* man winced — "youse guys can tell the cock-eyed world dat I put it over on Lindbergh, see? Yeh — an' made fools o' them two frogs." The "two frogs" was a reference to a pair of gallant French fliers who, in attempting a flight only halfway round the world, had, two weeks before, unhappily been lost at sea. The *Times* man was bold enough, at this point, to sketch out for Smurch the accepted formula for interviews in cases of this kind; he explained that there should be no arrogant statements belittling the achievements of other heroes, particularly heroes of foreign nations. "Ah, enough of that," said Smurch. "I did it, see? I did it, an' I'm talkin' about it." And he did talk about it.

None of this extraordinary interview was, of course, printed. On the contrary, the newspapers, already under the disciplined direction of a secret directorate created for the occasion and composed of statesmen and editors, gave out to a panting and restless world that "Jacky," as he had been arbitrarily nicknamed, would consent to say only that he was very happy and that anyone could have done what he did. "My achievement has been, I fear, slightly exaggerated," the *Times* man's article had him protest, with a modest smile. These newspaper stories were kept from the hero, a restriction which did not serve to abate the rising malevolence of his temper. The situation was, indeed, extremely grave, for Pal Smurch was, as he kept insisting, "rarin' to go." He could not much longer be kept from a nation clamorous to lionize him. It was the most desperate crisis the United States of America had faced since the sinking of the *Lusitania*.[4]

On the afternoon of the twenty-seventh of July, Smurch was spirited away to a conference room in which were gathered mayors, governors, government officials, behaviorist psychologists, and editors. He gave them each a limp, moist paw and a brief, unlovely grin. "Hah ya?" he said. When Smurch was seated, the Mayor of New York arose and, with obvious pessimism, attempted to explain what he must say and how he must act when presented to the

---

4 *Lusitania*: British ship sunk by the Germans during World War I.

world, ending his talk with a high tribute to the hero's courage and integrity. The Mayor was followed by Governor Fanniman of New York, who, after a touching declaration of faith, introduced Cameron Spottiswood, Second Secretary of the American Embassy in Paris, the gentleman selected to coach Smurch in the amenities of public ceremonies. Sitting in a chair, with a soiled yellow tie in his hand and his shirt open at the throat, unshaved, smoking a rolled cigarette, Jack Smurch listened with a leer on his lips. "I get ya, I get ya," he cut in nastily. "Ya want me to ack like a softy, huh? Ya want me to ack like that —— —— baby-faced Lindbergh, huh? Well, nuts to that, see?" Everyone took in his breath sharply; it was a sigh and a hiss. "Mr. Lindbergh," began a United States Senator, purple with rage, "and Mr. Byrd — " Smurch, who was paring his nails with a jackknife, cut in again. "Byrd!" he exclaimed. "Aw, *dat* big — " Somebody shut off his blasphemies with a sharp word. A newcomer had entered the room. Everyone stood up, except Smurch, who, still busy with his nails, did not even glance up. "Mr. Smurch," said someone sternly, "the President of the United States!" It had been thought that the presence of the Chief Executive might have a chastening effect upon the young hero, and the former had been, thanks to the remarkable cooperation of the press, secretly brought to the obscure conference room.

A great, painful silence fell. Smurch looked up, waved a hand at the President. "How ya comin'?" he asked, and began rolling a fresh cigarette. The silence deepened. Someone coughed in a strained way. "Geez, it's hot, ain't it?" said Smurch. He loosened two more shirt buttons, revealing a hairy chest and the tattooed word "Sadie" enclosed in a stenciled heart. The great and important men in the room, faced by the most serious crisis in recent American history, exchanged worried frowns. Nobody seemed to know how to proceed. "Come awn, come awn," said Smurch. "Let's get out of here! When do I start cuttin' in on de parties, huh? And what's they goin' to be *in* it?" He rubbed a thumb and forefinger together meaningly. "Money!" exclaimed a state senator, shocked, pale. "Yeh, money," said Pal, flipping his cigarette out of a window. "An' big money." He began rolling a fresh cigarette. "Big money," he repeated, frowning over the rice paper. He tilted back in his chair and leered at each gentleman, separately, the leer of an animal that knows its power, the leer of a leopard loose in a bird-and-dog shop. "Aw, let's get some place where it's cooler," he said. "I been cooped up plenty for three weeks!"

Smurch stood up and walked over to an open window, where he stood staring down into the street, nine floors below. The faint shouting of newsboys floated up to him. He made out his name. "Hot dog!" he cried, grinning, ecstatic. He leaned out over the sill. "You tell 'em, babies!" he shouted down. "Hot diggity dog!" In the tense little knot of men standing behind him, a quick, mad impulse flared up. An unspoken word of appeal, of command, seemed to ring through the room. Yet it was deadly silent. Charles K. L. Brand, secretary to the Mayor of New York City, happened to be standing nearest Smurch; he looked inquiringly at the President of the United States. The President, pale, grim, nodded shortly. Brand, a tall, powerfully built man, once a tackle at Rutgers, stepped forward, seized the greatest man in the world by his left shoulder and the seat of his pants, and pushed him out the window.

"He's fallen out the window!" cried a quick-witted editor.

"Get me out of here!" cried the President. Several men sprang to his side, and he was hurriedly escorted out of a door toward a side entrance of the building. The editor of the Associated Press took charge, being used to such things. Crisply he ordered certain men to leave, others to stay; quickly he outlined a story which all the papers were to agree on, sent two men to the street to handle that end of the tragedy, commanded a Senator to sob and two Congressmen to go to pieces nervously. In a word, he skillfully set the stage for the gigantic task that was to follow, the task of breaking to a grief-stricken world the sad story of the untimely, accidental death of its most illustrious and spectacular figure.

The funeral was, as you know, the most elaborate, the finest, the solemnest, and the saddest ever held in the United States of America. The monument in Arlington Cemetery, with its clean white shaft of marble and the simple device of a tiny plane carved on its base, is a place for pilgrims, in deep reverence, to visit. The nations of the world paid lofty tributes to little Jacky Smurch, America's greatest hero. At a given hour there were two minutes of silence throughout the nation. Even the inhabitants of the small, bewildered town of Westfield, Iowa, observed this touching ceremony; agents of the Department of Justice saw to that. One of them was especially assigned to stand grimly in the doorway of a little shack restaurant on the edge of the tourists' camping ground just outside the town. There, under his stern scrutiny, Mrs. Emma Smurch bowed her head above two hamburger steaks sizzling on her grill — bowed her head and turned away, so that the Secret Service man could not see the twisted, strangely familiar, leer on her lips.

VII. THE HERO AND THE MASS MEDIA

In this section from an essay on one of America's true heroes, Charles Lindbergh, the author makes a distinction which sometimes becomes lost in an age of publicity.

From Hero to Celebrity

DANIEL BOORSTIN

As other pseudo-events [1] in our day tend to overshadow spontaneous events, so celebrities (who are human pseudo-events) tend to overshadow heroes. They are more up-to-date, more nationally advertised, and more apt to have press agents. And there are far more of them. Celebrities die quickly, but they are still more quickly replaced. Every year we experience a larger number than the year before.

Just as real events tend to be cast in the mold of pseudo-events, so in our society heroes survive by acquiring the qualities of celebrities. The best publicized seems the most authentic experience. If someone does a heroic deed in our time, all the machinery of public information — press, pulpit, radio, and television — soon transform him into a celebrity. If they cannot succeed in this, the would-be hero disappears from public view.

A dramatic, a tragic, example is the career of Charles A. Lindbergh. He performed singlehanded one of the heroic deeds of this century. His deed was heroic in the best epic mold. But he became degraded into a celebrity. He then ceased to symbolize the virtues to which his heroic deed gave him a proper claim. He became filled with emptiness; then he disappeared from view. How did this happen?

---

[1] *pseudo-events:* the author defines a pseudo-event as a man-made synthetic happening, as opposed to a real event. Pseudo-events are planned or planted, primarily to be reported in the news media.

On May 21, 1927, Charles A. Lindbergh made the first nonstop solo flight from Roosevelt Field, New York, to Le Bourget Air Field, Paris, in a monoplane, *The Spirit of St. Louis*. This was plainly a heroic deed in the classic sense; it was a deed of valor — alone against the elements. In a dreary, unheroic decade Lindbergh's flight was a lightning flash of individual courage. Except for the fact of his flight, Lindbergh was a commonplace person. Twenty-five years old at the time, he had been born in Detroit and raised in Minnesota. He was not a great inventor or a leader of men. He was not extraordinarily intelligent, eloquent, or ingenious. Like many other young man in those years, he had a fanatical love of flying. The air was his element. There he showed superlative skill and extraordinary courage — even to foolhardiness.

He was an authentic hero. Yet this was not enough. Or perhaps it was too much. For he was destined to be made into a mere celebrity, and he was to be the American celebrity par excellence. His rise and fall as a hero, his tribulations, his transformation, and his rise and decline as a celebrity are beautifully told in Kenneth S. Davis's biography.

Lindbergh himself had not failed to predict that his exploit would put him in the news. Before leaving New York he had sold to *The New York Times* the exclusive story of his flight. A supposedly naive and diffident boy, on his arrival in Paris he was confronted by a crowd of newspaper reporters at a press conference in Ambassador Myron T. Herrick's residence. But he would not give out any statement until he had clearance from the *Times* representative. He had actually subscribed to a newspaper-clipping service, the clippings to be sent to his mother, who was then teaching school in Minnesota. With uncanny foresight, however, he had limited his subscriptions to clippings to the value of fifty dollars.

Lindbergh's newspaper success was unprecedented. The morning after his flight *The New York Times*, a model of journalistic sobriety, gave him the whole of its first five pages, except for a few ads on page 5. Other papers gave as much or more. Radio commentators talked of him by the hour. But there was not much hard news available. The flight was a relatively simple operation, lasting only thirty-three and a half hours. Lindbergh had told reporters in Paris just about all there was to tell. During his twenty-five years he had led a relatively uneventful life. He had few quirks of face, of figure, or of personality; little was known about his character. Some young women called him "tall and handsome," but his physical averageness was striking. He was the boy next door. To tell about this young man on the day after his flight, the nation's newspapers used 25,000 tons of newsprint more than usual. In many places sales were two to five times normal and might have been higher if the presses could have turned out more papers.

When Lindbergh returned to New York on June 13, 1927, *The New York Times* gave its first sixteen pages the next morning almost exclusively to news about him. At the testimonial dinner in Lindbergh's honor at the Hotel Commodore (reputed to be the largest for an individual "in modern history") Charles Evans Hughes, former Secretary of State, and about to become Chief Justice of the United States, delivered an extravagant eulogy. With unwitting precision he characterized the American hero-turned-celebrity: "We measure heroes as we do ships, by their displacement. Colonel Lindbergh has displaced everything."

Lindbergh was by now the biggest human pseudo-event of modern times. His achievement, actually because it had been accomplished so neatly and with such spectacular simplicity, offered little spontaneous news. The biggest news about Lindbergh was that he was such big news. Pseudo-events multiplied in more than the usual geometric progression, for Lindbergh's well-knownness was so sudden and so overwhelming. It was easy to make stories about what a big celebrity he was: how this youth, unknown a few days before, was now a household word, how he was received by presidents and kings and bishops. There was little else one could say about him. Lindbergh's singularly impressive heroic deed was soon far overshadowed by his even more impressive publicity. If well-knownness made a celebrity, here was the greatest. Of course, it was remarkable to fly the ocean by oneself but far more remarkable thus to dominate the news. His stature as hero was nothing compared with his stature as celebrity. All the more because it had happened, literally, overnight.

Among the most highly-prized sculptures in world art are the
Benin bronzes such as this of a musician. Mastery of the difficult
art of casting in bronze attests to the high degree of civilization
attained in the 15th century in this West African nation.

BOOK FOUR

READINGS IN WORLD LITERATURE

Part One: Drama

Shakespeare's Julius Caesar is a play set in the classical past. Jean Anouilh's Antigone is another. It is a modern version of a play which has been in existence for hundreds of years — the Antigone of Sophocles, a Greek playwright who died in 406 B.C.

Because Roman history is much more clearly documented than Greek history, most of the events in Julius Caesar may be said to have actually happened. The historical events on which Antigone is based, however, had faded into the past even in Sophocles's time. Thebes, the city-state where the play is set, existed. But did Antigone's father, Oedipus, actually live? Was the terrible fate that he and his children suffered really a matter of history? We do not know. Scholars once believed that Homer's Iliad was an invented tale; then the German archeologist Schliemann discovered the ruins of Troy and what had been called legend became history. It is possible that in the dim past the family of Oedipus did exist and met a terrible doom.

Classical Greek literature has always exercised a strong appeal on the French imagination. Earlier in this book, you read some animal fables by La Fontaine, who copied the form from the Greek Aesop. The modern French writer Jean Cocteau wrote a play about Oedipus called The Infernal Machine. The great playwright Jean Racine, called the "French Shakespeare," used Greek stories for the plots of all his plays. So Anouilh followed a French tradition in writing a modern version of a classical play.

Antigone was written in 1943, when Paris had been occupied for two years by German soldiers. The Germans held the country in an iron grip in spite of efforts by the French Resistance, an underground organization dedicated to the liberation of their country. Everything was controlled, from the administration of government to the selection of plays to be presented in French theaters.

When Anouilh presented Antigone to the German censors, they passed it, and the play was produced. Perhaps the censors thought that the play had no bearing on modern times, since it was based on an ancient Greek play. Perhaps they simply did not see the dangerous ideas in it. Whatever their reasons, the play became a sensation. French audiences saw a clear and immediate meaning in the story of a girl who placed her conscience above the law of the State and who resisted all efforts by the head of the State to force her cooperation. Watching Antigone, the French took secret courage to endure and to resist the enemies seated next to them in the theater.

Antigone

JEAN ANOUILH

CHARACTERS

CHORUS	FIRST GUARD (*Jonas*)
ANTIGONE	SECOND GUARD (*a Corporal*)
NURSE	THIRD GUARD
ISMENE	MESSENGER
HAEMON	PAGE
CREON	EURYDICE

ANTIGONE,[1] *her hands clasped round her knees, sits on the top step. The* THREE GUARDS *sit on the steps, in a small group, playing cards. The* CHORUS *stands on the top step.* EURYDICE [2] *sits on the top step, just left of center, knitting. The* NURSE *sits on the second step, left of* EURYDICE. ISMENE [3] *stands in front of arch, left, facing* HAEMON,[4] *who stands left of her.* CREON *sits in the chair at right end of the table, his arm over the shoulder of his* PAGE, *who sits on the stool beside his chair. The* MESSENGER *is leaning against the downstage portal of the right arch.*

[*The curtain rises slowly; then the* CHORUS *turns and moves downstage.*]

CHORUS. Well, here we are.

These people are about to act out for you the story of Antigone.

That thin little creature sitting by herself, staring straight ahead, seeing nothing, is Antigone. She is thinking. She is thinking that the instant I finish telling you who's who and what's what in this play, she will burst forth as the tense, sallow, willful girl whose family would never take her seriously and who is about to rise

---

[1] *Antigone* (an·tig′ə·nē).

[2] *Eurydice* (ōō·rid′ə·sē).

[3] *Ismene* (is·mē′nē).

[4] *Haemon* (hē′mən).

up alone against Creon, her uncle, the King.

Another thing that she is thinking is this: she is going to die. Antigone is young. She would much rather live than die. But there is no help for it. When your name is Antigone, there is only one part you can play; and she will have to play hers through to the end.

From the moment the curtain went up, she began to feel that inhuman forces were whirling her out of this world, snatching her away from her sister Ismene, whom you see smiling and chatting with that young man; from all of us who sit or stand here, looking at her, not in the least upset ourselves — for we are not doomed to die tonight. [CHORUS *turns and indicates* HAEMON.]

The young man talking to Ismene — to the gay and beautiful Ismene — is Haemon. He is the King's son, Creon's son. Antigone and he are engaged to be married. You wouldn't have thought she was his type. He likes dancing, sports, competition; he likes women, too. Now look at Ismene again. She is certainly more beautiful than Antigone. She is the girl you'd think he'd go for. Well. . . . There was a ball one night. Ismene wore a new evening frock. She was radiant. Haemon danced every dance with her. And yet, that same night, before the dance was over, suddenly he went in search of Antigone, found her sitting alone — like that, with her arms clasped round her knees — and asked her to marry him. We still don't know how it happened. It didn't seem to surprise Antigone in the least. She looked up at him out of those solemn eyes of hers, smiled sort of sadly and said "yes." That was all. The band struck up another dance. Ismene, surrounded by a group of young men, laughed out loud. And . . . well, here is Haemon expecting to marry Antigone. He won't, of course. He didn't know, when he asked her, that the earth wasn't meant to hold a husband of Antigone and that this princely distinction was to earn him no more than the right to die sooner than he might otherwise have done. [CHORUS *turns toward* CREON.]

That gray-haired, powerfully built man sitting lost in thought, with his little page at his side, is Creon, the King. His face is lined. He is tired. He practices the difficult art of a leader of men. When he was younger, when Oedipus [5] was King and Creon was no more than the King's brother-in-law, he was different. He

---

[5] *Oedipus* (ed′ə·pəs).

loved music, bought rare manuscripts, was a kind of art patron. He would while away whole afternoons in the antique shops of this city of Thebes. But Oedipus died. Oedipus's sons died. Creon had to roll up his sleeves and take over the kingdom. Now and then, when he goes to bed weary with the day's work, he wonders whether this business of being a leader of men is worth the trouble. But when he wakes up, the problems are there to be solved; and like a conscientious workman, he does his job.

Creon has a wife, a Queen. Her name is Eurydice. There she sits, the old lady with the knitting, next to the Nurse who brought up the two girls. She will go on knitting all through the play, till the times comes for her to go to her room and die. She is a good woman, a worthy, loving soul. But she is no help to her husband. Creon has to face the music alone. Alone with his Page, who is too young to be of any help.

The others? Well, let's see. [*He points toward the* MESSENGER.]

That pale young man leaning against the wall is the Messenger. Later on he will come running in to announce that Haemon is dead. He has a premonition of catastrophe. That's what he is brooding over. That's why he won't mingle with the others.

As for those three red-faced card players — they are the guards. One smells of garlic, another of beer; but they're not a bad lot. They have wives they are afraid of, kids who are afraid of them; they're bothered by the little day-to-day worries that beset us all. At the same time — they are policemen: eternally innocent, no matter what crimes are committed; eternally indifferent, for nothing that happens can matter to them. They are quite prepared to arrest anybody at all, including Creon himself, should the order be given by a new leader.

That's the lot. Now for the play.

Oedipus, who was the father of the two girls, Antigone and Ismene, had also two sons, Eteocles and Polynices.[6] After Oedipus died, it was agreed that the two sons should share his throne, each to reign over Thebes in alternate years.

[*Gradually, the lights on the stage have been dimmed.*]

But when Eteocles, the elder son, had reigned a full year, and time had come for him to step down, he refused to yield up the throne

---

6 *Eteocles* (i·tē′ə·klez), *Polynices* (pol′i·nī·sēz).

to his younger brother. There was civil war. Polynices brought up allies — six foreign princes; and in the course of the war he and his foreigners were defeated, each in front of one of the seven gates of the city. The two brothers fought, and they killed one another in single combat just outside the city walls. Now Creon is King.

[CHORUS *is leaning, at this point, against the left proscenium arch. By now the stage is dark, with only the cyclorama bathed in dark blue. A single spot lights up the face of* CHORUS.]

Creon has issued a solemn edict that Eteocles, with whom he had sided, is to be buried with pomp and honors, and that Polynices is to be left to rot. The vultures and the dogs are to bloat themselves on his carcass. Nobody is to go into mourning for him. No gravestone is to be set up in his memory. And above all, any person who attempts to give him religious burial will himself be put to death.

[*While* CHORUS *has been speaking the characters have gone out one by one.* CHORUS *disappears through the left arch.*]

It is dawn, gray and ashen, in a house asleep. ANTIGONE *steals in from out-of-doors, through the arch, right. She is carrying her sandals in her hand. She pauses, looking off through the arch, taut, listening, then turns and moves across downstage. As she reaches the table, she sees the* NURSE *approaching through the arch, left. She runs quickly toward the exit. As she reaches the steps, the* NURSE *enters through arch and stands still when she sees* ANTIGONE.

NURSE. Where have you been?

ANTIGONE. Nowhere. It was beautiful. The whole world was gray when I went out. And now — you wouldn't recognize it. It's like a postcard: all pink, and green, and yellow. You'll have to get up earlier, Nurse, if you want to see a world without color.

NURSE. It was still pitch black when I got up. I went to your room, for I thought you might have flung off your blanket in the night. You weren't there.

ANTIGONE (*comes down the steps*). The garden was lovely. It was still asleep. Have you ever thought how lovely a garden is when it is not yet thinking of men?

ANTIGONE   589

NURSE. You hadn't slept in your bed. I couldn't find you. I went to
the back door. You'd left it open.

ANTIGONE. The fields were wet. They were waiting for something to
happen. The whole world was breathless, waiting. I can't tell
you what a roaring noise I seemed to make alone on the road. It
bothered me that whatever was waiting wasn't waiting for me. I
took off my sandals and slipped into a field. [*She moves down to
the stool and sits.*]

NURSE (*kneels at* ANTIGONE's *feet to chafe them and put on the
sandals*). You'll do well to wash your feet before you go back to
bed, Miss.

ANTIGONE. I'm not going back to bed.

NURSE. Don't be a fool! You get some sleep! And me, getting up to
see if she hasn't flung off her blanket; and I find her bed cold and
nobody in it!

ANTIGONE. Do you think that if a person got up every morning like
this, it would be just as thrilling every morning to be the first
girl out-of-doors?

[NURSE *puts* ANTIGONE's *left foot down, lifts her other foot and
chafes it.*]

NURSE. Morning my grandmother! It was night. It still is. And now,
my girl, you'll stop trying to squirm out of this and tell me what
you were up to. Where've you been?

ANTIGONE. That's true. It was still night. There wasn't a soul out of
doors but me, who thought that it was morning. Don't you think
it's marvelous — to be the first person who is aware that it is
morning?

NURSE. Oh, my little flibbertigibbet! Just can't imagine what I'm
talking about, can she? Go on with you! I know that game.
Where have you been, wicked girl?

ANTIGONE (*soberly*). No. Not wicked.

NURSE. You went out to meet someone, didn't you? Deny it if you
can.

ANTIGONE. Yes. I went out to meet someone.

NURSE (*stands up; bursting out*). Ah, that's very nice now, isn't it?
Such goings-on! You, the daughter of a king. And we work our
fingers to the bone for you, we slave to bring you up like young
ladies! [*She sits on chair, right of table.*] You're all alike, all of

you. Even you — who never used to stop to primp in front of a looking glass, or smear your mouth with rouge, or dindle and dandle to make the boys ogle you, and you ogle back. How many times I'd say to myself, "Now that one, now: I wish she was a little more of a coquette — always wearing the same dress, her hair tumbling round her face. One thing's sure," I'd say to myself, "none of the boys will look at her while Ismene's about, all curled and cute and tidy and trim. I'll have this one on my hands for the rest of my life." And now, you see? Just like your sister, after all. Only worse: a hypocrite. Who is the lad? Some little scamp, eh? Somebody you can't bring home and show to your family, and say, "Well, this is him, and I mean to marry him and no other. That's how it is, is it? Answer me!

ANTIGONE (*smiling faintly*). That's how it is. Yes, Nurse.

NURSE. Yes, says she! God save us! I took her when she wasn't that high. I promised her poor mother I'd make a lady of her. And look at her! But don't you go thinking this is the end of this, my young 'un. I'm only your nurse and you can play deaf and dumb with me; I don't count. But your Uncle Creon will hear of this! That, I promise you.

ANTIGONE (*a little weary*). Yes. Creon will hear of this.

NURSE. And we'll hear what he has to say when he finds out that you go wandering alone o' nights. Not to mention Haemon. For the girl's engaged! Going to be married! Do you know what I ought to do to you? Take you over my knee the way I used to do when you were little.

ANTIGONE. Please, Nurse, I want to be alone.

NURSE. And if you so much as speak of it, she says she wants to be alone!

ANTIGONE. Nanny, you shouldn't scold, dear. This isn't a day when you should be losing your temper.

NURSE. Not scold, indeed! Along with the rest of it, I'm to like it. Didn't I promise your mother? What would she say if she was here? "Old Stupid!" That's what she'd call me. "Old Stupid. Spend your life making them behave, watching over them like a mother hen, running after them with mufflers and sweaters to keep them warm, and eggnogs to make them strong; and then at four o'clock in the morning, you who always complained you never could sleep a wink, snoring in your bed and letting them slip out."

That's what she'd say, your mother. And I'd stand there, dying of shame if I wasn't dead already. And all I could do would be not to dare look her in the face; and "That's true," I'd say. "That's all true what you say, Your Majesty."

ANTIGONE. Nanny, dear. Dear Nanny. Don't cry. You'll be able to look Mamma in the face when it's your time to see her. And she'll say, "Good morning, Nanny. Thank you for my little Antigone. You did look after her so well." She knows why I went out this morning.

NURSE. Well, you've a queer way of teasing me, I must say! Not to know when she's teasing me! [*Rises to stand behind* ANTIGONE.] I must be getting awfully old, that's what it is. But if you loved me, you'd tell me the truth. You'd tell me why your bed was empty when I went along to tuck you in. Wouldn't you?

ANTIGONE. Please, Nanny, don't cry any more. [ANTIGONE *turns partly toward* NURSE, *puts an arm up to* NURSE's *shoulder. With her other hand,* ANTIGONE *caresses* NURSE's *face.*] There now, my sweet red apple. Do you remember how I used to rub your cheeks to make them shine? My dear, wrinkled red apple! I didn't do anything tonight that was worth sending tears down the little gullies of your dear face. Save your tears, Nanny, save them, Nanny dear; you may still need them. When you cry like that, I become a little girl again; and I mustn't be a little girl today.

[ANTIGONE *rises and moves upstage.*]

[ISMENE *enters through arch, left. She pauses in front of arch.*]

ISMENE. Antigone! What are you doing up at this hour? I've just been to your room.

NURSE. The two of you, now! You're both going mad, to be up before the kitchen fire has been started. Do you like running about without a mouthful of breakfast? Do you think it's decent for the daughters of a king? [*She turns to* ISMENE.] And look at you, with nothing on, and the sun not up! I'll have you both on my hands with colds before I know it.

ANTIGONE. Nanny dear, go away now. It's not chilly, really. Summer's here. Go and make us some coffee. Please, Nanny, I'd love some coffee. It would do me so much good.

NURSE. My poor baby! Her head's swimming, what with nothing on her stomach, and me standing here like an idiot when I could be getting her something hot to drink. [*Exit* NURSE.]

[A *pause.*]

ISMENE. Aren't you well?

ANTIGONE. Of course I am. Just a little tired. I got up too early.

[ANTIGONE *sits on a chair, suddenly tired.*]

ISMENE. I couldn't sleep, either.

ANTIGONE. Ismene, you ought not to go without your beauty sleep.

ISMENE. Don't make fun of me.

ANTIGONE. I'm not, Ismene, truly. This particular morning, seeing how beautiful you are makes everything easier for me. Wasn't I a miserable little beast when we were small? I used to fling mud at you, and put worms down your neck. I remember tying you to a tree and cutting off your hair. Your beautiful hair! How easy it must be never to be unreasonable with all that smooth, silken hair so beautifully set round your head.

ISMENE (*abruptly*). Why do you insist upon talking about other things?

ANTIGONE (*gently*). I am not talking about other things.

ISMENE. Antigone, I've thought about it a lot.

ANTIGONE. Have you?

ISMENE. I thought about it all night long. Antigone, you're mad.

ANTIGONE. Am I?

ISMENE. We cannot do it.

ANTIGONE. Why not?

ISMENE. Creon will have us put to death.

ANTIGONE. Of course he will. That's what he's here for. He will do what he has to do, and we will do what we have to do. He is bound to put us to death. We are bound to go out and bury our brother. That's the way it is. What do you think we can do to change it?

ISMENE (*releases* ANTIGONE's *hand; draws back a step*). I don't want to die.

ANTIGONE. I'd prefer not to die, myself.

ISMENE. Listen to me, Antigone. I thought about it all night. I'm older than you are. I always think things over, and you don't. You are impulsive. You get a notion in your head and you jump up and do the thing straight off. And if it's silly, well, so much the worse for you. Whereas, *I* think things out.

ANTIGONE. Sometimes it is better not to think too much.

ISMENE. I don't agree with you! [ANTIGONE *looks at* ISMENE, *then turns and moves to chair behind table.* ISMENE *leans on end of table top, toward* ANTIGONE.] Oh, I know it's horrible. And I pity Polynices just as much as you do. But all the same, I sort of see what Uncle Creon means.

ANTIGONE. I don't want to "sort of see" anything.

ISMENE. Uncle Creon is the king. He has to set an example!

ANTIGONE. But *I* am not the king; and I don't have to set people examples. Little Antigone gets a notion in her head — the nasty brat, the willful, wicked girl; and they put her in a corner all day, or they lock her up in the cellar. And she deserves it. She shouldn't have disobeyed!

ISMENE. There you go, frowning, glowering, wanting your own stubborn way in everything. Listen to me. I'm right oftener than you are.

ANTIGONE. I don't want to be right!

ISMENE. At least you can try to understand.

ANTIGONE. Understand! The first word I ever heard out of any of you was that word "understand." Why didn't I "understand" that I must not play with water — cold, black, beautiful, flowing water — because I'd spill it on the palace tiles. Or with earth, because earth dirties a little girl's frock. Why didn't I "understand" that nice children don't eat out of every dish at once or give everything in their pockets to beggars or run in the wind so fast that they fall down or ask for a drink when they're perspiring or want to go swimming when it's either too early or too late, merely because they happen to feel like swimming. Understand! I don't want to understand. There'll be time enough to understand when I'm old. . . . If I ever *am* old. But not now.

ISMENE. He is stronger than we are, Antigone. He is the king. And the whole city is with him. Thousands and thousands of them, swarming through all the streets of Thebes.

ANTIGONE. I am not listening to you.

ISMENE. His mob will come running, howling as it runs. A thousand arms will seize our arms. A thousand breaths will breathe into our faces. Like one single pair of eyes, a thousand eyes will stare at us. We'll be driven in a tumbrel through their hatred, through the smell of them and their cruel, roaring laughter. We'll be dragged to the scaffold for torture, surrounded by guards with their idiot faces all bloated, their animal hands clean-washed for the sacrifice, their beefy eyes squinting as they stare at us. And we'll know that no shrieking and no begging will make them understand that we want to live, for they are like slaves who do exactly as they've been told, without caring about right or wrong. And we shall suffer, we shall feel pain rising in us until it becomes so unbearable that we *know* it must stop. But it won't stop; it will go on rising and rising, like a screaming voice. Oh, I can't, I can't, Antigone!

[A *pause*.]

ANTIGONE. How well have you thought it all out.

ISMENE. I thought of it all night long. Didn't you?

ANTIGONE. Oh, yes.

ISMENE. I'm an awful coward, Antigone.

ANTIGONE. So am I. But what has that to do with it?

ISMENE. But, Antigone! Don't you want to go on living?

ANTIGONE. Go on living! Who was it that was always the first out of bed because she loved the touch of the cold morning air on her bare skin? Who was always the last to bed because nothing less than infinite weariness could wean her from the lingering night? Who wept when she was little because there were too many grasses in the meadow, too many creatures in the field, for her to know and touch them all?

ISMENE (*clasps* ANTIGONE's *hands, in a sudden rush of tenderness*). Darling little sister!

ANTIGONE (*repulsing her*). No! For heaven's sake! Don't paw me! And don't let us start sniveling! You say you've thought it all out. The howling mob — the torture — the fear of death. . . . They've made up your mind for you. Is that it?

ISMENE. Yes.

ANTIGONE. All right. They're as good excuses as any.

ISMENE. Antigone, be sensible. It's all very well for men to believe in ideas and die for them. But you are a girl!

ANTIGONE. Don't I know I'm a girl? Haven't I spent my life cursing the fact that I was a girl?

ISMENE (*with spirit*). Antigone! You have everything in the world to make you happy. All you have to do is reach out for it. You are going to be married; you are young; you are beautiful —

ANTIGONE. I am not beautiful.

ISMENE. Yes, you are! Not the way other girls are. But it's always you that the little boys turn to look back at when they pass us in the street. And when you go by, the little girls stop talking. They stare and stare at you, until we've turned a corner.

ANTIGONE (*a faint smile*). "Little boys — little girls."

ISMENE (*challengingly*). And what about Haemon?

[A *pause*.]

ANTIGONE. I shall see Haemon this morning. I'll take care of Haemon. You always said I was mad; and it didn't matter how little I was or what I wanted to do. Go back to bed now, Ismene. The sun is coming up, and, as you see, there is nothing I can do today. Our brother Polynices is as well guarded as if he had won the war and were sitting on his throne. Go along. You are pale with weariness.

ISMENE. What are you going to do?

NURSE (*calls from off-stage*). Come along, my dove. Come to breakfast.

ANTIGONE. I don't feel like going to bed. However, if you like, I'll promise not to leave the house till you wake up. Nurse is getting me breakfast. Go and get some sleep. The sun is just up. Look at you: you can't keep your eyes open. Go.

ISMENE. And you will listen to reason, won't you? You'll let me talk to you about this again? Promise?

ANTIGONE. I promise. I'll let you talk. I'll let all of you talk. Go to bed, now. [ISMENE *goes to arch; exit.*] Poor Ismene!

NURSE (*enters through arch, speaking as she enters*). Come along, my dove. I've made you some coffee and toast and jam. [*She turns toward arch as if to go out.*]

ANTIGONE. I'm not really hungry, Nurse.

[NURSE *stops, looks at* ANTIGONE, *then moves behind her.*]

NURSE (*very tenderly*). Where is your pain?

ANTIGONE. Nowhere, Nanny dear. But you must keep me warm and safe, the way you used to do when I was little. Nanny! Stronger than all fever, stronger than any nightmare, stronger than the shadow of the cupboard that used to snarl at me and turn into a dragon on the bedroom wall. Stronger than the thousand insects gnawing and nibbling in the silence of the night. Stronger than the night itself, with the weird hooting of the night birds that frightened me even when I couldn't hear them. Nanny, stronger than death. Give me your hand, Nanny, as if I were ill in bed, and you sitting beside me.

NURSE. My sparrow, my lamb! What is it that's eating your heart out?

ANTIGONE. Oh, it's just that I'm a little young still for what I have to go through. But nobody but you must know that.

NURSE (*places her other arm around* ANTIGONE'*s shoulder*). A little young for what, my kitten?

ANTIGONE. Nothing in particular, Nanny. Just — all this. Oh, it's so good that you are here. I can hold your callused hand, your hand that is so prompt to ward off evil. You are very powerful, Nanny.

NURSE. What is it you want me to do for you, my baby?

ANTIGONE. There isn't anything to do, except put your hand like this against my cheek. [*She places the* NURSE'*s hand against her cheek. A pause, then, as* ANTIGONE *leans back, her eyes shut.*] There! I'm not afraid any more. Not afraid of the wicked ogre, nor of the sandman, nor of the dwarf who steals little children. [*A pause.* ANTIGONE *resumes on another note.*] Nanny . . .

NURSE. Yes?

ANTIGONE. My dog, Puff . . .

NURSE (*straightens up, draws her hand away*). Well?

ANTIGONE. Promise me that you will never scold her again.

NURSE. Dogs that dirty up a house with their filthy paws deserve to be scolded.

ANTIGONE. I know. Just the same, promise me.

NURSE. You mean you want me to let her make a mess all over the place and not say a thing?

ANTIGONE. Yes, Nanny.

NURSE. You're asking a lot. The next time she wets my living-room carpet, I'll —

ANTIGONE. Please, Nanny, I beg of you!

NURSE. It isn't fair to take me on my weak side, just because you look a little peaked today. . . . Well, have it your own way. We'll mop up and keep our mouth shut. You're making a fool of me, though.

ANTIGONE. And promise me that you will talk to her. That you will talk to her often.

NURSE (*turns and looks at* ANTIGONE). Me, talk to a dog!

ANTIGONE. Yes. But mind you: you are not to talk to her the way people usually talk to dogs. You're to talk to her the way I talk to her.

NURSE. I don't see why both of us have to make fools of ourselves. So long as you're here, one ought to be enough.

ANTIGONE. But if there was a reason why I couldn't go on talking to her —

NURSE (*interrupting*). Couldn't go on talking to her! And why couldn't you go on talking to her? What kind of poppycock — ?

ANTIGONE. And if she got too unhappy, if she moaned and moaned, waiting for me with her nose under the door as she does when I'm out all day, then the best thing, Nanny, might be to have her mercifully put to sleep.

NURSE. Now what *has* got into you this morning? [HAEMON *enters through arch*]. Running around in the darkness, won't sleep, won't eat — [ANTIGONE *sees* HAEMON.] — and now it's her dog she wants killed. I never.

ANTIGONE (*interrupting*). Nanny! Haemon is here. Go inside, please. And don't forget that you've promised me. [NURSE *goes to arch; exit.* ANTIGONE *rises.*] Haemon, Haemon! Forgive me for quarreling with you last night. [*She crosses quickly to* HAEMON *and they embrace.*] Forgive me for everything. It was all my fault. I beg you to forgive me.

HAEMON. You know that I've forgiven you. You had hardly slammed the door, your perfume still hung in the room, when I had already forgiven you. [*He holds her in his arms and smiles at her. Then draws slightly back.*] You stole that perfume. From whom?

ANTIGONE. Ismene.

HAEMON. And the rouge? and the face powder? and the frock? Whom did you steal them from?

ANTIGONE. Ismene.

HAEMON. And in whose honor did you get yourself up so elegantly?

ANTIGONE. I'll tell you everything. [*She draws him closer.*] Oh, darling, what a fool I was! To waste a whole evening! A whole, beautiful evening!

HAEMON. We'll have other evenings, my sweet.

ANTIGONE. Perhaps we won't.

HAEMON. And other quarrels, too. A happy love is full of quarrels, you know.

ANTIGONE. A happy love, yes. Haemon, listen to me.

HAEMON. Yes?

ANTIGONE. Don't laugh at me this morning. Be serious.

HAEMON. I am serious.

ANTIGONE. And hold me tight. Tighter than you have ever held me. I want all your strength to flow into me.

HAEMON. There! With all my strength.

[A *pause.*]

ANTIGONE (*breathless*). That's good. [*They stand for a moment, silent and motionless.*] Haemon! I wanted to tell you. You know — the little boy we were going to have when we were married?

HAEMON. Yes?

ANTIGONE. I'd have protected him against everything in the world.

HAEMON. Yes, dearest.

ANTIGONE. Oh, you don't know how I should have held him in my arms and given him my strength. He wouldn't have been afraid of anything, I swear he wouldn't. Not of the falling night, nor of the terrible noonday sun, nor of all the shadows, or all the walls in the world. Our little boy, Haemon! His mother wouldn't have been very imposing: her hair wouldn't always have been brushed; but she would have been strong where he was concerned, so much stronger than all those real mothers with their real bosoms and their aprons around their middle. You believe that, don't you, Haemon?

HAEMON (*soothingly*). Yes, yes, my darling.

ANTIGONE. And you believe me when I say that you would have had a real wife?

HAEMON. Darling, you *are* my real wife.

ANTIGONE (*pressing against him and crying out*). Haemon, you loved me! You did love me that night, didn't you? You're sure of it!

HAEMON (*rocking her gently*). What night, my sweet?

ANTIGONE. And you are very sure, aren't you, that that night, at the dance, when you came to the corner where I was sitting, there was no mistake? It was me you were looking for? It wasn't another girl? And you're sure that never, not in your most secret heart of hearts, have you said to yourself that it was Ismene you ought to have asked to marry you?

HAEMON (*reproachfully*). Antigone, you are idiotic. You might give me credit for knowing my own mind. It's you I love, and no one else.

ANTIGONE. But you love me as a woman — as a woman wants to be loved, don't you? Your arms around me aren't lying, are they? Your hands, so warm against my back — they're not lying? This warmth that's in me; this confidence, this sense that I am safe, secure, that flows through me as I stand here with my cheek in the hollow of your shoulder: they are not lies, are they?

HAEMON. Antigone, darling, I love you exactly as you love me. With all of myself.

[*They kiss.*]

ANTIGONE. I'm sallow, and I'm scrawny. Ismene is pink and golden. She's like a fruit.

HAEMON. Look here, Antigone —

ANTIGONE. Ah, dearest, I am ashamed of myself. But this morning, this special morning, I must know. Tell me the truth! I beg you to tell me the truth! When you think about me, when it strikes you suddenly that I am going to belong to you — do you have the feeling that — that a great empty space is being hollowed out inside you, that there is something inside you that is just — dying?

HAEMON. Yes, I do, I do.

[*A pause.*]

ANTIGONE. That's the way I feel. And another thing. I wanted you to know that I should have been very proud to be your wife — the woman whose shoulder you would put your hand on as you sat down to table, absent-mindedly, as upon a thing that belonged to you. [*After a moment, draws away from him. Her tone changes.*] There! Now I have two things more to tell you. And when I have told them to you, you must go away instantly, without asking any questions. However strange they may seem to you. However much they may hurt you. Swear that you will!

HAEMON (*beginning to be troubled*). What are these things that you are going to tell me?

ANTIGONE. Swear, first, that you will go away without one word.

Without so much as looking at me. [*She looks at him, wretched-ness in her face.*] You hear me, Haemon. Swear it, please. This is the last mad wish that you will ever have to grant me.

[*A pause.*]

HAEMON. I swear it, since you insist. But I must tell you that I don't like this at all.

ANTIGONE. Please, Haemon. It's very serious. You must listen to me and do as I ask. First, about last night, when I came to your house. You asked me a moment ago why I wore Ismene's dress and rouge. It was because I was stupid. I was trying to be more like other girls.

HAEMON. Was *that* the reason? My poor —

ANTIGONE. Yes. And you laughed at me. And we quarreled; and my awful temper got the better of me and I flung out of the house. . . .

HAEMON. Oh, my darling —

ANTIGONE (*shuts him off*). You swore you wouldn't ask any ques-tions. You swore, Haemon. [*Turns her face away and goes on in a hard voice.*] As a matter of fact, I'll tell you why. Oh, my darling, my darling, forgive me; I'm going to cause you quite a lot of pain. [*She draws away from him.*] I shall never, never be able to marry you, never! [HAEMON *is stupefied and mute; then he moves a step toward her.*] Haemon! You took a solemn oath! You swore! Leave me quickly! Tomorrow the whole thing will be clear to you. Even before tomorrow: this afternoon. If you please, Haemon, go now. It is the only thing left that you can do for me if you still love me. [*A pause as* HAEMON *stares at her. Then he turns and goes out through the arch,* ANTIGONE *stands motionless, then moves to a chair at end of table and lets herself gently down on it. In a mild voice, as of calm after storm.*] Well, it's over for Haemon, Antig-one.

[ISMENE *enters through arch, pauses for a moment in front of it when she sees* ANTIGONE, *then crosses behind table.*]

ISMENE. I can't sleep. I'm terrified. I'm so afraid that, even though it is daylight, you'll still try to bury Polynices. Antigone, little sis-ter, we all want to make you happy — Haemon, and Nurse, and I, and Puff whom you love. We love you, we are alive, we need you.

And you remember what Polynices was like. He was our brother, of course. But he's dead, and he never loved you. He was a bad brother. He was like an enemy in the house. He never thought of you. Why should you think of him? What if his soul does have to wander through endless time without rest or peace? Don't try something that is beyond your strength. You are always defying the world, but you're only a girl, after all. Stay at home tonight. Don't try to do it, I beg you. It's Creon's doing, not ours.

ANTIGONE. You are too late, Ismene. When you first saw me this morning, I had just come in from burying him.

[*Exit* ANTIGONE *through arch.*]

The lighting, which by this time has reached a point of early morning sun, is quickly dimmed out, leaving the stage bathed in a light blue color. ISMENE *runs out after* ANTIGONE. *On* ISMENE'S *exit the lights are brought up suddenly to suggest a later period of the day.* CREON *and* PAGE *enter through curtain upstage.* CREON *stands on the top step; his* PAGE *stands at his right side.*

CREON. A private of the guards, you say? One of those standing watch over the body? Show him in.

[*The* PAGE *crosses to arch; exit.* CREON *moves down to end of table.* PAGE *re-enters, preceded by the* FIRST GUARD, *livid with fear.* PAGE *remains on upstage side of arch.* GUARD *salutes.*]

GUARD. Private Jonas, Second Battalion.
CREON. What are you doing here?
GUARD. It's like this, sir. Soon as it happened, we said: "Got to tell the chief about this before anybody else spills it. He'll want to know right away." So we tossed a coin to see which one would come up and tell you about it. You see, sir, we thought only one man had better come, because, after all, you don't want to leave the body without a guard. Right? I mean, there's three of us on duty, guarding the body.
CREON. What's wrong about the body?
GUARD. Sir, I've been seventeen years in the service. Volunteer. Wounded three times. Two mentions. My record's clean. I know my business and I know my place. I carry out orders. Sir, ask any officer in the battalion; they'll tell you. "Leave it to Jonas. Give

him an order: he'll carry it out." That's what they'll tell you, sir. Jonas, that's me — that's my name.

CREON. What's the matter with you, man? What are you shaking for?

GUARD. By rights it's the corporal's job, sir. I've been recommended for a corporal, but they haven't put it through yet. June, it was supposed to go through.

CREON (interrupts). Stop chattering and tell me why you are here. If anything has gone wrong, I'll break all three of you.

GUARD. Nobody can say we didn't keep our eye on that body. We had the two o'clock watch — the tough one. You know how it is, sir. It's nearly the end of the night. Your eyes are like lead. You've got a crick in the back of your neck. There's shadows, and the fog is beginning to roll in. A fine watch they give us! And me, seventeen years in the service. But we was doing our duty all right. On our feet, all of us. Anybody says we were sleeping is a liar. First place, it was too cold. Second place — [CREON makes a gesture of impatience.] Yes, sir. Well, I turned around and looked at the body. We wasn't only ten feet away from it, but that's how I am. I was keeping my eye on it. (Shouts.) Listen, sir, I was the first man to see it! Me! They'll tell you. I was the one let out that yell!

CREON. What for? What was the matter?

GUARD. Sir, the body! Somebody had been there and buried it. [CREON comes down a step on the stair. The GUARD becomes more frightened.] It wasn't much, you understand. With us three there, it couldn't have been. Just covered over with a little dirt, that's all. But enough to hide it from the buzzards.

CREON. By God, I'll — ! [He looks intently at the GUARD.] You are sure that it couldn't have been a dog, scratching up the earth?

GUARD. Not a chance, sir. That's kind of what we hoped it was. But the earth was scattered over the body just like the priests tell you you should do it. Whoever did that job knew what he was doing, all right.

CREON. Who could have dared? [He turns and looks at the GUARD.] Was there anything to indicate who might have done it?

GUARD. Not a thing, sir. Maybe we heard a footstep — I can't swear to it. Of course we started right in to search, and the corporal found a shovel, a kid's shovel no bigger than that, all rusty and everything. Corporal's got the shovel for you. We thought maybe a kid did it.

CREON (*to himself*). A kid! [*He looks away from the* GUARD.] I broke the back of the rebellion; but like a snake, it is coming together again. Polynices' friends, with their gold, blocked by my orders in the banks of Thebes. The leaders of the mob, stinking of garlic and allied to envious princes. And the temple priests, always ready for a bit of fishing in troubled waters. A kid! I can imagine what he is like, their kid: a baby-faced killer, creeping in the night with a toy shovel under his jacket. [*He looks at his* PAGE.] Though why shouldn't they have corrupted a real child? Very touching! Very useful to the party, an innocent child. A martyr. A real white-faced baby of fourteen who will spit with contempt at the guards who kill him. A free gift to their cause: the precious, innocent blood of a child on my hands. [*He turns to the* GUARD.] They must have accomplices in the Guard itself. Look here, you. Who knows about this?

GUARD. Only us three, sir. We flipped a coin, and I came right over.

CREON. Right. Listen, now. You will continue on duty. When the relief squad comes up, you will tell them to return to barracks. You will uncover the body. If another attempt is made to bury it, I shall expect you to make an arrest and bring the person straight to me. And you will keep your mouths shut. Not one word of this to a human soul. You are all guilty of neglect of duty, and you will be punished; but if the rumor spreads through Thebes that the body received burial, you will be shot — all three of you.

GUARD (*excitedly*). Sir, we never told nobody, I swear we didn't! Anyhow, I've been up here. Suppose my pals spilled it to the relief; I couldn't have been with them and here too. That wouldn't be my fault if they talked. Sir, I've got two kids. You're my witness, sir, it couldn't have been me. I was here with you. I've got a witness! If anybody talked, it couldn't have been me! I was —

CREON (*interrupting*). Clear out! If the story doesn't get around, you won't be shot. [*The* GUARD *salutes, turns, and exits at the double.* CREON *turns and paces upstage, then comes down to end of the table.*] A child! [*He looks at* PAGE.] Come along, my lad. Since we can't hope to keep this to ourselves, we shall have to be the first to give out the news. And after that, we shall have to clean up the mess. [PAGE *crosses to side of* CREON. CREON *puts his hand on*

PAGE's *shoulder*.] Would you be willing to die for me? Would you defy the Guard with your little shovel? [PAGE *looks up at* CREON.] Of course you would. You would do it, too. [*A pause.* CREON *looks away from* PAGE *and murmurs.*] A child! [CREON *and* PAGE *go slowly upstage center to top step.* PAGE *draws aside the curtain, through which exit* CREON *with* PAGE *behind him.*]

As soon as CREON and PAGE have disappeared, CHORUS enters and leans against the upstage portal or arch, left. The lighting is brought up to its brightest point to suggest mid-afternoon. CHORUS allows a pause to indicate that a crucial moment has been reached in the play, then moves slowly downstage, center. He stands for a moment silent, reflecting, and then smiles faintly.

CHORUS. The spring is wound up tight. It will uncoil of itself. That is what is so convenient in tragedy. The least little turn of the wrist will do the job. Anything will set it going: a glance at a girl who happens to be lifting her arms to her hair as you go by; a feeling when you wake up on a fine morning that you'd like a little respect paid to you today, as if it were as easy to order as a second cup of coffee; one question too many, idly thrown out over a friendly drink — and the tragedy is on.

The rest is automatic. You don't need to lift a finger. The machine is in perfect order; it has been oiled ever since time began, and it runs without friction. Death, treason, and sorrow are on the march; and they move in the wake of storm, of tears, of stillness. Every kind of stillness. The hush when the executioner's ax goes up at the end of the last act. The unbreathable silence when, at the beginning of the play, the two lovers, their hearts bared, stand for the first time face to face in the darkened room, afraid to stir. The silence inside you when the roaring crowd acclaims the winner — so that you think of a film without a sound track, mouths agape and no sound coming out of them, a clamor that is no more than a picture; and you, the victor, already vanquished, alone in the desert of your silence. That is tragedy.

Tragedy is clean, it is restful, it is flawless. It has nothing to do with melodrama — with wicked villains, persecuted maidens, avengers, sudden revelations, and eleventh-hour repentances. Death, in a melodrama, is really horrible because it is never inevitable. The dear old father might so easily have been saved; the honest young man might so easily have brought in the police five minutes earlier.

In a tragedy, nothing is in doubt and everyone's destiny is known. That makes for tranquillity. There is a sort of fellow-feeling among characters in a tragedy: he who kills is as innocent as he who gets killed: it's all a matter of what part you are playing. Tragedy is restful; and the reason is that hope, that foul, deceitful thing, has no part in it. There isn't any hope. You're trapped. The whole sky has fallen on you, and all you can do about it is to shout.

Don't mistake me: I said "shout": I did not say groan, whimper, complain. That, you cannot do. But you can shout aloud; you can get all those things said that you never thought you'd be able to say — or never even knew you had it in you to say. And you don't say these things because it will do any good to say them: you know better than that. You say them for their own sake; you say them because you learn a lot from them.

In melodrama you argue and struggle in the hope of escape. That is vulgar; it's practical. But in tragedy, where there is no temptation to try to escape, argument is gratuitous: it's kingly.

[Voices of the GUARDS and scuffling sound heard through the archway. CHORUS looks in that direction; then, in a changed tone:]

The play is on. Antigone has been caught. For the first time in her life, little Antigone is going to be able to be herself.

[Exit CHORUS through arch. A pause, while the offstage voices rise in volume, then the FIRST GUARD enters, followed by SECOND and THIRD GUARDS, holding the arms of ANTIGONE and dragging her along. The FIRST GUARD, speaking as he enters, crosses swiftly to end of the table.

The TWO GUARDS and ANTIGONE stop downstage.]

FIRST GUARD (recovered from his fright). Come on, now, Miss, give it a rest. The chief will be here in a minute and you can tell him about it. All I know is my orders. I don't want to know what you were doing there. People always have excuses; but I can't afford to listen to them, see. Why, if we had to listen to all the people who want to tell us what's the matter with this country, we'd never get our work done. (To the GUARDS.) You keep hold of her and I'll see that she keeps her face shut.

ANTIGONE. They are hurting me. Tell them to take their dirty hands off me.

FIRST GUARD. Dirty hands, eh? The least you can do is try to be polite, Miss. Look at me: I'm polite.

ANTIGONE. Tell them to let me go. I shan't run away. My father was King Oedipus. I am Antigone.

FIRST GUARD. King Oedipus's little girl! Well, well, well! Listen, Miss, the night watch never picks up a lady but they say, you better be careful: I'm a friend of the police commissioner.

[*The* GUARDS *laugh.*]

ANTIGONE. I don't mind being killed, but I don't want them to touch me.

FIRST GUARD. And what about stiffs, and dirt, and such like? You wasn't afraid to touch them, was you? "Their dirty hands!" Take a look at your own hands. [ANTIGONE, *handcuffed, smiles despite herself as she looks down at her hands. They are grubby.*] You must have lost your shovel, didn't you? Had to go at it with your fingernails the second time, I'll bet. By God, I never saw such nerve! I turn my back for about five seconds; I ask a pal for a chew; I say "thanks"; I get the tobacco stowed away in my cheek — the whole thing don't take ten seconds; and there she is, clawing away like a hyena. Right out in broad daylight! And did she scratch and kick when I grabbed her! Straight for my eyes with them nails she went. And yelling something fierce about, "I haven't finished yet; let me finish!" She ain't got all her marbles!

SECOND GUARD. I pinched a nut like that the other day.

FIRST GUARD. Listen, we're going to get a bonus out of this. What do you say we throw a party, the three of us?

SECOND GUARD. At the old woman's? Behind Market Street?

THIRD GUARD. Suits me. Sunday would be a good day. We're off duty Sunday. What do you say we bring our wives?

FIRST GUARD. No. Let's have some fun this time. Bring your wife, there's always something goes wrong. First place, what do you do with the kids? Bring them, they always want to go to the bathroom just when you're right in the middle of a game of cards or something. Listen, who would have thought an hour ago that us three would be talking about throwing a party now? The way I felt when the old man was interrogating me, we'd be lucky if we

got off with being docked a month's pay. I want to tell you, I was
scared.

SECOND GUARD. You sure we're going to get a bonus?

FIRST GUARD. Yes. Something tells me this is big stuff.

THIRD GUARD (*to* SECOND GUARD). What's-his-name, you know — in
the Third Battalion? He got an extra month's pay for catching a
firebug.

SECOND GUARD. If we get an extra month's pay, I vote we throw the
party at the Arabian's.

FIRST GUARD. You're crazy! He charges twice as much for liquor as
anybody else in town.

THIRD GUARD. Well, we can't keep this from our wives, no matter
how you work it out. You get an extra month's pay, and what happens? Everybody in the battalion knows it, and your wife knows
it too. They might even line up the battalion and give it to you
in front of everybody, so how could you keep your wife from finding out?

FIRST GUARD. Well, we'll see about that. If they do the job out in
the barrack yard — of course that means women, kids, everything.

ANTIGONE. I should like to sit down, if you please.

[A *pause, as the* FIRST GUARD *thinks it over.*]

FIRST GUARD. Let her sit down. But keep hold of her. [*The two*
GUARDS *start to lead her toward the chair at end of table. The cur-
tain upstage opens, and* CREON *enters, followed by his* PAGE. FIRST
GUARD *turns and moves upstage a few steps, sees* CREON.] 'Tenshun!

[*The three* GUARDS *salute.* CREON, *seeing* ANTIGONE *handcuffed to*
THIRD GUARD, *stops on the top step, astonished.*]

CREON. Antigone! (*To the* FIRST GUARD.) Take off those handcuffs!
[FIRST GUARD *crosses above table to left of* ANTIGONE.] What is
this? [CREON *and his* PAGE *come down off the steps.*]

[FIRST GUARD *takes key from his pocket and unlocks the cuff on*
ANTIGONE'S *hand.* ANTIGONE *rubs her wrist as she crosses below
table toward chair at end of table.* SECOND *and* THIRD GUARDS *step
back to front of arch.* FIRST GUARD *turns upstage toward* CREON.]

FIRST GUARD. The watch, sir. We all came this time.

CREON. Who is guarding the body?

FIRST GUARD. We sent for the relief.

[CREON *comes down.*]

CREON. But I gave orders that the relief was to go back to barracks and stay there! [ANTIGONE *sits on chair at left of table.*] I told you not to open your mouth about this!

FIRST GUARD. Nobody's said anything, sir. We made this arrest and brought the party in, the way you said we should.

CREON (*to* ANTIGONE). Where did these men find you?

FIRST GUARD. Right by the body.

CREON. What were you doing near your brother's body? You knew what my orders were.

FIRST GUARD. What was she doing? Sir, that's why we brought her in. She was digging up the dirt with her nails. She was trying to cover up the body all over again.

CREON. Do you realize what you are saying?

FIRST GUARD. Sir, ask these men here. After I reported to you, I went back, and first thing we did, we uncovered the body. The sun was coming up and it was beginning to smell, so we moved it up on a little rise to get him in the wind. Of course, you wouldn't expect any trouble in broad daylight. But just the same, we decided one of us had better keep his eye peeled all the time. About noon, what with the sun and the smell, and as the wind dropped and I wasn't feeling none too good, I went over to my pal to get a chew. I just had time to say "thanks" and stick it in my mouth, when I turned round and there she was, clawing away at the dirt with both hands. Right out in broad daylight! Wouldn't you think when she saw me come running she'd stop and leg it out of there? Not her! She went right on digging as fast as she could, as if I wasn't there at all. And when I grabbed her, she scratched and bit and yelled to leave her alone, she hadn't finished yet, the body wasn't all covered yet, and the like of that.

CREON (*to* ANTIGONE). Is this true?

ANTIGONE. Yes, it is true.

FIRST GUARD. We scraped the dirt off as fast as we could, then we sent for the relief and we posted them. But we didn't tell them a thing, sir. And we brought in the party so's you could see her. And that's the truth, so help me God.

CREON [*to* ANTIGONE.] And was it you who covered the body the first time? In the night?

ANTIGONE. Yes, it was. With a toy shovel we used to take to the sea-shore when we were children. It was Polynices' own shovel; he had cut his name in the handle. That was why I left it with him. But these men took it away; so the next time, I had to do it with my hands.

FIRST GUARD. Sir, she was clawing away like a wild animal. Matter of fact, first minute we saw her, what with the heat haze and every-thing, my pal says, "That must be a dog," he says. "Dog!" I says, "that's a girl, that is!" And it was.

CREON. Very well. [*Turns to the* PAGE.] Show these men to the ante-room. [*The* PAGE *crosses to the arch, stands there, waiting.* CREON *moves behind the table. To the* FIRST GUARD.] You three men will wait outside. I may want a report from you later.

FIRST GUARD. Do I put the cuffs back on her, sir?

CREON. No. [*The three* GUARDS *salute, do an about-turn, and exeunt through arch, right.* PAGE *follows them out. A pause.*] Had you told anybody what you meant to do?

ANTIGONE. No.

CREON. Did you meet anyone on your way — coming or going?

ANTIGONE. No, nobody.

CREON. Sure of that, are you?

ANTIGONE. Perfectly sure.

CREON. Very well. Now listen to me. You will go straight to your room. When you get there, you will go to bed. You will say that you are not well and that you have not been out since yesterday. Your nurse will tell the same story. [*He looks toward arch, through which the* GUARDS *have gone out.*] And I'll get rid of those three men.

ANTIGONE. Uncle Creon, you are going to a lot of trouble for no good reason. You must know that I'll do it all over again tonight.

[*A pause. They look one another in the eye.*]

CREON. Why did you try to bury your brother?

ANTIGONE. I owed it to him.

CREON. I had forbidden it.

ANTIGONE. I owed it to him. Those who are not buried wander eter-nally and find no rest. If my brother were alive, and he came home weary after a long day's hunting, I should kneel down and unlace his boots, I should fetch him food and drink, I should see that his

bed was ready for him. Polynices is home from the hunt. I owe it
to him to unlock the house of the dead in which my father and my
mother are waiting to welcome him. Polynices has earned his rest.

CREON. Polynices was a rebel and a traitor, and you know it.

ANTIGONE. He was my brother.

CREON. You heard my edict. It was proclaimed throughout Thebes.
You read my edict. It was posted up on the city walls.

ANTIGONE. Of course I did.

CREON. You knew the punishment I decreed for any person who at-
temped to give him burial.

ANTIGONE. Yes, I knew the punishment.

CREON. Did you by any chance act on the assumption that a daughter
of Oedipus, a daughter of Oedipus's stubborn pride, was above
the law?

ANTIGONE. No, I did not act on that assumption.

CREON. Because if you had acted on that assumption, Antigone, you
would have been deeply wrong. Nobody has a more sacred obligation to obey the law than those who make the law. You are a
daughter of lawmakers, a daughter of kings, Antigone. You must
observe the law.

ANTIGONE. Had I been a scullery maid washing my dishes when that
law was read aloud to me, I should have scrubbed the greasy water
from my arms and gone out in my apron to bury my brother.

CREON. What nonsense! If you had been a scullery maid, there would
have been no doubt in your mind about the seriousness of that
edict. You would have known that it meant death; and you would
have been satisfied to weep for your brother in your kitchen. But
you! You thought that because you come of the royal line, because
you were my niece and were going to marry my son, I shouldn't
dare have you killed.

ANTIGONE. You are mistaken. Quite the contrary. I never doubted
for an instant that you would have me put to death.

[A *pause, as* CREON *stares fixedly at her.*]

CREON. The pride of Oedipus! Oedipus and his headstrong pride all
over again. I can see your father in you — and I believe you. Of
course you thought that I should have you killed! Proud as you
are, it seemed to you a natural climax in your existence. Your
father was like that. For him as for you human happiness was

meaningless; and mere human misery was not enough to satisfy his passion for torment. [*He sits on stool behind the table.*] You come of people for whom the human vestment is a kind of strait-jacket: it cracks at the seams. You spend your lives wriggling to get out of it. Nothing less than a cozy tea party with death and destiny will quench your thirst. The happiest hour of your father's life came when he listened greedily to the story of how, unknown to himself, he had killed his own father and dishonored the bed of his own mother. Drop by drop, word by word, he drank in the dark story that the gods had destined him first to live and then to hear. How avidly men and women drink the brew of such a tale when their names are Oedipus — and Antigone! And it is so simple, afterwards, to do what your father did, to put out one's eyes and take one's daughter begging on the highways.

Let me tell you, Antigone: those days are over for Thebes. Thebes has a right to a king without a past. My name, thank God, is only Creon. I stand here with both feet firm on the ground; with both hands in my pockets; and I have decided that so long as I am king — being less ambitious than your father was — I shall merely devote myself to introducing a little order into this absurd kingdom; if that is possible.

Don't think that being a king seems to me romantic. It is my trade, a trade a man has to work at every day; and like every other trade, it isn't all beer and skittles. But since it is my trade, I take it seriously. And if, tomorrow, some wild and bearded messenger walks in from some wild and distant valley — which is what happened to your dad — and tells me that he's not quite sure who my parents were but thinks that my wife Eurydice is actually my mother, I shall ask him to do me the kindness to go back where he came from; and I shan't let a little matter like that persuade me to order my wife to take a blood test and the police to let me know whether or not my birth certificate was forged. Kings, my girl, have other things to do than to surrender themselves to their private feelings. [*He looks at her and, smiles.*] Hand *you* over to be killed! [*He rises, moves to end of table and sits on the top of table.*] I have other plans for you. You're going to marry Haemon, and I want you to fatten up a bit so that you can give him a sturdy boy. Let me assure you that Thebes needs that boy a good deal more than it needs your death. You will go to your room, now, and do as you have been told; and you won't say a word about this to anybody. Don't fret about the guards: I'll see that their mouths are shut. And don't annihilate me with those eyes. I know that you think I am a brute, and I'm sure you must consider me very prosaic. But the fact is, I have always been fond of you, stubborn though you always were. Don't forget that the first doll you ever had came from me. [A *pause.* ANTIGONE *says nothing, rises, and crosses slowly below the table toward the arch.* CREON *turns and watches her; then*] Where are you going?

ANTIGONE (*stops downstage. Without any show of rebellion*). You know very well where I am going.

CREON (*after a pause*). What sort of game are you playing?

ANTIGONE. I am not playing games.

CREON. Antigone, do you realize that if, apart from those three guards, a single soul finds out what you have tried to do, it will be impossible for me to avoid putting you to death? There is still a chance that I can save you; but only if you keep this to yourself and give up your crazy purpose. Five minutes more, and it will be too late. You understand that?

ANTIGONE. I must go and bury my brother. Those men uncovered him.

CREON. What good will it do? You know that there are other men standing guard over Polynices. And even if you did cover him over with earth again, the earth would again be removed.

ANTIGONE. I know all that. I know it. But that much, at least, I can do. And what a person can do, a person ought to do.

[*Pause.*]

CREON. Tell me, Antigone, do you believe all that flummery about religious burial? Do you really believe that a so-called shade of your brother is condemned to wander forever homeless if a little earth is not flung on his corpse to the accompaniment of some priestly abracadabra? Have you ever listened to the priests of Thebes when they were mumbling their formula? Have you ever watched those dreary bureaucrats while they were preparing the dead for burial — skipping half the gestures required by the ritual, swallowing half their words, hustling the dead into their graves out of fear that they might be late for lunch?

ANTIGONE. Yes, I have seen all that.

CREON. And did you never say to yourself as you watched them, that if someone you really loved lay dead under the shuffling, mumbling ministrations of the priests, you would scream aloud and beg the priests to leave the dead in peace?

ANTIGONE. Yes, I've thought all that.

CREON. And you still insist upon being put to death — merely because I refuse to let your brother go out with that grotesque passport, because I refuse his body the wretched consolation of that mass-production jibber-jabber, which you would have been the first to be embarrassed by if I had allowed it. The whole thing is absurd!

ANTIGONE. Yes, it's absurd.

CREON. Then why, Antigone, why? For whose sake? For the sake of them that believe in it? To raise them against me?

ANTIGONE. No.

CREON. For whom then if not for them and not for Polynices either?

ANTIGONE. For nobody. For myself.

[A pause as they stand looking at one another.]

CREON. You must want very much to die. You look like a trapped animal.

ANTIGONE. Stop feeling sorry for me. Do as I do. Do your job. But if you are a human being, do it quickly. That is all I ask of you. I'm not going to be able to hold out forever.

CREON (takes a step toward her). I want to save you, Antigone.

ANTIGONE. You are the king, and you are all-powerful. But that you cannot do.

CREON. You think not?

ANTIGONE. Neither save me nor stop me.

CREON. Prideful Antigone! Little Oedipus!

ANTIGONE. Only this can you do: have me put to death.

CREON. Have you tortured, perhaps?

ANTIGONE. Why would you do that? To see me cry? To hear me beg for mercy? Or swear whatever you wish, and then begin over again?

[A pause.]

CREON. You listen to me. You have cast me for the villain in this little play of yours and yourself for the heroine. And you know it, you damned little mischief-maker! But don't you drive me too far!

If I were one of your preposterous little tyrants that Greece is
full of, you would be lying in a ditch this minute with your tongue
pulled out and your body drawn and quartered. But you can see
something in my face that makes me hesitate to send for the
guards and turn you over to them. Instead, I let you go on arguing;
and you taunt me, you take the offensive. [*He grasps her left
wrist.*] What are you driving at, you she devil?

ANTIGONE. Let me go. You are hurting my arm.

CREON (*gripping her tighter*). I will not let you go.

ANTIGONE (*moans*). Oh!

CREON. I was a fool to waste words. I should have done this from the
beginning. [*He looks at her.*] I may be your uncle — but we are
not a particularly affectionate family. Are we, eh? (*Through his
teeth, as he twists.*) Are we? [CREON *propels* ANTIGONE *around below him to his side.*] What fun for you, eh? To be able to spit in
the face of a king who has all the power in the world; a man who
has done his own killing in his day; who has killed people just as
pitiable as you are — and who is still soft enough to go to all this
trouble in order to keep you from being killed.

[A *pause.*]

ANTIGONE. Now you are squeezing my arm too tightly. It doesn't hurt
any more.

[CREON *stares at her, then drops her arm.*]

CREON. I shall save you yet. [*He goes below the table to the chair
at end of table, takes off his coat, and places it on the chair.*]
God knows, I have things enough to do today without wasting my
time on an insect like you. There's plenty to do, I assure you,
when you've just put down a revolution. But urgent things can
wait. I am not going to let politics be the cause of your death.
For it is a fact that this whole business is nothing but politics: the
mournful shade of Polynices, the decomposing corpse, the sentimental weeping, and the hysteria that you mistake for heroism —
nothing but politics.

Look here. I may not be soft, but I'm fastidious. I like things clean,
shipshape, well scrubbed. Don't think that I am not just as offended as you are by the thought of that meat rotting in the sun.
In the evening, when the breeze comes in off the sea, you can

smell it in the palace, and it nauseates me. But I refuse even to
shut my window. It's vile, and I can tell you what I wouldn't tell
anybody else: it's stupid, monstrously stupid. But the people of
Thebes have got to have their noses rubbed into it a little longer.
My God! If it was up to me, I should have had them bury your
brother long ago as a mere matter of public hygiene. I admit that
what I am doing is childish. But if the featherheaded rabble I
govern are to understand what's what, that stench has got to fill
the town for a month!

ANTIGONE (*turns to him*). You are a loathsome man!

CREON. I agree. My trade forces me to be. We could argue whether
I ought or ought not to follow my trade; but once I take on the
job, I must do it properly.

ANTIGONE. Why do you do it at all?

CREON. My dear, I woke up one morning and found myself King of
Thebes. God knows, there were other things I loved in life more
than power.

ANTIGONE. Then you should have said no.

CREON. Yes, I could have done that. Only, I felt that it would have
been cowardly. I should have been like a workman who turns
down a job that has to be done. So I said yes.

ANTIGONE. So much the worse for you, then. I didn't say yes. I can
say no to anything I think vile, and I don't have to count the
cost. But because you said yes, all that you can do, for all your
crown and your trappings, and your guards — all that you can do
is to have me killed.

CREON. Listen to me.

ANTIGONE. If I want to. I don't have to listen to you if I don't want
to. You've said your *yes*. There is nothing more you can tell me
that I don't know. You stand there, drinking in my words. [*She
moves behind chair.*] Why is it that you don't call your guards?
I'll tell you why. You want to hear me out to the end; that's why.

CREON. You amuse me.

ANTIGONE. Oh, no, I don't. I frighten you. That is why you talk about
saving me. Everything would be so much easier if you had a
docile, tongue-tied little Antigone living in the palace. I'll tell you
something, Uncle Creon: I'll give you back one of your own
words. You are too fastidious to make a good tyrant. But you are
going to have to put me to death today, and you know it. And

that's what frightens you. God! Is there anything uglier than a frightened man!

CREON. Very well. I am afraid, then. Does that satisfy you? I am afraid that if you insist upon it, I shall have to have you killed. And I don't want to.

ANTIGONE. I don't have to do things that I think are wrong. If it comes to that, you didn't really want to leave my brother's body unburied, did you? Say it! Admit that you didn't.

CREON. I have said it already.

ANTIGONE. But you did it just the same. And now, though you don't want to do it, you are going to have me killed. And you call that being a king!

CREON. Yes, I call that being a king.

ANTIGONE. Poor Creon! My nails are broken, my fingers are bleeding, my arms are covered with the welts left by the paws of your guards — but I am a queen!

CREON. Then why not have pity on me, and live? Isn't your brother's corpse, rotting there under my windows, payment enough for peace and order in Thebes? My son loves you. Don't make me add your life to the payment. I've paid enough.

ANTIGONE. No, Creon! You said yes, and made yourself king. Now you will never stop paying.

CREON. But God in heaven! Won't you try to understand me! I'm trying hard enough to understand you! There had to be one man who said yes. Somebody had to agree to captain the ship. She had sprung a hundred leaks; she was loaded to the water line with crime, ignorance, poverty. The wheel was swinging with the wind. The crew refused to work and were looting the cargo. The officers were building a raft, ready to slip overboard and desert the ship. The mast was splitting, the wind was howling, the sails were beginning to rip. Every man jack on board was about to drown — and only because the only thing they thought of was their own skins and their cheap little day-to-day traffic. Was that a time, do you think, for playing with words like yes and no? Was that a time for a man to be weighing the pros and cons, wondering if he wasn't going to pay too dearly later on; if he wasn't going to lose his life, or his family, or his touch with other men? You grab the wheel, you right the ship in the face of a mountain of water. You shout an order, and if one man refuses to obey, you shoot straight into the mob. Into the mob, I say! The beast as nameless as the wave that crashes down upon your deck; as nameless as the whipping wind. The thing that drops when you shoot may be someone who poured you a drink the night before; but it has no name. And you, braced at the wheel, you have no name, either. Nothing has a name — except the ship, and the storm. [A *pause as he looks at her*.] Now do you understand?

ANTIGONE. I am not here to understand. That's all very well for you. I am here to say no to you, and die.

CREON. It is easy to say no.

ANTIGONE. Not always.

CREON. It is easy to say no. To say yes, you have to sweat and roll up your sleeves and plunge both hands into life up to the elbows. It is easy to say no, even if saying no means death. All you have to do is to sit still and wait. Wait to go on living; wait to be killed. That is the coward's part. No is one of your man-made words. Can you imagine a world in which trees say *no* to the sap? In which beasts say *no* to hunger or to propagation? Animals are good, simple, tough. They move in droves, nudging one another onward, all traveling the same road. Some of them keel over, but the rest go on; and no matter how many may fall by the wayside, there are always those few left that go on bringing their young into the world, traveling the same road with the same obstinate will, unchanged from those who went before.

ANTIGONE. Animals, eh, Creon! What a king you could be if only men were animals!

[A *pause*. CREON *turns and looks at her*.]

CREON. You despise me, don't you? [ANTIGONE *is silent*. CREON *goes on, as if to himself*.] Strange. Again and again, I have imagined myself holding this conversation with a pale young man I have never seen in the flesh. He would have come to assassinate me, and would have failed. I would be trying to find out from him why he wanted to kill me. But with all my logic and all my powers of debate, the only thing I could get out of him would be that he despised me. Who would have thought that the white-faced boy would turn out to be you? And that the debate would arise out of something so meaningless as the burial of your brother?

ANTIGONE (*repeats contemptuously*). Meaningless!

CREON (*earnestly, almost desperately*). And yet, you must hear me out. My part is not an heroic one, but I shall play my part. I shall have you put to death. Only, before I do, I want to make one last appeal. I want to be sure that you know what you are doing as well as I know what I am doing. Antigone, do you know what you are dying for? Do you know the sordid story to which you are going to sign your name in blood, for all time to come?

ANTIGONE. What story?

CREON. The story of Eteocles and Polynices, the story of your brothers. You think you know it, but you don't. Nobody in Thebes knows that story but me. And it seems to me, this afternoon, that you have a right to know it too. [*A pause as* ANTIGONE *moves to chair and sits.*] It's not a pretty story. [*He turns, gets stool from behind the table and places it between the table and the chair.*] You'll see. [*He looks at her for a moment.*] Tell me, first. What do you remember about your brothers? They were older than you, so they must have looked down on you. And I imagine that they tormented you — pulled your pigtails, broke your dolls, whispered secrets to each other to put you in a rage.

ANTIGONE. They were big and I was little.

CREON. And later on, when they came home wearing evening clothes, smoking cigarettes, they would have nothing to do with you; and you thought they were wonderful.

ANTIGONE. They were boys and I was a girl.

CREON. You didn't know why, exactly, but you knew that they were making your mother unhappy. You saw her in tears over them, and your father would fly into a rage because of them. You heard them come in, slamming doors, laughing noisily in the corridors — insolent, spineless, unruly, smelling of drink.

ANTIGONE (*staring outward*). Once, it was very early and we had just got up. I saw them coming home and hid behind a door. Polynices was very pale, and his eyes were shining. He was so handsome in his evening clothes. He saw me and said: "Here, this is for you," and he gave me a big paper flower that he had brought home from his night out.

CREON. And of course you still have that flower. Last night, before you crept out, you opened a drawer and looked at it for a time, to give yourself courage.

ANTIGONE. Who told you so?

CREON. Poor Antigone! With her night club flower. Do you know what your brother was?

ANTIGONE. Whatever he was, I know that you will say vile things about him.

CREON. A cheap, idiotic bounder, that is what he was. A cruel, vicious little voluptuary.[7] A little beast with just wit enough to drive a car faster and throw more money away than any of his pals. I was with your father one day when Polynices, having lost a lot of money gambling, asked him to settle the debt; and when your father refused, the boy raised his hand against him and called him a vile name.

ANTIGONE. That's a lie!

CREON. He struck your father in the face with his fist. It was pitiful. Your father sat at his desk with his head in his hands. His nose was bleeding. He was weeping with anguish. And in a corner of your father's study, Polynices stood sneering and lighting a cigarette.

ANTIGONE. That's a lie.

[A pause.]

CREON. When did you last see Polynices alive? When you were twelve years old. That's true, isn't it?

ANTIGONE. Yes, that's true.

CREON. Now you know why. Oedipus was too chicken-hearted to have the boy locked up. Polynices was allowed to go off and join the Argive [8] army. And as soon as he reached Argos, the attempts upon your father's life began — upon the life of an old man who couldn't make up his mind to die, couldn't bear to be parted from his kingship. One after another, men slipped into Thebes from Argos for the purpose of assassinating him, and every killer we caught always ended by confessing who had put him up to it, who had paid him to try it. And it wasn't only Polynices. That is really what I am trying to tell you. I want you to know what went on in the back room, in the kitchen of politics; I want you to know what took place in the wings of this drama in which you are burning to play a part.

Yesterday, I gave Eteocles a state funeral, with pomp and honors. Today, Eteocles is a saint and a hero in the eyes of all Thebes. The

---

[7] *voluptuary:* one given to sensual, luxurious pleasures.

[8] *Argive:* Greek.

whole city turned out to bury him. The schoolchildren emptied their saving boxes to buy wreaths for him. Old men, orating in quavering, hypocritical voices, glorified the virtues of the great-hearted brother, the devoted son, the loyal prince. I made a speech myself, and every temple priest was present with an appropriate show of sorrow and solemnity in his stupid face. And military honors were accorded the dead hero.

Well, what else could I have done? People had taken sides in the civil war. Both sides couldn't be wrong; that would be too much. I couldn't have made them swallow the truth. Two gangsters was more of a luxury than I could afford. [*He pauses for a moment.*] And this is the whole point of my story. Eteocles, that virtuous brother, was just as rotten as Polynices. That great-hearted son had done his best, too, to procure the assassination of his father. That loyal prince had also offered to sell out Thebes to the highest bidder.

Funny, isn't it? Polynices lies rotting in the sun while Eteocles is given a hero's funeral and will be housed in a marble vault. Yet I have absolute proof that everything that Polynices did, Eteocles had plotted to do. They were a pair of blackguards — both engaged in selling out Thebes, and both engaged in selling out each other, and they died like the cheap gangsters they were, over a division of the spoils.

But, as I told you a moment ago, I had to make a martyr of one of them. I sent out to the holocaust for their bodies; they were found clasped in one another's arms — for the first time in their lives, I imagine. Each had been spitted [9] on the other's sword, and the Argive cavalry had trampled them down. They were mashed to a pulp, Antigone. I had the prettier of the two carcasses brought in and gave it a state funeral, and I left the other to rot. I don't know which was which. And I assure you, I don't care.

[*Long silence, neither looking at the other.*]

ANTIGONE (*in a mild voice*). Why do you tell me all this?

CREON. Would it have been better to let you die a victim to that obscene story?

ANTIGONE. It might have been. I had my faith.

---

[9] *spitted:* impaled, stabbed.

CREON. What are you going to do now?

ANTIGONE (*rises to her feet in a daze*). I shall go up to my room.

CREON. Don't stay alone. Go and find Haemon. And get married quickly.

ANTIGONE (*in a whisper*). Yes.

CREON. All this is really beside the point. You have your whole life ahead of you — and life is a treasure.

ANTIGONE. Yes.

CREON. And you were about to throw it away. Don't think me fatuous if I say that I understand you and that at your age I should have done the same thing. A moment ago, when we were quarreling, you said I was drinking in your words. I was. But it wasn't you I was listening to; it was a lad named Creon who lived here in Thebes many years ago. He was thin and pale, as you are. His mind, too, was filled with thoughts of self-sacrifice. Go and find Haemon. And get married quickly, Antigone. Be happy. Life flows like water, and you young people let it run away through your fingers. Shut your hands; hold on to it, Antigone. Life is not what you think it is. Life is a child playing around your feet, a tool you hold firmly in your grip, a bench you sit down upon in the evening, in your garden. People will tell you that that's not life, that life is something else. They will tell you that because they need your strength and your fire, and they will want to make use of you. Don't listen to them. Believe me, the only poor consolation that we have in our old age is to discover that what I have just said to you is true. Life is nothing more than the happiness that you get out of it.

ANTIGONE (*murmurs, lost in thought*). Happiness . . .

CREON (*suddenly a little self-conscious*). Not much of a word, is it?

ANTIGONE (*quietly*). What kind of happiness do you foresee for me? Paint me the picture of your happy Antigone. What are the unimportant little sins that I shall have to commit before I am allowed to sink my teeth into life and tear happiness from it? Tell me: to whom shall I have to lie? Upon whom shall I have to fawn? To whom must I sell myself? Whom do you want me to leave dying, while I turn away my eyes?

CREON. Antigone, be quiet.

ANTIGONE. Why do you tell me to be quiet when all I want to know is what I have to do to be happy? This minute, since it is this very minute that I must make my choice. You tell me that life is so wonderful. I want to know what I have to do in order to be able to say that myself.

CREON. Do you love Haemon?

ANTIGONE. Yes, I love Haemon. The Haemon I love is hard and young, faithful and difficult to satisfy, just as I am. But if what I love in Haemon is to be worn away like a stone step by the tread of the thing you call life, the thing you call happiness, if Haemon reaches the point where he stops growing pale with fear when I grow pale, stops thinking that I must have been killed in an accident when I am five minutes late, stops feeling that he is alone on earth when I laugh and he doesn't know why — if he too has to learn to say yes to everything — why, no, then, no! I do not love Haemon!

CREON. You don't know what you are talking about!

ANTIGONE. I do know what I am talking about! Now it is you who have stopped understanding. I am too far away from you now, talking to you from a kingdom you can't get into with your quick tongue and your hollow heart. [Laughs.] I laugh, Creon, because I see you suddenly as you must have been at fifteen: the same look of impotence in your face and the same inner conviction that there was nothing you couldn't do. What has life added to you, except those lines in your face, and that fat on your stomach?

CREON. Be quiet, I tell you!

ANTIGONE. Why do you want me to be quiet? Because you know that I am right? Do you think I can't see in your face that what I am saying is true? You can't admit it, of course; you have to go on growling and defending the bone you call happiness.

CREON. It is your happiness, too, you little fool!

ANTIGONE. I spit on your happiness! I spit on your idea of life — that life must go on, come what may. You are all like dogs that lick everything they smell. You with your promise of a humdrum happiness — provided a person doesn't ask too much of life. I want everything of life, I do; and I want it now! I want it total, complete: otherwise I reject it! I will *not* be moderate. I will *not* be satisfied with the bit of cake you offer me if I promise to be a good little girl. I want to be sure of everything this very day; sure that everything will be as beautiful as when I was a little girl. If not, I want to die!

CREON. Scream on, daughter of Oedipus! Scream on, in your father's own voice!

ANTIGONE. In my father's own voice, yes! We are of the tribe that asks questions, and we ask them to the bitter end. Until no tiniest chance of hope remains to be strangled by our hands. We are of the tribe that hates your filthy hope, your docile, female hope; hope, your —

CREON (*grasps her by her arms*). Shut up! If you could see how ugly you are, shrieking those words!

ANTIGONE. Yes, I am ugly! Father was ugly, too. [CREON *releases her arms, turns and moves away. Stands with his back to* ANTIGONE.] But Father became beautiful. And do you know when? [*She follows him to behind the table.*] At the very end. When all his questions had been answered. When he could no longer doubt that he *had* killed his own father, that he *had* gone to bed with his own mother. When all hope was gone, stamped out like a beetle. When it was absolutely certain that nothing, nothing could save him. Then he was at peace; then he could smile, almost; then he became beautiful. . . . Whereas you! Ah, those faces of yours, you candidates for election to happiness! It's you who are the ugly ones, even the handsomest of you — with that ugly glint in the corner of your eyes, that ugly crease at the corner of your mouths. Creon, you spoke the word a moment ago: the kitchen of politics. You look it and you smell of it.

CREON (*struggles to put his hand over her mouth*). I order you to shut up! Do you hear me?

ANTIGONE. *You* order me? Cook! Do you really believe that you can give me orders?

CREON. Antigone! The anteroom is full of people! Do you want them to hear you?

ANTIGONE. Open the doors! Let us make sure that they can hear me!

CREON. By God! You shut up, I tell you!

[ISMENE *enters through arch.*]

ISMENE (*distraught*). Antigone!

ANTIGONE (*turns to* ISMENE). You, too? What do you want?

ISMENE. Oh, forgive me, Antigone. I've come back. I'll be brave. I'll go with you now.

ANTIGONE. Where will you go with me?

ISMENE (*to* CREON). Creon! If you kill her, you'll have to kill me too.

ANTIGONE. Oh, no, Ismene. Not a bit of it. I die alone. You don't think I'm going to let you die with me after what I've been through? You don't deserve it.

ISMENE. If you die, I don't want to live. I don't want to be left behind, alone.

ANTIGONE. You chose life and I chose death. Now stop blubbering. You had your chance to come with me in the black night, creeping on your hands and knees. You had your chance to claw up the earth with your nails, as I did, to get yourself caught like a thief, as I did. And you refused it.

ISMENE. Not any more. I'll do it alone tonight.

ANTIGONE (*turns around toward* CREON). You hear that, Creon? The thing is catching! Who knows but that lots of people will catch the disease from me! What are you waiting for? Call in your guards! Come on, Creon! Show a little courage! It only hurts for a minute! Come on, cook!

CREON (*turns toward arch and calls*). Guard!

[GUARDS *enter through arch.*]

ANTIGONE (*in a great cry of relief*). At last, Creon!

[CHORUS *enters through left arch.*]

CREON (*to the* GUARDS). Take her away! [CREON *goes up on top step.*]

[GUARDS *grasp* ANTIGONE *by her arms, turn and hustle her toward the arch, right, and exeunt.* ISMENE *mimes horror, backs away toward the arch, left, then turns and runs out through the arch. A long pause, as* CREON *moves slowly downstage.*]

CHORUS (*behind* CREON. *Speaks in a deliberate voice*). You are out of your mind, Creon. What have you done?

CREON (*his back to* CHORUS). She had to die.

CHORUS. You must not let Antigone die. We shall carry the scar of her death for centuries.

CREON. She insisted. No man on earth was strong enough to dissuade her. Death was her purpose, whether she knew it or not. Polynices was a mere pretext. When she had to give up that pretext, she found another one — that life and happiness were tawdry things and not worth possessing. She was bent upon only one thing: to reject life and to die.

CHORUS. She is a mere child, Creon.

CREON. What do you want me to do for her? Condemn her to live?

HAEMON (*calls from offstage*). Father! [HAEMON *enters through arch, right.* CREON *turns toward him.*]

CREON. Haemon, forget Antigone. Forget her, my dearest boy.

HAEMON. How can you talk like that?

CREON (*grasps* HAEMON *by the hands*). I did everything I could to save her, Haemon. I used every argument. I swear I did. The girl doesn't love you. She could have gone on living for you, but she refused. She wanted it this way; she wanted to die.

HAEMON. Father! The guards are dragging Antigone away! You've got to stop them! [*He breaks away from* CREON.]

CREON (*looks away from* HAEMON). I can't stop them. It's too late. Antigone has spoken. The story is all over Thebes. I cannot save her now.

CHORUS. Creon, you must find a way. Lock her up. Say that she has gone out of her mind.

CREON. Everybody will know it isn't so. The nation will say that I am making an exception of her because my son loves her. I cannot.

CHORUS. You can still gain time and get her out of Thebes.

CREON. The mob already knows the truth. It is howling for her blood. I can do nothing.

HAEMON. But, Father, you are master in Thebes!

CREON. I am master under the law. Not above the law.

HAEMON. You cannot let Antigone be taken from me. I am your son!

CREON. I cannot do anything else, my poor boy. She must die, and you must live.

HAEMON. Live, you say! Live a life without Antigone? A life which I am to go on admiring you as you busy yourself about your kingdom, make your persuasive speeches, strike your attitudes? Not without Antigone. I love Antigone. I will not live without Antigone!

CREON. Haemon — you will have to resign yourself to life without Antigone. [*He moves to left of* HAEMON.] Soonor or later there comes a day of sorrow in each man's life when he must cease to be a child and take up the burden of manhood. That day has come for you.

HAEMON (*backs away a step*). That giant strength, that courage.

That massive god who used to pick me up in his arms and shelter me from shadows and monsters — was that you, Father? Was it of you I stood in awe? Was that man you?

CREON. For God's sake, Haemon, do not judge me! Not you, too!

HAEMON (*pleading now*). This is all a bad dream, Father. You are not yourself. It isn't true that we have been backed up against a wall, forced to surrender. We don't have to say *yes* to this terrible thing. You are still king. You are still the father I revered. You have no right to desert me, to shrink into nothingness. The world will be too bare, I shall be too alone in the world, if you force me to disown you.

CREON. The world *is* bare, Haemon, and you *are* alone. You must cease to think your father all-powerful. Look straight at me. See your father as he is. That is what it means to grow up and be a man.

HAEMON (*stares at* CREON *for a moment*). I tell you that I will not live without Antigone. [*Turns and goes quickly out through arch.*]

CHORUS. Creon, the boy will go mad.

CREON. Poor boy! He loves her.

CHORUS. Creon, the boy is wounded to death.

CREON. We are all wounded to death.

[FIRST GUARD *enters through arch, right, followed by* SECOND *and* THIRD GUARDS *pulling* ANTIGONE *along with them.*]

FIRST GUARD. Sir, the people are crowding into the palace!

ANTIGONE. Creon, I don't want to see their faces. I don't want to hear them howl. You are going to kill me; let that be enough. I want to be alone until it is over.

CREON. Empty the palace! Guards at the gates!

CREON *quickly crosses toward the arch; exit. Two* GUARDS *release* ANTIGONE; *exeunt behind* CREON. CHORUS *goes out through arch, left. The lighting dims so that only the area about the table is lighted. The cyclorama is covered with a dark blue color. The scene is intended to suggest a prison cell, filled with shadows and dimly lit.* ANTIGONE *moves to stool and sits. The* FIRST GUARD *stands upstage. He watches* ANTIGONE, *and as she sits, he begins pacing slowly downstage, then upstage. A pause.*

ANTIGONE [*turns and looks at the* GUARD]. It's you, is it?

GUARD. What do you mean, me?

ANTIGONE. The last human face that I shall see. [A *pause as they look at each other, then* GUARD *paces upstage, turns, and crosses behind table.*] Was it you that arrested me this morning?

GUARD. Yes, that was me.

ANTIGONE. You hurt me. There was no need for you to hurt me. Did I act as if I was trying to escape?

GUARD. Come on now, Miss. It was my business to bring you in. I did it. [A *pause. He paces to and fro upstage. Only the sound of his boots is heard.*]

ANTIGONE. How old are you?

GUARD. Thirty-nine.

ANTIGONE. Have you any children?

GUARD. Yes. Two.

ANTIGONE. Do you love your children?

GUARD. What's that got to do with you? [A *pause. He paces upstage and downstage.*]

ANTIGONE. How long have you been in the Guard?

GUARD. Since the war. I was in the army. Sergeant. Then I joined the Guard.

ANTIGONE. Does one have to have been an army sergeant to get into the Guard?

GUARD. Supposed to be. Either that or on special detail. But when they make you a guard, you lose your stripes.

ANTIGONE (*murmurs*). I see.

GUARD. Yes. Of course, if you're a guard, everybody knows you're something special; they know you're an old N.C.O. Take pay, for instance. When you're a guard you get your pay, and on top of that you get six months' extra pay, to make sure you don't lose anything by not being a sergeant any more. And of course you do better than that. You get a house, coal, rations, extras for the wife and kids. If you've got two kids, like me, you draw better than a sergeant.

ANTIGONE (*barely audible*). I see.

GUARD. That's why sergeants, now, they don't like guards. Maybe you noticed they try to make out they're better than us? Promotion, that's what it is. In the army, anybody can get promoted. All you need is good conduct. Now in the Guard, it's slow, and you have to know your business — like how to make out a report and the like of that. But when you're an N.C.O. in the Guard, you've got something that even a sergeant-major ain't got. For instance —

ANTIGONE (*breaking him off*). Listen.

GUARD. Yes, Miss.

ANTIGONE. I'm going to die soon.

[*The* GUARD *looks at her for a moment, then turns and moves away.*]

GUARD. For instance, people have a lot of respect for guards, they have. A guard may be a soldier, but he's kind of in the civil service, too.

ANTIGONE. Do you think it hurts to die?

GUARD. How would I know? Of course, if somebody sticks a saber in your guts and turns it around, it hurts.

ANTIGONE. How are they going to put me to death?

GUARD. Well, I'll tell you. I heard the proclamation all right. Wait a minute. How did it go now? [*He stares into space and recites from memory.*] "In order that our fair city shall not be pol-luted with her sinful blood, she shall be im-mured — immured." That means, they shove you in a cave and wall up the cave.

ANTIGONE. Alive?

GUARD. Yes. . . . [*He moves away a few steps.*]

ANTIGONE (*murmurs*). O tomb! O bridal bed! Alone!

[ANTIGONE *sits there, a tiny figure in the middle of the stage. You would say she felt a little chilly. She wraps her arms around herself.*]

GUARD. Yes! Outside the southeast gate of the town. In the Cave of Hades. In broad daylight. Some detail, eh, for them that's on the job! First they thought maybe it was a job for the army. Now it looks like it's going to be the Guard. There's an outfit for you! Nothing the Guard can't do. No wonder the army's jealous.

ANTIGONE. A pair of animals.

GUARD. What do you mean, a pair of animals?

ANTIGONE. When the winds blow cold, all they need do is to press close against one another. I am all alone.

GUARD. Is there anything you want? I can send out for it, you know.

ANTIGONE. You are very kind. [*A pause.* ANTIGONE *looks up at the* GUARD.] Yes, there is something I want. I want you to give someone a letter from me, when I am dead.

GUARD. How's that again? A letter?

ANTIGONE. Yes, I want to write a letter; and I want you to give it to someone for me.

GUARD (*straightens up*). Now, wait a minute. Take it easy. It's as much as my job is worth to go handing out letters from prisoners.

ANTIGONE (*removes a ring from her finger and holds it out toward him*). I'll give you this ring if you will do it.

GUARD. Is it gold? [*He takes the ring from her.*]

ANTIGONE. Yes, it is gold.

GUARD (*shakes his head*). Uh-uh. No can do. Suppose they go through my pockets. I might get six months for a thing like that. [*He stares at the ring, then glances off right to make sure that he is not being watched.*] Listen, tell you what I'll do. You tell me what you want to say, and I'll write it down in my book. Then, afterward, I'll tear out the pages and give them to the party, see? If it's in my handwriting, it's all right.

ANTIGONE (*winces*). In your handwriting? [*She shudders slightly.*] No. That would be awful. The poor darling! In your handwriting.

GUARD (*offers back the ring*). O.K. It's no skin off my nose.

ANTIGONE (*quickly*). Of course, of course. No, keep the ring. But hurry. Time is getting short. Where is your notebook? [*The GUARD pockets the ring, takes his notebook and pencil from his pocket, puts his foot up on chair, and rests the notebook on his knee, licks his pencil.*] Ready? [*He nods.*] Write, now. "My darling . . ."

GUARD (*writes as he mutters*). The boy friend, eh?

ANTIGONE. "My darling. I wanted to die, and perhaps you will not love me any more . . ."

GUARD (*mutters as he writes*). ". . . will not love me any more."

ANTIGONE. "Creon was right. It is terrible to die."

GUARD (*repeats as he writes*). ". . . terrible to die."

ANTIGONE. "And I don't even know what I am dying for. I am afraid . . ."

GUARD (*looks at her*). Wait a minute! How fast do you think I can write?

ANTIGONE (*takes hold of herself*). Where are you?

GUARD (*reads from his notebook*). "And I don't even know what I am dying for."

ANTIGONE. No. Scratch that out. Nobody must know that. They

have no right to know. It's as if they saw me naked and touched me, after I was dead. Scratch it all out. Just write: "Forgive me."

GUARD (*looks at* ANTIGONE). I cut out everything you said there at the end, and I put down, "Forgive me"?

ANTIGONE. Yes. "Forgive me, my darling. You would all have been so happy except for Antigone. I love you."

GUARD (*finishes the letter*). ". . . I love you." [*He looks at her.*] Is that all?

ANTIGONE. That's all.

GUARD (*straightens up, looks at notebook*). Damn funny letter.

ANTIGONE. I know.

GUARD (*looks at her*). Who is it to? [*A sudden roll of drums begins and continues until after* ANTIGONE's *exit. The* FIRST GUARD *pockets the notebook and shouts at* ANTIGONE.] O.K. That's enough out of you! Come on!

At the sound of the drum roll, SECOND and THIRD GUARDS enter through the arch. ANTIGONE rises. GUARDS seize her and exeunt with her. The lighting moves up to suggest late afternoon. CHORUS enters.

CHORUS. And now it is Creon's turn.

[MESSENGER *runs through the arch, right.*]

MESSENGER. The Queen . . . the Queen! Where is the Queen?

CHORUS. What do you want with the Queen? What have you to tell the Queen?

MESSENGER. News to break her heart. Antigone had just been thrust into the cave. They hadn't finished heaving the last block of stone into place when Creon and the rest heard a sudden moaning from the tomb. A hush fell over us all, for it was not the voice of Antigone. It was Haemon's voice that came forth from the tomb. Everybody looked at Creon, and he howled like a man demented: "Take away the stones! Take away the stones!" The slaves leaped at the wall of stones, and Creon worked with them, sweating and tearing at the blocks with his bleeding hands. Finally a narrow opening was forced, and into it slipped the smallest guard.

Antigone had hanged herself by the cord of her robe, by the red and golden twisted cord of her robe. The cord was around her neck like a child's collar. Haemon was on his knees, holding her in his arms and moaning, his face buried in her robe. More stones were removed, and Creon went into the tomb. He tried to raise Haemon to his feet. I could hear him begging Haemon to rise to his feet. Haemon was deaf to his father's voice, till suddenly he stood up of his own accord, his eyes dark and burning. Anguish was in his face, but it was the face of a little boy. He stared at his father. Then suddenly he struck him — hard, and he drew his sword. Creon leaped out of range. Haemon went on staring at him, his eyes full of contempt — a glance that was like a knife and that Creon couldn't escape. The King stood trembling in the far corner of the tomb, and Haemon went on staring. Then, without a word, he stabbed himself and lay down beside Antigone, embracing her in a great pool of blood.

[A *pause as* CREON *and* PAGE *enter through arch on the* MESSENGER's *last words.* CHORUS *and the* MESSENGER *both turn to look at* CREON; *then exit the* MESSENGER *through curtain.*]

CREON. I have had them laid out side by side. They are together at last and at peace. Two lovers on the morrow of their bridal. Their work is done.

CHORUS. But not yours, Creon. You have still one thing to learn. Eurydice, the Queen, your wife —

CREON. A good woman. Always busy with her garden, her preserves, her sweaters — those sweaters she never stopped knitting for the poor. Strange, how the poor never stop needing sweaters. One would almost think that was all they needed.

CHORUS. The poor in Thebes are going to be cold this winter, Creon. When the Queen was told of her son's death, she waited carefully until she had finished her row, then put down her knitting calmly — as she did everything. She went up to her room, her lavender-scented room, with its embroidered doilies and its pictures framed in plush; and there, Creon, she cut her throat. She is laid out now in one of those two old-fashioned twin beds, exactly where you went to her one night when she was still a maiden. Her smile is still the same, scarcely a shade more melancholy. And if it were not for that great red blot on the bed linen by her neck, one might think she was asleep.

CREON (*in a dull voice*). She, too. They are all asleep. [*Pause.*] It must be good to sleep.

CHORUS. And now you are alone, Creon.

CREON. Yes, all alone. (*To* PAGE.) My lad.

PAGE. Sir?

CREON. Listen to me. They don't know it, but the truth is the work is there to be done, and a man can't fold his arms and refuse to do it. They say it's dirty work. But if we didn't do it, who would?

PAGE. I don't know, sir.

CREON. Of course you don't. You'll be lucky if you never find out. In a hurry to grow up, aren't you?

PAGE. Oh, yes, sir.

CREON. I shouldn't be if I were you. Never grow up if you can help it. [*He is lost in thought as the hour chimes.*] What time is it?

PAGE. Five o'clock, sir.

CREON. What have we on at five o'clock?

PAGE. Cabinet meeting, sir.

CREON. Cabinet meeting. Then we had better go along to it.

[*Exeunt* CREON *and* PAGE *slowly through arch, left, and* CHORUS *moves downstage.*]

CHORUS. And there we are. It is quite true that if it had not been for Antigone they would all have been at peace. But that is over now. And they are all at peace. All those who were meant to die have died: those who believed one thing, those who believed the contrary thing, and even those who believed nothing at all, yet were caught up in the web without knowing why. All dead: stiff, useless, rotting. And those who have survived will now begin quietly to forget the dead: they won't remember who was who or which was which. It is all over. Antigone is calm tonight, and we shall never know the name of the fever that consumed her. She has played her part.

[*Three* GUARDS *enter, resume their places on steps as at the rise of the curtain, and begin to play cards.*]

A great melancholy wave of peace now settles down upon Thebes, upon the empty palace, upon Creon, who can now begin to wait for his own death.

Only the guards are left, and none of this matters to them. It's no skin off their noses. They go on playing cards.

[CHORUS *walks toward the arch, left, as the curtain falls.*]

Part Two: Short Stories

The following short stories come from the literature of three countries separated in both distance and time. Each story reflects the values and ideas of a particular nation. At the same time, the hopes, fears, conflicts, and passions in each tale have a universal appeal, helping us to see — sometimes by contrast — our own culture and values.

V. S. Naipaul is a writer from the small island of Trinidad in the Caribbean. His story takes place in the capital, Port of Spain, a city that has a wonderful mixture of peoples. Most of the people of Trinidad are either Negro or (like Naipaul) East Indian, the descendants of Hindus and Moslems who came to Trinidad when it was a British colony. There are also many Chinese and people of English, Spanish, and Portuguese backgrounds.

English is the native language of Trinidad, but it is an English which is transformed into a beautifully musical dialect. This speech has gone into Trinidad's most famous export, the calypso song. Its peculiar lilt and grammar ("it have a man outside here") can be heard in the dialogue of this story.

B. Wordsworth

V. S. NAIPAUL

Three beggars called punctually every day at the hospitable houses in Miguel Street. At about ten an Indian came in his dhoti [1] and white jacket, and we poured a tin of rice into the sack he carried on his back. At twelve an old woman smoking a clay pipe came, and she got a cent. At two a blind man led by a boy called for his penny.

[1] *dhoti:* loin cloth.

Sometimes we had a rogue.[2] One day a man called and said he was hungry. We gave him a meal. He asked for a cigarette and wouldn't go until we had lit it for him. That man never came again.

The strangest caller came one afternoon at about four o'clock. I had come back from school and was in my home clothes. The man said to me, "Sonny, may I come inside your yard?"

He was a small man, and he was tidily dressed. He wore a hat, a white shirt, and black trousers.

I asked, "What you want?"

He said, "I want to watch your bees."

We had four small gru-gru palm trees and they were full of uninvited bees.

I ran up the steps and shouted, "Ma, it have a man outside here. He say he want to watch the bees."

My mother came out, looked at the man and asked in an unfriendly way, "What you want?"

The man said, "I want to watch your bees."

His English was so good it didn't sound natural, and I could see my mother was worried.

She said to me, "Stay here and watch him while he watch the bees."

The man said, "Thank you, madam. You have done a good deed today."

He spoke very slowly and very correctly, as though every word was costing him money.

We watched the bees, this man and I, for about an hour, squatting near the palm trees.

The man said, "I like watching bees. Sonny, do you like watching bees?"

I said, "I ain't have the time."

He shook his head sadly. He said, "That's what I do, I just watch. I can watch ants for days. Have you ever watched ants? And scorpions, and centipedes — have you watched those?"

I shook my head.

I said, "What you does do, mister?"

He got up and said, "I am a poet."

I said, "A good poet?"

He said, "The greatest in the world."

---

[2] *rogue* (rōg): a dishonest person.

"What your name, mister?"

"B. Wordsworth."

"B for Bill?"

"Black. Black Wordsworth. White Wordsworth [3] was my brother. We share one heart. I can watch a small flower like the morning glory and cry."

I said, "Why you does cry?"

"Why, boy? Why? You will know when you grow up. You're a poet, too, you know. And when you're a poet you can cry for everything."

I couldn't laugh.

He said, "You like your mother?"

"When she not beating me."

He pulled out a printed sheet from his hip pocket and said, "On this paper is the greatest poem about mothers and I'm going to sell it to you at a bargain price. For four cents."

I went inside and I said, "Ma, you want to buy a poetry for four cents?"

My mother said, "Tell that blasted man to get away from my yard, you hear."

I said to B. Wordsworth, "My mother say she ain't have four cents."

B. Wordsworth said, "It is the poet's tragedy."

And he put the paper back in his pocket. He didn't seem to mind.

I said, "Is a funny way to go round selling poetry like that. Only calypsonians do that sort of thing. A lot of people does buy?"

He said, "No one has yet bought a single copy."

"But why you does keep on going round, then?"

He said, "In this way I watch many things, and I always hope to meet poets."

I said, "You really think I is a poet?"

"You're as good as me," he said.

And when B. Wordsworth left, I prayed I would see him again.

About a week later, coming back from school one afternoon, I met him at the corner of Miguel Street.

He said, "I have been waiting for you for a long time."

---

[3] *Wordsworth:* Poems by the English Romantic poet William Wordsworth appear on pages 208 and 215.

I said, "You sell any poetry yet?"

He shook his head.

He said, "In my yard I have the best mango tree in Port of Spain. And now the mangoes are ripe and red and very sweet and juicy. I have waited here for you to tell you this and to invite you to come and eat some of my mangoes."

He lived in Alberto Street in a one-roomed hut placed right in the center of the lot. The yard seemed all green. There was the big mango tree. There was a coconut tree, and there was a plum tree. The place looked wild, as though it wasn't in the city at all. You couldn't see all the big concrete houses in the street.

He was right. The mangoes were sweet and juicy. I ate about six, and the yellow mango juice ran down my arms to my elbows and down my mouth to my chin and my shirt was stained.

My mother said when I got home, "Where you was? You think you is a man now and could go all over the place? Go cut a whip for me."

She beat me rather badly, and I ran out of the house swearing that I would never come back. I went to B. Wordsworth's house. I was so angry, my nose was bleeding.

B. Wordsworth said, "Stop crying, and we will go for a walk."

I stopped crying, but I was breathing short. We went for a walk. We walked down St. Clair Avenue to the Savannah, and we walked to the racecourse.

B. Wordsworth said, "Now, let us lie on the grass and look up at the sky, and I want you to think how far those stars are from us."

I did as he told me, and I saw what he meant. I felt like nothing, and at the same time I had never felt so big and great in all my life. I forgot all my anger and all my tears and all the blows.

When I said I was better, he began telling me the names of the stars, and I particularly remember the constellation of Orion the Hunter, though I don't really know why. I can spot Orion even today, but I have forgotten the rest.

Then a light was flashed into our faces, and we saw a policeman. We got up from the grass.

The policeman said, "What you doing here?"

B. Wordsworth said, "I have been asking myself the same question for forty years."

We became friends, B. Wordsworth and I. He told me, "You

must never tell anybody about me and about the mango tree and the coconut tree and the plum tree. You must keep that a secret. If you tell anybody, I will know, because I am a poet."

I gave him my word and I kept it.

I liked his little room. But it looked lonely.

One day I asked him, "Mr. Wordsworth, why you does keep all this bush in your yard? Ain't it does make the place damp?"

He said, "Listen, and I will tell you a story. Once upon a time a boy and girl met each other and they fell in love. They loved each other so much they got married. They were both poets. He loved words. She loved grass and flowers and trees. They lived happily in a single room, and then one day, the girl poet said to the boy poet, 'We are going to have another poet in the family.' But this poet was never born, because the girl died, and the young poet died with her. And the girl's husband was very sad, and he said he would never touch a thing in the girl's garden. And so the garden remained and grew high and wild."

I looked at B. Wordsworth, and as he told me this lovely story, he seemed to grow older. I understood his story.

We went for long walks together. We went to the Botanical Gardens and the Rock Gardens. We climbed Chancellor Hill in the late afternoon and watched the darkness fall on Port of Spain and watched the lights go on in the city and on the ships in the harbor.

He did everything as though he were doing it for the first time in his life. He did everything as though he were doing some church rite.

He would say to me, "Now, how about having some ice cream?"

And when I said yes, he would grow very serious and say, "Now, which café shall we patronize?" As though it were a very important thing. He would think for some time about it and finally say, "I think I will go and negotiate the purchase with that shop."

The world became a most exciting place.

One day, when I was in his yard, he said to me, "I have a great secret which I am now going to tell you."

I said, "It really secret?"

"At the moment, yes."

I looked at him, and he looked at me. He said, "This is just between you and me, remember. I am writing a poem."

"Oh." I was disappointed.

He said, "But this is a different sort of poem. This is the greatest poem in the world."

I whistled.

He said, "I have been working on it for more than five years now. I will finish it in about twenty-two years from now, that is, if I keep on writing at the present rate."

"You does write a lot, then?"

He said, "Not any more. I just write one line a month. But I make sure it is a good line."

I asked, "What was last month's good line?"

He looked up at the sky, and said, "*The past is deep.*"

I said, "It is a beautiful line."

B. Wordsworth said, "I hope to distill the experiences of a whole month into that single line of poetry. So, in twenty-two years, I shall have written a poem that will sing to all humanity."

I was filled with wonder.

Our walks continued. We walked along the seawall at Docksite one day, and I said, "Mr. Wordsworth, if I drop this pin in the water, you think it will float?"

He said, "This is a strange world. Drop your pin, and let us see what will happen."

The pin sank.

I said, "How is the poem this month?"

But he never told me any other line. He merely said, "Oh, it comes, you know. It comes."

Or we would sit on the seawall and watch the liners come into the harbor.

But of the greatest poem in the world I heard no more.

I felt he was growing older.

"How you does live, Mr. Wordsworth?" I asked him one day.

He said, "You mean how I get money?"

When I nodded, he laughed in a crooked way.

He said, "I sing calypso in the calypso season."

"And that last you the rest of the year?"

"It is enough."

"But you will be the richest man in the world when you write the greatest poem?"

He didn't reply.

One day when I went to see him in his little house, I found him lying on his little bed. He looked so old and so weak that I found myself wanting to cry.

He said, "The poem is not going well."

He wasn't looking at me. He was looking through the window at the coconut tree, and he was speaking as though I wasn't there. He said, "When I was twenty I felt the power within myself." Then, almost in front of my eyes, I could see his face growing older and more tired. He said, "But that — that was a long time ago."

And then — I felt it so keenly, it was as though I had been slapped by my mother. I could see it clearly on his face. It was there for everyone to see. Death on the shrinking face.

He looked at me and saw my tears and sat up.

He said, "Come." I went and sat on his knees.

He looked into my eyes, and he said, "Oh, you can see it, too. I always knew you had the poet's eye."

He didn't even look sad, and that made me burst out crying loudly.

He pulled me to his thin chest, and said, "Do you want me to tell you a funny story?" and he smiled encouragingly at me.

But I couldn't reply.

He said, "When I have finished this story, I want you to promise that you will go away and never come back to see me. Do you promise?"

I nodded.

He said, "Good. Well, listen. That story I told you about the boy poet and the girl poet, do you remember that? That wasn't true. It was something I just made up. All this talk about poetry and the greatest poem in the world, that wasn't true, either. Isn't that the funniest thing you have heard?"

But his voice broke.

I left the house, and ran home crying, like a poet, for everything I saw.

I walked along Alberto Street a year later, but I could find no sign of the poet's house. It hadn't vanished, just like that. It had been pulled down, and a big two-storied building had taken its place. The mango tree and the plum tree and the coconut tree had all been cut down, and there was brick and concrete everywhere.

It was just as though B. Wordsworth had never existed.

The Decameron *by Giovanni Boccaccio is one of the most famous books ever written. Boccaccio lived in Florence, Italy, in the fourteenth century, a time when plagues often drove people from the city. In writing the* Decameron, *Boccaccio imagined that a group of noblemen and noblewomen had fled from the plague to a villa on one of the hills overlooking Florence. Here they told stories to pass the time until it was safe to return. As the book's title suggests, the refugees told stories for ten days, at the rate of ten stories a day. "The Falcon" is the ninth story told on the fifth day.*

The Falcon

GIOVANNI BOCCACCIO

There once lived in Florence a young man named Federigo. In all the countryside around, he was held in high esteem for his skill in arms and his many accomplishments. This young man fell deeply in love with a lady named Monna Giovanna, famous in her time as one of the most beautiful and charming women of Florence. In order to capture her attention and her love, Federigo gave a series of tournaments and banquets and spared no expense in his entertainments. But the lady, who was as discreet as she was beautiful, paid no attention to him.

Federigo spent all his money on these entertainments, and at last he had nothing left but one small farm, from which he scraped a living. He also managed to keep one favorite falcon, a bird of such qualities that no other falcon could compare with her. Since he had no more money, he could not afford to live in the city. He retired to his farm and lived there in poverty with only his falcon to amuse him.

Shortly after Federigo left town, Monna Giovanna's husband fell sick and died. In his will he left his fortune, which was very great, to the young son; but if the son were to die, everything would go to Monna Giovanna, whom he loved very dearly. Monna Giovanna, then, followed the custom of the time, which was that a widow should retire for a while from the city and carry on her mourning in the country. And so she moved to an estate which was very near the farm of Federigo.

Her young son, who went with her to the country estate, took to visiting Federigo's farm and became very fond of the famous falcon. He longed to have the falcon for his own, but he did not dare ask for it because he knew how dear it was to its owner.

A short time later, the boy became sick. His mother, who had no other child, loved him very much; she stayed with him all day as he lay sick and asked him if there was anything in the world he wanted. Whatever it was, she would get it for him. After she had asked him many times what he wanted, the boy finally said, "My dear mother, if you could get me Federigo's falcon, I think it would make me well again."

The lady had no idea how to go about fulfilling the boy's wish. It seemed to her beyond her power to obtain the falcon for him. She knew that Federigo loved her, but she had never repaid his attention with so much as one kind look.

"How then," she thought to herself, "can I go and ask for this falcon? They say it is one of the most prized birds that ever flew. And Federigo depends on it for his hunting. How can I be so rude as to ask a poor gentleman to give up the last thing he has and his only pleasure?"

But her love for her son was so strong that at last she decided to go to Federigo. She said to her son, "My dear son, get well, and I promise you that first thing in the morning I will go to Federigo and bring you back the falcon." Her promise made the boy beam with joy, and the same day he showed signs of improvement.

The next morning Monna Giovanna, with another lady as her companion, went to Federigo's humble farm and inquired for him. He was greatly surprised when he heard that Monna Giovanna was asking for him and ran in joy to meet her. As soon as she saw him, she gracefully and respectfully saluted him, saying, "Federigo, I am come to repay you in some way for the evil you have received from me at a time when you loved me more than was wise on your part. I intend to make myself and my companion your guests at dinner today."

Federigo replied with great humility, "Alas, madam, I do not remember any evil from you but instead so much good that I would spend my fortune a second time in your honor." Saying this, he respectfully led her into his house and, not having anyone else to introduce to her, said, "Madame, this good woman, the wife of my overseer, will wait on you while I prepare our table."

Because of his extreme poverty, Federigo was seldom able to entertain anyone in his house, and this morning he was less well prepared than usual. He ran back and forth like a madman, finding neither money nor food. Then, the hour being late, he happened to glance at his favorite falcon on her perch. Seeing no other solution, he seized the poor bird, killed it, and gave it to the cook to roast. He then spread a white tablecloth, and, after some time, he cheerfully returned to the lady and told her that the best dinner he could provide was prepared.

At this, the lady and her companion sat down at the table, and Federigo waited on them with great courtesy while they unknowingly ate his favorite bird. After the meal was over, Monna Giovanna decided the time had come to reveal the purpose of her visit. Turning politely to Federigo, she said, "When you recall your past life, Federigo, and remember my reserve toward you, which you perhaps thought hard-hearted and cruel, you will no doubt wonder at my boldness when I tell you the purpose of my visit. But I know that if you had children or knew the strength of parental love, you would pardon me. My love for my son forces me to ask you for the gift of a possession which I know is very dear to you. The gift I ask is your falcon. If I do not bring the falcon to my son, who is gravely ill, I fear I shall lose him. I ask you to help me preserve the life of my son not because you love me but because you have such a generous character."

Hearing this request, Federigo began to weep most bitterly and could not speak. The lady, thinking he grieved because he could not part with the falcon, prepared herself for the worst.

"From the moment I met you," began Federigo, "fate has been cruel to me. But this is the cruelest blow. You have at last come to my house and have asked for such a small gift, but fate will not let me grant it. When you honored me by coming to dinner, I wanted to honor you with every delicacy in my power. Therefore, I served you the falcon at dinner. Now I have so much grief that I shall never be happy again."

Monna Giovanna reprehended him for killing so fine a falcon for a lady's dinner, at the same time thinking to herself what a generous man Federigo was. With all hope gone, she thanked Federigo for the honor done her and left greatly depressed. Her son died a few days later.

After Monna Giovanna had mourned for some time, her brothers, seeing that she was still young and extremely rich, urged her to marry again. After much urging, she said to her brothers, "I would rather not marry again, but if you insist I marry, it shall be to Federigo."

Her brothers smiled at the news. "What folly is this? Would you marry a beggar?"

She answered, "Brothers, I know he is poor, but I would rather choose a man who needs wealth than wealth that needs a man."

The brothers saw that her mind was made up and, knowing Federigo was a good man, they gave their blessings to Monna Giovanna. Federigo thus found himself united to a beautiful lady whom he had long dearly loved and passed the rest of his days in peace and happiness.

The Colombian diplomat, Hernando Téllez, has closely observed revolutions which have divided the citizens of South American countries. As a storyteller, he presents this kind of division dramatically as two individuals with opposing views confront each other in the quiet of a barbershop.

Just Lather, That's All

HERNANDO TÉLLEZ

He said nothing when he entered. I was passing the best of my razors back and forth on a strop. When I recognized him I started to tremble. But he didn't notice. Hoping to conceal my emotion, I continued sharpening the razor. I tested it on the meat of my thumb and then held it up to the light. At that moment he took off the bullet-studded belt that his gun holster dangled from. He hung it up on a wall hook and placed his military cap over it. Then he turned to me, loosening the knot of his tie, and said, "It's hot. Give me a shave." He sat in the chair.

I estimated he had a four-day beard. The four days taken up by the latest expedition in search of our troops. His face seemed reddened, burned by the sun. Carefully, I began to prepare the soap. I cut off a few slices, dropped them into the cup, mixed in a bit of warm water, and began to stir with the brush. Immediately the foam began to rise. "The other boys in the group should have this much beard, too." I continued stirring the lather.

"But we did all right, you know. We got the main ones. We brought back some dead, and we've got some others still alive. But pretty soon they'll all be dead."

"How many did you catch?" I asked.

"Fourteen. We had to go pretty deep into the woods to find them. But we'll get even. Not one of them comes out of this alive, not one."

He leaned back on the chair when he saw me with the lather-covered brush in my hand. I still had to put the sheet on him. No doubt about it, I was upset. I took a sheet out of a drawer and knotted it around my customer's neck. He wouldn't stop talking. He probably thought I was in sympathy with his party.

"The town must have learned a lesson from what we did the other day," he said.

"Yes," I replied, securing the knot at the base of his dark, sweaty neck.

"That was a fine show, eh?"

"Very good," I answered, turning back for the brush. The man closed his eyes with a gesture of fatigue and sat waiting for the cool caress of the soap. I had never had him so close to me. The day he ordered the whole town to file into the patio of the school to see the four rebels hanging there, I came face to face with him for an instant. But the sight of the mutilated bodies kept me from noticing the face of the man who had directed it all, the face I was now about to take into my hands. It was not an unpleasant face, certainly. And the beard, which made him seem a bit older than he was, didn't suit him badly at all. His name was Torres. Captain Torres. A man of imagination, because who else would have thought of hanging the naked rebels and then holding target practice on their bodies? I began to apply the first layer of soap. With his eyes closed, he continued. "Without any effort I could go straight to sleep," he said, "but there's plenty to do this afternoon." I stopped the lathering and asked with a feigned lack of interest: "A firing squad?" "Something like that, but a little slower." I got on with the job of lathering his beard. My hands started trembling again. The man could not possibly realize it, and this was in my favor. But I would have preferred that he hadn't come. It was likely that many of our faction had seen him enter. And an enemy under one's roof imposes certain conditions. I would be obliged to shave that beard like any other one, carefully, gently, like that of any customer, taking pains to see that no single pore emitted a drop of blood. Being careful to see that the little tufts of hair did not lead the blade astray. Seeing that his skin ended up clean, soft, and healthy, so that passing the back of my hand over it I couldn't feel a hair. Yes, I was secretly a rebel, but I was also a conscientious barber and proud of the preciseness of my profession. And this four days' growth of beard was a fitting challenge.

I took the razor, opened up the two protective arms, exposed the blade and began the job, from one of the sideburns downward. The razor responded beautifully. His beard was inflexible and hard, not too long, but thick. Bit by bit the skin emerged. The razor rasped along, making its customary sound as fluffs of lather mixed with bits of hair gathered along the blade. I paused a moment to clean it, then took up the strop again to sharpen the razor, because I'm a barber who does things properly. The man, who had kept his eyes closed, opened them now, removed one of his hands from under the sheet, felt the spot on his face where the soap had been cleared off, and said, "Come to the school today at six o'clock." "The same thing as the other day?" I asked horrified. "It could be better," he replied. "What do you plan to do?" "I don't know yet. But we'll amuse ourselves." Once more he leaned back and closed his eyes. I approached him with the razor poised. "Do you plan to punish them all?" I ventured timidly. "All." The soap was drying on his face. I had to hurry. In the mirror I looked toward the street. It was the same as ever: the grocery store with two or three customers in it. Then I glanced at the clock: two-twenty in the afternoon. The razor continued on its downward stroke. Now from the other sideburn down. A thick, blue beard. He should have let it grow as some poets or priests do. It would suit him well. A lot of people wouldn't recognize him. Much to his benefit, I thought, as I attempted to cover the neck area smoothly. There, for sure, the razor had to be handled masterfully, since the hair, although softer, grew into little swirls. A curly beard. One of the tiny pores could be opened up and issue forth its pearl of blood. A good barber such as I prides himself on never allowing this to happen to a client. And this was a first-class client. How many of us had he ordered shot? How many of us had he ordered mutilated? It was better not to think about it. Torres did not know that I was his enemy. He did not know it nor did the rest. It was a secret shared by very few, precisely so that I could inform the revolutionaries of what Torres was doing in the town and of what he was planning each time he undertook a rebel-hunting excursion. So it was going to be very difficult to explain that I had him right in my hands and let him go peacefully — alive and shaved.

The beard was now almost completely gone. He seemed younger,

less burdened by years than when he had arrived. I suppose this always happens with men who visit barbershops. Under the stroke of
my razor Torres was being rejuvenated — rejuvenated because I am
a good barber, the best in the town, if I may say so. A little more
lather here, under his chin, on his Adam's apple, on this big vein.
How hot it is getting! Torres must be sweating as much as I. But
he is not afraid. He is a calm man, who is not even thinking about
what he is going to do with the prisoners this afternoon. On the
other hand, I, with this razor in my hands, stroking and restroking
this skin, trying to keep blood from oozing from these pores, can't
even think clearly. I'm a revolutionary and not a murderer. And
how easy it would be to kill him. And he deserves it. Does he? No!
What the devil! No one deserves to have someone else make the
sacrifice of becoming a murderer. What do you gain by it? Nothing. Others come along and still others, and the first ones kill the
second ones and they the next ones, and it goes on like this until
everything is a sea of blood. I could cut this throat just so, zip! zip!
I wouldn't give him time to complain, and since he has his eyes
closed, he wouldn't see the glistening knife blade or my glistening
eyes. But I'm trembling like a real murderer. Out of his neck a
gush of blood would spout onto the sheet, on the chair, on my
hands, on the floor. I would have to close the door. And the blood
would keep inching along the floor, warm, ineradicable, uncontain-
able, until it reached the street, like a little scarlet stream. I'm sure
that one solid stroke, one deep incision, would prevent any pain.
He wouldn't suffer. But what would I do with the body? Where
would I hide it? I would have to flee, leaving all I have behind, and
take refuge far away, far, far away. But they would follow until
they found me. "Captain Torres's murderer. He slit his throat
while he was shaving him — a coward." And then on the other side.
"The avenger of us all. A name to remember. (And here they would
mention my name.) He was the town barber. No one knew he was
defending our cause."

And what of all this? Murderer or hero? My destiny depends on
the edge of this blade. I can turn my hand a bit more, press a little
harder on the razor, and sink it in. The skin would give way like
silk, like rubber, like the strop. There is nothing more tender than
human skin, and the blood is always there, ready to pour forth. A
blade like this doesn't fail. It is my best. But I don't want to be a

murderer, no sir. You came to me for a shave. And I perform my work honorably. . . . I don't want blood on my hands. Just lather, that's all. You are an executioner and I am only a barber. Each person has his own place in the scheme of things. That's right. His own place.

Now his chin had been stroked clean and smooth. The man sat up and looked into the mirror. He rubbed his hands over his skin and felt it fresh, like new.

"Thanks," he said. He went to the hanger for his belt, pistol and cap. I must have been very pale; my shirt felt soaked. Torres finished adjusting the buckle, straightened his pistol in the holster, and after automatically smoothing down his hair, he put on the cap. From his pants pocket he took out several coins to pay me for my services. And he began to head toward the door. In the doorway he paused for a moment, and turning to me he said:

"They told me that you'd kill me. I came to find out. But killing isn't easy. You can take my word for it." And he headed on down the street.

Part Three: African Voices

Africa has for too long been thought of as a "dark continent." It has been called a sleeping giant. But today the giant is full of wakeful, vibrant life.

And the giant has an important past. Long before there was any contact with Europe, Africa saw the rise of great kingdoms with highly developed trade and culture. Such basic discoveries of civilization as the calendar, the alphabet, and the counting system were known and used in Africa at early dates. Elements of African culture reached North and South America and Europe, where they have influenced music, dance, theater, painting, and literature.

As Americans, we have an African as well as a European heritage. It has often been claimed that the most distinctive American contribution to the arts is jazz. Jazz developed from blues and ragtime, which in turn sprang from the spirituals and work songs which retained a strong element of African music. Many modern "classical" composers such as Stravinsky, Ravel, Dvořák, Weill, and Gershwin were influenced by the music of black peoples.

In literature, African folktales were modified and became part of American Negro folklore. The African folktale of the Talking Skull (page 677) has been found in strikingly similar versions in the American South.

Perhaps nowhere else in the world do old customs and new ways coexist as they do in Africa today. The selections which follow are taken from both modern and traditional sources and indicate strongly that Africa is a continent of change, growth, and progress. The reader can enjoy freshness of style and, most of all, can experience a sense of adventure and discovery in reading about people, places, and things that may be foreign and unfamiliar.

This is a chapter from Camara Laye's autobiography, The Dark Child. *The author, who was educated in France, looks back at his childhood in a West African village. He tells of things which he cannot now explain. His parents seemed to possess supernatural powers and were protected by guiding spirits in the forms of a snake and a crocodile.*

The Snake and the Crocodile

CAMARA LAYE

I

I was a little boy playing around my father's hut. How old would I have been at that time? I cannot remember exactly. I must still have been very young: five, maybe six years old. My mother was in the workshop with my father, and I could just hear their familiar voices above the noise on the anvil and the conversation of the customers.

Suddenly I stopped playing, my whole attention fixed on a snake that was creeping around the hut. After a moment I went over to him. I had taken in my hand a reed that was lying in the yard — there were always some lying around; they used to get broken off the fence of plaited reeds that marked the boundary of our concession [1] — and I thrust it into his mouth. The snake did not try to get away; he was beginning to enjoy our little game; he was slowly swallowing the reed; he was devouring it, I thought, as if it were some delicious prey, his eyes glittering with voluptuous bliss; and inch by inch his head was drawing nearer to my hand.

---

[1] *concession:* the section of an African village that belongs to one family.

At last the reed was almost entirely swallowed, and the snake's jaws were terribly close to my fingers.

I was laughing. I had not the slightest fear, and I feel sure that the snake would not have hesitated much longer before burying his fangs in my fingers if, at that moment, Damany, one of the apprentices, had not come out of the workshop. He called my father, and almost at once I felt myself lifted off my feet: I was safe in the arms of one of my father's friends.

Around me there was a great commotion. My mother was shouting hardest of all, and she gave me a few sharp slaps. I wept, more upset by the sudden uproar than by the blows. A little later, when I was somewhat calmer and the shouting had ceased, my mother solemnly warned me never to play that game again. I promised, although the game still didn't seem dangerous to me.

My father's hut was near the workshop, and I often played beneath the veranda that ran around the outside. It was his private hut and like all our huts built of mud bricks that had been pounded and molded with water; it was round and proudly helmeted with thatch. It was entered by a rectangular doorway. Inside, a tiny window let in a thin shaft of daylight. On the right was the bed, made of beaten earth like the bricks and spread with a simple wickerwork mat on which lay a pillow stuffed with kapok. At the rear, right under the window where the light was strongest, were the toolboxes. On the left were the *boubous* and the prayer-rugs.[2] At the head of the bed, hanging over the pillow and watching over my father's slumber, stood a row of pots that contained extracts from plants and the bark of trees. These pots all had metal lids and were profusely and curiously garlanded; it did not take long to discover that they were the most important things in the hut; they contained magic charms — those mysterious liquids that keep the evil spirits at bay and, if smeared on the body, make it invulnerable to every kind of black magic. My father, before going to bed, never failed to smear his body with a little of each liquid, first one, then another, for each charm had its own particular property but exactly *what* property I did not know: I had left my father's house too soon.

From the veranda under which I played, I could keep an eye on the workshop opposite, and the adults for their part could keep an

---

[2] *boubous and prayer-rugs:* Moslems wear *boubous* for prayer and kneel upon the prayer-rugs.

eye on me. This workshop was the main building in our concession, and my father was generally to be found there, looking after the work, forging the most important items himself or repairing delicate mechanisms; there he received his friends and his customers, and the place resounded with noise from morning to night. Moreover, everyone who entered or left our concession had to cross the workshop. There was a perpetual coming and going, though no one seemed to be in any particular hurry; each had his bit of gossip; each lingered at the forge to watch. Sometimes I came near the door, but I rarely went in; everyone there frightened me, and I would run away as soon as anyone tried to touch me. It was not until very much later that I got into the habit of crouching in a corner of the workshop to watch the fire blazing in the forge.

My private domain at that time was the veranda that encircled my father's hut, my mother's hut, and the orange tree that grew in the middle of the concession.

As soon as you crossed the workshop and went through the door at the back, you would see the orange tree. Compared with the giants of our native forests, the tree was not very big, but its mass of glossy leaves cast a dense shade that kept the heat at bay. When it was in flower, a heady perfume pervaded the entire concession. When the fruit first appeared, we were only allowed to look: we had to wait patiently until it was ripe. Then my father, who as head of the family — and a very large family it was — governed the concession, gave the order to pick the fruit. The men who did the picking brought their baskets one by one to my father, who portioned them out among the people who lived in the concession and among his neighbors and customers. After that we were permitted to help ourselves from the baskets, and we were allowed as much as we liked! My father was open-handed, in fact, a lavish giver. Any visitor, no matter who he was, shared our meals; since I could never keep up with the speed at which such guests ate, I might have remained forever hungry if my mother had not taken the precaution of putting my share aside.

"Sit here," she would say, "and eat, for your father's mad."

She did not look upon such guests with a kindly eye. There were too many for her liking, all bent on filling their bellies at her expense. My father, for his part, ate very little; he was an extremely temperate man.

We lived beside a railroad. The trains skirted the reed fence of the concession so closely that sparks thrown off from the locomotive set fire to it every now and then, which had to be quickly extinguished so that the whole concession would not go up in smoke. These alarms, frightening yet exciting, made me aware of the passing trains. And even when there were no trains — for in those days the railroad was dependent on a most irregular water traffic — much of my time was spent watching the iron rails. They glistened cruelly in a light which nothing in that place could relieve. Baking since dawn, the roadbed was so hot that oil which dropped from the locomotives evaporated immediately, leaving no trace. Was it the ovenlike heat or the smell of oil — for the smell remained in spite of everything — which attracted the snakes? I do not know. But often I came upon them crawling in that hot roadbed. It would have been fatal if they had gotten into the concession.

Ever since the day when I had been forbidden by my mother to play with snakes, I ran to her as soon as I saw one.

"There's a snake!" I would cry.

"What? Another?"

And she would come running to see what sort of snake it was. If it was just a snake like any other snake — actually they were all quite different — she would immediately beat it to death; and, like all the women of our country, she would work herself into a frenzy, beating the snake to a pulp. The men contented themselves with a single hard blow, neatly struck.

One day, however, I noticed a little black snake with a strikingly marked body. He was proceeding slowly in the direction of the workshop. I ran to warn my mother, as usual. But as soon as she saw the black snake, she said to me gravely:

"My son, this one must not be killed: he is not like other snakes, and he will not harm you; you must never interfere with him."

Everyone in our concession knew that this snake must not be killed — everyone except myself, and, I suppose, my little playmates, who were still ignorant children.

"This snake," my mother added, "is your father's guiding spirit."

I gazed dumbfounded at the little snake. He was proceeding calmly toward the workshop, gracefully, very sure of himself, and almost as if conscious of his immunity; his body, black and brilliant, glittered in the harsh light of the sun. When he reached the workshop, I noticed for the first time a small hole in the wall, cut out level with the ground. The snake disappeared through this hole.

"Look," said my mother, "the snake is going to pay your father a visit."

Although I was familiar with the supernatural, this sight filled me with such astonishment that I was struck dumb. What business would a snake have with my father? And why this particular snake? No one was to kill him because he was my father's guiding spirit! At any rate, that was the explanation my mother had given me. But what exactly *was* a "guiding spirit"? What were these guiding spirits that I encountered almost everywhere, forbidding one thing, commanding another to be done? I could not understand it at all, though their presences surrounded me as I grew to manhood. There were good spirits, and there were evil ones, and more evil than good ones, it seemed. And how was I to know that this snake was harmless? He was a snake like the others: black, to be sure, with extraordinary markings — but for all that a snake. I was completely perplexed, but I did not question my mother: I had decided that I must ask my father about it, as if this were a mystery to be discussed only between men, a mystery in which women had no part. I decided to wait until evening to speak to him.

Immediately after the evening meal, when the palavers were over, my father bade his friends farewell and sat under the veranda of his hut; I seated myself near him. I began questioning him in a dilatory [3] manner, as all children do, regarding every subject under the sun. Actually I was no more talkative than on other evenings. Only this evening I withheld what troubled me, waiting for the opportunity when — my face betraying nothing — I might ask the question which had worried me so deeply from the moment when I first saw the black snake going toward the workshop. Finally, unable to restrain myself any longer, I asked:

"My father, what is that little snake that comes to visit you?"

"What snake do you mean?"

"Why, the little black snake that my mother forbids us to kill."

"Ah!" he said.

He gazed at me for a long while. He seemed to be considering whether to answer or not. Perhaps he was thinking about how old

---

[3] *dilatory*: slow, tardy.

I was, perhaps he was wondering if it was not a little too soon to confide such a secret to a twelve-year-old boy. Then suddenly he made up his mind.

"That snake," he said, "is the guiding spirit of our race. Can you understand that?"

"Yes," I answered, although I did not understand very well.

"That snake," he went on, "has always been with us; he has always made himself known to one of us. In our time, it is to me that he has made himself known."

"Yes," I said.

And I said it with all my heart, for it seemed obvious to me that the snake could have made himself known to no one but my father. Was not my father the head man in our concession? Was it not my father who had authority over all the blacksmiths in our district? Was he not the most skilled? Was he not, after all, my father?

"How did he make himself known?" I asked.

"First of all, he made himself known in the semblance of a dream. He appeared to me several times in sleep and told me the day on which he would appear to me in reality: he gave me the precise time and place. But when I really saw him for the first time, I was filled with fear. I took him for a snake like any other snake, and I had to keep myself under control or I would have tried to kill him. When he saw that I did not receive him kindly, he turned away and departed the way he had come. And there I stood, watching him depart, wondering all the time if I should not simply have killed him there and then; but a power greater than I stayed my hand and prevented me from pursuing him. I stood watching him disappear. And even then, at that very moment, I could easily have overtaken him; a few swift strides would have been enough; but I was struck motionless by a kind of paralysis. Such was my first encounter with the little black snake."

He was silent a moment, then went on:

"The following night, I saw the snake again in my dream. 'I came as I foretold,' he said, 'but thou didst not receive me kindly; nay, rather I did perceive that thou didst intend to receive me unkindly: I did read it thus in thine eyes. Wherefore dost thou reject me? Lo, I am the guiding spirit of thy race, and it is even as the guiding spirit of thy race that I make myself known to thee, as to the most worthy. Therefore, forbear to look with fear upon me, and beware that thou dost not reject me, for behold, I bring thee good fortune.' After that, I received the snake kindly when he made himself known to me a second time; I received him without fear, I received him with loving kindness, and he brought me nothing but good."

My father again was silent for a moment, then he said:

"You can see for yourself that I am not more gifted than other men, that I have nothing which other men have not also, and even that I have less than others, since I give everything away, and would even give away the last thing I had, the shirt on my back. Nevertheless, I am better known. My name is on everyone's tongue, and it is I who have authority over all the blacksmiths in the five cantons.[4] If these things are so, it is by virtue of this snake alone, who is the guiding spirit of our race. It is to this snake I owe everything; it is he who gives me warning of all that is to happen. Thus I am never surprised, when I awake, to see this or that person waiting for me outside my workshop: I already know that he will be there. No more am I surprised when this or that motorcycle or bicycle breaks down, or when an accident happens to a clock: because I have had foreknowledge of what would come to pass. Everything is transmitted to me in the course of the night, together with an account of all the work I shall have to perform, so that from the start, without having to cast about in my mind, I know how to repair whatever is brought to me. These things have established my renown as a craftsman. But all this — let it never be forgotten — I owe to the snake, I owe it to the guiding spirit of our race."

He was silent; and then I understood why, when my father came back from a walk, he would enter the workshop and say to the apprentices: "During my absence, this or that person has been here, he was dressed in such and such a way, he came from such and such a place, and he brought with him such and such a piece of work to be done." And all marveled at this curious knowledge. When I raised my eyes, I saw that my father was watching me.

"I have told you all these things, little one, because you are my son, the eldest of my sons, and because I have nothing to hide from you. There is a certain form of behavior to observe and certain ways of acting in order that the guiding spirit of our race may approach you also. I, your father, was observing that form of be-

---

[4] *canton:* a political subdivision or district.

havior which persuades our guiding spirit to visit us. Oh, perhaps not consciously: but nevertheless it is true that if you desire the guiding spirit of our race to visit you one day, if you desire to inherit it in your turn, you will have to conduct yourself in the self-same manner; from now on, it will be necessary for you to be more and more in my company."

He gazed at me with burning eyes, then suddenly he heaved a sigh.

"I fear, I very much fear, little one, that you are not often enough in my company. You are all day at school, and one day you will depart from that school for a greater one. You will leave me, little one. . . ."

And again he heaved a sigh. I saw that his heart was heavy within him. The hurricane lamp hanging on the veranda cast a harsh glare on his face. He suddenly seemed to me an old man.

"Father!" I cried.

"Son . . ." he whispered.

And I was no longer sure whether I ought to continue to attend school or whether I ought to remain in the workshop: I felt unutterably confused.

"Go now," said my father.

I went to my mother's hut. The night was full of sparkling stars; an owl was hooting nearby. Ah! what was the right path for me? Did I know yet where that path lay? My perplexity was boundless as the sky, and mine was a sky, alas, without any stars. . . . I entered my mother's hut, which at that time was mine also, and went to bed at once. But sleep did not come, and I tossed restlessly on my bed.

"What's the matter with you?" asked my mother.

"Nothing."

No. I couldn't find anything to say.

"Why don't you go to sleep?" my mother continued.

"I don't know."

"Go to sleep!" she said.

"Yes," I said.

"Sleep. . . . Nothing can resist sleep," she said sadly.

Why did she, too, appear so sad? Had she divined my distress? Anything that concerned me she sensed very deeply. I was trying to sleep, but I shut my eyes and lay still in vain: the image of my father under the hurricane lamp would not leave me: my father who had suddenly seemed so old and who was so young, so lively — younger and livelier than the rest of us, a man no one could out-run, who was swifter of limb than any of us. . . . "Father! . . . Father! . . ." I kept repeating. "What must I do if I am to do the right thing?" And I wept silently and fell asleep still weeping.

After that we never mentioned the little black snake again: my father had spoken to me about him for the first and last time. But from that time on, as soon as I saw the little snake, I would run and sit in the workshop. I would watch him glide through the little hole in the wall. As if informed of his presence, my father at that very instant would turn his eyes to the hole and smile. The snake would go straight to him, opening his jaws. When he was within reach, my father would stroke him, and the snake would accept the caress with a quivering of his whole body. I never saw the little snake attempt to do the slightest harm to my father. That caress and the answering tremor — but I ought to say: that appealing caress and that answering tremor — threw me each time into an inexpressible confusion. I imagined I know not what mysterious conversations: the hand inquired, and the tremor replied. . . .

Yes. It was like a conversation. Would I too converse that way some day? No. I would continue to attend school. Yet I should have liked so much to place my hand, my own hand, on that snake and to understand and listen to that tremor too; but I did not know whether the snake would have accepted my hand, and I felt now that he would have nothing to tell me. I was afraid that he would never have anything to tell me.

When my father felt that he had stroked the snake enough, he left him alone. Then the snake coiled himself under the edge of one of the sheepskins on which my father, facing his anvil, was seated.

II

Of all the different kinds of work my father engaged in, none fascinated me so much as his skill with gold. No other occupation was so noble, no other needed such a delicate touch. And then, every time he worked in gold it was like a festival — indeed it *was* a festival — that broke the monotony of ordinary working days.

So, if a woman, accompanied by a go-between, crossed the threshold of the workshop, I followed her in at once. I knew what she wanted: she had brought some gold, and had come to ask my father to transform it into a trinket. She had collected it in the placers of Siguiri,[5] where, crouching over the river for months on end, she had patiently extracted grains of gold from the mud.

These women never came alone. They knew my father had other things to do than make trinkets. And even when he had the time, they knew they were not the first to ask a favor of him and that, consequently, they would not be served before others.

Generally they required the trinket for a certain date, for the festival of Ramadan[6] or the Tabaski[7] or some other family ceremony or dance.

Therefore, to enhance their chances of being served quickly and to more easily persuade my father to interrupt the work before him, they used to request the services of an official praise-singer, a go-between, arranging in advance the fee they were to pay him for his good offices.

The go-between installed himself in the workshop, tuned up his *cora*, which is our harp, and began to sing my father's praises. This was always a great event for me. I heard recalled the lofty deeds of my father's ancestors and their names from the earliest times. As the couplets were reeled off, it was like watching the growth of a great genealogical tree that spread its branches far and wide and flourished its boughs and twigs before my mind's eye. The harp played an accompaniment to this vast utterance of names, expanding it with notes that were now soft, now shrill.

I could sense my father's vanity being inflamed, and I already knew that after having sipped this milk-and-honey, he would lend a favorable ear to the woman's request. But I was not alone in my knowledge. The woman also had seen my father's eyes gleaming with contented pride. She held out her grains of gold as if the whole matter were settled. My father took up his scales and weighed the gold.

"What sort of trinket do you want?" he would ask.

---

[5] *placers of Siguiri*: places where gold is washed from the river at Siguiri, a town in the Republic of Guinea.
[6] *Ramadan*: the ninth month of the Mohammedan year, which is observed as a sacred month.
[7] *Tabaski*: a Moslem religious holiday.

"I want . . ."

And then the woman would not know any longer exactly what she wanted because desire kept making her change her mind and because she would have liked all the trinkets at once. But it would have taken a pile of gold much larger than she had brought to satisfy her whim, and from then on her chief purpose in life was to get hold of it as soon as she could.

"When do you want it?"

Always the answer was that the trinket was needed for an occasion in the near future.

"So! You are in that much of a hurry? Where do you think I shall find the time?"

"I am in a great hurry, I assure you."

"I have never seen a woman eager to deck herself out who wasn't in a great hurry! Good! I shall arrange my time to suit you. Are you satisfied?"

He would take the clay pot that was kept specially for smelting gold and would pour the grains into it. He would then cover the gold with powdered charcoal, a charcoal he prepared by using plant juices of exceptional purity. Finally, he would place a large lump of the same kind of charcoal over the pot.

As soon as she saw that the work had been duly undertaken, the woman, now quite satisfied, would return to her household tasks, leaving her go-between to carry on with the praise-singing which had already proved so advantageous.

At a sign from my father the apprentices began working two sheepskin bellows. The skins were on the floor, on opposite sides of the forge, connected to it by earthen pipes. While the work was in progress, the apprentices sat in front of the bellows with crossed legs. That is, the younger of the two sat, for the elder was sometimes allowed to assist. But the younger — this time it was Sidafa — was only permitted to work the bellows and watch while waiting his turn for promotion to less rudimentary tasks. First one and then the other worked hard at the bellows: the flame in the forge rose higher and became a living thing, a genie implacable and full of life.

Then my father lifted the clay pot with his long tongs and placed it on the flame.

Immediately all activity in the workshop almost came to a halt.

During the whole time that the gold was being smelted, neither copper nor aluminum could be worked nearby, lest some particle of these base metals fall into the container which held the gold. Only steel could be worked on such occasions, but the men whose task that was hurried to finish what they were doing or left it abruptly to join the apprentices gathered around the forge. There were so many, and they crowded so around my father, that I, the smallest person present, had to come near the forge in order not to lose track of what was going on.

If he felt he had inadequate working space, my father had the apprentices stand well away from him. He merely raised his hand in a simple gesture; at that particular moment he never uttered a word, and no one else would; no one was allowed to utter a word. Even the go-between's voice was no longer raised in song. The silence was broken only by the panting of the bellows and the faint hissing of the gold. But if my father never actually spoke, I know that he was forming words in his mind. I could tell from his lips, which kept moving, while, bending over the pot, he stirred the gold and charcoal with a bit of wood that kept bursting into flame and had constantly to be replaced by a fresh one.

What words did my father utter? I do not know. At least I am not certain what they were. No one ever told me. But could they have been anything but incantations? On these occasions was he not invoking the genies of fire and gold, of fire and wind, of wind blown by the blast-pipes of the forge, of fire born of wind, of gold married to fire? Was it not their assistance, their friendship, their espousal that he besought? Yes. Almost certainly he was invoking these genies, all of whom are equally indispensable for smelting gold.

The operation going on before my eyes was certainly the smelting of gold, yet something more than that: a magical operation that the guiding spirits could regard with favor or disfavor. That is why, all around my father, there was absolute silence and anxious expectancy. Though only a child, I knew there could be no craft greater than the goldsmith's. I expected a ceremony; I had come to be present at a ceremony, and it actually was one, though very protracted. I was still too young to understand why, but I had an inkling as I watched the almost religious concentration of those who followed the mixing process in the clay pot.

When finally the gold began to melt, I could have shouted aloud — and perhaps we all would have if we had not been forbidden to make a sound. I trembled, and so did everyone else watching my father stir the mixture — it was still a heavy paste — in which the charcoal was gradually consumed. The next stage followed swiftly. The gold now had the fluidity of water. The genies had smiled on the operation!

"Bring me the brick!" my father would order, thus lifting the ban that until then had silenced us.

The brick, which an apprentice would place beside the fire, was hollowed out, generously greased with Galam butter. My father would take the pot off the fire and tilt it carefully, while I would watch the gold flow into the brick, flow like liquid fire. True, it was only a very sparse trickle of fire, but how vivid, how brilliant! As the gold flowed into the brick, the grease sputtered and flamed and emitted a thick smoke that caught in the throat and stung the eyes, leaving us all weeping and coughing.

But there were times when it seemed to me that my father ought to turn this task over to one of his assistants. They were experienced, had assisted him hundreds of times, and could certainly have performed the work well. But my father's lips moved, and those inaudible, secret words, those incantations he addressed to one we could not see or hear, were the essential part. Calling on the genies of fire, of wind, of gold and exorcising the evil spirits — this was a knowledge he alone possessed.

By now the gold had been cooled in the hollow of the brick, and my father began to hammer and stretch it. This was the moment when his work as a goldsmith really began. I noticed that before embarking on it he never failed to stroke the little snake stealthily as it lay coiled up under the sheepskin. I can only assume that this was his way of gathering strength for what remained to be done, the most trying part of his task.

But was it not extraordinary and miraculous that on these occasions the little black snake was always coiled under the sheepskin? He was not always there. He did not visit my father every day. But he was always present whenever there was gold to be worked. His presence was no surprise to *me*. After that evening when my father had spoken of the guiding spirit of his race, I was no longer astonished. The snake was there intentionally. He knew what the future held. Did he tell my father? I think that he most certainly did. Did he tell him everything? I have another reason for believing firmly that he did.

The craftsman who works in gold must first of all purify himself. Great respecter of ceremony as he was, it would have been impossible for my father to ignore these rules. Now, I never saw him make these preparations. I saw him address himself to his work without any apparent preliminaries. From that moment it was obvious that, forewarned in a dream by his black guiding spirit of the task which awaited him in the morning, my father must have prepared for it as soon as he arose, entering his workshop in a state of purity, his body smeared with the secret potions hidden in his numerous pots of magical substances; or perhaps he always came into his workshop in a state of ritual purity. I am not trying to make him out a better man than he was — he was a man and had his share of human frailties — but he was always uncompromising in his respect for ritual observance.

The woman for whom the trinket was being made, and who had come often to see how the work was progressing, would arrive for the final time, not wanting to miss a moment of this spectacle — as marvelous to her as to us — when the gold wire, which my father had succeeded in drawing out from the mass of molten gold and charcoal, was transformed into a trinket.

There she would be. Her eyes would devour the fragile gold wire, following it in its tranquil and regular spiral around the little slab of metal which supported it. My father would catch a glimpse of her and I would see him slowly beginning to smile. Her avid attention delighted him.

"Are you trembling?" he would ask.

"Am I trembling?"

And we would all burst out laughing at her. For she would be trembling! She would be trembling with covetousness for the spiral pyramid in which my father would be inserting, among the convolutions, tiny grains of gold. When he had finally finished by crowning the pyramid with a heavier grain, she would dance in delight.

No one — no one at all — would be more enchanted than she as my father slowly turned the trinket back and forth between his fingers to display its perfection. Not even the praise-singer whose business it was to register excitement would be more excited than she. Throughout this metamorphosis he did not stop speaking faster and ever faster, increasing his tempo, accelerating his praises and flatteries as the trinket took shape, shouting to the skies my father's skill.

For the praise-singer took a curious part — I should say rather that it was direct and effective — in the work. He was drunk with the joy of creation. He shouted aloud in joy. He plucked his *cora* like a man inspired. He sweated as if he were the trinket-maker, as if he were my father, as if the trinket were his creation. He was no longer a hired censer-bearer,[8] a man whose services anyone could rent. He was a man who created his song out of some deep inner necessity. And when my father, after having soldered the large grain of gold that crowned the summit, held out his work to be admired, the praise-singer would no longer be able to contain himself. He would begin to intone the *douga*, the great chant which is sung only for celebrated men and which is danced for them alone.

But the *douga* is a formidable chant, a provocative chant, a chant which the praise-singer dared not sing and which the man for whom it is sung dared not dance before certain precautions had been taken. My father had taken them as soon as he woke, since he had been warned in a dream. The praise-singer had taken them when he concluded his arrangements with the woman. Like my father, he had smeared his body with magic substances and had made himself invulnerable to the evil genies whom the *douga* inevitably set free; these potions made him invulnerable also to rival praise-singers, perhaps jealous of him, who awaited only this song and the exaltation and loss of control which attended it, in order to begin casting their spells.

At the first notes of the *douga* my father would arise and emit a cry in which happiness and triumph were equally mingled; and brandishing in his right hand the hammer that was the symbol of his profession and in his left a ram's horn filled with magic substances, he would dance the glorious dance.

No sooner had he finished, than workmen and apprentices, friends and customers in their turn, not forgetting the woman for whom the trinket had been created, would flock around him, con-

---

[8] *censer-bearer:* a man who carries the vessel for burning incense in religious ceremonies.

gratulating him, showering praises on him and complimenting the praise-singer at the same time. The latter found himself laden with gifts — almost his only means of support, for the praise-singer leads a wandering life after the fashion of the troubadours of old. Aglow with dancing and the praises he had received, my father would offer everyone cola nuts, that small change of Guinean courtesy.

Now all that remained to be done was to redden the trinket in a little water to which chlorine and sea salt had been added. I was at liberty to leave. The festival was over! But often as I came out of the workshop, my mother would be in the court, pounding millet or rice, and she would call to me:

"Where have you been?" although she knew perfectly well where I had been.

"In the workshop."

"Of course. Your father was smelting gold. Gold! Always gold!"

And she would beat the millet or rice furiously with her pestle.

"Your father is ruining his health!"

"He danced the *douga*."

"The *douga*! The *douga* won't keep him from ruining his eyes. As for you, you would be better off playing in the courtyard instead of breathing dust and smoke in the workshop."

My mother did not like my father to work in gold. She knew how dangerous it was: a trinket-maker empties his lungs blowing on the blow-pipe, and his eyes suffer from the fire. Perhaps they suffer even more from the microscopic precision which the work requires. And even if there had been no such objections involved, my mother would scarcely have relished this work. She was suspicious of it, for gold cannot be smelted without the use of other metals, and my mother thought it was not entirely honest to put aside for one's own use the gold which the alloy had displaced. However, this was a custom generally known, and one which she herself had accepted when she took cotton to be woven and received back only a piece of cotton cloth half the weight of the original bundle.

III

I realize that my mother's authoritarian attitudes may appear surprising; generally the role of the African woman is thought to be a ridiculously humble one, and indeed there are parts of the continent where it is insignificant; but Africa is vast, with a diversity equal to its vastness. The woman's role in our country is one of fundamental independence, of great inner pride. We despise only those who allow themselves to be despised, and our women very seldom give cause for that. My father would never have dreamed of despising anyone, least of all my mother. He had the greatest respect for her too, and so did our friends and neighbors. That was due, I am sure, to my mother's character, which was impressive; it was due also to the strange powers she possessed.

I hesitate to say what these powers were, and I do not wish to describe them all. I know that what I say will be greeted with skeptical smiles. And today, now that I come to remember them, even I hardly know how I should regard them. They seem to be unbelievable; they *are* unbelievable. Nevertheless, I can only tell you what I saw with my own eyes. How can I disown the testimony of my own eyes? Those unbelievable things. I saw them. I see them again as I saw them then. Are there not things around us, everywhere, which are inexplicable? In our country there were mysteries without number, and my mother was familiar with them all.

One day — it was toward evening — I saw some men request her to use her powers to get a horse on his feet after he had resisted all attempts to make him rise. He was out at pasture, but he was lying down, and his owner wanted to bring him back to the stable before nightfall. The horse obstinately refused to move, although there was no apparent reason why he should disobey. But his inclination was otherwise, though it might have been a magic spell that immobilized him. I heard the men telling my mother about it and asking her help.

"Well, then, let's go and have a look at this horse," said my mother.

She called the eldest of my sisters and told her to look after the cooking of the evening meal and then went off with the men. I followed her. When we arrived at the pasture, we saw the horse: he was lying in the grass, gazing at us unconcernedly. His owner tried again to make him get up and spoke to him in honeyed tones, but the horse remained deaf to all entreaty. His master raised a hand to strike him.

"Do not strike him," said my mother. "It won't do any good."

She went up to the horse and, lifting her own hand, declaimed in a solemn tone: "I command you, horse, rise up!"

And we all saw the horse get up at once and follow his master quietly away. I have told in very simple words, and very exact words, what I saw then, with my own eyes, and to my mind it is unbelievable; but the event was just as I have described it: the horse got up without any further delay and followed his master: if he had refused to follow him, my mother's intervention would once more have had its effect.

Where did these powers come from? Well, my mother was the next child born after my twin uncles in Tindican. Now, they say that twin brothers are wiser than other children and are practically magicians. As for the child that follows them, and who receives the name *sayon*, that is, the younger brother of twins, he too is endowed with the gift of magic, and he is even considered to be more powerful and more mysterious than the twins, in whose lives he plays a very important role.

I have given one example of my mother's supernatural powers; I could give many others, equally strange, equally mysterious. How many times I have seen her, at daybreak, walk a few steps into the yard and turn her head in one direction or another to shout at the top of her voice:

"If this business goes any further, I shall not hesitate to expose you. That's my final word!"

In the early morning her voice traveled far: it was intended to reach the ears of the witch doctor, for whom the warning had been uttered. He understood that if he did not stop his nocturnal activities, my mother would denounce him in public; and this threat always worked: from then on, the witch doctor kept quiet. My mother used to receive warning of these activities while she was asleep. We never wakened her, for fear of interrupting the course of the revelations that flowed through her dreams. This power was well known by our neighbors and by the whole community: no one ever doubted it.

Though my mother could see what evil was being hatched and could denounce the author of it, her power went no further. Even if she had wished, her power to cast spells did not allow her to do any evil on her own account. She was never suspect. If people made themselves pleasant to her, it was not at all out of fear. They were pleasant because they thought she deserved it and because they respected her power to cast spells from which nothing was to be feared. On the contrary, much was to be hoped from them.

As well as this gift, or rather part-gift, of magic, my mother had other powers that she had inherited in the same way. At Tindican her father had been a skillful blacksmith, and my mother possessed the usual powers of that caste from which the majority of soothsayers are drawn. It was in my mother that the spirit of her caste was most visibly — I was going to say ostensibly — manifested. I don't pretend that she was more faithful to it than my uncles were, but she alone demonstrated her fidelity. Finally, she had inherited, as a matter of course, my grandfather's totem, which is the crocodile. This totem allowed all Damans to draw water from the Niger without running any danger of harm.

Normally, everyone draws water from the river. The Niger flows slowly and abundantly; it can be forded, and the crocodiles, which keep to the deep water upstream or downstream from where the water is drawn, are not to be feared. You can bathe quite freely on the banks of pale sand and do your washing there.

But when the water rises, the volume of the river is increased threefold. The water is deep, and the crocodiles are dangerous. One can see their triangular heads breaking the surface. Everyone, therefore, keeps away from the river and instead draws water from the little streams.

My mother used to continue to draw water from the river. I watched her draw it from the place where the crocodiles were. Naturally I watched her from a distance, for my totem is not my mother's. And I had every reason to fear those voracious beasts; but my mother could draw water without fear, and no one warned her of the danger, because everyone knew that the danger did not exist for her. Whoever else had ventured to do what my mother used to do would inevitably have been knocked down by a blow from a powerful tail, seized in the terrible jaws, and dragged into deep water. But the crocodiles could do no harm to my mother, and this privilege is quite understandable: the totem is identified with its possessor; this identification is absolute and of such a nature that its possessor has the power to take on the form of the totem itself; it follows quite obviously that the totem cannot devour itself. My uncles at Tindican enjoyed the same prerogative.

I do not wish to say more, and I have told you only what I saw with my own eyes. These miracles — they were miracles indeed — I think about now as if they were the fabulous events of a far-off past. That past is, however, still quite near: it was only yesterday. But the world rolls on, the world changes, my own world perhaps more rapidly than anyone else's; so that it appears as if we are ceasing to be what we were, and that truly we are no longer what we were, and that we were not exactly ourselves even at the time when these miracles took place before our eyes. Yes, the world rolls on, the world changes; it rolls on and changes, and the proof of it is that my own totem — I too have my totem — is still unknown to me.

Many stories are written from the point of view of a young person who makes discoveries about the adult world. In "The Last Lesson" (page 151), Franz not only discovers that he loves his native language but also comes to better understand his teacher. Chig, in "A Visit to Grandmother" (page 513), discovers jealousy and weakness among adults. Here, the young narrator witnesses his grandfather's treatment of a neighbor and discovers the meaning of greed. The story takes place in the Sudan, where most of the people are Moslems, or members of the Mohammedan religion.

A Handful of Dates

TAYEB SALIH

I must have been very young at the time. While I don't remember exactly how old I was, I do remember that when people saw me with my grandfather, they would pat me on the head and give my cheek a pinch — things they didn't do to my grandfather. The strange thing was that I never used to go out with my father, rather it was my grandfather who would take me with him wherever he went, except for the mornings when I would go to the mosque [1] to learn the Koran. [2] The mosque, the river, and the fields — these were the landmarks in our life. While most of the children of my age grumbled at having to go to the mosque to learn the Koran, I used to love it. The reason was, no doubt, that I was quick at learning by heart and the Sheikh always asked me to stand up and recite the *Chapter of the Merciful* whenever we had a visitor, and the visitors would pat me on my head and cheek just as people did when they saw me with my grandfather. Yes, I used to love the mosque, and I loved the river too. Directly we finished our Koran reading in the morning, I would throw down my wooden slate and dart off, with the quickness of a genie, to my mother, hurriedly swallow down my breakfast, and run off for a plunge in the river. When

---

[1] *mosque:* Mohammedan temple.
[2] *Koran:* Mohammedan sacred book.

tired of swimming about, I would sit on the bank and gaze at the
strip of water that wound away eastward and hid behind a thick
wood of acacia trees. I loved to give rein to my imagination and
picture to myself a tribe of giants living behind that wood, a people tall and thin with white beards and sharp noses, like my grandfather's. Before my grandfather ever replied to my many questions,
he would rub the tip of his nose with his forefinger; as for his beard,
it was soft and luxuriant and as white as cotton wool — never in my
life have I seen anything of a purer whiteness or greater beauty.
My grandfather must also have been extremely tall, for never did
I see anyone in the whole area address him without having to look
up at him, nor did I see him enter a house but that he had to so
bend his back that I was put in mind of the way the river bent
around behind the wood of acacia trees. I loved him and would
imagine myself, when I grew to be a man, tall and slender like him,
walking along with great strides.

I believe that I was his favorite grandchild: no wonder, for my
cousins were a stupid bunch and I — so they say — was an intelligent child. I used to know when my grandfather wanted me to
laugh, when to be silent; also I would remember the times for his
prayers and would bring him his prayer-rug and fill the ewer for his
ablutions without his having to ask me. When he had nothing else
to do he enjoyed listening to me reciting to him from the Koran in
a lilting voice, and I could tell from his face that he was moved.

One day I asked him about our neighbor Masood. I said to my
grandfather: "I think you don't like our neighbor Masood?" to
which he answered, having rubbed the tip of his nose: "He's an
indolent man and I don't like such people." I said to him: "What's
an indolent man?" My grandfather lowered his head for a moment,
then looking across at the wide expanse of field, he said: "Do you
see it stretching from the edge of the desert up to the Nile bank?
A hundred feddans.³ Do you see all those date palms? And those
trees — sant, acacia, and sayal? All this fell into Masood's lap, was
inherited by him from his father."

Taking advantage of the silence that had descended upon my
grandfather, I turned my gaze from him to the vast area defined by
his words. "I don't care," I told myself, "who owns those date

---

³ feddan: a land area equivalent to 1.3 acres.

palms, those trees or this black, cracked earth, all I know is that it's the arena for my dreams and my playground."

My grandfather then continued: "Yes, my boy, forty years ago all this belonged to Masood — two thirds of it is now mine."

This was news to me, for I had imagined that the land had belonged to my grandfather ever since God's creation.

"I didn't own a single feddan when I first set foot in this village. Masood was then the owner of all these riches. The position has changed now, though, and I think that before Allah calls me to him I shall have bought the remaining third as well."

I do not know why it was I felt fear at my grandfather's words — and pity for our neighbor Masood. How I wished my grandfather wouldn't do what he'd said! I remembered Masood's singing, his beautiful voice and powerful laugh that resembled the gurgling of water. My grandfather never used to laugh.

I asked my grandfather why Masood had sold his land.

"Women," and from the way my grandfather pronounced the word I felt that "women" was something terrible. "Masood, my boy, was a much-married man. Each time he married, he sold me a feddan or two," and I made the quick calculation that Masood must have married some ninety women. Then I remembered his three wives, his shabby appearance, his lame donkey and its dilapidated saddle, his *galabia* with the torn sleeves. I had all but rid my mind of the thoughts that jostled in it when I saw the man approaching us, and my grandfather and I exchanged glances.

"We'll be harvesting the dates today," said Masood. "Don't you want to be there?"

I felt, though, that he did not actually want my grandfather to attend. My grandfather, however, jumped to his feet, and I saw that his eyes sparkled momentarily with an intense brightness. He pulled me by the hand, and we went off to the harvesting of Masood's dates.

Someone brought my grandfather a stool covered with an oxhide, while I remained standing. There was a vast number of people there, but though I knew them all, I began, for some reason, to watch Masood. Standing aloof from that great gathering of people, it was as though it were no concern of his, despite the fact that the date palms to be harvested were his own. Sometimes his attention would be caught by the sound of a huge clump of dates crashing down from on high. Once he shouted up at the boy perched on the very summit of the date palm, who had begun hacking at a clump with his long, sharp sickle: "Be careful you don't cut the heart of the palm."

No one paid any attention to what he said, and the boy seated at the very summit of the date palm continued, quickly and energetically, to work away at the branch with his sickle until the clump of dates began to drop like something descending from the heavens.

I, however, had begun to think about Masood's phrase "the heart of the palm." I pictured the palm tree as something with feeling possessed of a heart that throbbed. I remembered Masood's remark to me when he had once seen me playing about with the branch of a young palm tree: "Palm trees, my boy, like humans, experience joy and suffering," and I had felt an inward embarrassment for which I found no reason.

When I again looked at the expanse of ground stretching before me, I saw my young companions swarming like ants around the trunks of the palm trees, gathering up dates and eating most of them. The dates were collected up into high mounds. I saw people coming along and weighing them into measuring bins and pouring them into sacks, of which I counted thirty. The crowd of people broke up except for Hussein the merchant, Mousa the owner of the field next to ours on the east, and two men I'd never seen before.

I heard a low whistling sound and saw that my grandfather had fallen asleep. Then I noticed that Masood had not changed his stance except that he had placed a stalk in his mouth and was munching at it like someone surfeited with food who doesn't know what to do with the mouthful he still has.

Suddenly my grandfather woke up, jumped to his feet, and walked toward the sacks of dates. He was followed by Hussein the merchant, Mousa the owner of the field next to ours, and the two strangers. I glanced at Masood and saw that he was making his way toward us with extreme slowness, like a man who wants to retreat but whose feet insist on going forward. All of them made a circle around the sacks of dates and began examining them, some taking a date or two to eat. My grandfather gave me a fistful, which I began munching. I saw Masood filling the palms of both hands with dates and bringing them up close to his nose, then returning them.

Then I saw them dividing up the sacks between them. Hussein the merchant took ten, each of the strangers took five. Mousa, the owner of the field next to ours on the eastern side, took five, and my grandfather took five. Understanding nothing, I looked at Masood and saw that his eyes were darting about to left and right like two mice that have lost their way home.

"You're still fifty pounds in debt to me," said my grandfather to Masood. "We'll talk about it later."

Hussein called his assistants and they brought along donkeys, the two strangers produced camels, and the sacks of dates were loaded on to them. One of the donkeys let out a braying which set the camels frothing at the mouth and complaining noisily. I felt myself drawing close to Masood, felt my hand stretch out toward him as though I wanted to touch the hem of his garment. I heard him make a noise in his throat like the rasping of a lamb being slaughtered. For some unknown reason, I experienced a sharp sensation of pain in my chest.

I ran off into the distance. Hearing my grandfather call after me, I hesitated a little, then continued on my way. I felt at that moment that I hated him. Quickening my pace, I felt as though I carried within me a secret I wanted to rid myself of. I reached the river bank near the bend it made behind the wood of acacia trees. Then, without knowing why, I put my finger into my throat and spewed up the dates I'd eaten.

Like animal fables, Africa's folk tales often combine humor and wisdom. This folk tale comes from the Nupe tribe of Nigeria. It is written as nearly as possible in the way it was once told by word of mouth.

The Talking Skull

ANONYMOUS

A hunter goes into the bush. He finds an old human skull. The hunter says: "What brought you here?" The skull answers: "Talking brought me here." The hunter runs off. He runs to the king. He tells the king: "I found a dry human skull in the bush. It asks you how its father and mother are."

The king says: "Never since my mother bore me have I heard that a dead skull can speak." The king summons the Alkali, the Saba, and the Degi and asks them if they have ever heard the like. None of the wise men has heard the like, and they decide to send a guard out with the hunter into the bush to find out if his story is true and, if so, to learn the reason for it. The guard accompany the hunter into the bush with the order to kill him on the spot should he have lied. The guard and the hunter come to the skull. The hunter addresses the skull: "Skull, speak." The skull is silent. The hunter asks as before: "What brought you here?" The skull does not answer. The whole day long the hunter begs the skull to speak, but it does not answer. In the evening the guard tell the hunter to make the skull speak, and when he cannot, they kill him in accordance with the king's command. When the guard are gone, the skull opens its jaws and asks the dead hunter's head: "What brought you here?" The dead hunter's head replies: "Talking brought me here!"

"The Fetish Tree" is based on the belief that certain objects — a tree, a river, a stone, or an animal — are inhabited by spirits which have the power to influence man's destiny. These objects, called fetishes, are treated with great respect: advice is often sought from the spirit dwelling within, and special offerings are left for it.

The theme of this story is similar to that of "The New Road" (page 79*).*

The Fetish Tree

JEAN PLIYA

In the history of African Negro civilization, the name Abomey, the historical capital of Dahomey, occupies a special place. To explain its past importance, writers often refer to its artistic wealth and the remarkable political and military organization of the kings, but they forget the occult forces of ancestral customs and fetishes. Colonization introduced into Dahomeyan society a division which is developing more and more at the expense of tradition.

The tarred Bohicon Road is like a real backbone along which the essential contributions of the new order are arranged: the schools, the hospital, the post office, the water tower, the police station, and finally the cemetery, where about a hundred white tombstones blaze in the sun. In the old days, the dead were buried in their houses, because they belonged body and soul to their families. Loyalty to their memory had become a cult. Their present isolation is a sign of a slow but painful breakup.

Running from west to east, the road suddenly comes to a stop. It then broadens out into a splendid square, in the center of which the war memorial stands like an obelisk. All around are grouped the administrative buildings, in either the colonial or the modern style: the Prefecture, the Law Courts, the Council Chambers.

The Houndjro Market, right in the center of the town, forms a rather dismal ensemble. Halls with corrugated iron roofs stand there next to ramshackle straw huts.

On both sides of the main street, old Abomey, the Abomey of the craftsmen and the princes, vegetates, clinging to the remains of a once brilliant civilization. The royal palace, converted into a historical museum, now offers its treasures only to anonymous crowds of tourists. At the very most, a few dances are organized outside the tiered house of Ghézo, on the occasion of the traditional festivals, which the kings' descendants faithfully commemorate.

The life which animates the city along the main street seems to set the tone of the place. However, in the secrecy of the fetishist covens,[1] and in the old men's heads weighed down with wisdom, the mysterious force which sustained the fervor of the kings lives on. If you go for a walk in the districts scattered in the scrub, you will notice that the dusty alleys take curious turns. They seem to take care to avoid certain tumbledown huts or isolated trees. And if, in your perplexity, you ask one of the countless children with intelligent eyes whom you meet everywhere for an explanation of these abrupt bends, he is sure to reply that the sordid hut shelters a fetish and that the sacred tree symbolizes an ancestor.

The making of a modern nation may call for the destruction of certain relics of the past. But the young men in authority are sometimes faced with insoluble dilemmas, especially as they know nothing of the local civilization except those of its antiquated vestiges which have survived.

Paul Lanta is one of these young men in authority. Cotonou, his native town, the biggest and busiest in Dahomey, is a town without a past. He lived there until he obtained his school-leaving certificate. After a rapid course in the topographical service, he was engaged as a government clerk and put in charge of certain town-planning operations. But Lanta liked to regard himself as a civil engineer. Modern to the fingertips, he thought that present-day youth should not be deterred by any obstacle. His professional diligence had earned him rapid promotion. He was posted to Abomey to help with the execution of the plan prepared by the town council.

He always dressed with studied elegance: terylene [2] trousers with knife-edge creases, a nylon shirt with a red silk tie, and shoes with horseshoe buckles. A short man, he walked with a firm step, his head held high, and seemed to be full of his own importance. He

---

[1] *fetishist covens*: secret groups which worship fetishes.
[2] *terylene*: a synthetic cloth.

mixed only with young men of education, lived in the residential district, and scorned the company of his elders. What could anybody learn from those old people, he used to ask himself.

When he came into his office at the town hall that morning, Monsieur Lanta carefully dusted his desk and sat down. As a methodical man, he consulted his block-calendar and saw that the team whose work he was supervising was due to start that very day on the opening up of a new street. He picked up a little brass bell from his desk and shook it vigorously. A few moments later, an old orderly, dressed in a crumpled tight-fitting jacket which was fraying at the elbows, knocked at the office door, came in almost at once, and stiffened in a military salute.

"Go straight away to the camp of the Republican Guard," said Monsieur Lanta, "and ask for Anatole, the warder in charge of the prisoners detailed for opening up new streets."

"Yes, sir," replied the orderly.

"I want him to come along at once with his men."

"Yes, sir."

The orderly went out. The door, caught by a draft, shut with a bang behind him. After tidying up his desk, Monsieur Lanta stood up and went out in his turn. In the huge courtyard of the town hall with its neatly mown lawns, a dozen prisoners of all ages and all heights, dressed in blue shorts and sleeveless shirts without collars or buttons, were lined up in two columns. The scarred soles of their bare feet showed that they never wore shoes. Some of them were holding hoes or machetes, others rakes or wooden forks.

"We shall be working today on the Sinhoué Road," Monsieur Lanta explained to the warder Anatole, who had just finished straightening his cap with its gilt buttons and its silver-gray peak. "We are going to open up a street as quickly as possible at right-angles to the one that runs west of the Houndjro Market. Off you go!"

At a word of command from Anatole, the prisoners set off at a walking pace along the tarred road, whose edges had been furrowed by the torrential rains. Although it was early in the morning, the sun was already warming the smooth, black asphalt. But as yet there was no need to seek the refreshing shade of the acacias planted along both sides of the road. A certain sultriness in the air indicated the approach of stormy weather, which is very common in

March, at the end of the dry season, especially in this region of the Central Plateau.

They reached the market and turned right, following a track of rust-colored laterite[3] reinforced after a fashion with quartz gravel. A quarter of a mile farther on, a path branched off from this track: this was the Sinhoué Road. By taking short cuts, Monsieur Lanta had reached the crossroads first, and he was waiting.

The prisoners looked all the way along the winding path which had to be widened to the proportions of a street. They realized straight away that this was not going to be an easy day's work. For on the left, just after the first bend, there was a magnificent iroko, still known as a "loko": what the botanists call *chlorophora excelsa*. The foot of the tree, invisible from a distance, was surrounded by a tangle of bushes and shrubs from which there rose a bole as straight and powerful as a cathedral column, topped with dark green foliage. Creepers as thick as cables criss-crossed to weave a net which hung from the top of the tree to the undergrowth. Huge branches formed a leafy vault above the path, casting an unbroken shadow over the ground.

At the sight of this tree, one was filled in spite of oneself with a sense of awe.

A serious question immediately preoccupied the prisoners: Were they going to be forced to cut down this tree? In the meantime, without a word, they calmly began their work. With the help of a ten-meter measuring tape, and starting from the market road, two men measured out the width of the future street. A little farther on toward the tree, they planted marking stakes to which they tied lengths of string. Once the working area had been fixed in this way, they started clearing it. When the weeds were not too tough, the hoe dug them up and the rakes swept them away. But soon the prisoners could not put off any longer the problem which was worrying them. The warder Anatole, who was a native of Abomey and well aware of the situation, shared his men's fears. He did not look forward to ordering them to cut down the iroko. He therefore agreed to let them send a delegation to Monsieur Lanta, who was sitting on a rock a little way off.

"Boss, please don't be astonished at this question," said the

---

[3] *laterite:* clay.

spokesman. "My workmates and I want to know what we are to do with that tree."

"Why do you ask?" said the civil servant in surprise. "Have you ever heard of a tree being left right in the middle of the roadway? Our job, as part of the town-planning scheme, is to open up beautiful, clean, straight streets and to do that we have to clear, cut, and uproot everything in our way so that asphalt can be laid down later."

"But our tools aren't up to the job! We haven't any saws or axes, just machetes."

"Oh, get along with you!" cried Monsieur Lanta. "Is this the first time you've been told to cut down a tree?"

"No, Boss, but the other times they were just little trees, or at the very most shrubs. We've never had to cut down a tree as big as this. Our workmates have sent us to tell you that that tree over there is an iroko, a fetish tree, and that it would be very dangerous to try to fell it."

"Now, I don't want any nonsense of that sort, you bunch of idlers! Get on with your work, and stop worrying. Seeing that you say you haven't got the necessary tools, just clear the ground all around. Tomorrow we'll provide you with axes and handsaws so that you can cut down that iroko."

When the disappointed delegation returned and delivered this reply, there was consternation among the prisoners. Their shining, sweating faces, to which blades of green grass and tiny seeds were stuck, assumed scowling expressions. Muttering to themselves, they reluctantly resumed their work. Their progress slowed down, the nearer they got to the tree. Monsieur Lanta, who had not taken his eyes off them since their unexpected move, was puzzled. He got to his feet, went over to the working party, and questioned the warder Anatole. The latter seemed scarcely any easier in his mind than the prisoners. When his superior asked him to explain their attitude, he prudently shifted the responsibility on to their ringleader, a man who seemed to possess a certain authority over the team.

"That man," he said, pointing to an old prisoner, "claims that the tree over there is sacred and that it is forbidden to cut off even the smallest branch. He must have got his mates all worked up."

Sure enough, all the prisoners now seemed determined not to go any further. Reprimands and threats of punishment were of no avail. Monsieur Lanta decided to use persuasion to try to solve this problem. He took aside the man Anatole had accused, an old man called Mehou whose kapok-gray hair curled oddly into the shape of little balls. His face was remarkable for the breadth of his forehead and the sharpness of his eyes.

While the others continued their work unenthusiastically, Monsieur Lanta and Mehou walked about a stone's-throw away.

"Well," began the civil servant, "what's this cock-and-bull story you've been telling to discourage your workmates? We can't allow any rebels or saboteurs. The regulations are particularly strict about that sort of thing. What have you got to say to that?"

"Boss," replied Mehou, standing at a respectful distance, his head bowed and his fingers twined together behind his back, to keep himself in countenance, "it isn't a cock-and-bull story. I was born in Abomey, before King Béhanzin was taken prisoner and deported to the white men's country. My father was a great fetishist chieftain, and I pride myself on knowing the history of the sacred woods which in the old days used to shelter the covens. In the time of the kings, this part of the country was covered with forests of irokos. Nobody had the right to touch those fetish trees, under pain of severe punishment. But some time ago, people began cutting them down to make chairs, tables, and doors. Now there are very few left. The trees which have escaped the woodcutter's ax have become more precious as a result. Our sorcerers choose them as the center for their nocturnal celebrations. Any offering made to a god is placed at the foot of an iroko or at a crossroads, so that the effects can be spread to the four winds. It's dangerous to make fun of the sorcerers. To live in peace, to enjoy good health, and to have no trouble in our work, we have to seek their protection.

"The iroko you are ordering us to cut down has a history you must know. King Tégbessou is said to have been saved several times by a bird which lived in that tree and which warned him in wartime of the tricks of his enemies from Zà. In memory of these great services given to the kingdom of Dan, it has always been respected. That is why we ought to spare it. If you go up to it, you'll see that the lower part of the trunk is hollow. That is supposed to be the lair of a serpent which watches over the tree and to which any man threatened by an evil spell can offer up a sacrifice in order to be cured. Even without the serpent's presence, that iroko is a redoubtable fetish. Forgive us if we are unwilling to incur its vengeance."

Somewhat irritated by the lengthiness of the old man's explanations, Monsieur Lanta looked skeptical. He smiled sarcastically as he listened to these tales from another age. This was not the first time that well-meaning people had advised him to respect some fetish or to guard against the sorcerers. In his heart of hearts, he wondered how anybody could be alarmed by such unconvincing stories.

"That's all very fine," he said, "but hard to verify. In the second half of the twentieth century, we can't believe in fetishes any more. Otherwise, in spite of being independent, we should never succeed in building a modern civilized nation. We have to fell that tree for public purposes, and nothing is going to stop us. The old town of Abomey has to be given a new, up-to-date look."

Just then, another prisoner joined them and offered to find a woodcutter who would be sure to agree to fell the iroko. This providential individual was called Dossou.

Monsieur Lanta, being a realist, decided to call a halt to the day's work and to employ Dossou's services. The men returned to camp, their work half done.

At nightfall, Anatole got the prisoner who knew Dossou to take him to see the woodcutter. Dossou's house, which was in the district of the Houtondji blacksmiths, on the outskirts of the town, was a round hut without any windows. The mud walls were roughcast and whitewashed and covered with a thatched roof. Through the solitary rectangular opening, which was closed by a lattice-work rattan curtain, rays of dull yellow light were filtering. A little distance away, an apatam of wooden planks covered with palm leaves leaned against the enclosing wall. This was the kitchen. A wood fire was glowing in a crude hearth made of three blocks of dried clay. The smell of sauces floated in the air. Earthenware cooking-pots stood here and there. Clucking hens were looking for a roost for the night. The prisoner clapped his hands.

"Who's there?" asked a man's voice which was deep and very calm. Without waiting for a reply, it called out:

"Cossi! Go and see who's at the door."

The young man who answered to this name had a cotton pagne [4]

---

[4] *pagne:* a long, rectangular piece of cloth, worn in Africa in various ways.

knotted around his neck. He opened the rattan curtain a little way, smiling broadly, but he took fright at the sight of Anatole's new peaked cap. Wiping the smile off his face, he said politely:

"Good evening, sir."

"Good evening," replied the warder, conscious of the effect his uniform had produced. "I want to speak to your master."

"Right. I'll call him straight away."

When Dossou learned that a Republican Guard wanted to see him, he hurriedly searched his conscience, for he thought that his caller was a gendarme bearing a warrant. Trusting in his reputation as an honest workman and sure that he was innocent of any crime, he stood up without a word and asked his visitors indoors. Shaking hands with him, the warder noticed the exceptional strength of Dossou's grip.

The hut was divided in two by a wall. One half served as the bedroom, the other as the living room. The visitors were invited to sit down on low, three-legged stools, in crudely carved wood. On the wall there hung axes, handsaws, machetes, and thick coils of rope.

Dossou was a real athlete with a bull neck and long arms with knotty biceps. His eyes squinted and seemed to be perpetually laughing. He was dressed only in a coarse loincloth. He walked toward his stool. Anatole noticed that he limped with his right leg, which was less developed than the other. His strength had, as it were, been concentrated in his muscular arms.

Cossi squatted on his haunches near the door, determined to know the reason for such an impressive visit. Without standing on ceremony, and puffing himself up slightly, Anatole informed Dossou in a few words of what was wanted of him. He did not fail to emphasize the eventual danger he would be running by agreeing. He then asked him if he was willing to collaborate with the government. A relieved Dossou relaxed with a sudden laugh. Would he agree? Of course, and enthusiastically! Flattered that the "Governor," the Prefect himself, should appeal to him in his capacity as a feller of trees, Dossou could not contain himself for vanity and joy. Who could tell if he would not be appointed a civil servant one day? Besides, deep down, he had never doubted in his own destiny. He was a native of Allada. At the age of fourteen, accompanying his woodcutter father in the forest, he had fallen from a tree and broken his right leg. Since then, he had sworn never to ply any other trade than that of a woodcutter.

Henceforth, felling trees meant wreaking a personal revenge for him, settling scores with the instrument which fate had used to disable him. His hands could not wield anything but the ax. A freethinker who was afraid of nobody, he was hugely amused at the idea that a dozen able-bodied men had been unable to perform a task as easy as the one which was being asked of him.

"There hasn't been a single tree in living memory," he said, "that I've been unable to master. Do you remember the baobab at Covè which nobody but I could cut down? You don't? But you can't have failed to hear about that exploit of mine. It was five years ago, in the days of the white commanders. They congratulated me in public and promised me a medal."

Sensing a movement of impatience on the part of his distinguished visitor, Dossou pulled himself together.

"What day is it tomorrow?"

"It's market day, and Thursday," the prisoner replied.

"That's perfect! A good day for my job. Everything's fine. Do we meet on the Sinhoué Road?"

"Yes. Don't be late. In the civil service, time is important," Anatole concluded sententiously.[5]

"You can count on me."

It was completely dark when the two men came out of the hut. As they had just left the smoky light of a palm-oil lamp, the night struck them as darker by contrast. They groped about before finding their way. The sky had the cruel purity of those skies during the dry season when, for four or five months, the farmer dreams of the cool rains. The air was fresh. In the grass along both sides of the path, swarms of fireflies were intermittently lighting up their greenish phosphorus. Anatole was pleased with the success of his mission. As soon as he had taken the prisoner back to camp, he went to see Monsieur Lanta and gave him a full report.

The next day, early in the morning, Dossou informed his assistant Cossi that they were going to do a job which would stand out in his life and bring him a great deal of prestige and money, namely, felling the iroko on the Sinhoué Road for the "Governor." Cossi,

---

[5] *sententiously*: pompously formal.

who had known all about it since the warder's visit, had been thinking and worrying about the problem for part of the night. He ventured to reply timidly:

"Master, can't we refuse this deadly job?"

"Shut up, you little fool: you're talking nonsense! Who do you
take me for? You've lived such a long time with me. . . . What
fresh exploits have I got to perform to prove to you that I'm invulnerable?"

"Forgive me, Master, I'm not casting any doubts on your powers,
but people say that that iroko is a magic tree which can work evil.
It seems that . . ."

"That's enough! Don't you know that, as far as magic is concerned, I've taken precautions long ago? I wasn't born yesterday!
In any case, I'm not in the habit of arguing with cowards. Take my
best axes and go and sharpen them as usual."

Cossi unhooked the two heavy axes from the wall and made for
the kitchen. First of all he poured some palm oil on to a big mill-
stone made of Dassa-Zoumé granite, balanced on an oil drum filled
with sand to keep it steady. With a regular, rasping motion, he
carefully sharpened the steel until it could cut like a razor. Then,
with a glum expression on his face, he took the tools and set off in
front of his master.

As for Dossou, proudly draped in a brightly colored calico pagne,
he walked along calmly. But he had scarcely left his house before
he met one of his former neighbors coming the opposite way. He
scowled in irritation. "I don't like that at all," he said to himself.
He looked annoyed, for he regarded this as an evil omen. Dossou
did not believe in the host of fetishes which the old people worshiped, and consequently he did not observe their prohibitions. For
him, the only laws which counted were those of Dada Segbo, the
Supreme Being, the unique creator of day and night, of inanimate
objects and living creatures, who in the event of danger warned
men by means of signs intelligible only to the initiated. Thus, for
fear of offending him, he was careful to choose only working days
and avoided touching a tool or any metal on the days dedicated
to Gou, the guardian divinity of blacksmiths, warriors, and all
workers who handle sharp instruments. Similarly, according to
whether the first person he met after leaving home in the morning
was a woman or a man, he considered that he was going to have a

good or a bad day. Apart from that, Dossou was convinced that worshiping a serpent, a stone, or a tree was a superstition unworthy of him. In any case, the piece of luck which had come his way today was so exceptional that he had no doubt that the outstanding task which had been entrusted to him was a gift from Dada Segbo.

The morning sky had the same purity as that of the previous night, with the sole difference that the golden stars had disappeared, giving place to a sun of dull silver.

Soon Dossou and Cossi passed the Houndjro Market, which was already coming to life. They met merchants on bicycles, each carrying his wife on the luggage grid, a baby on her back and full baskets on her head. The pedestrians hugged the walls to avoid the vehicles filling the roadways. As a truck heavily laden with Indian potatoes went by, clouds of yellow dust enveloped Dossou and Cossi. To avoid breathing it in, they stopped, pinched their noses between their left thumbs and forefingers, and then continued on their way. Cossi said nothing. In his opinion, there had been far too many evil omens already. No more were required to make him feel pessimistic.

As soon as the woodcutter reached the working site, he made for the iroko. For a long time he eyed his powerful adversary supported by broad buttresses like ships' hulls. The ash-gray trunk, smooth in places, was peeling in others or cracked like crocodile skin. Straight away, Dossou took charge of operations and, like a real foreman, gave detailed orders to the prisoners who were to help him to clear the ground around the iroko. In a matter of moments the bushes and the weeds were cut down. They had to tug at the net of tangled creepers in order to strip certain branches. Some of the men piled up the brushwood, which would be burned later on when it had dried up.

Right against the tree there was a straw hut sheltering a crude dummy made of two balls of clay, the smaller representing the head and the other the body. This fetish, the Tolegba, a familiar feature of the Dahomeyan landscape, is very popular. It is sprinkled with palm oil when people bring it offerings. They had to smash it to smithereens.

When the base of the trunk was completely accessible, Dossou took off the pagne which he was wearing draped over his shoulders like a Roman toga, keeping on nothing but his loincloth. He stroked his thick biceps, spat into his hands, rubbed them together to obtain a better hold, and then seized one of the skillfully hafted axes in his wrestler's grip. Removing the bark with a series of little blows, he first of all girdled the trunk at a convenient height, ringing it with a notch into which the sacrilegious tool would bite. Refusing to send somebody up the tree to fasten a rope which would make it fall in a given direction, he calculated the angle of felling with a practiced eye.

Then the ax began to dance. As the first blows cut into the buttresses, some weaver birds which were building their nests in a nearby palm tree flew off in a twittering cloud. Red ants settled on the prisoners, who prudently withdrew. The entire frame of the giant shuddered under the rape of the ax. The brick-red flesh was opened. Chips of wood flew in every direction and littered the ground. The tempered steel described bluish circles in the air, with gleams of silver. Sweat streamed down Dossou's face, ran down his back, spread out, and drenched his loincloth. In the west, the sky was gradually covered with slate-gray clouds. The stormy atmosphere charged with electricity heightened the general tension. The man panted for breath as he threw himself into his task. Once, the ax sank so deep into the wooden flesh that the beveled edge was caught as if by a powerful vise. Dossou arched his body backward on his good leg and tugged vainly at the handle. He had to have help in order to free the tool.

"Never mind," swore Dossou. "I'll get the better of you yet!"

It was only grudgingly that he agreed to a break for the midday meal. When the prisoners and their leaders came back at the beginning of the afternoon, the tree was three quarters cut. By examining the gash, an expert could have told that the iroko was nearly three hundred years old.

The woodcutter's movements, which had been strong and calm at first, now became feverish. His eyes turned bloodshot. He was fighting the tree, as if the two of them were locked in single combat. As the support grew narrower, he seemed to be seized by a murderous frenzy and to feel that he was engaged in a pitiless struggle. He refused all offers of help and looked irritated when Monsieur Lanta urged him to take a rest. "Leave me alone," he muttered. And the blows went on striking the iroko at a breath-taking rate.

The others, now wonder-struck spectators, applauded the infectious self-assurance shown by the woodcutter, whose victory seemed certain. An improvised choir spontaneously sang Dossou's praises after the fashion of strolling minstrels. With a song accompanied by their hands beating time against their chests, they sustained the woodcutter's ardor.

When only a thin strip of wood still joined the trunk to its base, and a few feeble blows would have been enough to fell the tree, Dossou broke off his onslaught at last and straightened his pure ebony body with its perfect muscles.

"You can finish the job now," he said triumphantly to the prisoners.

Cossi and one of the prisoners began almost playfully to bring Dossou's task to completion. The woodcutter, with a certainty which was usually almost miraculous, had calculated that the iroko would fall in the opposite direction from the path on which the men were standing. Its trajectory, he had declared, did not involve the slightest risk. All the same, for safety's sake, Monsieur Lanta, Anatole, and the prisoners, who were divided into two groups on either side of the iroko, had left the immediate vicinity.

With his right forefinger hooked like a claw, Dossou cleaned his moist forehead and started walking about with the confident step of a victor. It never occurred to him that he might be threatened by any sort of danger. Convinced of his own powers and certain that the tree would fall in the direction he had imposed on it, he strutted about from one group to another, amused by the general consternation and apparently flattered by the admiring gaze of the prisoners. Some merchants on their way home to Sinhoué quickened their pace when they reached the iroko. They hurried away, calling upon the ancestral shades and crying: "Hélou!" — "Death to him who commits sacrilege!"

At last the iroko was cut in two. The foliage started swaying like a boat's mast in a storm. Spasms shook the giant in every limb. A dull, creaking sound like a death rattle indicated that the support had just given way. Dossou was standing on the path, just opposite the tree. The trunk suddenly started falling. The greenish-black parasol swayed unexpectedly in the direction of the path. Panic rooted the onlookers to the spot. At the anguished cry which came from their throats, Dossou swung around. He scarcely had time to realize the imminence of the danger threatening him. Dumbfounded by his adversary's deceit, he made a frantic effort to flee, but his crippled leg could not follow the impulse of his whole being as he tried to avoid the fatal blow. Before starting on his limping run, instead of looking to see which way the tree was going to fall, he turned his back on it. The force of impact being multiplied tenfold at the level of the branches, a terrible blow flattened him on the ground. The noise made by the fall of the tree and the crash of the branches drowned the inhuman cry he was about to utter. Torn leaves and frightened insects flew about in a mad whirlwind. Then, very suddenly, silence fell: a silence so absolute that the cackling of a toucan could be heard in the distance. Everybody seemed to be waiting in a daze for Dossou to emerge from under the branches. When it became obvious that nobody was going to hear even the slightest groan, the men all moved at once, like panic-stricken ants.

It was then that the storm which had been brewing all day finally burst, adding to the solemnity of the scene with explosions of thunder and blinding flashes of lightning. The thunder god Heviosso showed his anger by spitting fire. Under rain rattling down like hail, the rescuers, armed with axes and handsaws, had to cut dozens of thick branches to reach Dossou's unrecognizable body. They then grasped the full horror of the iroko's shattering riposte.[6] A knot in one branch, swollen until it looked like the head of a gigantic club, had struck the woodcutter in the back. The bowels had spurted out of the belly. The blood had turned black as it flowed away on all sides, as if the crumpled leaves had soaked in it. The skull had become an indescribable pulp, a mixture of whitish brain, dark hair, and crushed bone. Nobody dared to take charge of the remains of the foolhardy Dossou, not even Cossi, who was crying his heart out. The prisoners covered up the body again with branches and went off, silent and horror-stricken. Monsieur Lanta, dumbfounded by what had happened, did not understand. He could not understand.

At nightfall, the fetishists who worshiped the iroko came along in a procession to take possession of the human remains. They laid them on a bamboo hurdle and carried them through every district

---

[6] *riposte:* a return thrust, as in fencing.

in the town, to the sound of twin gongs and by the light of hurriedly devised torches. Inquisitive crowds gathered in the doorways, astonished by this nocturnal procession; but as soon as they saw the body, they understood the purpose of the ceremony. Within a few hours, the whole town was fully informed.

The funereal gongs rang out like a warning to anybody who might try to commit another sacrilegious act of this sort. Finally Dossou's corpse was thrown to the jackals and the vultures.

For the fetishists, death itself is not sufficient punishment for the crime of deicide.[7]

---

[7] *deicide*: the killing of a god.

Poetry has always been an important and natural part of African life. The following poems are traditional. That is, no one knows exactly who wrote them or when. In the absence of written language, such poems become the common property of all the people, with everyone feeling free to change lines or to add new ones.

In an African tribe, festivals, rituals, and celebrations are occasions for reciting poetry. Often the poetry is combined with the music of drums, flutes, and other instruments, and part of the meaning is conveyed by the music. Sometimes dancing accompanies the poetry as well.

Praise Songs for the Baboon

HOTTENTOT

I

Heretse!°
Heretse!
Thou thin-armed one,
Who hast thin hands!
Thou smooth bulrush mat,
Thou whose neck is bent.
Thou who are made so as to be lifted up (upon a tree),
Who liftest thyself up.
Thou who wilt not die even behind *that* hill
Which is yet beyond those hills,
That lie on the other side of this far-distant hill.

II

Thou hollow-cheeked son
Of a hollow-cheeked one,
My hollow-cheeked one!
Who hast two hip-bones,
High hip-bones.
With which thou sittest on the edge of the rock,
Thou whose face appears like the edge of a rock.

---

1. *Heretse:* imitates the voice of the baboon.

*The fear of spirits that attacked men by night gave rise to this song,
which is a song of atonement or expiation — an attempt to drive
the spirits away by singing about them.*

[handwritten: get spirits away.]

Song of Expiation

PYGMY

Spirits of the forest, night-walking ghosts
Who during the bright day,
Like bats that suck men's blood,
Hang hooked to the slippery walls of great caves,
Behind the green moss, behind the great white stones —
Tell us: Who has seen them, the night-walking ghosts?
Tell us: Who has seen them?

[handwritten: communicated thru drums —]
[handwritten: Lu-Chen — can't cope]
[handwritten: they want their own life style]

Song of the Telegraph

[handwritten: righting down message]

EWE

The European's hand goes into the book when the telegraph calls
him, the telegraph calls him.

Song of a Wandering Storyteller

BAULE

In times past lute and drum
were played together for dancing.
Now only I can play the lute to my storytelling.
I am a young man,
my lute is beautiful,
because of my lute I have planted no crop,
because of my lute I have nothing to eat.

Africa's history has long been a record of the intrusion of outsiders. Much contemporary African literature is a reaction to the injustices of those who came to Africa for selfish reasons; it is a search for values and traditions that are truly African.

The three modern poets represented here have freedom and individualism as their common theme.

"Up-Country" begins by expressing delight in the modern cities that line the coast of West Africa. But (the poem suggests) these cities — modeled after those of Europe and America — are not the real Africa. The poet finds joy as he anticipates a search for identity and his real self in the bush country.

Up-Country *(Inner Africa)*

ABIOSEH NICOL (Sierra Leone)

Then I came back
Sailing down the Guinea coast,
Loving the sophistication
Of your brave new cities:
Dakar, Accra, Cotonou,
Lagos, Bathhurst, and Bissau,
Freetown, Libreville.
Freedom is really in the mind.

Go up-country, they said,
To see the real Africa.
For whomsoever you may be,
That is where you come from.
Go for bush — inside the bush
You will find your hidden heart,
Your mute ancestral spirit.

And so I went,
Dancing on my way.

"Africa's Plea" is a protest against the suppression and frustration of colonial rule. It is also a fervent plea for acceptance of differences and for understanding.

Angry - want to leave them own their own life. Don't want to change.

Africa's Plea

ROLAND TOMBEKAI DEMPSTER (Liberia)

I am not you —
but you will not
give me a chance,
will not let me be *me*.

"If I were you" —
but you know
I am not you,
yet you will not
let me be *me*.

You meddle, interfere   10
in my affairs
as if they were yours
and you were me.

You are unfair, unwise,
foolish to think
that I can be you,
talk, act
and think like you.

God made me *me*.
He made you *you*.   20
For God's sake
Let me be *me*.

In this poem by a modern Nigerian writer, the images of a jungle beast and a jet airplane are united.

Around Us, Dawning

(Jet Flight)

WOLE SOYINKA

This beast was fashioned well; it prowls
The rare selective heights
And spurns companionship with bird

Wings are tipped in sulfurs
Scouring gray recesses of the void
To a linear flare of dawns

Red haloes through the ports wreathe us
Passive martyrs, bound to a will of rotors

Yielding ours,
To the alien mote
The hidden ache . . . when
Death makes a swift descent

The mountains range in spire on spire
Lances at the bold carbuncle
On the still night air. I am light honed

To a still point in the incandescent
Onrush, a fine ash in the beast's sudden
Dessication when the sun explodes.

Part Four: Poetry

Poetry is the most difficult form of literature to translate because it is the most closely tied to the sounds and rhythms of its language. The poems which follow have all been translated from the languages in which they were written. Careful attempts have been made to duplicate in English the meaning of each, yet part of every poem gets lost in translation.

Each language has its special way of suggesting the unique meanings that come from a poem. Certain words placed side by side suggest ideas, images, overtones that the same words, taken separately, do not suggest. The translator cannot merely make a literal, or direct, translation: he must search for the meaning that lies beyond dictionary definition.

Look at a specific problem one translator faced in attempting to put into English Lorca's poem "In a Poor Neighborhood: Córdoba." The last two lines in Spanish read:

> Las gentes van suspirando
> con las guitarras abiertas.

The most literal reading of these lines would be:

> The people go sighing
> with the guitars open.

But the translator has to ask himself: What does Lorca mean by abierta (open)? Open in what sense? A Spanish dictionary tells him that abierta means many things: "open," "candid," "outspoken," "full-blown." The line in Spanish has many suggestions: first, the guitars are open because they are being played — that is, they are not in their cases. They are open in the sense that the music they make at the girl's funeral reflects the open way in which the gypsies show their feelings. And they are open in the sense that they are not muffled — they are "wide open," "full-blown" like a flower. So from all these possibilities the translator took a chance, made a personal choice, knowing that his line in English would not have all of Lorca in it. He wrote:

> The people are sighing.
> The guitars are loud.

With works that are often translated, we find that the same line is rendered in many ways. Here are the opening lines of Homer's *Odyssey* in five versions:

Tell me, Muse, of the man of many ways, who was driven
far journeys, after he had sacked Troy's sacred citadel.

(Lattimore)

Tell me, O Muse, of that ingenious hero who traveled far and wide after he had sacked the famous town of Troy.

(Butler)

Sing me the RESTLESS MAN, O Muse, who roamed the world over, When, by his wondrous guile, he had sacked Troy's sacred fortress.

(Caulfield)

Recall for me, Muse, the toils of that man so ready of wit in every need, who wandered far and wide after he had sacked the sacred citadel of Troy.

(Epps)

This is the story of a man, one who was never at a loss. He had traveled far in the world, after the sack of Troy, the virgin fortress.

(Rouse)

All the translations say the same thing, more or less, but say it in such different ways that the underlying tone or attitude is changed in each case. The one word that the five translators can agree on is "sack(ed)."

Since it is impossible for us to know all the languages of the world, we are forced to rely on translations if we wish to know the literature of other cultures. As we read translations, then, we know that some are very close to their originals, some quite free. A translation should be approached with skepticism. Some poems — especially those that present definite visual images or tell stories — retain something in translation. Others vanish completely.

Chinese and Japanese are languages whose grammar and word order bear little relation to English, yet English translations of Chinese and Japanese poetry are surprisingly effective. The reason is that the short lyric poems of these languages are so concrete: their meanings spring from sharp visual images. The power of these poems is in their shortness — they flash across the reader's mind like lightning against a landscape.

The Ching-ting Mountain

LI PO

Flocks of birds have flown high and away;
A solitary drift of cloud, too, has gone, wandering on.
And I sit alone with the Ching-ting Peak, towering beyond.
We never grow tired of each other, the mountain and I.

In this Chinese poem, a girl picking plums from a tree worries that no suitor will come for her hand in marriage.

Anxiety of a Young Girl to Get Married

ANONYMOUS

Ripe, the plums fall from the bough;
Only seven tenths left there now!
Ye whose hearts on me are set,
Now the time is fortunate!

Ripe, the plums fall from the bough;
Only three tenths left there now!
Ye who wish my love to gain
Will not now apply in vain!

No more plums upon the bough!
All are in my basket now!
Ye who me with ardor seek,
Need the word but freely speak!

The seven poems which follow are written in a Japanese verse form called the haiku. It is a very strict form, allowing only seventeen syllables for an entire poem — five syllables for the first line, seven syllables for the second, and five syllables for the third. (The number of syllables in English translations may vary.) This form also demands that the poet express his feelings indirectly, without moralizing. Japanese poets capture a moment in some striking image, evoke a mood, suggest a meaning — and suddenly the poem is over.

Issa, who was born in the eighteenth century, was one of the best-loved haiku poets. Shiki, born a century later, was something of a rebel and often attacked the past masters of haiku.

Issa: Four Haiku

IN THE HOUSE

At the butterflies
    the caged bird gazes, envying —
        just watch its eyes!

THE GREAT BUDDHA AT NARA

Out from the hollow
    of Great Buddha's nose —
        comes a swallow.

THE MUSHROOM

Death it can bring,
    that kind of mushroom; and, of course,
        it's a pretty thing.

SPRING RAIN

Rain on a spring day:
  to the grove is blown a letter
    someone threw away.

Shiki: Three Haiku

AFTER THE FIREWORKS

The others go home.
  With the fireworks over,
    how dark it's become!

AT KAMAKURA

The Great Buddha! Not at all
  does he blink an eyelid —
    as the hailstones fall.

LONELINESS

No sky at all;
  no earth at all — and still
    the snowflakes fall. . . .

GREEK AND ROMAN POETRY

Many of the forms of literature that we prize in English had their origins in the poetry of the ancient Greeks and Romans. It is remarkable how much of this poetry, written from two to four thousand years ago, has survived as a living influence in modern times. Although there is a great deal of emotion in these poems, the poets do not "emote" in the sense of pouring out their feelings in a flood of words. There is a spare, hard, chiseled quality in classical poetry which preserves it from the erosion of time.

To honor the dead is an impulse common to men of all ages. From the greatest tombs ever built — the pyramids of the pharaohs of ancient Egypt — to the rows and rows of crosses that stand in today's military cemeteries, the purpose is the same: to give some lasting recognition to the dead. Following are three poems from ancient Greece written as epitaphs for tombstones.

Not all the Greek epitaphs were actually inscribed on stone, however. The brief epitaph became a literary convention which is still alive. See, for example, W. H. Auden's "Elegy for J.F.K." on page 210. Auden's lines are meant only as a poem, not as an actual inscription.

Inscription for the Grave of a Dog

SIMONIDES

Beneath this mound, my hound, my faithful huntress,
Rest by a hearth whose flames forever burn.
The hills around recall your barking valor;
The beasts we hunted fear, still, your return.

An Unknown Grave

PAUL THE SILENTIARY

My name, my country, what are they to you?
Or whether my birth was high or low.
Perhaps I was better than other men,
Perhaps not. What difference is it now?
Stranger, you can see that this is a tomb:
You know its purpose. It holds — no matter whom.

The Persian army under Xerxes invaded Greece in 480 B.C. A brave army of three hundred Spartans held off the invaders in the narrow pass at Thermopylae. After three days, the entire Spartan army had been killed. This epitaph was written for a monument erected to their memory at Thermopylae.

For the Spartans Who Died at Thermopylae

ANONYMOUS

Traveler, when you get to Sparta, tell them:
We lie here, obedient to their command.

Like the epitaphs, the pastoral is another convention of Greek literature which has had a long life. A pastoral is a poem about shepherds and shepherdesses, their music and dancing and love affairs. A pastoral is seldom about real shepherds and shepherdesses, however. It usually takes place in an artificial, prettied-up countryside. In the following pastoral, a shepherd appears about ready to give up the world because of a love affair that didn't go the way he wanted it.

A Gift for Pan

THEOCRITUS

Daphnis,° the herdsman, handsome Daphnis,
who used to play happy tunes on a homemade flute,
offers these gifts to the god Pan:
the reeds on which he made his music,
the javelin with which he hunted,
the crook with which he kept his sheep,
and the knapsack where he carried, once
before they went sour, the apples of Love.

---

1. *Daphnis* (daf′nis).

*Not all the short Greek poems from the Classical Age are epitaphs.
The Greek Anthology (a collection which is the source of most of the
Greek lyrics) also contains love poems and satirical squibs like this
verse on an aging beauty.*

Mycilla's Hair

LUCILIUS

Mycilla dyes her hair, they say.
Liars! She never dyes it!
Her hair is black. It comes that way —
And I know where she buys it.

*This poem by Catullus, a Roman who lived in the last century before
the birth of Christ, is also a graveside poem, but, unlike the Greek
epitaphs, here it is the poet's voice that speaks, not the voice of the
person buried.*

At the Grave of His Brother

CATULLUS

By ways remote and distant waters sped,
    Brother, to thy sad graveside am I come,
That I may give the last gifts° to the dead,
    And vainly parley with thine ashes dumb;
Since She who now bestows and now denies
    Have ta'en thee, hapless brother, from mine eyes.
But lo! These gifts, the heirlooms of past years,
    Are made sad things to grace thy coffin-shell;
Take them, all drenched with a brother's tears,
    And, brother, for all time, hail and farewell.

---

3. *gifts:* the Romans left offerings for the dead.

In the time of Martial, the first century after Christ, the Roman Empire was reaching its height of luxurious living, in which the seed of its own destruction was already growing. Affectation, dishonesty, and vice were already beginning to weaken Rome's hold on the civilized world. True to the spirit of his times, Martial scolded his contemporaries, not with solemn reminders of ancient virtues but with ridicule. His poems are satires, attacks upon the vanities and follies of his own time, similar to some of the animal fables earlier in this book.

To Chloë

MARTIAL

I could resign that eye of blue
   Howe'er its splendor used to thrill me;
And even that cheek of roseate° hue, —
   To lose it, Chloë, scarce would kill me.
That snowy neck I ne'er should miss,
   However much I've raved about it;
And sweetly as that lip can kiss,
   I *think* I could exist without it.
In short, so well I've learned to fast,
   That, sooth my love, I know not whether
I might not bring myself at last,
   To — do without you altogether.

A Hinted Wish

MARTIAL

You told me, Maro, whilst you live
You'd not a single penny give,
But that, whene'er you chanced to die,
You'd leave a handsome legacy:
You must be mad beyond redress,
If my next wish you cannot guess!

---

3. *roseate:* rosy.

Some of the following poets are famous, some are not. The poems have only one thing in common: each one presents a sharp image. With the exception of Villon, all are from the twentieth century.

François Villon, the most vigorous French poet of his time, was a revolutionary. Although our knowledge of his life is nearly as clouded as our knowledge of Shakespeare's, we do know that he was a rebellious student in Paris and, later in his life, a convicted criminal. How much of his life was spent in crime we do not know. But his poetry possesses an honesty, a freshness, so original that it still has the power to surprise and move us.

Villon, like the men in the ballad which follows, may have ended his life hanging from a gibbet at a place of public execution.

Ballad from the Gibbet

FRANÇOIS VILLON

Brothers, men that after us shall be,
    Look not with hardened hearts upon us:
Rather, take pity on our misery,
    That God in time to you be piteous.
    Observe the six who hang here thus,
Look at the flesh we dearly cherished,
How it is pecked by birds and perished,
    Dust and ashes starting to take its place.
Mock us not that now so helpless be,
    But pray God pardon us out of his grace.   10

Listen, we beg you, and look not in scorn,
    Though it is just we have been sent to die:
For never has a man been born
    Who kept his wisdom with him constantly.
    Be you then merciful and cry
To Mary's Son, who is all piteous,
That he with mercy take our stains from us
    And save us from hell's fiery place.
We have just died: let no man now deny
    To pray God pardon us out of his grace.   20

We are rinsed clean by rain from the skies;
 The sun has charred us black and bare;
Ravens and crows have pecked our eyes
 And lined their nests with our beards and hair.
 Hanging, swinging here and there,
This way and that at the wind's will,
Never a minute is my body still,
 And the birds are busy about my face.
Live not as we lived! Fare not as we fare!
 Pray God pardon us out of his grace! 30

Envoi

Prince Jesus, Master of all, to thee
We pray hell gain no mastery
 Upon us, that we may avoid that place.
Brothers, men that after us shall be,
 Pray God pardon us out of his grace.

The Spanish poet Juan Ramon Jiménez, born in 1881, was educated in Spain and later lived in France, Switzerland, the United States, and, after the Spanish Civil War began, in Puerto Rico. Like an impressionist painter, he is interested in the play of light and color upon natural objects.

Dawning

JUAN RAMON JIMÉNEZ

The sun gilds honey
on mauve and green fields —
rock and vineyard, hill and plain.
Breezes make the blue flower
fresh and soft on livid stone walls.
There is no one now, or not yet,
in the enormous readied fields
which the lark decorates
with crystal wings.
 Here, there, open and deserted,
the red dazzling towns.

All his life, Garcia Lorca was fascinated by the folklore of his country and especially by the songs and dances of the Spanish gypsies. In a way that no other poet has matched, he translated the spirit of his people into passionate, lyrical poems like the three which follow.

The Dance

FEDERICO GARCIA LORCA

Out in the garden
at night
six gypsies dressed in white
are dancing.

Out in the garden
at night
their heads are crowned with bright
paper roses.

Out in the garden
at night
their teeth are pearls that write
across burnt shadows.

And in the garden
at night
their long dark shadows reach right
up to the sky.

In a Poor Neighborhood: Córdoba

FEDERICO GARCIA LORCA

The house defends them
against the stars.
The night is upside-down.
Inside, there is a dead girl
with a blood-red rose
hidden in her hair.
Six nightingales are crying
on the window grating.
The people are sighing.
The guitars are loud.

The Horseman

FEDERICO GARCIA LORCA

Under the black
bandit moon
spurs ring out their song.

Black pony,
where are you taking your dead rider?

The sharp spurs belong
to a motionless bandit
who has dropped the reins,

Shivering pony,
smell the perfume of a flowering knife!

Under the black moon
blood runs down the side
of Sierra Morena.

Black pony,
where are you taking your dead rider?

The night digs spurs
into the ribs of its darkness
and shoots off stars.

Shivering pony,
smell the perfume of a flowering knife!

Under the black moon
a cry! and a horn of flame
spirals into the sky.

Black pony,
where are you taking your dead rider?

Gloria Fuertes, a contemporary Spanish poet, chose subjects less romantic than those of Lorca for her poem which follows. "The Picture" is filled with realistic details, made more vivid by rich color imagery.

The Picture

GLORIA FUERTES

The picture could never have painted itself.
Someone had to mix that green for the mountains;
and blue for the top part brighter than the blue below,
(and the sea — someone had to invent it);
black for the mouth of the mine;
white for the waves' blood;
brown for the rocks;
and this difficult yellow.
He covered the sheep with wool,
filled the cows with milk,
gypsies with lice,
and girls with love.
He sharpened the blackberry's brambles,
filled certain small bushes with surprises,
painted naked children in the streets,
put trout and women in the river,
chickens in the roadway,
water in the springs,
sleep in the lizards,
patience in all insects.
He painted the night black,
with a plate of rice for the moon.

The Panther

(Jardin des Plantes, Paris)*

RAINER MARIA RILKE

His sight from ever gazing through the bars
has grown so blunt that it sees nothing more.
It seems to him that thousands of bars are
before him, and behind them nothing merely.

The easy motion of his supple stride,
which turns about the very smallest circle,
is like a dance of strength about a center
in which a mighty will stands stupefied.

Only sometimes when the pupil's film
soundlessly opens . . . then one image fills
and glides through the quiet tension of the limbs
into the heart and ceases and is still.

The Dunce

JACQUES PRÉVERT

He says no with his head
but his heart says yes
he says yes to what he likes
he says no to the teacher
he is on his feet
to be questioned
to be asked all the problems
suddenly he shakes with uncontrollable mirth
and he rubs them all out
the figures and the words
the dates and the names
the sentences and the traps
and despite the threats from the master
amid the jeers of the child prodigies
with all the colored chalks
upon the miserable blackboard
he draws the face of happiness.

---

* The Jardin des Plantes is a zoo.

*Vladislav Khodasevich was a Russian poet who died in exile in 1939.
Compare his treatment of the monkey in this poem with Rilke's
picture of the panther (page 710).*

The Monkey

VLADISLAV KHODASEVICH

The day was hot. The forests were on fire.
Time dragged. Behind the country house next door
A cock was crowing. The gate swung behind me.
There on a bench, leaning against the fence,
A wandering Serb,° lean, swarthy, had dozed off.
A heavy cross, fashioned of silver, hung
On his half-naked breast, down which great drops
Of sweat were rolling. On the fence, close by,
A small red-skirted monkey crouched, and chewed
The dusty leaves of lilac overhead.   10
A leather collar on a heavy chain
That pulled her back pressed hard against her throat.
The Serb, roused by my step, awoke and wiped
His sweat, and begged some water for the creature.
He tasted it, to test how cold it was,
Then placed the saucer on the bench. At once
The monkey, wetting eager fingers, seized
The saucer in both hands. She leaned her elbows
Upon the bench, and crouching thus, she drank.
Her chin was almost resting on the boards,   20
And her back arched above her half-bald head.
Even so Darius,° centuries ago,
Fleeing the phalanxes of Alexander,
Must have leaned to a puddle in the road.
When she had drunk her water, casually
The monkey brushed the saucer off the bench,

---

5. *Serb:* a man from Serbia, formerly an independent country, now part of
Yugoslavia. 22. *Darius:* Darius III, king of ancient Persia, who fled from the
armies of Alexander the Great.

And standing up, with an immortal gesture
She offered me her small black horny hand
The moisture had left cool. . . .
Though I have pressed the hands of lovely women,   30
Of poets, and of men who led a nation,
Yet there was not one hand among them all
Had such a noble shape. Not any hand
Ever touched mine in such full comradeship!
I swear by God that no one ever looked
Into my eyes so wisely and so deeply;
Her soft gaze pierced me. That indigent° creature
Revived for me the sweetest lore bequeathed
By far antiquity to human hearts.
And in that moment life appeared so full,   40
It seemed to me the sun and moon, the waves
Of all the seas, the winds, the heavenly spheres,
Were choiring together, organ music
That rang as wonderfully in my ears
As in the days beyond man's memory.
And then the Serb, knuckling his tambourine,
Went off, the monkey perched on his left shoulder:
A maharajah on an elephant.
And in the heavens, wreathed in opal smoke,
A swollen, raspberry-colored sun was hanging.   50
Heat, with no hope of thunder, lay upon
The wheat fields that were wilting in the blaze.
That was the very day war was declared.

---

37. *indigent:* poor, needy.

Index

Adams, Franklin P., 146
Aesop, 113, 114, 117
Africa's Plea, 694
America the Beautiful — and Its Dese-
    craters, 315
Animal Farm, 1
Anouilh, Jean, 583
Ant, The, 145
Ant and the Grasshopper, The, 119
Antaeus, 267
Antigone, 583
Anxiety of a Young Girl to Get Mar-
    ried, 698
Armour, Richard, 145
Around Us, Dawning, 695
At the Grave of His Brother, 703
Auden, W. H., 206, 210, 524

B. Wordsworth, 633
Bad News, 196
Ballad from the Gibbet, 705
ballad of late Annie, The, 218
Bat, The, 211
Bean Eaters, The, 217
Beard of Joseph Palmer, The, 244
Bee!, 198
Benchley, Robert, 139
Bill Trapp's Silence, 259
Bird and the Machine, The, 306
Blake, William, 522
Boccaccio, Giovanni, 640
Boorstin, Daniel, 579
Booth, Philip, 205
Brooks, Gwendolyn, 217–19
Brooks, Gwendolyn, An Interview with,
    219
Buck, Pearl, 79
Bullet, Gerald, 207
Burnett, Whit, 411

Catullus, 703
Cavafy, C. P., 108
Chekhov, Anton, 129, 453
Ching-ting Mountain, The, 698
Come In, 183
Composed upon Westminster Bridge,
    215
Crab and Her Son, The, 114
Crane, Stephen, 522
Cuestas, Katherine, 212
Cummings, E. E., 190

Dance, The, 707
Dark House, The, 207
Daudet, Alphonse, 151
Dawning, 706
Day's Wait, A, 155
Deal, Borden, 267
De la Mare, Walter, 197
Demby, William, 259
Dempster, Roland Tombekai, 694
Desert Places, 180
Design, 173
Dickinson, Emily, 191, 198, 523
Dog and His Shadow, The, 113
Dream, The, 453
Dunce, The, 710
Dust of Snow, 170

Eaton, Sidney, 204
Edmund G. Ross, 233
Edwards, Dolton, 142
Eiseley, Loren, 306
Elegy for J.F.K., 210
Epitaph for a Dog, 199

Falcon, The, 640
Fetish Tree, The, 676
Fifteen, 199
Fight, The, 481
Figure in the Doorway, The, 174
First Lesson, 205
Flight, 494
For the Spartans Who Died at Ther-
    mopylae, 702
Fox and the Crow, The: Three Ver-
    sions, 117
Friendship, 419
From Hero to Celebrity, 579
Frost, Robert, 167–83
Frost, Robert, In Tribute to, 184
Fuertes, Gloria, 709

Galsworthy, John, 252
Gift for Pan, A, 702
Grasshopper and the Ant, The, 115
Graves, Robert, 216
Greatest Man in the World, The, 571

Haiku, 699–700
Hamilton, Edith, 529
Handful of Dates, A, 670
Happy Childhood Tales, 139

96

9

st, 155

...or, 293

...sh, A, 704

...ok, Stewart, 244

...ner, 537

Horseman, The, 708

Housman, A. E., 190, 211, 523

Howard, Eric, 92

Hughes, Langston, 147, 205

I Counsel You Beware, 190

Iliad, The, (Book 22), from, 537

In a Poor Neighborhood: Córdoba, 707

Indian Business, 92

Inscription for the Grave of a Dog, 701

Interior, 200

Iron Lady, The, 556

Island, 205

Issa, 699

Jiménez, Juan Ramón, 706

John and Jane, 196

John Henry, 554

Julius Caesar, 327

Just Lather, That's All, 644

Kelley, William Melvin, 513

Kennedy, John F., 184, 233

Khodasevich, Vladislav, 711

Kon-Tiki, 293

La Fontaine, Jean de, 115, 117, 123

Last Lesson, The, 151

Lattimore, Richmond, 201, 537

Laye, Camara, 650

Lessing, Doris, 484

Li Po, 698

Little Lyric (Of Great Importance), 147

London, Jack, 277

Lorca, Federico Garcia, 707–08

Loveliest of Trees, 211

Lucilius, 703

McGinley, Phyllis, 216

Man Said to the Universe, A, 522

Marquand, John P., 429

Martial, 704

Maugham, Somerset, 119

Maupassant, Guy de, 95

Meditatio, 209

Meihem in ce Klasrum, 142

Mending Wall, 176

Miles, Josephine, 207

Monkey, The, 711

Morte d'Arthur, 546

Moth and the Star, The, 116

Mother Goose, 202

Mouse from the City and the Mouse from the Country, The, 113

My Dreams Are of a Field Afar, 523

Mycilla's Hair, 703

Naipaul, V. S., 633

Napoleon, 197

Nash, Ogden, 145, 147, 194

Need of Being Versed in Country Things, The, 171

New Road, The, 79

Nicol, Abioseh, 693

No Longer Mourn for Me When I Am Dead, 215

O What Is That Sound, 524

O'Casey, Sean, 127

Of Robert Frost, 219

Old Man and His Donkey, The, 123

Old Man Traveling, 208

Old Mary, 218

On the High Upland Plain, 207

Once by the Pacific, 172

Orwell, George, 1, 100, 162

Packard, Vance, 315

Panther, The, 710

Parker, Dorothy, 200

Paul the Silentiary, 701

Perseus, 529

Picture, The, 709

Player Piano, 193

Pliya, Jean, 676

Poem, 202

Poison Tree, A, 522

Politics and the English Language, from, 162

Pound, Ezra, 209

Power of Laughter: Weapon Against Evil, The, 127

Praise Songs for the Baboon, 691

Prévert, Jacques, 710

Private Dining Room, The, 194

Purist, The, 147

Quality, 252

Rexroth, Kenneth, 202

Richter, Conrad, 556

Rilke, Ranier Maria, 710

Road Not Taken, The, 181

Roethke, Theodore, 211